COBOL
A Pragmatic Approach

COBOL
A Pragmatic Approach

ROBERT T. GRAUER
University of Miami

MARSHAL A. CRAWFORD
Programming Consultant

Prentice-Hall, Inc. Englewood Cliffs, New Jersey 07632

Library of Congress Cataloging in Publication Data

GRAUER, ROBERT T.   (date)
    COBOL: a pragmatic approach.

    Includes index.
    1. COBOL (Computer program language)   I. Crawford,
Marshal, A.,   (date)   joint author.   II. Title.
QA76.73.C25G7   001.6'424   77-23356
ISBN   0-13-139097-X

To Our Families

Printed in the United States of America

10   9   8   7   6   5   4

Prentice-Hall International, Inc., *London*
Prentice-Hall of Australia Pty. Limited, *Sydney*
Prentice-Hall of Canada, Ltd., *Toronto*
Prentice-Hall of India Private Limited, *New Delhi*
Prentice-Hall of Japan, Inc., *Tokyo*
Prentice-Hall of Southeast Asia Pte. Ltd., *Singapore*
Whitehall Books Limited, *Wellington, New Zealand*

The following information is reprinted from COBOL Edition 1965, published by the Conference on Data Systems Languages (CODASYL), and printed by the U.S. Government Printing Office:

The authors and copyright holders of the copyrighted material used herein:

FLOWMATIC (Trade mark of the Sperry Rand Corporation), Programming for the Univac (R) I and II, Data Automation Systems copyrighted 1958, 1959, by Sperry Rand Corporation; IBM Commercial Translator Form No. F28-8013, copyrighted 1959 by IBM; FACT, DSI 27A5260-2760, copyrighted 1960 by Minneapolis-Honeywell

have specifically authorized the use of this material in whole or in part, in the COBOL specifications. Such authorization extends to the reproduction and use of COBOL specifications in programming manuals of similar publications.

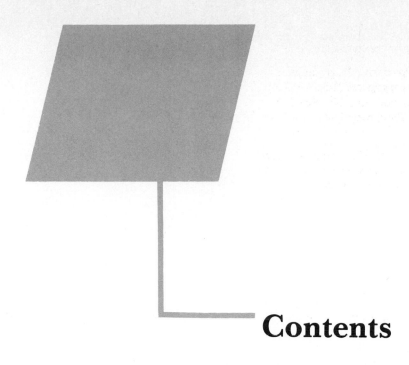

Contents

II   THE COBOL LANGUAGE

III MORE COBOL

IV   THE ROLE OF BAL IN DEEPER UNDERSTANDING

12   Necessary Background   *223*

13   Debugging, II   *237*

14   Insight into the COBOL Compiler   *254*

V   FILE PROCESSING

15   Magnetic Tape: Concepts and COBOL Implications   *273*

16   Magnetic Disk: Concepts and COBOL Implications   *295*

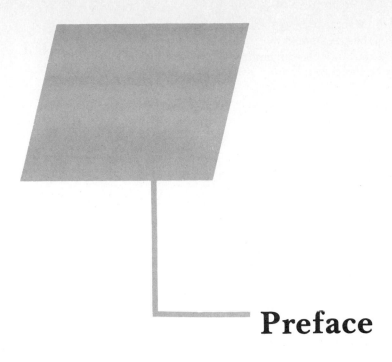

Preface

Why another book on COBOL? In recent years, universities have been criticized for failing to provide computer science and business graduates who are sufficiently versed in commercial data processing. This statement is partially justified for two reasons:

1. Most COBOL courses provide only "textbook" coverage and are sorely lacking in practical; i.e., commercial emphasis. Such subjects as JCL, file processing, debugging, structured programming, documentation, standards, and testing are glossed over or missed entirely.

2. College curricula traditionally treat COBOL and BAL in separate courses and do not provide an adequate link between the two. Although the COBOL programmer can and does exist without knowledge of Assembler, even a superficial understanding promotes superior capability to write efficient COBOL and is invaluable in debugging.

The primary objective of this book is to bridge the gap between traditional university curricula and the needs of industry. We address ourselves directly to the above statements and attempt to produce the well-rounded individual who can perform immediately and effectively in a third or fourth generation environment.

The scope of the book is extensive; ranging from an introduction to data processing to maintaining sequential and nonsequential files. A student may use this book without any previous exposure to data processing. Students with limited knowledge of COBOL can also use it since complete coverage will require two semesters. The text is modular in design so that Sections III, IV, and V may be covered in any order after Sections I and II are completed (see the accompanying diagram).

Modular Organization

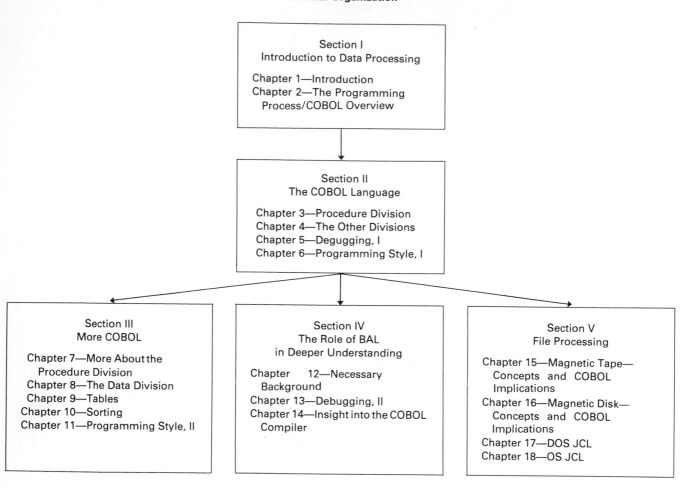

Programming style is introduced as soon as the rudiments of COBOL have been presented. Structured Programming is considered as one element of programming style, and is used exclusively after its introduction. We do believe, however, that a structured program is not necessarily, in and of itself, a good program nor is a nonstructured program necessarily a poor one. Other elements of programming style, e.g., coding standards, documentation, and efficiency, are also essential to a well-written program and are discussed within.

In addition to the material on standard COBOL, there are two chapters devoted to debugging, two to JCL, two to programming style, two to file processing, and two on the role of BAL in better understanding COBOL. Although some chapters pertain directly to IBM systems, ANS COBOL is emphasized, so that the majority of the text relates to non-IBM installations as well. Inclusion of the IBM material, however, should enable the book to be used as a "programmer's guide" in that it contains a wealth of information which is not usually found in one place.

The authors wish to thank Karl Karlstrom of Prentice-Hall for making possible *Preface* our entry into the world of publishing, and also Phyllis Springmeyer, our Production Editor for making it so pleasant. We thank our principle reviewers, Dr. Thomas DeLutis of Ohio State University and Dr. Jan L. Mize of Georgia State University for their help and continued encouragement. Steve Shatz and Art Cooper are to be commended for their thoroughness in proofreading the galleys. We thank our many colleagues for their fine suggestions. These include: Ken Anderson, Jeff Borow, Les Davidson, Don Dejewski, Giselle Goldschmidt, Sam Ryan, Sue and Steve Wain, and anyone else whom we inadvertantly omitted. Finally, we thank Francie Makoske who saw the project through from beginning to end, who typed and retyped the many revisions, and who never lost her sense of humor.

ROBERT T. GRAUER
MARSHAL A. CRAWFORD

COBOL

A Pragmatic Approach

Introduction
to Data Processing

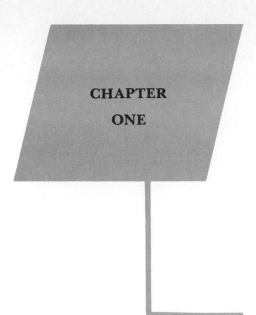

CHAPTER
ONE

Introduction

This book is about computer programming. In particular it is about COBOL, a widely used commercial programming language. Programming involves the translation of a precise means of problem solution into a form the computer can understand. Programming is necessary because, despite reports to the contrary, computers cannot think for themselves. Instead they do *exactly* what they have been instructed to do, and these instructions take the form of a computer program. The advantage of the computer stems from its speed and accuracy. It does not do anything that a human being could not if he/she were given sufficient time.

All computer applications consist of three phases: input, processing, and output. Information enters the computer, it is processed (i.e., calculations are performed), and the results are communicated to the user. Input can come from punched cards, magnetic tape or disk, computer terminals, or any of a variety of other devices. Processing encompasses the logic to solve a problem, but in actuality all a computer does is add, subtract, multiply, divide, or compare. All logic stems from these basic operations, and the power of the computer comes from its ability to alter a sequence of operations based on the results of a comparison. Output can take several forms. It may consist of the ubiquitous $11 \times 14\frac{7}{8}$ computer listing or printout, or it may be payroll checks, computer letters, mailing labels, magnetic tape, punched cards, etc.

We shall begin our study of computer programming by describing punched card input and printed output in some detail. We shall consider the structure of a computer and contrast machine- and problem-oriented languages. We shall pose a simple problem and construct the flowchart and COBOL program to solve it. The rapid entrance into COBOL is somewhat different from the approach followed by most textbooks, but we believe in learning by doing. There is nothing very mysterious about COBOL programming, so let's get started.

Punched Card Input

The punched card (Figure 1.1) has been around a long time. Its development was motivated by the U.S. Constitution (that is not a typographical error). Our Constitution requires that a federal census be taken every ten years. As the country expanded, processing of census data consumed increasing amounts of time (three years for the 1880 census), and the government needed a faster way of tabulating data. Dr. Herman Hollerith introduced the 80-column card in the late 1880s, and it has been with us ever since. (Mechanical devices, which are not computers, were available in the nineteenth century to process these cards.) Another interesting sidelight is the size of the punched card; it has the dimensions of the dollar bill of 1880.

The punched card has 80 vertical columns, each of which consists of 12 rows and contains a single character. Each character has its own unique combination of row punches. The letter A, for example, has a punch in row 12 and row 1 (see Figure 1.1). The letter B has a punch in row 12 and row 2. In Figure 1.1, A and B appear in columns 1 and 2, respectively. The upper three rows of the card (rows 12, 11, and 0) are known as zones, and the other rows as digits. Every letter has two punches; one zone and one digit. The letters A through I all have the same zone, i.e., row 12. The letters J through R all have a punch in row 11 and S through Z in row 0. The numbers 0 through 9 contain a single punch in the appropriate row. The bottom edge of the card indicates the column. The column indicator, in conjunction with the alphabetic information at the very top, indicates what is punched where; e.g., column 38 contains a zero.

As a test of your understanding, what character is punched in column 26 of Figure 1.1? (Answer: Z.) What punches are required for the letter X? (Answer: row 0 and row 7.) In what column does X appear? (Answer: column 24.)

The computer is colorblind, and hence it does not matter if information is punched on red, white, or blue cards. Some installations, however, require that the first or last card in a deck be a specified color. This is to delineate one deck from another and is totally for human convenience. The very top edge of the card in Figure 1.1 interprets the information on the card. Again this is for human convenience only. The card reader senses the holes that are punched and does not refer to the interpreted information. Indeed, the latter need not be present at all.

Printed Output

The most widely used medium for computer output is the $11 \times 14\frac{7}{8}$ printout (alias listing, readout, etc.). Just as a computer must be told which card columns contain incoming data, it must also be told where to print its output. The $11 \times 14\frac{7}{8}$ form typically contains 132 print positions per line and 66 lines per page. Figure 1.2 contains a print layout form commonly used by programmers to plan their output. As can be seen from Figure 1.2, "THIS IS A PRINT LAYOUT FORM" is to appear on the tenth line from the top, beginning in column 15 and extending to column 41.

It makes no difference to the computer if printing is on wide or narrow paper, single- or multiple-part forms, mailing labels, payroll checks, etc. The machine is only interested in knowing what information is to appear and where. This is accomplished via instructions in a program.

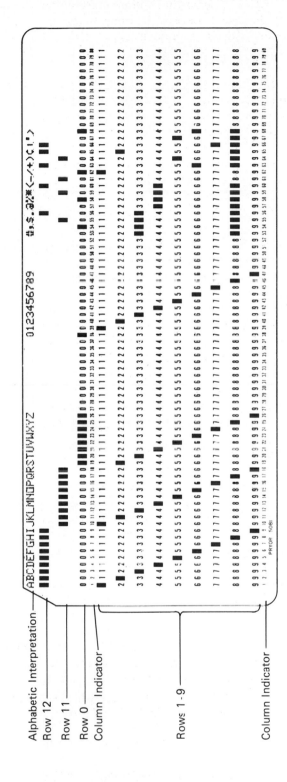

Figure 1.1 The 80-Column Card

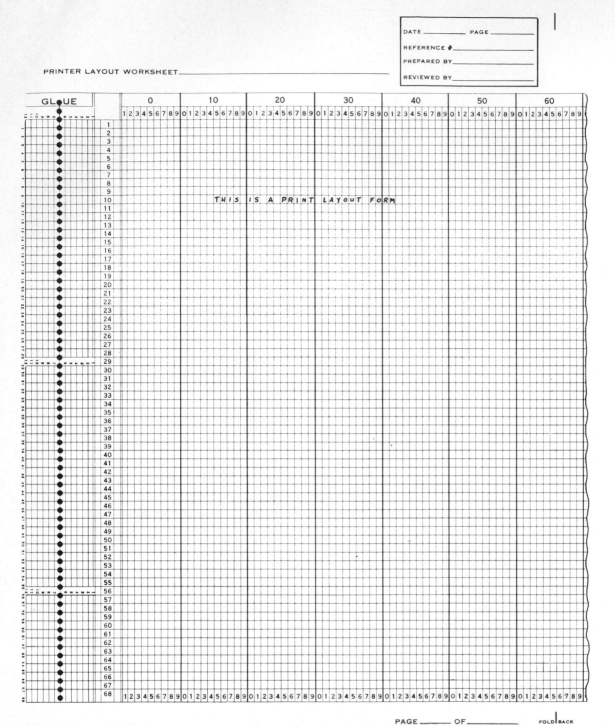

THIS IS A PRINT LAYOUT FORM

Figure 1.2 Print Layout Form

Structure of a Computer

A computer can be thought of as a collection of electronic devices which (1) accept data, (2) perform calculations, and (3) produce results. A functional representation is shown in Figure 1.3.

We have already spoken about input and output. Main storage, i.e., the computer's memory, stores instructions and data while they are being processed. The size of a computer is measured by the capacity of its memory. Large modern machines have memory capacities of several million characters.

The central processing unit (CPU) is the "brain" of the computer. It consists of an arithmetic and logical unit (ALU) and a control unit. The ALU

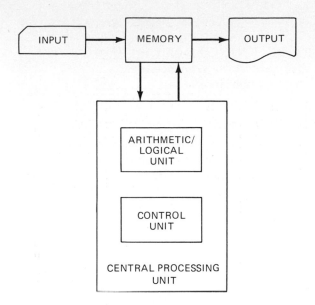

Figure 1.3 Functional Representation of a Computer

actually executes instructions; i.e., it adds, subtracts, multiplies, divides, and compares. The control unit monitors the transfer of data between main storage, input/output (I/O) devices, and the ALU. It decides which instruction will be executed next and is the "boss" of the computer.

Speed of execution is another way in which computers are measured. The ALU of a modern machine can execute millions of instructions per second. The time to execute a single instruction is expressed in microseconds (millionths of a second) or nanoseconds (billionths of a second).

Machine vs. Higher-Level Languages

Each computer has its own unique machine language tied to specific locations in its memory. Human beings, however, think in terms of problems and use quantities with mnemonic significance, e.g., HOURS, RATE, PAY, etc. We might say that a person thinks in a problem-oriented or higher-level language, while in actuality the computer functions in a machine-oriented or lower-level language. The two are related through a compiler, which is a computer program that translates a problem language into a machine language. COBOL is an example of a problem-oriented language for business systems. The COBOL compiler is itself a machine language program written in the language of the machine on which it is executed.

The wide availability of COBOL compilers provides tremendous flexibility for individual programs. A COBOL program written for an IBM computer can also execute on a Univac, Honeywell, NCR, or any other machine which has a COBOL compiler. In each instance the input to the compiler is the same, i.e., a COBOL program (in actuality there are slight variations from compiler to compiler). The output from the compiler is different. An IBM compiler produces an IBM machine language program, a Univac compiler produces Univac machine language, etc. However, this does not concern the COBOL programmer. All he need know, and indeed care about, is COBOL; the compiler does the rest.

Consider a simple COBOL statement, MULTIPLY HOURS BY RATE GIVING PAY. This takes HOURS, multiplies it by RATE, and puts the result into PAY. The values of HOURS and RATE are unchanged as a result of this instruction. For this instruction to execute, the compiler has to assign locations in its memory to HOURS, RATE, and PAY. It will multiply HOURS by

RATE in a work area (known as an accumulator or register) and put the result into PAY.

Assume that the compiler decides to store HOURS, RATE, and PAY in locations 1000, 2000, and 3000, respectively. It then generates a sequence of three machine instructions to accomplish the intended multiplication:

```
LOAD      1000
MULTIPLY 2000
STORE     3000
```

The first instruction, LOAD 1000, brings the contents of location 1000 (HOURS) into the accumulator. The next instruction multiplies the contents of the accumulator by the contents of location 2000 (RATE). The result remains in the accumulator. Finally the STORE instruction puts the contents of the accumulator into location 3000 (PAY). (Note that these instructions are typical of compilers in general and vary from computer to computer.) Table 1.1

Table 1.1 Machine Instructions to Multiply HOURS by RATE

| | Memory Contents | | | | | | | |
| | Before | | | | After | | | |
Instruction	1000 (HOURS)	2000 (RATE)	3000 (PAY)	ACCUM	1000 (HOURS)	2000 (RATE)	3000 (PAY)	ACCUM
LOAD 1000	40	5	?	?	40	5	?	40
MULTIPLY 2000	40	5	?	40	40	5	?	200
STORE 3000	40	5	?	200	40	5	200	200

illustrates what happens as a result of these three machine instructions. It assumes values of 40 and 5 for HOURS and RATE, respectively. It shows the contents of locations 1000, 2000, 3000, and the accumulator before and after each of the three machine language instructions are executed. Prior to the LOAD instruction the contents of both locations 3000 and the accumulator are immaterial. After the LOAD has been executed, the contents of location 1000 have been brought into the accumulator. After the MULTIPLY, the contents of the accumulator are 200, and after the STORE the contents of location 3000 are also 200. Note that the initial contents of locations 1000 and 2000 are unchanged throughout.

A single COBOL statement invariably expands to one or more machine language statements after compilation. This phenomenon is known as *instruction explosion* and is a distinguishing characteristic of compiler languages. Compare the three machine language statements to the single COBOL statement. Obviously the latter is shorter, but it is also easier to write, since the COBOL programmer need not remember which memory locations contain the data. In the early days of the computer age, there were no compilers, and all programs were written in machine language. Then someone had a remarkably simple yet powerful idea: Why not let the computer remember where data are kept; The compiler concept was born, and things have never been the same since.

The First Problem

We are ready for our first problem statement. Input is a set of student cards, one card per student. Each card contains the student's name (columns 1–25), number of completed credits (columns 26–28), and major (columns 29–43). Figure 1.4 contains the card of John Doe, an engineering major, who has completed 30 credits.

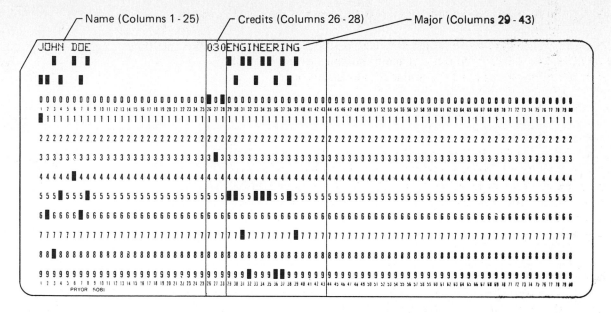

Figure 1.4 Data Card for First Problem

The registrar needs a list of engineering students who have completed at least 110 credits. This is easily accomplished by developing a COBOL program with the following logic:

1. Read a student card; stop after all cards have been read.
2. If the student has completed less than 110 credits, go back to step 1.
3. If the student is not an engineering major, go back to step 1.
4. Print the name of any student reaching this point.
5. Go back to step 1.

Before we can even begin to code a computer program, we first have to develop the logic that the program will follow; i.e., we must convert the verbal problem statement into a series of unambiguous steps that the machine can execute. The result of this effort is termed a flowchart.

A flowchart is a pictorial representation of the logic inherent in a program. In effect one takes a problem statement and constructs a logical blueprint which is subsequently incorporated into the COBOL program. A set of standard flowchart symbols has been adopted by the American National Standards Institute and is shown in Figure 1.5.

A flowchart to determine the engineering students with at least 110 credits is shown in Figure 1.6. To facilitate discussion, each block in Figure 1.6 has been numbered and is described in Table 1.2.

To better understand how a flowchart and subsequent program function, we shall concoct some test data for the problem statement and run it through the flowchart. Assume data cards have been prepared for four students as follows:

Student Name	Credits	Major
John Adams	90	Political science
Adam Smith	120	Economics
Orville Wright	115	Engineering
Francis Key	80	Music

The flowchart begins execution with the start and housekeeping blocks. The third block reads the first data card, John Adams. The end of file has not been

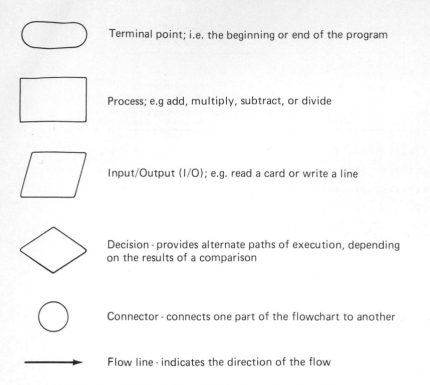

Terminal point; i.e. the beginning or end of the program

Process; e.g add, multiply, subtract, or divide

Input/Output (I/O); e.g. read a card or write a line

Decision - provides alternate paths of execution, depending on the results of a comparison

Connector - connects one part of the flowchart to another

Flow line - indicates the direction of the flow

Figure 1.5 American National Standards Institute Flowchart Symbols

Table 1.2 Block-by-Block Explanation of Flowchart in Figure 1.6

Block Number	Symbol	
1	Terminal	Every flowchart contains a START block indicating where the program begins.
2	Processing	As a rule, most programs require some initial processing, the nature of which is not always apparent in the problem statement. A good practice is to include a "HOUSEKEEPING" block at the beginning of a flowchart.
3	I/O	This block reads a card.
4	Decision	This block determines if the *end-of-file* condition (i.e., no more data cards) has been reached. If so, it terminates processing; if not, processing continues.
5	Decision	Are credits less than 110? If yes, go right, i.e., to the connector block directing flow to read another card. If credits are 110 or more, the flow is downward to check on the major.
6	Decision	Is the major engineering? If not, the flow is directed right; i.e. to the connector block directing flow to read another card. If the major is engineering, the flow is directed downward.
7	I/O	Write the name of the student being processed as he/she is an engineering major with at least 110 credits.
8	Terminal	Stop. Every program contains at least one such block to terminate processing.
A	Connector	Connector blocks appear at several points in a flowchart to direct program flow. In this example, they are all directed toward reading another card.

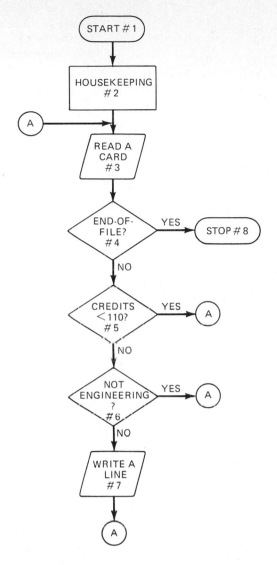

Figure 1.6 Flowchart to Select Engineering Majors
with 110 Credits or More

reached, so block 4 directs flow to block 5, the test for the number of credits. Since John Adams has not completed 110 credits, the program returns to block 3 to read another card.

The data for Adam Smith are now stored in the computer's memory. Again the end-of-file condition has not been reached, so the program "falls through" to the credits test. Smith has completed 120 credits, so processing continues with the major test, Smith, however, is an economics major, and program flow is again directed to read another card. So far the data for two students have been processed, but neither has passed both tests.

Orville Wright is now read into memory. Since Wright is an engineering major with 115 credits, we go through blocks 4, 5, 6, and 7. We write a line for Orville Wright (block 7) and return to read another card.

Francis Key enters the computer's memory and fails the credits test. The computer is directed to read another card, but the end of file has been reached. Processing is terminated via block 8. We should now begin to realize that program execution involves extensive repetition; i.e., the same instructions are continually executed for different data. It is helpful to tabulate the number of times each block in Figure 1.6 is executed:

Block Number	Times Executed	Explanation
1. Start	1	At beginning of program
2. Housekeeping	1	At beginning of program
3. Read	5	Once for each of four students; once to sense the end-of-file condition
4. End-of-file test	5	Explanation as above
5. Credits test	4	Once for each student
6. Major test	2	Executed only for those students who passed the credits test, i.e., SMITH and WRIGHT
7. Write	1	Executed only for WRIGHT since no one else passed both credits and major
8. Stop	1	Executed at program's end

We shall now proceed to COBOL. Figure 1.7 is a COBOL program written for the flowchart in Figure 1.6. The syntactical rules for COBOL are extremely precise, and we certainly *do not* expect you to remember them after a brief exposure to Figure 1.7. We do believe, however, that immediate exposure to a real program is extremely beneficial in terms of stripping the mystical aura which too often surrounds programming. Further, we believe Figure 1.7 will become conceptually clear after some brief explanation.

Figure 1.7 is made clearer when we realize that every COBOL program consists of four divisions which must be in a specified order:

IDENTIFICATION DIVISION—This division contains the program and author's name. It can also contain other identifying information such as date written, installation name, security, and general remarks to help explain the program.

ENVIRONMENT DIVISION—This portion mentions the computer on which the program is to be compiled and executed (usually one and the same). It also specifies the I/O devices to be used by the program.

DATA DIVISION—This division describes the data. In card and print files, for example, it specifies the incoming card columns and outgoing print positions, respectively.

PROCEDURE DIVISION—This division contains the program logic, i.e., the instructions the computer is to execute in solving the problem.

A line-by-line description of Figure 1.7 is given in Figure 1.8. We would hope the reader has a general understanding of the data and procedure divisions for Figure 1.7. If not, we expect to answer many of your questions in Chapter 2. Further, we believe that when you actually run your own programs in Chapter 2, everything will crystallize.

Assume the student cards for Adams, Smith, Wright, and Key were input to the COBOL program of Figure 1.7. Output would consist of a single line of output for Orville Wright. Can you examine the data division and determine in which print positions his name would appear? (Answer: positions 9–33.)

Obviously it doesn't pay to go through the effort described herein for a mere four students. The advantages of the computer are realized only when large amounts of data are processed.

```
00001          IDENTIFICATION DIVISION.
00002          PROGRAM-ID.     FIRSTTRY.
00003          AUTHOR.        CRAWFORD.
00004          REMARKS.   THIS IS A COBOL PROGRAM WHICH READS A DECK OF CARDS
00005             AND PRINTS THE NAMES OF ENGINEERING MAJORS WHO ARE ALSO
00006             SENIORS   (110 CREDITS OR MORE).
00007          ENVIRONMENT DIVISION.
00008          CONFIGURATION SECTION.
00009          SOURCE-COMPUTER.   IBM-370.
00010          OBJECT-COMPUTER.   IBM-370.
00011          INPUT-OUTPUT SECTION.
00012          FILE-CONTROL.
00013             SELECT CARD-FILE ASSIGN TO UR-2540R-S-SYSIN.
00014             SELECT PRINT-FILE ASSIGN TO UR-1403-S-SYSOUT.
00015          DATA DIVISION.
00016          FILE SECTION.
00017          FD  CARD-FILE
00018             LABEL RECORDS ARE OMITTED
00019             RECORD CONTAINS 80 CHARACTERS
00020             DATA RECORD IS CARD-IN.
00021          01  CARD-IN.
00022             05  CARD-NAME                 PICTURE IS A(25).
00023             05  CARD-CREDITS              PICTURE IS 9(3).
00024             05  CARD-MAJOR               PICTURE IS A(15).
00025             05  FILLER                    PICTURE IS X(37).
00026          FD  PRINT-FILE
00027             LABEL RECORDS ARE OMITTED
00028             RECORD CONTAINS 133 CHARACTERS
00029             DATA RECORD IS PRINT-LINE.
00030          01  PRINT-LINE.
00031             05  FILLER                    PICTURE IS X(8).
00032             05  PRINT-NAME               PICTURE IS X(25).
00033             05  FILLER                    PICTURE IS X(100).
00034          PROCEDURE DIVISION.
00035             OPEN INPUT CARD-FILE, OUTPUT PRINT-FILE.
00036          READ-A-CARD.
00037             READ CARD-FILE, AT END GO TO END-OF-JOB.
00038             IF CARD-CREDITS IS LESS THAN 110, GO TO READ-A-CARD.
00039             IF CARD-MAJOR IS NOT EQUAL 'ENGINEERING', GO TO READ-A-CARD.
00040          ******* NOW PRINT A LINE - ENGINEERING SENIOR *****
00041             MOVE SPACES TO PRINT-LINE.
00042             MOVE CARD-NAME TO PRINT-NAME.
00043             WRITE PRINT-LINE.
00044             GO TO READ-A-CARD.
00045          END-OF-JOB.
00046             CLOSE CARD-FILE, PRINT-FILE.
00047             STOP RUN.
```

Figure 1.7 The First COBOL Program

Summary

This chapter is intended as an introduction to COBOL programming and the text which follows. In reality, we have presented a substantial amount of material in terms of the fundamental concepts which were developed. We trust the true significance of this information will be better appreciated as you progress through the text. In the meantime, a recap should prove helpful:

1. Every computer application consists of input, processing, and output.
2. Input and output must be precisely specified as to content and location.
3. The computer cannot think for itself but must be told precisely what to do. This is done through a series of instructions known as a program.
4. The computer does not do anything that a human being could not do if given sufficient time. The advantages of a computer stem from its speed and accuracy.
5. Human beings think in terms of problem-oriented languages, while the computer functions in machine language. Compilation relates the two.
6. The flowchart is a pictorial representation of the logic embodied in a computer program.

00001	Header for IDENTIFICATION DIVISION.
00002	Names the program as FIRSTTRY.
00003	Identifies the author.
00004–00006	Descriptive information about the program.
00007	Header for ENVIRONMENT DIVISION.
00008	Beginning of CONFIGURATION SECTION.
00009	Identifies IBM-370 as SOURCE-COMPUTER, i.e., the machine on which the program will compile.
00010	Identifies IBM-370 as OBJECT-COMPUTER, i.e., the machine on which the program will execute.
00011	Beginning of INPUT-OUTPUT SECTION, which identifies I/O devices.
00012	Beginning of FILE-CONTROL paragraph, which connects file names to I/O devices.
00013	States that CARD-FILE is to come from a 2540 card reader.
00014	States that PRINT-FILE is to come from a 1403 printer.
00015	Header for DATA DIVISION.
00016	Beginning of FILE SECTION.
00017–00020	FD (File Description) for CARD-FILE, which was specified in the ENVIRONMENT DIVISION in line 00013.
00021–00025	Specification of which columns contain which data, as per program definition. Notice that only the first 43 columns contain data but that the last 37 columns contain FILLER.
00026–00029	FD (File Description) for PRINT-FILE, which was specified in the ENVIRONMENT DIVISION in line 00014.
00030–00033	Description of a line of output; PRINT-NAME is to appear in print positions 9–33.
00034	Header for PROCEDURE DIVISION.
00035	The OPEN statement makes the files CARD-FILE and PRINT-FILE available for processing. The former is input to the program, the latter is output created by the program. (Opening files is an example of housekeeping.)
00036	READ-A-CARD is the name of a paragraph in the PROCEDURE DIVISION. It is the paragraph to which we refer whenever a student card is to be read.
00037	Reads a student card. After all cards have been read, the program goes to the paragraph END-OF-JOB.
00038	Checks if the completed credits are less than 110. If so, the program goes to read another card.
00039	Checks if the major is not engineering; if not engineering, the program goes to read another card.
00040	A comment: If the program reaches this point, the student is an engineering major with at least 110 credits.
00041	Clears the print line.
00042	Moves the incoming name in columns 1–25 to the output area, positions 9–33.
00043	Writes a line.
00044	Directs the program to go back to read another card.
00045	Paragraph name where program is to go after all cards have been processed.
00046	Closes files.
00047	Terminates processing.

Figure 1.8 Line-by-Line Description of COBOL Program

TRUE	FALSE		
☐	☐	**1**	A compiler translates a machine-oriented language into a problem-oriented language.
☐	☐	**2**	A compiler translates a higher-level language into a lower-level language.
☐	☐	**3**	A compiler is a computer program.
☐	☐	**4**	The COBOL compiler for a Univac computer is identical to the COBOL compiler for an IBM computer.
☐	☐	**5**	The "instruction explosion" stems from the fact that a single machine language statement generates several COBOL statements.
☐	☐	**6**	A microsecond is one-billionth of a second.
☐	☐	**7**	It is realistic to expect the CPU of a large, modern computer to execute 60 million instructions per minute.
☐	☐	**8**	It is realistic to expect the memory of a large, modern computer to contain a million characters or more.
☐	☐	**9**	A single program, written in machine language, can run on a variety of computers.
☐	☐	**10**	A COBOL program can run on a variety of computers.
☐	☐	**11**	There are four divisions in a COBOL program.
☐	☐	**12**	The divisions of a COBOL program may appear in any order.
☐	☐	**13**	Data description appears in the identification division.
☐	☐	**14**	Computers can "think" for themselves.
☐	☐	**15**	The 80-column punched card is more than 50 years old.
☐	☐	**16**	A COBOL program must be punched on red, white, or blue cards.
☐	☐	**17**	The control unit is part of the ALU.
☐	☐	**18**	The ALU decides which instruction will be executed next.
☐	☐	**19**	No statement in a computer program may be executed more than once.
☐	☐	**20**	A rectangle is the standard flowchart symbol for a decision block.
☐	☐	**21**	Computer output must be directed onto $11 \times 14\frac{7}{8}$ sheets.
☐	☐	**22**	A LOAD instruction changes the contents of an accumulator (see Table 1.1).
☐	☐	**23**	A STORE instruction changes the contents of an accumulator (see Table 1.1).
☐	☐	**24**	A MULTIPLY instruction changes the contents of both an accumulator and a storage location (see Table 1.1).

1 Given the following sequence of machine language instructions,

LOAD   500
MULTIPLY 600
STORE   700

complete the following table of memory contents:

		Memory Contents							
		Before				After			
Instruction		500	600	700	ACC	500	600	700	ACC
LOAD	500	10	20	?	?	?	?	?	?
MULTIPLY	600	?	?	?	?	?	?	?	?
STORE	700	?	?	?	'?	?	?	?	?

2 Assume that our hypothetical computer also has a machine language ADD instruction in addition to the LOAD, MULTIPLY, and STORE instructions described in the text. Specifically, "ADD X" will add the contents of location X to the contents of the accumulator and leave the sum in the accumulator. Show the series of machine language instructions which would probably be generated for the COBOL instruction "ADD A, B, C GIVING D." Assume A, B, C, and D are in locations 100, 200, 300, and 400, respectively.

3 Given the flowchart of Figure 1.6 and the student data below,

Student Name	Credits	Major
Merriweather Lewis	115	Travel
John Kennedy	115	Political science
Alex Bell	90	Engineering
George Sand	85	Literature
John Roebling	115	Engineering

how many times, and for which students, will blocks 1–8 be executed?

4 Given the COBOL program of Figure 1.7, indicate what changes would have to be made if
(a) We wanted MUSIC students rather than ENGINEERING students?
(b) We wanted students with 60 or fewer credits?
(c) The student major was contained in columns 60–74 of the incoming card?
(d) We wanted engineering students *or* students with 110 credits or more? (Hint: You may want to insert an extra paragraph name.)
Note: Treat parts (a), (b), (c), and (d) independently.

5 Which DIVISION in a COBOL program contains
(a) The CONFIGURATION SECTION?
(b) The FILE SECTION?
(c) Statements to open and close files?
(d) The description of incoming data?
(e) The description of outgoing data?
(f) The author's name?
(g) The program's name?
(h) Statements to read information?
(i) Statements to write information?
Note: Use Figure 1.7 as a guide, and indicate specific line numbers where the information is found.

6 Your programming supervisor has drawn a flowchart for you to code. He left the flowchart on his dining room table at home and unfortunately his three-year-old son, Benjy, cut it up into pieces with a pair of scissors. Your supervisor collected the pieces (shown below) and has asked you to rearrange them properly into a correct flowchart; do so. The flowchart is to read a file of cards with each card containing three *unequal* numbers A, B, and C. Write out the *greater* of the two sums (A + B) and (B + C) for each card *only* if A is less than 50.

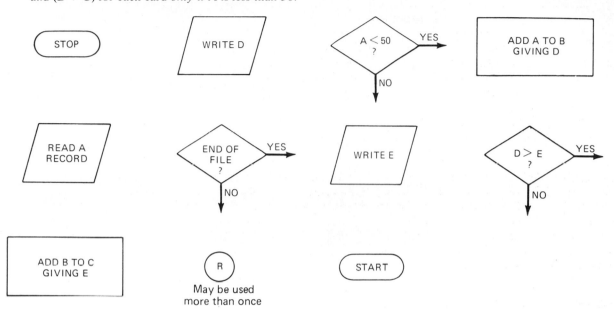

7 World Wide Sales, Inc. is looking to promote one of its employees to head the South American Division. The selected employee must speak Spanish, be younger than 40, and hold a college degree. The programming manager has prepared the necessary flowchart (see figure below), but unfortunately Benjy and his scissors got to it first (see Problem 6). Your job is to put the flowchart together. Note well that there may be more than one employee who qualifies for the position. Accordingly, the flowchart includes the necessary logic to count and print the number of qualified employees and to print the name of every such employee.

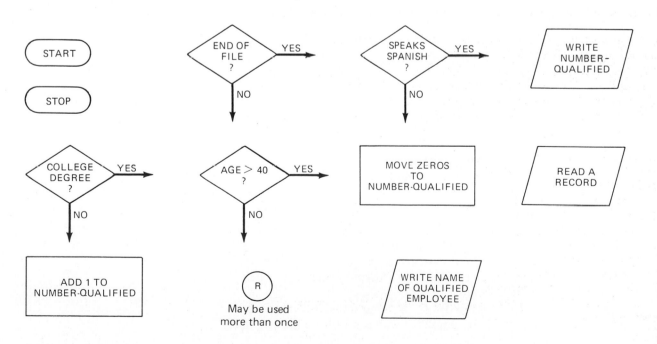

17

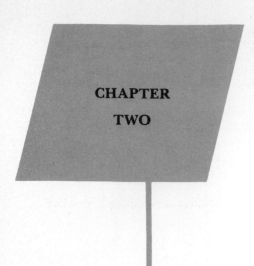

The Programming Process
COBOL Overview

One objective of this book is to teach you COBOL programming. A broader **Overview**
objective is to teach you how to solve problems using the computer. To this
end, we shall present a generally accepted problem-solving procedure consisting of six steps:

1. Problem statement and analysis
2. Flowcharting
3. Coding
4. Program testing—phase 1 (compilation)
5. Program testing—phase 2 (execution)
6. Documentation

You probably have a broad appreciation for this procedure from Chapter 1. In
this chapter we shall first expand the procedure in general fashion and then
cover specifics to enable you to run your own program. We shall discuss the
elements of COBOL, the COBOL coding form, keypunching, and finally
submission to the computer.

    At the end of Chapter 1 we presented a COBOL program which prints a
listing of engineering majors who had completed at least 110 credits. At the

conclusion of this chapter we shall ask you to keypunch the program of Chapter 1 and to submit it to your computer center. "Seeing is believing" is especially pertinent to data processing. We are very confident that after you have seen computer output from your own program, many of your questions will answer themselves. In other words, we would not be surprised if you were a bit confused after reading Chapter 1. *However, the sooner you get down to running a program, the sooner things will resolve themselves.* You could read this book until all hours of the night but to no avail unless you interact heavily with the computer.

A Problem-Solving Procedure

The first step is to obtain a clear statement of the problem containing a complete description of the input and desired output. The problem statement should also contain processing specifications. It is not enough to say calculate quality point average (QPA). Rather the method for calculating QPA must be given as well.

Once the input, output, and processing specifications have been enumerated, a flowchart is drawn. The flowchart is a graphical display of the logic used in solving the problem, and a good flowchart simplifies subsequent coding. Flowcharting is in accordance with the conventions of Chapter 1.

Coding is the translation of a flowchart into COBOL. Coding must be done within well-defined COBOL rules and coding conventions. In subsequent sections in this chapter we shall discuss the elements of COBOL and the COBOL coding form.

After the program is coded, it is keypunched and submitted to the computer. The first thing the machine has to do is translate the COBOL program into machine language. Initial attempts at compilation are apt to contain several errors, which may be due to misspellings, missing periods, misplaced parentheses, etc. Corrections are made, and the program is recompiled. Only after the compilation has been successfully completed can we proceed to the next step. Compilation errors are thoroughly discussed in Chapter 5.

After compilation, we begin program execution, where we are apt to encounter logical errors. In this step the computer does exactly what we instructed it to do, but we may have done so incorrectly. For example, assume the GO TO statement in line 44 of Figure 1.7 was omitted. The program would write at most one output line, after which it would come to end-of-job processing. The program would compile perfectly in that the COBOL syntax was correct. It would not, however, execute as intended. Corrections are made, the program is recompiled, and testing continues.

Documentation requires explicit explanation of a program's input, logic, and output. A program is well documented if a programmer, other than the original author, can step in and easily handle any desired modifications. Program documentation is particularly important in a commercial environment.

Figure 2.1 is a flowchart of the problem-solving procedure. Note the presence of two decision blocks which indicate the iterative nature of the entire process. Very few, if any, programs compile correctly on the first shot—hence the need to recode or rekeypunch specific statements. Similarly, very few programs execute properly on the first test and thus the need to reflowchart, recode, recompile, etc. Figure 2.1 also contains two dotted boxes for keypunching and preparation of job control language (JCL). These are definite steps to the beginner but not significant enough to merit explicit mention in the previous discussion.

We now return to the "engineering senior" problem of Chapter 1. In the introductory chapter we skipped over some of the blocks in Figure 2.1 and ended with a working COBOL program. Our purpose there was to provide a rapid introduction to COBOL to give the reader an immediate feeling of what

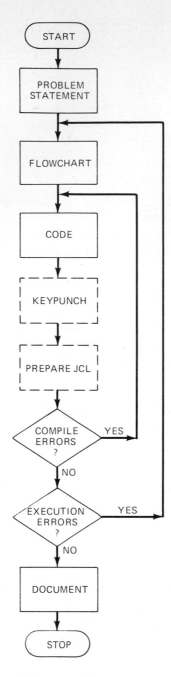

Figure 2.1 The Programming Process

programming is all about. Now we shall retrace our steps; in particular we shall discuss the elements of COBOL, the COBOL coding form, keypunching, and submission to the computer.

COBOL consists of six language elements: reserved words, programmer-supplied names, literals, symbols, level numbers, and pictures. Every COBOL statement contains at least one reserved word which gives the entire statement its meaning. Reserved words have special significance to the compiler and are used in a rigidly prescribed manner. They must be spelled correctly, or the compiler will not be able to recognize them. The list of reserved words varies from compiler to compiler, and a comprehensive list is given in Appendix B.

Elements of COBOL

The beginner is urged to refer frequently to this appendix for two reasons: (1) to ensure the proper spelling of reserved words used in his program, and (2) to avoid the inadvertent use of reserved words as programmer-supplied data names.

The programmer supplies his own names for paragraph, data, and file names. A paragraph name is a tag to which the program refers, e.g., READ-A-CARD or END-OF-JOB in Figure 1.7. File names are specified in several places throughout a COBOL program, but their initial appearance is in the environment division, e.g., CARD-FILE and PRINT-FILE in Figure 1.7. Data names are the elements on which instructions operate, e.g., CARD-NAME, CARD-CREDITS, and CARD-MAJOR in Figure 1.7. A programmer chooses his own names within the following rules:

1. A programmer-supplied name can contain the letters A–Z, the digits 0–9, and the hyphen (-). No other characters are permitted, not even blanks.

2. Data names must contain at least one letter. Paragraph and section names may be all numeric.

3. A programmer-supplied name cannot begin or end with a hyphen.

4. Reserved words may not be used as programmer-supplied names.

5. Programmer-supplied names must be 30 characters or less.

The examples below should clarify the rules associated with programmer-supplied names:

Programmer-Supplied Name	Explanation
SUM	Invalid—reserved word
SUM-OF-X	Valid
SUM OF X	Invalid—contains blanks
SUM-OF-X-	Invalid—ends with a hyphen
SUM-OF-ALL-THE-XS	Valid
SUM-OF-ALL-THE-XS-IN-ENTIRE-PROGRAM	Invalid—more than 30 characters
GROSS-PAY-IN-$	Invalid—contains a character other than a letter, number, or hyphen
12345	Valid as a paragraph name but invalid as a data name

A literal is an exact value or constant. It may be numeric, i.e., a number, or nonnumeric, i.e., enclosed in quotes. Literals appear throughout a program and are frequently used to compare the value of a data name to a specified constant. Consider lines 38 and 39 of Figure 1.7:

```
IF CARD-CREDITS IS LESS THAN 110,...
IF CARD-MAJOR IS NOT EQUAL 'ENGINEERING',...
```

In the first statement, CARD-CREDITS is compared to 110, a numeric literal. The second statement contains a nonnumeric literal, ENGINEERING. Nonnumeric literals are contained in quotes and may be up to 120 characters in length. Anything, including blanks, numbers, or reserved words, may appear in the quotes and be part of the literal. Numeric literals can be up to 18 digits and may begin with a leading (leftmost) plus or minus sign. The latter may contain a decimal point but cannot end on a decimal point. Examples are shown below:

Literal	*Explanation*
123.4	Valid numeric literal
'123.4'	Valid nonnumeric literal
+123	Valid numeric literal
'IDENTIFICATION DIVISION'	Valid nonnumeric literal
123.	Invalid numeric literal—cannot end on a decimal point
123–	Invalid numeric literal—the minus sign must be in the leftmost position

Symbols are of three types—punctuation, arithmetic, and relational—and are contained in Table 2.1.

Table 2.1 COBOL Symbols

Category	*Symbol*	*Meaning*
Punctuation	.	Denotes end of COBOL entry
	,	Delineates clauses
	;	Delineates clauses
	" " or ' '	Sets off nonnumeric literals
	( )	Encloses subscripts or expressions
Arithmetic	+	Addition
	–	Subtraction
	*	Multiplication
	/	Division
	**	Exponentiation
Relational	=	Equal to
	>	Greater than
	<	Less than

The use of relational and arithmetic symbols is described in detail later in the text, beginning in Chapter 3. Commas and semicolons are used to improve the legibility of a program, and their omission (or inclusion) does not constitute an error. Periods, on the other hand, should be used after a sentence, and their omission could cause difficulty. Thus, there are two rules with respect to punctuation symbols. The first is an absolute requirement; i.e., violation will cause compiler errors. The second is strongly recommended; i.e., violation will *not* cause compiler errors but could cause execution errors.

1. A space must follow and cannot precede a comma, semicolon, and period. (Thus a space is a valid and necessary symbol.)
2. All entries should be terminated by a period.

Consider these examples:

1. OPEN INPUT CARD-FILE, OUTPUT PRINT-FILE.
2. OPEN INPUT CARD-FILE OUTPUT PRINT-FILE.
3. OPEN INPUT CARD-FILE, OUTPUT PRINT-FILE
4. OPEN INPUT CARD-FILE , OUTPUT PRINT-FILE.
5. OPEN INPUT CARD-FILE,OUTPUT PRINT-FILE.

Examples 1 and 2 are perfect. Example 3 is missing a period; although that is not an error, it does violate our second guideline. In example 4, the comma is preceded by a space. Example 5 is missing a space after the comma.

Level numbers and pictures are discussed more fully in Chapter 4 under the data division. Level numbers describe the relationship of items in a record. For example, under CARD-FILE in Figure 1.7 there was a single 01-level entry and several 05 entries. In general, the higher (numerically) the level number, the less significant the entry; i.e., 05 is less important than 01. Entries with higher numeric values are said to belong to the levels above them. Thus, in Figure 1.7, the several 05-level entries belong to their respective 01-level entries.

Pictures describe the nature of incoming or outgoing data. Lines 23–25 in Figure 1.7 contain three types of picture entry: 9, A, and X. A picture of 9's means the entry is numeric, a picture of A's implies the entry is alphabetic, and a picture of X's says the entry can contain both alphabetic and numeric data. Note, however, that alphabetic pictures are seldom used; i.e., even names can contain apostrophes or hyphens which are alphanumeric rather than alphabetic in nature.

The COBOL Coding Form

The COBOL compiler is very particular about the information it receives; i.e., certain areas of the punched card are reserved for specific elements of COBOL. For example, division and section headers are required to begin in column 8, whereas most other statements may begin in or past column 12. Further, there are additional rules for continuation (what happens if a sentence doesn't fit on one card), comments, optional sequencing of source statements in columns 1–6, and program identification in columns 73–80. Rules of the coding sheet are summarized in Table 2.2 and illustrated in Figure 2.2. The latter shows completed forms for the engineering senior problem of Chapter 1.

Table 2.2 Rules for the COBOL Coding Form

Columns	Explanation and Use
1–6	Optional sequence numbers: If this field is coded, the compiler performs a sequence check on incoming COBOL statements by flagging any statements out of order. Most commercial installations encourage the use of this option. For students, however, we do not advocate its use if you are keypunching your own programs.
7	Used to indicate comments and for continuation of nonnumeric literals: A comment may appear anywhere in a COBOL program and is indicated by an * in column 7 (see line 40 in Figure 1.7). Comments appear on the source listing but are otherwise ignored by the compiler. We encourage their use to facilitate program documentation. Column 7 is also used to indicate continuation of nonnumeric literals, and this is more fully explained in Chapter 4.
8–11	Known as the "A margin": Division headers, section headers, paragraph names, FD's, and 01's all begin in the A margin. Division and section headers are followed immediately by a period, and the rest of the line is blank. Paragraph names are also followed by a period but may contain additional information on the line.
12–72	Known as the "B margin": All remaining entries begin in or past column 12. COBOL permits considerable flexibility here, but individual installations have their own requirements. We, for example, begin PICTURE clauses in column 48 for better legibility. (We shall discuss this further in Chapter 6.)
73–80	Program identification: a second optional field which is ignored by the compiler. Different installations have different standards. However, we suggest you omit these columns if keypunching your own programs.

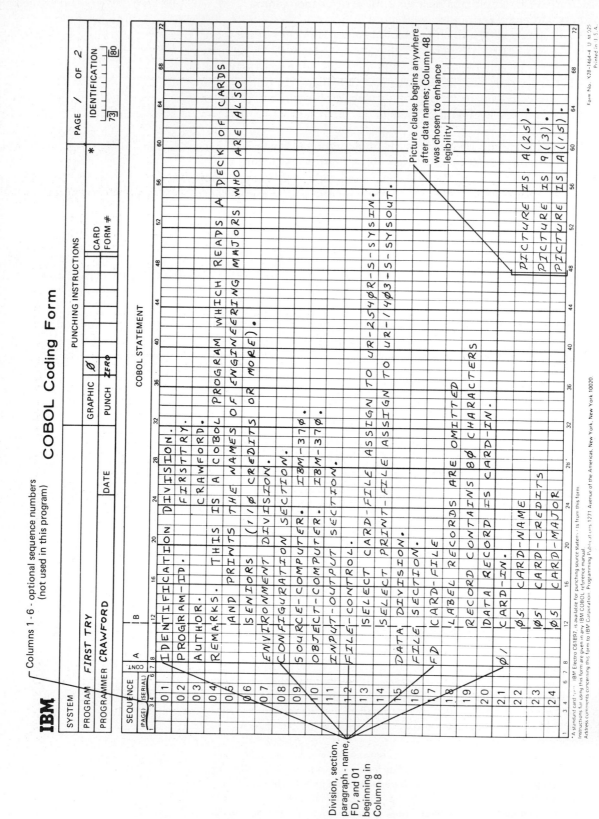

Figure 2.2 COBOL Coding Form for "Engineering Senior" Problem of Chapter 1 (Page 1)

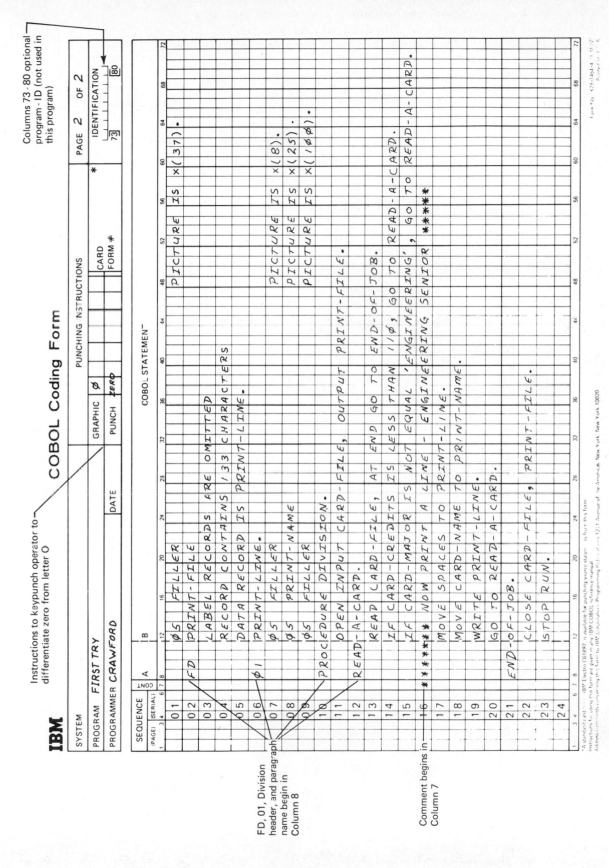

Figure 2.2 COBOL Coding Form for "Engineering Senior" Problem of Chapter 1 (Page 2)

25

Professional programmers generally have their programs keypunched by someone else. Students do not have this luxury, and, for this reason, we have included a brief section on keypunching. Figure 2.3 shows an IBM 029 keypunch, and Figure 2.4 shows the keyboard layout. As you can see, a keypunch bears a strong resemblance to a typewriter. Operating instructions are summarized on page 27. They may appear complicated now, but after you have punched a few cards by yourself, this material will become second nature.

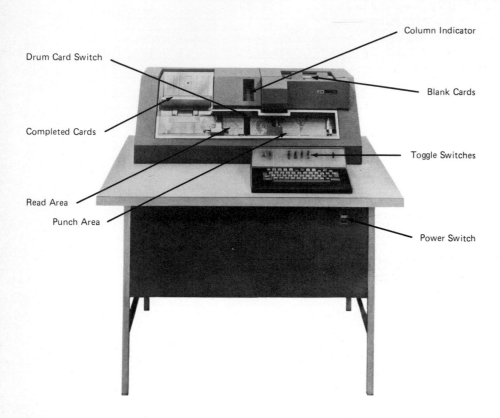

Figure 2.3 IBM 029 Keypunch (*Courtesy* of IBM.)

Figure 2.4 Keyboard for IBM 029 Keypunch (*Courtesy* of IBM.)

1. Turn the power switch on.
2. Place sufficient blank cards in the feed hopper. Cards must be placed with the 9 edge down.
3. Set all toggle switches to the off (down) position with the exception of two PRINT switches. Push the drum switch to the right.
4. Press the FEED key, causing a card from the feed hopper to drop.
5. Press the REG key, causing the card to register in the punch station.
6. Punch to your heart's content, keeping the following in mind:
   a. The space bar skips a space; i.e., it leaves a column blank.
   b. Most keys contain two characters (Figure 2.4). The lower character is punched by just hitting the appropriate key. The upper character is punched by holding the numeric shift and hitting the key simultaneously.
   c. The column indicator shows the next column to be punched.
7. When you have finished punching, hit the REL (release) key to move the completed card from the punch area.
8. Hit the FEED key to bring in another blank card and return to step 5.

Some hints at speeding up:

1. Use of the AUTO FEED switch: If this switch is turned on (up position), hitting the REL key also causes a new card to feed. In effect step 8 is eliminated from the above procedure.
2. Use of the DUP (duplicate) key: Very often we may punch 30 or 40 columns correctly and then make an error. Unlike a typewriter, where one can merely backspace and retype the correction, the entire card must be done over. The most expeditious procedure is to
   a. Place the incorrect card in the read station.
   b. FEED a blank card into the punch station and hit REG.
   c. Depress the DUP key until you reach the column containing the error (this will copy the information from the incorrect card to the blank card).
   d. Punch corrected information as normal. If possible, use the DUP key after the correction.
   e. Verify that the new card is correct.
   f. Thow away, immediately, the incorrect card.
3. Organization: We cannot overemphasize the need for preparation prior to the keypunch room. In our college, students are usually waiting for a machine, and it is difficult, and indeed unfair to those waiting, to take time to think under those circumstances. It is imperative that you be well organized and know precisely what you intend to punch *before* sitting down at the machine.

Submitting a Program to the Computer

Modern computers are highly sophisticated devices capable of executing many different kinds of programs. Accordingly, a computer must be told precisely what program to execute, where the program is coming from, and where to obtain the data. These tasks are accomplished through the operating system and JCL (job control language). An operating system consists of a series of programs, which include the COBOL compiler, that enable the computer to function. The operating system is supplied by the computer manufacturer because it is far too complex to be developed by individual installations. Job control language is the method of communication with the operating system.

In Chapters 17 and 18 we shall study in detail JCL for DOS and OS, the two most widely used operating systems. For the present, however, we shall cover only the minimum JCL which must accompany a COBOL program when it is submitted to the computer. Your instructor may want to embellish this material, or perhaps your computer center has a handout to make the information clearer. If not, much of what we say in this section must be "taken on faith" until you cover the JCL chapters.

OS JCL

A set of JCL statements is known collectively as a job stream. Figure 2.5 contains the job stream necessary to run a COBOL program under OS, but undoubtedly there will be minor variations at your installation. The JOB statement always starts a new job stream. The name of the job, GRAUER in Figure 2.5, can be no more than eight characters and immediately follows the //. The EXEC card invokes a procedure known as COBUCLG which calls the COBOL compiler. The next statement, //COB.SYSIN DD *, indicates that the COBOL deck follows immediately. The first /* signals the end of the COBOL deck. //GO.SYSIN DD * tells the computer that data follow next, and the second /* indicates the end of the data. The // signals the end of the job stream.

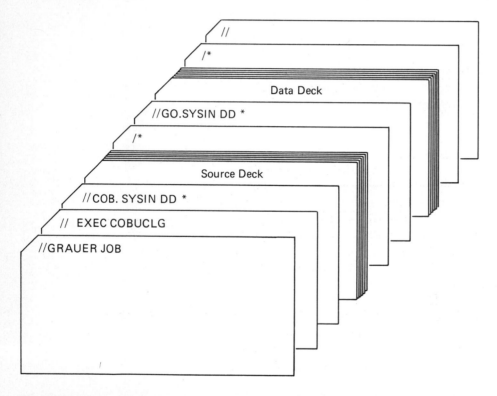

Figure 2.5 OS JCL for the First COBOL Program

DOS JCL

In Chapter 1 we learned that a COBOL program is first translated into machine language (compilation) and that the machine language program is subsequently executed. In reality there is an additional step known as linkage editing. The linkage editor is part of the operating system. It takes the output of the COBOL compiler and combines it with other routines in the operating system to enable the subsequent execution. Figure 2.6 illustrates the DOS JCL necessary and draws attention to the linkage editor.

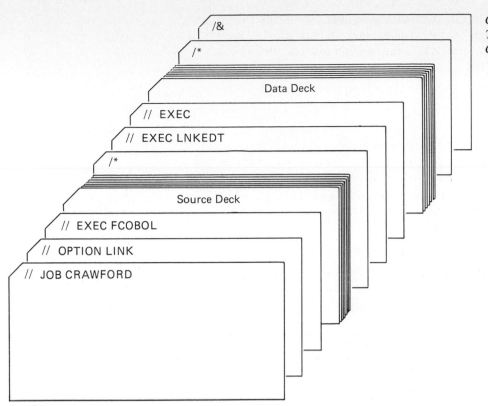

Figure 2.6 DOS JCL for the First COBOL Program

The JOB statement signals the start of a new job stream. The job name, CRAWFORD in Figure 2.6, must be eight characters or less. The OPTION statement allows the linkage editor to be called if compilation is successful. // EXEC FCOBOL invokes the COBOL compiler and is followed immediately by the COBOL source deck. The first /* signals the end of the COBOL program. // EXEC LNKEDT calls the linkage editor, and // EXEC executes the generated machine language program. The // EXEC statement is followed immediately by the data. The second /* indicates the end of the data, and the /& signals the end of the job stream.

Putting It Together

"One learns by doing." This time-worn axiom is especially true for programming. We have covered a lot of material since you first began reading Chapter 1. Now it is time to put everything together and actually run your first program. Keypunch the coding from Figure 2.2. Prepare the appropriate JCL. Make up your own test data and submit the job.

We believe, in fact we are very sure, that after you receive your first computer printout everything will fall into place.

Summary

The programming process was presented. It consisted of six steps: analysis, flowcharting, coding, compilation, execution, and documentation. Errors in compilation and execution are to be expected in the first several attempts; hence the procedure assumes an iterative nature.

The COBOL language consists of six elements: reserved words, programmer-supplied names, literals, symbols, level numbers, and pictures. Rules for the COBOL coding form were covered, and keypunching was discussed briefly.

Finally the procedure for submitting jobs to the computer was presented. All computers function through an operating system, which is a set of programs supplied by the manufacturers. Job control language (JCL) is the means of communication with the operating system. Elementary JCL to compile and execute COBOL programs under both DOS and OS was supplied.

TRUE	FALSE		
☐	☐	**1**	Nonnumeric literals may not contain numbers.
☐	☐	**2**	Numeric literals may not contain letters.
☐	☐	**3**	A data name cannot contain any characters other than letters or numbers.
☐	☐	**4**	Columns 1–6 are never used on the coding sheet.
☐	☐	**5**	The use of columns 73–80 is optional.
☐	☐	**6**	File names typically appear in three divisions.
☐	☐	**7**	Column 8 is used as a continuation column.
☐	☐	**8**	The rules for forming paragraph names and data names are exactly the same.
☐	☐	**9**	A data name cannot consist of more than 30 characters.
☐	☐	**10**	A nonnumeric literal cannot contain more than 30 characters.
☐	☐	**11**	A numeric literal can contain up to 18 digits.
☐	☐	**12**	Division headers must begin in the A margin.
☐	☐	**13**	Division headers must begin in column 8.
☐	☐	**14**	Section headers must begin in column 12.
☐	☐	**15**	Paragraph names must begin in column 8.
☐	☐	**16**	PICTURE clauses can appear in column 12 or after.
☐	☐	**17**	If a program compiles correctly, then it must execute correctly.
☐	☐	**18**	Reserved words may appear in a nonnumeric literal.
☐	☐	**19**	Reserved words may be used as data names.
☐	☐	**20**	JCL is used to communicate with the operating system.

1 Indicate whether the entries below are valid as data names. If any entry is invalid, **PROBLEMS** state the reason.
(a) NUMBER-OF-TIMES
(b) CODE
(c) 12345
(d) ONE TWO THREE
(e) IDENTIFICATION-DIVISION
(f) IDENTIFICATION
(g) HOURS-
(h) GROSS-PAY
(i) GROSS-PAY-IN-$

2 Classify the entries below as being valid or invalid literals. For each valid entry, indicate if it is numeric or nonnumeric; for each invalid entry, indicate the reason it is invalid.
(a) 567
(b) 567.
(c) −567
(d) +567
(e) +567.
(f) '567.'
(g) 'FIVE SIX SEVEN'

(h) '−567'
(i) 567−
(j) 567+
(k) '567+'

3 Indicate whether the following entries are acceptable according to the COBOL rules for punctuation. Correct any invalid entries.
(a) CLOSE CARD-FILE,PRINT-FILE.
(b) CLOSE CARD-FILE PRINT-FILE.
(c) CLOSE CARD-FILE, PRINT-FILE
(d) CLOSE CARD-FILE , PRINT-FILE.
(e) CLOSE CARD-FILE, PRINT-FILE.

4 (a) Which division(s) does not contain paragraph names?
(b) Which division(s) contains the SELECT statement(s)?
(c) Which division(s) contains level numbers?
(d) Which division(s) contains data names?
(e) Which division(s) contains reserved words?
(f) Which division(s) contains picture clauses?
(g) Which division(s) does not contain file names?

5 Modify the COBOL program of Figure 2.2 to accommodate *all* the following:
(a) Major is moved to columns 50–64 of the data card.
(b) Print the names of *all* students, regardless of major, who have completed 110 credits or more.
(c) Print the major in print positions 40–54 in addition to the student's name.
Code and then keypunch the necessary changes. Rerun the program.

6 Develop a COBOL program which will
(a) Read in a file of employee cards.
(b) Print the name, salary, age, and location of every employee who
    (i) Earns between $20,000 and $30,000,
    (ii) Works in New York or Chicago,
    (iii) Is 35 years or younger.
The data for each employee are punched according to the following format:

Field	Columns	Picture
Name	6–20	A(15)
Salary	25–29	9(5)
Location	40–50	X(11)
Age	51–52	9(2)

Use any appropriate print positions for your output. Draw a flowchart, keypunch, and run your program.

The COBOL Language

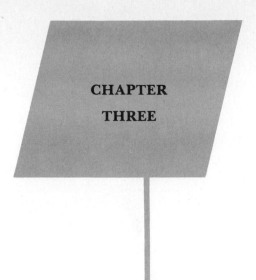

CHAPTER THREE

The Procedure Division

Overview

The procedure division is the portion of a COBOL program that contains the logic; it is the part of the program that "actually does something." In this chapter we shall cover several of the basic COBOL verbs. We shall begin with those which do arithmetic: ADD, SUBTRACT, MULTIPLY, DIVIDE, and COMPUTE. We shall look at the READ, WRITE, OPEN, and CLOSE verbs for use in I/O (input/output) operations. We shall study the MOVE verb which transfers data from one area of memory to another. We shall learn the IF and GO TO statements to alter the normal sequential path of execution. Finally we shall cover the STOP RUN to terminate program execution.

    All the above verbs have a variety of options. For the most part, we shall use only the more elementary formats and defer additional coverage to later chapters.

COBOL Notation

COBOL is an "English-like" language. As such, it has inherent flexibility in the way a particular entry may be expressed; i.e., there are a number of different, but equally acceptable ways to say the same thing. Accordingly, a standard notation is used to express permissible COBOL formats and is listed on the following page.

1. COBOL reserved words appear in uppercase (capital) letters.
2. Reserved words which are required are underlined; optional reserved words are not underlined.
3. Lowercase words denote programmer-supplied information.
4. Brackets ([ ]) indicate optional information.
5. Braces ({ }) indicate that one of the enclosed items must be chosen.
6. Three periods (...) mean that the last syntactical unit can be repeated an arbitrary number of times.

This notation is clarified by example; consider the IF statement:

$$\underline{\text{IF}} \left\{ \begin{matrix} \text{identifier-1} \\ \text{literal-1} \end{matrix} \right\} \left\{ \begin{matrix} \text{IS [\underline{NOT}] \underline{GREATER} THAN} \\ \text{IS [\underline{NOT}] \underline{LESS} THAN} \\ \text{IS [\underline{NOT}] \underline{EQUAL} \underline{TO}} \end{matrix} \right\} \left\{ \begin{matrix} \text{identifier-2} \\ \text{literal-2} \end{matrix} \right\}$$

The format for the IF statement has IF underlined and in uppercase letters; thus IF is a required reserved word. The first set of braces means that either a literal or identifier must appear; both are in lowercase letters, indicating they are programmer supplied. The next set of braces forces a choice among one of three relationships: greater then, less than, or equal to. In each case, IS appears in capital letters but is not underlined; hence its use is optional. Brackets denote NOT as an optional entry. THAN is an optional reserved word which may be added to improve legibility. Finally a choice must be made between literal-2 or identifier-2.

Additional flexibility is supplied in the IF statement in that $>$, $<$, and $=$ may be substituted for GREATER THAN, LESS THAN, and EQUAL TO, respectively. Returning to the engineering senior problem of Chapter 1, in which we compared CARD-MAJOR to engineering, all the following are acceptable:

```
IF CARD-MAJOR IS EQUAL TO 'ENGINEERING'...
IF CARD-MAJOR EQUAL TO 'ENGINEERING'...
IF 'ENGINEERING' IS EQUAL TO CARD-MAJOR...
IF CARD-MAJOR = 'ENGINEERING'...
```

Arithmetic Verbs

In this section we shall use the notation to study the COBOL verbs for arithmetic: ADD, SUBTRACT, MULTIPLY, DIVIDE, and COMPUTE. (The ROUNDED and SIZE ERROR options for these verbs are discussed in Chapter 7.)

ADD

The ADD verb has two basic formats:

$$\underline{\text{ADD}} \left\{ \begin{matrix} \text{identifier-1} \\ \text{literal-1} \end{matrix} \right\} \left[\begin{matrix} \text{identifier-2} \\ \text{literal-2} \end{matrix} \right] \ldots \underline{\text{TO}} \ \text{identifier-n}$$

and

$$\underline{\text{ADD}} \left\{ \begin{matrix} \text{identifier-1} \\ \text{literal-1} \end{matrix} \right\} \left\{ \begin{matrix} \text{identifier-2} \\ \text{literal-2} \end{matrix} \right\} \left[\begin{matrix} \text{identifier-3} \\ \text{literal-3} \end{matrix} \right] \ldots \underline{\text{GIVING}} \ \text{identifier-n}$$

Note that one or several identifiers (literals) may precede identifier-n. Regardless of which format is chosen, i.e., GIVING or TO, only the value of identifier-n is changed. In the "TO" option, the values of identifier-1, identifier-2, etc., are added to the initial contents of identifier-n. In the "GIVING" option, the sum does not include the initial value of identifier-n.

Simply stated, the "TO" option includes the initial value of identifier-n in the final sum, while the "GIVING" option ignores the initial value. Examples 3.1 and 3.2 illustrate both formats.

Example 3.1

ADD A B TO C.

Before execution: A [5]   B [10]   C [20]

After execution: A [5]   B [10]   C [35]

In Example 3.1, the initial values of A, B, and C are 5, 10, and 20, respectively. After execution the values are 5, 10, and 35. The instruction took the initial value of A (5), added the value of B (10), added the initial value of C (20), and put the sum (35) back into C.

Example 3.2

ADD A B GIVING C.

Before execution: A [5]   B [10]   C [20]

After execution: A [5]   B [10]   C [15]

In Example 3.2 the initial value of A (5) is added to the initial value of B (10), and the sum (15) replaces the initial value of C.

Table 3.1 contains additional examples of the ADD instruction. In each instance, the instruction is assumed to operate on the initial values of A, B, and C, (5, 10, and 30, respectively). Note that only the value of C changes.

Table 3.1   The ADD Instruction

Data name	A	B	C
Value *before* execution	5	10	30
Value *after* execution of			
ADD A TO C.	5	10	35
ADD A B TO C.	5	10	45
ADD A 18 B GIVING C.	5	10	33
ADD A 18 B TO C.	5	10	63
ADD 1 TO C.	5	10	31

SUBTRACT

The SUBTRACT verb also has two formats:

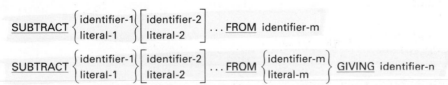

In the first format, the initial value of identifier-m is replaced by the result of the subtraction. In the second format, the initial value of either identifier-m or literal-m is unchanged as the result is stored in identifier-n. Regardless of which option is used, the value of only one data name is changed.

Example 3.3

Section II
The COBOL Language

SUBTRACT A FROM B.

Before execution:	A	5	B	15
After execution:	A	5	B	10

In Example 3.3, the SUBTRACT verb causes the value of A (5) to be subtracted from the initial value of B (15) and the result (10) to be stored in B. Only the value of B was changed.

Example 3.4

SUBTRACT A FROM B GIVING C.

Before execution:	A	5	B	15	C	100
After execution:	A	5	B	15	C	10

In the "FROM . . . GIVING" format of Example 3.4, the value of A (5) is subtracted from the value of B (15), and the result (10) is placed in C. The values of A and B are unchanged, and the initial value of C (100) is replaced by 10. Table 3.2 contains additional examples. In each example, the instruction is assumed to operate on the initial contents of A, B, and C.

Table 3.2 The SUBTRACT Instruction

Data name	A	B	C	D
Value *before* execution	5	10	30	100
Value *after* execution of				
SUBTRACT A FROM C.	5	10	25	100
SUBTRACT A B FROM C.	5	10	15	100
SUBTRACT A B FROM C GIVING D.	5	10	30	15
SUBTRACT 10 FROM C.	5	10	20	100

MULTIPLY

The MULTIPLY format is shown below:

$$\text{MULTIPLY} \begin{Bmatrix} \text{identifier-1} \\ \text{literal-1} \end{Bmatrix} \underline{\text{BY}} \begin{Bmatrix} \text{identifier-2} \\ \text{literal-2} \end{Bmatrix} [\underline{\text{GIVING}}\ \text{identifier-3}]$$

The use of GIVING is optional. If it is used, then the result of the multiplication is stored in identifier-3. If GIVING is omitted, then the result is stored in identifier-2. Either way, the value of only one data name is changed. Consider Examples 3.5 and 3.6.

Example 3.5

MULTIPLY A BY B.

Before execution:	A	10	B	20
After execution:	A	10	B	200

Example 3.6

Chapter 3
The Procedure Division

MULTIPLY A BY B GIVING C.

Before execution: A `10`   B `20`   C `345`

After execution: A `10`   B `20`   C `200`

Table 3.3 contains additional examples of the MULTIPLY verb.

Table 3.3 The MULTIPLY Instruction

Data name	A	B	C
Value *before* execution	5	10	30
Value *after* execution of			
MULTIPLY B BY A GIVING C.	5	10	50
MULTIPLY A BY B GIVING C.	5	10	50
MULTIPLY A BY B.	5	50	30
MULTIPLY B BY A.	50	10	30
MULTIPLY A BY 3 GIVING C.	5	10	15

DIVIDE

The DIVIDE verb has two formats:

$$\underline{\text{DIVIDE}} \left\{ \begin{array}{l} \text{identifier-1} \\ \text{literal-1} \end{array} \right\} \underline{\text{INTO}} \ \text{identifier-2}$$

$$\underline{\text{DIVIDE}} \left\{ \begin{array}{l} \text{identifier-1} \\ \text{literal-1} \end{array} \right\} \left\{ \begin{array}{l} \underline{\text{INTO}} \\ \underline{\text{BY}} \end{array} \right\} \left\{ \begin{array}{l} \text{identifier-2} \\ \text{literal-2} \end{array} \right\} \underline{\text{GIVING}} \ \text{identifier-3}$$

In the first format the quotient replaces the initial value of identifier-2. In the second format, the quotient replaces the initial value of identifier-3. In either case, the value of only one data name is changed. Consider Examples 3.7 and 3.8.

Example 3.7

DIVIDE A INTO B.

Before execution: A `10`   B `50`

After execution: A `10`   B `5`

Example 3.8

DIVIDE A INTO B GIVING C:

Before execution: A `10`   B `50`   C `13`

After execution: A `10`   B `50`   C `5`

In Example 3.7, the initial value of B (50) is divided by the value of A (10), and the quotient (5) replaces the initial value of B. In Example 3.8, which uses the "GIVING" option, the quotient goes into C and the values of A and B are unaffected.

Table 3.4 contains additional examples of the DIVIDE verb.

Table 3.4 The DIVIDE Instruction

Data name	A	B	C
Value *before* execution	5	10	30
Value *after* execution of			
DIVIDE 2 INTO B.	5	5	30
DIVIDE 2 INTO B GIVING C.	5	10	5
DIVIDE B BY 5 GIVING A.	2	10	30
DIVIDE B INTO C.	5	10	3
DIVIDE A INTO B GIVING C.	5	10	2

COMPUTE

Any operation which can be done in an ADD, SUBTRACT, MULTIPLY, or DIVIDE statement may also be done using the COMPUTE instruction. In addition, the COMPUTE statement can combine different arithmetic operations in the same statement. For example, consider the following algebraic statement: $X = 2(A + B)/C$. A and B are first added together, the sum is multiplied by 2, and the product is divided by C. The single algebraic statement requires three COBOL arithmetic statements as shown. (Note that the true value of X is not obtained until after the last statement is executed.)

```
ADD A B GIVING X.
MULTIPLY 2 BY X.
DIVIDE C INTO X.
```

The above statements can be combined into a single COMPUTE with obvious benefits:

```
COMPUTE X = 2 * (A + B) / C.
```

The general format of the COMPUTE statement is

$$\underline{\text{COMPUTE}} \text{ identifier-1} = \begin{cases} \text{identifier-2} \\ \text{literal-2} \\ \text{expression} \end{cases}$$

Expressions are formed according to the following rules:

1. The symbols $+$, $-$, $*$, $/$, and $**$ denote addition, subtraction, multiplication, division, and exponentiation, respectively.
2. An expression consists of data names, literals, arithmetic symbols, and parentheses. Spaces must precede and follow arithmetic symbols.
3. Parentheses are used to clarify and in some cases alter the sequence of operations within a COMPUTE. Anything contained within the parentheses must also be a valid expression. The left parenthesis is preceded by a space, and the right parenthesis is followed by a space.

The COMPUTE statement calculates the value on the right side of the equal sign and stores it in the data name to the left of the equal sign. Expressions are evaluated as follows:

1. Anything contained in parentheses is evaluated first as a separate expression.

2. Within the expression exponentiation is done first, then multiplication or division, then addition or subtraction.

3. If rule 2 results in a tie, e.g., both addition and subtraction are present, then evaluation proceeds from left to right.

Table 3.5 contains examples to illustrate the formation and evaluation of expressions in a compute statement.

Table 3.5 The COMPUTE Instruction

Data name	A	B	C	Comments
Value *before* execution	2	3	10	Initial values
Value *after* execution of				
COMPUTE C = A + B.	2	3	5	Simple addition
COMPUTE C = A + B * 2.	2	3	8	Multiplication done *before* addition
COMPUTE C = (A + B) * 2.	2	3	10	Parentheses evaluated first
COMPUTE C = A ** B.	2	3	8	Algebraically, $c = a^b$
COMPUTE C = B ** A.	2	3	9	Algebraically, $c = b^a$

Table 3.6 should further clarify evaluation of the COBOL COMPUTE. This table contains several algebraic expressions and the corresponding COMPUTE statements to accomplish the intended logic. Note that parentheses are often required in the COMPUTE which are not present in the algebraic counterpart. Parentheses may also be optionally used to clarify the intent of a COMPUTE statement; however, their use in Table 3.6 is mandatory in all instances.

Table 3.6 The COMPUTE Instruction Continued

Algebraic Expression	COBOL COMPUTE
$x = a + b$	COMPUTE X = A + B.
$x = \dfrac{a + b}{2}$	COMPUTE X = (A + B) / 2.
$x = \dfrac{(a + b)c}{2}$	COMPUTE X = (A + B) * C / 2.
$x = \dfrac{a + b}{2c}$	COMPUTE X = (A + B) / (2 * C).
$x = \sqrt{a}$	COMPUTE X = A ** .5.
$x = \dfrac{a^2 + b^2}{c^2}$	COMPUTE X = (A ** 2 + B ** 2) / C ** 2.

An abbreviated format of the READ verb is

> READ file-name AT END statement

As an example, consider line 37 of the engineering senior problem in Figure 1.7:

> READ CARD-FILE, AT END GO TO END-OF-JOB.

This statement causes a record (i.e., a card) to be read into main storage. If, however, the end-of-file condition has been reached, i.e., there are no more cards, then control passes to the paragraph END-OF-JOB. Thus the computer is directed to execute the first statement in the paragraph END-OF-JOB.

Look carefully at Figure 1.7. The file name (CARD-FILE) in the READ statement appears in four other lines in the COBOL program. It is in a SELECT statement in the environment division (line 13), in an FD in the data division (line 17), and in an OPEN and CLOSE in the procedure division (lines 35 and 46).

An abbreviated format of the WRITE verb is **WRITE**

$$\underline{\text{WRITE}} \text{ record-name} \left[\left\{ \begin{array}{l} \text{AFTER} \\ \text{BEFORE} \end{array} \right\} \underline{\text{ADVANCING}} \text{ integer LINES} \right]$$

The WRITE statement transfers data from main storage to an output device. The ADVANCING option controls line spacing on a printer; if omitted, single spacing occurs. If AFTER ADVANCING 3 LINES is used, the printer triple spaces (i.e., skips two lines and writes on the third). Logically enough, the BEFORE option causes the line to be written first, after which the specified number of lines are skipped.

Note that the WRITE statement contains a record name, whereas the READ statement contains a file name. The record name in the WRITE will appear as an 01 entry in the file section of the data division. The file in which it is contained will appear in SELECT, FD, OPEN, and CLOSE statements.

Every file in a COBOL program must be "opened" before it can be accessed. **OPEN** The OPEN verb causes the operating system to initiate action to make a file available for processing. For example, it can ensure that the proper reel of tape has been mounted.

The format of the OPEN is

$$\underline{\text{OPEN}} \left\{ \begin{array}{l} \underline{\text{INPUT}} \\ \underline{\text{I-O}} \\ \underline{\text{OUTPUT}} \end{array} \right\} \text{file-name-1} \text{ [,file-name-2 ...]}$$

Notice that one must specify the type of file in an OPEN statement. INPUT is used for a file that can be read only (e.g., a card file). OUTPUT is used for a file that can be written only (e.g., a print file). An I/O file can be both read or written, and such files are not discussed until Chapter 16.

Line 35 of the engineering senior problem contains an OPEN in which two files are opened in the same statement.

        OPEN INPUT CARD-FILE, OUTPUT PRINT-FILE.

An alternative way to accomplish the same thing is to use two OPEN statements:

        OPEN INPUT CARD-FILE.
        OPEN OUTPUT PRINT-FILE.

All files must be closed before processing terminates. The format of the **CLOSE** CLOSE is simply

        CLOSE file-name-1 [,file-name-2] ...

Notice that several files may be closed in the same statement. Further, the type of file, i.e., INPUT, OUTPUT, or I-O, is not specified. Statement 46 in the engineering senior problem provides an example:

        CLOSE CARD-FILE PRINT-FILE.

The MOVE statement accomplishes data transfer, i.e., the movement of data **MOVE** from one storage location to another. The format is

$$MOVE \begin{Bmatrix} \text{identifier-1} \\ \text{literal} \end{Bmatrix} \underline{TO} \text{ identifier-2 } [\text{identifier-3}]\dots$$

Consider the following three examples:

```
MOVE 80 TO PRICE-PER-CREDIT.
MOVE 'ABC UNIVERSITY' TO SCHOOL-NAME.
MOVE CARD-NAME TO PRINT-NAME.
```

The first example moves a numeric literal, 80, to the data name PRICE-PER-CREDIT. The second moves a nonnumeric literal, ABC UNIVERSITY, to SCHOOL-NAME. The third example is taken from line 42 of the engineering senior problem and transfers data from an input to an output area for subsequent printing.

The figurative constants, ZEROS and SPACES, are frequently used in a MOVE as shown:

```
MOVE SPACES TO PRINT-LINE.
MOVE ZEROS TO TOTAL-NUMBER,
```

The first statement moves spaces (i.e., blanks) to the data name PRINT-LINE. The second statement moves numeric zeros to TOTAL-NUMBER.

One final point: As can be seen from the MOVE format, a given quantity may be moved to several data names in the same statement. For example,

```
MOVE 10 TO FIELD-A FIELD-B FIELD-C.
```

is equivalent to

```
MOVE 10 TO FIELD-A.
MOVE 10 TO FIELD-B.
MOVE 10 TO FIELD-C.
```

The results of a MOVE depend on the picture of the receiving field; i.e., whenever the receiving field has a picture different from that of the sending field, a conversion must take place. Further, certain moves are not permitted. Table 3.7 summarizes the rules of the MOVE. (It is not necessary that the reader commit Table 3.7, or the discussion which follows, to memory. Instead he should be aware that certain restrictions exist and know where to turn when questions arise later. Numeric edited fields are discussed in Chapters 4 and 8.)

Inspection of Table 3.7 shows that an alphabetic field cannot be moved to a numeric field and vice versa. However, even Table 3.7 does not tell the whole

Table 3.7 Rules of the MOVE Statement

Source Field	Receiving Field				
	Group	Alphabetic	Alpha-numeric	Numeric	Numeric Edited
Group	Valid	Valid	Valid	Valid	Valid
Alphabetic	Valid	Valid	Valid	Invalid	Invalid
Alphanumeric	Valid	Valid	Valid	Invalid	Invalid
Numeric	Valid	Invalid	Integers only	Valid	Valid
Numeric edited	Valid	Invalid	Valid	Invalid	Invalid

story, e.g., what happens if a field with a picture of X(3) is moved to a picture of X(5) or vice versa? Two additional statements clarify the action of the move:

1. Data moved from an alphanumeric area to an alphanumeric area are moved one character at a time from left to right. If the receiving field is bigger than the sending field, it is padded on the right with blanks; if the receiving field is smaller than the sending field, the rightmost characters are truncated.
2. A numeric field moved to a numeric field is always aligned according to the decimal point. If the receiving field is larger than the sending field, high-order zeros are added. If the receiving field is smaller than the sending field, the high-order positions are truncated.

Statements 1 and 2 above are illustrated in Table 3.8:

Table 3.8 Illustration of the MOVE Statement

Source Field		Receiving Field	
Picture	Contents	Picture	Contents
X(5)	A B C D E	X(5)	A B C D E
X(5)	A B C D E	X(4)	A B C D
X(5)	A B C D E	X(6)	A B C D E
9(5)	1 2 3 4 5	9(5)	1 2 3 4 5
9(5)	1 2 3 4 5	9(4)	2 3 4 5
9(5)	1 2 3 4 5	9(6)	0 1 2 3 4 5

One final point: The above discussion pertains to elementary items only. *If the receiving field is a group item, the move takes place as though the receiving field were an alphanumeric item, with padding or truncation on the right as necessary.*

Transfer of Control

The instructions in a COBOL program are executed sequentially unless a transfer of control statement is encountered. In the engineering senior problem of Chapter 1, execution begins with the OPEN at line 35. The second executed instruction is the READ of line 37. Instructions are executed in sequential order until the IF statement in line 38 is reached. The next instruction after the IF depends on the result of the comparison in the IF statement; it will be either the READ in line 37 or the IF in line 39.

Since the IF statement varies the normal path of execution, depending on the result of a comparison, it is known as a conditional transfer of control statement. On the other hand, the GO TO statement always causes the same branch and is known as an unconditional transfer of control. The IF and GO TO statements are the subject of this section.

GO TO

The format of the GO TO is simply

GO TO procedure-name.

The procedure name denotes either a paragraph or section name. However, the present discussion is limited to paragraph names, and thus the object of our GO TO's will always be a paragraph name. Individual statements can be reached only by entering the paragraph in which they are contained; i.e., one does not branch to an individual statement per se but rather to the paragraph in which that statement is contained. In the engineering senior problem, for example, one branches to the paragraph READ-A-CARD, which contains the instructions to read a card.

IF

The IF statement is one of the more powerful in COBOL. For the present, our concern is only a few of the available options, and we shall defer additional discussion to Chapters 6 and 7. The format of the IF statement is

IF condition [THEN] statement-1 [ELSE statement-2]

The condition in the IF statement involves the comparison of two quantities. The syntax of the condition was presented under COBOL formats at the beginning of this chapter.

The IF statement may be used with or without the ELSE option. The action of the IF is best described with the aid of Figures 3.1 and 3.2.

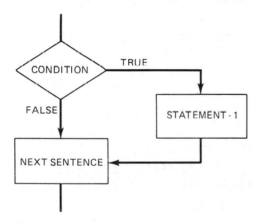

Figure 3.1 IF Statement without the ELSE Option

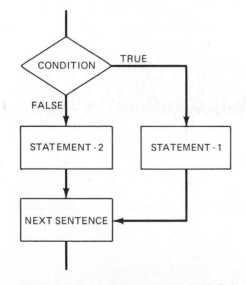

Figure 3.2 IF Statement with the ELSE Option

In Figure 3.1 a condition is tested. If the condition is true, then statement-1 is executed, after which execution continues with the block called next sentence. If the condition is false, execution continues immediately with the next sentence block.

A condition is tested in Figure 3.2. If true, then statement-1 is executed followed by the next sentence block. If the condition is false, then statement-2 is executed and followed by next sentence.

Figure 3.3 contains procedure division statements to illustrate transfer of control. Processing specifications are as follows:

1. Read a card file.
2. Calculate separate totals for qualified men and women who meet all the following:
   a. Have 10 years or less of service,
   b. Are 30 years old or younger,
   c. Earn $15,000 or more.

```
PROCEDURE DIVISION.
HOUSEKEEPING.
        .
        .
        .

READ-A-CARD.
    READ CARD-FILE, AT END GO TO END-OF-JOB-PROCESSING.
    IF SERVICE > 10 GO TO READ-A-CARD.
    IF AGE IS GREATER THAN 30 GO TO READ-A-CARD.
    IF SALARY LESS THAN 15000 GO TO READ-A-CARD.
    IF SEX = 'M' ADD 1 TO NUMBER-OF-MEN,
        ELSE ADD 1 TO NUMBER-OF-WOMEN.
    GO TO READ-A-CARD.
END-OF-JOB-PROCESSING.
        .
        .
        .

    STOP RUN.
```

Figure 3.3 Illustration of Transfer of Control

Note that an incoming employee must pass three tests, service, age, and salary, in order to qualify. If any of these conditions is not met, the employee is not counted, and another card is read. If the sex of a qualified employee is male, then the number of qualified men is incremented by 1; otherwise the number of qualified women is incremented.

Coding for the HOUSEKEEPING and END-OF-JOB-PROCESSING paragraphs is not shown. Finally, note the flexibility in the COBOL coding for the IF statements as discussed earlier.

Every program must have at least one STOP statement; the format is   **STOP**

$$\underline{STOP} \begin{Bmatrix} \text{literal} \\ \underline{RUN} \end{Bmatrix}$$

When STOP RUN is encountered, execution of the COBOL program terminates, and control passes back to the operating system. The literal option can be used to print a message to the operator, but its use is not encouraged at this time.

It is important to realize that STOP RUN need not be the last statement in the procedure division. Further, there may be more than one of these statements in a given program. STOP RUN means the programmer wants the job to end. The usual reason is that the program has finished its work; e.g., it ran out of data cards. There could, however, be other reasons, namely severe errors for which the program should terminate as well.

Several procedure division verbs were introduced as shown:

Summary

Arithmetic:
ADD
SUBTRACT
MULTIPLY
DIVIDE
COMPUTE

Input/output:
READ
WRITE
OPEN
CLOSE

Transfer of control:
IF
GO TO

Data transfer:
MOVE

Program termination:
STOP RUN

In the next chapter we shall study the other divisions in a COBOL program.

**REVIEW
EXERCISES**

TRUE	FALSE		
☐	☐	1	The ADD instruction changes the value of only one data name.
☐	☐	2	Both GIVING and TO may be present in the same ADD instruction.
☐	☐	3	A valid ADD instruction may contain neither GIVING nor TO.
☐	☐	4	Both FROM and GIVING may appear in the same SUBTRACT instruction.
☐	☐	5	The use of GIVING is optional in the MULTIPLY verb.
☐	☐	6	The reserved word INTO must appear in a DIVIDE statement.
☐	☐	7	In the DIVIDE statement, the dividend is always identifier-1.
☐	☐	8	Multiplication and division can be performed in the same MULTIPLY statement.
☐	☐	9	Multiplication and addition can be performed in the same COMPUTE statement.
☐	☐	10	In a COMPUTE statement, with no parentheses, multiplication is always done before subtraction.
☐	☐	11	In a COMPUTE statement, with no parentheses, multiplication is always done before division.
☐	☐	12	Parentheses are sometimes required in a COMPUTE statement.

TRUE	FALSE		
☐	☐	**13**	The COMPUTE statement changes the value of only one data name.
☐	☐	**14**	The IF statement must always contain the ELSE option.
☐	☐	**15**	The GO TO statement is known as an unconditional transfer of control statement.
☐	☐	**16**	A program may contain more than one STOP RUN statement.
☐	☐	**17**	STOP RUN must be the last statement in the procedure division.
☐	☐	**18**	The ADVANCING option is mandatory in the WRITE statement.
☐	☐	**19**	The READ statement contains a record name.
☐	☐	**20**	The WRITE statement contains a record name.
☐	☐	**21**	The OPEN and CLOSE statements are optional.

PROBLEMS

1 Some of the arithmetic statements below are invalid. Identify those which are invalid, and state why they are unacceptable to the COBOL compiler.
(a) ADD A B C.
(b) SUBTRACT 10 FROM A.
(c) SUBTRACT A FROM 10.
(d) ADD A TO B GIVING C.
(e) SUBTRACT A FROM B GIVING C.
(f) MULTIPLY A BY 10.
(g) MULTIPLY 10 BY A.
(h) MULTIPLY A BY 10 GIVING B.
(i) DIVIDE A BY B.
(j) DIVIDE A INTO B.
(k) DIVIDE A INTO B GIVING C.
(l) DIVIDE B BY A GIVING C.
(m) COMPUTE X = A + B.
(n) COMPUTE X = 2(A + B).
(o) COMPUTE V = 20 / A − C.

2 Complete the table below. In each instance, refer to the *initial* values of A, B, C, and D.

Data name	A	B	C	D
Value *before* execution	4	8	12	1
Value *after* execution of				
ADD 1 TO D.				
ADD A B C GIVING D.				
ADD A B C TO D.				
SUBTRACT A B FROM C.				
SUBTRACT A B FROM C GIVING D.				
MULTIPLY A BY B.				
MULTIPLY B BY A.				
DIVIDE A INTO C.				
DIVIDE C BY A.				
DIVIDE C BY A GIVING D.				
COMPUTE D = A + B / 2 * D.				
COMPUTE D = (A + B) / (2 * D).				
COMPUTE D = A + B / (2 * D).				
COMPUTE D = (A + B)/2 * D.				
COMPUTE D = A + (B / 2) * D.				

3 Complete the table below for valid statements only. In each instance, refer to the *initial* value of A, B, C, and D. If a MOVE statement is invalid, indicate it as such and state the reason why.

Data name	A	B	C	D
Value *before* execution	5	6	7	8

Value *after* execution of
   MOVE C TO SPACE.
   MOVE ZERO TO A, B, C.
   MOVE D TO B.
   MOVE SPACE TO A, B.
   MOVE 'X' TO A.
   MOVE A TO 'X'.

4 Develop a flowchart and procedure division code to calculate weekly withholding taxes as follows:

     16% on first $200.
     18% on amounts between $200 and $240.
     20% on anything over $240.

Thus if John Jones earned $300, his withholding tax would be

16% of $200	$= .16 \times 200 =$	32.00
+18% on amount between $200 and $240	$= .18 \times 40 \ =$	7.20
+20% on amount over $240	$= .20 \times 60 \ =$	12.00
TOTAL	$=$	$51.20

Assume that GROSS-PAY is already calculated. Further assume that the proper data division entries have been established to handle decimal points (more on this in Chapter 4).

5 Some of the following statements are invalid. Indicate those which are, and state why they are invalid. (Assume FILE-ONE and FILE-TWO are file names, RECORD-ONE is a record name, and PARAGRAPH-THREE is a paragraph name.)
(a) OPEN INPUT RECORD-ONE.
(b) OPEN INPUT FILE-ONE OUTPUT FILE-TWO.
(c) OPEN INPUT FILE-ONE.
(d) CLOSE OUTPUT FILE-ONE.
(e) READ FILE-ONE.
(f) READ FILE-ONE AT END GO TO PARAGRAPH-THREE.
(g) READ RECORD-ONE AT END GO TO PARAGRAPH-THREE.
(h) WRITE RECORD-ONE.
(i) WRITE RECORD-ONE AFTER ADVANCING TWO LINES.
(j) WRITE RECORD-ONE BEFORE ADVANCING TWO LINES.
(k) CLOSE FILE-ONE FILE-TWO.
(l) WRITE FILE-ONE.
(m) WRITE RECORD-ONE AT END GO TO PARAGRAPH-THREE.

6 Write COBOL COMPUTE statements to accomplish the intended logic:
(a) $x = a + b + c$

(b) $x = \dfrac{a + bc}{2}$

(c) $x = a^2 + b^2 + c^2$

(d) $x = \dfrac{a + b}{2} - c$

(e) $x = a + b$

(f) $x = \sqrt{\dfrac{a + b}{2c}}$

(g) $x = \sqrt{\dfrac{a^2 + b^2}{c^2 - d^2}} + 2e$

7 Write procedure division code for the following:

(a)
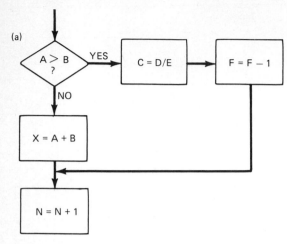

(b)
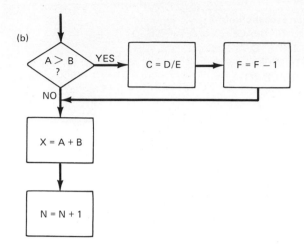

8 Write procedure division code for the following:

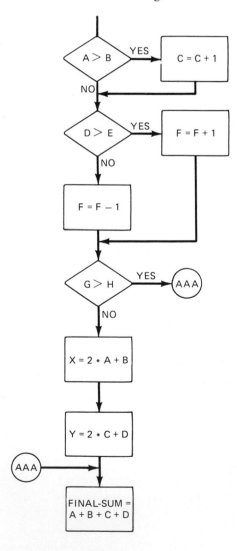

9 Complete the following table, showing the contents of the receiving field. If a particular move is invalid, indicate it as such (assume elementary moves only).

	Sending Field		Receiving Field	
	Picture	Contents	Picture	Contents
(a)	A(4)	H O P E	X(4)	
(b)	A(4)	H O P E	9(4)	
(c)	A(4)	H O P E	A(3)	
(d)	A(4)	H O P E	X(5)	
(e)	9(4)	6 7 8 9	A(4)	
(f)	9(4)	6 7 8 9	9(3)	
(g)	9(4)	6 7 8 9	9(5)	
(h)	999V9	6 7 8 9	9(4)	
(i)	999V9	6 7 8 9	9(4)V9	
(j)	999V9	6 7 8 9	9(3)V99	
(k)	999V9	6 7 8 9	99V99	

Note: The V in questions (h), (i), (j), and (k) indicates an assumed decimal point (see Chapter 4).

51

The Other Divisions

Chapter 1 began with a rapid introduction to COBOL. We learned that there **Overview** are four divisions in a COBOL program and that they must come in a specified order: IDENTIFICATION, ENVIRONMENT, DATA, and PROCEDURE. In the previous chapter we studied the procedure division, which contains the logic of a COBOL program. Now we shall look at the other divisions in order to write a complete COBOL program.

The emphasis in this chapter is on the data division. We shall begin with level numbers and picture clauses. Next we shall look at the file and working storage sections. Finally we shall learn how to edit data and "dress-up" printed reports.

The chapter ends with the development of a complete program for tuition billing. It is a substantial problem and will require you to use everything covered so far. However, at the conclusion of this chapter you will be well on your way toward writing meaningful programs.

The identification division is the first of the four divisions in a COBOL **Identification Division** program. Its function is to provide identifying information about the program, such as author, date written, security, etc. The division consists of a division header and up to seven paragraphs, as shown on the following page.

```
IDENTIFICATION DIVISION.
  PROGRAM-ID.        program-name.
  [AUTHOR.           comment-entry.]
  [INSTALLATION.     comment-entry.]
  [DATE-WRITTEN.     comment-entry.]
  [DATE-COMPILED.    comment-entry.]
  [SECURITY.         comment-entry.]
  [REMARKS.          comment-entry.]
```

Only the division header and PROGRAM-ID paragraph are required. The remaining paragraphs are optional and contain documentation about the program. The DATE-COMPILED paragraph is worthy of special mention. If it is used, the compiler will automatically insert the current date during program compilation. A completed identification division is shown below:

```
IDENTIFICATION  DIVISION.
PROGRAM-ID.     TUITION.
AUTHOR.         GRAUER AND CRAWFORD.
INSTALLATION.   GRAUER AND CRAWFORD SCHOOL OF DATA PROCESSING.
DATE-WRITTEN.   SEPTEMBER 1, 1976.
DATE-COMPILED.  The compiler will supply the date of compilation.
SECURITY.       TOP SECRET—INSTRUCTORS ONLY.
REMARKS.        THIS PARAGRAPH CONSISTS OF SEVERAL SENTENCES
                DESCRIBING THE PROGRAM. ONE SIMPLY WRITES SENTENCE
                AFTER SENTENCE UNTIL ONE RUNS OUT OF THINGS TO SAY.
```

Coding for the identification division follows the general rules described in Chapter 2. The division header and paragraph names begin in column 8 (A margin). All other entries begin in or past column 12 (B margin).

The environment division serves two functions:

Environment Division

1. It identifies the computer to be used for compiling and executing the program (usually one and the same). This is done in the configuration section.
2. It relates the files used in the program to I-O devices. This is done in the input-output section.
3. It can contain a special-names paragraph to establish carriage control for printed reports. (See Figure 4.8, COBOL lines 11, 12, and 93).

The nature of these functions makes the environment division heavily dependent on the computer on which one is working. Thus the environment division for a COBOL program on a Univac system is significantly different from that of a program for an IBM configuration. You should consult either your instructor or computer center for the proper entries at your installation. Our illustrations in this section are for an IBM OS system.

The configuration section has the format

```
CONFIGURATION SECTION.
SOURCE-COMPUTER.  computer-name.
OBJECT-COMPUTER.  computer-name.
```

The section header and paragraph names begin in the A margin. The computer name entries begin in or past column 12.

The input-output section relates the files known to the COBOL program to the files known to the operating system. A file is a collection of records of similar purpose. In the engineering senior problem of Chapter 1, each data card is a record, and the set of data cards is known collectively as a file. Similarly, each printed line of output is a record, and the set of print lines is a file.

Each file in a COBOL program has its own SELECT and ASSIGN clauses, which appear in the file-control paragraph of the input-output section of the environment division. The format of the ASSIGN clause varies from compiler to compiler. The coding below is taken from lines 11–14 in the engineering senior problem and is for an IBM OS system:

```
INPUT-OUTPUT SECTION.
FILE-CONTROL.
    SELECT CARD-FILE ASSIGN TO UR-2540R-S-SYSIN.
    SELECT PRINT-FILE ASSIGN TO UR-1403-S-SYSOUT.
```

As before, section headers and paragraph names begin in the A margin (column 8). SELECT statements begin in or past column 12. The OS SELECT statement has the format

<u>SELECT</u> file-name <u>ASSIGN</u> TO system-name-1

where the system name varies from installation to installation depending on the physical I/O devices. Our example is for a 2540 card reader and 1403 printer.

The dependence of the environment division on the individual computer installation bears repeating. You should consult either your instructor or computer center for the proper statements to use in your program.

Data Division

The data division describes all data fields used in the program. The number of characters in each data item are specified and also classified as to type, e.g., numeric or alphabetic. Finally the relationship among data is described. The description of data is accomplished through the picture clause and level numbers.

PICTURE Clause

All data names are described according to size and class. Size specifies the number of characters in a field. Class denotes the type of field. For the present we shall restrict type to alphabetic, numeric, or alphanumeric, denoted by A, 9, or X, respectively. The size of a field is indicated by the number of times the A, 9, or X is repeated. Thus a data name with a picture of AAAA or A(4) is a four-position alphabetic field. In similar fashion, 999 and X(5) denote a three-position numeric field and a five-position alphanumeric field, respectively.

Level Numbers

Data items in COBOL are classified as either elementary or group items. A group item is one which can be further divided, whereas an elementary item cannot be further divided. As an example, consider Figure 4.1, depicting a student exam card.

In Figure 4.1, student-name is considered a group item since it is divided into three fields: last-name, first-name, and initial. Last-name, first-name, and middle-initial are elementary items since they are not further divided. Social-security-number is an elementary item. Exam-scores is a group item, as are math and english. Algebra, geometry, reading, etc., are elementary items.

Level numbers are used to describe the hierarchy between group and elementary items; in effect they show which elementary items comprise a group

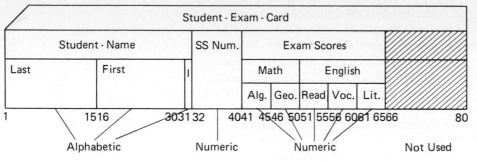

Figure 4.1 Student Exam Card

item. Level numbers can assume values of 01–49 inclusive, 66, 77, and 88. (Levels 66 and 88 have special meanings; 88-level entries are mentioned in Chapters 7 and 8; 66-level entries are not covered. 77-Level entries appear in the working-storage section of the data division and are discussed later in this chapter.) Level numbers and picture clauses are best described by example. Consider the data division statements of Figure 4.2, which correspond to the student exam card of Figure 4.1.

```
01   STUDENT-EXAM-CARD.
     05   STUDENT-NAME.
          10   LAST-NAME        PICTURE IS A(15).
          10   FIRST-NAME       PICTURE IS A(15).
          10   MID-INITIAL      PICTURE IS A.
     05   SOC-SEC-NUM           PICTURE IS 9(9).
     05   EXAM-SCORES.
          10   MATH.
               15   ALGEBRA     PICTURE IS 99999.
               15   GEOMETRY    PICTURE IS 9(5).
          10   ENGLISH.
               15   READING     PICTURE IS 99999.
               15   VOCABULARY  PICTURE IS 99999.
               15   LITERATURE  PICTURE IS 99999.
     05   FILLER                PICTURE IS X(15).
```

Figure 4.2 Data Division Code for Level Numbers and Picture Clauses

The data division code of Figure 4.2 is in accordance with basic rules pertaining to level numbers:

1. 01 is used to denote the record as a whole.
2. 02–49 are used for subfields in the record.
3. Only elementary items have picture clauses.

Level numbers need not be consecutive as long as elementary items have a numerically higher level number than the group item to which they belong.

In Figure 4.2 STUDENT-EXAM-CARD has a level number of 01. STUDENT-NAME is a subfield of STUDENT-EXAM-CARD, and hence it has a higher level number (05). LAST-NAME, FIRST-NAME, and MID-INITIAL are subfields of STUDENT-NAME, and all have the level number 10. SOC-SEC-NUM and EXAM-SCORES are also subfields of STUDENT-EXAM-CARD and have the same level number as STUDENT-NAME. EXAM-SCORES in turn is subdivided into two group items, MATH and ENGLISH, which in turn are further subdivided into elementary items.

Each elementary item must have a picture clause to describe the data it contains. LAST-NAME has "PICTURE IS A(15)," denoting a 15-position alphabetic field. However, there is no picture entry for STUDENT-NAME since that is a group item. The parentheses in a picture entry denote repetition; thus the entries of 9(5) and 99999 for ALGEBRA and GEOMETRY both depict 5-position numeric fields. Finally, note the FILLER entry with "PICTURE IS X(15)." FILLER denotes a field with no useful information, i.e., data that are not referenced in this program. X(15) denotes 15 positions of alphanumeric data. Since the student-exam-card of Figure 4.1 is presumed to contain 80 columns, all 80 columns must be accounted for. The last field (EXAM-SCORES, ENGLISH, or LITERATURE) ends in column 65—hence the need for an entry to account for the last 15 columns.

Considerable flexibility is permitted with level numbers and picture clauses. Any level numbers from 02 to 49 are permitted in describing subfields as long as the basic rules are followed. Thus 04, 08, and 12 could be used in lieu of 05, 10, and 15. Next the picture clause itself can assume any one of four forms: PICTURE IS, PICTURE, PIC IS, or PIC. Finally, parentheses may be used to signal repetition of a picture type; i.e., A(3) is equivalent to AAA. Figure 4.3 is an alternative way of coding Figure 4.2 with emphasis on the above flexibility.

```
01   STUDENT-EXAM-CARD.
     04   STUDENT-NAME.
          08   LAST-NAME        PIC           A(15).
          08   FIRST-NAME       PIC IS        A(15).
          08   MID-INITIAL      PICTURE IS A.
     04   SOC-SEC-NUM           PIC IS        9(9).
     04   EXAM SCORES.
          08   MATH.
               12   ALGEBRA     PIC           9(5).
               12   GEOMETRY    PIC           99999.
          08   ENGLISH.
               12   READING     PICTURE       9(5).
               12   VOCABULARY  PICTURE IS 99999.
               12   LITERATURE  PIC IS        99999.
     04   FILLER                PIC           X(15).
```

Figure 4.3 Data Division Code for Level Numbers and Picture Clauses: II

The file section is typically the first section in the data division. It describes every file mentioned in a SELECT statement in the environment division. (If, however, there are no input/output files, then there is no need for the file section.)

File Section

The file section contains both file description (FD) and record description entries (i.e., level number and picture clause). We have already discussed the latter. An abbreviated format for the file description (FD) entry is as follows:

```
FD   file-name
     [RECORDING MODE IS mode]
            ⎧RECORDS ARE⎫ ⎧OMITTED ⎫
     LABEL  ⎨RECORD  IS  ⎬ ⎨STANDARD⎬
            ⎩           ⎭ ⎩        ⎭
     [RECORD CONTAINS integer-1 CHARACTERS]
     [DATA RECORD IS data-name-1]
```

A SELECT statement is required for each file (FD) in the program. FD appears in the A margin, followed by the file name beginning in column 12. The FD may contain up to six clauses, four of which are shown. The clauses may appear in any order, and only the last clause has a period. The LABEL

RECORDS clause is the only required one, but it is accepted practice to code the others as well.

The FD provides information about the physical characteristics of a file. The RECORD CONTAINS clause specifies the number of characters per record (this entry should equal the sum of the picture clauses in the record description). The LABEL RECORDS clause has special meaning for tape and disk files (Chapters 15 and 16). For card and print files, however, we use the following entry: LABEL RECORDS ARE OMITTED. The RECORDING MODE clause indicates whether records are Fixed (i.e., every record has the same number of characters) or Variable (different records have different number of characters) length. For card and print files, we usually use RECORDING MODE IS F. Finally, the DATA RECORD clause specifies the name of the 01 entry for that file. A completed FD for the student-exam-card of Figure 4.1 is coded in Figure 4.4.

```
FD   CARD-FILE
     RECORDING MODE IS F    RECFM
     LABEL RECORDS ARE OMITTED
     RECORD CONTAINS 80 CHARACTERS   LRECL
     DATA RECORD IS STUDENT-EXAM-CARD.
```

Figure 4.4 FD for Student-Exam-Card

In Figure 4.4 CARD-FILE is the file name which would appear in a SELECT statement for the file (see environment division in this chapter). STUDENT-EXAM-CARD is the record name, i.e., the 01 entry in Figure 4.2 or 4.3.

Working Storage Section

The working storage section is used for storing intermediate results and/or constants needed by the program. In effect it defines data used by the program which are not read during program execution.

Working storage typically contains two types of entries. The first is for independent, elementary items, i.e., those data names that have no hierarchical relationship to one another. These entries are assigned level number 77 and precede all other entries in working storage. Group items, beginning with level 01, are the second type of entry appearing in working storage. Group items follow 77-level entries and use level numbers as discussed earlier.

An example of a working storage section appears in Figure 4.5.

```
WORKING-STORAGE SECTION.
77   TOTAL-STUDENTS     PIC 9(3)      VALUE ZEROS.
77   PRICE-PER-CREDIT   PIC 99        VALUE 80.
01   HEADING-LINE.
     05   FILLER        PIC X(5)      VALUE SPACES.
     05   FILLER        PIC X(12)     VALUE 'STUDENT NAME'.
     05   FILLER        PIC X(5)      VALUE SPACES.
     05   FILLER        PIC X(5)      VALUE 'MAJOR'.
     05   FILLER        PIC X(106)    VALUE SPACES.
```

Figure 4.5 An Example of the Working Storage Section

VALUE Clause

Figure 4.5 introduces the VALUE clause, which has the general form

VALUE IS literal

Literals are of three types: numeric (e.g., 80), nonnumeric (e.g., 'MAJOR'), and figurative constant (e.g., ZERO). Numeric and nonnumeric literals were discussed in Chapter 2 as a basic COBOL element. Figurative constants are COBOL reserved words with preassigned values. COBOL contains six of these constants, but only ZERO (equivalent forms are ZEROS and ZEROES) and SPACE (also SPACES) are discussed here.

The Value clause associated with a particular data name must be consistent with the corresponding picture clause. It is <u>incorrect</u> to use a nonnumeric literal with a numeric picture or a numeric literal with a nonnumeric picture. Consider

```
(correct)    77  FIELD-A    PIC 9    VALUE 2.
(incorrect)  77  FIELD-B    PIC X    VALUE 2.
(incorrect)  77  FIELD-C    PIC 9    VALUE '2'.
(correct)    77  FIELD-D    PIC X    VALUE '2'.
```

Only the entries for FIELD-A and FIELD-D are correct. FIELD-B has a nonnumeric picture but a numeric value. FIELD-C has a numeric picture but a nonnumeric value (remember, anything enclosed in quotes is a nonnumeric literal).

Assumed Decimal Point

Incoming numeric data are not allowed to contain actual decimal points. On first reading, that statement may be somewhat hard to take, so let's repeat it in different words. If incoming decimal data are contained on cards, no decimal points will be punched on the cards. Undoubtedly this should "bother" you. How, for example, does one read a field containing dollars and cents? The answer is an assumed decimal point.

Consider the COBOL entry

```
05  HOURLY-RATE    PICTURE IS 9V99.
```

Everything is familiar except the "V" imbedded in the picture clause. The "V" means an implied decimal point; i.e., HOURLY-RATE is a three-digit (there are three 9's) numeric field, with two of the digits coming after the decimal point.

To check your understanding, assume that 9876543210 is punched in columns 1–10 of an incoming data card and that the following data division entries apply:

```
01  INCOMING-DATA-CARD.
    05  FIELD-A        PIC 9V99.
    05  FIELD-B        PIC 99V9.
    05  FIELD-C        PIC 9.
    05  FIELD-D        PIC V999.
    05  FILLER         PIC X(70).
```

The values of FIELD-A, FIELD-B, FIELD-C, and FIELD-D are 9.87, 65.4, 3, and .210, respectively. FIELD-A is contained in the first three columns with two digits after the decimal point. FIELD-B is contained in the next three columns, i.e., in columns 4, 5, and 6, with one digit after the decimal point. FIELD-C is contained in column 7 with no decimal places. Finally, FIELD-D is contained in columns 8, 9, and 10, with three decimal places. The last 70 columns do not contain data, as indicated by the FILLER entry.

Incoming numeric fields typically do not contain anything other than digits. On the other hand, it is highly desirable to have dollar signs, commas, decimal points, etc., appear in printed reports. The problem is resolved by the use of editing symbols. Consider the two entries for FIELD-A and FIELD-A-EDITED:

```
05  FIELD-A          PIC 9V99.
05  FIELD-A-EDITED   PIC 9.99
```

FIELD-A is a three-digit numeric field, with two digits after the decimal point. FIELD-A-EDITED is a four-position edit field containing an actual decimal point. In a COBOL program all calculations would be done using FIELD-A. Then, just prior to printing, FIELD-A is moved to FIELD-A-EDITED, and the latter field is printed. For example,

Before MOVE:

V

FIELD-A | 7 | 8 | 3 | FIELD-A-EDITED | ? | . | ? | ? |

After execution of MOVE FIELD-A TO FIELD-A-EDITED.

V

FIELD-A | 7 | 8 | 3 | FIELD-A-EDITED | 7 | . | 8 | 3 |

Notice that the decimal point actually takes a position in FIELD-A-EDITED. However, it does not occupy a position in FIELD-A as it (the decimal point) is only implied.

There are many editing symbols in COBOL, and complete discussion is deferred to Chapter 8. For the present, we shall discuss the $, comma, and decimal point.

The appearance of a single $ causes a dollar sign to print in the indicated position.

```
05  FIELD-B          PIC 9(3)V99.
05  FIELD-B-EDITED   PIC $9(3).99.
```

Before MOVE:

V

FIELD-B | 6 | 5 | 4 | 3 | 2 | FIELD-B-EDITED | $ | ? | ? | ? | . | ? | ? |

After execution of MOVE FIELD-B TO FIELD-B-EDITED:

V

FIELD-B | 6 | 5 | 4 | 3 | 2 | FIELD-B-EDITED | $ | 6 | 5 | 4 | . | 3 | 2 |

Notice that the dollar sign and decimal point both take up a position in FIELD-B-EDITED.

It is also possible to obtain a "floating" dollar sign by using multiple dollar signs in the edited field. In this instance a single $ prints immediately to the left of the leftmost significant digit. Thus,

```
05  FIELD-C          PIC 9(3)V99.
05  FIELD-C-EDITED   PIC $$$$.99.
```

Before MOVE:

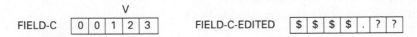

FIELD-C | 0 | 0 | 1 | 2 | 3 | FIELD-C-EDITED | $ | $ | $ | $ | . | ? | ? |

FIELD-C `0` `0` `1` `2` `3`   FIELD-C-EDITED ` ` ` ` `$` `1` `.` `2` `3`

A single dollar sign prints immediately before the leftmost digit in the field. FIELD-C-EDITED is a seven-position field, but the first two positions hold blanks.

The presence of a comma as an editing symbol causes a comma to print if it is preceded by a significant digit. If, however, a comma is preceded only by zeros, then it is suppressed. Consider

```
05   FIELD-D          PIC 9(4).
05   FIELD-D-EDITED   PIC $$,$$9.
```

Before MOVE:

FIELD-D `8` `7` `6` `5`   FIELD-D-EDITED `$` `$` `,` `$` `$` `?`

After execution of MOVE FIELD-D TO FIELD-D-EDITED:

FIELD-D `8` `7` `6` `5`   FIELD-D-EDITED `$` `8` `,` `7` `6` `5`

The comma prints in the indicated position. Suppose, however, that the contents of FIELD-D were 0087, instead of 8765. Now FIELD-D-EDITED would be

Before MOVE:

FIELD-D `0` `0` `8` `7`   FIELD-D-EDITED `$` `$` `,` `$` `$` `?`

After execution of MOVE FIELD-D TO FIELD-D-EDITED:

FIELD-D `0` `0` `8` `7`   FIELD-D-EDITED ` ` ` ` ` ` `$` `8` `7`

Notice that the dollar sign floats and that the comma is suppressed. Note also that all numeric moves are accomplished so that decimal alignment is maintained with truncation or addition of insignificant zeros. Information on editing is summarized in Table 4.1.

Table 4.1 Use of Editing Symbols

Source Field		Receiving Field	
PICTURE	*CONTENTS*	*PICTURE*	*CONTENTS*
9(4)	0678	9(4)	0678
9(4)	0678	$9(4)	$0678
9(4)	0678	$$$$	$678
9(4)V99	123456	9(4).99	1234.56
9(4)V99	123456	$9(4).99	$1234.56
9(4)V99	123456	$9,999.99	$1,234.56
9(4)	0008	$,$$$	$8
9(4)V9	12345	9(4)	1234
9(4)V9	12345	9(4).99	1234.50

Our text began with the presentation of a complete COBOL program in Chapter 1 (the engineering senior program). Our objective at that time was to remove the aura surrounding computer programming and to give the reader an immediate feel for COBOL. Since that time, we have come a long way. In Chapter 2 we learned the elements of COBOL, the rules of the coding sheet, and the procedure for problem solving. In Chapter 3 we studied the basic verbs of the procedure division. In this chapter we learned about the other divisions. Now we are ready to put this material together and solve a detailed problem about student billing.

Specifications for the student billing problem are as follows:

INPUT—A card has been prepared for every student in XYZ University with information as follows:

Field	Card Columns	Picture
Student name	1–20	A(20)
Social security #	21–29	9(9)
Credits	30–31	99
Union member	32	A
Scholarship	33–36	9(4)

PROCESSING—Student bills are to be calculated for every student as follows:

Tuition	$80 per credit
Union fee	$25 for members, $0 for nonmembers (members have a "Y" in column 32)
Activity fee	$25: 6 credits or less
	$50: 7–12 credits
	$75: more than 12 credits
Scholarship	Amount, if any, is punched in columns 33–36.
Student bill	Tuition + union fee
	+ activity fee
	− scholarship

In addition university-wide totals for each of these fields are required.

OUTPUT—Printed output is to be in accordance with Figure 4.6. Note the presence of literal information in the heading line and the dashed line after the heading line and before the total line. Also notice the use of edited data fields.

A page heading routine is *not* required; i.e., the heading line is required to appear only once before the first student record (see Problem 9).

Figure 4.7 contains a flowchart for the tuition billing problem. Note the presence of the HOUSEKEEPING block to remind us that certain tasks have to be done at the beginning of every program (e.g., open files). Realize also that blocks in the flowchart do not correspond one to one with statements in the procedure division. For example, computation of TUITION, UNION-FEE, and ACTIVITY-FEE take one block in the flowchart but will take several statements in the procedure division. This is as it should be. The flowchart is intended only as a guide in writing the program. It depicts the logic inherent in the program but at a higher level of aggregation; indeed if we insisted on one-to-one correspondence, we would in effect be writing the program twice.

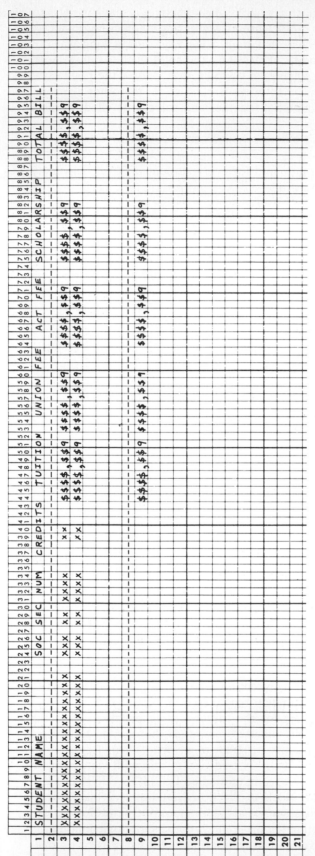

Figure 4.6 Required Output for Tuition Billing Problem

62

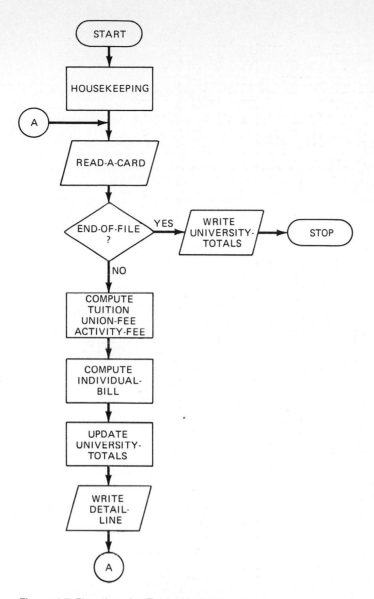

Figure 4.7 Flowchart for Tuition Billing Problem

Figure 4.8 contains the COBOL program for the tuition billing problem. It encompasses all the material covered to date and indeed is somewhat formidable the first time you see it. We suggest you take it in pieces and review those sections of the text as you need them. Some highlights:

1. The identification division: COBOL lines 1–3.
2. The environment division: COBOL lines 6–17. The two SELECT statements are applicable to our installation and may not be appropriate at yours.
3. The FD's for CARD-FILE and PRINT-FILE: COBOL lines 22–26 and 34–38.
4. The description for the incoming data cards: COBOL lines 27–33. Notice how this matches the problem description and the presence of the FILLER entry.
5. The use of edit symbols in a detail line: COBOL lines 39–56. The symbol "B" causes blanks to be inserted in the social security number (line 43). This is discussed further in Chapter 8.

```
00001          IDENTIFICATION DIVISION.
00002          PROGRAM-ID.  'TUITION'.
00003          AUTHOR.      THE BURSAR.
00004
00005
00006          ENVIRONMENT DIVISION.
00007
00008          CONFIGURATION SECTION.                    Used to cause printed output to
00009          SOURCE-COMPUTER.  IBM-370.                begin on new page (see COBOL
00010          OBJECT-COMPUTER.  IBM-370.                line 93)
00011          SPECIAL-NAMES.
00012              C01 IS TOP-OF-PAGE.
00013
00014          INPUT-OUTPUT SECTION.
00015          FILE-CONTROL.
00016              SELECT CARD-FILE ASSIGN TO UR-2540R-S-SYSIN.
00017              SELECT PRINT-FILE ASSIGN TO UR-1403-S-SYSOUT.
00018
00019                                           SELECT and FD for CARD-FILE
00020          DATA DIVISION.
00021          FILE SECTION.
00022          FD  CARD-FILE
00023              RECORDING MODE IS F
00024              LABEL RECORDS ARE OMITTED
00025              RECORD CONTAINS 80 CHARACTERS    FD for CARD-FILE
00026              DATA RECORD IS STUDENT-CARD.
00027          01  STUDENT-CARD.
00028              05  STUDENT-NAME     PICTURE IS A(20).
00029              05  SOC-SEC-NO       PICTURE IS 9(9).
00030   Incoming  05  CREDITS          PICTURE IS 9(2).
00031   record    05  UNION-MEMBER     PICTURE IS A.
00032              05  SCHOLARSHIP      PICTURE IS 9(4).
00033              05  FILLER           PICTURE IS X(44).
00034          FD  PRINT-FILE
00035              RECORDING MODE IS F
00036              LABEL RECORDS ARE OMITTED
00037              RECORD CONTAINS 133 CHARACTERS
00038              DATA RECORD IS PRINT-LINE.
00039          01  PRINT-LINE.
00040              05  FILLER                       PICTURE IS X.
00041              05  PRINT-STUDENT-NAME           PICTURE IS A(20).
00042              05  FILLER                       PICTURE IS X(2).
00043              05  PRINT-SOC-SEC-NO             PICTURE IS 999B99B9999.
00044              05  FILLER                       PICTURE IS X(4).
00045              05  PRINT-CREDITS                PICTURE IS 99.
00046              05  FILLER                       PICTURE IS X(3).
00047   Detail    05  PRINT-TUITION                PICTURE IS  $$$$,$$9.
00048   line      05  FILLER                       PICTURE IS X(1).
00049              05  PRINT-UNION-FEE              PICTURE IS  $$$$,$$9.
00050              05  FILLER                       PICTURE IS X(3).
00051              05  PRINT-ACTIVITY-FEE           PICTURE IS  $$$$,$$9.
00052              05  FILLER                       PICTURE IS X(3).
00053              05  PRINT-SCHOLARSHIP            PICTURE IS  $$$$,$$9.
00054              05  FILLER                       PICTURE IS X(5).
00055              05  PRINT-IND-BILL               PICTURE IS  $$$$,$$9.
00056              05  FILLER                       PICTURE IS X(38).
00057
00058          WORKING-STORAGE SECTION.
00059          77  TUITION           PICTURE IS 9(4)  VALUE IS ZEROS.
00060          77  ACTIVITY-FEE      PICTURE IS 9(2)  VALUE IS ZEROS.
00061          77  UNION-FEE         PICTURE IS 9(2)  VALUE IS ZEROS.
00062          77  INDIVIDUAL-BILL   PICTURE IS 9(4)  VALUE IS ZEROS.   Initialization
00063          77  TOTAL-TUITION     PICTURE IS 9(6)  VALUE IS ZEROS.   of 77 level
00064          77  TOTAL-SCHOLARSHIP PICTURE IS 9(6)  VALUE IS ZEROS.   entries
00065          77  TOTAL-ACTIVITY-FEE PICTURE IS 9(6) VALUE IS ZEROS.
00066          77  TOTAL-UNION-FEE   PICTURE IS 9(6)  VALUE IS ZEROS.
00067          77  TOTAL-IND-BILL    PICTURE IS 9(6)  VALUE IS ZEROS.
```

Figure 4.8 Student Billing Problem

```
00068              01  HEADER-LINE.
00069                  05  FILLER            PICTURE IS X.
00070                  05  HDG-NAME          PICTURE IS X(12) VALUE IS 'STUDENT NAME'.
00071                  05  FILLER            PICTURE IS X(10) VALUE IS SPACES.
00072                  05  HDG-SOC-SEC       PICTURE IS X(11) VALUE IS 'SOC SEC NUM'.
00073                  05  FILLER            PICTURE IS X(2)  VALUE IS SPACES.
00074                  05  HDG-CREDITS       PICTURE IS X(7)  VALUE IS 'CREDITS'.
C00075                 05  FILLER            PICTURE IS X(2)  VALUE IS SPACES.
00076                  05  HDG-TUITION       PICTURE IS X(7)  VALUE IS 'TUITION'.
00077                  05  FILLER            PICTURE IS X(2)  VALUE IS SPACES.
00078                  05  HDG-UNION-FEE     PICTURE IS X(9)  VALUE IS 'UNION FEE'.
00079                  05  FILLER            PICTURE IS X(2)  VALUE IS SPACES.
00080                  05  HDG-ACTIVITY      PICTURE IS X(7)  VALUE IS 'ACT FEE'.
00081                  05  FILLER            PICTURE IS X(2)  VALUE IS SPACES.
00082                  05  HDG-SCHOLAR       PICTURE IS X(11) VALUE IS 'SCHOLARSHIP'.
00083                  05  FILLER            PICTURE IS X(2)  VALUE IS SPACES.
00084                  05  HDG-TOTAL-BILL    PICTURE IS X(10) VALUE IS 'TOTAL BILL'.
00085                  05  FILLER            PICTURE IS X(36) VALUE IS SPACES.
00086
00087
00088         PROCEDURE DIVISION.
00089
00090         HOUSEKEEPING.
00091             OPEN INPUT CARD-FILE, OUTPUT PRINT-FILE.
00092             MOVE HEADER-LINE TO PRINT-LINE.
00093             WRITE PRINT-LINE AFTER ADVANCING TOP-OF-PAGE LINES.
00094             MOVE SPACES TO PRINT-LINE.
00095             MOVE '------------------------------------------------
00096         '-----------------------------------------' TO PRINT-LINE.
00097             WRITE PRINT-LINE AFTER ADVANCING 1 LINES.
00098
00099         READ-A-CARD.
00100             READ CARD-FILE AT END GO TO WRITE-UNIVERSITY-TOTALS.
00101             COMPUTE TUITION = 80 * CREDITS.
00102             IF UNION-MEMBER IS EQUAL TO 'Y' MOVE 25 TO UNION-FEE
00103                 ELSE MOVE ZERO TO UNION-FEE.
00104             IF CREDITS IS GREATER THAN 6 GO TO MORE-THAN-6-CREDITS.
00105             MOVE 25 TO ACTIVITY-FEE.
00106             GO TO ADD-TOTAL-BILL.
00107
00108         MORE-THAN-6-CREDITS.
00109             IF CREDITS IS GREATER THAN 12 MOVE 75 TO ACTIVITY-FEE
00110             ELSE MOVE 50 TO ACTIVITY-FEE.
00111
00112         ADD-TOTAL-BILL.
00113             COMPUTE INDIVIDUAL-BILL = TUITION + UNION-FEE + ACTIVITY-FEE
00114                 - SCHOLARSHIP.
00115
00116         UPDATE-UNIVERSITY-TOTALS.
00117             ADD TUITION TO TOTAL-TUITION.
00118             ADD UNION-FEE TO TOTAL-UNION-FEE.
00119             ADD ACTIVITY-FEE TO TOTAL-ACTIVITY-FEE.
00120             ADD INDIVIDUAL-BILL TO TOTAL-IND-BILL.
00121             ADD SCHOLARSHIP TO TOTAL-SCHOLARSHIP.
00122
00123         WRITE-DETAIL-LINE.
00124             MOVE SPACES TO PRINT-LINE.
00125             MOVE STUDENT-NAME      TO PRINT-STUDENT-NAME.
00126             MOVE SOC-SEC-NO        TO PRINT-SOC-SEC-NO.
00127             MOVE CREDITS           TO PRINT-CREDITS.
00128             MOVE TUITION           TO PRINT-TUITION.
00129             MOVE UNION-FEE         TO PRINT-UNION-FEE.
00130             MOVE ACTIVITY-FEE      TO PRINT-ACTIVITY-FEE.
00131             MOVE SCHOLARSHIP       TO PRINT-SCHOLARSHIP.
00132             MOVE INDIVIDUAL-BILL   TO PRINT-IND-BILL.
00133             WRITE PRINT-LINE AFTER ADVANCING 1 LINES.
00134             GO TO READ-A-CARD.
00135
00136         WRITE-UNIVERSITY-TOTALS.
00137             MOVE SPACES TO PRINT-LINE.
00138             MOVE '------------------------------------------------
00139         '-----------------------------------------' TO PRINT-LINE.
00140             WRITE PRINT-LINE AFTER ADVANCING 1 LINES.
00141             MOVE SPACES TO PRINT-LINE.
00142             MOVE TOTAL-TUITION       TO PRINT-TUITION.
00143             MOVE TOTAL-UNION-FEE     TO PRINT-UNION-FEE.
00144             MOVE TOTAL-ACTIVITY-FEE TO PRINT-ACTIVITY-FEE.
00145             MOVE TOTAL-SCHOLARSHIP   TO PRINT-SCHOLARSHIP.
00146             MOVE TOTAL-IND-BILL      TO PRINT-IND-BILL.
00147             WRITE PRINT-LINE AFTER ADVANCING 2 LINES.
00148
00149         END-OF-JOB-ROUTINE.
00150             CLOSE CARD-FILE, PRINT-FILE.
00151             STOP RUN.
```

Heading line

Writing the heading line

Incrementing university totals

Building detail line

Non-numeric literal continued in column 7

Figure 4.8 *(Continued)*

65

6. 77-Level entries in WORKING-STORAGE: COBOL lines 59–67. Notice how all quantities are initialized to zero.

7. 01 entry in WORKING-STORAGE: COBOL lines 68–85. This is done to establish a heading line.

8. Use of column 7 for continuation of a nonnumeric literal: COBOL lines 96 and 139. An alternative way of establishing a line of hyphens is to use the figurative constant ALL as follows:

```
MOVE ALL ' – ' TO DASHED-LINE.
```

This would require establishment of a second heading line in working storage to correspond to print positions 2–97 in Figure 4.6. For example,

```
01   HEADING-LINE-TWO.
     05   FILLER          PIC X.
     05   DASHED-LINE     PIC X(96).
     05   FILLER          PIC X(36).
```

9. The SPECIAL-NAMES paragraph in the environment division to place the heading line on a new page: COBOL lines 11–12 and 93. This requires the WRITE AFTER ADVANCING option and the inclusion of a one-position field for carriage control in each print line; see COBOL lines 40 and 69.

10. Calculation of university totals: COBOL lines 117–121.

11. Writing a detail line for each student: COBOL lines 123–133.

12. Return to read another card: COBOL line 134.

The COBOL program of Figure 4.8 was tested, and sample output appears in Figure 4.9.

STUDENT NAME	SOC SEC NUM	CREDITS	TUITION	UNION FEE	ACT FEE	SCHOLARSHIP	TOTAL BILL
JOHN SMITH	123 45 6789	15	$1,200	$25	$75	$0	$1,300
HENRY JAMES	987 65 4321	15	$1,200	$0	$75	$500	$775
SUSAN BAKER	111 22 3333	09	$720	$0	$50	$500	$270
JOHN PART-TIMER	456 21 3546	03	$240	$25	$25	$0	$290
PEGGY JONES	456 45 6456	15	$1,200	$25	$75	$0	$1,300
H. HEAVY-WORKER	789 52 1234	18	$1,440	$0	$75	$0	$1,515
BENJAMINE LEE	876 87 6876	18	$1,440	$0	$75	$0	$1,515
			$7,440	$75	$450	$1,000	$6,965

Figure 4.9 Sample Output of Tuition Billing Problem

Summary

We certainly have covered a lot of material since we began. No doubt your head is swimming with vaguely familiar terms: A-margin, division-header, paragraph-name, etc. Our objective is for you to write meaningful COBOL programs, not to have you memorize what must appear to be an endless list of rules. You must eventually remember certain things, but we have found the best approach is to pattern your first few COBOL programs after existing

examples. To that end, we have spent considerable time developing the
engineering senior and tuition billing problems. Everything you need to know
to get started is contained in those listings (Figures 1.7 and 4.8) if only you will
take the time to look. As a further aid, see Figure 4.10, which contains a
skeleton outline of a COBOL program and some helpful hints.

```
IDENTIFICATION DIVISION.
PROGRAM-ID.      8-Character name.
AUTHOR.          Your name.
REMARKS.         A sentence or two stating what the program does.
ENVIRONMENT DIVISION.
CONFIGURATION SECTION.
SOURCE-COMPUTER.    Computer name.
OBJECT-COMPUTER.    Computer name.
SPECIAL-NAMES.
    C01 IS TOP-OF-PAGE.      Used to get printed output to begin on new page.
INPUT-OUTPUT SECTION.
FILE-CONTROL.
    SELECT CARD-FILE ASSIGN TO.......
    SELECT PRINT-FILE ASSIGN TO......
DATA DIVISION.
FILE SECTION.
FD  CARD-FILE
    RECORDING MODE IS F
    LABEL RECORDS ARE OMITTED
    RECORD CONTAINS 80 CHARACTERS     Typical FD for a card file.
    DATA RECORD IS STUDENT-CARD.
01  STUDENT-CARD.
    05  etc.
FD  PRINT-FILE
    RECORDING MODE IS F
    LABEL RECORDS ARE OMITTED
    RECORD CONTAINS 133 CHARACTERS    Typical FD for a print file.
    DATA RECORD IS PRINT-LINE.
01  PRINT-LINE.
    05  etc.
WORKING-STORAGE SECTION.
77  .......
77  .......
01  entries (if any)
PROCEDURE DIVISION.
HOUSEKEEPING.                         Good idea to have a housekeeping
    OPEN INPUT CARD-FILE              paragraph. Don't forget to open
        OUTPUT PRINT-FILE.           files.

       .  .
       .
          your logic here
       .  .
       .

END-OF-JOB.                           Good idea for end-of-job routine.
    CLOSE CARD-FILE, PRINT-FILE.      Don't forget to close files and
    STOP RUN.                         stop run.
```

Figure 4.10 Skeleton Outline of a COBOL Program

Finally, we shall present a list of guidelines for writing COBOL programs:

1. The four divisions must appear in specified order: identification, environment, data, and procedure. Division headers begin in column 8 and always appear on a line by themselves.

2. The environment and data divisions contain sections with fixed names. The identification division does not contain any sections. (The procedure division may contain programmer-defined sections; however, this is usually not done in beginning programs.) Section headers begin in column 8 and are on a line by themselves.

3. The data division is the only division without paragraph names. In the identification and environment divisions the paragraph names are fixed. In the procedure division, they are determined by the programmer. Paragraph names begin in column 8.

4. Any entry not required to begin in column 8 may begin in or past column 12.

5. The COBOL program executes instructions sequentially as they appear in the procedure division, unless a transfer of control is encountered.

6. Every file must be opened and closed. A file name will appear in at least four statements: SELECT, FD, OPEN, and CLOSE. In addition, the READ statement will contain the file name of an input file, whereas the WRITE statement contains the record name of an output file.

7. Every program must contain at least one STOP RUN statement.

One final word: *Programming is learned by doing.* You can read forever, but reading alone will not teach you COBOL. You *must write* programs for this material to have real meaning. The true learning experience comes when you pick up your own listings in the machine room.

**REVIEW
EXERCISES**

TRUE	FALSE		
☐	☐	**1**	The identification division may contain up to seven paragraphs.
☐	☐	**2**	The PROGRAM-ID paragraph is the only required paragraph in the identification division.
☐	☐	**3**	The REMARKS paragraph may contain several sentences.
☐	☐	**4**	A COBOL program which runs successfully on a UNIVAC system would also run successfully on an IBM system with no modification whatsoever.
☐	☐	**5**	Level numbers may go from 1 to 77 inclusive.
☐	☐	**6**	An 01-level entry cannot have a picture clause.
☐	☐	**7**	All elementary items have a picture clause.
☐	☐	**8**	77-Level entries may appear anywhere in the data division.
☐	☐	**9**	01-Level entries may appear in both the FILE and WORKING-STORAGE sections of the data division.
☐	☐	**10**	A data name at the 10 level will always be an elementary item.
☐	☐	**11**	A data name at the 05 level may or may not have a picture clause.
☐	☐	**12**	PICTURE, PICTURE IS, PIC, and PIC IS are *all* acceptable forms of the picture clause.
☐	☐	**13**	"PICTURE IS 9(3)" and "PICTURE IS 999" are equivalent entries.
☐	☐	**14**	The file section is required in every COBOL program.
☐	☐	**15**	The working-storage section is required in every COBOL program.
☐	☐	**16**	Blocks in a flowchart should correspond one to one with statements in the procedure division.

1 Consider the accompanying time card. Show an appropriate record description for **PROBLEMS** this information in COBOL; use any picture clauses which you think appropriate.

TIME-CARD							
NAME			NUMBER	DATE			HOURS
FIRST	MIDDLE	LAST		MO	DA	YR	

2 In which division do we find
   (a) PROGRAM-ID paragraph?
   (b) FILE-CONTROL paragraph?
   (c) CONFIGURATION SECTION?
   (d) WORKING-STORAGE SECTION?
   (e) FILE SECTION?
   (f) FD's?
   (g) AUTHOR paragraph?
   (h) REMARKS paragraph?
   (i) INPUT-OUTPUT SECTION?
   (j) File names?
   (k) Level numbers?
   (l) Paragraph names?
   (m) STOP RUN statements?
   (n) SELECT statements?
   (o) VALUE clauses?
   (p) PICTURE clauses?

3 Given the following record layout for incoming data cards,

```
01  EMPLOYEE-CARD.
    05  SOC-SEC-NUMBER          PICTURE IS 9(9).
    05  EMPLOYEE-NAME.
        10  LAST-NAME           PICTURE IS A(12).
        10  FIRST-NAME          PICTURE IS A(10).
        10  MIDDLE-INIT         PICTURE IS A.
    05  FILLER                  PICTURE IS X.
    05  BIRTH-DATE.
        10  BIRTH-MONTH         PICTURE IS 99.
        10  BIRTH-DAY           PICTURE IS 99.
        10  BIRTH-YEAR          PICTURE IS 99.
    05  FILLER                  PICTURE IS X(3).
    05  EMPLOYEE-ADDRESS.
        10  NUMBER-AND-STREET.
            15  HOUSE-NUMBER    PICTURE IS X(6).
            15  STREET-NAME     PICTURE IS X(10).
        10  CITY-STATE-ZIP.
            15  CITY            PICTURE IS X(10).
            15  STATE           PICTURE IS X(4).
            15  ZIP             PICTURE IS 9(5).
    05  FILLER                  PICTURE IS X(3).
```

   (a) List all group items.
   (b) List all elementary items.
   (c) State the columns in which the following fields are found:

69

1. SOC-SEC-NUMBER
2. EMPLOYEE-NAME
3. LAST-NAME
4. FIRST-NAME
5. MIDDLE-INIT
6. BIRTH-DATE
7. BIRTH-MONTH
8. BIRTH-DAY
9. BIRTH-YEAR
10. EMPLOYEE-ADDRESS
11. NUMBER-AND-STREET
12. HOUSE-NUMBER
13. STREET-NAME
14. CITY-STATE-ZIP
15. CITY
16. STATE
17. ZIP

4 Given the following record layout (assume that FIELD-I is the last entry under FIELD-A),

```
01  FIELD-A
    05  FIELD-B
        10  FIELD-C
        10  FIELD-D
    05  FIELD-E
    05  FIELD-F
        10  FIELD-G
        10  FIELD-H
        10  FIELD-I
```

answer true or false:
(a) FIELD-C is an elementary item.
(b) FIELD-E is an elementary item.
(c) FIELD-E should have a picture.
(d) FIELD-F should have a picture.
(e) FIELD-B must be larger than FIELD-C.
(f) FIELD-C must be larger than FIELD-D.
(g) FIELD-C must be larger than FIELD-H.
(h) FIELD-B and FIELD-D end in the same column.
(i) FIELD-A and FIELD-I end in the same column.
(j) FIELD-E could be larger than FIELD-F.
(k) FIELD-D could be larger than FIELD-E.
(l) FIELD-F and FIELD-G start in the same column.

5 Show the value of the edited result for each of the following entries:

	Sending Field		Receiving Field	
	PICTURE	CONTENTS	PICTURE	CONTENTS
(a)	9(6)	123456	9(6)	
(b)	9(6)	123456	9(8)	
(c)	9(6)	123456	9(6).99	
(d)	9(4)V99	123456	9(6)	
(e)	9(4)V99	123456	9(4)	
(f)	9(4)V99	123456	$$$$$9.99	
(g)	9(4)V99	123456	$$$,$$9.99	
(h)	9(6)	123456	$$$$,$$9.99	

6 Modify the tuition billing problem to account for *all* the following:

(a) The grade point average (GPA) is in columns 33–36 of each data card as a 9V999 number.

(b) The scholarship award is a function of grade point average rather than a flat amount as follows:

GPA	Scholarship
>3.500	20% reduction in tuition
3.001–3.500	15% reduction in tuition
2.500–3.000	10% reduction in tuition
<2.500	No scholarship

(c) Calculate and print the total number of credits taken.

(d) Calculate and print the *average* GPA (weigh the GPA of each student equally).

7 Write a COBOL program to calculate the gross pay for the XYZ Widget Company. A single data card has been prepared for every employee according to the format

Columns	Field	Picture
1–25	Name	A(25)
26–30	Hours worked	999V99
31–35	Hourly rate	9(3)V99

Gross pay is computed as follows:

1. Straight time for the first 40 hours;

2. Time and a half for the next 8 hours (i.e., hours 41–48);

3. Double time for anything over 48 hours.

Print an appropriate heading line. Print a detail line for every employee. Maintain and print a company total for gross pay.

8 Modify Problem 7 to compute the federal withholding tax for each employee as per the instructions in Problem 4 of Chapter 3. Compute the net pay for each employee as well. (Net pay = gross pay − federal withholding tax.). Add the tax and net pay columns to your output. Also maintain and print company totals for these amounts.

9 Modify the tuition billing problem to accommodate a page heading routine as follows: A maximum of 50 students is to appear on each page, and the heading line and row of dashes are to appear on top of each succeeding page. Thus if there were 178 data cards, 4 heading lines would appear (before the 1st, 51st, 101st, and 151st students). There will still be only one total line.

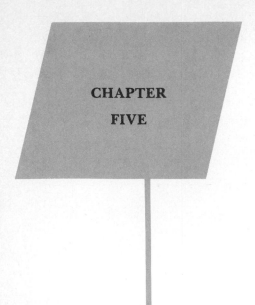

Debugging, I

Very few computer programs run successfully on the first attempt. Indeed the programmer is realistically expected to make errors, and an important "test" of a good programmer is not whether he/she makes mistakes but how quickly he can detect and correct the errors that invariably occur. Since this process is such an integral part of programming, two entire chapters are devoted to debugging. In the present chapter we shall consider errors in compilation and errors in execution in which the program goes to a normal end of job. In a later chapter we shall consider errors resulting in an "ABEND," or abnormal end-of-job, condition.

Compilation errors occur in the translation of COBOL to machine language and result because the programmer has violated a rule of the COBOL grammar, e.g., a missing period, a misspelled word, an entry in a wrong column, etc. Execution errors result after the program has been successfully translated to machine language and are generally of two types:

1. The computer was able to execute the entire program, but the calculated results are different from that which the programmer expected or intended, *or*

2. The computer is unable to execute a particular instruction and comes to an abnormal end of job, e.g., division by zero, addition of nonnumeric data, etc.

Execution errors of the first type may be caused by an incorrect translation of the flowchart to the programming language or by a correct translation of an incorrect flowchart. In either case, there is an error in logic which is generating incorrect output.

Execution errors of the second type are generally more difficult to correct, and consideration of these is deferred to Chapter 13. At that point we shall introduce the memory print or core dump as an important debugging tool. For the present, however, we shall restrict our discussion to compilation errors and execution errors of the first type.

There are four types of COBOL compiler error messages or diagnostics; they are listed in order of increasing severity:

Errors in Compilation

w—Warning diagnostic: calls attention to what may cause a potential problem. A program can compile and execute with several W-level diagnostics present; however, ignoring these messages could lead to errors in execution.

c—Conditional diagnostic: requires the compiler to make an assumption in order to complete the compilation. Execution is typically suppressed, and if not, usually inaccurate.

e—Error diagnostic: a severe error in the sense the compiler cannot make corrections and therefore cannot generate object instructions. Execution will not take place. Any statement flagged as an E-level error is ignored and treated as if it were not present in the program.

d—Disaster diagnostic: an error of such severity that the compiler does not know what to do and cannot continue. D-Level diagnostics are extremely rare, and one practically has to submit a FORTRAN program to the COBOL compiler to cause a D-level message.

The COBOL compiler tends to rub salt in a wound in the sense that an error in one statement can cause error messages in other statements which appear correct. For example, should you have an E-level error in a SELECT statement, the compiler will flag the error, ignore the SELECT statement, and then flag any other statement which references that file even though those other statements are otherwise correct. (See Figure 5.2.)

Often simple mistakes such as omitting a card or misspelling a reserved word can lead to a long and sometimes confusing set of error messages. The only consolation is that compiler errors can disappear as quickly as they occurred. Correction of the misspelled word or insertion of the missing card will often eliminate several errors at once.

Proficiency in debugging comes from experience; the more programs you write, the better you become. To give you a truer feel as to what to expect in your own programs, we have taken the tuition billing problem from Chapter 4 and deliberately changed several of the statements to cause compilation errors.

Consider the three pages of COBOL code and the one page of diagnostics in Figure 5.1. The COBOL compiler first lists the source program and then summarizes the compiler errors which have occurred. Each message references a card number, an IBM message number, and contains a brief explanation of the error. Some of the error causes will be immediately obvious; others may require you to seek help. As you progress through this book and gain practical experience you will become increasingly self-sufficient.

Let us examine the errors below:

CARD 16   w   LABEL RECORDS CLAUSE MISSING...
                Card 16 is the SELECT statement for CARD-FILE. The diagnostic, however, refers to the FD for this field in cards

```
00001          IDENTIFICATION DIVISION.
00002          PROGRAM-ID.  'TUITION'.
00003          AUTHOR.       THE BURSAR.
00004
00005
00006          ENVIRONMENT DIVISION.
00007
00008          CONFIGURATION SECTION.
00009          SOURCE-COMPUTER.  IBM-370.
00010          OBJECT-COMPUTER.  IBM-370.
00011          SPECIAL-NAMES.
00012              C01 IS TOP-OF-PAGE.                    ┌─ LABEL RECORDS clause
00013                                                     │  missing in this FD
00014          INPUT-OUTPUT SECTION.
00015          FILE-CONTROL.
00016              SELECT CARD-FILE  ASSIGN TO UR-2540R-S-SYSIN.
00017              SELECT PRINT-FILE ASSIGN TO UR-1403-S-SYSOUT.
00018
00019
00020          DATA DIVISION.                             ┌─ PICTURE clauses do not
00021          FILE SECTION.                              │  sum to 133 in this FD
00022          FD  CARD-FILE
00023              RECORDING MODE IS F
00024              RECORD CONTAINS 80 CHARACTERS
00025              DATA RECORD IS STUDENT-CARD.
00026          01  STUDENT-CARD.
00027              05  STUDENT-NAME    PICTURE IS A(20).
00028              05  SOC-SEC-NO      PICTURE IS 9(9).
00029              05  CREDITS         PICTURE IS 9(2).
00030              05  UNION-MEMBER    PICTURE IS A.
00031              05  SCHOLARSHIP     PICTURE IS 9(4).
00032              05  FILLER          PICTURE IS X(44).
00033          FD  PRINT-FILE
00034              RECORDING MODE IS F
00035              LABEL RECORDS ARE OMITTED
00036              RECORD CONTAINS 133 CHARACTERS         ┌─ Missing PRINT
00037              DATA RECORD IS PRINT-LINE.
00038          01  PRINT-LINE.
00039              05  FILLER                  PICTURE IS X.
00040              05  PRINT-STUDENT-NAME      PICTURE IS A(20).
00041              05  FILLER                  PICTURE IS X(2).
00042              05  PRINT-SOC-SEC-NO        PICTURE IS 999B99B9999.
00043              05  FILLER                  PICTURE IS X(4).
00044              05      CREDITS             PICTURE IS 99.
00045              05  FILLER                  PICTURE IS X(3).
00046              05  PRINT-TUITION           PICTURE IS  $$$$,$$9.
00047              05  FILLER                  PICTURE IS X(1).
00048              05  PRINT-UNION-FEE         PICTURE IS  $$$$,$$9.
00049              05  FILLER                  PICTURE IS X(3).
```

Figure 5.1 COBOL Listing with Diagnostics

74

```
00050          05   PRINT-ACTIVITY-FEE         PICTURE IS  $$$$,$$9.
00051          05   FILLER                     PICTURE IS  X(3).
00052          05   PRINT-SCHOLARSHIP          PICTURE IS  $$$$,$$9.
00053          05   FILLER                     PICTURE IS  X(5).        ——— Missing $ signs
00054          05   PRINT-IND-BILL             PICTURE IS  │ $$,$$9. │
00055          05   FILLER                     PICTURE IS  X(38).
00056
00057      WORKING-STORAGE SECTION.
00058      77   TUITION               PICTURE IS 9(4)   VALUE IS ZEROS.
00059      77   ACTIVITY-FEE          PICTURE IS 9(2)   VALUE IS ZEROS.
00060      77   UNION-FEE             PICTURE IS 9(2)   VALUE IS ZEROS.
00061      77   INDIVIDUAL-BILL       PICTURE IS 9(4)   VALUE IS ZEROS.
00062      77   TOTAL-TUITION         PICTURE IS 9(6)   VALUE IS ZEROS.
00063      77   TOTAL-SCHOLARSHIP     PICTURE IS 9(6)   VALUE IS ZEROS.
00064      77   TOTAL-ACTIVITY-FEE    PICTURE IS 9(6)   VALUE IS ZEROS.
00065      77   │ TOTAL UNION FEE │   PICTURE IS 9(6)   VALUE IS ZEROS.
00066      77   TOTAL-IND-BILL        PICTURE IS X(6)   VALUE IS ZEROS.
00067      01   HEADER-LINE.                             ┌─ Missing period
00068          05   FILLER            PICTURE IS X.
00069          05   HDG-NAME          PICTURE IS X(12)  VALUE IS 'STUDENT NAME'.
00070          05   FILLER            PICTURE IS X(10)  │ VALUE IS SPACES │
00071          05   HDG-SOC-SEC       PICTURE IS X(11)  VALUE IS 'SOC SEC NUM'.
00072          05   FILLER            PICTURE IS X(2)   VALUE IS SPACES.
00073          05   HDG-CREDITS       PICTURE IS X(7)   VALUE IS 'CREDITS'.
00074          05   FILLER            PICTURE IS X(2)   VALUE IS SPACES.
00075          05   HDG-TUITION       PICTURE IS X(7)   VALUE IS 'TUITION'.
00076          05   FILLER            PICTURE IS X(2)   VALUE IS SPACES.
00077          05   HDG-UNION-FEE     PICTURE IS X(9)   VALUE IS 'UNION FEE'.
00078          05   FILLER            PICTURE IS X(2)   VALUE IS SPACES.
00079          05   HDG-ACTIVITY      PICTURE IS X(7)   VALUE IS 'ACT FEE'.
00080          05   FILLER            PICTURE IS X(2)   VALUE IS SPACES.
00081          05   HDG-SCHOLAR       PICTURE IS X(11)  VALUE IS 'SCHOLARSHIP'.
00082          05   FILLER            PICTURE IS X(2)   VALUE IS SPACES.
00083          05   HDG-TOTAL-BILL    PICTURE IS X(10)  VALUE IS 'TOTAL BILL'.
00084          05   FILLER            PICTURE IS X(36)  VALUE IS SPACES.
00085
00086
00087      PROCEDURE DIVISION.              ——— Reserved word used as paragraph name
00088
00089      │ START. │
00090          OPEN INPUT CARD-FILE, OUTPUT PRINT-FILE.
00091          MOVE HEADER-LINE TO PRINT-LINE.
00092          WRITE PRINT-LINE AFTER ADVANCING TOP-OF-PAGE LINES.
00093          MOVE SPACES TO PRINT-LINE.
00094          MOVE '--------------------------------------------------
00095     -        '----------------------------------------------' TO PRINT-LINE.
00096          WRITE PRINT-LINE AFTER ADVANCING 1 LINES.
00097
00098      READ-A-CARD.            ——— Misspelled file name, should be CARD-FILE
00099          READ │ CRD-FILE │ AT END GO TO WRITE-UNIVERSITY-TOTALS.
00100          COMPUTE TUITION = │ 80* │ │ CREDITS │.
00101          IF UNION-MEMBER IS EQUAL TO 'Y' MOVE 25 TO UNION-FEE
```

Missing hyphens (pointing to line 00065 TOTAL UNION FEE)

Missing space before * ——┘   └── Multiple definition in
                                              lines 29 and 44

Figure 5.1 *(Continued)*

75

```
00102                    ELSE MOVE ZERO TO UNION-FEE.
00103               IF CREDITS IS GREATER THAN 6 GO TO MORE-THAN-6-CREDITS.
00104               MOVE 25 TO ACTIVITY-FEE.
00105               GO TO ADD-TOTAL-BILL.
00106
00107          MORE-THAN-6-CREDITS.
00108               IF CREDITS IS GREATER THAN 12 MOVE 75 TO ACTIVITY-FEE
00109               ELSE MOVE 50 TO ACTIVITY-FEE.
00110
00111          ADD-TOTAL-BILL.
00112               COMPUTE INDIVIDUAL-BILL = TUITION + UNION-FEE + ACTIVITY-FEE
00113                   - SCHOLARSHIP.
00114                                              ── TO does not belong
00115          UPDATE-UNIVERSITY-TOTALS.
00116               ADD TUITION  TO  TOTAL-TUITION GIVING TOTAL-TUITION.
00117               ADD UNION-FEE TO  TOTAL-UNION-FEE.
00118               ADD ACTIVITY-FEE TO TOTAL-ACTIVITY-FEE.        ── Put hyphen in
00119               ADD INDIVIDUAL-BILL TO  TOTAL-IND-BILL.           W.S. definition
00120               ADD SCHOLARSHIP TO TOTAL-SCHOLARSHIP.             in line 65
00121
00122          WRITE-DETAIL-LINE.                                     ── PICTURE X(6)
00123               MOVE SPACES TO PRINT-LINE.                           incorrectly used
00124               MOVE STUDENT-NAME        TO PRINT-STUDENT-NAME. in definition on
00125               MOVE SOC-SEC-NO          TO PRINT-SOC-SEC-NO.    line 66
00126               MOVE  CREDITS            TO PRINT-CREDITS.
00127               MOVE TUITION             TO PRINT-TUITION.
00128               MOVE UNION-FEE           TO PRINT-UNION-FEE.
00129               MOVE ACTIVITY-FEE        TO PRINT-ACTIVITY-FEE.
00130               MOVE SCHOLARSHIP         TO PRINT-SCHOLARSHIP.
00131               MOVE INDIVIDUAL-BILL     TO PRINT-IND-BILL.
00132               WRITE  PRINT-FILE AFTER ADVANCING 1 LINES.
00133               GO TO READ-A-CARD.
00134                                          ── Multiple definition in
00135          WRITE-UNIVERSITY-TOTALS.              lines 29 and 44
00136               MOVE SPACES TO PRINT-LINE. ── Should be PRINT-LINE
00137               MOVE '------------------------------------------------
00138          -    '------------------------------------------------' TO PRINT-LINE.
00139               WRITE PRINT-LINE AFTER ADVANCING 1 LINES.
00140               MOVE SPACES TO PRINT-LINE.
00141               MOVE TOTAL-TUITION       TO PRINT-TUITION.
00142               MOVE  TOTAL-UNION-FEE     TO PRINT-UNION-FEE.
00143               MOVE TOTAL-ACTIVITY-FEE TO PRINT-ACTIVITY-FEE.
00144               MOVE TOTAL-SCHOLARSHIP  TO PRINT-SCHOLARSHIP.
00145               MOVE TOTAL-IND-BILL      TO  PRINT-IND-BILL.
00146               WRITE PRINT-LINE AFTER ADVANCING 2 LINES.
00147                                                   ── PICTURE of PRINT-IND-BILL
00148          END-OF-JOB-ROUTINE.                         is too small to contain
00149               CLOSE CARD-FILE, PRINT-FILE. ── Put hyphens in W.S.   TOTAL-IND-BILL
00150               STOP RUN.                       definition in line 65
```

Figure 5.1 *(Continued)*

CARD	ERROR MESSAGE	
16	IKF2133I-W	LABEL RECORDS CLAUSE MISSING. DD CARD OPTION WILL BE TAKEN.
17	IKF2146I-C	RECORD SIZE IN RECORD-CONTAINS CLAUSE DISAGREES WITH COMPUTED RECORD SIZE. 00131 ASSUMED.
65	IKF1037I-E	UNION INVALID IN DATA DESCRIPTION. SKIPPING TO NEXT CLAUSE.
71	IKF1043I-W	END OF SENTENCE SHOULD PRECEDE 05 . ASSUMED PRESENT.
89	IKF1087I-W	' START ' SHOULD NOT BEGIN A-MARGIN.
89	IKF4050I-E	SYNTAX REQUIRES QISAM-FILE WITH NOMINAL KEY . FOUND END-OF-SENT . STATEMENT DISCARDED.
99	IKF3001I-E	CRD-FILE NOT DEFINED. STATEMENT DISCARDED.
100	IKF1007I-W	ASTERISK NOT PRECEDED BY A SPACE. ASSUME SPACE.
100	IKF3002I-E	CREDITS NOT UNIQUE. DISCARDED.
103	IKF3002I-E	CREDITS NOT UNIQUE. TEST DISCARDED.
108	IKF3002I-E	CREDITS NOT UNIQUE. TEST DISCARDED.
116	IKF4008I-W	SUPERFLUOUS TO FOUND IN ADD STATEMENT. IGNORED.
117	IKF3001I-E	TOTAL-UNION-FEE NOT DEFINED. SUBSTITUTING TALLY .
119	IKF4019I-E	DNM=2-479 (AN) MAY NOT BE USED AS ARITHMETIC OPERAND IN ADD STATEMENT. ARBITRARILY SUBSTITUTING TALLY .
126	IKF3002I-E	CREDITS NOT UNIQUE. DISCARDED.
126	IKF3001I-E	PRINT-CREDITS NOT DEFINED.
132	IKF4050I-E	SYNTAX REQUIRES RECORD-NAME . FOUND DNM=1-370 . STATEMENT DISCARDED.
142	IKF3001I-E	TOTAL-UNION-FEE NOT DEFINED. DISCARDED.
145	IKF5011I-W	AN INTERMEDIATE RESULT OR A SENDING FIELD MIGHT HAVE ITS HIGH ORDER DIGIT POSITION TRUNCATED.

ERROR MESSAGE	
IKF6006I-E	SUPMAP SPECIFIED AND E-LEVEL DIAGNOSTIC HAS OCCURRED. PMAP CLIST LOAD DECK STATE FLOW SYMDMP IGNORED/

Figure 5.1 (Continued)

22–25 and, sure enough, the LABEL RECORDS CLAUSE has been omitted. Since this is a W-level diagnostic, the compiler indicates what action it is taking; in this case it will extract the necessary information from the DD card, a JCL statement.

Correction: Insert a card LABEL RECORDS ARE OMITTED between lines 23 and 24.

CARD 17 c RECORD SIZE IN RECORD-CONTAINS CLAUSE DISAGREES WITH COMPUTED RECORD SIZE...
Card 17 points to the SELECT statement for PRINT-FILE, and as before the error is actually in the FD for this file. Card 36 states there are 133 characters in a record, but the actual computed record size from lines 39 to 55 is 131—hence the message.

Correction: Error will disappear after card 145 is fixed (see explanation under card 145).

CARD 65 e 'UNION' INVALID IN DATA DESCRIPTION...
Note the occurrence of TOTAL UNION FEE in line 65; the -'s between the parts of the name are missing. In COBOL a data name is followed by a blank, and the compiler does not know how to handle what it thinks are three data names in a row (TOTAL, UNION, FEE) in line 65.

Correction: Insert -'s to read TOTAL-UNION-FEE.

CARD 71 w END OF SENTENCE SHOULD PRECEDE 05...
Any level number must follow a completed statement, but the period ending line 70 has been removed. In this instance, the compiler assumes that the period is present, so no harm is done, but it is poor programming to permit such W-level diagnostics to remain. Moreover, there are situations in which a missing period can be very damaging.

Correction: Insert a period at the end of card 70.

CARD 89 e 'START' SHOULD NOT BEGIN A-MARGIN.
A subtle error and one which typically sends the beginner for help. START is intended as a paragraph name, and paragraph names must begin in the A-MARGIN, so what's the problem? START, however, is a reserved word in COBOL (see Appendix B), and its usage is severely restricted; it may not be used as a paragraph name.

Correction: Choose another paragraph name, e.g., START-THE-PROGRAM.

CARD 89 e SYNTAX REQUIRES QISAM-FILE WITH NOMINAL KEY...
A most perplexing error and an example of how one mistake can cause several other diagnostics to appear. This error stems from the previous error concerning the word START.

Correction: No action required other than the previous correction.

CARD 99 E CRD-FILE NOT DEFINED. STATEMENT DISCARDED.
Perhaps your initial reaction is that the compiler made a mistake. CARD-FILE is defined with a SELECT statement in line 16 and an FD beginning in line 22. Take another look. Lines 16 and 22 define CARD-FILE, not CRD-FILE. You know they are the same, but the compiler does not.
Correction: Change to CARD-FILE in statement 99.

CARD 100 W ASTERISK NOT PRECEDED BY A SPACE. ASSUME SPACE.
An easy error to fix; remember all arithmetic operators, +, −, *, /, and **, must be preceded and followed by a blank. Correction: Insert a space before the *.

CARD 100 E CREDITS NOT UNIQUE...
103
108
126
A message of "not unique" means that there is more than one data item with the same name. In this case we find CREDITS is defined in line 29 and again in line 44 (it should be PRINT CREDITS as in Chapter 4), and the compiler does not know which is which.
Correction: Restore uniqueness to the data name, e.g., PRINT-CREDITS in line 44 or use qualification. (See Chapter 7.)

CARD 116 W SUPERFLUOUS TO FOUND IN ADD STATEMENT. IGNORED.
Check the syntax of the COBOL ADD verb in Chapter 3 and observe that the TO option is not permitted with the GIVING option.
Correction: Eliminate TO in line 116.

CARD 117 E TOTAL-UNION-FEE NOT DEFINED...
142
Another example of how one error can cause several others. In line 65 the -'s were omitted in the definition of TOTAL-UNION-FEE; thus insofar as the compiler is concerned this data name (i.e., TOTAL-UNION-FEE) does not exist.
Correction: This diagnostic will disappear with the correction to line 65.

CARD 119 E DNM-2-479 MAY NOT BE USED AS AN ARITHMETIC OPERAND IN ADD STATEMENT...
This error becomes easy to understand once we guess that DNM-2-479 refers to TOTAL-IND-BILL in line 119. (In Chapter 13, we shall introduce the data division map, which relates compiler names, e.g., DNM-2-479, to programmer-defined data names.) Observe that in the definition of TOTAL-IND-BILL in line 66 a picture of X(6) was specified; this is not a numeric picture which is required in arithmetic operations—hence the error.
Correction: Change X(6) to 9(6) in line 66.

CARD 126   E   PRINT-CREDITS NOT DEFINED.
This diagnostic pertains to the nonunique message from lines 100, 103, 108, and 126.
Correction: If we eliminate that diagnostic by distinguishing between CREDITS and PRINT-CREDITS, then this message will also disappear.

CARD 132   E   SYNTAX REQUIRES RECORD-NAME...
Statement 132 is WRITE PRINT-FILE.... The problem here is that PRINT-FILE is a file name, not a record name. Remember, in COBOL, read a file name but write a record name.
Correction: Statement 132 should read WRITE PRINT-LINE....

CARD 145   W   AN INTERMEDIATE RESULT OR A SENDING FIELD MIGHT HAVE ITS HIGH ORDER DIGIT POSITION TRUNCATED.
Statement 145 is MOVE TOTAL-IND-BILL TO PRINT-IND-BILL. The PICTURE associated with the sending field is X(6), and the receiving field has a picture of $$,$$9. (Ignore the improper picture for TOTAL-IND-BILL which has already been flagged.) The sending field is a six-position field, but the receiving field can accommodate only four numeric digits—thus the warning message.
Correction: Change line 54 to read as follows: PRINT-IND-BILL PICTURE IS $$$$,$$9.

A Second Example

Let us return to the tuition billing program of Chapter 4 and make one very slight change. Statement 17 will now read "SERECT PRINT-FILE..." instead of "SELECT PRINT-FILE...." Consider the COBOL listing and associated diagnostics of Figure 5.2; the latter are reproduced below:

CARD 17   E   INVALID WORD SERECT...
This is to be expected; the compiler does not recognize the word SERECT.
Correction: Substitute SELECT for SERECT.

CARD 38   E   FILE-NAME NOT DEFINED IN A SELECT...
While there is nothing wrong with the COBOL FD in lines 34–38, the SELECT statement for these lines had been previously flagged by an E-level error and consequently discarded. Thus it appears to the compiler as though there is no SELECT statement for PRINT-FILE.
Correction: None required beyond fixing card 17.

CARD 91   E   ...NOT DEFINED. DISCARDED.
      92   What do these 28 errors have in common? Each one contains a
     ETC.   data name initially defined in the FD for PRINT-FILE. However, since the SELECT statement was in error and subsequently discarded, the FD is also ignored, and all these data names are effectively undefined—a definite case of the COBOL compiler "rubbing it in."
Correction: None required beyond fixing card 17.

The point of this example is that a seemingly simple error in one statement can lead to a large number of errors in other related statements that disappear when the initial error is corrected. However, don't expect all errors you don't understand to just go away. There is always a logical explanation for everything a computer does, and sometimes it may take quite a while to find it.

```
00001          IDENTIFICATION DIVISION.
00002          PROGRAM-ID.  'TUITION'.
00003          AUTHOR.       THE BURSAR.
00004
00005
00006          ENVIRONMENT DIVISION.
00007
00008          CONFIGURATION SECTION.
00009          SOURCE-COMPUTER.  IBM-370.
00010          OBJECT-COMPUTER.  IBM-370.
00011          SPECIAL-NAMES.
00012              C01 IS TOP-OF-PAGE.
00013
00014          INPUT-OUTPUT SECTION.
00015          FILE-CONTROL.
00016              SELECT CARD-FILE ASSIGN TO UR-2540R-S-SYSIN.
00017              SERECT PRINT-FILE ASSIGN TO UR-1403-S-SYSOUT.
00018                            ┌─── Misspelling - causes
00019                                 all errors
00020          DATA DIVISION.
00021          FILE SECTION.
00022          FD  CARD-FILE
00023              RECORDING MODE IS F
00024              LABEL RECORDS ARE OMITTED
00025              RECORD CONTAINS 80 CHARACTERS
00026              DATA RECORD IS STUDENT-CARD.
00027          01  STUDENT-CARD.
00028              05  STUDENT-NAME    PICTURE IS A(20).
00029              05  SOC-SEC-NO      PICTURE IS 9(9).
00030              05  CREDITS         PICTURE IS 9(2).
00031              05  UNION-MEMBER    PICTURE IS A.
00032              05  SCHOLARSHIP     PICTURE IS 9(4).
00033              05  FILLER          PICTURE IS X(44).
00034          FD  PRINT-FILE
00035              RECORDING MODE IS F
00036              LABEL RECORDS ARE OMITTED
00037              RECORD CONTAINS 133 CHARACTERS
00038              DATA RECORD IS PRINT-LINE.
00039          01  PRINT-LINE.
00040              05  FILLER                   PICTURE IS X.
00041              05  PRINT-STUDENT-NAME       PICTURE IS A(20).
00042              05  FILLER                   PICTURE IS X(2).
00043              05  PRINT-SOC-SEC-NO         PICTURE IS 999B99B9999.
00044              05  FILLER                   PICTURE IS X(4).
00045              05  PRINT-CREDITS            PICTURE IS 99.
00046              05  FILLER                   PICTURE IS X(3).
00047              05  PRINT-TUITION            PICTURE IS  $$$$,$$9.
00048              05  FILLER                   PICTURE IS X(1).
00049              05  PRINT-UNION-FEE          PICTURE IS  $$$$,$$9.
00050              05  FILLER                   PICTURE IS X(3).
00051              05  PRINT-ACTIVITY-FEE       PICTURE IS  $$$$,$$9.
00052              05  FILLER                   PICTURE IS X(3).
00053              05  PRINT-SCHOLARSHIP        PICTURE IS  $$$$,$$9.
00054              05  FILLER                   PICTURE IS X(5).
00055              05  PRINT-IND-BILL           PICTURE IS  $$$$,$$9.
00056              05  FILLER                   PICTURE IS X(38).
00057
```

Figure 5.2 COBOL Listing with Invalid SELECT Statement

```
00058            WORKING-STORAGE SECTION.
00059            77   TUITION             PICTURE IS 9(4)   VALUE IS ZEROS.
00060            77   ACTIVITY-FEE        PICTURE IS 9(2)   VALUE IS ZEROS.
00061            77   UNION-FEE           PICTURE IS 9(2)   VALUE IS ZEROS.
00062            77   INDIVIDUAL-BILL     PICTURE IS 9(4)   VALUE IS ZEROS.
00063            77   TOTAL-TUITION       PICTURE IS 9(6)   VALUE IS ZEROS.
00064            77   TOTAL-SCHOLARSHIP   PICTURE IS 9(6)   VALUE IS ZEROS.
00065            77   TOTAL-ACTIVITY-FEE  PICTURE IS 9(6)   VALUE IS ZEROS.
00066            77   TOTAL-UNION-FEE     PICTURE IS 9(6)   VALUE IS ZEROS.
00067            77   TOTAL-IND-BILL      PICTURE IS 9(6)   VALUE IS ZEROS.
00068            01   HEADER-LINE.
00069                 05   FILLER         PICTURE IS X.
00070                 05   HDG-NAME       PICTURE IS X(12) VALUE IS 'STUDENT NAME'.
00071                 05   FILLER         PICTURE IS X(10) VALUE IS SPACES.
00072                 05   HDG-SOC-SEC    PICTURE IS X(11) VALUE IS 'SOC SEC NUM'.
00073                 05   FILLER         PICTURE IS X(2)  VALUE IS SPACES.
00074                 05   HDG-CREDITS    PICTURE IS X(7)  VALUE IS 'CREDITS'.
00075                 05   FILLER         PICTURE IS X(2)  VALUE IS SPACES.
00076                 05   HDG-TUITION    PICTURE IS X(7)  VALUE IS 'TUITION'.
00077                 05   FILLER         PICTURE IS X(2)  VALUE IS SPACES.
00078                 05   HDG-UNION-FEE  PICTURE IS X(9)  VALUE IS 'UNION FEE'.
00079                 05   FILLER         PICTURE IS X(2)  VALUE IS SPACES.
00080                 05   HDG-ACTIVITY   PICTURE IS X(7)  VALUE IS 'ACT FEE'.
00081                 05   FILLER         PICTURE IS X(2)  VALUE IS SPACES.
00082                 05   HDG-SCHOLAR    PICTURE IS X(11) VALUE IS 'SCHOLARSHIP'.
00083                 05   FILLER         PICTURE IS X(2)  VALUE IS SPACES.
00084                 05   HDG-TOTAL-BILL PICTURE IS X(10) VALUE IS 'TOTAL BILL'.
00085                 05   FILLER         PICTURE IS X(36) VALUE IS SPACES.
00086
00087
00088            PROCEDURE DIVISION.
00089
00090            HOUSEKEEPING.
00091                OPEN INPUT CARD-FILE, OUTPUT PRINT-FILE.
00092                MOVE HEADER-LINE TO PRINT-LINE.
00093                WRITE PRINT-LINE AFTER ADVANCING TOP-OF-PAGE LINES.
00094                MOVE SPACES TO PRINT-LINE.
00095                MOVE '--------------------------------------------------------
00096           -    '---------------------------------------' TO PRINT-LINE.
00097                WRITE PRINT-LINE AFTER ADVANCING 1 LINES.
00098
00099            READ-A-CARD.
00100                READ CARD-FILE AT END GO TO WRITE-UNIVERSITY-TOTALS.
00101                COMPUTE TUITION = 80 * CREDITS.
00102                IF UNION-MEMBER IS EQUAL TO 'Y' MOVE 25 TO UNION-FEE
00103                    ELSE MOVE ZERO TO UNION-FEE.
00104                IF CREDITS IS GREATER THAN 6 GO TO MORE-THAN-6-CREDITS.
00105                MOVE 25 TO ACTIVITY-FEE.
00106                GO TO ADD-TOTAL-BILL.
00107
00108            MORE-THAN-6-CREDITS.
00109                IF CREDITS IS GREATER THAN 12 MOVE 75 TO ACTIVITY-FEE
00110                ELSE MOVE 50 TO ACTIVITY-FEE.
00111
00112            ADD-TOTAL-BILL.
00113                COMPUTE INDIVIDUAL-BILL = TUITION + UNION-FEE + ACTIVITY-FEE
00114                    - SCHOLARSHIP.
00115
00116            UPDATE-UNIVERSITY-TOTALS.
00117                ADD TUITION TO TOTAL-TUITION.
00118                ADD UNION-FEE TO TOTAL-UNION-FEE.
00119                ADD ACTIVITY-FEE TO TOTAL-ACTIVITY-FEE.
00120                ADD INDIVIDUAL-BILL TO TOTAL-IND-BILL.
00121                ADD SCHOLARSHIP TO TOTAL-SCHOLARSHIP.
00122
```

Figure 5.2 *(Continued)*

```
00123          WRITE-DETAIL-LINE.
00124              MOVE SPACES TO PRINT-LINE.
00125              MOVE STUDENT-NAME        TO PRINT-STUDENT-NAME.
00126              MOVE SOC-SEC-NO          TO PRINT-SOC-SEC-NO.
00127              MOVE CREDITS             TO PRINT-CREDITS.
00128              MOVE TUITION             TO PRINT-TUITION.
00129              MOVE UNION-FEE           TO PRINT-UNION-FEE.
00130              MOVE ACTIVITY-FEE        TO PRINT-ACTIVITY-FEE.
00131              MOVE SCHOLARSHIP         TO PRINT-SCHOLARSHIP.
00132              MOVE INDIVIDUAL-BILL     TO PRINT-IND-BILL.
00133              WRITE PRINT-LINE AFTER ADVANCING 1 LINES.
00134              GO TO READ-A-CARD.
00135
00136          WRITE-UNIVERSITY-TOTALS.
00137              MOVE SPACES TO PRINT-LINE.
00138              MOVE '-----------------------------------------------------
00139        -      '---------------------------------------' TO PRINT-LINE.
00140              WRITE PRINT-LINE AFTER ADVANCING 1 LINES.
00141              MOVE SPACES TO PRINT-LINE.
00142              MOVE TOTAL-TUITION       TO PRINT-TUITION.
00143              MOVE TOTAL-UNION-FEE     TO PRINT-UNION-FEE.
00144              MOVE TOTAL-ACTIVITY-FEE TO PRINT-ACTIVITY-FEE.
00145              MOVE TOTAL-SCHOLARSHIP   TO PRINT-SCHOLARSHIP.
00146              MOVE TOTAL-IND-BILL      TO PRINT-IND-BILL.
00147              WRITE PRINT-LINE AFTER ADVANCING 2 LINES.
00148
00149          END-OF-JOB-ROUTINE.
00150              CLOSE CARD-FILE, PRINT-FILE.
00151              STOP RUN.
```

```
CARD   ERROR MESSAGE

17     IKF1004I-E      INVALID WORD SERECT . SKIPPING TO NEXT RECOGNIZABLE WORD.
38     IKF1056I-E      FILE-NAME NOT DEFINED IN A SELECT. DESCRIPTION IGNORED.
91     IKF3001I-E      PRINT-FILE NOT DEFINED. DELETING TILL LEGAL ELEMENT FOUND.
92     IKF3001I-E      PRINT-LINE NOT DEFINED. DISCARDED.
93     IKF3001I-E      PRINT-LINE NOT DEFINED. STATEMENT DISCARDED.
93     IKF3001I-E      TOP-OF-PAGE NOT DEFINED.
94     IKF3001I-E      PRINT-LINE NOT DEFINED. DISCARDED.
95     IKF3001I-E      PRINT-LINE NOT DEFINED. DISCARDED.
97     IKF3001I-E      PRINT-LINE NOT DEFINED. STATEMENT DISCARDED.
124    IKF3001I-E      PRINT-LINE NOT DEFINED. DISCARDED.
125    IKF3001I-E      PRINT-STUDENT-NAME NOT DEFINED. DISCARDED.
126    IKF3001I-E      PRINT-SOC-SEC-NO NOT DEFINED. DISCARDED.
127    IKF3001I-E      PRINT-CREDITS NOT DEFINED. DISCARDED.
128    IKF3001I-E      PRINT-TUITION NOT DEFINED. DISCARDED.
129    IKF3001I-E      PRINT-UNION-FEE NOT DEFINED. DISCARDED.
130    IKF3001I-E      PRINT-ACTIVITY-FEE NOT DEFINED. DISCARDED.
131    IKF3001I-E      PRINT-SCHOLARSHIP NOT DEFINED. DISCARDED.
132    IKF3001I-E      PRINT-IND-BILL NOT DEFINED. DISCARDED.
133    IKF3001I-E      PRINT-LINE NOT DEFINED. STATEMENT DISCARDED.
137    IKF3001I-E      PRINT-LINE NOT DEFINED. DISCARDED.
138    IKF3001I-E      PRINT-LINE NOT DEFINED. DISCARDED.
140    IKF3001I-E      PRINT-LINE NOT DEFINED. STATEMENT DISCARDED.
141    IKF3001I-E      PRINT-LINE NOT DEFINED. DISCARDED.
142    IKF3001I-E      PRINT-TUITION NOT DEFINED. DISCARDED.
143    IKF3001I-E      PRINT-UNION-FEE NOT DEFINED. DISCARDED.
144    IKF3001I-E      PRINT-ACTIVITY-FEE NOT DEFINED. DISCARDED.
145    IKF3001I-E      PRINT-SCHOLARSHIP NOT DEFINED. DISCARDED.
146    IKF3001I-E      PRINT-IND-BILL NOT DEFINED. DISCARDED.
147    IKF3001I-E      PRINT-LINE NOT DEFINED. STATEMENT DISCARDED.
150    IKF3001I-E      PRINT-FILE NOT DEFINED. DELETING TILL LEGAL ELEMENT FOUND.

       ERROR MESSAGE

       IKF6006I-E      SUPMAP SPECIFIED AND E-LEVEL DIAGNOSTIC HAS OCCURRED. PMAP CLIST LOAD DECK STATE
                       FLOW SYMDMP IGNORED/
```

Figure 5.2 *(Continued)*

After a program has been successfully compiled, it proceeds to execute and **Errors in Execution** therein lie the strength and weakness of the computer. The primary attractiveness of the machine is its ability to perform a fantastic number of operations in infinitesimal amounts of time; its weakness stems from the fact it does exactly what it has been instructed to do. The machine cannot think for itself. The programmer must think for the machine. If you were to inadvertently instruct the computer to compute tuition by charging $8 instead of $80 per credit, then that is what it would do.

To give you an idea of what can happen, we have deliberately removed one statement from the tuition billing problem of Chapter 4 to produce Figure 5.3.

```
00001              IDENTIFICATION DIVISION.
00002              PROGRAM-ID.  'TUITION'.
00003              AUTHOR.      THE BURSAR.
00004
00005
00006              ENVIRONMENT DIVISION.
00007
00008              CONFIGURATION SECTION.
00009              SOURCE-COMPUTER.  IBM-370.
00010              OBJECT-COMPUTER.  IBM-370.
00011              SPECIAL-NAMES.
00012                  C01 IS TOP-OF-PAGE.
00013
00014              INPUT-OUTPUT SECTION.
00015              FILE-CONTROL.
00016                  SELECT CARD-FILE ASSIGN TO UR-2540R-S-SYSIN.
00017                  SELECT PRINT-FILE ASSIGN TO UR-1403-S-SYSOUT.
00018
00019
00020              DATA DIVISION.
00021              FILE SECTION.
00022              FD  CARD-FILE
00023                  RECORDING MODE IS F
00024                  LABEL RECORDS ARE OMITTED
00025                  RECORD CONTAINS 80 CHARACTERS
00026                  DATA RECORD IS STUDENT-CARD.
00027              01  STUDENT-CARD.
00028                  05   STUDENT-NAME    PICTURE IS A(20).
00029                  05   SOC-SEC-NO      PICTURE IS 9(9).
00030                  05   CREDITS         PICTURE IS 9(2).
00031                  05   UNION-MEMBER    PICTURE IS A.
00032                  05   SCHOLARSHIP     PICTURE IS 9(4).
00033                  05   FILLER          PICTURE IS X(44).
00034              FD  PRINT-FILE
00035                  RECORDING MODE IS F
00036                  LABEL RECORDS ARE OMITTED
00037                  RECORD CONTAINS 133 CHARACTERS
00038                  DATA RECORD IS PRINT-LINE.
00039              01  PRINT-LINE.
00040                  05   FILLER                 PICTURE IS X.
00041                  05   PRINT-STUDENT-NAME     PICTURE IS A(20).
00042                  05   FILLER                 PICTURE IS X(2).
00043                  05   PRINT-SOC-SEC-NO       PICTURE IS 999B99B9999.
00044                  05   FILLER                 PICTURE IS X(4).
00045                  05   PRINT-CREDITS          PICTURE IS 99.
00046                  05   FILLER                 PICTURE IS X(3).
00047                  05   PRINT-TUITION          PICTURE IS $$$$,$$9.
00048                  05   FILLER                 PICTURE IS X(1).
00049                  05   PRINT-UNION-FEE        PICTURE IS $$$$,$$9.
00050                  05   FILLER                 PICTURE IS X(3).
00051                  05   PRINT-ACTIVITY-FEE     PICTURE IS $$$$,$$9.
00052                  05   FILLER                 PICTURE IS X(3).
00053                  05   PRINT-SCHOLARSHIP      PICTURE IS $$$$,$$9.
00054                  05   FILLER                 PICTURE IS X(5).
00055                  05   PRINT-IND-BILL         PICTURE IS $$$$,$$9.
00056                  05   FILLER                 PICTURE IS X(38).
00057
```

Figure 5.3 Errors in Execution (Use of TRACE and EXHIBIT)

```
00058          WORKING-STORAGE SECTION.
00059          77  TUITION              PICTURE IS 9(4)  VALUE IS ZEROS.
00060          77  ACTIVITY-FEE         PICTURE IS 9(2)  VALUE IS ZEROS.
00061          77  UNION-FEE            PICTURE IS 9(2)  VALUE IS ZEROS.
00062          77  INDIVIDUAL-BILL      PICTURE IS 9(4)  VALUE IS ZEROS.
00063          77  TOTAL-TUITION        PICTURE IS 9(6)  VALUE IS ZEROS.
00064          77  TOTAL-SCHOLARSHIP    PICTURE IS 9(6)  VALUE IS ZEROS.
00065          77  TOTAL-ACTIVITY-FEE   PICTURE IS 9(6)  VALUE IS ZEROS.
00066          77  TOTAL-UNION-FEE      PICTURE IS 9(6)  VALUE IS ZEROS.
00067          77  TOTAL-IND-BILL       PICTURE IS 9(6)  VALUE IS ZEROS.
00068          01  HEADER-LINE.
00069              05  FILLER           PICTURE IS X.
00070              05  HDG-NAME         PICTURE IS X(12) VALUE IS 'STUDENT NAME'.
00071              05  FILLER           PICTURE IS X(10) VALUE IS SPACES.
00072              05  HDG-SOC-SEC      PICTURE IS X(11) VALUE IS 'SOC SEC NUM'.
00073              05  FILLER           PICTURE IS X(2)  VALUE IS SPACES.
00074              05  HDG-CREDITS      PICTURE IS X(7)  VALUE IS 'CREDITS'.
00075              05  FILLER           PICTURE IS X(2)  VALUE IS SPACES.
00076              05  HDG-TUITION      PICTURE IS X(7)  VALUE IS 'TUITION'.
00077              05  FILLER           PICTURE IS X(2)  VALUE IS SPACES.
00078              05  HDG-UNION-FEE    PICTURE IS X(9)  VALUE IS 'UNION FEE'.
00079              05  FILLER           PICTURE IS X(2)  VALUE IS SPACES.
00080              05  HDG ACTIVITY     PICTURE IS X(7)  VALUE IS 'ACT FEE'.
00081              05  FILLER           PICTURE IS X(2)  VALUE IS SPACES.
00082              05  HDG-SCHOLAR      PICTURE IS X(11) VALUE IS 'SCHOLARSHIP'.
00083              05  FILLER           PICTURE IS X(2)  VALUE IS SPACES.
00084              05  HDG-TOTAL-BILL   PICTURE IS X(10) VALUE IS 'TOTAL BILL'.
00085              05  FILLER           PICTURE IS X(36) VALUE IS SPACES.
00086
00087
00088          PROCEDURE DIVISION.
00089
00090          HOUSEKEEPING.                    ┌─ Trace statement
00091              ┌READY TRACE.┐
00092              OPEN INPUT CARD-FILE, OUTPUT PRINT-FILE.
00093              MOVE HEADER-LINE TO PRINT-LINE.
00094              WRITE PRINT-LINE AFTER ADVANCING TOP-OF-PAGE LINES.
00095              MOVE SPACES TO PRINT-LINE.
00096              MOVE '------------------------------------------------
00097              '----------------------------------------' TO PRINT-LINE.
00098              WRITE PRINT-LINE AFTER ADVANCING 1 LINES.
00099
00100          READ-A-CARD.
00101              READ CARD-FILE AT END GO TO WRITE-UNIVERSITY-TOTALS.
00102              COMPUTE TUITION = 80 * CREDITS.
00103              IF UNION-MEMBER IS EQUAL TO 'Y' MOVE 25 TO UNION-FEE
00104                  ELSE MOVE ZERO TO UNION-FEE.
00105              IF CREDITS IS GREATER THAN 6 GO TO MORE-THAN-6-CREDITS.
00106              MOVE 25 TO ACTIVITY-FEE.
00107              ┌──────────────────────┐── GO TO statement missing
00108          MORE-THAN-6-CREDITS.
00109              IF CREDITS IS GREATER THAN 12 MOVE 75 TO ACTIVITY-FEE
00110              ELSE MOVE 50 TO ACTIVITY-FEE.
00111
00112          ADD-TOTAL-BILL.
00113              COMPUTE INDIVIDUAL-BILL = TUITION + UNION-FEE + ACTIVITY-FEE
00114                  - SCHOLARSHIP.
00115
00116          UPDATE-UNIVERSITY-TOTALS.
00117              ADD TUITION TO TOTAL-TUITION.
00118              ADD UNION-FEE TO TOTAL-UNION-FEE.
```

Figure 5.3 *(Continued)*

```
00119              ADD ACTIVITY-FEE TO TOTAL-ACTIVITY-FEE.
00120              ADD INDIVIDUAL-BILL TO TOTAL-IND-BILL.
00121              ADD SCHOLARSHIP TO TOTAL-SCHOLARSHIP.
00122
00123          WRITE-DETAIL-LINE.                                        Exhibit statement
00124              EXHIBIT NAMED STUDENT-NAME CREDITS ACTIVITY-FEE.      for debugging
00125              MOVE SPACES TO PRINT-LINE.
00126              MOVE STUDENT-NAME        TO PRINT-STUDENT-NAME.
00127              MOVE SOC-SEC-NO          TO PRINT-SOC-SEC-NO.
00128              MOVE CREDITS             TO PRINT-CREDITS.
00129              MOVE TUITION             TO PRINT-TUITION.
00130              MOVE UNION-FEE           TO PRINT-UNION-FEE.
00131              MOVE ACTIVITY-FEE        TO PRINT-ACTIVITY-FEE.
00132              MOVE SCHOLARSHIP         TO PRINT-SCHOLARSHIP.
00133              MOVE INDIVIDUAL-BILL     TO PRINT-IND-BILL.
00134              WRITE PRINT-LINE AFTER ADVANCING 1 LINES.
00135              GO TO READ-A-CARD.
00136
00137          WRITE-UNIVERSITY-TOTALS.
00138              MOVE SPACES TO PRINT-LINE.
00139              MOVE '----------------------------------------------------
00140          -    '-------------------------------------------' TO PRINT-LINE.
00141              WRITE PRINT-LINE AFTER ADVANCING 1 LINES.
00142              MOVE SPACES TO PRINT-LINE.
00143              MOVE TOTAL-TUITION       TO PRINT-TUITION.
00144              MOVE TOTAL-UNION-FEE     TO PRINT-UNION-FEE.
00145              MOVE TOTAL-ACTIVITY-FEE  TO PRINT-ACTIVITY-FEE.
00146              MOVE TOTAL-SCHOLARSHIP   TO PRINT-SCHOLARSHIP.
00147              MOVE TOTAL-IND-BILL      TO PRINT-IND-BILL.
00148              WRITE PRINT-LINE AFTER ADVANCING 2 LINES.
00149
00150          END-OF-JOB-ROUTINE.
00151              CLOSE CARD-FILE, PRINT-FILE.
00152              STOP RUN.
```

Figure 5.3 *(Continued)*

Computed results are shown in Table 5.1.

Table 5.1 Incorrect Activity Fee Calculation

STUDENT NAME	SOC SEC NUM	CREDITS	TUITION	UNION FEE	ACT FEE	SCHOLARSHIP	TOTAL BILL
JOHN SMITH	123 45 6789	15	$1,200	$25	$75	$0	$1,300
HENRY JAMES	987 65 4321	15	$1,200	$0	$75	$500	$775
SUSAN BAKER	111 22 3333	09	$720	$0	$50	$500	$270
JOHN PART-TIMER	456 21 3546	03	$240	$25	$50	$0	$315
PEGGY JONES	456 45 6456	15	$1,200	$25	$75	$0	$1,300
H. HEAVY-WORKER	789 52 1234	18	$1,440	$0	$75	$0	$1,515
BENJAMINE LEE	876 87 6876	18	$1,440	$0	$75	$0	$1,515
			$7,440	$75	$475	$1,000	$6,990

The computed table is suitably presentable, and all calculations are as they should be with the exception of the activity fee. According to the specifications given in Chapter 4, the activity fee is computed according to the following table:

Credits Taken	Activity Fee
0–6	$25
7–12	$50
13 or more	$75

JOHN PART-TIMER is taking only three credits but is being charged $50, which is $25 too high. The computer is doing exactly what we told it to do; unfortunately for John, we made a mistake. The activity fee is computed in statements 105–112, and you could probably determine the problem by inspection. However, we are going to expend some effort in finding the cause of the problem in the hope you will develop your own systematic procedures for locating and correcting logic errors.

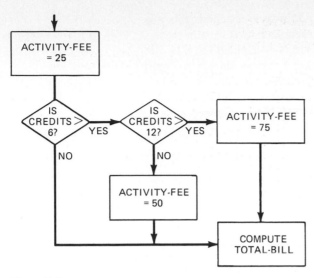

Figure 5.4

The activity fee should be calculated according to the flowchart in Figure 5.4. Note there is *exact* correspondence between the flowchart and activity fee specifications.

In Figure 5.3 COBOL statements 105–112 are used to calculate activity fee. COBOL statements 105–112 are intended to produce the logic of Figure 5.4 and are listed below:

```
        IF CREDITS IS GREATER THAN 6 GO TO MORE-THAN-6-CREDITS.
        MOVE 25 TO ACTIVITY-FEE.
    MORE-THAN-6-CREDITS.
        IF CREDITS IS GREATER THAN 12 MOVE 75 TO ACTIVITY-FEE
        ELSE MOVE 50 TO ACTIVITY-FEE.
    ADD-TOTAL-BILL.
```

Unfortunately the flowchart and COBOL code do not correspond completely. In particular, if CREDITS is not greater than 6, ACTIVITY-FEE is set equal to 25, but then, instead of skipping to ADD-TOTAL-BILL, the program falls through to the paragraph MORE-THAN-6-CREDITS, which resets ACTIVITY-FEE to either 50 or 75. The solution is obvious; insert a statement in line 107, GO TO ADD-TOTAL-BILL.

In this particular instance, it was very easy to determine the *actual* sequence of statements executed and to contrast that to the *intended* logic flow. It is not always this easy, however, and the programmer can then take advantage of additional COBOL statements which facilitate debugging. These include the TRACE, EXHIBIT, and ON statements.

READY TRACE

Insertion of the READY TRACE statement in a COBOL program enables one to trace the actual program flow as each paragraph is executed. In Figure 5.3, READY TRACE was inserted as statement 91. Immediately upon execution of this statement, the statement numbers (or in some systems paragraph names) of all subsequent paragraph names are listed as the paragraphs are executed. The next paragraph to be executed after the READY TRACE is

87

READ-A-CARD, line 100. If the end-of-file condition is reached, the program is to branch to WRITE-UNIVERSITY-TOTALS, line 137; otherwise it should continue to the next paragraph MORE-THAN-6-CREDITS, line 108. The statement numbers of the paragraph names are listed as shown in Figure 5.5. Notice that every time except the last time, paragraph 100 (READ-A-CARD) is followed by paragraph 108 (MORE-THAN-6-CREDITS), which is the problem associated with calculation of ACTIVITY-FEE. Observe further

```
100    ,108    ,112    ,116    ,123    ,
STUDENT-NAME = JOHN SMITH              CREDITS = 15 ACTIVITY-FEE = 75
100    ,108    ,112    ,116    ,123    ,
STUDENT-NAME = HENRY JAMES             CREDITS = 15 ACTIVITY-FEE = 75
100    ,108    ,112    ,116    ,123    ,
STUDENT-NAME = SUSAN BAKER             CREDITS = 09 ACTIVITY-FEE = 50
100    ,108    ,112    ,116    ,123    ,
STUDENT-NAME = JOHN PART-TIMER         CREDITS = 03 ACTIVITY-FEE = 50
100    ,108    ,112    ,116    ,123    ,
STUDENT-NAME = PEGGY JONES             CREDITS = 15 ACTIVITY-FEE = 75
100    ,108    ,112    ,116    ,123    ,
STUDENT-NAME = H. HEAVY-WORKER         CREDITS = 18 ACTIVITY-FEE = 75
100    ,108    ,112    ,116    ,123    ,
STUDENT-NAME = BENJAMINE LEE           CREDITS = 18 ACTIVITY-FEE = 75
100    ,137    ,150    ,
```
└ Incorrect value of ACTIVITY-FEE

Figure 5.5 Output of TRACE and EXHIBIT Statements

that after the last time paragraph 100 was executed, i.e., when the end of file was reached, the program next executed line 137 (WRITE-UNIVERSITY-TOTALS) and then line 150 (END-OF-JOB-ROUTINE). Line 100 was executed eight times in all, once for each of seven data cards and once for the end of file.

RESET TRACE

Assume, for example, that there were 2000 statements in the program instead of 150. Execution of the READY TRACE command would result in many more paragraphs being listed, yet the additional information is not apt to be helpful if we already have an idea of where the error is occurring. We would still want the capability of the READY TRACE, but we would not need it for the entire program. RESET TRACE suppresses the TRACE feature until the next READY TRACE statement is encountered. READY TRACE and RESET TRACE can each appear several times in the program, and a prudent mix can effectively isolate a program bug.

EXHIBIT

Very often we would like to see the value of various data names as they change during execution. Interspersion of DISPLAY statements can accomplish this, but the EXHIBIT statement is particularly well suited to this purpose. Syntactically the EXHIBIT statement is as follows:

$$\text{EXHIBIT} \left\{ \begin{matrix} \text{NAMED} \\ \text{CHANGED NAMED} \\ \text{CHANGED} \end{matrix} \right\} \left\{ \begin{matrix} \text{data-name-1} \\ \text{literal-1} \end{matrix} \right\} \left\{ \begin{matrix} \text{data-name-2} \\ \text{literal-2} \end{matrix} \right\} \dots$$

There are three ways in which the EXHIBIT statement can be used:

EXHIBIT NAMED—Whenever this statement is encountered, the data names and their values are printed.

EXHIBIT CHANGED NAMED—The first time this statement is executed, the data
names and corresponding values of all listed vari-
ables are printed. Every subsequent time only
those data names whose values changed are listed.

Chapter 5
Debugging, I

EXHIBIT CHANGED—This works exactly like EXHIBIT CHANGED
NAMED except that only the value of the data
name, and not the data name itself, is printed.

The EXHIBIT NAMED statement was inserted in Figure 5.3 as statement 124. Thus, every time the READY TRACE indicates the paragraph at statement 123 was executed, the EXHIBIT statement causes the printing of STUDENT-NAME, CREDITS, and ACTIVITY-FEE. Note how the EXHIBIT NAMED statement highlights the incorrect calculation for JOHN PART-TIMER (see Figure 5.5).

ON

Returning to the realm of the practical, suppose we had 7000 data records instead of 7. While we would like the capabilities of the EXHIBIT or TRACE statement, we may not require them for every single input record. Admittedly we could insert our own counters, switches, etc., but the ON statement does this automatically.

Syntactically,

ON integer-1 [AND EVERY integer-2] [UNTIL integer-3] any statement...

Each time an ON statement is encountered in the program flow, a hidden counter is incremented. If, for example, we wanted to use the TRACE feature only after the first 500 cards have been processed, i.e., we want to begin with the 501st card, we would use the following statement: ON 501 READY TRACE. Or perhaps we want to use the EXHIBIT statement for every 10th card; simply use ON 10 AND EVERY 10 EXHIBIT....

Don't be discouraged if you have many compilation errors in your first few attempts, and don't be surprised if you have several pages of diagnostics. Remember that a single error in a COBOL program can result in many error messages and that the errors can be made to disappear in bunches. (Recall the invalid SELECT statement of Figure 5.2.)

Summary

Before leaving the subject of compilation errors, it is worthwhile to review a list of common errors and suggested ways to avoid them:

1. *Nonunique data names.* Occurs because the same data name is defined in two different records or twice within the same record. For example, CREDITS might be specified as input data in a CARD-FILE and printed as output in a PRINT-FILE. To avoid the problem of nonunique data names, it is best to prefix every data name within a file by a short prefix. CARD could be established as a prefix for CARD-FILE, and PRINT as the prefix for PRINT-FILE, as shown below; this also helps locate data names while writing and debugging programs (see Chapter 6):

```
FD  CARD-FILE
```

```
        DATA RECORD IS CARD-RECORD.
    01  CARD-RECORD.
        05  CARD-NAME           PIC A(20).
        05  CARD-SOC-SEC-NO     PIC 9(9).
                .
                .
                .

    FD  PRINT-FILE
                .
                .
                .

        DATA RECORD IS PRINT-RECORD.
    01  PRINT-RECORD.
        05  PRINT-NAME          PIC A(20).
        05  FILLER              PIC X(5).
        05  PRINT-SOC-SEC-NO    PIC 9(9).
                .
                .
                .
```

2. *Omitted periods*. Every COBOL sentence should have a period; omission usually results in the compiler's assumption of a period.

3. *Omitted space before/after an arithmetic operator*. The arithmetic operators **, *, /, + , and − all require a blank before and after (a typical error for FORTRAN or PL/I programmers since the space is not required in those languages).

4. *Invalid picture for numeric entry*. All data names used in arithmetic statements must have numeric pictures consisting of 9's and V only. Any other entry in the picture clause is invalid.

5. *Conflicting picture and value clause*. Numeric pictures must have numeric values (no quotes); nonnumeric data pictures must have nonnumeric values (must be enclosed in quotes). Both entries below are *invalid*:

```
    77  TOTAL        PIC 9(3)    VALUE '123'.
    77  TITLE-WORD   PIC X(3)    VALUE 123.
```

Another common error is to use value and picture clauses of different lengths. The entry

```
    77  EMPLOYEE-NAME    PIC X(4)    VALUE 'R BAKER'.
```

causes a diagnostic for just that reason.

6. *Inadvertent use of COBOL reserved words*. COBOL has a list of some 300 reserved words which can only be used in their designated sense; any other use results in one or several diagnostics. Some reserved words are obvious, e.g., WORKING-STORAGE, IDENTIFICATION, ENVIRONMENT, DATA, and PROCEDURE. Others such as CODE, DATE, START, and REPORT are less obvious. Instead of memorizing the list or continually referring to it, we suggest this simple rule of thumb. Always use a hyphen in every data name you create. This will work better than 99% of the time.

7. *Conflicting RECORD CONTAINS clause and FD record description*. A recurrent error, even for established programmers. It stems from sometimes careless addition in that the sum of the pictures in an FD does not equal the number of characters in the RECORD CONTAINS clause. It can also result from other errors within the data division, namely when an entry containing a picture clause is flagged. If an E-level diagnostic is present, that entry will be ignored, and the count is thrown off. This is often one of the last errors to disappear before a clean compile.

8. *Receiving field too small to accommodate sending field.* An extremely common error, often associated with edited pictures. Consider the entries

```
05   PRINT-TOTAL-PAY      PIC $$,$$$.
          .
          .
          .
77   WS-TOTAL-PAY         PIC 9(5).
          .
          .
          .
     MOVE WS-TOTAL-PAY TO PRINT-TOTAL-PAY.
```

The MOVE statement would generate the warning that the receiving field may be too small to accommodate the sending field. The greatest possible value for WS-TOTAL-PAY is 99,999; the largest possible value that could be printed by PRINT-TOTAL-PAY is $9,999. Even though the print field contains five $'s, one $ must always print and hence the warning.

9. *Omitted hyphen in a data name.* A careless error but one that occurs entirely too often. If in the data division we define PRINT-TOTAL-PAY and then try to reference PRINT TOTAL-PAY, the compiler objects violently. It doesn't state that a hyphen was omitted, but it flags both PRINT and TOTAL-PAY as undefined.

10. *Misspelled data names or reserved words.* Too many COBOL students are poor spellers. Sound strange? How do you spell environment? One or many errors can result, depending on which word was spelled incorrectly.

11. *Reading a record name or writing a file name.* The COBOL rule is very simple. One is supposed to read a file and write a record; many people get it confused. The entries below should clarify the situation:

```
FD   CARD-FILE
        .
        .
     DATA RECORD IS CARD-RECORD.
        .
        .
        .
FD   PRINT-FILE
        .
        .
     DATA RECORD IS PRINT-RECORD.
```
Correct entries:
```
     READ CARD-FILE, . . . . .
     WRITE PRINT-RECORD . . . .
```
Incorrect entries:
```
     READ CARD-RECORD . . . .
     WRITE PRINT-FILE . . .
```

12. *Going past column 72.* This error can cause any of the above errors as well as a host of others. A COBOL statement must end in column 72 or before; columns 73–80 are left blank or used for program identification. If one goes past column 72 in a COBOL statement, it is very difficult to catch because the COBOL listing contains columns 1–80 although the compiler interprets only columns 1–72. (The 72-column restriction does not apply to data cards.)

TRUE	FALSE		
☐	☐	**1**	If a program compiles with no diagnostics, it must execute correctly.
☐	☐	**2**	If a program compiles with warning diagnostics, execution will be suppressed.
☐	☐	**3**	If READY TRACE is used in a program, RESET TRACE must be used also.
☐	☐	**4**	READY TRACE can appear only once in a program.
☐	☐	**5**	An error in one COBOL statement can cause errors in several other, apparently correct, statements.
☐	☐	**6**	There are four distinct levels of compiler diagnostics.
☐	☐	**7**	A C-level diagnostic is more severe than a W-level diagnostic.
☐	☐	**8**	Paragraph names begin in the A margin.
☐	☐	**9**	Spaces are required before and after arithmetic symbols.
☐	☐	**10**	Spaces are required before and after punctuation symbols.
☐	☐	**11**	A data name which appears in a COMPUTE statement can be defined with a picture of X's.
☐	☐	**12**	Data names may contain blanks.
☐	☐	**13**	The contents of columns 73–80 are ignored by the compiler.
☐	☐	**14**	In a COBOL program, one reads a record name and writes a file name.

PROBLEMS

1 *Desk checking.* The coding in Figure 5.6 represents a COBOL program after initial coding. However, it should be *desk-checked* prior to submission to the computer. Accordingly, list all errors you see. (There are *over* 20.)

2 Figure 5.7 contains our first try at the engineering senior problem. Indicate the necessary corrections to eliminate compiler diagnostics.

3 ACME Widgets is computerizing its company payroll and is preparing a data card for each employee with the following information:

Columns	Field	Picture
1–20	Name	A(20)
21–29	Soc. Sec. #	9(9)
30–32	Hours	99V9
33–36	Rate	99V99
37–40	Pension	99V99

Individual pay is computed as follows: straight time up to 40 hours, time and a half for anything over 40 but less than 48, and double time for anything over 48. Net pay is equal to gross pay less taxes (assumed 25% for simplicity) and less pension. A program is to be developed which will compute and print the relevant information for each individual. Company totals are to be computed and printed as well, and the information is to appear in tabular form under appropriate headings.

(a) The program has been assigned to Thomas T. Trainee, who is new on the job and requires help with debugging. As group leader, explain how to correct each of the compilation errors in the program (Figure 5.8).

(b) Unfortunately, Tom also has several logic errors in the program, so that even after it compiles properly, it will not execute correctly. State the logic errors, and indicate necessary corrections.

COBOL Coding Form

IBM

SYSTEM:

PROGRAM:

PROGRAMMER JOHN SMITH   DATE 8/17/76

PUNCHING INSTRUCTIONS — GRAPHIC / PUNCH

CARD FORM #

PAGE 1 OF 2   IDENTIFICATION [73] ... [80]

COBOL STATEMENT

```
01   IDENTIFICATION DIVISION.
02   PROGRAM ID.  'CHECK'.
03   AUTHOR.  JOHN SMITH.
04   REMARKS.
05      THIS PROGRAM READS IN CARDS. COUNTS THEM, AND PRINTS THE
06      NAME FIELD OF EVERY CARD READ IN. IT ALSO PRINTS THE TOTAL
07      NUMBER OF CARDS. IT HAS LOTS OF ERRORS.
08   ENVIRONMENT DIVISION.
09   CONFIGURATION SECTION.
10   SOURCE COMPUTER.  IBM-370.
11   OBJECT-COMPUTER.  IBM-370.
12   INPUT-OUTPUT SECTION.
13      SELECT CARD-FILE ASSIGN TO UR-2540R-S-SYSIN.
14      SELECT PRINT-FILE ASSIGN TO UR-1403-S-SYSOUT.
15   DATA DIVISION.
16   FILE SECTION.
17   FD CARD-FIL
18      LABEL RECORDS ARE OMITTED
19      RECORD CONTAINS 80 CHARACTERS
20      DATA RECORD IS CARD-IN.
21   01 CARD-FILE.
22      05 STUDENT-NAME.
23      05 STUDENT-ADDRESS.
24         10 LINE-ONE        PICTURE IS X(20).
```

Figure 5.6 Problem 1

IBM

COBOL Coding Form

SYSTEM						
PROGRAM			PUNCHING INSTRUCTIONS			PAGE 2 OF 2
PROGRAMMER JOHN SMITH	DATE 8/17/76	GRAPHIC	PUNCH	CARD FORM #		IDENTIFICATION 73 [80] *

SEQUENCE (PAGE) (SERIAL)	CONT A B	COBOL STATEMENT
01		10 LINE-TWO PICTURE IS X(20).
02		05 FILLER PICTURE IS X(40).
03	FD	PRINT-FILE
04		LABEL RECORDS ARE OMITTED
05		RECORD CONTAINS 133 CHARACTERS
06		DATA RECORD IS PRINT-LINE.
07		01 PRINT-LINE PICTURE IS X(133).
08		WORKING-STORAGE SECTION.
09		77 TOTAL-CARDS PICTURE IS 9(3) VALUE IS ZEROS.
10		PROCEDURE-DIVISION.
11		OPEN INPUT CARD-FILE, PRINT-FILE.
12		READ-A-CARD.
13		READ CARD-IN, AT END GO TO NO-MORE-CARDS.
14		ADD 1 TO TOTAL-CARDS.
15		MOVE SPACES TO PRINT-LINE.
16		MOVE CARD-NAME PRINT-NAME.
17		WRITE PRINT-FILE AFTER ADVANCING TWO LINES.
18		GO BACK TO READ-A-CARD.
19		NO MORE-CARDS.
20		MOVE SPACES TO PRINT LINE.
21		MOVE TOTAL-CARDS TO PRINT TOTAL-CARDS.
22		WRITE PRINT-LINE AFTER ADVANCING 2 LINES.
23		CLOSE CARD-FILE.
24		STOP.

*A standard card form — IBM Electro C61897 is available for punching source statements from this form
Instructions for using this form are given in any IBM COBOL reference manual
Address comments concerning this form to IBM Corporation, Programming Publications, 1271 Avenue of the Americas, New York, New York 10020

Form No. X28-1464-4 U/M 025
Printed in U.S.A.

Figure 5.6 *(Continued)*

```
00001          IDENTIFICATION DIVISION.
00002          PROGRAM-ID.      FIRSTTRY.
00003          AUTHOR.          CRAWFORD.
00004          REMARKS.   THIS IS A COBOL PROGRAM WHICH READS A DECK OF CARDS
00005             AND PRINTS THE NAMES OF ENGINEERING MAJORS WHO ARE ALSO
00006             SENIORS  (110 CREDITS OR MORE).
00007          ENVIRONMENT DIVISION.
00008          CONFIGURATION SECTION.
00009          SOURCE-COMPUTER.  IBM-370.
00010          OBJECT-COMPUTER.  IBM-370.
00011          INPUT-OUTPUT SECTION.
00012          FILE-CONTROL.
00013             SELECT CARD-FILE ASSIGN TO UR-2540R-S-SYSIN.
00014             SELECT PRINT-FILE ASSIGN TO UR-1403-S-SYSOUT.
00015          DATA DIVISION.
00016          FILE SECTION.
00017          FD  CARD-FILE
00018             LABEL RECORDS ARE OMITTED
00019             RECORD CONTAINS 80 CHARACTERS
00020             DATA RECORD IS CARD-IN.
00021          01  CARD-IN.
00022             05  CARD-NAME               PICTURE IS A(25).
00023             05  CARD-CREDITS            PICTURE IS 9(3).
00024             05  CARD-MAJOR              PICTURE IS A(15).
00025             05  FILLER                  PICTURE IS X(27).
00026          FD  PRINT-FILE
00027             LABEL RECORDS ARE OMITTED
00028             RECORD CONTAINS 133 CHARACTERS
00029             DATA RECORD IS PRINT-LINE.
00030          01  PRINT-LINE.
00031             05  FILLER                  PICTURE IS X(8).
00032             05  PRINT-NAME              PICTURE IS X(25).
00033             05  FILLER                  PICTURE IS X(100).
00034          PROCEDURE DIVISION.
00035             OPEN INPUT CARD-FILE, OUTPUT PRINT-FILE.
00036          READ-A-CARD.
00037             READ CARD-IN, AT END GO TO END-OF-JOB.
00038             IF CARD-CREDITS IS LESS THAN 110, GO TO READ-A-CARD.
00039             IF CARD-MAJOR IS NOT EQUAL 'ENGINEERING', GO TO READ-A-CARD.
00040          ******* NOW PRINT A LINE - ENGINEERING SENIOR *****
00041             MOVE SPACES TO PRINT-LINE.
00042             MOVE CARD-NAME TO.
00043             WRITE PRINT-FILE.
00044             GO TO READ-A-CARD.
00045          END-OF-JOB.
00046             CLOSE CARD-FILE, PRINT-FILE.
00047             STOP RUN.
```

CARD ERROR MESSAGE

13	IKF2146I-C	RECORD SIZE IN RECORD-CONTAINS CLAUSE DISAGREES WITH COMPUTED RECORD SIZE. 00070 ASSUMED.
37	IKF4050I-E	SYNTAX REQUIRES FILE-NAME . FOUND DNM=1-89 . STATEMENT DISCARDED.
37	IKF3001I-E	END-OF NOT DEFINED. STATEMENT DISCARDED.
37	IKF3001I-E	JOB NOT DEFINED.
42	IKF4004I-E	END-OF-SENT (AL) IS ILLEGALLY USED IN MOVE STATEMENT. DISCARDED.
43	IKF4050I-E	SYNTAX REQUIRES RECORD-NAME . FOUND DNM=1-181 . STATEMENT DISCARDED.

ERROR MESSAGE

| | IKF6006I-E | SUPMAP SPECIFIED AND E-LEVEL DIAGNOSTIC HAS OCCURRED. PMAP CLIST LOAD DECK STATE FLOW SYMDMP IGNORED/ |

Figure 5.7 Problem 2

```
00001          IDENTIFICATION DIVISION.
00002             PROGRAM-ID.  'PAYROLL'.
00003             AUTHOR.       THOMAS T TRAINEE.
00004
00005
00006          ENVIRONMENT DIVISION.
00007          CONFIGURATION SECTION.
00008          SOURCE-COMPUTER.  IBM-370.
00009          OBJECT-COMPUTER.  IBM-370.
00010          SPECIAL-NAMES.
00011             C01 IS TOP-OF-PAGE.
00012
00013          INPUT-OUTPUT SECTION.
00014          FILE-CONTROL.
00015             SELECT CARD-FILE ASSIGN TO UR-2540R-S-SYSIN.
00016             SELECT PRINT-FILE ASSIGN TO UR-1403-S-SYSOUT.
00017
00018
00019          DATA DIVISION.
00020          FILE SECTION.
00021          FD  CARD-FILE
00022              RECORDING MODE IS F
00023              LABEL RECORDS ARE OMITTED
00024              RECORD CONTAINS 80 CHARACTERS
00025              DATA RECORD IS EMPLOYEE-CARD.
00026          01  EMPLOYEE-CARD.
00027              05  NAME                PICTURE IS A(20).
00028              05  SOC-SEC-NO          PICTURE IS 9(9).
00029              05  HOURS               PICTURE IS  99V9.
00030              05  RATE                PICTURE IS 99V99.
00031              05  PENSION-DEDUCTION   PICTURE IS 99V99.
00032          FD  PRINT-FILE
00033              RECORDING MODE IS F
00034              LABEL RECORDS ARE OMITTED
00035              RECORD CONTAINS 133 CHARACTERS
00036              DATA RECORD IS PRINT-LINE.
00037          01  PRINT-LINE.
00038              05  FILLER              PICTURE IS X(1).
00039              05  PRINT-NAME          PICTURE IS A(20).
00040              05  FILLER              PICTURE IS X(2).
00041              05  PRINT-SOC-SEC-NO    PICTURE IS 9(9).
00042              05  FILLER              PICTURE IS X(2).
00043              05  PRINT-HOURS         PICTURE IS 99.99
00044              05  FILLER              PICTURE IS X(2).
00045              05  PRINT-RATE          PICTURE IS $$9.99.
00046              05  FILLER              PICTURE IS X(2).
00047              05  PRINT-GROSS-PAY     PICTURE IS $$,$$$.99.
00048              05  FILLER              PICTURE ISX(2).
00049              05  PRINT-TAXES         PICTURE IS $$.$$$.99.
00050              05  FILLER              PICTURE IS X(2).
00051              05  PRINT-PENSION       PICTURE IS $$,$$$.99.
00052              05  FILLER              PICTURE IS X(2).
00053              05  PRINT-NET-PAY       PICTURE IS $$,$$$.99.
00054              05  FILLER              PICTURE IS X(42).
00055
00056          WORKING-STORAGE SECTION.
00057          77  GROSS-PAY               PICTURE IS 9(4)V99.
00058          77  TAXES                   PICTURE IS 9(4)V99.
00059          77  NET-PAY                 PICTURE IS 9(4)V99.
00060          77  TOTAL-GROSS-PAY         PICTURE IS 9(4) VALUE IS ZEROS.
00061          77  TOTAL-PENSION           PICTURE IS 9(4) VALUE IS ZEROS.
00062          77  TOTAL-TAXES             PICTURE IS 9(4) VALUE IS ZEROS.
00063          77  TOTAL-NET-PAY           PICTURE IS 9(4) VALUE IS ZEROS.
00064
00065
```

Figure 5.8 Thomas T. Trainee Program (Problem 3)

```
00066          PROCEDURE DIVISION.
00067              OPEN INPUT CARD-FILE OUTPUT PRINT-FILE.
00068
00069          READ-A-CARD.
00070              READ EMPLOYEE-CARD, AT END GO TO WRITE-TOTALS.
00071              MULTIPLY HOURS BY RATE GIVING GROSS-PAY.
00072              IF HOURS NOT GREATER THAN 40 GO TO CALCULATE-NET-PAY.
00073              IF HOURS NOT GREATER THAN 48 GO TO TIME-AND-A-HALF.
00074
00075          DOUBLE-TIME.
00076              COMPUTE GROSS-PAY = GROSS-PAY + 2 * RATE * (HOURS - 48).
00077                  + 1.5 * RATE * 8.
00078              GO TO COMPUTE-NET-PAY.
00079
00080          TIME-AND-A-HALF.
00081              COMPUTE GROSS-PAY = GROSS-PAY + 1.5 * RATE * (HOURS - 40).
00082
00083          COMPUTE-NET-PAY.
00084              COMPUTE NET-PAY = GROSS-PAY - PENSION-DEDUCTION
00085          TOTALING.
00086                  - .25 * GROSS-PAY.
00087              ADD GROSS-PAY TO TOTAL-GROSS-PAY.
00088              ADD TAXES TO TOTAL-TAXES.
00089              ADD PENSION-DEDUCTION TO TOTAL-PENSION.
00090
00091          WRITE-DETAIL-LINE.
00092              MOVE SPACES TO PRINT-LINE.
00093              MOVE NAME                TO PRINT-NAME.
00094              MOVE SOC-SEC-NO     TO PRINT-SOC-SEC-NO.
00095              MOVE HOURS TO PRINT-HOURS.
00096              MOVE RATE            TO PRINT-RATE.
00097              MOVE GROSS-PAY       TO PRINT-GROSS-PAY.
00098              MOVE TAXES           TO PRINT-TAXES.
00099              MOVE PENSION-DEDUCTION TO PRINT-PENSION.
00100              MOVE NET-PAY         TO PRINT-NET-PAY.
00101              WRITE PRINT-LINE AFTER ADVANCING 1 LINES.
00102
00103          WRITE-TOTALS.
00104              MOVE SPACES TO PRINT-LINE.
00105              MOVE '----------------------------------------------------
00106          -    '------------------------------' TO PRINT-LINE.
00107              WRITE PRINT-LINE.
00108              MOVE SPACES TO PRINT-LINE.
00109              MOVE TOTAL-GROSS-PAY TO PRINT-GROSS-PAY.
00110              MOVE TOTAL-TAXES TO PRINT-TAXES.
00111              MOVE TOTAL-PENSION TO PRINT-PENSION.
00112              MOVE TOTAL-NET-PAY TO PRINT-NET-PAY.
00113              WRITE PRINT-LINE AFTER ADVANCING 1 LINES.
00114              CLOSE PRINT-FILE, CARD-FILE.   STOP RUN.
```

CARD   ERROR MESSAGE

15	IKF2146I-C	RECORD SIZE IN RECORD-CONTAINS CLAUSE DISAGREES WITH COMPUTED RECORD SIZE. 00040 ASSUMED.
16	IKF2146I-C	RECORD SIZE IN RECORD-CONTAINS CLAUSE DISAGREES WITH COMPUTED RECORD SIZE. 00132 ASSUMED.
44	IKF1043I-W	END OF SENTENCE SHOULD PRECEDE 05 . ASSUMED PRESENT.
48	IKF1007I-W	(2) NOT PRECEDED BY A SPACE. ASSUME SPACE.
48	IKF1037I-E	(2) INVALID IN DATA DESCRIPTION. SKIPPING TO NEXT CLAUSE.
48	IKF2039I-C	PICTURE CONFIGURATION ILLEGAL. PICTURE CHANGED TO 9 UNLESS USAGE IS 'DISPLAY-ST', THEN L(6)BDZ9BDZ9.
70	IKF4050I-E	SYNTAX REQUIRES FILE-NAME . FOUND DNM=1-180 . STATEMENT DISCARDED.
72	IKF3001I-E	CALCULATE-NET-PAY NOT DEFINED. STATEMENT DISCARDED.
76	IKF4003I-E	EXPECTING NEW STATEMENT. FOUND PLUS SIGN . DELETING TILL NEXT VERB OR PROCEDURE-NAME.
85	IKF1091I-C	TOTALING IN A-MARGIN NOT VALID AS PROC-NM. ASSUME B-MARGIN.
84	IKF4003I-E	EXPECTING NEW STATEMENT. FOUND TOTALING . DELETING TILL NEXT VERB OR PROCEDURE-NAME.
84	IKF4003I-E	EXPECTING NEW STATEMENT. FOUND MINUS SIGN . DELETING TILL NEXT VERB OR PROCEDURE-NAME.
107	IKF4093I-C	ALL WRITE STATEMENTS FOR DNM=1-299 SHOULD HAVE ADVANCING OPTION. AFTER ADVANCING 1 LINE ASSUMED.
112	IKF3001I-E	TOTAL NOT DEFINED. DISCARDED.

ERROR MESSAGE

	IKF6006I-E	SUPMAP SPECIFIED AND E-LEVEL DIAGNOSTIC HAS OCCURRED. PMAP CLIST LOAD DECK STATE FLOW SYMDMP IGNORED/

Figure 5.8 *(Continued)*

CHAPTER SIX

Programming Style, I

As a beginning student, your objective should simply be a working program. **Overview**
As an advanced student or professional, your objective is enlarged, namely an
"efficient" program which is easily read and maintained by someone other than
yourself. Further, the professional's program should conform to his installation's standards. It must be tested under a variety of conditions, including
obviously improper data, and should include programming checks to flag
potential invalid transactions. In short, while the beginner is concerned with
merely translating a working flowchart into COBOL, the professional requires
a better flowchart, straightforward logic, easy-to-read COBOL code, and a
well-tested program.

Over time, an individual develops a collection of techniques, i.e., a style, to
accomplish his objectives. Most introductory texts omit programming style
entirely, or at best devote only a few pages to the subject near the end of the
book. We believe that the topic is so important that it merits two entire
chapters and further that coverage should begin as soon as basic programming
concepts have been established. We have found that an early awareness of
"style" is highly beneficial to both student and professional. Individuals con-
scious of style tend to write programs that are easier to read, easier to debug,
and more apt to be correct.

In this chapter we are concerned with two elements of programming style: coding standards and structured programming. There are no absolute truths, i.e., no right or wrong, insofar as programming style is concerned. Different programmers develop slightly or even radically different styles that are consistent within the rules of COBOL and within the programmer's objective. Accordingly, the discussion which follows here and in Chapter 11 reflects the viewpoints of the authors and is necessarily subjective in parts.

Coding Standards

In spite of what you may think of the COBOL compiler, COBOL is a relatively free-form language. There is considerable flexibility as to starting column for most entries (i.e., in or beyond column 12). The rules for paragraph and data names make for easy-to-write, but not necessarily easy-to-read, programs.

In a commercial installation, it is absolutely essential that programs be well documented, as the person who writes a program today may not be here tomorrow. Indeed, continuing success depends on someone other than the author being able to maintain a program. Accordingly, most installations impose a set of coding standards, such as those described herein, which go beyond the requirements of COBOL. Such standards are optional for the student. However, they are typical of what is required in the real world.

Data Division

1. *Begin all PICTURE clauses in the same column*—usually between columns 36 and 52, but the choice is arbitrary. Further, choose one form of the PICTURE clause (PIC, PIC IS, PICTURE, or PICTURE IS) and follow it consistently. The actual starting column and form chosen are immaterial, but consistency is essential. Vertical alignment of the PICTURE clause greatly improves the overall appearance of a COBOL program. (Similar guidelines apply to the VALUE and USAGE clauses as well.)

2. *Prefix all data names within the same FD*, e.g., two characters unique to the FD: CD-LAST-NAME, CD-FIRST-NAME, CD-ADDRESS, etc. The utility of this guideline becomes apparent in the procedure division if it is necessary to refer back to the definition of a data name. The prefix points you immediately to the proper FD.

3. *Prefix all 77-level entries by WS and list them in alphabetical order.* The reasoning is similar to the previous suggestion. "WS" in front of a data name indicates its definition occurred in the working-storage section. Alphabetical listing speeds references, particularly in long (i.e., real-world) application programs.

4. *Indent successive level numbers in an FD by a consistent amount*, e.g., two or four columns. Use the same level numbers from FD to FD and leave numerical gaps between successive levels: 05, 10, 15, 20 or 03, 07, 11, 15, etc.

5. *Choose mnemonically significant data names.* COBOL allows data names up to 30 characters, but 2- and 3-character cryptic names are used frequently. Use meaningful data-names!

6. *Indent successive lines of the same entry.* If a given statement contains several clauses, it is usually not possible to fit the entire entry on one line. In those instances the continued line should be indented. Further, a clause should not be split over two lines (not always possible with VALUE clauses).

The COBOL code below summarizes these suggestions:

```
01  STUDENT-INPUT-RECORD.
    05  SR-STUDENT-NAME.
        10  SR-STUDENT-LAST-NAME      PICTURE IS A(20).
        10  SR-STUDENT-FIRST-NAME     PICTURE IS A(10).
```

```
05  SR-BIRTH-DATE.
    10  SR-BIRTH-MONTH        PICTURE IS 99.
    10  SR-BIRTH-YEAR         PICTURE IS 99.
            .
            .
            .

  WORKING-STORAGE SECTION.
  77  WS-STUDENT-COUNT        PICTURE IS 9(4)
          VALUE IS ZERO.
  77  WS-TOTAL-TUITION        PICTURE IS 9(6)
          VALUE IS ZERO.
```

Procedure Division

1. *Do not put more than one statement on a line.* The COBOL compiler accepts a period as the delimiter between statements, but a new line is much easier for the eye to follow. Further, if a sentence extends past column 72, then continued lines should be indented by a consistent amount, e.g., four columns.

2. *Paragraph and section headers should be the only entries on a line.* Thus, the first statement in a section or paragraph should always begin a new line. In addition a blank line before each paragraph or section name helps the entry to further stand out. IBM compilers permit SKIP1, SKIP2, and SKIP3 (beginning in or past column 12) to skip one, two, or three lines, respectively.

3. *Sequence all section and paragraph names*, e.g., 0010-HOUSEKEEPING, 0020-READ-A-CARD, etc. This technique makes it easy to locate paragraphs and/or section headers quickly and is particularly important for large programs.

4. *Highlight important verbs or clauses by indenting or inserting a blank line.* We like to indent all nested IF statements and also precede them by a blank line. Additional verbs, clauses, etc., are at programmer discretion.

5. *Align IF/ELSE statements with the ELSE portion under the relevant IF.* This can be tricky, particularly with nested IF's required for structured programming (see the next section). The compiler does not interpret ELSE clauses as the programmer writes them but *associates the ELSE clause with the closest unpaired previous IF.* Incorrect indentation in a listing conveys a programmer's intention, which is not recognized by the compiler. Consider the *misleading* example

```
IF CD-SEX IS EQUAL TO 'M'
    IF CD-AGE IS GREATER THAN 30
        MOVE CD-NAME TO MALE-OVER-30,
ELSE MOVE CD-NAME TO REJECT.
```

The indentation implies that CD-NAME should be moved to REJECT if CD-SEX is not equal to 'M'. This is *not* the compiler interpretation. *The ELSE clause is associated with the closest previous IF which is not already paired with another ELSE.* Therefore the compiler will move CD-NAME to REJECT if CD-SEX equals 'M' but CD-AGE is not greater than 30.

Two or more IF's within the same sentence are known as a nested IF statement. Such statements are difficult to interpret, and consequently some installations avoid them entirely. However, nested IF statements are required for structured programming. Indeed the pros and cons of the nested IF demonstrate how programming style is an individual (or installation) concern and how "one man's meat is another's poison."

6. *Stack, i.e., vertically align, similar portions of a statement or group of statements.* The MOVE statement provides a good example:

```
MOVE CD-NAME          TO PR-NAME.
MOVE CD-STUDENT-ID    TO PR-STUDENT-ID.
MOVE CD-AGE           TO PR-AGE.
MOVE CD-ADDRESS       TO PR-ADDRESS.
                                etc.
```

Both Divisions

1. *Use blank lines, SKIP's, and EJECT's freely.* EJECT (restricted to IBM systems) causes the next statement in a COBOL listing to begin on top of a new page. SKIP1, SKIP2, and SKIP3 (also restricted to IBM) cause the listing to space one, two, or three lines, respectively, before the next statement. Blank lines, SKIP's, and EJECT's should be freely used prior to section and division headers, FD's, 01's, etc.

2. *Use comments and set them off by boxing with ****s.* Free use of comments increases the self-documentation capability of COBOL. A comment is indicated by an * in column 7; the remainder of the line is listed, but ignored by the compiler. Comments may be boxed in the following manner:

```
*****************************************************************
*                                                             *
*                 THIS IS A COMMENT                           *
*                                                             *
*****************************************************************
```

Structured Programming

Structured programming, whatever it is, fills much of the current literature in data processing. Strong proponents say it is the greatest thing since the invention of the wheel, or at least the most significant development since the digital computer itself. Opponents contend it is nothing special and that good programs have always been structured. Proponents say that structured programs are easy to read; opponents argue that "GO TO less" programs are unnatural and difficult to follow. Very few people are indifferent about the subject.

In this discussion, structured programming is considered as only one element in programming style. We do not believe that a structured program is in and of itself a good program or that a nonstructured program is necessarily a poor one. We define the term, use structured programming throughout the text, and *encourage* its use. (The advantages of the technique are well presented by the file maintenance programs in Chapters 11, 15 and 16).

A structured program can be written using only the three logic structures of Figure 6.1:

1. Sequence
2. Selection (IF THEN ELSE)
3. Iteration (DO WHILE)

An additional structure, CASE, (GO TO DEPENDING), is presented in Chapter 11. The essential idea is that there is exactly one entry and one exit point for any of these structures.

The *sequence* structure formally specifies that program statements are executed sequentially, i.e., in the order in which they appear unless otherwise specified. The two blocks, A and B, may denote anything from single statements to complete programs.

Selection is the choice between two actions. A condition (known as a predicate) is tested. If the predicate is true, THEN block A is executed; ELSE

(a) SEQUENCE

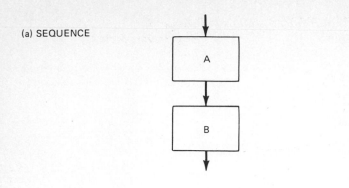

(b) SELECTION (IF THEN ELSE)

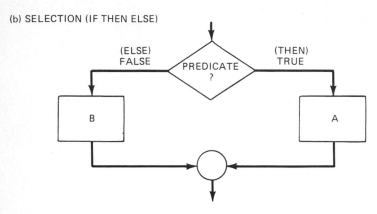

(c) ITERATION (DO WHILE)

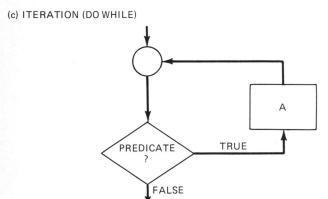

Figure 6.1 The Logic Structures of a "Proper" Program

if it is false, then block B is executed. A and B join in a single exit point from the structure. The predicate itself is the single entry point.

Iteration calls for repeated execution of code while a condition is true. The condition (predicate) is tested. If it holds true, block A is executed; if false, the structure relinquishes control to the next sequential statement. Again, there is exactly one entry point and exit point from the structure.

Conspicuous by its absence in Figure 6.1 is the unconditional transfer of control, i.e., the GO TO statement, and hence the term "GO TO less" program. In conventional, i.e., nonstructured programs, the GO TO statement often occupies 10% of the procedure division. This causes the program flow to "jump around" and often obscures the logic. Proponents believe therefore that structured programs are inherently easier to follow.

The logic structures of Figure 6.1 can be combined in a limitless variety of ways to produce any required logic. This is possible because an entire structure may be substituted anywhere block A or B appears. Figure 6.2 contains such a

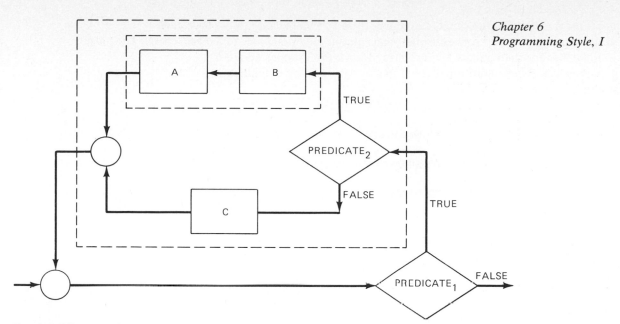

Figure 6.2 Combination of Logic Structures

combination. The iteration structure contains a selection structure, which in turn contains a sequence. Each of the structures contains one entry and one exit point.

Implementation in COBOL

The sequence structure is implemented by coding statements sequentially, and no further explanation is necessary. The selection structure is implemented by the COBOL "IF THEN ELSE" statement, and the iteration structure by the COBOL "PERFORM UNTIL."

IF THEN ELSE Structure

The COBOL "IF THEN ELSE" has the general format

```
IF condition
    statement 1
ELSE
    statement 2.
```

The condition generally tests the relationship between two items, e.g., equal, less than, etc. Statements 1 and 2 denote any COBOL statement (or group of statements) which are to be executed if the condition is true or false, respectively.

For example, consider the computation of the student union fee in the tuition billing problem. Union members (denoted by a 'Y' on the input card) are to be charged a fee of $25; nonmembers are not charged anything. This is coded as follows:

```
IF UNION-MEMBER IS EQUAL TO 'Y'
    MOVE 25 TO UNION-FEE
ELSE
    MOVE ZERO TO UNION-FEE.
```

The predicate tests whether 'Y' is contained in the field UNION-MEMBER. If so, 25 is moved to UNION-FEE; if not, 0 is moved to UNION-FEE.

In the general form of the IF statement, statements 1 and 2 can each denote a series of statements. Suppose, for example, that union members are to receive season tickets to football games and are also to have their names added to a member mailing list. These additional requirements are met by extending the code of statement 1 above as shown:

```
IF UNION-MEMBER IS EQUAL TO 'Y'
     MOVE 25               TO UNION-FEE
     MOVE STUDENT-NAME     TO FOOTBALL-TICKET-LIST
     MOVE STUDENT-NAME     TO MEMBER-MAILING-LIST
ELSE
     MOVE ZERO             TO UNION-FEE.
```

Statements 1 and 2 can also denote additional IF statements. Consider the specification for calculating the activity fee in the tuition billing example:

Credits Taken	Activity Fee
0–6	$25
7–12	$50
13 or more	$75

These instructions are represented by combining two selection structures as shown in Figure 6.3. (Note that credits must be less than 7 for a fee of $25.) It is now a simple matter to establish the correct COBOL code:

```
IF CREDITS < 7
     MOVE 25 TO ACTIVITY-FEE
ELSE
     IF CREDITS > 12
          MOVE 75 TO ACTIVITY-FEE
     ELSE
          MOVE 50 TO ACTIVITY-FEE.
```

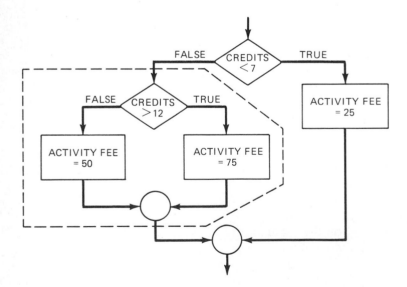

Figure 6.3 Nested IF Structure

Note that the IF and its associated ELSE have similar indentations for clarity, as described in the section on coding standards. This is not a COBOL requirement but rather a technique to improve clarity.

The PERFORM verb is one of the more powerful in COBOL. We shall discuss a simplified format in this section and defer additional material on the PERFORM verb until Chapters 7 and 9. The general format is as follows:

```
PERFORM paragraph-name-1 [THRU paragraph-name-2]
    [UNTIL condition]
```

The PERFORM statement causes a portion of code to be executed. It transfers control to the paragraph specified, continues execution from that point until another paragraph is encountered, and then returns control to the statement immediately following the perform statement.

If the UNTIL clause is specified, the condition in the UNTIL clause is tested *prior* to any transfer of control. The performed paragraph is executed until the condition is met; i.e., if the condition is not satisfied, transfer takes place as described in the preceding paragraph. When the condition is satisfied, control passes to the statement following the PERFORM.

Iteration is accomplished by using the UNTIL clause, specifying a condition, and modifying that condition during execution of the performed paragraph. Two examples are shown:

```
MOVE 'NO' TO END-OF-FILE-SWITCH.
PERFORM READ-A-CARD
    UNTIL END-OF-FILE-SWITCH = 'YES'.
    .
    .
    .

READ-A-CARD.
    .
    .
    .
    READ CARD-FILE, AT END MOVE 'YES' TO END-OF-FILE-SWITCH.
```

The paragraph READ-A-CARD will be performed until END-OF-FILE-SWITCH equals 'YES', i.e., until there are no more data cards. When the end of file is reached, the END-OF-FILE-SWITCH is set to YES. This causes the next test of the UNTIL condition to fail and prevents the READ-A-CARD paragraph from further execution. (Care must be taken in using this technique, for unless one is very careful, the last card is processed twice. This point is made clearer in Figure 6.4, discussed in the next section.)

A second example involves the establishment of a counter.

```
MOVE 1 TO COUNTER.
PERFORM PARAGRAPH-A UNTIL COUNTER > 20.
    .
    .
    .

PARAGRAPH-A.
    ADD 1 TO COUNTER.
    .
    .
    .
```

PARAGRAPH-A will be executed 20 times. Remember, the condition is tested *prior* to performing the specified paragraph.

The PERFORM statement is frequently used with the THRU option to delineate the range of the PERFORM, e.g.,

```
PERFORM PARAGRAPH-A THRU PARAGRAPH-A-EXIT.
```

The latter paragraph should consist of a single entry, EXIT, which merely denotes the end of the PERFORM.

The tuition billing example of Figure 4.8 has been rewritten to reflect the ideas of this chapter. Although no objections were raised to Figure 4.8 at the time of its development, Figure 6.4 is superior because of the attention to programming style.

COBOL statements 91–96 are the *mainline* portion of the program. Execution beings at line 91, which performs 010-HOUSEKEEPING. Control is returned to line 92, which reads and processes student cards until the end of file is reached (note the use of the THRU option to delineate the range of this perform). Control next passes to line 94 for university totals and finally to lines 95 and 96 for end-of-job processing.

Note well the two READ statements, lines 100 and 161. Both are required, and must be placed as shown, for the program to execute correctly as a structured program. Explanation is facilitated by the assumption of only one data card. The READ of line 100 is part of housekeeping and is done once.

```
00001              IDENTIFICATION DIVISION.
00002              PROGRAM-ID.  'TUITION'.
00003              AUTHOR.      THE BURSAR.
00004
00005
00006              ENVIRONMENT DIVISION.
00007
00008              CONFIGURATION SECTION.
00009              SOURCE-COMPUTER.  IBM-370.
00010              OBJECT-COMPUTER.  IBM-370.
00011              SPECIAL-NAMES.
00012                   C01 IS TOP-OF-PAGE.
00013
00014              INPUT-OUTPUT SECTION.
00015              FILE-CONTROL.
00016                   SELECT CARD-FILE ASSIGN TO UR-2540R-S-SYSIN.
00017                   SELECT PR-FILE ASSIGN TO UR-1403-S-SYSOUT.
00018
00019
00020              DATA DIVISION.
00021              FILE SECTION.
00022              FD  CARD-FILE
00023                   RECORDING MODE IS F
00024                   LABEL RECORDS ARE OMITTED
00025                   RECORD CONTAINS 80 CHARACTERS
00026                   DATA RECORD IS STUDENT-CARD.        — Prefix STUDENT-CARD entries
00027              01  STUDENT-CARD.
00028                   05  SC-STUDENT-NAME     PIC A(20).
00029                   05  SC-SOC-SEC-NO       PIC 9(9).
00030                   05  SC-CREDITS          PIC 9(2).
00031                   05  SC-UNION-MEMBER     PIC A.
00032                   05  SC-SCHOLARSHIP      PIC 9(4).
00033                   05  FILLER              PIC X(44).
00034              FD  PR-FILE
00035                   RECORDING MODE IS F
00036                   LABEL RECORDS ARE OMITTED
00037                   RECORD CONTAINS 133 CHARACTERS
00038                   DATA RECORD IS PRINT-LINE.
00039              01  PRINT-LINE.                              Vertical alignment of
00040                   05  FILLER          PIC X.            PICTURE clause
00041                   05  PR-STUDENT-NAME PIC A(20).
00042                   05  FILLER          PIC X(2).
00043                   05  PR-SOC-SEC-NO   PIC 999B99B9999.
00044                   05  FILLER          PIC X(4).
00045                   05  PR-CREDITS      PIC 99.
00046                   05  FILLER          PIC X(3).
00047                   05  PR-TUITION      PIC  $$$$,$$9.
00048                   05  FILLER          PIC X(1).
00049                   05  PR-UNION-FEE    PIC  $$$$,$$9.
```

Figure 6.4 Tuition Billing as a Structured Program

```
00050              05   FILLER              PIC X(3).
00051              05   PR-ACTIVITY-FEE     PIC   $$$$,$$9.
00052              05   FILLER              PIC X(3).
00053              05   PR-SHOLARSHIP       PIC   $$$$,$$9.
00054              05   FILLER              PIC X(5).
00055              05   PR-IND-BILL         PIC   $$$$,$$9.
00056              05   FILLER              PIC X(38).          ── Vertical alignment of
00057                                                              PICTURE clause
00058          WORKING-STORAGE SECTION.
00059          77   WS-ACTIVITY-FEE         PIC 9(2)    VALUE ZEROS.
00060          77   WS-END-OF-FILE-INDICATOR PIC X      VALUE SPACES.
00061          77   WS-INDIVIDUAL-BILL      PIC 9(4)    VALUE ZEROS.
00062  WS prefix  77   WS-TOTAL-ACTIVITY-FEE   PIC 9(6)    VALUE ZEROS.
00063          77   WS-TOTAL-IND-BILL       PIC 9(6)    VALUE ZEROS.
00064          77   WS-TOTAL-SCHOLARSHIP    PIC 9(6)    VALUE ZEROS.
00065          77   WS-TOTAL-TUITTON        PIC 9(6)    VALUE ZEROS.
00066          77   WS-TUTAL-UNION-FEE      PIC 9(6)    VALUE ZEROS.
00067          77   WS-TUITION              PIC 9(4)    VALUE ZEROS.
00068          77   WS-UNION-FEE            PIC 9(2)    VALUE ZEROS.
00069          01   HEADER-LINE.                                ── Vertical alignment of
00070              05   FILLER              PIC X.                  VALUE clause
00071              05   HDG-NAME            PIC X(12)   VALUE 'STUDENT NAME'.
00072              05   FILLER              PIC X(10)   VALUE SPACES.
00073              05   HDG-SOC-SEC         PIC X(11)   VALUE 'SOC SEC NUM'.
00074              05   FILLER              PIC X(2)    VALUE SPACES.
00075              05   HDG-CREDITS         PIC X(7)    VALUE 'CREDITS'.
00076              05   FILLER              PIC X(2)    VALUE SPACES.
00077              05   HDG-TUITION         PIC X(7)    VALUE 'TUITION'.
00078              05   FILLER              PIC X(2)    VALUE SPACES.
00079              05   HDG-UNION-FEE       PIC X(9)    VALUE 'UNION FEE'.
00080              05   FILLER              PIC X(2)    VALUE SPACES.
00081              05   HDG-ACTIVITY        PIC X(7)    VALUE 'ACT FEE'.
00082              05   FILLER              PIC X(2)    VALUE SPACES.
00083              05   HDG-SCHOLAR         PIC X(11)   VALUE 'SCHOLARSHIP'.
00084              05   FILLER              PIC X(2)    VALUE SPACES.
00085              05   HDG-TOTAL-BILL      PIC X(10)   VALUE 'TOTAL BILL'.
00086              05   FILLER              PIC X(36)   VALUE SPACES.
00087
00088
00089          PROCEDURE DIVISION.
00090
00091          PERFORM 010-HOUSEKEEPING.
00092  Mainline routine  PERFORM 020-READ-A-CARD THRU 020-READ-A-CARD-EXIT
00093              UNTIL WS-END-OF-FILE-INDICATOR = 'Y'.
00094          PERFORM 070-WRITE-UNIVERSITY-TOTALS.          Use of THRU option
00095          CLOSE CARD-FILE, PR-FILE.                     to delineate range of PERFORM
00096          STOP RUN.
00097
00098          010-HOUSEKEEPING.
00099              OPEN INPUT CARD-FILE, OUTPUT PR-FILE.
00100              READ CARD-FILE, AT END MOVE 'Y' TO WS-END-OF-FILE-INDICATOR.
00101              MOVE HEADER-LINE TO PRINT-LINE.
```

Figure 6.4 *(Continued)*

```
00102              WRITE PRINT-LINE AFTER ADVANCING TOP-OF-PAGE LINES.
00103              MOVE SPACES TO PRINT-LINE.
00104              MOVE '----------------------------------------------
00105          -   '----------------------------------------' TO PRINT-LINE.
00106              WRITE PRINT-LINE AFTER ADVANCING 1 LINES.
00107
00108          020-READ-A-CARD.
00109              COMPUTE WS-TUITION = 80 * SC-CREDITS.
00110
00111              IF SC-UNION-MEMBER IS EQUAL TO 'Y'
00112                  MOVE 25 TO WS-UNION-FEE
00113              ELSE
00114                  MOVE ZERO TO WS-UNION-FEE.
00115
00116              IF SC-CREDITS < 7
00117                  MOVE 25 TO WS-ACTIVITY-FEE
00118              ELSE
00119                  IF SC-CREDITS IS > 12
C0120                      MOVE 75 TO WS-ACTIVITY-FEE
00121                  ELSE
00122                      MOVE 50 TO WS-ACTIVITY-FEE.
```

Nested IF with appropriate indentation

```
00123
00124          ****************************************************************
00125          *                                                              *
00126          *            COMPUTE INDIVIDUAL BILL                           *
00127          *                                                              *
00128          ****************************************************************
00129
00130              COMPUTE WS-INDIVIDUAL-BILL = WS-TUITION + WS-UNION-FEE
00131                  + WS-ACTIVITY-FEE - SC-SCHOLARSHIP.
00132
00133          ****************************************************************
00134          *                                                              *
00135          *            UPDATE UNIVERSITY TOTALS                          *
00136          *                                                              *
00137          ****************************************************************
```

"Boxed" comment

```
00138
00139              ADD WS-TUITION              TO WS-TOTAL-TUITION.
00140              ADD WS-UNION-FEE            TO WS-TOTAL-UNION-FEE.
00141              ADD WS-ACTIVITY-FEE         TO WS-TOTAL-ACTIVITY-FEE.
00142              ADD WS-INDIVIDUAL-BILL      TO WS-TOTAL-IND-BILL.
00143              ADD SC-SCHOLARSHIP          TO WS-TOTAL-SCHOLARSHIP.
00144
00145          ****************************************************************
00146          *                                                              *
00147          *            WRITE INDIVIDUAL LINE                             *
00148          *                                                              *
00149          ****************************************************************
00150
00151              MOVE SPACES TO PRINT-LINE.
00152              MOVE SC-STUDENT-NAME        TO PR-STUDENT-NAME.
00153              MOVE SC-SOC-SEC-NO          TO PR-SOC-SEC-NO.
00154              MOVE SC-CREDITS             TO PR-CREDITS.
00155              MOVE WS-TUITION             TO PR-TUITION.
00156              MOVE WS-UNION-FEE           TO PR-UNION-FEE.
00157              MOVE WS-ACTIVITY-FEE        TO PR-ACTIVITY-FEE.
00158              MOVE SC-SCHOLARSHIP         TO PR-SHOLARSHIP.
00159              MOVE WS-INDIVIDUAL-BILL     TO PR-IND-BILL.
00160              WRITE PRINT-LINE AFTER ADVANCING 1 LINES.
00161              READ CARD-FILE, AT END MOVE 'Y' TO WS-END-OF-FILE-INDICATOR.
00162
00163          020-READ-A-CARD-EXIT.
00164              EXIT.
00165
00166          070-WRITE-UNIVERSITY-TOTALS.
00167              MOVE SPACES TO PRINT-LINE.
00168              MOVE '----------------------------------------------
00169          -   '----------------------------------------' TO PRINT-LINE.
00170              WRITE PRINT-LINE AFTER ADVANCING 1 LINES.
00171              MOVE SPACES                 TO PRINT-LINE.
00172              MOVE WS-TOTAL-TUITION       TO PR-TUITION.
00173              MOVE WS-TOTAL-UNION-FEE     TO PR-UNION-FEE.
00174              MOVE WS-TOTAL-ACTIVITY-FEE  TO PR-ACTIVITY-FEE.
00175              MOVE WS-TOTAL-SCHOLARSHIP   TO PR-SHOLARSHIP.
00176              MOVE WS-TOTAL-IND-BILL      TO PR-IND-BILL.
00177              WRITE PRINT-LINE AFTER ADVANCING 2 LINES.
```

Numerical sequence for paragraph names

Figure 6.4 *(Continued)*

When 020-READ-A-CARD is initially entered via the PERFORM of line 92, that first data card is processed. At the end of that perform, CARD-FILE is accessed again. Since there is only one data card, 'Y' is moved to the end-of-file switch. This causes the next test of the until condition to fail, and control passes to line 94. This reasoning is easily extended to 'n' data cards.

Coding standards are used throughout Figure 6.4. CARD-FILE and PRINT-FILE are prefixed by SC (Student-Card) and PR, respectively. All 77-level entries are prefixed by WS and listed in alphabetical order. Paragraph names begin with a numerical sequence. PICTURE and VALUE clauses are vertically aligned. Blank lines are inserted before IF's, and the ELSE portion is coded under the associated IF. Comments are included and boxed.

Figure 6.5 is a structured flowchart for the tuition billing program. It contains logic identical to the nonstructured flowchart of Figure 4.7 but is considerably shorter. An identifying trait of a structured flowchart is the presence of rectangular blocks with vertical lines, which denote a performed procedure. This is essential to the *top-down modular* approach of structured programming.

Documentation of a Structured Program

The flowchart in Figure 6.5 depicts only the mainline logic of the program and corresponds to COBOL statements 91–96 in Figure 6.4. Each of the modules (i.e., performed procedures) would typically have their own flowcharts and be developed separately. The advantage to this approach is that the highest level of program logic is made clearer, and further it allows several programmers to develop individual modules. This is in direct contrast to the more traditional *bottom-up* approach, which begins with the detailed logic and leaves the mainline for last.

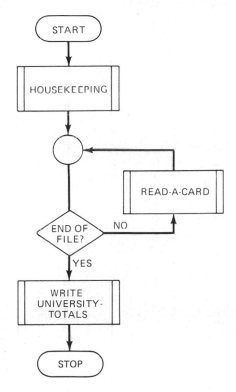

Figure 6.5 Structured Flowchart for Tuition Billing Program

A well-written program should be easily understood by someone other than the original author. Its logical flow should be readily apparent, and the program itself should be as self-documenting as possible. Legibility is one of the key aspects of a good program.

Summary

Structured programming and coding standards are both designed to accomplish this objective. These techniques can be used simultaneously, as in Figure 6.4, or individually (nondevotees of structured programming will use coding standards). Accordingly, a structured program is not in and of itself a good program, nor is a nonstructured program necessarily a poor one. Programming style is discussed further in Chapter 11.

1 Given the accompanying flowchart,

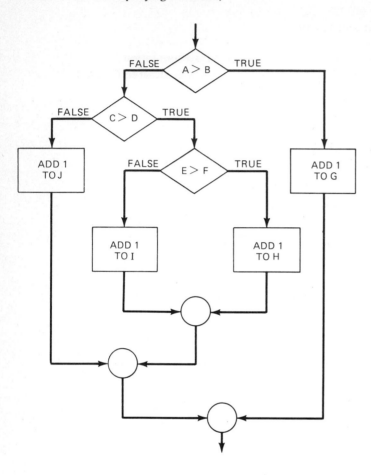

(a) Construct a nested COBOL IF to accomplish this logic.
(b) Respond true or false to the following based on the flowchart:
  1. If A > B and C > D, then *always* add 1 to J.
  2. If A > B, then *always* add 1 to G.
  3. If E > F, then *always* add 1 to H.
  4. If A < B and C < D, then *always* add 1 to J.
  5. There are no conditions under which 1 will be added to both G and J simultaneously.
  6. If C > D and E < F, then *always* add 1 to I.

2 Given the following procedure division,

```
PROCEDURE DIVISION.
    PERFORM 010-FIRST.
    PERFORM 020-SECOND THRU 030-THIRD.
    PERFORM 040-FOURTH UNTIL FINAL-SUM > 20.
    STOP RUN.
010-FIRST.
    MOVE 1 TO N.
    MOVE ZERO TO FINAL-SUM.
```

```
020-SECOND.
    COMPUTE M = N * 2.
    COMPUTE X = N * 3.
    ADD 1 TO N.
030-THIRD.
    COMPUTE SUM = M + N + X.
040-FOURTH.
    ADD SUM TO FINAL-SUM.
050-FIFTH.
    ADD 1 TO N.
    ADD 1 TO X.
```

(a) What is the final value of SUM?

(b) What is the final value of FINAL-SUM?

(c) How many times is the paragraph 040-FOURTH executed?

(d) Are there any paragraphs which are not executed?

(e) Are there any paragraphs which are executed more than once?

3 Given the COBOL statement,

```
IF A > 100 MOVE 20 TO N, ELSE IF A = 100 MOVE 19 TO N,
ELSE IF B = 100 MOVE 30 TO N, ELSE MOVE 40 TO N.
```

(a) Rewrite the COBOL statement indenting the ELSE under the associated IF.

(b) Determine the value of N for the following pairs of A and B:

    1. A = 101, B = 100; N = ?

    2. A = 100, B = 100; N = ?

    3. A = 99, B = 100; N = ?

    4. A = 99, B = 99; N = ?

(c) Draw the flowchart corresponding to the intended logic.

4 Draw a flowchart corresponding to the following COBOL statements (use only the logic structures of Figure 6.1):

(a)
```
    IF A > B
        IF C > D
            MOVE E TO F
            MOVE G TO H
        ELSE
            ADD I TO J
    ELSE
        ADD K TO L
        ADD M TO N.
```

(b)
```
        MOVE ZERO TO SUM.
        MOVE 1 TO WS-COUNTER.
        PERFORM 010-TOTALS UNTIL WS-COUNTER > 10.
        STOP RUN.
    010-TOTALS.
        ADD 1 TO N.
        COMPUTE SUM = SUM + N * N.
        ADD 1 TO WS-COUNTER.
```

(c)
```
    IF A > B
        IF C > D
            IF E > F
                MOVE 1 TO G
            ELSE
                ADD 1 TO H.
```

More COBOL

**CHAPTER
SEVEN**

More About
the Procedure Division

This chapter begins the third section in our text. Section I (Chapters 1 and 2) **Overview** consisted of a general introduction to computers and the programming process. In Section II (Chapters 3–6) we learned the rudiments of programming. We learned how to write a COBOL program, how to debug it, and were made aware of programming style. Now we are concerned with becoming proficient in COBOL.

This chapter is devoted entirely to the procedure division. Its objective is to introduce a somewhat disjoint set of procedure division elements to increase one's overall capability in COBOL. We shall study the IF and PERFORM statements in detail. We shall learn some new verbs to make life easier, e.g., ACCEPT, DISPLAY, and EXAMINE. We shall learn new options for statements we already know something about, e.g., READ INTO, WRITE FROM, and MOVE CORRESPONDING. We shall also cover the ROUNDED and SIZE ERROR options of the arithmetic verbs.

There is so much material in this chapter that it is not possible to master it all in a first reading. We suggest you read initially for general content only and leave the details for later. Try to get a "feel" for the overall power of the material but do not attempt to memorize all the options. Instead, return to specific portions in the chapter as you need the material in your projects.

The IF Statement is often used incorrectly. Its importance is obvious, yet the large number of options make it one of the more difficult statements to master. The IF statement was introduced in Chapter 3. Now we shall extend the condition portion to include class tests, sign tests, and condition names (88-level entries). Next we shall consider compound IF's via AND and OR. Finally, we shall take a good look at the NEXT SENTENCE and ELSE options and nested IF's.

Class Tests

If you haven't already realized, improper data are a frequent cause of a program's failure to execute. A numeric field can contain only the digits 0–9 (a sign is optional), while an alphabetic field can contain only the letters A–Z and/or blanks. Alphanumeric fields can contain anything, e.g., combinations of letters and numbers or special characters, e.g., +, &, etc.

The presence of nonnumeric data in a numeric field used for computation can cause some rather unpleasant results (see Chapter 13 on dump reading and the data exception). Class tests are an excellent way to ensure that numeric data are numeric, alphabetic data are alphabetic, etc. The general format is

$$\text{IF identifier IS [\underline{NOT}]} \begin{Bmatrix} \text{NUMERIC} \\ \text{ALPHABETIC} \end{Bmatrix}$$

The class test cannot be used indiscriminately. Specifically, a numeric test is used for data names defined with a numeric picture (i.e., a picture of 9's). An alphabetic test is valid for data names defined with a picture of A. However, either test may be performed on alphanumeric items. The validity of class tests is summarized in Table 7.1 and by examples in Figure 7.1.

Table 7.1 Valid Forms of Class Test

Data Type and Pictures	Valid Tests
Numeric (9)	NUMERIC, NOT NUMERIC
Alphabetic (A)	ALPHABETIC, NOT ALPHABETIC
Alphanumeric (X)	NUMERIC, NOT NUMERIC, ALPHABETIC, NOT ALPHABETIC

```
        05  NUMERIC-FIELD        PIC 9(5).
        05  ALPHABETIC-FIELD     PIC A(5).
        05  ALPHANUMERIC-FIELD   PIC X(5).

(valid)     IF NUMERIC-FIELD IS NUMERIC.....
(valid)     IF NUMERIC-FIELD IS NOT NUMERIC.....
(invalid)   IF NUMERIC-FIELD IS NOT ALPHABETIC.....
(invalid)   IF ALPHABETIC-FIELD IS NOT NUMERIC.....
(valid)     IF ALPHANUMERIC-FIELD IS NOT NUMERIC.....
(valid)     IF ALPHANUMERIC-FIELD IS NOT ALPHABETIC.....
```

Figure 7.1 Examples of Class Test

116

The relational test was first discussed in Chapter 3 when we introduced the IF statement. The general form of the relational test is

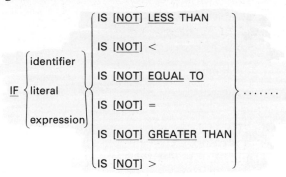

The action of the relational test is easily predictable when only numeric quantities are involved, but more explanation is required concerning alphabetic or alphanumeric items. Assume BAKER is compared to BROWN. BAKER is considered smaller since it is alphabetically before BROWN. Comparison proceeds from left to right one letter at a time. Both names begin with B, but the A in BAKER precedes the R in BROWN.

Now compare GREEN to GREENFIELD. GREEN is considered smaller. Comparison again proceeds from left to right. The first five characters, G, R, E, E, and N, are the same in both names. The shorter field, GREEN, is extended with blanks so that comparison may continue. A blank, however, is always considered smaller than any other letter so that GREEN is the smaller of the two names.

Comparison is possible on alphanumeric fields as well as alphabetic fields. In this instance, determination of the smaller field depends on the collating sequence of the machine. Collating sequence is defined as the ordered list (from low to high) of all valid characters. Collating sequence is a function of manufacturer; IBM uses EBCDIC, while most others use ASCII. Both sequences are shown in Figure 7.2 for selected characters.

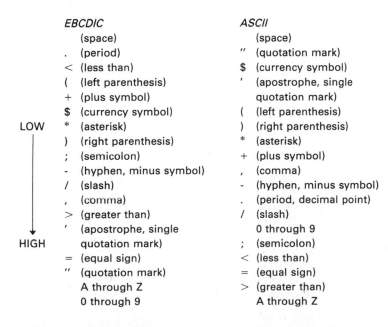

Figure 7.2 Collating Sequences

As can be seen from Figure 7.2, 1 is greater than A for EBCDIC. Under ASCII, however, 1 is less than A. It is certainly not necessary for you to memorize either collating sequence. Simply learn which one applies to your machine and be aware of the conceptual significance.

Sign Test

The sign test determines the sign of a numeric data field; the general format is

$$\text{IF} \begin{Bmatrix} \text{identifier} \\ \text{arithmetic expression} \end{Bmatrix} \text{IS [NOT]} \begin{Bmatrix} \underline{\text{POSITIVE}} \\ \underline{\text{NEGATIVE}} \\ \underline{\text{ZERO}} \end{Bmatrix}$$

A value is positive if it is greater than zero and negative if it is less than zero. This test is frequently used to validate incoming data or to verify the results of a calculation. Consider these examples:

```
IF NET-PAY IS NOT POSITIVE PERFORM TOO-MUCH-TAXES.
IF CHECK-BALANCE IS NEGATIVE PERFORM OVERDRAWN.
```

Condition Name Tests

The condition in the IF statement often tests the value of an incoming code, e.g., IF YEAR-CODE = '1'. . . . While such coding is quite permissible, and indeed commonplace, the meaning of the value '1' in YEAR-CODE is not immediately apparent. An alternative form of coding, condition names (88-level entries), provides superior documentation. 88-Level entries appear in the data division and can be applied only to elementary items.

```
05  YEAR-CODE    PIC    X.
    88 FRESHMAN   VALUE  '1'.
    88 SOPHOMORE  VALUE  '2'.
    88 JUNIOR     VALUE  '3'.
    88 SENIOR     VALUE  '4'.
```

if the above entries were made in the data division, we can code

```
IF FRESHMAN
```

as equivalent to

```
IF YEAR-CODE = '1'
```

The advantage of condition names is twofold. First, they provide improved documentation; i.e., FRESHMAN is inherently clearer than YEAR-CODE = '1.' Second, they facilitate maintenance in that addition and/or changes to existing codes need be made in only one place. For example, suppose the code for freshman is subsequently changed to 'F'. Only a single change is required in the 88-level entry. If, however, condition names are not used, then we must find all occurrences of YEAR-CODE = '1' in the procedure division, and the chance of error is much greater.

Condition names are discussed again in Chapter 8.

Compound Tests

Any two "simple" tests (i.e., relational, class, condition name, or sign) may be combined to form a compound test. This is accomplished through the logical operators AND and OR. AND means both; i.e., two conditions must be satisfied for the IF to be considered true. OR means either; i.e., only one of the two conditions needs to be satisfied for the IF to be considered true. A flowchart and corresponding COBOL code is shown in Figure 7.3 depicting the AND condition. (Note that while we do not generally approve of the GO TO in a program, its use is pedagodically helpful in illustrating the concept of compound tests; i.e., OR and AND).

The flowchart in Figure 7.3 requires that *both* A be greater than B *and* C be greater than D in order to proceed to TRUE. If either of these tests fail, processing is directed to FALSE. This logic can be accomplished in a number of ways, two of which are shown in Figure 7.3. Method 1 uses the compound condition and in addition has the ELSE option if the test fails. Method 2 consists of three separate statements.

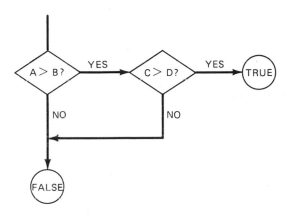

Illustrative Code:

Method 1:
```
    IF A > B AND C > D GO TO TRUE,
    ELSE GO TO FALSE.
```

Method 2:
```
    IF A NOT > B GO TO FALSE.
    IF C NOT > D GO TO FALSE.
    GO TO TRUE.
```

Figure 7.3 Flowchart and COBOL Code for the Compound AND

Figure 7.4 contains a flowchart and corresponding COBOL code for a compound OR. As can be seen from Figure 7.4, *only* one of two conditions needs to be met for the IF to be considered true. If either A is greater than B *or* C is greater than D, processing is directed to TRUE. In other words, the OR provides a second chance in that the first test can fail but the IF can still be considered true.

Beginning programmers are often carried away with compound conditions. Consider the statement

IF X > Y OR X = Z AND X < W...

Surely the programmer knew what he intended at the time he first wrote this statement. A day later, however, he is apt to stare at it and wonder what will happen first, i.e., which takes precedence, AND or OR? To provide an unequivocal evaluation of compound conditions the following hierarchy is established by COBOL:

1. Arithmetic expressions
2. Relational operators
3. NOT condition
4. AND (from left to right if more than one)
5. OR (from left to right if more than one)

119

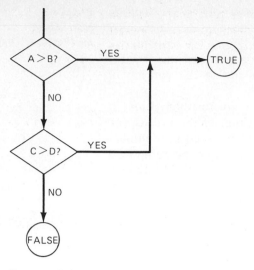

Illustrative Code:

```
Method 1:
    IF A >B OR C >D GO TO TRUE,
    ELSE GO TO FALSE.

Method 2:
    IF A >B GO TO TRUE.
    IF C >D GO TO TRUE.
    GO TO FALSE.
```

Figure 7.4 Flowchart and COBOL Code for the Compound OR

Thus, for the statement to be true either

$$X > Y$$

or

$$(X = Z) \quad \underline{\text{and}} \quad (X < W)$$

However, parentheses can and should be used to clarify the programmer's intent. The meaning of the above statement is made clearer if it is rewritten as

$$\text{IF } (X > Y) \text{ OR } (X = Z \text{ AND } X < W)\dots$$

Note well that parentheses can also *alter* meaning. Thus the statement below is *logically different* from the original code:

$$\text{IF } (X > Y \text{ OR } X = Z) \text{ AND } X < W\dots$$

Nested IF's

Nested IF's (several IF statements in one sentence) are possible in COBOL. Advocates of structured programming use them extensively, whereas other installations discourage (and even prohibit) their use. We like the capability, but suggest beginners do not *nest* more than three levels, as the resulting code can become difficult to follow.

The general format of the IF statement is

$$\underline{\text{IF}} \text{ condition} \left\{ \begin{array}{l} \text{statement-1} \\ \underline{\text{NEXT SENTENCE}} \end{array} \right\} \left[\underline{\text{ELSE}} \left\{ \begin{array}{l} \text{statement-2} \\ \underline{\text{NEXT SENTENCE}} \end{array} \right\} \right]$$

The condition may be any of the tests we have discussed, namely class, condition name, relational, sign, or compound. NEXT SENTENCE directs the computer to continue execution with the first statement following the period.

120

Nested IF's stem from the fact that either statement-1 or statement-2 may in turn be another IF statement. Consider Figure 7.5, which shows a flowchart and corresponding COBOL code to determine the largest of three quantities A, B, and C. (They are assumed to be unequal numbers.)

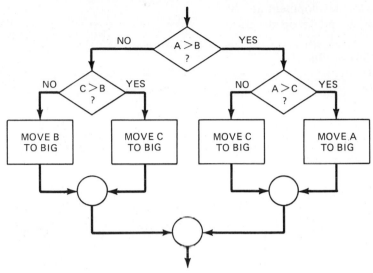

Illustrative Code:

```
IF A>B
       IF A>C
              MOVE A TO BIG
       ELSE
              MOVE C TO BIG
ELSE
       IF C>B
              MOVE C TO BIG
       ELSE
              MOVE B TO BIG.
```

Figure 7.5 Flowchart and COBOL Code for Nested IF's

Interpretation of the code in Figure 7.5 is tricky and can pose problems even for experienced programmers. Note well, however, that implementation of a nested IF is facilitated by the IF THEN ELSE logic structure of Chapter 6. Specifically, if the flowchart is drawn so that each block has only one entry and one exit point, subsequent coding is indeed simplified.

We would never attempt to use nested IF's without the indentation convention of Chapter 6; namely, align the ELSE clause under the associated IF. The rule for computer interpretation bears repeating: *The ELSE clause is associated with the closest previous IF which is not already paired with another ELSE.* Consider also the following COBOL statement:

IF A > B, IF C > D, MOVE X TO Y, ELSE ADD 1 TO Z.

The above should be recoded with appropriate indentation to clarify the programmer's intent. Thus,

```
IF A > B,
       IF C > D
              MOVE X TO Y
       ELSE
              ADD 1 TO Z.
```

Note that if the first condition fails, i.e., if A is not greater than B, control passes to the next sentence. Nested IF's can be tricky, but they can also be used to great advantage.

The PERFORM statement is one of the most powerful in COBOL. It enables transfer of control to and from a procedure (e.g., a paragraph) elsewhere in the program. The significance of this capability is that a complex program can be divided into a series of clear and straightforward routines. The mainline portion of the program consists essentially of a series of PERFORM statements. This style of programming is known as *top-down* development and has the immediate benefit of easy legibility. (See Chapters 6 and 11 on structured programming.)

The PERFORM statement has multiple forms and is so important that it is discussed in several places (see Chapters 6, 8, and 9).

Consider the simplest form and the following code:

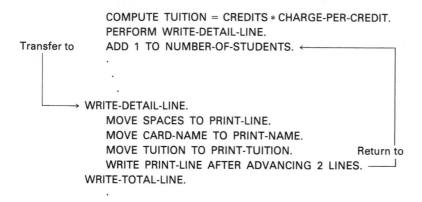

```
                 COMPUTE TUITION = CREDITS * CHARGE-PER-CREDIT.
                 PERFORM WRITE-DETAIL-LINE.
Transfer to      ADD 1 TO NUMBER-OF-STUDENTS.  ←─────────┐
                   .                                      │
                                                          │
                   .                                      │
                                                          │
                   .                                      │
              ┌─→ WRITE-DETAIL-LINE.                      │
                   MOVE SPACES TO PRINT-LINE.             │
                   MOVE CARD-NAME TO PRINT-NAME.          │
                   MOVE TUITION TO PRINT-TUITION.    Return to
                   WRITE PRINT-LINE AFTER ADVANCING 2 LINES. ─┘
                 WRITE-TOTAL-LINE.

                   .

                   .
```

The statement PERFORM WRITE-DETAIL-LINE transfers control to the first statement in the procedure WRITE-DETAIL-LINE. When every statement in WRITE-DETAIL-LINE has been executed (i.e., when the next paragraph name is encountered), control returns to the statement immediately after the PERFORM, i.e., to the ADD statement.

The procedure name in the PERFORM statement can be either a paragraph name or a section name. We already know what a paragraph is. A section consists of one or more paragraphs. If the procedure name in the PERFORM refers to a section name, then every paragraph in the section will be executed prior to returning control. Consider

```
                 PERFORM 010-READ-PROCESS-WRITE.
                   .                ←─────────────────┐
Transfer to        .                                  │
              ┌─→ 010-READ-PROCESS-WRITE SECTION.      │
                 011-READ.                             │
                   .                                   │
                                                       │
                   .                                   │
                                                       │
                 012-PROCESS.                          │
                   .                                   │
                                                       │
                   .                                   │
                                                       │
                 013-WRITE.                       Return to
                   .                                   │
                                                       │
                   .  ─────────────────────────────────┘
                 020-CONTINUE-PROCESSING SECTION.
```

When the PERFORM statement references a section-name, control is transferred to the first sentence in the section. Control will not return to the sentence after the PERFORM until the last statement in the section was executed. Notice that this results in the execution of several paragraphs. How does the compiler know when the section ends? Simply when a new section name is encountered. We tend to PERFORM sections rather than paragraphs, but either method is acceptable.

It is possible to enter a performed procedure and *not* return to the statement following the PERFORM. This happens if the performed procedure contains a 'GO TO' statement which transfers control out of the procedure. This is a decidedly poor practice and should *not* be attempted. Consider

```
PERFORM 010-READ-CARDS.
ADD 1 TO CARD-COUNTER.
   .
   .
   .
010-READ-CARDS.
   .
   .
   .
   IF CARD-CODE = 'F', GO TO 030-ERROR-ROUTINE.
   .
   .
   .
020-WRITE-DETAIL-LINE.
   .
   .
   .
030-ERROR-ROUTINE.
```

The PERFORM statement causes entry into 010-READ-CARDS. When that paragraph is finished, we expect to return to the statement after the PERFORM; i.e. to the ADD statement. However, if CARD-CODE = 'F', we never complete 010-READ-CARDS. Instead, we are directed to 030-ERROR-ROUTINE at which point execution continues sequentially. The program flow is badly obscured. Worse yet, subsequent execution of the routine 010-READ-CARDS may be invalid. Hence a cardinal rule, *never branch out of a performed routine via a GO TO*.

Obviously there will be situations where it is necessary to cease performing a given routine. The way to accomplish this is *not* by a GO TO out of the procedure, but via the THRU option of the PERFORM and the EXIT statement. Consider an extended format of the PERFORM:

PERFORM procedure-name-1 [THRU procedure-name-2].

The THRU option causes all statements between the two procedure names to be executed. Common practice is to make procedure-name-2 a single sentence paragraph consisting of the word EXIT. The EXIT statement causes no action to be taken; its function is to delineate the end of the PERFORM. Consider

PERFORM 010-READ-PROCESS THRU 020-READ-EXIT.

```
010-READ-PROCESS.
        .

        .

        .
        IF CARD-CODE = 'F', GO TO 020-READ-EXIT.
015-ANOTHER-PARAGRAPH.
        .

        .

        .
        IF CARD-CODE = 'G', GO TO 020-READ-EXIT.
018-STILL-ANOTHER-PARAGRAPH.
        .

        .

        IF CARD-CODE = 'H', GO TO 020-READ-EXIT.
020-READ-EXIT.
        EXIT.
```

Range
of
PERFORM

The PERFORM nominally causes execution of all statements within the two procedures. However, at various points within the PERFORM, we wish to return control to the statement after the PERFORM. This is readily accomplished by GO TO 020-READ-EXIT. The GO TO does *not* leave the PERFORM, but it does jump forward to the end of the PERFORM, i.e., to the EXIT statement. The PERFORM is terminated, and control returns to the statement after the PERFORM. Although the strictest definition of structured programming does not permit the use of GO TO, we believe its use in this fashion is completely permissible and indeed consistent with the overall goal of structured programming, namely greater legibility; i.e., we permit the use of GO TO provided it is a *forward* branch to an exit paragraph.

Another form of the PERFORM includes the UNTIL condition:

<u>PERFORM</u> procedure-name-1 [<u>THRU</u> procedure-name-2][<u>UNTIL</u> condition]

The specified procedure(s) are performed until the condition is satisfied. *The condition is tested prior to performing the procedure.* Thus, if the condition is satisfied initially, the procedure is never performed. For example,

```
MOVE 10 TO N.
PERFORM PAR-A UNTIL N = 10.
```

Since the condition is satisfied immediately (i.e., N = 10) PAR-A will never be performed. Consider this example:

```
MOVE 1 TO N.
PERFORM PAR-A THRU PAR-A-EXIT UNTIL N = 5.
    .

    .

    .
PAR-A.
    ADD 1 TO N.
    .

    .

    .
PAR-A-EXIT.
    EXIT.
```

PAR-A will be performed four times, not five. After the fourth time through PAR-A, N = 5. Thus when the condition is next tested, N = 5, and

PAR-A is not performed. (If we want the paragraph to be performed five times, change the condition to N > 5. An alternative way to accomplish the same thing is to retain N = 5 but MOVE ZERO TO N.)

The EXAMINE verb is used to accomplish two things:

1. To count the number of times a specified character appears within a field, and
2. To replace one character by another within a field.

The EXAMINE verb has two formats: consider the first:

$$\text{EXAMINE identifier \underline{REPLACING}} \left\{ \begin{array}{l} \text{\underline{UNTIL FIRST}} \\ \text{\underline{ALL}} \\ \text{\underline{LEADING}} \\ \text{\underline{FIRST}} \end{array} \right\} \text{literal-1 \underline{BY} literal-2}$$

This format is extremely useful for editing reports and is often used in conjunction with the edit characters of Chapters 4 and 8. Assume, for example, that the social security number is stored as a nine-position field (i.e., with no hyphens) but we wish it to appear with hyphens in a printed report. This is accomplished as follows:

```
01  CARD-IN.
      .
      .

    05  SOC-SEC-NUM                   PIC 9(9).
01  PRINT-LINE.
      .
      .

    05  SOC-SEC-NUM-OUT               PIC 999B99B9999.

PROCEDURE DIVISION.
      .
      .

        MOVE SOC-SEC-NUM TO SOC-SEC-NUM-OUT.
        EXAMINE SOC-SEC-NUM-OUT REPLACING ALL ' ' BY '–'.
```

The MOVE statement transfers the incoming social security number to an 11-position field containing two blanks (denoted by B in the PICTURE clause). The EXAMINE statement replaces every occurrence of a blank in SOC-SEC-NUM-OUT by the desired hyphen. (This technique is also used to insert /'s in date fields.)

Another frequent use of the EXAMINE verb is the elimination of leading blanks in numeric fields. Numeric fields in COBOL should not contain anything other than the digits 0–9 and a sign over the rightmost (low-order) position, although the latter is infrequently used. Let us assume a lazy keypuncher did not punch the leading zeros but left blanks instead. Such data cards might not be acceptable in subsequent numeric calculations, and corrective action must be taken. (IBM systems will, however, accept blanks as leading zeros.) One alternative is to repunch the data; our choice is to use the EXAMINE verb as follows:

```
EXAMINE FIELD-WITH-BLANKS REPLACING LEADING ' ' BY '0'.
```

A second format of the EXAMINE verb includes the TALLYING option:

$$\text{EXAMINE identifier } \underline{\text{TALLYING}} \begin{Bmatrix} \underline{\text{UNTIL FIRST}} \\ \underline{\text{ALL}} \\ \underline{\text{LEADING}} \end{Bmatrix} \text{ literal-1 } [\underline{\text{REPLACING BY}} \text{ literal-2}]$$

The TALLYING option counts the number of times a designated character appears. The count is contained in the data name TALLY, which is a COBOL reserved word. The programmer *must not* define TALLY in his data division. This form can contain the REPLACING option as well; indeed it can do everything the other format can except that FIRST is not permitted as an option before literal-1.

The EXAMINE verb is summarized in Table 7.2.

Table 7.2 Use of the EXAMINE Verb

	FIELD-A Before Execution	FIELD-A After Execution	Value of TALLY
EXAMINE FIELD-A REPLACING ALL ' ' BY '/'.	10 31 73	10/31/73	N/A
EXAMINE FIELD-A TALLYING ALL ' ' REPLACING BY '/'.	10 31 73	10/31/73	2
EXAMINE FIELD-A TALLYING UNTIL FIRST '1'.	32110	32110	2
EXAMINE FIELD-A TALLYING LEADING '1'.	32110	32110	0
EXAMINE FIELD-A TALLYING LEADING ' ' REPLACING BY '0'.	___123	000123	3
EXAMINE FIELD-A REPLACING LEADING ' ' BY '0'.	___123	000123	N/A

Notes: 1. N/A denotes not applicable.
2. TALLY does *not* maintain a running total: i.e., the value is reset to zero prior to each EXAMINE statement.

Duplicate Data Names

Most programs require that the output contain some of the input, e.g., name, social security number, etc. COBOL permits duplicate data names to be defined in the data division provided all procedure division references to duplicate data names use qualification. We prefer not to use duplicate names in that they violate the prefix coding standard of Chapter 6. However, duplicate names are often used by others since they are conducive to the CORRESPONDING option, which results in fewer statements in the procedure division. Both qualification and the CORRESPONDING option are discussed in accordance with Figure 7.6.

Qualification

The coding in Figure 7.6 has several data names contained in both CARD-IN and PRINT-LINE, e.g., CREDITS, and it is confusing to reference any of these data names in the Procedure Division.

Consider the statement

MULTIPLY CREDITS BY COST-PER-CREDIT GIVING CHARGE.

The use of CREDITS is ambiguous; i.e., the compiler does not know which CREDITS (i.e., in CARD-IN or PRINT-LINE) we are talking about. The solution is to qualify the data name, using OF or IN to clarify the reference.

```
01  CARD-IN.
    05  STUDENT-NAME          PIC A(20).
    05  SOCIAL-SECURITY-NUM   PIC 9(9).
    05  STUDENT-ADDRESS.
        10  STREET            PIC A(15).
        10  CITY-STATE        PIC A(15).
    05  ZIP-CODE              PIC X(5).
    05  CREDITS               PIC 999.
    05  MAJOR                 PIC X(10).
    05  FILLER                PIC X(3).
             .
             .
01  PRINT-LINE.
    10  STUDENT-NAME          PIC A(20).
    10  FILLER                PIC X(2).
    10  CREDITS               PIC ZZ9.
    10  FILLER                PIC X(2).
    10  TUITION               PIC $$,$$9.99.
    10  FILLER                PIC X(2).
    10  STUDENT-ADDRESS.
        15  STREET            PIC A(15).
        15  CITY-STATE        PIC A(15).
        15  ZIP-CODE          PIC X(5).
    10  FILLER                PIC X(2).
    10  SOCIAL-SECURITY-NUM   PIC 999B99B9999.
    10  FILLER                PIC X(47).
```

Figure 7.6 Data Division Code for Duplicate Data Names

Thus the statement is rewritten as:

MULTIPLY CREDITS OF CARD-IN BY COST-PER-CREDIT GIVING CHARGE.

Qualifications may be required over several levels. For example, this statement is still ambiguous:

MOVE STREET OF STUDENT-ADDRESS TO OUTPUT-AREA.

Both STREET and STUDENT-ADDRESS are duplicate data names, so the qualification didn't help. We could use two levels to make our intent clear, e.g.,

MOVE STREET OF STUDENT-ADDRESS OF CARD-IN...

We could also skip the intermediate level and code

MOVE STREET IN CARD-IN...

Notice that OF and IN can be used interchangeably. What advantage can duplicate data names offer? Only one; they permit the CORRESPONDING option.

CORRESPONDING Option

The general form of the CORRESPONDING option is

$$\text{MOVE} \begin{Bmatrix} \underline{\text{CORRESPONDING}} \\ \underline{\text{CORR}} \end{Bmatrix} \text{identifier-1} \ \underline{\text{TO}} \ \text{identifier-2.}$$

Notice that CORR is the abbreviated form of CORRESPONDING (analogous to PIC and PICTURE). Consider the record description in Figure 7.6 and the statement

MOVE CORRESPONDING CARD-IN TO PRINT-LINE.

127

The MOVE CORRESPONDING statement is equivalent to several individual MOVES. It takes every data name of CARD-IN and looks for a duplicate data name in PRINT-LINE. Whenever a "match" is found, an individual MOVE is generated. Thus the above MOVE CORRESPONDING is equivalent to

```
MOVE STUDENT-NAME OF CARD-IN        TO STUDENT-NAME OF PRINT-LINE.
MOVE SOCIAL-SECURITY-NUM OF CARD-IN TO SOCIAL-SECURITY-NUM OF PRINT-LINE.
MOVE STREET OF CARD-IN              TO STREET OF PRINT-LINE.
MOVE CITY-STATE OF CARD-IN          TO CITY-STATE OF PRINT-LINE.
MOVE CREDITS OF CARD-IN             TO CREDITS OF PRINT-LINE.
```

Notice that the level numbers of the duplicate data names do not have to match; it is only the data names themselves which must be the same in each record. Further, notice that the order of the data names is immaterial; e.g., SOCIAL-SECURITY-NUM is the second field in CARD-IN and the next to last on PRINT-LINE.

There are several restrictions pertaining to the use of the CORRESPONDING option. In particular,

1. At least one item in each pair of CORRESPONDING items must be an elementary item for the MOVE to be effective. Thus, in the example, STUDENT-ADDRESS of CARD-IN is *not* moved to STUDENT-ADDRESS of PRINT-LINE. (The elementary items STREET and CITY-STATE are moved instead.)

2. Corresponding elementary items will be moved only if they have the same name and qualifications up to but not including identifier-1 and identifier-2. Thus ZIP-CODE will *not* be moved.

3. Any elementary item containing a REDEFINES, RENAMES, OCCURS, or USAGE IS INDEX clause is not moved.

One additional point: The CORRESPONDING option is also available with the ADD and SUBTRACT statements (see COBOL formats, Appendix B). We shall not discuss this feature in the text and suggest you consult a COBOL manual at your installation for additional information.

The DISPLAY verb is a convenient way of printing information without having to format a record description in the data division. The general form is **DISPLAY**

$$\underline{\text{DISPLAY}} \begin{Bmatrix} \text{identifier-1} \\ \text{literal-1} \end{Bmatrix} \begin{bmatrix} \begin{Bmatrix} \text{identifier-2} \\ \text{literal-2} \end{Bmatrix} \end{bmatrix} \dots [\underline{\text{UPON}} \ \text{mnemonic-name}]$$

Some examples:

1. DISPLAY EMPLOYEE-NAME.
2. DISPLAY 'NAME = ' EMPLOYEE-NAME.
3. DISPLAY EMPLOYEE-NAME, EMPLOYEE-NUMBER.
4. DISPLAY 'IDENTIFICATION ', EMPLOYEE-NAME, EMPLOYEE-NUMBER.

Example 1 causes the value of the data name EMPLOYEE-NAME to print. Example 2 causes the literal 'NAME = ' to print, prior to the value of EMPLOYEE-NAME. Example 3 prints the values of two data names, and example 4 prints one literal and two data names.

The "UPON mnemonic-name" is an optional clause. If it is omitted, the information is displayed on the printer. If a mnemonic name is specified, then output goes to the referenced device, and the mnemonic name must have been defined in the SPECIAL-NAMES paragraph of the environment division. (Note, however, that IBM computers establish CONSOLE and SYSOUT as reserved words, so that one may display directly on these devices *without* defining a mnemonic name.) Consider

```
SPECIAL-NAMES.
    SYSOUT IS LINE-PRINTER.
    CONSOLE IS KEYBOARD.
    .
    .
    .

PROCEDURE DIVISION.
    DISPLAY FIELD-A.
    DISPLAY FIELD-B UPON LINE-PRINTER.
    DISPLAY FIELD-C UPON KEYBOARD.
    DISPLAY FIELD-D UPON CONSOLE.
```

Both FIELD-A and FIELD-B would appear on the printer. FIELD-C and FIELD-D would appear on the console typewriter. It should be noted that many installations frown on sending messages to the operator. Indeed, within medium and large configurations, the operator is apt to miss or ignore such messages.

The ACCEPT statement is a convenient way to "read" information without having to define the entire record. The general form is

ACCEPT

ACCEPT identifier [FROM mnemonic-name]

As with the DISPLAY statement, the mnemonic name is optional. If the mnemonic name is omitted, then the input is taken from the card reader. If the mnemonic name is used, then it must be defined in the SPECIAL-NAMES paragraph. However, taking input directly from the operator via the console is specifically discouraged. First, the operator may not know the required response. Second, execution of the program is delayed waiting for the operator's response.

The general form of the READ statement is

READ INTO

READ file-name RECORD [INTO identifier] AT END imperative statement.

The READ INTO option stores the input record in the specified area and, in addition, moves it to the designated identifier following INTO. Consider

```
FD CARD-FILE
    .
    .
    .

    DATA RECORD IS CARD-IN.
01  CARD-IN                 PIC X(80).
    .
    .
    .

WORKING-STORAGE SECTION.
01  WS-CARD-AREA            PIC X(80).
    .
    .
    .

PROCEDURE DIVISION.
    READ CARD-FILE INTO WS-CARD-AREA,
        AT END PERFORM END-OF-JOB-ROUTINE.
```

The input data will be available in both CARD-IN and WS-CARD-AREA. Thus the single READ INTO statement is equivalent to both

```
        READ CARD-FILE,
            AT END PERFORM END-OF-JOB-ROUTINE.
```

and

```
        MOVE CARD-IN TO WS-CARD-AREA.
```

WRITE FROM

WRITE FROM is analogous to READ INTO in that it combines a MOVE and WRITE statement into one. Note, however, that after a WRITE is executed, one may not access the data in the FD area. In other words, do all your work on a given record *prior* to writing it out. Do not expect the record in the FD area to contain the current record after writing, as system I/O routines alter pointers. The general form of the WRITE statement is

$$\underline{\text{WRITE}} \text{ record-name } [\underline{\text{FROM}} \text{ identifier-1}] \left[\left\{ \begin{array}{l} \underline{\text{BEFORE}} \\ \underline{\text{AFTER}} \end{array} \right\} \underline{\text{ADVANCING}} \left\{ \begin{array}{l} \text{identifier-2 LINES} \\ \text{integer LINES} \\ \text{mnemonic-name} \end{array} \right\} \right]$$

WRITE FROM is particularly useful when writing heading lines. Consider

```
    FD PRINT-FILE
        .
        .
        .
        DATA RECORD IS PRINT-LINE.
    01  PRINT-LINE                        PIC X(133).
        .
        .
        .
    WORKING-STORAGE SECTION.
    01  HEADING-LINE.
        05  FILLER     VALUE SPACES        PIC X(20).

        05  FILLER     VALUE 'ACME WIDGETS'  PIC X(12).
        .
        .
        .
        WRITE PRINT-LINE FROM HEADING-LINE
            AFTER ADVANCING TOP-OF-PAGE LINES.
```

The single WRITE FROM statement is equivalent to

```
        MOVE HEADING-LINE TO PRINT-LINE.
        WRITE PRINT-LINE AFTER ADVANCING TOP-OF-PAGE LINES.
```

Note well that TOP-OF-PAGE must be defined in the SPECIAL-NAMES paragraph of the environment division (see Figure 7.8).

ROUNDED and SIZE ERROR Options

The ROUNDED and SIZE ERROR options are available for the five arithmetic verbs ADD, SUBTRACT, MULTIPLY, DIVIDE, and COMPUTE. Both options are frequently used. Consider the general form of the COMPUTE statement:

$$\underline{\text{COMPUTE}} \text{ identifier-1 } [\underline{\text{ROUNDED}}] = \left\{ \begin{array}{l} \text{identifier-2} \\ \text{literal-2} \\ \text{arithmetic expression} \end{array} \right\} \dots [\text{ON } \underline{\text{SIZE}} \text{ } \underline{\text{ERROR}} \text{ imperative-statement}]$$

The SIZE ERROR option is used to signal when the result of a calculation is too large for the designated field. Consider

```
77   HOURLY-RATE                          PIC 99.
77   HOURS-WORKED                         PIC 99.
77   GROSS-PAY                            PIC 999.
     .
     .
     .
```

```
COMPUTE GROSS-PAY = HOURLY-RATE * HOURS-WORKED.
```

Assume that HOURLY-RATE and HOURS-WORKED are 25 and 40, respectively. The result of the multiplication should be 1000. Unfortunately, GROSS-PAY is defined as a three-position numeric field. Only the three rightmost digits are retained, and GROSS-PAY becomes 000. The computer goes merrily on its way, for it does not sense any kind of error. Indeed, the director of data processing will first be made aware of this happening only when the burly construction worker pounds on his door asking about his check.

The situation is prevented by the inclusion of the SIZE ERROR option:

```
COMPUTE GROSS-PAY = HOURLY-RATE * HOURS-WORKED
    ON SIZE ERROR PERFORM ERROR-ROUTINE.
```

Whenever the calculated result is too large, the SIZE ERROR clause will perform ERROR-ROUTINE. The latter consists of programmer-specified logic which should cause a warning message to print.

Realize also that SIZE ERROR can be activated by zero division since any attempt to divide by zero results in a quotient of infinity.

The ROUNDED clause causes the last decimal place to be rounded. Consider

```
COMPUTE GROSS-PAY ROUNDED = HOURLY-RATE * HOURS-WORKED
    ON SIZE ERROR PERFORM ERROR-ROUTINE.
```

If GROSS-PAY is defined to two decimal places [e.g., PIC 9(4)V99], then .005 is added to the result, and the third decimal place is truncated.

Summary and a Complete Example

In this chapter we covered several advanced procedure division capabilities. We began with the IF statement and all its ramifications. We studied the EXAMINE verb and saw its use in editing data. We took another look at I/O statements, namely ACCEPT, DISPLAY, READ INTO, and WRITE FROM. We learned about nonunique data names, qualification, and the CORRESPONDING option. Arithmetic statements were expanded to include the ROUNDED and SIZE ERROR options. Finally we took a second look at the PERFORM verb.

While we hope the material in this chapter has been understandable, we readily admit it can make for dry reading. Our fundamental approach throughout the text is to learn by doing. To that end we have developed a complete COBOL program which incorporates most of the material in this chapter. In addition, the program includes three "aspects of reality," namely validation of incoming data, dating the report, and a page heading routine. Further, the program is a structured program and follows the techniques of Chapter 6.

Our illustrative program computes customer bills for Stacey Car Rental. Specifications are as follows:

INPUT—A deck of cards, one card for each customer, in the following format:

Columns	Field	Picture
1–9	Soc-Sec-Num	9(9)
10–34	Name	A(25)
35–40	Date-Returned	9(6)
41	Car-Type	X
42–43	Days-Rented	99
44–47	Miles-Driven	9(4)

PROCESSING—Compute the money owed for each customer card. The amount due is a function of car type, days rented, and miles driven. Compact cars (C in column 41) are billed at 8 cents per mile and $7.00 a day. Intermediate cars (I in column 41) cost 10 cents per mile and $8.00 per day. Full-size cars (F in column 41) cost 12 cents per mile and $10.00 per day. Each incoming card is to be checked for valid data. Car type must be C, I, or F, and both miles driven and days rented must be positive numbers. If any of these conditions is not met, the card should be bypassed and an appropriate error message indicated.

OUTPUT—One line of information is required for each valid card. Output is to be double-spaced, and a maximum of 25 customers are to appear on each page. Further, each page of output is to have an appropriate heading, including the date on which the program was executed.

A flowchart for the car billing problem is shown in Figure 7.7. Notice that the flowchart consists entirely of the structured building blocks of Chapter 6: sequence, selection, and iteration. Further, the flowchart depicts only the overall logic of the program in that several COBOL statements can correspond to a single block, e.g., VALIDATE-DATA or COMPUTE-BILL. Finally, the vertical lines in the PAGE-HEADING block indicate this is a performed procedure.

The COBOL program is shown in Figure 7.8, and sample output is shown in Figure 7.9. Let us begin with the PAGE-HEADING-ROUTINE. Two counters, WS-LINE-COUNT and WS-PAGE-COUNT, are established in working storage. Every time the PAGE-HEADING-ROUTINE is executed, WS-PAGE-COUNT is incremented by 1 so that the proper page number prints at the top of each page. Every time a detail line is written, WS-LINE-COUNT is incremented by 2 (COBOL line 148). The PAGE-HEADING-ROUTINE is performed only if WS-LINE-COUNT is greater than 50 (COBOL line 140) so that 25 customers will be printed per page. Note that WS-LINE-COUNT is reset to zero each time the heading routine is entered (COBOL line 158).

The PAGE-HEADING-ROUTINE causes three heading lines to be printed: WS-HEADING-LINE-ONE, TWO, and THREE. The constant portions of heading lines 1 and 3 are established directly in working storage via the VALUE clause (e.g., COBOL lines 79–92). The constant portion of line 2 is established via the move of a nonnumeric literal (COBOL line 164). Both techniques are equally acceptable. COBOL line 165 is of special interest in that it contains the reserved word CURRENT-DATE. This is a special eight-character area which contains the date of execution in the form mm/dd/yy. To have the date of execution appear on a report, simply move CURRENT-DATE to an 8-byte alphanumeric field defined by the programmer (COBOL line 165).

The mainline portion of the program appears in COBOL statements 96–103. Compound IF's, condition names, and class tests are used to validate incoming data (COBOL lines 109–117). Notice that each IF has two

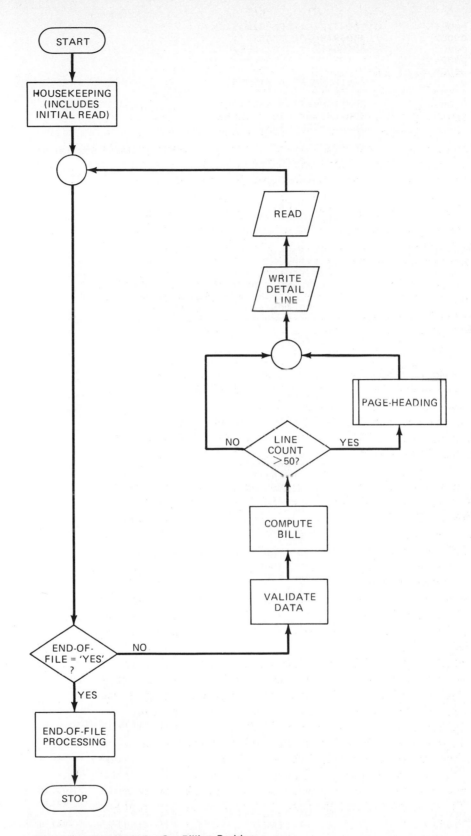

Figure 7.7 Flowchart for Car Billing Problem

```
00001          IDENTIFICATION DIVISION.
00002          PROGRAM-ID.   'CARS'.
00003          AUTHOR.       GRAUER.
00004
00005
00006          ENVIRONMENT DIVISION.
00007
00008          CONFIGURATION SECTION.
00009          SOURCE-COMPUTER.   IBM-370.
00010          OBJECT-COMPUTER.   IBM-370.
00011
00012          SPECIAL-NAMES.                        ── Use of SPECIAL-NAMES paragraph
00013              C01 IS TOP-OF-PAGE.
00014
00015          INPUT-OUTPUT SECTION.
00016          FILE-CONTROL.
00017              SELECT CARD-FILE ASSIGN TO UR-2540R-S-SYSIN.
00018              SELECT PRINT-FILE ASSIGN TO UR-1403-S-SYSOUT.
00019
00020
00021          DATA DIVISION.
00022          FILE SECTION.
00023          FD  CARD-FILE
00024              RECORDING MODE IS F
00025              LABEL RECORDS ARE OMITTED
00026              RECORD CONTAINS 80 CHARACTERS
00027              DATA RECORD IS CARD-IN.
00028          01  CARD-IN                PIC X(80).
00029          FD  PRINT-FILE
00030              RECORDING MODE IS F
00031              LABEL RECORDS ARE OMITTED
00032              RECORD CONTAINS 133 CHARACTERS
00033              DATA RECORD IS PRINT-LINE.
00034          01  PRINT-LINE             PIC X(133).  ── Line-counter
00035                                                  ── Page-counter
00036          WORKING-STORAGE SECTION.
00037          77  WS-END-OF-FILE         PIC X(3)           VALUE 'NO'.
00038          77  WS-LINE-COUNT          PIC 99             VALUE 51.
00039          77  WS-PAGE-COUNT          PIC 99             VALUE ZERO.
00040          77  WS-MILEAGE-RATE        PIC 9V99.
00041          77  WS-DAILY-RATE          PIC 99V99.
00042          77  WS-CUSTOMER-BILL       PIC 9999V99.
00043          01  WS-CARD-IN.
00044              05   SOC-SEC-NUM       PIC 9(9).
00045              05   NAME-FIELD        PIC A(25).
00046              05   DATE-RETURNED     PIC 9(6).
00047              05   CAR-TYPE          PIC X.
00048                   88   COMPACT                         VALUE 'C'.
00049                   88   INTERMEDIATE                    VALUE 'I'.
00050                   88   FULL-SIZE                       VALUE 'F'.
00051              05   DAYS-RENTED       PIC 99.
00052              05   MILES-DRIVEN      PIC 9999.
00053              05   FILLER            PIC X(33).
00054          01  WS-PRINT-LINE.
00055              05   FILLER            PIC X(4).
00056              05   SOC-SEC-NUM       PIC 999B99B9999.
00057              05   FILLER            PIC X(4).
00058              05   NAME-FIELD        PIC A(25).
00059              05   FILLER            PIC X(2).
00060              05   CAR-TYPE          PIC X.
00061              05   FILLER            PIC X(4).
00062              05   DAYS-RENTED       PIC Z9.
00063              05   FILLER            PIC X(4).
00064              05   MILES-DRIVEN      PIC ZZZ9.
00065              05   FILLER            PIC X(4).
00066              05   CUSTOMER-BILL     PIC $$,$$9.99.
00067              05   FILLER            PIC X(59).
00068          01  WS-HEADING-LINE-ONE.
00069              05   FILLER            PIC X(65)          VALUE SPACES.
00070              05   FILLER            PIC X(5)           VALUE 'PAGE '.
00071              05   WS-PAGE-PRINT     PIC ZZ9.
00072              05   FILLER            PIC X(60)          VALUE SPACES.
```

Figure 7.8 Car Billing Problem

```
00073          01   WS-HEADING-LINE-TWO.
00074               05   FILLER             PIC X(20).
00075               05   TITLE-INFO         PIC X(33).
00076               05   FILLER             PIC X(2).
00077               05   TITLE-DATE         PIC X(8).
00078               05   FILLER             PIC X(70).
00079          01   WS-HEADING-LINE-THREE.
00080               05   FILLER             PIC X(8)           VALUE SPACES.
00081               05   FILLER             PIC X(11)          VALUE ' ACCT #'.
00082               05   FILLER             PIC X(2)           VALUE SPACES.
00083               05   FILLER             PIC X(4)           VALUE 'NAME'.
00084               05   FILLER             PIC X(19)          VALUE SPACES.
00085               05   FILLER             PIC X(4)           VALUE 'TYPE'.
00086               05   FILLER             PIC X(2)           VALUE SPACES.
00087               05   FILLER             PIC X(4)           VALUE 'DAYS'.
00088               05   FILLER             PIC X(2)           VALUE SPACES.
00089               05   FILLER             PIC X(5)           VALUE 'MILES'.
00090               05   FILLER             PIC X(4)           VALUE SPACES.
00091               05   FILLER             PIC X(6)           VALUE 'AMOUNT'.
00092               05   FILLER             PIC X(60)          VALUE SPACES.
00093
00094
00095          PROCEDURE DIVISION.
00096              OPEN INPUT CARD-FILE,
00097                   OUTPUT PRINT-FILE.
00098              READ CARD-FILE INTO WS-CARD-IN
00099                   AT END MOVE 'YES' TO WS-END-OF-FILE.
00100              PERFORM 020-CUSTOMER-CARDS THRU 028-CUSTOMER-CARDS-EXIT
00101                   UNTIL WS-END-OF-FILE = 'YES'.
00102              CLOSE CARD-FILE, PRINT-FILE.
00103              STOP RUN.
00104
00105          020-CUSTOMER-CARDS.
00106          *********************************************************
00107          *        CHECK INCOMING DATA                            *
00108          *********************************************************
00109              IF NOT FULL-SIZE AND NOT COMPACT AND NOT INTERMEDIATE
00110                   DISPLAY ' ERROR IN DATA ' NAME-FIELD OF WS-CARD-IN
00111                   GO TO 025-READ-ANOTHER-CARD.
00112              IF MILES-DRIVEN OF WS-CARD-IN IS NOT POSITIVE
00113                   DISPLAY ' ERROR IN DATA ' NAME-FIELD OF WS-CARD-IN
00114                   GO TO 025-READ-ANOTHER-CARD.
00115              IF DAYS-RENTED OF WS-CARD-IN IS NOT POSITIVE
00116                   DISPLAY ' ERROR IN DATA ' NAME-FIELD OF WS-CARD-IN
00117                   GO TO 025-READ-ANOTHER-CARD.
00118          *********************************************************
00119          *    MILEAGE RATE AND DAILY RATE BOTH DEPEND ON TYPE CAR
00120          *********************************************************
00121              IF COMPACT
00122                   MOVE .08 TO WS-MILEAGE-RATE
00123                   MOVE 7.00 TO WS-DAILY-RATE
00124              ELSE
00125                   IF INTERMEDIATE
00126                        MOVE .10 TO WS-MILEAGE-RATE
00127                        MOVE 8.00 TO WS-DAILY-RATE
00128                   ELSE
00129                        MOVE .12 TO WS-MILEAGE-RATE
00130                        MOVE 10.00 TO WS-DAILY-RATE.
00131              COMPUTE WS-CUSTOMER-BILL ROUNDED
00132                   = MILES-DRIVEN OF WS-CARD-IN * WS-MILEAGE-RATE
00133                   + DAYS-RENTED OF WS-CARD-IN * WS-DAILY-RATE
00134              ON SIZE ERROR
00135                   DISPLAY ' RECEIVING FIELD TOO SMALL FOR BILL',
00136                   NAME-FIELD OF WS-CARD-IN.
00137          *********************************************************
00138          *    WRITE DETAIL LINE
00139          *********************************************************
00140              IF WS-LINE-COUNT > 50 PERFORM 060-PAGE-HEADING-ROUTINE.
00141              MOVE SPACES TO WS-PRINT-LINE.
00142              MOVE CORRESPONDING WS-CARD-IN TO WS-PRINT-LINE.
00143              EXAMINE SOC-SEC-NUM OF WS-PRINT-LINE
00144                   REPLACING ALL ' ' BY '-'.
00145              MOVE WS-CUSTOMER-BILL TO CUSTOMER-BILL.
00146              WRITE PRINT-LINE FROM WS-PRINT-LINE
00147                   AFTER ADVANCING 2 LINES.
00148              ADD 2 TO WS-LINE-COUNT.
00149
```

Annotations:
- THRU option with PERFORM verb (pointing to line 00100)
- Validate incoming data (pointing to lines 00109–00117)
- Nested IF (pointing to lines 00121–00130)
- SIZE ERROR option (pointing to lines 00134–00136)
- Check for PAGE-HEADING (pointing to line 00140)

Figure 7.8 (Continued)

```
00150        025-READ-ANOTHER-CARD.
00151            READ CARD-FILE INTO WS-CARD-IN
00152                AT END MOVE 'YES' TO WS-END-OF-FILE.
00153
00154        028-CUSTOMER-CARDS-EXIT.          EXIT paragraph
00155            EXIT.
00156
00157        060-PAGE-HEADING-ROUTINE SECTION.
00158            MOVE ZEROS TO WS-LINE-COUNT.
00159            ADD 1 TO WS-PAGE-COUNT.
00160            MOVE WS-PAGE-COUNT TO WS-PAGE-PRINT.
00161            WRITE PRINT-LINE FROM WS-HEADING-LINE-ONE
00162                AFTER ADVANCING TOP-OF-PAGE LINES.
00163            MOVE SPACES TO WS-HEADING-LINE-TWO.
00164            MOVE ' STACEY CAR RENTALS - REPORT DATE ' TO TITLE-INFO.
00165            MOVE CURRENT-DATE TO TITLE-DATE.
00166            WRITE PRINT-LINE FROM WS-HEADING-LINE-TWO
00167                AFTER ADVANCING 1 LINES.
00168            WRITE PRINT-LINE FROM WS-HEADING-LINE-THREE
00169                AFTER ADVANCING 1 LINES.
```
EXIT paragraph

Use of CURRENT-DATE

PAGE-HEADING routine

Figure 7.8 (*Continued*)

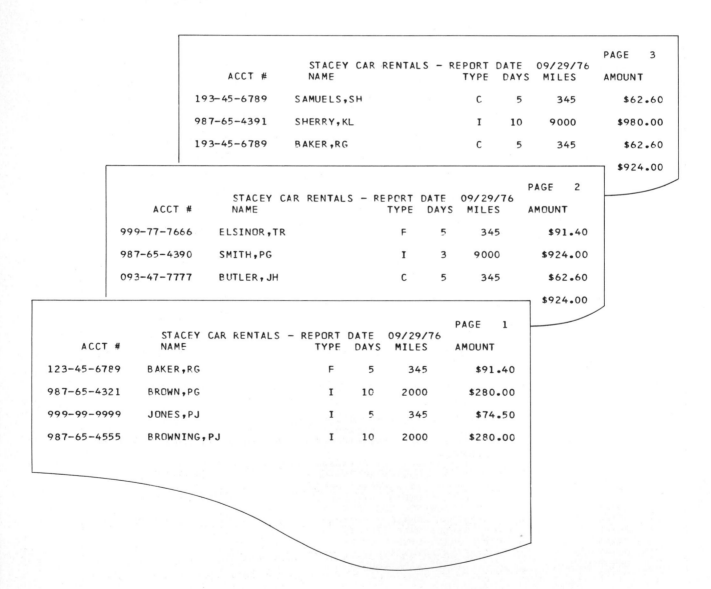

```
                                                              PAGE    3
                    STACEY CAR RENTALS - REPORT DATE  09/29/76
        ACCT #      NAME                TYPE  DAYS  MILES   AMOUNT

   193-45-6789     SAMUELS,SH            C      5    345     $62.60

   987-65-4391     SHERRY,KL            I     10   9000    $980.00

   193-45-6789     BAKER,RG             C      5    345     $62.60

                                                            $924.00
```

```
                                                              PAGE    2
                    STACEY CAR RENTALS - REPORT DATE  09/29/76
        ACCT #      NAME                TYPE  DAYS  MILES   AMOUNT

   999-77-7666     ELSINOR,TR           F      5    345     $91.40

   987-65-4390     SMITH,PG             I      3   9000    $924.00

   093-47-7777     BUTLER,JH            C      5    345     $62.60

                                                            $924.00
```

```
                                                              PAGE    1
                    STACEY CAR RENTALS - REPORT DATE  09/29/76
     ACCT #         NAME                TYPE  DAYS  MILES  AMOUNT

 123-45-6789      BAKER,RG              F      5    345     $91.40

 987-65-4321      BROWN,PG              I     10   2000    $280.00

 999-99-9999      JONES,PJ             I      5    345     $74.50

 987-65-4555      BROWNING,PJ          I     10   2000    $280.00
```

Figure 7.9 Illustrative Output for Car Rental Problem

statements after the condition (a DISPLAY and GO TO, e.g., COBOL lines 116–117). Both will be done if the condition is met since there is only one period; i.e., after the GO TO. The presence of the GO TO is itself interesting, especially in view of the fact that this is a structured program. We are not disturbed, however, *because the goal of structured programming is to make programs clearer, not necessarily to eliminate the GO TO.* There are certain instances in which the GO TO can enhance, rather than detract from, overall clarity. If so, it should be used, but only in a certain manner. (Notice how the GO TO only branches forward.) We shall discuss this further in Chapter 11.

Observe the nested IF/ELSE statement to determine appropriate rates (COBOL lines 121–130). Note the indentation conventions and the multiple statements after a condition is met. Finally, note the ROUNDED and SIZE ERROR options in the COMPUTE statement (COBOL lines 131–136), the MOVE CORRESPONDING (COBOL line 142), and the EXAMINE REPLACING (COBOL lines 143–144).

REVIEW EXERCISES

TRUE	FALSE		
☐	☐	**1**	The EXAMINE statement must contain the reserved word REPLACING.
☐	☐	**2**	If the TALLYING form of the EXAMINE statement is used, the programmer must define TALLY in his data division.
☐	☐	**3**	The value of TALLY is a running total.
☐	☐	**4**	The numeric class test can be applied to alphanumeric data.
☐	☐	**5**	The alphabetic class test can be applied to alphanumeric data.
☐	☐	**6**	The numeric class test can be applied to alphabetic data.
☐	☐	**7**	The alphabetic class test can be applied to numeric data.
☐	☐	**8**	Every machine has the same collating sequence.
☐	☐	**9**	BLOOM will be considered less than BLOOMBERG, independent of collating sequence.
☐	☐	**10**	XYZ will always be considered less than 123, independent of collating sequence.
☐	☐	**11**	Several data names can appear in the same DISPLAY statement.
☐	☐	**12**	Several data names can appear in the same ACCEPT statement.
☐	☐	**13**	Both literals and data names can appear in a DISPLAY statement.
☐	☐	**14**	COBOL requires that the DISPLAY statement direct its output to the printer.
☐	☐	**15**	COBOL requires that the ACCEPT statement receive its input from the console typewriter.
☐	☐	**16**	Either OF or IN may be used to qualify data names.
☐	☐	**17**	Qualification over a single level will always remove ambiguity of duplicate data names.
☐	☐	**18**	CORRESPONDING is allowed only in the MOVE statement.
☐	☐	**19**	ROUNDED and SIZE ERROR are allowed only in the COMPUTE statement.
☐	☐	**20**	ROUNDED and SIZE ERROR are mandatory in the COMPUTE statement.
☐	☐	**21**	CORR is permitted instead of CORRESPONDING.
☐	☐	**22**	For the CORRESPONDING option to work, both duplicate names must be at the same level.

1 Recode the following statements to show the ELSE indented under the relevant IF. **PROBLEMS**
Draw appropriate flowcharts, using the structures of Chapter 6.
(a) IF A > B, IF C > D, MOVE E TO F,
    ELSE MOVE G TO H.
(b) IF A > B, IF C > D, MOVE E TO F,
    ELSE MOVE G TO H, ELSE MOVE X TO Y.
(c) IF A > B, IF C > D, MOVE E TO F,
    ADD 1 TO E, ELSE MOVE G TO H,
    ADD 1 TO G.
(d) IF A > B, MOVE X TO Y, MOVE Z TO W,
    ELSE IF C > D MOVE 1 TO N,
    ELSE MOVE 2 TO Y, ADD 3 TO Z.

2 Code COBOL statements to correspond to the accompanying flowcharts.

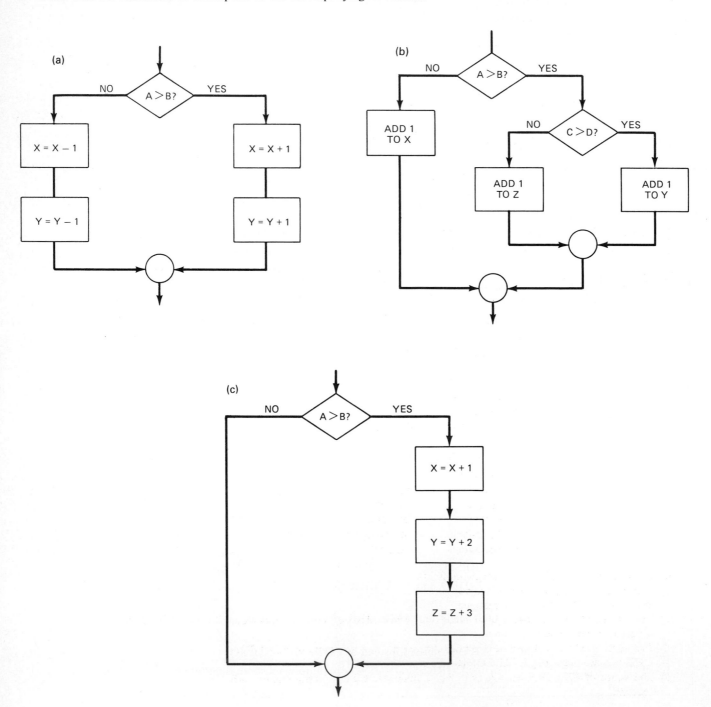

138

```
PROCEDURE DIVISION.
    PERFORM SEC-A.
    PERFORM PAR-C THRU PAR-E.
    MOVE 1 TO N.
    PERFORM PAR-G UNTIL N > 3.
    STOP RUN.

SEC-A SECTION.
    ADD 1 TO X.
    ADD 1 TO Y.
    ADD 1 TO Z.
PAR-B.
    ADD 2 TO X.
PAR-C.
    ADD 10 TO X.
PAR-D.
    ADD 10 TO Y.
    ADD 20 TO Z.
PAR-E.
    EXIT.
PAR-F.
    MOVE 2 TO N.
PAR-G.
    ADD 1 TO N.
    ADD 5 TO X.
```

(a) How many times is each paragraph executed?

(b) What is the final value of X, Y, and Z? (Assume they were all initialized to 0.)

(c) What would happen if the statement ADD 1 TO N were removed from PAR-G?

4 Given the data division entries below and the procedure division statement MOVE CORRESPONDING RECORD-ONE TO RECORD-TWO:

```
01  RECORD-ONE.
    05  FIELD-A         PIC X(4).
    05  FIELD-B         PIC X(4).
    05  FIELD-C.
        10  C-ONE       PIC X(4).
        10  C-TWO       PIC X(4).
    05  FIELD-D.
        10  D-ONE       PIC X(6).
        10  D-TWO       PIC X(6).
        10  D-THREE     PIC X(6).

01  RECORD-TWO.
    15  FIELD-E         PIC X(8).
    15  FIELD-D         PIC X(18).
    15  FIELD-C         PIC X(8).
    15  FIELD-B         PIC X(2).
    15  FIELD-A         PIC X(4).
```

answer true or false (refer to the receiving field):

(a) The value of FIELD-E is unchanged.

(b) The value of FIELD-D is unchanged.

(c) No moves at all will take place since the corresponding level numbers are different in both records.

(d) The value of FIELD-A will be unchanged since it is the first entry in RECORD-ONE but the last entry in RECORD-TWO.

(e) The value of FIELD-B will be unchanged since the length is different in both records.

5 Take the tuition billing problem of Chapter 6 (Figure 6.4) and modify it to include a page heading routine (print 45 lines per page). Print the current date at the top of each page.

6 Modify the tuition billing problem of Chapter 6 (Figure 6.4) to include an error-processing routine which will flag invalid data. We leave the decision of which errors to check for in your hands.

7 Write a COBOL program to read in a paragraph of English text and compute
(a) The average number of words per sentence.
(b) The average number of letters per word.
The paragraph continues from one data card to the next until the end of file is reached. For simplicity, assume that words are not split from card to card and that no punctuation (other than periods) are present. The EXAMINE verb should be most helpful.

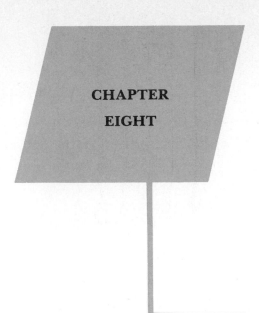

CHAPTER
EIGHT

The Data Division

Overview

We return to the data division to cover some of the fine points used by professional programmers. We shall begin with an extended discussion of editing and condition names. We shall cover multiple record definitions for the same file and the COPY clause. We shall introduce tables (in this chapter we shall cover only one dimension; in Chapter 9 we shall discuss two and three dimensions). We shall present the OCCURS and REDEFINES clauses. We shall show how to establish a table of constant values and how to do a *table lookup*. We shall conclude with a discussion of subprograms and the linkage section.

Editing

Editing involves a change in data format. We may add commas, insert a dollar sign, suppress leading zeros, indicate negative values by a credit sign, etc. Regardless of what we do, our purpose is to make reports easier to read.

The tuition billing problem of Chapter 4 introduced the concept of editing. Now we shall present a more complete discussion, beginning with Table 8.1, which contains the set of editing characters.

The blank (B) can be associated with any type of source field, i.e., alphabetic, numeric, or alphanumeric. The zero (0) is restricted to numeric or alphanumeric fields. All other symbols are for numeric source fields only.

Table 8.1 Editing Characters

Symbol	Meaning
.	Actual decimal point
Z	Zero suppress
*	Check protection
CR	Credit symbol
DB	Debit symbol
+	Plus sign
−	Minus sign
$	Dollar sign
,	Comma
0	Zero
B	Blank

Realize, however, that any MOVE statement involving edited pictures is also affected by the rules discussed in Chapter 3 with regard to decimal alignment, truncation, etc.

The use of various editing characters is best explained by direct example. Consider Table 8.2.

Table 8.2 The $, Z, and * Edit Characters

	Source Field		Receiving Field	
	Picture	Value	Picture	Edited Result
(a)	9999V99	000123	9999.99	0001.23
(b)	9999V99	000123	ZZZZ.99	1.23
(c)	9999V99	000123	$$$$.99	$1.23
(d)	9999V99	000123	$ZZZZ.99	$ 1.23
(e)	9999V99	000123	$****.99	$*** 1.23

The concepts of source field, receiving field, and actual and assumed decimal point were covered in Chapter 4. The character Z will zero-suppress; i.e., it replaces leading zeros by blanks. The $ causes a dollar sign to print. If several dollar signs are strung together [example (c) in Table 8.2], the effect is a floating dollar sign; i.e., a dollar sign prints immediately to the left of the first significant digit. The $ can be used in conjunction with Z to cause a fixed dollar sign as in example (d) in Table 8.2. For obvious reasons example (d) is not sound practice when "cutting" checks, and the asterisk is used for check protection as shown in example (e). The asterisks appear in the edited result in lieu of leading zeros.

Signed Numbers

Frequently the picture of a numeric source field is preceded by an S to indicate a signed field. The S is immaterial if only positive numbers can occur but absolutely essential any time a negative number results as the consequence of an arithmetic operation. If the S is omitted, the result of the arithmetic operation will always assume a positive sign. Consider

```
77   FIELD-A          PIC S99     VALUE −20.
77   FIELD-B          PIC 99      VALUE 15.
77   FIELD-C          PIC S99     VALUE −20.
77   FIELD-D          PIC 99      VALUE 15.

     ADD FIELD-B TO FIELD-A.
     ADD FIELD-C TO FIELD-D.
```

Numerically we expect the sum of −20 and +15 to be −5. If the result is
stored in FIELD-A, there is no problem. However, if the sum is stored in FIELD-D (an unsigned field), it will assume a value of +5. Many programmers adopt the habit of always using signed fields to avoid any difficulty.

Additional difficulties can arise if one attempts to print the contents of signed fields without first moving to an unsigned field. Consider the following example:

```
77  FIELD-C   PIC 9    VALUE 2.
77  FIELD-D   PIC S9   VALUE 3.
77  FIELD-E   PIC 9    VALUE 2.
77  FIELD-F   PIC S9   VALUE 3.

    ADD FIELD-D TO FIELD-C.
    EXHIBIT NAMED FIELD-C.
    ADD FIELD-E TO FIELD-F.
    EXHIBIT NAMED FIELD-F.
```

Numerically we expect both FIELD-C and FIELD-F to exhibit as the number 5. There is no problem with FIELD-C, but FIELD-F will show up as an E. The explanation has to do with the assembler instructions generated to retain (or remove) the sign and is meaningful only after the discussion in Chapters 12–14. We mention it here only to prepare the reader for a stunning surprise, when and if it happens to him.

Table 8.3 illustrates the use of floating plus and minus signs. If a plus sign is used, the sign of the edited field will appear if the number is either positive, negative, or zero [examples (a), (b), and (c)]. However, if a minus sign is used, the sign appears only when the edited result is negative. Note also that the receiving field must be at least one character longer than the sending field to accommodate the sign; otherwise a compiler warning message results.

Table 8.3 Floating + and − Characters

Source Field		Receiving Field	
Picture	*Value*	*Picture*	*Edited Result*
(a) S9(4)	1234	++,+++	+1,234
(b) S9(4)	0123	++,+++	+123
(c) S9(4)	−1234	++,+++	−1,234
(d) S9(4)	1234	−−,−−−	1,234
(e) S9(4)	0123	−−,−−−	123
(f) S9(4)	−1234	−−,−−−	−1,234

Financial statements usually contain either the credit (CR) or debit (DB) symbol to indicate a negative number. The use of these characters is illustrated in Table 8.4.

Table 8.4 CR and DB Symbols

Source Field		Receiving Field	
Picture	*Value*	*Picture*	*Value*
(a) S9(5)	98765	$$$,999CR	$98,765
(b) S9(5)	−98765	$$$,999CR	$98,765CR
(c) S9(5)	98765	$$$,999DB	$98,765
(d) S9(5)	−98765	$$$,999DB	$98,765DB

CR and DB appear only when the sending field is negative [examples (b) and (d)]. If the field is positive or zero, the symbols are replaced by blanks.

Condition names

In Chapter 7 we introduced 88-level entries. Now we shall consider them in greater detail by using the VALUES ARE option. The general format is

$$88 \text{ data-name} \begin{Bmatrix} \underline{\text{VALUE}} \text{ IS} \\ \underline{\text{VALUES}} \text{ ARE} \end{Bmatrix} \text{literal-1 } [\underline{\text{THRU}} \text{ literal-2}][\text{literal-3 } [\underline{\text{THRU}} \text{ literal-4}]] \dots$$

The power of condition names is illustrated below. Note that certain values may appear under more than one classification; e.g., records containing a 3 are classified as both JUNIOR and UPPER-CLASSMAN.

```
05  YEAR-IN-SCHOOL         PIC 9.
    88  FRESHMAN                   VALUE 1.
    88  SOPHOMORE                  VALUE 2.
    88  JUNIOR                     VALUE 3.
    88  SENIOR                     VALUE 4.
    88  GRAD-STUDENT               VALUES ARE 5 THRU 8.
    88  UNDER-CLASSMAN             VALUES ARE 1, 2.
    88  UPPER-CLASSMAN             VALUES ARE 3, 4.
    88  ERROR-CODES                VALUES ARE 0, 9.
```

In addition to documentation advantages, the VALUES ARE clause eliminates the need for compound conditions in an IF statement. Thus,

    IF GRAD-STUDENT...

is equivalent to

    IF YEAR-IN-SCHOOL > 4 AND YEAR-IN-SCHOOL < 9...

Further, the VALUES ARE clause makes it very easy to test for error conditions by grouping all invalid codes together as shown.

Multiple Records

The commercial programmer frequently finds himself in situations where the same file contains different record formats. A card file may contain two types of cards, e.g., a single master card and several transaction cards. A print file may contain several print lines, e.g., heading, detail, and total lines. One way to handle this is to use the READ INTO and WRITE FROM options which were discussed in Chapter 7 and then define multiple 01 entries in working storage. A widely used alternative is to use the DATA RECORDS ARE clause in the COBOL FD as shown in Figure 8.1.

Only one card is contained in storage at any given instant. The type of card is indicated by a code in column 80 (MAST-CARD-CODE and DET-CARD-CODE). If 'M' and 'D' denote a master and detail, respectively, we might find procedure division code of the form

    IF MAST-CARD-CODE = 'M' PERFORM MASTER-PROCESSING.
    IF DET-CARD-CODE = 'D' PERFORM DETAIL-PROCESSING.

It does not matter if we test MAST-CARD-CODE or DET-CARD-CODE, as both data names refer to position 80 in an incoming card. Thus, the two statements below are completely equivalent:

    IF DET-CARD-CODE = 'D' PERFORM DETAIL-PROCESSING.
    IF MAST-CARD-CODE = 'D' PERFORM DETAIL-PROCESSING.

Of course it is possible, and indeed desirable, to modify Figure 8.1 to accommodate 88-level entries.

```
FD  CARD-FILE
    RECORDING MODE IS F
    RECORD CONTAINS 80 CHARACTERS
    LABEL RECORDS ARE OMITTED
    DATA RECORDS ARE MASTER-RECORD, DETAIL-RECORD.
01  MASTER-RECORD.
    05  MAST-NAME                         PIC A(25).
    05  MAST-ACCT-NUMBER                  PIC 9(9).
    05  MAST-ADDRESS.
        10  MAST-ADDRESS-LINE-ONE         PIC A(20).
        10  MAST-ADDRESS-LINE-TWO         PIC A(20).
    05  MAST-NUMBER-OF-DETAILS            PIC 99.
    05  FILLER                            PIC X(3).
    05  MAST-CARD-CODE                    PIC X.
01  DETAIL-RECORD.
    05  DET-ACCT-NUMBER                   PIC 9(9).
    05  DET-ITEM-DESCRIPTION              PIC A(25).
    05  DET-AMOUNT                        PIC S99999V99.
    05  DET-TYPE                          PIC X.
        88  PURCHASE        VALUE IS 'P'.
        88  CREDIT          VALUE IS 'C'.
    05  DET-DATE                          PIC 9(6).
    05  FILLER                            PIC X(31).
    05  DET-CARD-CODE                     PIC X.
```

Figure 8.1 Use of Multiple Records

Commercial applications are frequently classified into systems, e.g., inventory, **COPY Clause** accounting, payroll, etc. Each system in turn consists of several programs, the files of which are interrelated. Indeed, the same file may appear in several programs. The COPY clause enables an installation to build a library of record descriptions and offers the following advantages:

1. Individual programmers need not code the extensive data division entries which can make COBOL so tedious. (This is particularly helpful in commercial programs where record descriptions run into hundreds of lines.) Instead, a programmer codes an appropriate COPY clause. The COBOL compiler then searches a library and brings the proper entries into the COBOL program as though the programmer had written them himself.

2. Changes are made only in one place, i.e., in the library version. Although changes in a file or record description occur infrequently, they do happen. However, only the library version need be altered explicitly, as individual programs will automatically bring in the corrected version during compilation.

3. Programming errors are reduced, and standardization is promoted. Since an individual is coding fewer lines, his program will contain fewer errors. More importantly, all fields are defined correctly. Further, there is no chance of omitting an existing field or erroneously creating a new one. Finally, all programmers will be using identical record descriptions.

The general form of the COPY clause is shown below:

$$\underline{\text{COPY}} \text{ library-name [SUPPRESS]} \left[\underline{\text{REPLACING}} \text{ word-1 } \underline{\text{BY}} \left\{ \begin{array}{l} \text{word-2} \\ \text{literal-1} \\ \text{identifier-1} \end{array} \right\} \dots \right]$$

The SUPPRESS option is restricted to IBM. It suppresses the data names in the library and is used to condense the size of program listings.

The REPLACING option allows the programmer to substitute his data names for those in the library.

The COPY clause can be used virtually anywhere in a COBOL program. The most common use is to bring in FD's and record descriptions in the data division. However, it can also be used in the environment division (in both the configuration and input-output sections) and in the procedure division to bring in entire sections and/or paragraphs. Some common formats are shown below:

1. Environment division:

    SOURCE-COMPUTER.   COPY library-name.
    OBJECT-COMPUTER.   COPY library-name.
    SPECIAL-NAMES.   COPY library-name.
    FILE-CONTROL.   COPY library-name.
    I-O-CONTROL.   COPY library-name.

2. Data division:

    FD file-name   COPY library-name.
    SD file-name   COPY library-name.
    01 data-name   COPY library-name.

3. Procedure division:

    section-name SECTION.   COPY library-name.
    paragraph-name.   COPY library name.

Use of the COPY clause is shown in Figure 8.2.

Thus far we have discussed the COPY clause, multiple records, condition names, signed fields, and report editing. The significance of these important capabilities is best illustrated in a complete COBOL program. Specifications are as follows:

A Complete Example

INPUT—There are two types of incoming cards, a master and detail, denoted by 'M' and 'D', respectively, in column 80. The single master card contains the customer name and address and the number of detail cards. Each transaction card represents either a purchase (P in column 42) or a credit (C in column 42) and contains an item description, date, and amount.

PROCESSING—A customer's balance is to be calculated for each set of master and detail cards. The balance is computed by subtracting the sum of the credit transactions from the sum of the purchases. For example, if John Smith made two purchases of $100 and $200 and one payment (i.e., credit) of $50, his balance due should show as $250.

OUTPUT—Individual statements, one per page in suitable format.

The logic is straightforward, and the COBOL listing is contained in Figure 8.2. The sample output is shown in Figure 8.3.

Figure 8.2 illustrates several features discussed thus far. The FD for CARD-FILE is contained within the COBOL program, yet it was not coded explicitly by the COBOL programmer. COBOL line 16 contains the clause COPY CARDFD, which causes the computer to bring in lines 17–42 from a user library. Note the presence of a C in each of lines 17–42, denoting a copied entry.

```
00001          IDENTIFICATION DIVISION.
00002          PROGRAM-ID.       COPYEDIT.
00003          AUTHOR.           CRAWFORD.
00004          ENVIRONMENT DIVISION.
00005          CONFIGURATION SECTION.
00006          SOURCE-COMPUTER.   IBM-370.
00007          OBJECT-COMPUTER.   IBM-370.              ⌐ Statement to bring in
00008          SPECIAL-NAMES.                             FD from library
00009              C01 IS TOP-OF-PAGE.
00010          INPUT-OUTPUT SECTION.
00011          FILE-CONTROL.
00012              SELECT CARD-FILE ASSIGN TO UR-2540R-S-SYSIN.
00013              SELECT PRINT-FILE ASSIGN TO UR-1403-S-PRINT.
00014          DATA DIVISION.
00015          FILE SECTION.                                      'Copied' entry
00016          FD   CARD-FILE           COPY CARDFD.
00017 C             RECORDING MODE IS F
00018 C             LABEL RECORDS ARE OMITTED
00019 C             RECORD CONTAINS 80 CHARACTERS
00020 C             DATA RECORDS ARE MASTER-RECORD, DETAIL-RECORD.
00021 C        01   MASTER-RECORD.
00022 C             05   MAST-NAME                      PIC A(25).
00023 C             05   MAST-ACCT-NUMBER               PIC 9(9).
00024 C             05   MAST-ADDRESS.
00025 C                  10   MAST-ADDRESS-LINE-ONE     PIC A(20).
00026 C                  10   MAST-ADDRESS-LINE-TWO     PIC A(20).
00027 C             05   MAST-NUMBER-OF-DETAILS         PIC 99.
00028 C             05   FILLER                         PIC X(3).
00029 C             05   MAST-CARD-CODE                 PIC X.
00030 C        01   DETAIL-RECORD.
00031 C             05   DET-ACCT-NUMBER                PIC 9(9).
00032 C             05   DET-ITEM-DESCRIPTION           PIC A(25).
00033 C             05   DET-AMOUNT                     PIC S99999V99.
00034 C             05   DET-TYPE                       PIC X.
00035 C                  88   PURCHASE                  VALUE IS 'P'.
00036 C                  88   CREDIT                    VALUE IS 'C'.
00037 C             05   DET-DATE                       PIC 9(6).
00038 C             05   FILLER                         PIC X(31).
00039 C             05   DET-CARD-CODE                  PIC X.
00040 C                  88   VALID-CODES               VALUES ARE 'D', 'M'.
00041 C                  88   MASTER-CODE               VALUE IS 'M'.
00042 C                  88   DETAIL-CODE               VALUE IS 'D'.
00043          FD   PRINT-FILE
00044               RECORDING MODE IS F
00045               LABEL RECORDS ARE OMITTED
00046               RECORD CONTAINS 133 CHARACTERS
00047               DATA RECORDS ARE PRINT-LINE, PRINT-LINE-ONE, PRINT-LINE-TWO
00048               PRINT-LINE-THREE, PRINT-LINE-FOUR.
00049          01   PRINT-LINE                          PIC X(133).
00050          01   PRINT-LINE-ONE.     ⌐ Multiple records clause
00051               05   FILLER                         PIC X(5).          ⌐ Use of blank
00052               05   PRINT-NAME                     PIC A(25).           editing character
00053               05   FILLER                         PIC X(5).
00054               05   PRINT-ACCT-NUMBER              PIC 999B99B9999.
00055               05   FILLER                         PIC X(87).
00056          01   PRINT-LINE-TWO.
00057               05   FILLER                         PIC X(5).
00058               05   PRINT-ADDRESS                  PIC X(20).
00059               05   FILLER                         PIC X(108).
00060          01   PRINT-LINE-THREE.
00061               05   FILLER                         PIC X(13).
00062               05   PRINT-DATE-HDG                 PIC X(15).
00063               05   FILLER                         PIC X.
00064               05   PRINT-CURRENT-DATE             PIC X(8).
00065               05   FILLER                         PIC X(96).
00066          01   PRINT-LINE-FOUR.
00067               05   FILLER                         PIC X(5).
00068               05   PRINT-DESCRIPTION              PIC A(25).
00069               05   FILLER                         PIC X(2).
00070               05   PRINT-DATE                     PIC 99B99B99.
00071               05   FILLER             Fixed dollar PIC X(2).
00072               05   PRINT-AMOUNT       sign with zero PIC $ZZZZ9.99CR.
00073               05   FILLER             suppression  PIC X(80).
```

Figure 8.2 COBOL Listing to Illustrate Data Division Features

147

```
00074          WORKING-STORAGE SECTION.
00075          77  WS-END-OF-FILE                     PIC X(3)
00076                                        VALUE IS 'NO '.
00077          77  WS-RECORD-TOTAL                    PIC S9(6)V99.
00078          01  WS-TOTAL-LINE.
00079              05  FILLER                         PIC X(28)
00080                                        VALUE SPACES.
00081              05  FILLER                         PIC X(12)
00082                                        VALUE IS 'BALANCE DUE '.
00083              05  WS-EDIT-TOTAL                  PIC $***,***.99CR.
00084              05  FILLER                         PIC X(80)
00085                                        VALUE SPACES.
00086          01  WS-HEADING-LINE.
00087              09  FILLER                         PIC X(9)
00088                                        VALUE SPACES.
00089              05  FILLER                         PIC X(16)
00090                                        VALUE IS 'ITEM DESCRIPTION'.
00091              05  FILLER                         PIC X(14)
00092                                        VALUE IS '        DATE '.
00093              05  FILLER                         PIC X(14)
00094                                        VALUE IS '     AMOUNT    '.
00095              05  FILLER                         PIC X(80)
00096                                        VALUE SPACES.
00097          PROCEDURE DIVISION.
00098
00099          MAINLINE.
00100              OPEN INPUT CARD-FILE,
00101                  OUTPUT PRINT-FILE.
00102              READ CARD-FILE,
00103                  AT END MOVE 'YES' TO WS-END-OF-FILE.
00104              PERFORM 020-PROCESS-CARDS THRU 025-CARD-PROCESSING-EXIT
00105                  UNTIL WS-END-OF-FILE = 'YES'.
00106              CLOSE CARD-FILE, PRINT-FILE.
00107              STOP RUN.
00108
00109          020-PROCESS-CARDS.
00110              IF MASTER-CODE
00111                  PERFORM 030-NEW-MASTER-RECORD
00112                  PERFORM 040-DETAIL-RECORD MAST-NUMBER-OF-DETAILS TIMES
00113                  PERFORM 050-TOTAL-LINE
00114
00115              ELSE
00116                  DISPLAY 'FIRST CARD NOT MASTER', MAST-NAME,
00117                  STOP RUN.
00118
00119              READ CARD-FILE,
00120                  AT END MOVE 'YES' TO WS-END-OF-FILE.
00121
00122          025-CARD-PROCESSING-EXIT.
00123              EXIT.
00124
00125          030-NEW-MASTER-RECORD.
00126              MOVE ZEROS                 TO WS-RECORD-TOTAL.
00127              MOVE SPACES                TO PRINT-LINE-ONE.
00128              MOVE MAST-NAME             TO PRINT-NAME.
00129              MOVE MAST-ACCT-NUMBER      TO PRINT-ACCT-NUMBER.
00130              EXAMINE PRINT-ACCT-NUMBER REPLACING ALL ' ' BY '-'.
00131              WRITE PRINT-LINE-ONE AFTER ADVANCING TOP-OF-PAGE LINES.
00132              MOVE SPACES                TO PRINT-LINE-TWO.
00133              MOVE MAST-ADDRESS-LINE-ONE TO PRINT-ADDRESS.
00134              WRITE PRINT-LINE-TWO AFTER ADVANCING 1 LINES.
00135              MOVE SPACES                TO PRINT-LINE-TWO.
00136              MOVE MAST-ADDRESS-LINE-TWO TO PRINT-ADDRESS.
00137              WRITE PRINT-LINE AFTER ADVANCING 1 LINES.
00138              MOVE SPACES                TO PRINT-LINE-THREE.
00139              MOVE 'STATEMENT DATE'      TO PRINT-DATE-HDG.
00140              MOVE CURRENT-DATE          TO PRINT-CURRENT-DATE.
00141              WRITE PRINT-LINE-THREE AFTER ADVANCING 1 LINES.
00142              MOVE SPACES                TO PRINT-LINE.
00143              MOVE WS-HEADING-LINE       TO PRINT-LINE
00144              WRITE PRINT-LINE AFTER ADVANCING 3 LINES.
```

Use of CR to indicate negative number

*Fill character

Use of a variable to control a performed procedure

Use of SPECIAL-NAMES entry to begin on new page

Use of CURRENT-DATE

Figure 8.2 *(Continued)*

```
00145
00146          040-DETAIL-RECORD.
00147             READ CARD-FILE,
00148                AT END MOVE 'YES' TO WS-END-OF-FILE.
00149             IF CREDIT,
00150                COMPUTE DET-AMOUNT = DET-AMOUNT * (-1).
00151             ADD DET-AMOUNT                TO WS-RECORD-TOTAL.
00152             MOVE SPACES                   TO PRINT-LINE-FOUR.
00153             MOVE DET-ITEM-DESCRIPTION     TO PRINT-DESCRIPTION.
00154             MOVE DET-DATE                 TO PRINT-DATE.
00155             EXAMINE PRINT-DATE REPLACING ALL ' ' BY '/'.
00156             MOVE DET-AMOUNT               TO PRINT-AMOUNT.
00157             WRITE PRINT-LINE-FOUR AFTER ADVANCING 1 LINES.
00158
00159          050-TOTAL-LINE.
00160             MOVE WS-RECORD-TOTAL          TO WS-EDIT-TOTAL.
00161             MOVE WS-TOTAL-LINE            TO PRINT-LINE.
00162             WRITE PRINT-LINE AFTER ADVANCING 2 LINES.
```
— Use of EXAMINE REPLACING option

Figure 8.2 *(Continued)*

Multiple records are present in PRINT-FILE, as indicated by the DATA RECORDS ARE clause in COBOL lines 47–48. Note that each one of the multiple records has an 01 record entry and appropriate record description.

Multiple record formats are also present in CARD-FILE; i.e., there is a single master card and a variable number of detail cards signified by MAST-NUMBER-OF-DETAILS. Note the use of this field to control a performed procedure in COBOL line 112. [This is rather dangerous in that we are assuming the value of MAST-NUMBER-OF-DETAILS is correct. It would be preferable, indeed mandatory, in a commercial situation to include some type of defensive checks. However, the necessary logic is somewhat involved, and we shall not discuss the concept further until Chapter 15; see Figure 15.6.]

Various editing characters are used (COBOL lines 54, 72, and 83). In particular, note the asterisk fill character in line 83 and the use of CR to indicate negative numbers in lines 72 and 83. Figure 8.3 shows that M. A. CRAWFORD made a purchase of $123.45 on 8/17 and a payment of $200.00 on 8/21. Thus he has a credit of $76.55. Study COBOL lines 149–151 to see how the proper arithmetic sign is obtained for purchase, credit, and balance.

Numeric data almost always come in unsigned. However, it is possible to punch the sign over the low-order (rightmost) digit, although we believe this is not good practice.

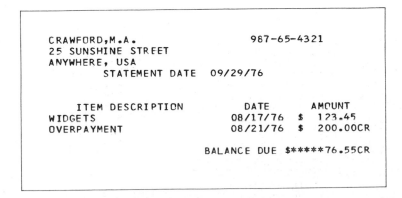

```
CRAWFORD,M.A.                   987-65-4321
25 SUNSHINE STREET
ANYWHERE, USA
          STATEMENT DATE   09/29/76


     ITEM DESCRIPTION          DATE       AMOUNT
WIDGETS                     08/17/76   $   123.45
OVERPAYMENT                 08/21/76   $   200.00CR

                      BALANCE DUE  $*****76.55CR
```

Figure 8.3 Output of Illustrative Data Division Program

A table is a grouping of similar data. The values in a table are stored in **Tables** consecutive storage locations and assigned a single data name. Reference to individual items within a table is accomplished by subscripts which identify the location of the particular item.

For example, assume company XYZ tabulates its sales on a monthly basis and that the sales of each month have to be referenced within a COBOL program. Without tables, 12 data names are required: SALES-FOR-JANUARY, SALES-FOR-FEBRUARY, etc. With tables, however, we define only a single data name, e.g., SALES, and refer to individual months by an appropriate subscript. Thus SALES (2) would indicate sales for the second month, i.e., February.

In COBOL, tables may contain one, two, or three dimensions. Let us further assume that company XYZ has 5 departments and that monthly sales totals are maintained for each department. There are thus 60 required entries (5 departments × 12 months). We shall construct a two-dimension table in which individual entries have two subscripts; the first is for month and the second for department. Thus SALES (10, 1) denotes the sales for month 10 in department 1. One- and two-dimension tables are illustrated in Tables 8.5 and 8.6, respectively.

In this chapter we shall consider one-dimension tables only. However, in Chapter 9 we shall consider both two- and three-dimension tables.

Table 8.5 One-Dimension Table

Month	Sales
Jan.	$1000
Feb.	$2000
Mar.	$3000
April	$4000
May	$5000
June	$4000
July	$3000
Aug.	$2000
Sept.	$1000
Oct.	$2000
Nov.	$3000
Dec.	$6000

Note: SALES (3) = sales for 3rd month = $3000.

Table 8.6 Two-Dimension Table

Month	Department				
	1	2	3	4	5
Jan.	$ 500	$ 400	$ 100	$ 0	$ 0
Feb.	0	0	1000	0	1000
Mar.	600	600	600	1200	0
April	2000	2000	0	0	0
May	3000	0	0	2000	0
June	1000	800	800	0	1400
July	600	0	0	1200	1200
Aug.	400	400	1200	0	0
Sept.	0	0	0	1000	0
Oct.	0	1500	500	0	0
Nov.	3000	0	0	0	0
Dec.	2000	2000	1000	500	500

Notes: 1. Sales (3, 4) = sales for 3rd month, 4th department = $1200.
2. The sum of five department sales equals the monthly total in Table 8.5.

OCCURS Clause

The OCCURS clause specifies the number of entries in a table. The format of the OCCURS clause is simply

<u>OCCURS</u> integer <u>TIMES</u>

Thus, for the one-dimension table of Table 8.5, we might have the entry

05 SALES   OCCURS 12 TIMES   PIC 9(6).

The above entry would cause a 72-position table (12 entries × 6 positions per entry) to be established in the computer's memory, as shown:

SALES					
SALES (1)	SALES (2)			SALES (12)	
		• • •			

There may be instances in which the OCCURS clause functions as a group item and does not contain a PICTURE clause. Consider

```
05  SALES-TABLE OCCURS 12 TIMES.
    10  VOLUME          PIC 9(6).
    10  MONTH           PIC A(10).
```

SALES-TABLE as shown contains 192 (12 × 16) positions:

SALES-TABLE							
SALES-TABLE (1)		SALES-TABLE (2)				SALES-TABLE (12)	
Vol	Month	Vol	Month	• • •		Vol	Month

We could reference either VOLUME (1) to refer to the sales volume of the first month, MONTH (1) to refer to the name of the first month, or SALES-TABLE (1) to refer collectively to the 16 positions of the first month.

Processing a Table

Once Table 8.5 has been established (via an OCCURS clause), we shall want to sum the 12 monthly totals and produce an annual total. We shall illustrate two approaches.

The first is brute force, i.e.,

```
COMPUTE ANNUAL-SALES = SALES (1)  + SALES (2)  + SALES (3)
                     + SALES (4)  + SALES (5)  + SALES (6)
                     + SALES (7)  + SALES (8)  + SALES (9)
                     + SALES (10) + SALES (11) + SALES (12).
```

This technique is cumbersome to code, but it does explicitly illustrate the concept of table processing. A more elegant procedure is to establish a *loop* through the use of a variable subscript. Consider the following:

```
MOVE ZERO TO ANNUAL-SALES.
MOVE 1 TO SUBSCRIPT.
PERFORM ANNUAL-TOTALS UNTIL SUBSCRIPT > 12.
    .
    .

ANNUAL-TOTALS.
    ADD SALES (SUBSCRIPT) TO ANNUAL-SALES.
    ADD 1 TO SUBSCRIPT.
```

The reader should convince himself that this code produces the same numeric result as the brute force technique. Even so, he/she is probably wondering why bother with the more complex code of a loop when a single

151

COMPUTE statement is apparently shorter? Suppose, however, that instead of monthly sales we had weekly or even daily totals—end of debate. (A second argument in favor of a loop is the increased generality it provides, a subject to which we shall return in Chapter 11.)

There are two basic ways to control the value of a subscript within a loop. The first is for the programmer to explicitly vary the value as was already shown. The second is to use the VARYING option of the PERFORM verb. Consider

```
MOVE ZERO TO ANNUAL-SALES.
PERFORM ANNUAL-TOTALS
    VARYING SUBSCRIPT FROM 1 BY 1
    UNTIL SUBSCRIPT > 12.



ANNUAL-TOTALS.
    ADD SALES (SUBSCRIPT) TO ANNUAL-SALES.
```

The value of SUBSCRIPT is initialized to 1 and automatically incremented by 1 every time ANNUAL-TOTALS is executed. In the next chapter, we shall consider this format in much greater detail.

Rules for Subscripts

COBOL subscripts may be either variable or constant. Either way, subscripts *must* adhere to the following rules:

1. A space may not precede the right parenthesis or follow the left parenthesis.

    ```
      VALID:  SALES (SUB)
      VALID:  SALES (2)
    INVALID:  SALES ( 2)
    INVALID:  SALES (2 )
    ```

2. At least one space is required between the data name and left parenthesis.

    ```
    INVALID:  SALES(SUB)
      VALID:  SALES (2)
    INVALID:  SALES(2)
    ```

3. Multiple subscripts are separated by commas. The comma must be followed by, but cannot be preceded by, a space. A maximum of three subscripts is allowed.

    ```
      VALID:  SALES (1, 3)
    INVALID:  SALES (1,3)
    INVALID:  SALES (1, 2, 3, 4)      (limit 3 dimensions)
    ```

4. Subscript values must be positive (nonzero) integers. Violation will probably not cause compile errors but will cause difficulty during execution.

Suggestions

When defining a variable subscript in working storage, make it binary via the USAGE clause. (In Chapter 9 we shall modify this suggestion through the introduction of indexes.) This will not affect the correctness of a program but strongly affects execution efficiency. The USAGE clause used to specify a

```
77  SUBSCRIPT-1    PIC 99    USAGE IS COMPUTATIONAL.
77  SUBSCRIPT-2    PIC 99    COMPUTATIONAL.
77  SUBSCRIPT-3    PIC 99    USAGE IS COMP.
77  SUBSCRIPT-4    PIC S9(4) COMP.
```

The fourth example, SUBSCRIPT-4, specifies a picture of S9(4). This should be standard practice under IBM, but this suggestion has to be taken on faith until the discussion on COBOL from the viewpoint of BAL in Section IV.

REDEFINES Clause

The REDEFINES clause is frequently used to establish constant values for a table. Assume, for example, that we wish to refer to the 12 months of the year by name. We know that MONTH (1) refers to January, MONTH (2) to February, etc., but the computer must be made aware of this explicitly. The OCCURS and REDEFINES clauses are used in conjunction with one another in working storage as shown in Figure 8.4.

```
WORKING-STORAGE SECTION.
   .
   .
   .
01  MONTH-TABLE.
    05  MONTH-NAMES.
        10  FILLER               PIC X(10) VALUE 'JANUARY    '.
        10  FILLER               PIC X(10) VALUE 'FEBRUARY   '.
        10  FILLER               PIC X(10) VALUE 'MARCH      '.
        10  FILLER               PIC X(10) VALUE 'APRIL      '.
        10  FILLER               PIC X(10) VALUE 'MAY        '.
        10  FILLER               PIC X(10) VALUE 'JUNE       '.
        10  FILLER               PIC X(10) VALUE 'JULY       '.
        10  FILLER               PIC X(10) VALUE 'AUGUST     '.
        10  FILLER               PIC X(10) VALUE 'SEPTEMBER  '.
        10  FILLER               PIC X(10) VALUE 'OCTOBER    '.
        10  FILLER               PIC X(10) VALUE 'NOVEMBER   '.
        10  FILLER               PIC X(10) VALUE 'DECEMBER   '.
    05  MONTH-SUB REDEFINES MONTH-NAMES.
        10  MONTH OCCURS 12 TIMES  PIC X(10).
```

Figure 8.4 Initialization of a Table Using OCCURS and REDEFINES

The group item MONTH-NAMES has 12 FILLER entries, each 10 characters long. The VALUE clause is used with each FILLER entry to establish an initial value.

The REDEFINES clause says that MONTH-SUB is another name for the 120 positions of MONTH-NAMES. However, MONTH-SUB consists of a table, MONTH, with 12 entries. Thus, MONTH (1) refers to the first 10 positions in MONTH-NAMES ('JANUARY   '), MONTH (2) to the next 10 positions ('FEBRUARY   '), etc. This may appear somewhat confusing. However, it is made mandatory by a language restriction in COBOL, namely that a VALUE clause cannot be used in the same statement as an OCCURS clause.

Note that an alternative way to accomplish the initialization is to define MONTH as a 12-element table and then use 12 MOVE statements in the procedure division, i.e.,

```
        MOVE 'JANUARY   ' TO MONTH (1).
        MOVE 'FEBRUARY  ' TO MONTH (2).
                        etc.
```

However, the latter approach requires additional machine instructions. Further, it is not so clear from the viewpoint of documentation. Hence it is seldom used by sophisticated programmers.

Table Lookups

Data are almost invariably stored in coded rather than expanded format. The obvious advantage is that less space is required in the storage medium be it punched cards, magnetic tape, etc. Printed reports, however, rarely contain coded information. Thus, somewhere along the way, a conversion from a code

```
WORKING-STORAGE SECTION.
   .
   .
   .
77  WS-SUB                   PIC S9(4)   USAGE IS COMPUTATIONAL.
77  WS-FOUND-MAJOR-SWITCH  PIC X(3)    VALUE 'NO'.
01  MAJOR-VALUE.
    05  FILLER                PIC X(14)   VALUE '1234ACCOUNTING'.
    05  FILLER                PIC X(14)   VALUE '1400BIOLOGY'.
    05  FILLER                PIC X(14)   VALUE '1976CHEMISTRY'.
    05  FILLER                PIC X(14)   VALUE '2100CIVIL ENG'.
    05  FILLER                PIC X(14)   VALUE '2458E. D. P.'.
    05  FILLER                PIC X(14)   VALUE '3245ECONOMICS'.
    05  FILLER                PIC X(14)   VALUE '3960FINANCE'.
    05  FILLER                PIC X(14)   VALUE '4321MANAGEMENT'.
    05  FILLER                PIC X(14)   VALUE '4999MARKETING'.
    05  FILLER                PIC X(14)   VALUE '5400STATISTICS'.
01  MAJOR-TABLE REDEFINES MAJOR-VALUE.
    05  MAJORS     OCCURS 10 TIMES.
        10  MAJOR-CODE      PIC X(4).
        10  MAJOR-NAME      PIC X(10).

* DETERMINE MAJOR
    MOVE 1 TO WS-SUB.
    MOVE 'NO' TO WS-FOUND-MAJOR-SWITCH.
    PERFORM 030-FIND-MAJOR THRU 030-FIND-MAJOR-EXIT
        UNTIL WS-FOUND-MAJOR-SWITCH = 'YES'.
   .
   .
   .
030-FIND-MAJOR.
    IF WS-SUB > 10
        MOVE 'YES' TO WS-FOUND-MAJOR-SWITCH
        MOVE 'UNKNOWN' TO HDG-MAJOR
        GO TO 030-FIND-MAJOR-EXIT.
    IF ST-MAJOR-CODE = MAJOR-CODE (WS-SUB)
        MOVE 'YES' TO WS-FOUND-MAJOR-SWITCH
        MOVE MAJOR-NAME (WS-SUB) TO HDG-MAJOR
        GO TO 030-FIND-MAJOR-EXIT
    ELSE
        ADD 1 TO WS-SUB.
030-FIND-MAJOR-EXIT.
    EXIT.
```

Figure 8.5 Table Lookup

to an expanded value has to take place. The conversion is known as a *table lookup* and is illustrated in Figure 8.5. In the next chapter we shall introduce the SEARCH verb, which simplifies the procedure division code of Figure 8.5. However, the logic in processing a table is so basic that the reader is well advised to study Figure 8.5 before looking for any shortcuts.

The coding in Figure 8.5 is extracted from the listing in Figure 8.7, which appears at the end of the chapter. The objective of Figure 8.5 is to take a four-digit code for major and convert it to an expanded value which will subsequently appear in a printed report. The table of codes and expanded values is established in working storage using the OCCURS, REDEFINES, and VALUE clauses discussed earlier. (Note that we are using a REDEFINES on the 01 level in working storage. REDEFINES *cannot* appear on the 01 level in the file section, where multiple records are used instead; i.e., the clause DATA RECORDS ARE corresponds conceptually to a REDEFINES at the 01 level. Nor can the VALUE clause appear in the file section except for 88-level entries.)

The logic in Figure 8.5 begins by setting a subscript to 1 and a switch to 'NO'. When the incoming code, ST-MAJOR-CODE, matches a code in the table, the switch, WS-FOUND-MAJOR-SWITCH, is set to 'YES' and processing is finished. Notice that we test the value of the subscript, WS-SUB, against the number of entries in the table. If we have gone through the entire table without finding a match, we signify an unknown major and terminate processing in the loop. This type of error checking is extremely important and is one way of distinguishing the professional from the student. If the check were not included and an unknown code did appear, the subscript would be incremented indefinitely until some type of fatal error occurred.

Subprograms and the Linkage Section

The PERFORM statement can be utilized to divide a program into a series of routines which are called by the mainline portion of the program. In effect the PERFORM invokes a subroutine in a COBOL program. As such the called routine must be coded, compiled, and debugged *within* the main program. There is, however, a way to make the subroutine an entirely separate entity from the main program. This technique requires the CALL and USING statements in the procedure division and the linkage section in the data division.

A subprogram (i.e., one which is independent of the main program) contains the four divisions of a regular program. In addition it contains a linkage section in its data division that passes information to and from the main program. The same program may call several subprograms, and a subprogram may in turn call another subprogram.

Consider Figure 8.6, which contains code extracted from the listings at the end of the chapter. *The two programs are developed independently of one another.* The main program contains a CALL statement somewhere in its procedure division. At that point control is transferred from the main program to the subroutine. The CALL statement contains a USING clause which specifies the data on which the subprogram is to operate. The subprogram in turn contains a USING clause in its procedure division header indicating which data it is to receive from an external program. Note that the data names in the two USING clauses are different. However, the *order* of data names within the USING clause is absolutely critical. The first item in the USING clause of the main program (STUDENT-RECORD) corresponds to the first item in the USING clause of the subprogram (DATA-PASSED-FROM-MAIN); both are 01 records with 80 characters. The second item in the main program (WS-GRADE-AVERAGE) matches the second item in the subroutine (LS-GRADE-AVERAGE), etc. Data names in the main program are defined in either the file section or working storage, whereas data names in the

```
         ┌─  IDENTIFICATION DIVISION.
         │   PROGRAM-ID. 'MAINPROG'.
         │       .
         │       .
         │       .
         │   DATA DIVISION.
         │   FILE SECTION.
         │       .
         │       .
         │       .
         │   FD  CARD-FILE
         │       .
         │       .
         │       .
         │   01  STUDENT-RECORD                        PIC X(80).
         │       .
         │       .
         │       .
         │   WORKING-STORAGE SECTION.
  MAIN   │       .
PROGRAM  │       .
         │   77  WS-GRADE-AVERAGE                      PIC S9V99.
         │       .
         │       .
         │   PROCEDURE DIVISION.
         │       .
         │       .
         │       .
         │       CALL 'SUBRTN'
         │           USING STUDENT-RECORD, WS-GRADE-AVERAGE.
         │       .
         │       .
         └─      .


         ┌─  IDENTIFICATION DIVISION.
         │   PROGRAM-ID. 'SUBRTN'.
         │       .
         │       .
         │   DATA DIVISION.
         │       .
         │       .
         │   WORKING-STORAGE SECTION.
         │       .
   SUB   │       .
PROGRAM  │   LINKAGE SECTION.
         │       .
         │       .
         │       .
         │   77  LS-CALCULATED-AVERAGE                 PIC S9V99.
         │       .
         │       .
         │   01  DATA-PASSED-FROM-MAIN                 PIC X(80).
         │       .
         │       .
         │   PROCEDURE DIVISION
         │       USING DATA-PASSED-FROM-MAIN, LS-CALCULATED-AVERAGE.
         │       .
         │       .
         │   RETURN-TO-MAIN.
         └─      EXIT PROGRAM.
```

Figure 8.6 Illustration of Subprogram

156

subprogram (which are passed from the main program) are defined in the linkage section.

When the CALL statement in the main program is executed, the subprogram is entered at the beginning of its procedure division. It executes exactly as a regular COBOL program except that it contains an EXIT PROGRAM statement instead of a STOP RUN. The EXIT PROGRAM terminates processing of the subprogram and returns control to the main program to the statement immediately after the CALL. (Note that it is possible for a subprogram to contain a STOP RUN statement as well. However, this would tend to obscure the mainline logic, as it would be difficult to tell where execution terminates.)

The data names passed to the subprogram are known as arguments. The main program is also known as the calling program, and the subprogram as the called program. The subprogram may also contain an 'ENTRY' statement instead of a procedure division USING, but that is not covered here.

Table initialization, table lookups, and subprograms are illustrated in Figures 8.7, 8.8, and 8.9. The program specifications are as follows:

INPUT—A file of student cards containing name, major code, and number of courses taken and, for each course, the course number, credits, and grade.

PROCESSING—Calculate a grade point average for each data card. A four-point system is used in which A, B, C, D, and F are worth 4, 3, 2, 1, and 0, respectively. A subprogram is to be written which calculates the grade point average.

OUTPUT—A separate transcript is to be printed for each student card. The transcript should show each course taken, the number of credits, and the grade received. It should also show the calculated average and the student's major.

Figure 8.7 contains the main (calling) program, and Figure 8.8 contains the subprogram (called program). The main program calls the subprogram in COBOL lines 105–107 and passes two arguments, STUDENT-RECORD and WS-GRADE-AVERAGE. The subprogram in turn knows these arguments as DATA-PASSED-FROM-MAIN and LS-CALCULATED-AVERAGE (subprogram lines 33–34). It defines these data names in its linkage section (subprogram lines 21–30).

The subprogram is concerned exclusively with calculating the grade point average. Notice the four simple IF statements in lines 57–60. These could of course have been written as a single nested IF, but we have chosen to use the four statements for greater clarity. Which is preferable? There is no unequivocal answer. Some installations disallow nested IF's on the grounds they are too difficult to read. Other installations encourage their use. We use both techniques in the text to give as broad exposure as possible.

The subprogram also illustrates table processing via the PERFORM VARYING option (lines 45–47). Each student card contains a variable number of courses (LS-NUMBER-OF-COURSES), and hence the routine to include each course in the overall average must be performed a variable number of times. The VARYING option increments WS-SUB by 1 prior to entering 010-COMPUTE-QUALITY-POINTS. The UNTIL clause terminates the PERFORM when all courses have been processed. Finally, note the running total of quality points in 010-COMPUTE-QUALITY-POINTS and the use of subscripting in conjunction with the table of student courses.

After the subprogram has been executed, control returns to the main program (line 109) where generation of output begins. Notice the table lookup (lines 135–148), which again illustrates subscripts and table processing. Also

```
00001          IDENTIFICATION DIVISION.
00002          PROGRAM-ID.  'MAINPROG'.
00003          AUTHOR.       GRAUER.
00004
00005
00006          ENVIRONMENT DIVISION.
00007
00008          CONFIGURATION SECTION.
00009          SOURCE-COMPUTER.  IBM-370.
00010          OBJECT-COMPUTER.  IBM-370.
00011          SPECIAL-NAMES.
00012              C01 IS TOP-OF-PAGE.
00013
00014          INPUT-OUTPUT SECTION.
00015          FILE-CONTROL.
00016              SELECT CARD-FILE ASSIGN TO UR-2540R-S-CARDS.
00017              SELECT PRINT-FILE ASSIGN TO UR-1403-S-SYSOUT.
00018
00019
00020          DATA DIVISION.
00021          FILE SECTION.
00022          FD   CARD-FILE
00023               RECORDING MODE IS F
00024               LABEL RECORDS ARE OMITTED
00025               RECORD CONTAINS 80 CHARACTERS            ┌─Copied entry
00026               DATA RECORD IS STUDENT-RECORD.          │
00027          01   STUDENT-RECORD          COPY STUDREC.  ╱
00028 C        01   STUDENT-RECORD.
00029 C             05   ST-NAME                     PIC A(15).
00030 C             05   ST-MAJOR-CODE               PIC X(4).
00031 C             05   ST-NUMBER-OF-COURSES        PIC 9(2).
00032 C             05   ST-COURSE-TABLE OCCURS 8 TIMES.
00033 C                  10   ST-COURSE-NUMBER       PIC X(3).
00034 C                  10   ST-COURSE-GRADE        PIC A.
00035 C                  10   ST-COURSE-CREDITS      PIC 9.
00036 C             05   FILLER                      PIC X(19).
00037          FD   PRINT-FILE
00038               RECORDING MODE IS F
00039               LABEL RECORDS ARE OMITTED
00040               RECORD CONTAINS 133 CHARACTERS
00041               DATA RECORD IS PRINT-LINE.            ┌─Binary subscript for
00042          01   PRINT-LINE      PIC X(133).          │  efficient processing
00043          WORKING-STORAGE SECTION.               ╱
00044          77   WS-SUB               PIC S9(4)     COMP.
00045          77   WS-END-OF-FILE       PIC X(3)   VALUE 'NO '.
00046          77   WS-FOUND-MAJOR-SWITCH PIC X(3)  VALUE 'NO '.
00047          77   WS-GRADE-AVERAGE     PIC S9V99.
00048          01   HEADING-LINE-ONE.
00049               05   FILLER          PIC X(20)   VALUE SPACES.
```

Figure 8.7 Main (Calling) Program

```
00050              05   FILLER              PIC X(10)    VALUE 'TRANSCRIPT'.
00051              05   FILLER              PIC X(103) VALUE SPACES.
00052         01  HEADING-LINE-TWO.
00053              05   FILLER              PIC X(6)     VALUE ' NAME:'.
00054              05   HDG-NAME            PIC A(15).
00055              05   FILLER              PIC X(5)     VALUE SPACES.
00056              05   FILLER              PIC X(6)     VALUE 'MAJOR:'.
00057              05   HDG-MAJOR           PIC X(10).
00058              05   FILLER              PIC X(91)    VALUE SPACES.
00059         01  HEADING-LINE-THREE.
00060              05   FILLER              PIC X(10)    VALUE SPACES.
00061              05   FILLER              PIC X(9)     VALUE 'COURSE#   '.
00062              05   FILLER              PIC X(9)     VALUE 'CREDITS   '.
00063              05   FILLER              PIC X(5)     VALUE 'GRADE'.
00064              05   FILLER              PIC X(100) VALUE SPACES.
00065         01  DETAIL-LINE.
00066              05   FILLER              PIC X(13)    VALUE SPACES.
00067              05   DET-COURSE          PIC X(3).
00068              05   FILLER              PIC X(9)     VALUE SPACES.
00069              05   DET-CREDITS         PIC 9.
00070              05   FILLER              PIC X(5)     VALUE SPACES.
00071              05   DET-GRADE           PIC A.
00072              05   FILLER              PIC X(101) VALUE SPACES.
00073         01  TOTAL-LINE.
00074              05   FILLER              PIC X(16)    VALUE SPACES.
00075              05   FILLER              PIC X(9)     VALUE 'AVERAGE: '.
00076              05   TOT-GPA             PIC 9.99.
00077              05   FILLER              PIC X(104) VALUE SPACES.
00078         01  MAJOR-VALUE.
00079              05   FILLER              PIC X(14)    VALUE '1234ACCOUNTING'.
00080              05   FILLER              PIC X(14)    VALUE '1400BIOLOGY   '.
00081              05   FILLER              PIC X(14)    VALUE '1976CHEMISTRY '.
00082              05   FILLER              PIC X(14)    VALUE '2100CIVIL ENG '.
00083              05   FILLER              PIC X(14)    VALUE '2458E. D. P.  '.
00084              05   FILLER              PIC X(14)    VALUE '3245ECONOMICS '.
00085              05   FILLER              PIC X(14)    VALUE '3960FINANCE   '.
00086              05   FILLER              PIC X(14)    VALUE '4321MANAGEMENT'.
00087              05   FILLER              PIC X(14)    VALUE '4999MARKETING '.
00088              05   FILLER              PIC X(14)    VALUE '5400STATISTICS'.
00089         01  MAJOR-TABLE REDEFINES MAJOR-VALUE.
00090              05   MAJORS      OCCURS 10 TIMES.
00091                   10   MAJOR-CODE     PIC X(4).
00092                   10   MAJOR-NAME     PIC X(10).
00093         PROCEDURE DIVISION.
00094         MAINLINE.
00095              OPEN INPUT CARD-FILE,
00096                   OUTPUT PRINT-FILE.
00097              READ CARD-FILE,
00098                   AT END MOVE 'YES' TO WS-END-OF-FILE.
00099              PERFORM 020-PROCESS-CARDS THRU 025-PROCESS-CARDS-EXIT
00100                   UNTIL WS-END-OF-FILE = 'YES'.
00101              CLOSE CARD-FILE, PRINT-FILE.
00102              STOP RUN.
00103
```

Establishing a table

Figure 8.7 *(Continued)*

```
00104          020-PROCESS-CARDS.
00105              CALL 'SUBRTN'
00106                   USING STUDENT-RECORD              ─── Call to subprogram, 'SUBRTN'
00107                         WS-GRADE-AVERAGE.
00108      *WRITE HEADING LINES
00109              WRITE PRINT-LINE FROM HEADING-LINE-ONE
00110                   AFTER ADVANCING TOP-OF-PAGE LINES.
00111      *DETERMINE MAJOR
00112              MOVE 1 TO WS-SUB.
00113              MOVE 'NO ' TO WS-FOUND-MAJOR-SWITCH.
00114              PERFORM 030-FIND-MAJOR THRU 030-FIND-MAJOR-EXIT
00115                   UNTIL WS-FOUND-MAJOR-SWITCH = 'YES'.
00116              MOVE ST-NAME TO HDG-NAME.
00117              WRITE PRINT-LINE FROM HEADING-LINE-TWO
00118                   AFTER ADVANCING 2 LINES.
00119              WRITE PRINT-LINE FROM HEADING-LINE-THREE
00120                   AFTER ADVANCING 2 LINES.
00121      *WRITE DETAIL LINES - 1 PER COURSE
00122              PERFORM 040-WRITE-DETAIL-LINE
00123                   VARYING WS-SUB FROM 1 BY 1
00124                   UNTIL WS-SUB > ST-NUMBER-OF-COURSES.
00125      *WRITE GRADE POINT AVERAGE
00126              MOVE WS-GRADE-AVERAGE TO TOT-GPA.
00127              WRITE PRINT-LINE FROM TOTAL-LINE
00128                   AFTER ADVANCING 2 LINES.
00129              READ CARD-FILE,
00130                   AT END MOVE 'YES' TO WS-END-OF-FILE.
00131
00132          025-PROCESS-CARDS-EXIT.
00133              EXIT.                                  ─── Routine to find major
00134
00135          030-FIND-MAJOR.
00136              IF WS-SUB > 10
00137                   MOVE 'YES' TO WS-FOUND-MAJOR-SWITCH
00138                   MOVE 'UNKNOWN    ' TO HDG-MAJOR
00139                   GO TO 030-FIND-MAJOR-EXIT.
00140              IF ST-MAJOR-CODE = MAJOR-CODE (WS-SUB)
00141                   MOVE 'YES' TO WS-FOUND-MAJOR-SWITCH
00142                   MOVE MAJOR-NAME (WS-SUB) TO HDG-MAJOR
00143                   GO TO 030-FIND-MAJOR-EXIT
00144              ELSE
00145                   ADD 1 TO WS-SUB.
00146
00147          030-FIND-MAJOR-EXIT.
00148              EXIT.
00149
00150          040-WRITE-DETAIL-LINE.
00151              MOVE ST-COURSE-NUMBER (WS-SUB) TO DET-COURSE.
00152              MOVE ST-COURSE-CREDITS (WS-SUB) TO DET-CREDITS.
00153              MOVE ST-COURSE-GRADE (WS-SUB) TO DET-GRADE.
00154              WRITE PRINT-LINE FROM DETAIL-LINE
00155                   AFTER ADVANCING 1 LINES.
```

Figure 8.7 *(Continued)*

```
00001          IDENTIFICATION DIVISION.
00002          PROGRAM-ID.  'SUBRTN'.        Program ID matches COBOL entry
00003          AUTHOR.      GRAUER.          in main program
00004
00005
00006          ENVIRONMENT DIVISION.
00007
00008          CONFIGURATION SECTION.
00009          SOURCE-COMPUTER.   IBM-370.
00010          OBJECT-COMPUTER.   IBM-370.
00011
00012                                        Designation of a binary
00013          DATA DIVISION.                subscript for efficient
00014          WORKING-STORAGE SECTION.      object code
00015          77   WS-TOTAL-CREDITS           PIC 999.
00016          77   WS-QUALITY-POINTS          PIC 999.
00017          77   WS-MULTIPLIER              PIC 9.
00018          77   WS-SUB                     PIC S9(4)      COMP.
00019          ****************************************************
00020          LINKAGE SECTION.
00021          77   LS-CALCULATED-AVERAGE      PIC S9V99.
00022          01   DATA-PASSED-FROM-MAIN.
00023               05   LS-NAME               PIC A(15).       Linkage
00024               05   LS-MAJOR-CODE         PIC X(4).        section
00025               05   LS-NUMBER-OF-COURSES  PIC 99.
00026               05   LS-COURSE-TABLE OCCURS 8 TIMES.
00027                    10   LS-COURSE-NUMBER  PIC X(3).       Table of
00028                    10   LS-COURSE-GRADE   PIC A.          student courses
00029                    10   LS-COURSE-CREDITS PIC 9.
00030               05   FILLER                PIC X(19).
00031          ****************************************************
00032          PROCEDURE DIVISION
00033              USING DATA-PASSED-FROM-MAIN    Arguments passed to and
00034                    LS-CALCULATED-AVERAGE.   from main program
00035          ****************************************************
00036          * ROUTINE TO COMPUTE GRADE POINT AVERAGE
00037          * WEIGHTS:   A=4, B=3, C=2, D=1, F=0
00038          * NO PLUS OR MINUS GRADES
00039          * QUALITY POINTS FOR A GIVEN COURSE = WEIGHT X CREDITS
00040          * GRADE POINT AVERAGE = TOTAL QUALITY POINTS / TOTAL CREDITS
00041          ****************************************************
00042          MAINLINE.
00043              MOVE ZERO TO WS-QUALITY-POINTS.      PERFORM VARYING option
00044              MOVE ZERO TO WS-TOTAL-CREDITS.
00045              PERFORM 010-COMPUTE-QUALITY-POINTS
00046                  VARYING WS-SUB FROM 1 BY 1
00047                  UNTIL WS-SUB > LS-NUMBER-OF-COURSES.
00048              COMPUTE LS-CALCULATED-AVERAGE ROUNDED
00049                  = WS-QUALITY-POINTS / WS-TOTAL-CREDITS.
00050          005-RETURN-TO-MAIN.
00051              EXIT PROGRAM.       Return to main program
00052
00053          010-COMPUTE-QUALITY-POINTS.
00054              MOVE ZERO TO WS-MULTIPLIER.
00055          * NESTED IF COULD BE USED, BUT ISN'T IN ORDER TO OBTAIN
00056          * GREATER CLARITY.
00057              IF LS-COURSE-GRADE (WS-SUB) = 'A', MOVE 4 TO WS-MULTIPLIER.
00058              IF LS-COURSE-GRADE (WS-SUB) = 'B', MOVE 3 TO WS-MULTIPLIER.
00059              IF LS-COURSE-GRADE (WS-SUB) = 'C', MOVE 2 TO WS-MULTIPLIER.
00060              IF LS-COURSE-GRADE (WS-SUB) = 'D', MOVE 1 TO WS-MULTIPLIER.
00061              COMPUTE WS-QUALITY-POINTS =  WS-QUALITY-POINTS
00062                  + LS-COURSE-CREDITS (WS-SUB) * WS-MULTIPLIER.
00063              ADD LS-COURSE-CREDITS (WS-SUB) TO WS-TOTAL-CREDITS.
               Use of four simple IF statements in lieu
               of a nested IF for greater clarity
```

Figure 8.8 Subprogram (Called Program)

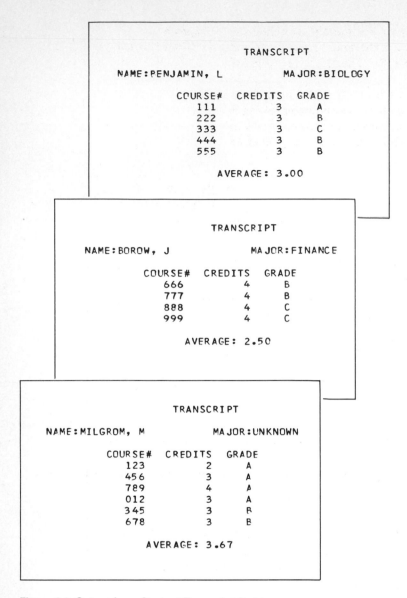

Figure 8.9 Output from Student Transcript Problem

note the use of the SPECIAL-NAMES paragraph to cause each transcript to begin a new page. (Undoubtedly special forms would be mounted on which to print the transcripts.)

Summary

This chapter has dealt exclusively with the data division. We began by amplifying points introduced in earlier chapters, namely editing and condition names. We then moved to new material: multiple records, COPY, tables, and subprograms.

Multiple records are used in the file section when there are different formats in a given file (e.g., a master card and several detail cards). They are not a requirement. Many programmers prefer to use the READ INTO and WRITE FROM options and define multiple records in working storage.

The advantages of the COPY clause are obvious. Earlier versions of COBOL limited the use of the COPY, but now it is permitted anywhere within the COBOL program. A direct consequence is the use of COPY to duplicate procedure division code. In this way entire modules may be copied directly from a library. The REPLACING option of the COPY verb is used to make the data names in the library version conform to those of the specific program.

Tables are extremely important, and this chapter has merely scratched the surface. In the next chapter we shall introduce two- and three-dimension tables. In Chapter 9 we shall also present the SEARCH verb, in an extended discussion on table processing.

Subprograms are an important concept and are extremely useful in modular programming. A primary advantage of this technique in a commercial setting is the capability to divide a large program into several smaller ones. These may in turn be divided among several programmers, who can work independently according to common specifications.

REVIEW EXERCISES

TRUE	FALSE		
☐	☐	**1**	The COPY clause is permitted only in the data division.
☐	☐	**2**	The VALUE clause cannot be used in the file section.
☐	☐	**3**	Several record descriptions are permitted for the same file.
☐	☐	**4**	Tables in COBOL may contain one, two, or three dimensions.
☐	☐	**5**	The REDEFINES clause must be used when defining a table.
☐	☐	**6**	The same entry may not contain both an OCCURS clause and a PICTURE clause.
☐	☐	**7**	The same entry may not contain both an OCCURS clause and a VALUE clause.
☐	☐	**8**	The REDEFINES clause cannot be used at the 01 level.
☐	☐	**9**	The USAGE clause is required when defining a subscript in working-storage.
☐	☐	**10**	Subscripts can assume a zero value.
☐	☐	**11**	The edit characters $ and * may not appear in the same PICTURE clause.
☐	☐	**12**	The linkage section appears in the main program.
☐	☐	**13**	The linkage section appears in the called program.
☐	☐	**14**	Data names in 'CALL...USING' and 'PROCEDURE DIVISION USING...' must be the same.
☐	☐	**15**	A subprogram contains only the data and procedure divisions.
☐	☐	**16**	The COPY clause can be used on an FD only.
☐	☐	**17**	Subscripts may be constant or variable.
☐	☐	**18**	A program can contain only one CALL statement.
☐	☐	**19**	The same program may be simultaneously considered a "called" and a "calling" program.
☐	☐	**20**	88-Level entries are allowed in the file section.

1 Indicate which entries are incorrectly subscripted. Assume SUB1 = 5 and that the following entry applies: **PROBLEMS**

          05   SALES-TABLE   OCCURS 12 TIMES   PIC 9(5).

(a) SALES-TABLE (1)
(b) SALES-TABLE (15)
(c) SALES-TABLE (0)
(d) SALES-TABLE (SUB1)
(e) SALES-TABLE(SUB1)
(f) SALES-TABLE (5)
(g) SALES-TABLE (SUB1, SUB2)
(h) SALES-TABLE (3)
(i) SALES-TABLE (3)

2 Show the edited results for each entry:

	Source Field		Receiving Field	
	Picture	Value	Picture	Edited Result
(a)	S9(4)V99	−45600	$$$$$.99CR	
(b)	S9(4)V99	45600	$$,$$$.99DB	
(c)	S9(4)	4567	$$,$$$.00	
(d)	S9(6)	122577	99B99B99	
(e)	S9(6)	123456	++++,+++	
(f)	S9(6)	−123456	++++,+++	
(g)	S9(6)	123456	−−−−,−−−	
(h)	S9(6)	−123456	−−−−,−−−	
(i)	9(6)V99	567890	$$$$,$$$.99	
(j)	9(6)V99	567890	$ZZZ,ZZZ.99	
(k)	9(6)V99	567890	$***,***.99	

3 Rewrite the car billing problem of Figure 7.8 to contain a subprogram which calculates the customer bills. The following arguments are to be passed: car type, mileage driven, days rented, and calculated bill.

4 Write a subprogram to accept a 2-position abbreviation for state name and return a 20-position expanded name. Include the table of abbreviations and state names in your subprogram.

AL — Alabama
AK — Alaska
AZ — Arizona
AR — Arkansas
CA — California
CO — Colorado
CT — Connecticut
DE — Delaware
DC — District of Columbia
FL — Florida
GA — Georgia
HI — Hawaii
ID — Idaho
IL — Illinois
IN — Indiana
IA — Iowa
KS — Kansas
KY — Kentucky
LA — Lousiana
ME — Maine
MD — Maryland
MA — Massachusetts
MI — Michigan
MN — Minnesota
MS — Mississippi
MO — Missouri
MT — Montana
NB — Nebraska
NV — Nevada
NH — New Hampshire
NJ — New Jersey
NM — New Mexico
NC — North Carolina
NY — New York
ND — North Dakota
OH — Ohio
OK — Oklahoma
OR — Oregon
PA — Pennsylvania
RI — Rhode Island
SC — South Carolina
SD — South Dakota
TN — Tennessee
TX — Texas
UT — Utah
VT — Vermont
VA — Virginia
WA — Washington
WV — West Virginia
WI — Wisconsin
WY — Wyoming

5 Modify the input for the car billing problem of Figure 7.8 to include a three-position field denoting the car type on the incoming data card (e.g., CHE for Chevrolet, PON for Pontiac, etc.). Include a table lookup routine which will print expanded car type on each line of output. Use your own table of abbreviations.

6 Write procedure division statements to do a table lookup in a table called CODE-NAME-TABLE for an entry that matches THIS-CODE. If a match is found perform paragraph FOUND; if no match is found, perform paragraph NO-MATCH.

```
77  THIS-CODE          PIC 9(5).
77  SUB                PIC S9(4)  COMP.
01  CODE-NAME-TABLE.
    02  TABLE-VALUES OCCURS 100 TIMES.
        03  CODE-TAB PIC 9(5).
        03  NAME-TAB PIC X(20).
```

7 Assume that STATE-TAX-TABLE contains 50 entries of the form 9V99. Write procedure division code and appropriate data division entries to
(a) Print the 50 values in a single column, i.e., 1 value per line, 50 lines in all.
(b) Print 10 values per line, 5 lines in all.
(c) Print 5 values per line, 10 lines in all.

8 Company XYZ has four corporate functions: manufacturing, marketing, financial, and administrative. Each function in turn has several departments, as shown:

Function	Departments
MANUFACTURING	10, 12, 16, 17–29, 30, 41, 56
MARKETING	6–9, 15, 31–33
FINANCIAL	60–62, 75
ADMINISTRATIVE	1–4, 78

Establish condition name entries so that given a value of EMPLOYEE-DEPARTMENT we can determine the function. Include an 88-level entry, VALID-CODES, to verify that the incoming department is indeed a valid department (any department number not shown is invalid).

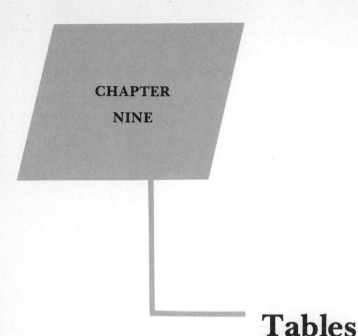

CHAPTER
NINE

Tables

Tables are of paramount importance. In the previous chapter, we introduced subscripts and one-dimension tables. In this chapter we shall extend those concepts to two- and three-dimension tables. We shall also introduce indexes, which are conceptually the same as subscripts; however, the use of indexes in lieu of subscripts leads to more efficient machine code.

    We shall present two distinct search techniques, namely linear and binary. We shall also discuss direct access to table entries and various means of initializing a table. Finally we shall present the necessary COBOL to implement these procedures. We shall cover the SEARCH, SEARCH ALL, and SET verbs as well as associated clauses in the data division.

Overview

Figure 8.5 contained a table lookup routine to determine a student major given a major code. Although the table lookup of Figure 8.5 is logically correct, it is not efficient in terms of the generated object code. Execution speed is increased if indexes and the SEARCH verb are used in lieu of subscripting. Consider Figure 9.1.

    Let us highlight the differences between Figure 8.5 and 9.1. Figure 8.5 uses a *subscript*, WS-SUB; Figure 9.1 uses an *index*, MAJOR-INDEX. The subscript is defined in working-storage, the index is defined with the table. Figure 8.5 uses the PERFORM verb for the table lookup; Figure 9.1 uses the

Subscripting Versus Indexing

```
01  MAJOR-VALUE.
    05  FILLER              PIC X(14)  VALUE  '1234ACCOUNTING'.
    05  FILLER              PIC X(14)  VALUE  '1400BIOLOGY'.
    05  FILLER              PIC X(14)  VALUE  '1976CHEMISTRY'.
    05  FILLER              PIC X(14)  VALUE  '2100CIVIL ENG'.
    05  FILLER              PIC X(14)  VALUE  '2458E. D. P.'.
    05  FILLER              PIC X(14)  VALUE  '3245ECONOMICS'.
    05  FILLER              PIC X(14)  VALUE  '3960FINANCE'.
    05  FILLER              PIC X(14)  VALUE  '4321MANAGEMENT'.
    05  FILLER              PIC X(14)  VALUE  '4999MARKETING'.
    05  FILLER              PIC X(14)  VALUE  '5400STATISTICS'.
01  MAJOR-TABLE REDEFINES MAJOR-VALUE.
    05  MAJORS      OCCURS 10 TIMES
                    INDEXED BY MAJOR-INDEX.
        10  MAJOR-CODE    PIC 9(4).
        10  MAJOR-NAME    PIC X(10).
*   DETERMINE MAJOR
    SET MAJOR-INDEX TO 1.
    SEARCH MAJORS
        AT END
            MOVE 'UNKNOWN   ' TO HDG-MAJOR
        WHEN ST-MAJOR-CODE = MAJOR-CODE (MAJOR-INDEX)
            MOVE MAJOR-NAME (MAJOR-INDEX) TO HDG-MAJOR.
```

Figure 9.1 Illustration of the SEARCH Verb (Linear Search)

SEARCH verb. In actuality, however, the most significant difference is in the generated machine code, and this is not overtly visible from a simple comparison of the two figures. We must further differentiate between a subscript and an index.

A subscript and an index are conceptually the same in that they both reference an entry in a table. An index, however, represents a *displacement* into the table, whereas a subscript is an *occurrence*. Consider the following sketch with respect to Figure 9.1:

MAJORS						
OCCURRENCE (1)		OCCURRENCE (2)			OCCURRENCE (10)	
MAJOR CODE	MAJOR NAME	MAJOR CODE	MAJOR NAME		MAJOR CODE	MAJOR NAME
				· · ·		

Figure 9.1 establishes a table with 10 entries, MAJORS, occupying a total of 140 positions. Valid *subscripts* for MAJOR-CODE are $1, 2, 3, \ldots, 10$; i.e., MAJOR-CODE can occur 10 times. Valid *displacements* for MAJOR-CODE are $0, 14, 28, \ldots, 126$; e.g., the second value of MAJOR-CODE begins in position 15, a displacement of 14 positions into the table, etc. Thus the first value in the table is denoted by a subscript of 1 or a displacement (i.e., an index) of 0, the second value by a subscript of 2 or an index of 14, the last value by a subscript of 10 or an index of 126. The COBOL programmer, however, explicitly codes index values of 1, 2, etc. which correspond to internal displacements of 0, 14, etc.

In most instances, the COBOL programmer need not concern himself with the actual value of an index; instead he should regard it conceptually as a subscript. Accordingly, COBOL provides the capability to adjust an index to its proper value through the SET, SEARCH, and PERFORM verbs. Indeed these are the *only* verbs which can be used to modify an index. The only time a programmer need be concerned with the actual value of an index is in debugging (i.e., dump reading).

167

Let us return to Figure 9.1 and consider the action of the SET and SEARCH verbs. The statement SET MAJOR-INDEX TO 1 is analogous to MOVE 1 TO WS-SUB and initiates the point in the table where the search is to begin. The SET verb must be used to modify an index; i.e., it is *incorrect* to say MOVE 1 TO MAJOR-INDEX.

When the SEARCH verb is executed, it compares in sequence the entries in the MAJORS table to ST-MAJOR-CODE. If no match is found, i.e., the AT END condition is reached, then UNKNOWN is moved to HDG-MAJOR. However, if a match does occur, i.e., ST-MAJOR-CODE = MAJOR-CODE (MAJOR-INDEX), the appropriate major is moved to HDG-MAJOR, and the search is terminated, with control passing to the statement following the SEARCH.

Binary Search

The coding in both Figures 8.5 and 9.1 represents a linear or sequential search. The incoming code is compared to the first entry in the table, then the second entry, the third entry, etc. The number of comparisons that have to be made depends on where in the table we find our match. Obviously if the incoming code is near the beginning of the table, fewer comparisons are needed than if the code is at the end of the table.

A binary search is a way to reduce the number of necessary comparisons and further to make the number of comparisons "relatively" independent of where in the table the match occurs. *It requires, however, that the entries in the table be in sequence (either ascending or descending).* The action of a binary search is illustrated in Figure 9.2.

Note: Incoming value is 3960

Position	Table Entries	
1	1234	
2	1400	
3	1976	
4	2100	
5	2458 ←——— 1st guess	
6	3245	
7	3960 ←————————— 3rd guess	
8	4321 ←——— 2nd guess	
9	4999	
10	5400	

Figure 9.2 Illustration of a Binary Search

A binary search eliminates half the table with every comparison. In Figure 9.2 there are ten entries in the table and we are looking for a match on 3960. We begin in the middle of the table at the fifth entry; the logic flow is as follows:

1. There are ten entries in the table; examine the middle (i.e., fifth entry). Is the incoming entry (3960) greater than the fifth entry (2458)? Yes; therefore eliminate table entries 1–5.

2. There are five remaining entries (positions 6, 7, 8, 9, and 10). Select the middle (i.e., the eighth entry). Is incoming entry (3960) greater than the eighth entry (4321)? No; therefore eliminate table entries 9 and 10.

3. There are three remaining entries (positions 6, 7, and 8). Select the middle (i.e., the seventh) entry; with a value of 3960, a match is found, and the search is terminated.

Individual programmers vary the implementation of a binary search as to the type of test, i.e., high or low. Further, it is sometimes necessary to include a second test (equal) at a given guess. Indeed steps 1, 2, and 3 are perhaps a little hazy in that we skip over this completely, for our objective is to present only the flavor of a binary search. However, it is a good exercise to try to program these considerations into your own binary search routine in COBOL.

Notice that a total of three comparisons was required to match 3960. (If 3245 had been the incoming entry, four comparisons would have been needed, but this is the *maximum* number that would ever be required for a ten-position table; see Table 9.1.) A linear search, on the other hand, would require seven comparisons until a match was found on 3960. Thus, if all ten entries in the table have an equal chance of occurring, the *average* number of comparisons for a linear search on a table of ten entries is five, which is greater than the *maximum* number for a binary search. Indeed, as table size increases, the advantage of the binary search increases dramatically. Table 9.1 shows the maximum number of comparisons for tables with 8 to 4095 entries.

Table 9.1 Required Number of Comparisons for Binary Search

Number of Elements		Maximum Number of Comparisons
8–15	(less than 2^4)	4
16–31	(less than 2^5)	5
32–63	(less than 2^6)	6
64–127	(less than 2^7)	7
128–255	(less than 2^8)	8
256–511	(less than 2^9)	9
512–1023	(less than 2^{10})	10
1024–2047	(less than 2^{11})	11
2048–4095	(less than 2^{12})	12

Although the number of comparisons is less for a binary search, additional machine time is required for individual comparisons. Thus, as a rule of thumb, the binary search should not be used for small tables, i.e., those with 25 elements or less.

Figure 9.3 illustrates the implementation of a binary search in COBOL. The differences between Figures 9.1 and 9.3 are slight. SEARCH ALL is used in lieu of SEARCH to denote a binary search. Further, the ASCENDING KEY clause is needed in the table definition to indicate that MAJORS is in ascending sequence by MAJOR-CODE. Remember, a table *must* be in sequence (either ascending or descending) if a binary search is to be applied. Finally, the SET verb is not needed to initiate a binary search, as SEARCH ALL calculates its own starting position.

Direct Access to Table Entries

The *binary* search is a substantial improvement over the *linear* search, as it reduces the number of required comparisons. *Direct* access to table entries is better yet in that it requires no comparisons whatsoever. It is not really a search but rather a table lookup that uses the key of a record to indicate its position in a table. Consider the table of student majors used to illustrate the linear and binary searches of Figures 9.1 and 9.3. MAJOR-CODE is a four-digit numeric code, presumably with values of 1 to 9999. Both the linear and binary searches vary MAJOR-INDEX and compare the incoming code, ST-MAJOR-CODE, to various codes in the table until a match is found. Suppose, however, that the MAJORS table is defined to occur 9999 times. We

```
01  MAJOR-VALUE
    05  FILLER              PIC X(14)   VALUE   '1234ACCOUNTING'.
    05  FILLER              PIC X(14)   VALUE   '1400BIOLOGY'.
    05  FILLER              PIC X(14)   VALUE   '1976CHEMISTRY'.
    05  FILLER              PIC X(14)   VALUE   '2100CIVIL ENG'.
    05  FILLER              PIC X(14)   VALUE   '2458E. D. P.'.
    05  FILLER              PIC X(14)   VALUE   '3245ECONOMICS'.
    05  FILLER              PIC X(14)   VALUE   '3960FINANCE'.
    05  FILLER              PIC X(14)   VALUE   '4321MANAGEMENT'.
    05  FILLER              PIC X(14)   VALUE   '4999MARKETING'.
    05  FILLER              PIC X(14)   VALUE   '5400STATISTICS'.
01  MAJOR-TABLE REDEFINES MAJOR-VALUE.
    05  MAJORS OCCURS 10 TIMES
            ASCENDING KEY IS MAJOR-CODE
            INDEXED BY MAJOR-INDEX.
        10  MAJOR-CODE    PIC 9(4).
        10  MAJOR-NAME    PIC X(10).
*  DETERMINE MAJOR
        SEARCH ALL MAJORS
            AT END
                MOVE 'UNKNOWN   ' TO HDG-MAJOR
            WHEN ST-MAJOR-CODE = MAJOR-CODE (MAJOR-INDEX)
                MOVE MAJOR-NAME (MAJOR-INDEX) TO HDG-MAJOR.
```

Figure 9.3 Illustration of the SEARCH ALL Verb (Binary Search)

no longer have to search for the matching code but instead can look it up directly. The SEARCH can be replaced by a single statement:

```
        MOVE MAJOR-NAME (ST-MAJOR-CODE) TO HDG-MAJOR.
```

The above assumes ST-MAJOR-CODE is a valid subscript; i.e. with a value from 1 to 9999. ST-MAJOR-CODE could also be defined as an index, instead of a subscript, provided:

1. The OCCURS clause for the table MAJOR-NAME contains the clause INDEXED BY ST-MAJOR-CODE, and
2. The value of ST-MAJOR-CODE has been established by a SET statement.

Direct access is desirable in that it eliminates a search entirely. Its primary drawback is one of storage requirements; e.g., the major code example requires a table of 9999 entries even though there are only a few valid codes. Tables of this size are apt to be prohibitive in terms of storage requirements. The table would be defined as shown:

```
        01  MAJOR-TABLE.
            05  MAJOR-NAME OCCURS 9999 TIMES    PIC X(10).
```

Notice that the MAJOR-CODE is not defined explicitly in the table, as the position in the table corresponds to the code. A second requirement of the direct search is that the incoming code be strictly numeric so that it can be treated as a subscript. Even with these constraints, the direct "search" is a widely used technique and should be utilized where possible.

COBOL Formats

We have established three common approaches for searching, i.e., linear, binary, and direct. We have also discussed the difference between a subscript and an index. In this section we shall discuss the necessary COBOL for searching and indexing.

170

The general format of the OCCURS clause is

$$\text{OCCURS} \quad \begin{Bmatrix} \text{integer-1 } \underline{\text{TO}} \text{ integer-2 TIMES [\underline{DEPENDING} ON data-name-1]} \\ \text{integer-2 TIMES} \end{Bmatrix}$$

$$\begin{bmatrix} \begin{Bmatrix} \underline{\text{ASCENDING}} \\ \underline{\text{DESCENDING}} \end{Bmatrix} \text{KEY IS data-name-2 [data-name-3]} \dots \end{bmatrix}$$

$$[\underline{\text{INDEXED}} \text{ BY index-name-1 [index-name-2]} \dots]$$

The OCCURS clause defines a table as explained in Chapter 8. Until now, all tables have been fixed length; i.e., they contained a constant number of entries. The DEPENDING ON option provides for variable-length tables. For example, consider the entries:

```
05  BILLING-TABLE OCCURS 1 TO 7 TIMES
                  DEPENDING ON NUMBER-OF-BILLS-SENT
                  INDEXED BY BILL-INDEX.
    10  INVOICE-NUMBER          PIC 9(4).
    10  INVOICE AMOUNT          PIC 9(3)V99.
```

The above establishes a variable-length table with 1 to 7 entries, depending on the number of bills sent. The table length will vary from 9 to 63 positions.

The ASCENDING (DESCENDING) KEY is required for tables which will utilize a binary search. The INDEXED BY clause denotes an index and is required anytime a table is processed with an index (either through the SEARCH verb and/or through indexing). Data names referenced in this clause are not defined elsewhere in the Data Division.

SET Verb

The SET verb is used to manipulate indexes. Two formats are available:

1. Format 1:

$$\text{SET} \quad \begin{Bmatrix} \text{index-name-1 [index-name-2]} \\ \text{identifier-1 [identifier-2]} \end{Bmatrix} \dots \underline{\text{TO}} \begin{Bmatrix} \text{index-name-3} \\ \text{identifier-3} \\ \text{literal-1} \end{Bmatrix}$$

2. Format 2:

$$\text{SET} \quad \text{index-name-1 [index-name-2]} \dots \begin{Bmatrix} \underline{\text{UP BY}} \\ \underline{\text{DOWN BY}} \end{Bmatrix} \begin{Bmatrix} \text{identifier-1} \\ \text{literal-1} \end{Bmatrix}$$

The SET verb can convert an index to an occurrence (i.e. subscript) and vice versa. However, the rules for such conversion can get tricky, and we refer the reader to an appropriate COBOL manual. We use the SET verb primarily to initialize an index and increment its value (see Figures 9.5 and 9.7).

The following code is a simple illustration of the SET verb, and its use in processing a table. Assume BILLING-TABLE was previously defined to contain a variable number of entries, and to be indexed by BILL-INDEX. The total amount due is to be computed and stored in the entry WS-TOTAL-BILL-AMOUNT. Note the use of the SET verb to both initialize and increment the index, BILL-INDEX.

```
      MOVE ZERO TO WS-TOTAL-BILL-AMOUNT.
      SET BILL-INDEX TO 1.
      PERFORM COMPUTE-INVOICE-AMOUNT NUMBER-OF-BILLS TIMES.



   COMPUTE-INVOICE-AMOUNT.
      ADD INVOICE-AMOUNT (BILL-INDEX) TO WS-TOTAL-BILL-AMOUNT.
      SET BILL-INDEX UP BY 1.
```

USAGE Clause

The general format of the USAGE clause is:

$$\underline{\text{USAGE IS}} \begin{Bmatrix} \underline{\text{DISPLAY}} \\ \underline{\text{COMPUTATIONAL}} \\ \underline{\text{COMPUTATIONAL-3}} \\ \underline{\text{INDEX}} \end{Bmatrix}$$

The differences among DISPLAY, COMPUTATIONAL, and COMPUTATIONAL-3 are fully discussed in Chapters 12 and 14 under internal representation of data (the reader should consult a vendor's manual for information on additional forms of the USAGE clause; e.g. COMPUTATIONAL-1, COMPUTATIONAL-2). USAGE IS INDEX designates indexes rather than subscripts. Appropriate specification in the USAGE clause causes more efficient object code to be generated. However, the clause does not affect a program's logic and thus it is often ignored by those unconcerned with machine efficiency, e.g., students. We shall say no more about the subject until Chapters 12 and 14.

SEARCH Verb

There are two formats of the SEARCH verb, for linear and binary searches respectively:

1. Format 1:

$$\underline{\text{SEARCH}} \quad \text{identifier-1} \left[\underline{\text{VARYING}} \begin{Bmatrix} \text{index-name-1} \\ \text{identifier-2} \end{Bmatrix} \right]$$

$$[\underline{\text{AT}} \ \underline{\text{END}} \quad \text{imperative-statement-1}]$$

$$\underline{\text{WHEN}} \ \text{condition-1} \begin{Bmatrix} \text{imperative-statement-2} \\ \underline{\text{NEXT}} \ \underline{\text{SENTENCE}} \end{Bmatrix}$$

$$\left[\underline{\text{WHEN}} \ \text{condition-2} \begin{Bmatrix} \text{imperative-statement-3} \\ \underline{\text{NEXT}} \ \underline{\text{SENTENCE}} \end{Bmatrix} \right] \dots$$

2. Format 2:

$$\underline{\text{SEARCH}} \ \underline{\text{ALL}} \ \text{identifier-1}$$

$$[\underline{\text{AT}} \ \underline{\text{END}} \quad \text{imperative-statement-1}]$$

$$\underline{\text{WHEN}} \ \text{condition-1} \begin{Bmatrix} \text{imperative-statement-2} \\ \underline{\text{NEXT}} \ \underline{\text{SENTENCE}} \end{Bmatrix}$$

SEARCH ALL denotes a binary search; SEARCH by itself specifies a linear search. Identifier-1, in both formats, designates a table defined in the data division containing OCCURS and INDEXED BY clauses. If a binary search is specified (i.e., SEARCH ALL), then identifier-1 must also contain an ASCENDING (DESCENDING) KEY clause.

The AT END clause is optional in both formats. If it is omitted, control passes to the next sentence following the SEARCH if the end of the table has been reached and no match was found. If the AT END clause is supplied but it does not contain a GO TO, control will also pass to the next sentence.

The WHEN clause specifies a condition and imperative sentence. Note that more than one of these clauses may be contained in a linear search; e.g. we are searching a table for one of two keys and the required action depends on which key is matched. If the WHEN clause does not contain a GO TO statement, control will pass to the statement immediately following the SEARCH whenever the WHEN condition is satisfied.

A VARYING option is also possible with a linear search but is not discussed here.

Two-Dimension Tables

Two-dimension tables require two subscripts to specify a particular entry. Consider Figure 9.4 which shows a two-dimension table to determine entry-level salaries in Company X. Personnel has established a policy that starting salary is a function of both responsibility level (values 1–10) and experience

Experience

Responsibility	1	2	3	4	5
1	6,000	7,000	8,000	9,000	10,000
2	7,000	8,000	9,000	10,000	11,000
3	8,000	9,000	10,000	11,000	12,000
4	10,000	12,000	14,000	16,000	18,000
5	12,000	14,000	16,000	18,000	20,000
6	14,000	16,000	18,000	20,000	22,000
7	16,000	19,000	22,000	25,000	28,000
8	19,000	22,000	25,000	28,000	31,000
9	22,000	25,000	28,000	31,000	34,000
10	26,000	30,000	34,000	38,000	42,000

Responsibility level = 4
Experience level = 1

Responsibility level = 1
Experience level = 4

Figure 9.4 Entry-Level Salary (Illustration of Two-Dimension Table)

(values 1–5). Thus an employee with responsibility level of 4 and experience level of 1 would receive $10,000. An employee with responsibility of 1 and experience of 4 would receive $9,000.

Establishment of space for this table in COBOL requires data division entries as follows:

```
01  SALARY-TABLE.
    05  SALARY-RESPONSIBILITY OCCURS 10 TIMES.
        10  SALARY-EXPERIENCE OCCURS 5 TIMES    PIC 9(5).
```

173

These entries would cause a total of 250 consecutive storage positions to be allocated (10 × 5 × 5) as shown:

SALARY - TABLE									
SALARY − RESPONSIBILITY (1)					SALARY − RESPONSBILITY (2)				
Exp 1	Exp 2	Exp 3	Exp 4	Exp 5	Exp 1	Exp 2	Exp 3	Exp 4	Exp 5

•••

Each of the 10 salary responsibility levels has 5 experience levels associated with it. Once we realize that the first 25 storage positions refer to the first responsibility level, the next 25 to the second responsibility level, etc., we know how to initialize the table using the VALUE and REDEFINES clauses. (See the COBOL listing in Figure 9.5.) Note that the level number for experience (10) is higher than for responsibility (05), indicating that experience belongs to responsibility. Indeed, if the level numbers were the same, SALARY-TABLE would not be two-dimensional.

Any reference to SALARY-EXPERIENCE in a program requires two subscripts, e.g., SALARY-EXPERIENCE (4, 1). Realize that SALARY-EXPERIENCE (10, 5) is a valid reference but that SALARY-EXPERIENCE (5, 10) is invalid. The former denotes responsibility and experience levels of 10 and 5, respectively. However, the latter denotes a responsibility level of 5 and an experience level of 10.

Table Lookups: A Complete Example

We are ready to incorporate the discussion on searching and two-dimension tables into a complete COBOL program. We shall utilize three table lookup techniques: linear search, binary search, and direct access to table entries. We shall also illustrate three ways of initializing a table: reading it from a file, redefinition and VALUE clauses, and use of the COPY clause. Specifications are as follows:

> INPUT—A file of employee records containing name, location code, job code, and two salary determinants—experience and responsibility. There is also a second file containing data to initialize the table of job codes and expanded values.

> PROCESSING—Establish tables for location, title, and salary determinants. For each employee record, determine expanded values of job title and location using a binary and linear search, respectively. Determine starting salary as a function of responsibility and experience (via a direct search) as per the two-level table in Figure 9.4.

> OUTPUT—One line per employee containing name, location, job title, and starting salary. Headings, page counts, line counts, etc., are not required.

Figure 9.5 contains the COBOL listing to illustrate table lookups. Three distinct tables are established and searched. The values for location codes and expanded names are brought in via a COPY clause (COBOL lines 63–73). The locations table itself is established in COBOL lines 74–78 and searched via a linear search in lines 142–148. Notice the SET verb in line 144, immediately prior to the SEARCH instruction, used to establish the starting position for the search.

The titles table is defined in COBOL lines 79–85, with the OCCURS DEPENDING clause used to indicate a variable-length table. Observe the ASCENDING KEY clause to subsequently enable a binary search. The titles table is initialized by reading a file of title records (FD in lines 21–29). After each record is read, the number of titles is incremented by 1 in an ADD statement (COBOL line 127) and TITLE-INDEX is also incremented by 1 in a SET statement (line 126). The table itself is searched (via a binary search) in COBOL lines 136–139.

The table of starting salaries is initialized in lines 88–97. SALARY-TABLE contains 250 positions (10 responsibilities × 5 experience levels × 5 positions per elementary item) and is initialized one row per COBOL line. Verify the correspondence with Figure 9.4. Study COBOL line 152 to see the implementation of a direct table lookup; i.e., the incoming values EMP-RESPONSIBILITY and EMP-EXPERIENCE are used as subscripts, and no search is required.

Notice that incoming data are coming from two distinct files (CARD-FILE and TAPE-FILE) and that two distinct end-of-file switches are established in working storage (lines 59–60). The first file contains the values to initialize the title table; the second contains the employee data.

```
00001          IDENTIFICATION DIVISION.
00002          PROGRAM-ID.  'SEARCH'.
00003          AUTHOR.      GRAUER.
00004
00005
00006          ENVIRONMENT DIVISION.
00007
00008          CONFIGURATION SECTION.
00009          SOURCE-COMPUTER.   IBM-370.
00010          OBJECT-COMPUTER.   IBM-370.
00011
00012          INPUT-OUTPUT SECTION.
00013          FILE-CONTROL.
00014              SELECT CARD-FILE ASSIGN TO UR-S-SYSIN.
00015              SELECT PRINT-FILE ASSIGN TO UR-S-SYSOUT.
00016              SELECT TAPE-FILE ASSIGN TO UT-S-TAPE.
00017
00018
00019          DATA DIVISION.
00020          FILE SECTION.
00021          FD  CARD-FILE
00022              RECORDING MODE IS F
00023              LABEL RECORDS ARE OMITTED
00024              RECORD CONTAINS 80 CHARACTERS
00025              DATA RECORD IS CARD-IN.
00026          01  CARD-IN.
00027              05  CARD-TITLE-CODE          PIC X(4).
00028              05  CARD-TITLE-NAME          PIC X(15).
00029              05  FILLER                   PIC X(61).
00030          FD  TAPE-FILE
00031              RECORDING MODE IS F
00032              LABEL RECORDS ARE OMITTED
00033              RECORD CONTAINS 80 CHARACTERS
00034              DATA RECORD IS EMPLOYEE-RECORD.
00035          01  EMPLOYEE-RECORD.
00036              05  EMP-NAME                 PIC A(20).
00037              05  EMP-TITLE-CODE           PIC X(4).
00038              05  EMP-LOC-CODE             PIC X(3).
00039              05  EMP-SALARY-DETERMINANTS.
00040                  10  EMP-RESPONSIBILITY   PIC 99.
00041                  10  EMP-EXPERIENCE       PIC 9.
00042              05  FILLER                   PIC X(50).
```

Figure 9.5 Illustration of Search Techniques

```
00043          FD  PRINT-FILE
00044              RECORDING MODE IS F
00045              LABEL RECORDS ARE OMITTED
00046              RECORD CONTAINS 133 CHARACTERS
00047              DATA RECORD IS PRINT-LINE.
00048          01  PRINT-LINE.
00049              05  FILLER                    PIC X(1).
00050              05  DET-NAME                  PIC A(20).
00051              05  FILLER                    PIC X(2).
00052              05  DET-LOCATION              PIC X(13).
00053              05  FILLER                    PIC X(2).
00054              05  DET-TITLE                 PIC X(14).
00055              05  FILLER                    PIC X(2).
00056              05  DET-SALARY                PIC $ZZ,ZZZ.00.
00057              05  FILLER                    PIC X(69).
00058          WORKING-STORAGE SECTION.
00059              77  WS-END-OF-TITLE-FILE       PIC X(3)    VALUE 'NO '.
00060              77  WS-END-OF-EMPLOYEE-FILE    PIC X(3)    VALUE 'NO '.
00061              77  WS-NUMBER-OF-TITLES        PIC 999     VALUE ZEROS.
00062          01  LOCATION-VALUE        COPY LOCVAL.
00063 C        01  LOCATION-VALUE.
00064 C            05  FILLER              PIC X(16)   VALUE 'ATLATLANTA      '.
00065 C            05  FILLER              PIC X(16)   VALUE 'BOSBOSTON       '.
00066 C            05  FILLER              PIC X(16)   VALUE 'CHICHICAGO      '.
00067 C            05  FILLER              PIC X(16)   VALUE 'DETDETROIT      '.
00068 C            05  FILLER              PIC X(16)   VALUE 'KC KANSAS CITY  '.
00069 C            05  FILLER              PIC X(16)   VALUE 'LA LOSANGELES   '.
00070 C            05  FILLER              PIC X(16)   VALUE 'MINMINEAPOLIS   '.
00071 C            05  FILLER              PIC X(16)   VALUE 'NY NEW YORK     '.
00072 C            05  FILLER              PIC X(16)   VALUE 'PHIPHILADELPHIA '.
00073 C            05  FILLER              PIC X(16)   VALUE 'SF SAN FRANCISCO'.
00074 C        01  LOCATION-TABLE REDEFINES LOCATION-VALUE.
00075 C            05  LOCATIONS OCCURS 10 TIMES
00076 C                INDEXED BY LOCATION-INDEX.
00077 C                10  LOCATION-CODE     PIC X(3).
00078 C                10  LOCATION-NAME     PIC X(13).
00079          01  TITLE-TABLE.
00080              05  TITLES OCCURS 1 TO 999 TIMES
00081                  DEPENDING ON WS-NUMBER-OF-TITLES
00082                  ASCENDING KEY IS TITLE-CODE
00083                  INDEXED BY TITLE-INDEX.
00084                  10  TITLE-CODE      PIC X(4).
00085                  10  TITLE-NAME      PIC X(15).
00086
00087          01  SALARY-MIDPOINTS.
00088              05  FILLER    PIC X(25)   VALUE '0600007000080009000100000'.
00089              05  FILLER    PIC X(25)   VALUE '0700008000090001000011000'.
00090              05  FILLER    PIC X(25)   VALUE '0800009000100001100012000'.
00091              05  FILLER    PIC X(25)   VALUE '1000012000140001600018000'.
00092              05  FILLER    PIC X(25)   VALUE '1200014000160001800020000'.
00093              05  FILLER    PIC X(25)   VALUE '1400016000180002000022000'.
00094              05  FILLER    PIC X(25)   VALUE '1600019000220002500028000'.
00095              05  FILLER    PIC X(25)   VALUE '1900022000250002800031000'.
00096              05  FILLER    PIC X(25)   VALUE '2200025000280003100034000'.
00097              05  FILLER    PIC X(25)   VALUE '2600030000340003800042000'.
00098          01  SALARY-TABLE REDEFINES SALARY-MIDPOINTS.
00099              05  SALARY-RESPONSIBILITY OCCURS 10 TIMES.
00100                  10  SALARY-EXPERIENCE OCCURS 5 TIMES   PIC 9(5).
00101
```

Initialization of
locations table
via COPY

ASCENDING KEY clause

Initialization of two
dimension table

Indexed by
clauses

Figure 9.5 (Continued)

176

```
00102
00103
00104          PROCEDURE DIVISION.
00105              OPEN INPUT CARD-FILE, TAPE-FILE,
00106                  OUTPUT PRINT-FILE.
00107              READ CARD-FILE,
00108                  AT END MOVE 'YES' TO WS-END-OF-TITLE-FILE.
00109              SET TITLE-INDEX TO 1.
00110              MOVE 1 TO WS-NUMBER-OF-TITLES
00111              PERFORM 010-INITIAL-TITLES
00112                  UNTIL WS-END-OF-TITLE-FILE = 'YES'.
00113              READ TAPE-FILE,
00114                  AT END MOVE 'YES' TO WS-END-OF-EMPLOYEE-FILE.
00115              PERFORM 020-PROCESS-EMPLOYEE-RECORDS
00116                  UNTIL WS-END-OF-EMPLOYEE-FILE = 'YES'.
00117              CLOSE CARD-FILE, PRINT-FILE, TAPE-FILE.
00118              STOP RUN.
00119
00120          010-INITIAL-TITLES SECTION.
00121              MOVE CARD TITLE-CODE TO TITLE-CODE (TITLE-INDEX).
00122              MOVE CARD-TITLE-NAME TO TITLE-NAME (TITLE-INDEX).
00123              READ CARD-FILE,
00124                  AT END MOVE 'YES' TO WS-END-OF-TITLE-FILE
00125                      GO TO 010-EXIT.                               Initialization of table
00126              SET TITLE-INDEX UP BY 1.                              by reading in values
00127              ADD 1 TO WS-NUMBER-OF-TITLES.
00128
00129          010-EXIT.
00130              EXIT.
00131
00132          020-PROCESS-EMPLOYEE-RECORDS SECTION.
00133          *CLEAR PRINT LINE
00134              MOVE SPACES TO PRINT-LINE.                   Binary search
00135          *DETERMINE TITLE USING BINARY SEARCH
00136              SEARCH ALL TITLES
00137                  AT END MOVE 'UNKNOWN' TO DET-TITLE
00138                  WHEN EMP-TITLE-CODE = TITLE-CODE (TITLE-INDEX)
00139                      MOVE TITLE-NAME (TITLE-INDEX) TO DET-TITLE.
00140
00141
00142          030-LOCATION-SEARCH.
00143          *DETERMINE LOCATION USING LINEAR SEARCH          Linear search
00144              SET LOCATION-INDEX TO 1.
00145              SEARCH LOCATIONS
00146                  AT END MOVE 'UNKNOWN' TO DET-LOCATION
00147                  WHEN EMP-LOC-CODE = LOCATION-CODE (LOCATION-INDEX)
00148                      MOVE LOCATION-NAME (LOCATION-INDEX) TO DET-LOCATION.
00149
00150          *USE DIRECT TABLE LOOKUP - NO SEARCH
00151          040-SALARY-MIDPOINT.                             Direct search
00152              MOVE SALARY-EXPERIENCE (EMP-RESPONSIBILITY, EMP-EXPERIENCE)
00153                  TO DET-SALARY.
00154          * WRITE DETAIL LINE
00155              MOVE EMP-NAME TO DET-NAME.
00156              WRITE PRINT-LINE AFTER ADVANCING 2 LINES.
00157              READ TAPE-FILE,
00158                  AT END MOVE 'YES' TO WS-END-OF-EMPLOYEE-FILE.
```

Figure 9.5 *(Continued)*

Three-dimension tables require three subscripts to specify a particular entry.
Consider a university with three colleges, five schools (e.g., engineering, business, etc.) within each college, and four years within each school. We define a three-dimension table of enrollments as follows:

```
01  ENROLLMENTS.
    05  COLLEGE OCCURS 3 TIMES.
        10  SCHOOL OCCURS 5 TIMES.
            15  YEAR OCCURS 4 TIMES     PIC S9(4).
```

There are 60 ($3 \times 5 \times 4$) elements in the table. Note that YEAR is the only elementary item, and hence it is the only entry with a PICTURE clause. The COBOL compiler allocates a total of 240 positions (60 elements $\times$ 4 positions per element), as indicated in Figure 9.6.

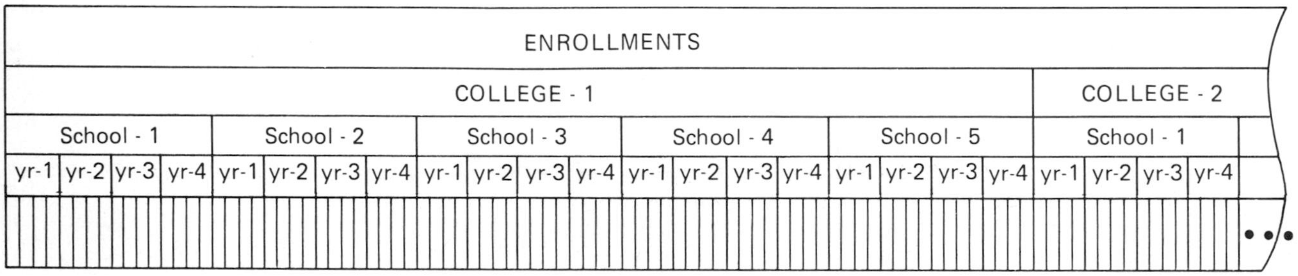

Figure 9.6 Storage Allocation for a Three-Dimension Table

As can be implied from Figure 9.6, table positions 1–80 refer to the first college, positions 81–160 to the second college, and positions 161–240 to the third college. Positions 1–16 refer to the first school in the first college, positions 81–96 refer to the first school in the second college, and positions 161–176 refer to the first school in the third college. Finally positions 1–4 refer to the first year in the first school in the first college, positions 81–84 refer to the first year in the first school in the second college, and so on.

Returning to the COBOL definition of the three-dimension table,

YEAR (1, 2, 3) refers to the enrollment in the first college,
    second school, third year.
YEAR (4, 3, 2) is incorrect since there are only 3 colleges
    (i.e., COLLEGE OCCURS 3 TIMES).

COBOL provides additional flexibility to reference data at different hierarchical levels. In effect definition of a three-dimension table automatically allows reference to one- and two-dimension tables as well. Thus,

SCHOOL (1, 2)   refers to the enrollment in college 1, school 2; in effect it references the four years of college 1, school 2 collectively. SCHOOL must always be used with two subscripts.

COLLEGE (3)   refers to the enrollment in the third college; it references the 20 fields of the third college collectively. COLLEGE must always be used with one subscript.

ENROLLMENTS   refers to the entire table of 60 elements. ENROLLMENTS may not be referenced with a subscript.

178

The VARYING option of the PERFORM verb is extremely convenient for manipulating subscripts and/or indexes. It was used in Figure 8.7 for one-dimension tables; it is extended below to two and three dimensions:

$$\underline{PERFORM}\ procedure\text{-}name\text{-}1\ [\underline{THRU}\ procedure\text{-}name\text{-}2]$$

$$\underline{VARYING} \left\{\begin{matrix} identifier\text{-}1 \\ index\text{-}1 \end{matrix}\right\} \underline{FROM} \left\{\begin{matrix} identifier\text{-}2 \\ literal\text{-}2 \\ index\text{-}2 \end{matrix}\right\} \underline{BY} \left\{\begin{matrix} identifier\text{-}3 \\ literal\text{-}3 \end{matrix}\right\} \underline{UNTIL}\ condition\text{-}1$$

$$\left[\ \underline{AFTER} \left\{\begin{matrix} identifier\text{-}4 \\ index\text{-}4 \end{matrix}\right\} \underline{FROM} \left\{\begin{matrix} identifier\text{-}5 \\ literal\text{-}5 \\ index\text{-}5 \end{matrix}\right\} \underline{BY} \left\{\begin{matrix} identifier\text{-}6 \\ literal\text{-}6 \end{matrix}\right\} \underline{UNTIL}\ condition\text{-}2\ \right]$$

$$\left[\ \underline{AFTER} \left\{\begin{matrix} identifier\text{-}7 \\ index\text{-}7 \end{matrix}\right\} \underline{FROM} \left\{\begin{matrix} identifier\text{-}8 \\ literal\text{-}8 \\ index\text{-}8 \end{matrix}\right\} \underline{BY} \left\{\begin{matrix} identifier\text{-}9 \\ literal\text{-}9 \end{matrix}\right\} \underline{UNTIL}\ condition\text{-}3\ \right]$$

As an illustration, consider the PERFORM statement below, which was extracted from the COBOL listing of Figure 9.7 (lines 88–94):

```
PERFORM 010-READ-CARDS
    VARYING COLLEGE-SUB
        FROM 1 BY 1 UNTIL COLLEGE-SUB > 3
    AFTER SCHOOL-SUB
        FROM 1 BY 1 UNTIL SCHOOL-SUB > 5
    AFTER YEAR-SUB
        FROM 1 BY 1 UNTIL YEAR-SUB > 4.
```

The procedure 010-READ-CARDS will be performed a total of 60 times. Initially COLLEGE-SUB, SCHOOL-SUB, and YEAR-SUB are all set to 1, and the first perform is done. Then YEAR-SUB is incremented by 1 and becomes 2 (COLLEGE-SUB and SCHOOL-SUB remain at 1), and a second perform is done. YEAR-SUB is incremented to 3 and then to 4, resulting in two additional performs. YEAR-SUB temporarily becomes 5, but no perform is realized since YEAR-SUB > 4. SCHOOL-SUB is then incremented to 2, YEAR-SUB drops to 1, and we go merrily on our way. (See Figure 9.8 for further illustration.)

Three-Dimension Tables: A Complete Example

Figure 9.7 is a COBOL listing containing a three-dimension table and the PERFORM VARYING option. It utilizes the enrollments table defined earlier. Figure 9.8 depicts the input, and Figure 9.9 has generated output.

INPUT—A file of data cards; each card contains the enrollment for a specific year, in a given school and college. There are 60 (3 colleges × 5 schools × 4 years) data cards in all. The cards are arranged by college, school, and year; i.e., the first 4 cards contain enrollments for the first school in the first college, the next 4 cards contain the enrollments for the second school in the first college, etc. Thus the order of the data cards corresponds directly to the storage arrangement of Figure 9.6.

PROCESSING—Read the file of enrollment cards. Compute the total enrollment for each school in each college.

OUTPUT—Display the enrollments in each college, one college per page. Show the calculated totals for each school as well.

```
00001          IDENTIFICATION DIVISION.
00002          PROGRAM-ID.  'SUBS'.
00003          AUTHOR.      GRAUER.
00004
00005
00006          ENVIRONMENT DIVISION.
00007
00008          CONFIGURATION SECTION.
00009          SOURCE-COMPUTER.  IBM-370.
00010          OBJECT-COMPUTER.  IBM-370.
00011          SPECIAL-NAMES.
00012               C01 IS TOP-OF-PAGE.
00013
00014          INPUT-OUTPUT SECTION.
00015          FILE-CONTROL.
00016               SELECT CARD-FILE ASSIGN TO UR-2540R-S-SYSIN.
00017               SELECT PRINT-FILE ASSIGN TO UR-1403-S-SYSOUT.
00018
00019
00020          DATA DIVISION.
00021          FILE SECTION.
00022          FD  CARD-FILE
00023              RECORDING MODE IS F
00024              LABEL RECORDS ARE OMITTED
00025              RECORD CONTAINS 80 CHARACTERS
00026              DATA RECORD IS CARD-IN.
00027          01  CARD-IN.
00028              05  CARD-TOTAL              PIC 9(4).
00029              05  FILLER                  PIC X(76).
00030          FD  PRINT-FILE
00031              RECORDING MODE IS F
00032              LABEL RECORDS ARE OMITTED
00033              RECORD CONTAINS 133 CHARACTERS
00034              DATA RECORD IS PRINT-LINE.
00035          01  PRINT-LINE                  PIC X(133).      ┌─ COMPUTATIONAL subscripts
00036          WORKING-STORAGE SECTION.
00037              ┌─ 77  COLLEGE-SUB   COMP    PIC S9(4). ─┐
00038              │  77  SCHOOL-SUB    COMP    PIC S9(4).  │
00039              └─ 77  YEAR-SUB      COMP    PIC S9(4). ─┘
00040          ┌─ 01  ENROLLMENTS.
00041          │      05  COLLEGE OCCURS 3 TIMES.               ┌─ Three dimension
00042          │          10  SCHOOLS  OCCURS 5 TIMES.          │   table
00043          │              15  YEAR  OCCURS 4 TIMES  PIC S9(4).
00044          ├─ 01  TOTALS.
00045          │      05  COL-TOTAL OCCURS 3 TIMES.             ── Two dimension table
00046          └─     10  SCH-TOTAL OCCURS 5 TIMES PIC S9(6).
00047          01  SCHOOL-VALUES.
00048              05  FILLER                  PIC X(12) VALUE 'BUSINESS     '.
00049              05  FILLER                  PIC X(12) VALUE 'EDUCATION    '.
00050              05  FILLER                  PIC X(12) VALUE 'ENGINEERING '.
00051              05  FILLER                  PIC X(12) VALUE 'FINE ARTS    '.
00052              05  FILLER                  PIC X(12) VALUE 'LIBERAL ARTS'.
00053          01  SCHOOL-NAMES REDEFINES SCHOOL-VALUES.
00054              05  SCH-NAME   OCCURS 5 TIMES  PIC X(12).
00055          01  COLLEGE-VALUES.
00056              05  FILLER                  PIC X(8) VALUE 'ATLANTIC'.
00057              05  FILLER                  PIC X(8)  VALUE 'MID-WEST'.
00058              05  FILLER                  PIC X(8) VALUE 'PACIFIC '.
00059          01  COLLEGE-NAME REDEFINES COLLEGE-VALUES.
00060              05  COL-NAME OCCURS 3 TIMES  PIC X(8).
00061          01  HEADING-LINE.
00062              05  FILLER                  PIC X(12) VALUE '  SCHOOL    '.
00063              05  FILLER                  PIC X(12) VALUE '  FRESHMAN  '.
00064              05  FILLER                  PIC X(12) VALUE '  SOPHOMORE '.
00065              05  FILLER                  PIC X(12) VALUE '  JUNIOR    '.
00066              05  FILLER                  PIC X(12) VALUE '  SENIOR    '.
00067              05  FILLER                  PIC X(12) VALUE '  TOTAL     '.
00068              05  FILLER                  PIC X(12) VALUE SPACES.
```

Figure 9.7 COBOL Program for Three-Dimension Table

```
00069          01   DETAIL-LINE.
00070               05   FILLER                    PIC X(1).
00071               05   DET-NAME                  PIC X(12).
00072               05   DET-OUTPUT   OCCURS 4 TIMES.
00073                    10   DET-YEAR             PIC ZZZZ,999.
00074                    10   FILLER               PIC X(4).
00075               05   DET-TOTAL                 PIC ZZZZ,999.
00076               05   FILLER                    PIC X(64).
00077          01   COLLEGE-LINE.
00078               05   FILLER                    PIC X(20) VALUE SPACES.
00079               05   FILLER                    PIC X(9)  VALUE 'COLLEGE: '.
00080               05   COL-LINE-NAME             PIC X(8).
00081               05   FILLER                    PIC X(96) VALUE SPACES.
00082
00083
00084          PROCEDURE DIVISION.
00085          MAINLINE.
00086               OPEN INPUT CARD-FILE,
00087                    OUTPUT PRINT-FILE.
00088               PERFORM 010-READ-CARDS
00089                   VARYING COLLEGE-SUB
00090                       FROM 1 BY 1 UNTIL COLLEGE-SUB > 3
00091                   AFTER SCHOOL-SUB
00092                       FROM 1 BY 1 UNTIL SCHOOL-SUB > 5
00093                   AFTER  YEAR-SUB
00094                       FROM 1 BY 1 UNTIL YEAR-SUB > 4.
00095
00096               PERFORM 015-COLLEGE-TOTALS
00097                   VARYING COLLEGE-SUB
00098                       FROM 1 BY 1 UNTIL COLLEGE-SUB > 3.
00099               CLOSE CARD-FILE, PRINT-FILE.
00100               STOP RUN.
00101
00102          010-READ-CARDS.
00103               READ CARD-FILE,
00104                   AT END DISPLAY 'ERROR - RAN OUT OF DATA'
00105                           STOP RUN.
00106               MOVE CARD-TOTAL TO YEAR (COLLEGE-SUB, SCHOOL-SUB, YEAR-SUB).
00107          015-COLLEGE-TOTALS SECTION.
00108          *WRITE HEADINGS FOR EACH COLLEGE
00109               MOVE COL-NAME (COLLEGE-SUB) TO COL-LINE-NAME.
00110               WRITE PRINT-LINE FROM COLLEGE-LINE
00111                   AFTER ADVANCING TOP-OF-PAGE LINES.
00112               WRITE PRINT-LINE FROM HEADING-LINE
00113                   AFTER ADVANCING 2 LINES.
00114               PERFORM 020-SCHOOL-TOTALS
00115                   VARYING SCHOOL-SUB
00116                       FROM 1 BY 1 UNTIL SCHOOL-SUB > 5.
00117
00118
00119          020-SCHOOL-TOTALS SECTION.
00120               MOVE ZERO TO SCH-TOTAL (COLLEGE-SUB, SCHOOL-SUB).
00121               ADD YEAR (COLLEGE-SUB, SCHOOL-SUB, 1),
00122                   YEAR (COLLEGE-SUB, SCHOOL-SUB, 2),
00123                   YEAR (COLLEGE-SUB, SCHOOL-SUB, 3),
00124                   YEAR (COLLEGE-SUB, SCHOOL-SUB, 4),
00125               GIVING SCH-TOTAL (COLLEGE-SUB, SCHOOL-SUB).
00126
00127          *WRITE DETAIL LINE-LINE.
00128               MOVE SPACES TO DETAIL-LINE.
00129               MOVE SCH-NAME (SCHOOL-SUB) TO DET-NAME.
00130               MOVE YEAR (COLLEGE-SUB, SCHOOL-SUB, 1) TO DET-YEAR (1).
00131               MOVE YEAR (COLLEGE-SUB, SCHOOL-SUB, 2) TO DET-YEAR (2).
00132               MOVE YEAR (COLLEGE-SUB, SCHOOL-SUB, 3) TO DET-YEAR (3).
00133               MOVE YEAR (COLLEGE-SUB, SCHOOL-SUB, 4) TO DET-YEAR (4).
00134               MOVE SCH-TOTAL (COLLEGE-SUB, SCHOOL-SUB) TO DET-TOTAL.
00135               WRITE PRINT-LINE FROM DETAIL-LINE
00136                   AFTER ADVANCING 2 LINES.
```

PERFORM VARYING statement for three variables

Figure 9.7 *(Continued)*

181

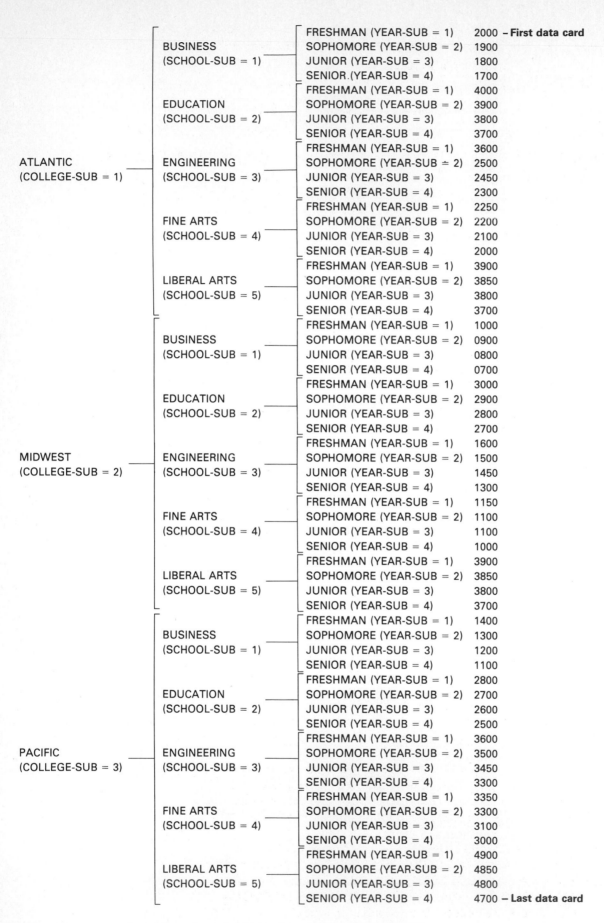

Figure 9.8 Input for Three-Dimension Table (Illustration of PERFORM VARYING)

```
                    COLLEGE: PACIFIC

     SCHOOL      FRESHMAN    SOPHOMORE    JUNIOR    SENIOR      TOTAL

    BUSINESS       1,400       1,300       1,200     1,100      5,000

    EDUCATION      2,800       2,700       2,600     2,500     10,600

    ENGINEERING    3,600       3,500       3,450     3,300     13,850

    FINE ARTS      3,350       3,300       3,100     3,000     12,750

    LIBERAL ARTS   4,900       4,850       4,800     4,700     19,250
```

```
                    COLLEGE: MID-WEST

     SCHOOL      FRESHMAN    SOPHOMORE    JUNIOR    SENIOR      TOTAL

    BUSINESS       1,000        900         800       700      3,400

    EDUCATION      3,000       2,900       2,800     2,700     11,400

    ENGINEERING    1,600       1,500       1,450     1,300      5,850

    FINE ARTS      1,150       1,100       1,100     1,000      4,350

    LIBERAL ARTS   3,900       3,850       3,800     3,700     15,250
```

```
                    COLLEGE: ATLANTIC

     SCHOOL      FRESHMAN    SOPHOMORE    JUNIOR    SENIOR      TOTAL

    BUSINESS       2,000       1,900       1,800     1,700      7,400

    EDUCATION      4,000       3,900       3,800     3,700     15,400

    ENGINEERING    3,600       2,500       2,450     2,300     10,850

    FINE ARTS      2,250       2,200       2,100     2,000      8,550

    LIBERAL ARTS   3,900       3,850       3,800     3,700     15,250
```

Figure 9.9 Output from Three-Dimension Table Program

A three-dimension enrollments table is established in COBOL lines 40–43. Subscripts are defined as binary (i.e., COMPUTATIONAL) entries in working storage in lines 37–39. The PERFORM VARYING statement of lines 88-94 reads the 60 elements of the table. Year is varied first, followed by school, then college. The variation in subscripts is depicted by Figure 9.8. Note well the correspondence between the input data of Figure 9.8 and the output in Figure 9.9.

A two-dimension table with 15 entries (3 colleges × 5 schools) is established for school-enrollment totals in lines 44–46. One-dimension tables are defined for school and college names. Note also the OCCURS clause in the detail line and the use of editing characters for printing enrollments (lines 73 and 75).

Notice the PERFORM VARYING statements in lines 96-98 and 114-116. The former statement invokes 015-COLLEGE-TOTALS 3 times. The second perform is contained within the 015-COLLEGE-TOTALS procedure and calls 020-SCHOOL-TOTALS 5 times. Thus the procedure 020-SCHOOL-TOTALS is effectively called 15 (3 colleges × 5 schools) times in all.

The output of Figure 9.9 is straightforward and should contain no surprises. The reader should, however, be able to verify the numbers in Figure 9.9 as being derived from the input of Figure 9.8.

Summary

An entire chapter has been devoted to table processing. In COBOL, tables may be one, two, or three dimensions. Individual elements are accessed by either subscripts or indexes. An index is conceptually the same as a subscript but results in more efficient machine code. If indexes are established, they can be referenced only by a SET, SEARCH, or PERFORM verb.

Three distinct methods for table lookups—linear, binary, and direct—were covered with associated COBOL implementation. The SEARCH and SEARCH ALL verbs are available for linear and binary searches, respectively.

Three distinct means of initializing a table were presented through the COBOL listing of Figure 9.5. These included use of the COPY clause, reading values from a file, and use of REDEFINES and VALUE clauses.

REVIEW EXERCISES

TRUE	FALSE		
☐	☐	**1**	A binary search over a table of 500 elements requires 10 or less comparisons.
☐	☐	**2**	A linear search over a table of 500 elements could require 500 comparisons.
☐	☐	**3**	Direct access to table entries requires no comparisons.
☐	☐	**4**	The SEARCH verb requires an index.
☐	☐	**5**	SEARCH ALL denotes a binary search.
☐	☐	**6**	There are no additional requirements of table organization in order to implement a binary rather than linear search.
☐	☐	**7**	An index of zero refers to the first element in a table.
☐	☐	**8**	A subscript of zero refers to the first element in a table.
☐	☐	**9**	An index cannot be manipulated by a MOVE statement.
☐	☐	**10**	PERFORM VARYING can manipulate both indexes and subscripts.
☐	☐	**11**	The working size of a table can be adjusted at execution time to be less than its maximum allotted size.
☐	☐	**12**	A SEARCH verb can contain only a single WHEN clause.
☐	☐	**13**	The ASCENDING (DESCENDING) KEY clause is required whenever the SEARCH verb is applied to a table.
☐	☐	**14**	The INDEXED BY clause is required whenever the SEARCH verb is applied to a table.

PROBLEMS

1 Write out the 12 pairs of values that will be assumed by SUB-1 and SUB-2 as a result of the statement

```
PERFORM 10-READ-CARDS
    VARYING SUB-1 FROM 1 BY 1
        UNTIL SUB-1 > 4
    AFTER SUB-2 FROM 1 BY 1
        UNTIL SUB-2 > 3.
```

2 Write out the 24 pairs of values that will be assumed by SUB-1, SUB-2, and SUB-3 as a result of the statement

```
PERFORM 10-READ-CARDS
    VARYING SUB-3 FROM 1 BY 1
        UNTIL SUB-3 > 3
    AFTER SUB-2 FROM 1 BY 1
        UNTIL SUB-2 > 2
    AFTER SUB-1 FROM 1 BY 1
        UNTIL SUB-1 > 4.
```

3 How many storage positions are allocated for each of the following table definitions? Show an appropriate schematic indicating storage assignment for each table.

```
(a)  01  STATE-TABLE.
         05  STATE-NAME OCCURS 50 TIMES        PIC A(15).
         05  STATE-POPULATION OCCURS 50 TIMES  PIC 9(8).

(b)  01  STATE-TABLE.
         05  NAME-POPULATION OCCURS 50 TIMES.
             10  STATE-NAME                    PIC A(15).
             10  STATE-POPULATION              PIC 9(8).

(c)  01  ENROLLMENTS.
         05  COLLEGE OCCURS 4 TIMES.
             10  SCHOOL OCCURS 5 TIMES.
                 15  YEAR OCCURS 4 TIMES       PIC 9(4).

(d)  01  ENROLLMENTS.
         05  COLLEGE OCCURS 4 TIMES.
             10  SCHOOL OCCURS 5 TIMES         PIC 9(4).
             10  YEAR OCCURS 4 TIMES           PIC 9(4).
```

4 Show procedure division code to determine the largest and smallest population in POPULATION-TABLE. Move these values to BIGGEST and SMALLEST, respectively. Move the state names to BIG-STATE and SMALL-STATE, respectively. POPULATION-TABLE is defined below:

```
01  POPULATION-TABLE.
    05  POPULATION-AND-NAME OCCURS 50 TIMES INDEXED BY POP-INDEX.
        10  POPULATION            PIC 9(8).
        10  STATE-NAME            PIC A(15).
```

5 Modify the COBOL listing in Figure 8.7 to use the SEARCH verb to determine the student major, given the student major code. Further modify the program to initialize the table of student majors by reading a file of codes, rather than initializing directly in the program.

6 Modify Problem 4 of Chapter 8 to utilize a binary search on the table of state abbreviations.

7 Acme Widgets Inc. has branch offices in New York, Los Angeles, and Miami (locations 1, 2, and 3, respectively). Each location has five departments: 10, 11, 12, 13, and 14. A deck of cards has been prepared for each employee in Acme containing the following information:

Field	Columns
Name	1–20
Location	21
Dept.	22–23

Write a COBOL program to read the file of data cards and compute and print

1. The total number of employees in each location.
2. The total number of employees in each department throughout the company (five totals in all).

185

3. The total number of employees in each department in each location.

Use any suitable format to print the totals.

8 A survey consisting of ten questions has been distributed, answered, and keypunched. Every question had three possible answers: yes, no, or not sure (denoted by Y, N, or X, respectively). The answers to all questions on a given survey were punched in columns 1–10 of a data card; i.e., there are as many data cards as surveys. Write a COBOL program to tabulate and print the total number of responses to each question; print the tabulations as a two-dimension table as shown:

Question #	Yes	Response No	Not sure
1			
2			
3			
4			
5			
6			
7			
8			
9			
10			

9 Modify Problem 8 above to determine the question with the most positive responses (i.e., the highest number of yes answers). Also determine the question with the most negative responses. (For simplicity, assume no ties.)

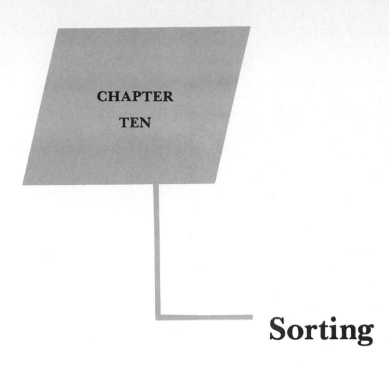

**CHAPTER
TEN**

Sorting

Sorting, i.e., the rearrangement of data, is one of the most frequent operations **Overview** in data processing. Reports are presented in a variety of ways, depending on the analysis required. Transactions may be listed alphabetically, alphabetically within location, numerically, etc.

Sorting is typically accomplished in one of three ways:

1. Internal sort, in which the programmer develops his own logic within his application program;
2. Utility sort, in which the sort program is called independently of the application program as a separate job step; and
3. COBOL SORT verb, in which the utility sort program is called directly from a COBOL program.

Regardless of which method is used, the objective is the same, namely to rearrange a file according to the requirements of a particular application. Our discussion deals exclusively with the third approach, i.e., the COBOL SORT verb.

We shall begin the chapter by developing necessary vocabulary. Next we shall consider COBOL requirements. Finally we shall present two complete programs to illustrate the concepts of the chapter and the variations within the COBOL SORT verb.

Vocabulary

A sort *key* is a field within a record that determines how the file is to be arranged. Several keys may be specified in a single sort. For example, assume an unsorted file is to be used in preparing a department census in which employees are to appear alphabetically within department. In other words, the file is to be rearranged, i.e. sorted, so that all employees in the same department appear together, and further that employees in a given department appear alphabetically. Department is a more important key than employee-name; thus department is considered the *major* key and employee-name the *minor* key. (Other, equally correct, terminology refers to department as the *primary* key and name as the *secondary* key.)

Sorting is done in one of two sequences: *ascending* (low to high) or *descending* (high to low). Generally, if the sequence is not specified, an ascending sort is assumed. Thus, employees listed alphabetically is an *ascending* sort on name. However, employees listed by age, with the oldest first, denotes a *descending* sort on age.

To be absolutely sure of this terminology, consider Figure 10.1. Figure 10.1(a) lists unsorted data for 12 students. Figure 10.1(b) sorts these records by name only; i.e., students with different majors and different years are mixed

Name	Year	Major
Smith	1	Liberal arts
Jones	4	Engineering
Adams	3	Business
Howe	2	Liberal arts
Frank	1	Engineering
Epstein	2	Engineering
Zev	4	Business
Benjamin	4	Business
Grauer	3	Liberal arts
Crawford	2	Engineering
Deutsch	4	Business
Makoske	1	Business

Figure 10.1(a) Unsorted Data

Primary Sort—Name (Ascending)

Name	Year	Major
Adams	3	Business
Benjamin	4	Business
Crawford	2	Engineering
Deutsch	4	Business
Epstein	2	Engineering
Frank	1	Engineering
Grauer	3	Liberal arts
Howe	2	Liberal arts
Jones	4	Engineering
Makoske	1	Business
Smith	1	Liberal arts
Zev	4	Business

Figure 10.1(b) Sorted Data

Primary Sort—Year (Descending)
Secondary Sort—Name (Ascending)

Name	Year	Major
Benjamin	4	Business
Deutsch	4	Business
Jones	4	Engineering
Zev	4	Business
Adams	3	Business
Grauer	3	Liberal arts
Crawford	2	Engineering
Epstein	2	Engineering
Howe	2	Liberal arts
Frank	1	Engineering
Makoske	1	Business
Smith	1	Liberal arts

Figure 10.1(c) Sorted Data

Primary Sort—Major (Ascending)
Secondary Sort—Year (Descending)
Tertiary Sort—Name (Ascending)

Name	Year	Major
Benjamin	4	Business
Deutsch	4	Business
Zev	4	Business
Adams	3	Business
Makoske	1	Business
Jones	4	Engineering
Crawford	2	Engineering
Epstein	2	Engineering
Frank	1	Engineering
Grauer	3	Liberal arts
Howe	2	Liberal arts
Smith	1	Liberal arts

Figure 10.1(d) Sorted Data

together in a single list. Figure 10.1(c) shows a primary sort on year (descending) and a secondary sort on name. Thus all students in year 4 are listed first (in alphabetical order), then all students in year· 3, etc. Finally, Figure 10.1(d) illustrates primary, secondary, and tertiary sorts. All business majors are listed first, then all engineering majors, and finally all liberal arts majors. Within a major, students are listed by year in descending order and listed alphabetically within year.

We shall now introduce four COBOL statements used exclusively with sorting: SD (sort description), SORT, RELEASE, and RETURN. The SD is present in the data division, and the other three are procedure division verbs. Implementation revolves around the SORT verb, which has the general form:

COBOL Implementation

SORT file-name-1

ON { DESCENDING / ASCENDING } KEY data-name-1 [data-name-2] ...

[ON { DESCENDING / ASCENDING } KEY data-namo 3 [dota-name-4] ...] ...

{ INPUT PROCEDURE IS section-name-1 [THRU section-name-2] / USING file-name-2 }

{ OUTPUT PROCEDURE IS section-name-3 [THRU section-name-4] / GIVING file-name-3 }

As can be seen, the word SORT is always required. Multiple keys are listed in the order of importance. Thus the statement

SORT file-name-1 ASCENDING MAJOR
DESCENDING YEAR
ASCENDING NAME ...

corresponds to the keys of Figure 10.1(d) (MAJOR is the primary sort and NAME the tertiary sort). File-name-1 refers to the file designated by an SD (sort description) in the data division.

The SORT verb has several formats. One can use INPUT PROCEDURE in combination with OUTPUT PROCEDURE or USING in conjunction with GIVING. Both methods are equally valid and are illustrated through sample programs (Figures 10.2 and 10.3). *However, the INPUT PROCEDURE/OUTPUT PROCEDURE is a more general technique in that it permits sorting on a calculated field.* For example, assume an incoming record has both an employee's present and previous salary. The USING/GIVING option permits a sort on either field but not on percent salary increase. The latter field is a calculated field; i.e., it is not contained in an incoming record per se but is calculated from two fields which are.

It is also possible to use INPUT PROCEDURE with GIVING or USING with OUTPUT PROCEDURE. However, these combinations are not illustrated with sample programs. The former combination permits sorting on a calculated field; the latter does not.

The RELEASE and RETURN verbs are required with the INPUT PROCEDURE/OUTPUT PROCEDURE format. The RELEASE verb appears in the INPUT PROCEDURE and has the format:

RELEASE record-name [FROM identifier]

We shall see in the sample program in Figure 10.2 that RELEASE is analogous to WRITE.

The RETURN statement appears in the OUTPUT PROCEDURE and has the form:

> RETURN file-name [INTO identifier] AT END statement

We shall see in Figure 10.2 that RETURN is analogous to READ.

File-name-1 of the SORT verb requires an SD in the data division which has the format:

$$\text{SD file-name} \left[\text{DATA} \left\{ \begin{array}{l} \underline{\text{RECORD}} \text{ IS} \\ \underline{\text{RECORDS}} \text{ ARE} \end{array} \right\} \text{data-name-1 [data-name-2]} \right]$$

$$\left[\underline{\text{RECORD}} \text{ CONTAINS } \text{[integer-1} \underline{\text{TO}}\text{] integer-2 CHARACTERS} \right]$$

Now that you are aware of the COBOL statements used in connection with sorting, we shall incorporate this material in actual programs and have chosen the car billing problem of Chapter 7 for this purpose. In the initial listing (Figure 7.8) customer bills were listed in the order they came in. The SORT verb will be used to list customers in order of decreasing bill (Figure 10.2) and in alphabetical order (Figure 10.3). Since the customer bill is a calculated field, Figure 10.2 utilizes the INPUT PROCEDURE/OUTPUT PROCEDURE option of the SORT verb. However, since NAME is contained on the input record and is therefore not a calculated field, the USING/GIVING option is shown in Figure 10.3.

Regardless of which option is chosen, the COBOL program must accomplish three things:

1. Read incoming data (e.g., from a card file) and transfer it to a sort file,
2. Rearrange the sort file, and
3. Read the sorted data and transfer it to an output file (e.g., a print file).

SORT Verb: INPUT PROCEDURE/OUTPUT PROCEDURE

Figure 10.2 is a modified version of the car billing problem in Chapter 7. COBOL lines 112–116 contain the SORT statement itself in which SORT-FILE (line 112) is the file actually used for sorting. It requires a SELECT statement (COBOL line 19) and an SD (COBOL lines 24–26). The INPUT PROCEDURE specifies a *section name*, 010-SORT-INPUT, which processes incoming data and writes records to the sort file. The OUTPUT PROCEDURE also specifies a section name, 030-SORT-OUTPUT, which reads records from the sorted file and writes records to the print file.

The mainline of the COBOL program is contained in lines 106–119. The program begins by opening CARD-FILE and PRINT-FILE (SORT-FILE is *not* opened explicitly in the program). The SORT verb transfers control to the INPUT PROCEDURE, which does the input and calculates the bills. After the individual bill has been computed, information is first moved to the SORT-FILE (lines 158–159) and then written to the SORT-FILE via the RELEASE statement in line 160.

When the entire CARD-FILE has been processed and the INPUT PROCEDURE is completed, control passes to the sort utility, which rearranges records in the SORT-FILE. After the sort is completed, control passes to the OUTPUT PROCEDURE, which reads data from the sort file via the RETURN statement and prints them. After the entire sort file has been read, control passes to the statement after the SORT verb. The files are closed (line 118), and the processing is terminated (line 119).

```
00001          IDENTIFICATION DIVISION.
00002          PROGRAM-ID.  'CARSORT'.
00003          AUTHOR.     GRAUER.
00004
00005
00006          ENVIRONMENT DIVISION.
00007
00008          CONFIGURATION SECTION.
00009          SOURCE-COMPUTER.  IBM-370.
00010          OBJECT-COMPUTER.  IBM-370.
00011
00012          SPECIAL-NAMES.
00013               C01 IS TOP-OF-PAGE.                    ┌─ SELECT for sort file
00014                                                      │
00015          INPUT-OUTPUT SECTION.                       │
00016          FILE-CONTROL.                               │
00017               SELECT CARD-FILE ASSIGN TO UR-2540R-S-SYSIN.
00018               SELECT PRINT-FILE ASSIGN TO UR-1403-S-PRINT.
00019          ┌─────────────────────────────────────────────────┐
               │  SELECT SORT-FILE ASSIGN TO UT-S-SORTOUT.        │
               └─────────────────────────────────────────────────┘
00020
00021
00022          DATA DIVISION.
00023          FILE SECTION.
00024     ┌──SD    SORT-FILE                              ┌─ SD for sort file
00025     │  RECORD CONTAINS 53 CHARACTERS               │
00026     │  DATA RECORD IS SORT-RECORD.                 │
          └────────────────────────────────────┘
00027          01    SORT-RECORD.
00028                05    SOC-SEC-NUM       PIC 9(9).
00029                05    NAME-FIELD        PIC A(25).
00030                05    DATE-RETURNED     PIC 9(6).
00031                05    CAR-TYPE          PIC X.
00032                05    DAYS-RENTED       PIC 99.
00033                05    MILES-DRIVEN      PIC 9999.
00034                05    CUSTOMER-BILL     PIC 9(4)V99.
00035          FD    CARD-FILE
00036                RECORDING MODE IS F
00037                LABEL RECORDS ARE OMITTED
00038                RECORD CONTAINS 80 CHARACTERS
00039                DATA RECORD IS CARD-IN.
00040          01    CARD-IN               PIC X(80).
00041          FD    PRINT-FILE
00042                RECORDING MODE IS F
00043                LABEL RECORDS ARE OMITTED
00044                RECORD CONTAINS 133 CHARACTERS
00045                DATA RECORD IS PRINT-LINE.
00046          01    PRINT-LINE            PIC X(133).
00047
00048          WORKING-STORAGE SECTION.
00049          77    WS-END-OF-FILE        PIC X(3)        VALUE 'NO'.
00050          77    WS-LINE-COUNT         PIC 99          VALUE 51.
00051          77    WS-PAGE-COUNT         PIC 99          VALUE ZERO.
00052          77    WS-MILEAGE-RATE       PIC 9V99.
00053          77    WS-DAILY-RATE         PIC 99V99.
00054          77    WS-CUSTOMER-BILL      PIC 9999V99.
00055          01    WS-CARD-IN.
00056                05    SOC-SEC-NUM       PIC 9(9).
00057                05    NAME-FIELD        PIC A(25).
00058                05    DATE-RETURNED     PIC 9(6).
00059                05    CAR-TYPE          PIC X.
00060                      88    COMPACT                   VALUE 'C'.
00061                      88    INTERMEDIATE              VALUE 'I'.
00062                      88    FULL-SIZE                 VALUE 'F'.
00063                05    DAYS-RENTED       PIC 99.
00064                05    MILES-DRIVEN      PIC 9999.
00065                05    FILLER            PIC X(19).
00066          01    WS-PRINT-LINE.
00067                05    FILLER            PIC X(4).
00068                05    SOC-SEC-NUM       PIC 999B99B9999.
00069                05    FILLER            PIC X(4).
00070                05    NAME-FIELD        PIC A(25).
00071                05    FILLER            PIC X(2).
00072                05    CAR-TYPE          PIC X.
00073                05    FILLER            PIC X(4).
00074                05    DAYS-RENTED       PIC Z9.
00075                05    FILLER            PIC X(4).
00076                05    MILES-DRIVEN      PIC ZZZ9.
```

Figure 10.2 SORT Verb (INPUT PROCEDURE/OUTPUT PROCEDURE)

```
00077                05   FILLER              PIC X(4).
00078                05   CUSTOMER-BILL       PIC $$,$$9.99.
00079                05   FILLER              PIC X(59).
00080           01   WS-HEADING-LINE-ONE.
00081                05   FILLER              PIC X(65)        VALUE SPACES.
00082                05   FILLER              PIC X(5)         VALUE 'PAGE '.
00083                05   WS-PAGE-PRINT       PIC ZZ9.
00084                05   FILLER              PIC X(60)        VALUE SPACES.
00085           01   WS-HEADING-LINE-TWO.
00086                05   FILLER              PIC X(20).
00087                05   TITLE-INFO          PIC X(33).
00088                05   FILLER              PIC X(2).
00089                05   TITLE-DATE          PIC X(8).
00090                05   FILLER              PIC X(70).
00091           01   WS-HEADING-LINE-THREE.
00092                05   FILLER              PIC X(8)         VALUE SPACES.
00093                05   FILLER              PIC X(11)        VALUE ' ACCT #'.
00094                05   FILLER              PIC X(2)         VALUE SPACES.
00095                05   FILLER              PIC X(4)         VALUE 'NAME'.
00096                05   FILLER              PIC X(19)        VALUE SPACES.
00097                05   FILLER              PIC X(4)         VALUE 'TYPE'.
00098                05   FILLER              PIC X(2)         VALUE SPACES.
00099                05   FILLER              PIC X(4)         VALUE 'DAYS'.
00100                05   FILLER              PIC X(2)         VALUE SPACES.
00101                05   FILLER              PIC X(5)         VALUE 'MILES'.
00102                05   FILLER              PIC X(4)         VALUE SPACES.
00103                05   FILLER              PIC X(6)         VALUE 'AMOUNT'.
00104                05   FILLER              PIC X(60)        VALUE SPACES.
00105
00106      PROCEDURE DIVISION.
00107          OPEN INPUT CARD-FILE,
00108               OUTPUT PRINT-FILE.
00109          READ CARD-FILE INTO WS-CARD-IN
00110               AT END MOVE 'YES' TO WS-END-OF-FILE.
00111
00112          ┌─────────────────────────────────────────────────┐
00113          │ SORT SORT-FILE                                   │
00114          │    ON DESCENDING KEY CUSTOMER-BILL OF SORT-RECORD│
00115          │    ON ASCENDING KEY NAME-FIELD OF SORT-RECORD    │────── SORT statement
00116          │ INPUT PROCEDURE IS 010-SORT-INPUT                │
               │ OUTPUT PROCEDURE IS 030-SORT-OUTPUT.             │
               └─────────────────────────────────────────────────┘
00117
00118          CLOSE CARD-FILE, PRINT-FILE.
00119          STOP RUN.
00120
00121      010-SORT-INPUT SECTION.
00122          PERFORM 020-CUSTOMER-CARDS THRU 025-READ-ANOTHER-CARD
00123               UNTIL WS-END-OF-FILE = 'YES'.
00124          GO TO 028-INPUT-EXIT.
00125
00126      020-CUSTOMER-CARDS.
00127      **********************************************************
00128      *      CHECK INCOMING DATA                               *
00129      **********************************************************
00130          IF NOT FULL-SIZE AND NOT COMPACT AND NOT INTERMEDIATE
00131               DISPLAY ' ERROR IN DATA' NAME-FIELD OF WS-CARD-IN
00132               GO TO 025-READ-ANOTHER-CARD.
00133          IF MILES-DRIVEN OF WS-CARD-IN IS NOT POSITIVE
00134               DISPLAY ' ERROR IN DATA' NAME-FIELD OF WS-CARD-IN
00135               GO TO 025-READ-ANOTHER-CARD.
00136          IF DAYS-RENTED OF WS-CARD-IN IS NOT POSITIVE
00137               DISPLAY ' ERROR IN DATA' NAME-FIELD OF WS-CARD-IN
00138               GO TO 025-READ-ANOTHER-CARD.
00139      **********************************************************
00140      *     MILEAGE RATE AND DAILY RATE BOTH DEPEND ON TYPE CAR
00141      **********************************************************
00142          IF COMPACT
00143               MOVE .08 TO WS-MILEAGE-RATE
00144               MOVE 7.00 TO WS-DAILY-RATE
00145          ELSE
00146               IF INTERMEDIATE
00147                    MOVE .10 TO WS-MILEAGE-RATE
00148                    MOVE 8.00 TO WS-DAILY-RATE
00149               ELSE
00150                    MOVE .12 TO WS-MILEAGE-RATE
00151                    MOVE 10.00 TO WS-DAILY-RATE.
00152          COMPUTE WS-CUSTOMER-BILL ROUNDED
00153               = MILES-DRIVEN OF WS-CARD-IN * WS-MILEAGE-RATE
```

Figure 10.2 *(Continued)*

192

```
00154                          + DAYS-RENTED OF WS-CARD-IN * WS-DAILY-RATE
00155                      ON SIZE ERROR
00156                          DISPLAY ' RECEIVING FIELD TOO SMALL FOR BILL',
00157                          NAME-FIELD OF WS-CARD-IN.
00158                      MOVE CORRESPONDING WS-CARD-IN TO SORT-RECORD.
00159                      MOVE WS-CUSTOMER-BILL TO CUSTOMER-BILL OF SORT-RECORD.
00160                    ┌ RELEASE SORT-RECORD. ┐
00161                    └──────────────────────┘ ── Release records
00162                  025-READ-ANOTHER-CARD.             to sort file
00163                      READ CARD-FILE INTO WS-CARD-IN
00164                          AT END MOVE 'YES' TO WS-END-OF-FILE.
00165                  028-INPUT-EXIT.
00166                      EXIT.
00167
00168                  030-SORT-OUTPUT SECTION.
00169                      MOVE 'NO ' TO WS-END-OF-FILE.
00170                    ┌ RETURN SORT-FILE
00171                    │     AT END MOVE 'YES' TO WS-END-OF-FILE. │
00172                      PERFORM 040-WRITE-LINE
00173                          UNTIL WS-END-OF-FILE = 'YES'.
00174                      GO TO 070-OUTPUT-EXIT.
00175
00176                  040-WRITE-LINE.
00177      *******************************************************
00178      *      WRITE DETAIL LINE
00179      *******************************************************
00180                      IF WS-LINE-COUNT > 50 PERFORM 060-PAGE-HEADING-ROUTINE.
00181                      MOVE SPACES TO WS-PRINT-LINE.
00182                      MOVE CORRESPONDING SORT-RECORD TO WS-PRINT-LINE.
00183                      EXAMINE SOC-SEC-NUM OF WS-PRINT-LINE
00184                          REPLACING ALL ' ' BY '-'.
00185                      WRITE PRINT-LINE FROM WS-PRINT-LINE
00186                          AFTER ADVANCING 2 LINES.            Returns
00187                      ADD 2 TO WS-LINE-COUNT.                 records from
00188                    ┌ RETURN SORT-FILE                        sort file
00189                    │     AT END MOVE 'YES' TO WS-END-OF-FILE. │
00190
00191                  060-PAGE-HEADING-ROUTINE .
00192                      MOVE ZEROS TO WS-LINE-COUNT.
00193                      ADD 1 TO WS-PAGE-COUNT.
00194                      MOVE WS-PAGE-COUNT TO WS-PAGE-PRINT.
00195                      WRITE PRINT-LINE FROM WS-HEADING-LINE-ONE
00196                          AFTER ADVANCING TOP-OF-PAGE LINES.
00197                      MOVE SPACES TO WS-HEADING-LINE-TWO.
00198                      MOVE ' STACEY CAR RENTALS - REPORT DATE ' TO TITLE-INFO.
00199                      MOVE CURRENT-DATE TO TITLE-DATE.
00200                      WRITE PRINT-LINE FROM WS-HEADING-LINE-TWO
00201                          AFTER ADVANCING 1 LINES.
00202                      WRITE PRINT-LINE FROM WS-HEADING-LINE-THREE
00203                          AFTER ADVANCING 1 LINES.
00204                  070-OUTPUT-EXIT.
00205                      EXIT.
```

Figure 10.2 *(Continued)*

The USING/GIVING format simplifies the job of the COBOL programmer in
that COBOL automatically does the I/O to and from the SORT. The price we
pay is twofold. First, the option cannot sort on a calculated field. Second, an
extra file is required. Thus Figure 10.3 contains SELECT statements for four
files (COBOL lines 17–20) and sorts on a noncalculated field.

SORT Verb: USING/GIVING

The PROCEDURE DIVISION begins immediately with the SORT statement (COBOL lines 118–121). Notice that CARD-FILE is not opened explicitly since the SORT verb itself performs the necessary I/O. The data in
CARD-FILE is read, written, and returned in sorted sequence in the file
OUTSORT. The mainline logic continues in the paragraph AFTER-SORT and
closely parallels the original listing in Figure 7.8. The essential difference
between this program and the one in Figure 7.8 is that data are read from a file
which has been sorted. Thus, the program in Figure 10.3 will cause bills to
print alphabetically, while in Figure 7.8 bills were printed in the order they
came in.

```
00001          IDENTIFICATION DIVISION.
00002          PROGRAM-ID.  'CARSORT'.
00003          AUTHOR.       GRAUER.
00004
00005
00006          ENVIRONMENT DIVISION.
00007
00008          CONFIGURATION SECTION.
00009          SOURCE-COMPUTER.  IBM-370.
00010          OBJECT-COMPUTER.  IBM-370.
00011
00012          SPECIAL-NAMES.
00013              CO1 IS TOP-OF-PAGE.
00014                                              ┌─ SELECT statements
00015          INPUT-OUTPUT SECTION.
00016          FILE-CONTROL.
00017         ┌─────────────────────────────────────────────────────┐
              │ SELECT CARD-FILE ASSIGN TO UR-2540R-S-SYSIN.         │
00018         │ SELECT PRINT-FILE ASSIGN TO UR-1403-S-PRINT.         │
00019         │ SELECT OUTSORT ASSIGN TO UT-S-ORDER.                 │
00020         │ SELECT SORT-FILE ASSIGN TO UT-S-SORTOUT.             │
              └─────────────────────────────────────────────────────┘
00021
00022
00023          DATA DIVISION.                      ┌─ SORT work file
00024          FILE SECTION.
00025         ┌──────────────────────────────────────┐
              │ SD  SORT-FILE                        │
00026         │     RECORD CONTAINS 80 CHARACTERS    │
00027         │     DATA RECORD IS SORT-RECORD.      │
00028         │ 01  SORT-RECORD.                     │
00029         │     05  FILLER          PIC 9(9).    │
00030         │     05  NAME-FIELD      PIC A(25).   │
00031         │     05  FILLER          PIC X(46).   │
              └──────────────────────────────────────┘
00032          FD  CARD-FILE
00033              RECORDING MODE IS F
00034              LABEL RECORDS ARE OMITTED
00035              RECORD CONTAINS 80 CHARACTERS
00036              DATA RECORD IS CARD-IN.
00037          01  CARD-IN.
00038              05  SOC-SEC-NUM      PIC 9(9).
00039              05  NAME-FIELD       PIC A(25).
00040              05  DATE-RETURNED    PIC 9(6).
00041              05  CAR-TYPE         PIC X.
00042              05  DAYS-RENTED      PIC 99.
00043              05  MILES-DRIVEN     PIC 9999.
00044              05  FILLER           PIC X(33).
00045          FD  PRINT-FILE
00046              RECORDING MODE IS F
00047              LABEL RECORDS ARE OMITTED
00048              RECORD CONTAINS 133 CHARACTERS
00049              DATA RECORD IS PRINT-LINE.
00050          01  PRINT-LINE           PIC X(133).
00051          FD  OUTSORT
00052              RECORDING MODE IS F
00053              LABEL RECORDS ARE OMITTED
00054              RECORD CONTAINS 80 CHARACTERS
00055              DATA RECORD IS ORDERED-RECORD.
00056          01  ORDERED-RECORD       PIC X(80).
00057
00058          WORKING-STORAGE SECTION.
00059          77  WS-END-OF-FILE        PIC X(3)        VALUE 'NO'.
00060          77  WS-LINE-COUNT         PIC 99          VALUE 51.
00061          77  WS-PAGE-COUNT         PIC 99          VALUE ZERO.
00062          77  WS-MILEAGE-RATE       PIC 9V99.
00063          77  WS-DAILY-RATE         PIC 99V99.
00064          77  WS-CUSTOMER-BILL      PIC 9999V99.
00065          01  WS-CARD-IN.
00066              05  SOC-SEC-NUM       PIC 9(9).
00067              05  NAME-FIELD        PIC A(25).
00068              05  DATE-RETURNED     PIC 9(6).
00069              05  CAR-TYPE          PIC X.
00070                  88  COMPACT                       VALUE 'C'.
00071                  88  INTERMEDIATE                  VALUE 'I'.
00072                  88  FULL-SIZE                     VALUE 'F'.
00073              05  DAYS-RENTED       PIC 99.
00074              05  MILES-DRIVEN      PIC 9999.
00075              05  FILLER            PIC X(33).
00076          01  WS-PRINT-LINE.
00077              05  FILLER            PIC X(4).
```

Figure 10.3 SORT Verb (USING/GIVING)

```
00078              05   SOC-SEC-NUM           PIC 999B99B9999.
00079              05   FILLER                PIC X(4).
00080              05   NAME-FIELD            PIC A(25).
00081              05   FILLER                PIC X(2).
00082              05   CAR-TYPE              PIC X.
00083              05   FILLER                PIC X(4).
00084              05   DAYS-RENTED           PIC 29.
00085              05   FILLER                PIC X(4).
00086              05   MILES-DRIVEN          PIC ZZ79.
00087              05   FILLER                PIC X(4).
00088              05   CUSTOMER-BILL         PIC $$,$$9.99.
00089              05   FILLER                PIC X(59).
00090         01   WS-HEADING-LINE-ONE.
00091              05   FILLER                PIC X(65)         VALUE SPACES.
00092              05   FILLER                PIC X(5)          VALUE 'PAGE '.
00093              05   WS-PAGE-PRINT         PIC ZZ9.
00094              05   FILLER                PIC X(60)         VALUE SPACES.
00095         01   WS-HEADING-LINE-TWO.
00096              05   FILLER                PIC X(20).
00097              05   TITLE-INFO            PIC X(33).
00098              05   FILLER                PIC X(2).
00099              05   TITLE-DATE            PIC X(8).
00100              05   FILLER                PIC X(70).
00101         01   WS-HEADING-LINE-THREE.
00102              05   FILLER                PIC X(8)          VALUE SPACES.
00103              05   FILLER                PIC X(11)         VALUE ' ACCT #'.
00104              05   FILLER                PIC X(2)          VALUE SPACES.
00105              05   FILLER                PIC X(4)          VALUE 'NAME'.
00106              05   FILLER                PIC X(19)         VALUE SPACES.
00107              05   FILLER                PIC X(4)          VALUE 'TYPE'.
00108              05   FILLER                PIC X(2)          VALUE SPACES.
00109              05   FILLER                PIC X(4)          VALUE 'DAYS'.
00110              05   FILLER                PIC X(2)          VALUE SPACES.
00111              05   FILLER                PIC X(5)          VALUE 'MILES'.
00112              05   FILLER                PIC X(4)          VALUE SPACES.
00113              05   FILLER                PIC X(6)          VALUE 'AMOUNT'.
00114              05   FILLER                PIC X(60)         VALUE SPACES.
00115
00116
00117         PROCEDURE DIVISION.
00118             SORT SORT-FILE
00119                 ASCENDING NAME-FIELD OF SORT-RECORD ─── SORT statement
00120             USING CARD-FILE
00121             GIVING OUTSORT.
00122         AFTER-SORT.
00123             OPEN INPUT OUTSORT
00124                 OUTPUT PRINT-FILE.
00125             READ OUTSORT INTO WS-CARD-IN
00126                 AT END MOVE 'YES' TO WS-END-OF-FILE.
00127             PERFORM 020-CUSTOMER-CARDS THRU 025-READ-ANOTHER-CARD
00128                 UNTIL WS-END-OF-FILE = 'YES'.
00129             CLOSE OUTSORT, PRINT-FILE.
00130             STOP RUN.
00131
00132         020-CUSTOMER-CARDS.
00133         ***************************************************************
00134         *     CHECK INCOMING DATA                                     *
00135         ***************************************************************
00136             IF NOT FULL-SIZE AND NOT COMPACT AND NOT INTERMEDIATE
00137                 DISPLAY ' ERROR IN DATA' NAME-FIELD OF WS-CARD-IN
00138                 GO TO 025-READ-ANOTHER-CARD.
00139             IF MILES-DRIVEN OF WS-CARD-IN IS NOT POSITIVE
00140                 DISPLAY ' ERROR IN DATA' NAME-FIELD OF WS-CARD-IN
00141                 GO TO 025-READ-ANOTHER-CARD.
00142             IF DAYS-RENTED OF WS-CARD-IN IS NOT POSITIVE
00143                 DISPLAY ' ERROR IN DATA' NAME-FIELD OF WS-CARD-IN
00144                 GO TO 025-READ-ANOTHER-CARD.
00145         ***************************************************************
00146         *     MILEAGE RATE AND DAILY RATE BOTH DEPEND ON TYPE CAR
00147         ***************************************************************
00148             IF COMPACT
00149                 MOVE .08 TO WS-MILEAGE-RATE
00150                 MOVE 7.00 TO WS-DAILY-RATE
00151             ELSE
00152                 IF INTERMEDIATE
00153                     MOVE .10 TO WS-MILEAGE-RATE
```

Figure 10.3 *(Continued)*

```
00154                    MOVE 8.00 TO WS-DAILY-RATE
00155                ELSE
00156                    MOVE .12 TO WS-MILEAGE-RATE
00157                    MOVE 10.00 TO WS-DAILY-RATE.
00158            COMPUTE WS-CUSTOMER-BILL ROUNDED
00159                = MILES-DRIVEN OF WS-CARD-IN * WS-MILEAGE-RATE
00160                + DAYS-RENTED OF WS-CARD-IN * WS-DAILY-RATE
00161            ON SIZE ERROR
00162                DISPLAY ' RECEIVING FIELD TOO SMALL FOR BILL',
00163                NAME-FIELD OF WS-CARD-IN.
00164        *****************************************************
00165        *    WRITE DETAIL LINE
00166        *****************************************************
00167            IF WS-LINE-COUNT > 50 PERFORM 060-PAGE-HEADING-ROUTINE.
00168            MOVE SPACES TO WS-PRINT-LINE.
00169            MOVE CORRESPONDING WS-CARD-IN TO WS-PRINT-LINE.
00170            MOVE WS-CUSTOMER-BILL TO CUSTOMER-BILL OF WS-PRINT-LINE.
00171            EXAMINE SOC-SEC-NUM OF WS-PRINT-LINE
00172                REPLACING ALL ' ' BY '-'.
00173            WRITE PRINT-LINE FROM WS-PRINT-LINE
00174                AFTER ADVANCING 2 LINES.
00175            ADD 2 TO WS-LINE-COUNT.
00176
00177        025-READ-ANOTHER-CARD.
00178            READ OUTSORT INTO WS-CARD-IN
00179                AT END MOVE 'YES' TO WS-END-OF-FILE.
00180
00181        060-PAGE-HEADING-ROUTINE SECTION.
00182            MOVE ZEROS TO WS-LINE-COUNT.
00183            ADD 1 TO WS-PAGE-COUNT.
00184            MOVE WS-PAGE-COUNT TO WS-PAGE-PRINT.
00185            WRITE PRINT-LINE FROM WS-HEADING-LINE-ONE
00186                AFTER ADVANCING TOP-OF-PAGE LINES.
00187            MOVE SPACES TO WS-HEADING-LINE-TWO.
00188            MOVE ' STACEY CAR RENTALS - REPORT DATE ' TO TITLE-INFO.
00189            MOVE CURRENT-DATE TO TITLE-DATE.
00190            WRITE PRINT-LINE FROM WS-HEADING-LINE-TWO
00191                AFTER ADVANCING 1 LINES.
00192            WRITE PRINT-LINE FROM WS-HEADING-LINE-THREE
00193                AFTER ADVANCING 1 LINES.
```

Figure 10.3 *(Continued)*

Figures 10.2 and 10.3 illustrate two versions of the SORT verb, and it is useful to highlight the differences:

INPUT PROCEDURE/OUTPUT PROCEDURE Versus USING/GIVING

1. Figure 10.2 sorts on CUSTOMER-BILL, a calculated field. Figure 10.3 sorts on NAME-FIELD, which is contained on the incoming record.

2. Figure 10.2 requires the programmer to do his own I/O to and from the SORT. In Figure 10.3, the SORT verb causes CARD-FILE to be opened, copied to SORT-FILE, and then closed.

3. Figure 10.2 uses the RELEASE and RETURN verbs to write to and read from SORT-FILE. These verbs are not used in Figure 10.3 since the USING/GIVING option does the I/O automatically.

4. Figure 10.2 requires only three files. Figure 10.3 uses four. (Compare SELECT statements.) The extra file is necessary since the sorted data are placed on a separate file (OUTSORT).

5. Record lengths in Figure 10.3 of CARD-FILE, OUTSORT, and SORT-FILE must be the same (80 bytes). The record lengths of SORT-FILE and CARD-FILE in Figure 10.2 are different.

6. Figure 10.2 *requires* section names for the INPUT PROCEDURE and OUTPUT PROCEDURE. Sections are optional in Figure 10.3.

Sorting is an integral part of data processing. If the COBOL SORT verb is used to accomplish this task, four formats are possible. INPUT PROCEDURE/OUTPUT PROCEDURE and USING/GIVING were

Summary

illustrated in Figures 10.2 and 10.3, respectively. However, we recommend the former technique because of its capacity to sort on calculated fields.

The chapter began with a definition of terms. Specifically, we discussed *key*, *ascending* vs. *descending* sorts, and *major* vs. *minor* sorts. Next we covered the COBOL implementation of sorting to include the SORT, SD, RELEASE, and RETURN statements.

We believe that the reader can readily adapt either Figure 10.2 or Figure 10.3 to any problem with which he is confronted. As an additional aid, however, we shall list three basic rules associated with COBOL implementation. Should any of these points appear unclear, return to the examples in the chapter.

1. File-name-1 of the SORT verb must be described in an SD. Further, each key (i.e., data-name) appearing in the SORT verb must be described in the sort record.

2. If the USING/GIVING option is used, file-name-2 and file-name-3 each require an FD. Further, the record sizes of file-names 1, 2, and 3 must all be the same.

3. If INPUT PROCEDURE/OUTPUT PROCEDURE is used, both must be section names. Further, the INPUT PROCEDURE must contain a RELEASE statement to transfer records to the sort; the OUTPUT PROCEDURE must contain a RETURN statement to read the sorted data.

REVIEW EXERCISES

TRUE	FALSE		
☐	☐	**1**	The SORT verb cannot be used on a calculated field.
☐	☐	**2**	If USING is specified in the SORT verb, then GIVING must be specified also.
☐	☐	**3**	If INPUT PROCEDURE is specified in the SORT verb, then OUTPUT PROCEDURE is also required.
☐	☐	**4**	Only one ascending and one descending key are permitted in the SORT verb.
☐	☐	**5**	Major sort and primary sort are synonymous.
☐	☐	**6**	The USING/GIVING option requires one less file than the INPUT PROCEDURE/OUTPUT PROCEDURE format.
☐	☐	**7**	RELEASE and RETURN are associated with the USING/GIVING option.
☐	☐	**8**	RELEASE is present in the INPUT PROCEDURE.
☐	☐	**9**	RETURN is specified in the OUTPUT PROCEDURE.
☐	☐	**10**	Both the INPUT and OUTPUT PROCEDURES must be paragraph names.
☐	☐	**11**	If a record is "released," it is written to the sort file.
☐	☐	**12**	If a record is "returned," it is read from the sort file.
☐	☐	**13**	If USING/GIVING is used, the sorted file *must* contain every record in the input file.
☐	☐	**14**	If INPUT PROCEDURE/OUTPUT PROCEDURE is used, the sorted file *must* contain every record in the input file.

1 Given the following data,

Name	Location	Department
Milgrom	New York	1000
Samuel	Boston	2000
Isaac	Boston	2000
Chandler	Chicago	2000
Lavor	Los Angeles	1000
Elsinor	Chicago	1000
Tater	New York	2000
Craig	New York	2000
Borow	Boston	2000
Kenneth	Boston	2000
Renaldi	Boston	1000
Gulfman	Chicago	1000

rearrange the data according to the following sorts:
(a) Major field—department (descending); minor field—name (ascending).
(b) Primary field—name; secondary field—location; tertiary field—department.
Note: If neither ascending nor descending is specified, an ascending sequence should be used.

2 Given the statement

```
SORT SORT-FILE
     ASCENDING KEY STUDENT-NAME
     DESCENDING YEAR-IN-SCHOOL
     ASCENDING MAJOR
  USING FILE-ONE
  GIVING FILE-TWO.
```

(a) What is the major key?
(b) What is the minor key?
(c) Which file will be specified in an SD?
(d) Which file will contain the sorted output?
(e) Which file(s) will be specified in a SELECT?
(f) Which file contains the input data?
(g) Which file must contain the data-names STUDENT-NAME, YEAR-IN-SCHOOL, and MAJOR?

3 Modify the tuition billing problem of Chapter 6 (Figure 6.4) to print students in alphabetical order.

4 Modify the tuition billing problem of Chapter 6 (Figure 6.4) to print students in order of computed charges (from high to low). Use name as the secondary sort.

5 Modify the program in Figure 8.2 to print customer statements in alphabetical order.

6 Modify the main and subprograms of Figures 8.7 and 8.8 to print a list of students in order of descending grade point average.

CHAPTER ELEVEN

Programming Style, II

Overview

Although the systems analyst is responsible for defining the "specs" of a program, a good programmer is more than just a computer that does only what it is told. Depending on the degree of standards enforcement, the programmer has varying leeway to determine how the problem is to be solved and what the final product will look like; in short, he has a definite opportunity to exert an influence.

In Chapter 6 we introduced programming style and presented structured programming and coding standards. Now that you are further along in your study of COBOL, we shall present additional elements of programming style. We shall offer specific COBOL techniques to facilitate debugging and improve efficiency and maintainability. We shall discuss what a "good" program should and should not do in terms of generality and error detection. We shall extend the discussion of structured programming to include (1) the case structure, (2) limited use of GO TO, (3) pseudocode, and (4) segmentation. Finally, we shall present two complete examples incorporating many of our ideas on programming style, and emphasizing the advantages of the structured technique.

We expect this chapter to be understandable to you now. However, the more you read, and the more programs you write, the clearer it will become. Indeed we hope that this is one chapter to which you will continually refer. Bear in mind that the techniques we offer are sound programming practices, but they need not be used 100% of the time. Undoubtedly situations will occur where techniques are not applicable and should be avoided.

We expect you and/or your instructor to disagree with some of our ideas on style. That is a perfectly acceptable, and perhaps even desirable, reaction. Our objective is to teach you COBOL, to expose you to a wide variety of practical situations, and to teach you to think your way through programming applications. If you have sound reasons against elements of our style, so be it; you are on your way toward developing your own. There are many ways to solve a problem, and that is one of the aspects which makes programming interesting.

Debugging

Debugging is a part of life, so much so that we include two entire chapters on the subject. In addition to the material in Chapters 5 and 13, we have adopted the following techniques as an integral part of our overall style:

1. *Always use the RECORD CONTAINS clause in the COBOL FD.* Although this clause is optional (e.g., the information can be entered through JCL under IBM OS as described in Chapter 18), its inclusion is highly desirable. The RECORD CONTAINS clause causes the compiler to indicate an error at compile time if the record description, i.e., the sum of the PICTURE clauses, does not match the RECORD CONTAINS entry. If the clause is omitted, such an error will not manifest itself until execution time when it is much more difficult to detect. Moreover, any future programmer is saved from the task of adding individual PICTURE clauses to determine record size.

2. *Include the two nonnumeric literals below as the first and last entries of the working-storage section:*

```
77  FILLER    PICTURE X(27)
        VALUE 'WORKING-STORAGE BEGINS HERE'.
        .
        .
        .
01  FILLER    PICTURE X(25)
        VALUE 'WORKING-STORAGE ENDS HERE'.
```

These entries will appear in all dumps of the program and will clearly delineate the working-storage section. (We shall discuss dumps further in Chapter 13.)

3. *Use READ INTO and WRITE FROM options and do all processing from working-storage.* First, this technique simplifies debugging since working-storage areas are generally easier to find in a dump than I/O buffer areas (especially if the above suggestion is followed). Second, if blocked records are processed (see Section V on file processing), it is much easier to determine the particular record in the block that was being processed. Next, the READ INTO option allows access to the last record after the end of file condition has been reached. Finally, since the WRITE FROM option specifies an area in working-storage, initial values can be assigned to output fields, and as a result it is often unnecessary to move spaces to the output area.

Maintainability

Programs can be more easily understood, and hence maintained, if techniques such as those listed below are practiced:

1. *Use condition names (88-level entries) for all codes that are checked.* This technique is absolutely essential. As a review of the material in Chapters 7 and 8, consider:

```
05  DEPARTMENT-CODE    PICTURE 99.
    88  ACCOUNTING                  VALUE IS 11.
    88  DATA-PROCESSING             VALUE IS 13.
    88  PERSONNEL                   VALUE IS 43.
                .
                .
                .
    88  VALID-CODES        VALUES ARE 11, 13, 43 THRU 99.
```

Use of condition names permits such procedure division statements as IF ACCOUNTING... or IF PERSONNEL..., etc. Omission of 88-level entries requires procedure division entries of the form IF DEPARTMENT-CODE IS EQUAL TO 11,... Obviously when condition names are used, the procedure division is easier to read. More importantly, if codes have to be changed, 88-level entries allow all changes to be made in only one easy-to-find place, the data division. If condition names were not used, changes would have to be made throughout the procedure division and the chance for error would be much higher, particularly if the same condition were tested more than once.

2. *Use the THRU option when performing paragraphs or PERFORM sections.* The THRU procedure should consist of a single sentence, EXIT, whose sole function is to signal the end of the perform. The paragraph name of the THRU option could be identical to the entry paragraph with –EXIT appended. Thus,

```
PERFORM 020-READ-A-CARD THRU 020-READ-A-CARD-EXIT.
        .
        .
        .
020-READ-A-CARD.
        .
        .
        .
020-READ-A-CARD-EXIT.
    EXIT.
```

The THRU option accomplishes two things. First, it makes the range of the perform explicitly clear. Second, it reduces the chance for error on subsequent maintenance. Consider, for example, omission of the EXIT paragraph and further that the entry paragraph subsequently had to be broken into two paragraphs. The maintenance programmer would have to examine the entire program to determine whether the original paragraph appeared in any perform statements (without the THRU clause), and if so, to modify those statements to include the THRU clause. Do it right the first time. Some programmers perform sections in lieu of paragraphs. The use of a section as a procedure name in the PERFORM statement accomplishes much the same thing as a PERFORM THRU. Thus additional paragraphs may be added to the performed section without affecting the range of the perform; i.e., the same section is still performed.

Error Processing

A well-written program is not limited to computing answers; it also includes checks for erroneous data. Indeed a sizable percentage of commercial programs is usually dedicated to error detection. The requirements of precisely what to check for are included in the specs given to the programmer, but in the course of coding other situations will suggest themselves. These should be brought to the attention of the analyst and included in the program.

Installations frequently develop program standards which specify overall requirements for error processing. We offer Murphy's law, namely "if something can go wrong, it will—and at the worst possible time," and suggest that you can't check too much. Incoming transactions are often processed by a separate edit program whose sole function is to "scrub the data." In this instance most of the programming checks suggested below are done in the edit program and need not be repeated. However, the essential point is that incoming data are apt to be in error and must be checked; when and how this is done is of secondary importance. The following are typical error checks:

1. *Check for proper order in sequenced files.* Do not assume a file is in order just because it is supposed to have been sorted. Print appropriate error messages for out-of-sequence records.

2. *Flag invalid codes.* If a table is searched, the at-end condition usually specifies a no-match condition and should branch to an error routine. If a code has two permissible values, do not assume the second if it is not the first. The field may have been left blank or miscoded; either way an error message should be printed.

3. *Numeric data should be numeric.* Use class tests prior to calculations and bypass invalid data, e.g.,

    IF CREDITS NOT NUMERIC PERFORM ERROR-ROUTINE.

    A strong advantage of this technique is the avoidance of data exceptions which prevent the normal end of job. Also many errors can be caught in one execution instead of the many individual jobs which would be required for each data exception and corresponding ABEND.

4. *Include checks on the range of computed values.* In a payroll problem, for example, one might check that net pay does not exceed a specified amount and print a warning message when this condition is violated. The excess amount need not signal an error, but better "safe than sorry."

5. *Eliminate duplicate transactions.* Often the same transaction is entered twice, either from different sources or twice from the same source at different times. This type of error is usually not caught in an edit program since it requires historical information from the master file.

6. *Check for invalid subscripts.* This is one of the most common, and indeed hardest to find, causes of a program's failure to execute. Consider

```
DATA DIVISION.
      .
      .
      .
    05  STATE-NAME    OCCURS 48 TIMES    PIC X(20).
      .
      .
      .
PROCEDURE DIVISION.
      .
      .
      .
    PERFORM STATE-PROCESSING VARYING SUB FROM 1 BY 1 UNTIL SUB > 50.
      .
      .
      .
STATE-PROCESSING.
      MOVE STATE-NAME (SUB) TO...
```

This apparently simple code will probably result in a fatal error and dump. STATE-NAME was defined as a table with 48 entries, yet in the procedure division we attempt to reference STATE-NAME (49) and (50). The compiler merely allocates sufficient storage for 48 entries in the table. During execution, the computer will reference the next contiguous locations for the 49th and 50th entries. Such situations occur frequently when table sizes are altered or subscripts are computed incorrectly. It is highly desirable to include additional code such as "IF SUB IS GREATER THAN 48 PERFORM ERROR-ROUTINE." as a check.

Obviously error checking requires additional time for both programming and execution. Is it worth it? We believe so, especially if you've ever received a call at home asking why your program didn't work.

Generality

In addition to checking for invalid data, a good program must most of all be a general program. It should be parameter driven, i.e., written in terms of variables rather than constants. Adherence to this technique simplifies maintenance and also minimizes the invalid subscript error which can be so damaging. Consider:

```
DATA DIVISION.
        .
        .
        .
    05  STATE-NAME    OCCURS 1 TO 50 TIMES
                      DEPENDING ON NUMBER-OF-STATES
        .             PIC X(20).
        .
        .
PROCEDURE DIVISION.
        .
        .
        .
    PERFORM STATE-PROCESSING NUMBER-OF-STATES TIMES.
```

Of course, if the number of states ever exceeds 50, the constant in the OCCURS clause must be altered. However, the procedure division entries need not be changed since all processing is a function of the variable NUMBER-OF-STATES, which can be input at execution. Indeed even the data division entry need not be altered if the table is initially made larger than necessary.

The desirability of generality cannot be overemphasized.

Efficiency

Commercial data processing imposes the additional requirement of efficiency, i.e., having programs run as quickly as possible. Suggestions on achieving efficiency are generally directed to coding techniques revolving around the USAGE clause, decimal alignment, etc. Indeed we do our share of "preaching" in this area in Chapter 14 when we discuss COBOL from the viewpoint of BAL. However, many people get carried away with machine considerations and neglect entirely algorithmic efficiency.

The algorithm employed to solve a problem is especially important in that it is machine independent. Further, an efficient algorithm, coded inefficiently, is often preferable to an inefficient algorithm painstakingly coded to take advantage of every machine idiosyncrasy. This is not to say that machine considerations are superfluous; they definitely are not, but there is a point of diminishing returns. We do believe that algorithmic considerations are entirely essential and certainly deserve more treatment than is commonly afforded them.

A general suggestion is "think before you code." After learning the requirements of a program, concentrate on the method you will use to solve it. Do no coding for a period of time, whether five minutes or five days. Determine first the best way to approach the problem. Then, and only then, should you begin to code. Two suggestions for achieving algorithmic efficiency are

1. *Use a linear search only as a last resort.* Direct and binary searches are quicker (see Chapter 9). The SEARCH ALL verb of ANS COBOL provides easy implementation of the binary search. The advantage of a binary search is obvious; it greatly reduces the number of comparisons, and hence the execution time, to find a match. For example, a linear search over a table of 500 entries requires an *average of 250* comparisons if each entry is equally likely. A binary search over the same table requires a *maximum of 9* comparisons.

2. *Test most likely conditions first.* Assume, for example, that in a file of 10,000 records three types of transaction codes are possible: A (addition), C (correction), and D (deletion). Further assume that 7000 records are corrections, 2500 are additions, and 500 are deletions and that this distribution remains fairly constant from run to run. If the most likely condition, i.e., corrections, are tested first, then a total of 13,500 comparisons are required, as shown:

```
IF IN-CODE = 'C' ...    (executed 10,000 times)
IF IN-CODE = 'A' ...    (executed  3,000 times)
IF IN-CODE = 'D' ...    (executed    500 times)
```

If, on the other hand, the least likely condition is tested first, then 26,500 comparisons are necessary:

```
IF IN-CODE = 'D' ...    (executed 10,000 times)
IF IN-CODE = 'A' ...    (executed  9,500 times)
IF IN-CODE = 'C' ...    (executed  7,000 times)
```

Although this technique requires some knowledge of file characteristics, it is used far too infrequently in our estimation.

Machine Efficiency

Techniques for machine efficiency are obviously machine dependent. Accordingly, these suggestions have to be accepted more or less on faith pending the discussion of COBOL from the viewpoint of BAL in Section IV. However, at the conclusion of that section, the reader should be able to provide his own explanations as to their validity.

1. *Specify USAGE IS INDEX for all subscripts.* As explained in Chapter 9, indexing is logically equivalent to subscripting but vastly more efficient in terms of generated code. Remember that the SET verb is used to manipulate indexes. If you do not use indexing, at least make all subscripts binary; i.e., specify USAGE IS COMPUTATIONAL.

2. *Specify all files in a single OPEN (CLOSE) statement.* This is distinctly preferable to several statements. Hence,

```
OPEN INPUT CARD-FILE
            OLD-MASTER-TAPE
     OUTPUT PRINT-FILE
            NEW-MASTER-TAPE.
```

is more efficient than

```
OPEN INPUT CARD-FILE.
OPEN INPUT OLD-MASTER-TAPE.
OPEN OUTPUT PRINT-FILE.
OPEN OUTPUT NEW-MASTER-TAPE.
```

3. *Make all numeric entries signed.* Use S in the picture description of any field that will be used in an arithmetic computation. However, do *not* follow this technique if negative values are to be converted to positive values or if the field itself is to be printed.

4. *Do not use the ROUNDED clause unless it is required.* Insertion of this clause causes additional machine code to be generated.

5. *Where possible, do arithmetic only on fields with similar decimal alignment.* If, for example a series of incoming fields all with a picture of S9(5)V9 are to be summed, then the picture of the total field should also contain a single decimal point.

6. *Input/Output.* System design considerations, e.g., blocking factors, are in the realm of the analyst rather than the programmer. However, these play a vital role in processing speed and the competent programmer should be aware of these concepts (see the discussion in Chapter 15).

Structured programming was first introduced in Chapter 6 as one element of programming style. Subsequently, all programs in Section III were written as per the guidelines in Chapter 6. Additional elements of the structured discipline are now introduced. These are the case structure, pseudocode, and top-down development. Finally, two complete programs are developed to firmly present the advantages of the technique.

More on Structured Programming

Case Structure (GO TO DEPENDING)

Structured programming is often referred to as 'GO TO-less' programming which, in fact, is a slight misrepresentation. No special effort is made to avoid the GO TO, even if there are valid reasons for not using it. The GO TO statement just never occurs if the three standard logic structures are adhered to. However, situations can occur in which the GO TO may actually improve clarity, as in the case structure.

Although all programs can be developed as a function of the three basic control structures, it is useful to include the case structure as a fourth permissible logic form. This structure conveniently expresses a multibranch situation. The value of a variable is tested to determine which of several routines is to be executed. Its flowchart is shown in Figure 11.1. As with the other building blocks of structured programming, there is exactly one entry and one exit point. Implementation is through the GO TO DEPENDING statement and is illustrated in Figure 11.2.

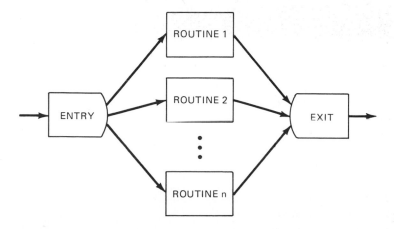

Figure 11.1 The Case Structure

```
YEAR-IN-COLLEGE.
    GO TO
        FRESHMAN
        SOPHOMORE
        JUNIOR
        SENIOR
        GRAD-SCHOOL
    DEPENDING ON INCOMING-YEAR-CODE.
    ... process error ...
    GO TO YEAR-IN-COLLEGE-EXIT.
FRESHMAN.
    ... process ...
    GO TO YEAR-IN-COLLEGE-EXIT.
SOPHOMORE.
    ... process ...
    GO TO YEAR-IN-COLLEGE-EXIT.
JUNIOR.
    ... process ...
    GO TO YEAR-IN-COLLEGE-EXIT.
SENIOR.
    ... process ...
    GO TO YEAR-IN-COLLEGE-EXIT.
GRAD-SCHOOL.
    ... process ...
YEAR-IN-COLLEGE-EXIT.
    EXIT.
```

Figure 11.2 COBOL Implementation of the Case Structure

The GO TO DEPENDING statement tests the value of a code, in this instance INCOMING-YEAR-CODE. If it is equal to 1, control passes to the first paragraph specified, i.e., FRESHMAN. If INCOMING-YEAR-CODE is equal to 2, control passes to the second paragraph, i.e., SOPHOMORE, etc. If the code has any value other than 1, 2, 3, 4, or 5 (since five paragraphs were specified), control passes to the next statement immediately following the GO TO DEPENDING, which should be an error routine. Indentation in the GO TO DEPENDING is strictly for legibility; it is not required by COBOL.

Figure 11.2 also contains five "villainous" GO TO statements, but their use is completely acceptable (to us, if not to the most rigid advocate of structured programming). If the GO TO statement is used in a structured program, it should appear only within the range of a perform statement and should always branch forward to the end of the perform. This in turn is a "dummy" paragraph consisting of a single EXIT statement. We believe that such usage adds to, rather than detracts from, clarity.

Of course the GO TO DEPENDING may be omitted entirely in favor of a series of 'IF THEN PERFORM' statements, but we opt for the case structure. Indeed the larger the number of acceptable codes the clearer the GO TO DEPENDING becomes, particularly if the paragraphs are stacked and an EXIT paragraph is used as in Figure 11.2.

Pseudocode

Pseudocode is a way of expressing a program's detailed logic. It is similar to a programming language but is not bound by syntactical rules. It uses indentation for clarity and is restricted to the basic logic structures. Everything else is at the discretion of the programmer. Pseudocode is widely used as associated documentation with structured programming in addition to, and sometimes in lieu of, the flowchart (see the Continental University example in the next section).

Top-Down Development

Structured programming emphasizes top-down development; i.e., it develops the highest levels of logic first and the details later. The mainline portion of a structured program contains the highest logic and consists of perform statements which invoke program segments. A program segment is a "chunk of code" to accomplish a particular piece of detail logic. Segmentation (i.e., the division of a program into distinct modules) is an integral part of structured programming and should follow these guidelines:

1. Segments should contain a maximum of 50 lines of code. In this way unnecessary page turning of the COBOL listing is avoided and it is relatively easy to determine the exact function of a segment. (The EJECT statement can be used to begin each segment on a new page for additional clarity.)

2. A program should be divided so that individual segments relate logically to each other in a hierarchy. A segment may call another segment, but not one on its own level in the hierarchy. (See Continental University example in next section.)

A Rationale for Structured Programming

Needless to say, structured programming has not gained unqualified acceptance in the programming community. Indeed, we would be less than honest if we said that the authors immediately embraced the concept and promptly rewrote all our old programs. Our initial skepticism (since departed), and no doubt your own, stemmed from several factors. First and foremost many people contend that PERFORM is another way of saying GO TO, and that structured programs jump around at least as much as conventional ones. This argument fails to recognize that a PERFORM, if properly used, always returns to the statement immediately under it. A GO TO, on the other hand, is a one way ticket, often over several pages of code.

The second argument against structured programming is that it requires substantially more time for initial coding. However, for some reason, structured programs are inherently easier to test and debug. Thus, since the commercial programmer spends at least as much time on these activities, as on coding, we believe the total time to program completion is not increased. More importantly, structured programs are less apt to contain bugs when they go into production.

Regardless of what we say now, the arguments for or against structured programming have a somewhat nebulous and perhaps unconvincing quality. Further, a primary advantage of the structured approach, namely that it facilitates the development of logically difficult problems, has not been adequately demonstrated. All of the illustrative programs to date suffer from the fact that they were "logically simple"; i.e., our objective in Sections I–III was to teach the COBOL language per se, not to present complex logical situations. Accordingly, any programming difficulties you have encountered should have been primarily restricted to COBOL problems, and once a "clean" compile was achieved, a completed program was not far behind.

We believe, therefore, that the most convincing argument for structured programming is presentation of problems with substantial logic requirements.

Accordingly, we consider two examples. The first is a program requiring two control breaks; the second accomplishes a match-merge operation.

Continental University consists of several colleges; each college has four levels of students; freshmen, sophomores, juniors, and seniors. A punched card, showing the number of students in a given major, year, and college has been prepared. These cards have been sorted by college (primary sort) and year (secondary sort). The problem is to:

1. Sum all the major totals in the same year to provide enrollment totals for each year.

2. Sum the four year totals in a college to provide a college total.

3. Sum all the college totals to provide a single university total.

4. For simplicity, page headings, line counts, etc., are not required.

The specifications call for two control breaks, on year and college. A running total will be maintained for all majors in a given year. When a new year is encountered, the previous year's total is printed, and then the year total is reinitialized to zero. When a new college is reached, there is a double break (on year and college). Both totals are printed and then zeroed out, and processing continues. The university total is printed after the end of file has been reached. This logic is represented in the pseudocode of Figure 11.3. As can be seen, pseudocode is nothing more than a systematic statement of the processing necessary to solve a problem. It is restricted to the basic logic structures, but everything else is left to the programmer.

```
Initialize
OPEN files
READ STUDENT-FILE at end of file indicate no more data
zero university total
PERFORM UNTIL there is no more data
    zero college total
    move CD-COLLEGE to WS-PREVIOUS-COLLEGE
    PERFORM UNTIL CD-COLLEGE is not equal to WS-PREVIOUS-COLLEGE
        or there is no more data
            zero year's total
            move CD-YEAR to WS-PREVIOUS-YEAR
            PERFORM UNTIL CD-COLLEGE is not equal to WS-PREVIOUS-COLLEGE
                or CD-YEAR is not equal to WS-PREVIOUS-YEAR
                or there is no more data
                    accumulate year's total
                    READ STUDENT-FILE at end of file indicate no more data
            ENDPERFORM
            print year's total
            accumulate college total
    ENDPERFORM
    print college total
    accumulate university total
ENDPERFORM
print university total
CLOSE files
STOP RUN
```

Figure 11.3 Pseudocode for Double Control Break Program

The logic for this program is adequately described by the pseudocode of Figure 11.3 and the hierarchical structure of Figure 11.5. In addition Figure

11.4 depicts the mainline logic. Flowcharts for the performed routines are not shown.

Chapter 11
Programming Style, II

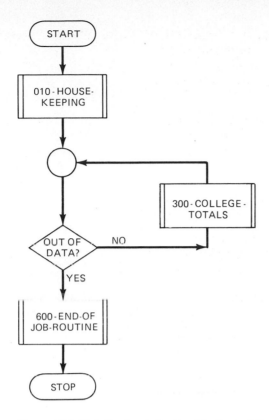

Figure 11.4 Mainline Logic for Double Control Break Program

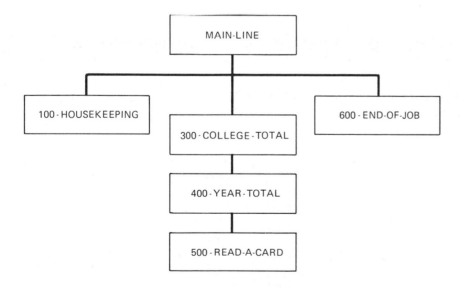

Figure 11.5 Hierarchy for Double Control Break Program

It is now an easy matter to develop the COBOL program of Figure 11.6 which produces output as shown in Figure 11.7. Figure 11.6 is a structured program as per our discussion in this chapter and in Chapter 6. The mainline performs three sections: 100-HOUSEKEEPING, 300-COLLEGE-TOTALS,

```
00001          IDENTIFICATION DIVISION.
00002          PROGRAM-ID.
00003             TOTALS.
00004          AUTHOR.
00005             GRAUER
00006          INSTALLATION.
00007             CITY UNIVERSITY OF NEW YORK.
00008          DATE-WRITTEN.
00009             MAY, 1976.
00010          ENVIRONMENT DIVISION.
00011          CONFIGURATION SECTION.
00012          SOURCE-COMPUTER.
00013             IBM-370.
00014          OBJECT-COMPUTER.
00015             IBM-370.
00016          INPUT-OUTPUT SECTION.
00017          FILE-CONTROL.
00018             SELECT STUDENT-FILE
00019                ASSIGN TO UR-2540R-S-SYSIN.
00020             SELECT PRINT-FILE
00021                ASSIGN TO UR-1403-S-SYSOUT.
00022          DATA DIVISION.
00023          FILE SECTION.
00024          FD  STUDENT-FILE
00025             RECORDING MODE IS F
00026             LABEL RECORDS ARE OMITTED
00027             RECORD CONTAINS 80 CHARACTERS
00028             DATA RECORD IS CARD.
00029          01  CARD                         PICTURE IS X(80).
00030          FD  PRINT-FILE
00031             RECORDING MODE IS F
00032             LABEL RECORDS ARE OMITTED
00033             RECORD CONTAINS 133 CHARACTERS
00034             DATA RECORD IS PRINT-LINE.
00035          01  PRINT-LINE                   PICTURE IS X(133).
00036          WORKING-STORAGE SECTION.
00037          77  FILLER                       PICTURE IS X(14)
00038                        VALUE IS 'WS BEGINS HERE'.
00039          77  WS-END-OF-FILE-INDICATOR     PICTURE IS X(3)
00040                        VALUE IS SPACES.
00041          77  WS-UNIVERSITY-TOTAL          PICTURE IS S9(6)
00042                        VALUE IS ZEROS.
00043          77  WS-COLLEGE-TOTAL             PICTURE IS S9(6)
00044                        VALUE IS ZEROS.
00045          77  WS-PREVIOUS-COLLEGE          PICTURE IS X(20)
00046                        VALUE IS SPACES.
00047          77  WS-YEAR-TOTAL                PICTURE IS S9(6)
00048                        VALUE IS ZEROS.
00049          77  WS-PREVIOUS-YEAR             PICTURE IS X(9)
00050                        VALUE IS SPACES.
00051          01  WS-PRINT-LINE.
00052                 10   FILLER               PICTURE IS X.
00053                 10   PR-YEAR              PICTURE IS X(9).
00054                 10   FILLER               PICTURE IS XXX.
00055                 10   PR-YEAR-TOTAL        PICTURE ZZZ,ZZ9.
00056                 10   FILLER               PICTURE IS X(9).
00057                 10   PR-COLLEGE           PICTURE IS X(10).
00058                 10   FILLER               PICTURE IS XX.
00059                 10   PR-COLLEGE-TOTAL     PICTURE ZZZ,ZZ9.
00060                 10   FILLER               PICTURE IS X(1).
00061                 10   PR-TOTAL             PICTURE IS X(26).
00062                 10   FILLER               PICTURE IS X.
00063                 10   PR-UNIVERSITY-TOTAL  PICTURE ZZZ,ZZ9.
00064                 10   FILLER               PICTURE IS X(50).
00065          01  WS-CARD-IN.
00066                 10   CD-YEAR              PICTURE IS X(9).
00067                 10   FILLER               PICTURE IS X(11).
00068                 10   CD-COLLEGE           PICTURE IS X(10).
00069                 10   FILLER               PICTURE IS X(19).
00070                 10   CD-MAJOR-TOTAL       PICTURE IS S9(6).
00071                 10   FILLER               PICTURE IS X(25).
00072          01  FILLER                       PICTURE IS X(12)
00073                        VALUE IS 'WS ENDS HERE'.
00074          PROCEDURE DIVISION.
00075             PERFORM 100-HOUSEKEEPING.
00076             PERFORM 300-COLLEGE-TOTALS
```

Figure 11.6 Structured Program for Two Control Breaks

```
00077                        UNTIL WS-END-OF-FILE-INDICATOR = 'YES'.
00078                   PERFORM 600-END-OF-JOB-ROUTINE.
00079                   CLOSE STUDENT-FILE,
00080                        PRINT-FILE.
00081                   STOP RUN.
00082
00083           100-HOUSEKEEPING SECTION.
00084                   OPEN INPUT STUDENT-FILE,
00085                        OUTPUT PRINT-FILE.
00086                   READ STUDENT-FILE INTO WS-CARD-IN,
00087                        AT END MOVE 'YES' TO WS-END-OF-FILE-INDICATOR.
00088                   MOVE ZEROS TO WS-UNIVERSITY-TOTAL.
00089
00090           300-COLLEGE-TOTALS SECTION.
00091                   MOVE ZEROS TO WS-COLLEGE-TOTAL.
00092                   MOVE CD-COLLEGE TO WS-PREVIOUS-COLLEGE.
00093                   PERFORM 400-YEAR-TOTAL
00094                        UNTIL CD-COLLEGE IS NOT EQUAL TO WS-PREVIOUS-COLLEGE
00095                        OR WS-END-OF-FILE-INDICATOR = 'YES'.
00096                   MOVE SPACES TO WS-PRINT-LINE.
00097                   MOVE WS-PREVIOUS-COLLEGE TO PR-COLLEGE.
00098                   MOVE WS-COLLEGE-TOTAL TO PR-COLLEGE-TOTAL.
00099                   WRITE PRINT-LINE FROM WS-PRINT-LINE.
00100                   ADD WS-COLLEGE-TOTAL TO WS-UNIVERSITY-TOTAL.
00101                   MOVE SPACES TO PRINT-LINE.
00102                   WRITE PRINT-LINE.
00103
00104           400-YEAR-TOTAL SECTION.
00105                   MOVE ZEROS TO WS-YEAR-TOTAL.
00106                   MOVE CD-YEAR TO WS-PREVIOUS-YEAR.
00107                   PERFORM 500-READ-A-CARD
00108                        UNTIL CD-COLLEGE IS NOT EQUAL TO WS-PREVIOUS-COLLEGE
00109                        OR CD-YEAR IS NOT EQUAL TO WS-PREVIOUS-YEAR
00110                        OR WS-END-OF-FILE-INDICATOR = 'YES'.
00111                   MOVE SPACES TO WS-PRINT-LINE.
00112                   MOVE WS-PREVIOUS-YEAR TO PR-YEAR.
00113                   MOVE WS-YEAR-TOTAL TO PR-YEAR-TOTAL.
00114                   WRITE PRINT-LINE FROM WS-PRINT-LINE.
00115                   ADD WS-YEAR-TOTAL TO WS-COLLEGE-TOTAL.
00116
00117           500-READ-A-CARD SECTION.
00118
00119                   IF CD-MAJOR-TOTAL IS NOT NUMERIC
00120                        DISPLAY CD-COLLEGE ' INVALID DATA',
00121                   ELSE
00122                        ADD CD-MAJOR-TOTAL TO WS-YEAR-TOTAL.
00123                   READ STUDENT-FILE INTO WS-CARD-IN,
00124                        AT END MOVE 'YES' TO WS-END-OF-FILE-INDICATOR.
00125
00126           600-END-OF-JOB-ROUTINE SECTION.
00127                   MOVE SPACES TO WS-PRINT-LINE.
00128                   MOVE ' *** UNIVERSITY TOTAL = ' TO PR-TOTAL.
00129                   MOVE WS-UNIVERSITY-TOTAL TO PR-UNIVERSITY-TOTAL.
00130                   WRITE PRINT-LINE FROM WS-PRINT-LINE.
```

Figure 11.6 *(Continued)*

```
FRESHMAN          300
SOPHOMORE         150
JUNIOR            228
SENIOR             54
                             ATLANTIC        732

FRESHMAN          400
SOPHOMORE         543
JUNIOR            199
SENIOR            220
                             MIDWEST       1,362

FRESHMAN          441
SOPHOMORE         400
JUNIOR            400
SENIOR             55
                             PACIFIC       1,296

                             *** UNIVERSITY TOTAL =      3,390
```

Figure 11.7 Output for Two Control Break Program

and 600-END-OF-JOB. 300-COLLEGE-TOTALS in turn invokes 400-
YEAR-TOTAL (a second-level routine) which in turn calls 500-READ-A-
CARD (a third-level routine). Note that each routine has exactly one entry
point (i.e., it is performed by a higher level routine). Further note that a
routine cannot invoke another routine on its own level, and that the entire
sequence of performs is consistent with Figure 11.5.

Section III
More COBOL

Figure 11.6 also demonstrates coding standards and other techniques of
sound programming. All 77 level entries are prefixed by WS; and 01 records in
working-storage have their own unique two-letter prefixes (PR and CD).
PICTURE and VALUE clauses are vertically aligned. Each section header is
preceded by a blank line. No line contains more than one statement, and
statements which carry over to a second line are indented for clarity.

The procedure division utilizes READ INTO and WRITE FROM options.
A class test for numeric entries is done prior to arithmetic computations in line
119. All performed procedures are sections. Finally, note the entries denoting
the start and end of working storage (lines 37, 38, 72, 73).

File maintenance is not formally discussed until Chapters 15 and 16. We take
this opportunity, however, to present an example of a match/merge operation.
The reader may want to defer consideration of this section until the concepts of
file processing are covered. However, we believe this to be such an excellent
example of the advantages of the structured approach that we have included it
at this time.

Example 2: Match/Merge

Specifications are as follows: Two sequential files, an old master and a
transaction file, are to be matched against one another. Each record in the old
master contains a part number and quantity on hand. Each record in the
transaction file contains a part number, quantity received, and quantity
shipped. A printed report is required showing updated quantities for any part
appearing in both files. A part number appearing in the master and not the
transaction file is to be flagged as inactive. A part number appearing in the
transaction file, but not the master is to be flagged as an error. Sample output is
shown in Figure 11.8. Note that the report of Figure 11.8 contains part names
as well as numbers. Accordingly a file of codes is to be initially stored, then
subsequently searched in the program.

PART	PART #	OLD-AMT	RECEIVED	SHIPPED	NEW-AMT	
LARGE WIDGET	111111	2000	1000	7000	4000	*BACKLOG*
LARGEST WIDGET	333333	500	8000	1000	7500	
SMALLER GADGET	555555	50000	500	0	50500	
SMALLEST GADGET	666666	4444	1000	0	5444	

Figure 11.8a Records Appearing in Both Files

Figure 11.8b Records Appearing in Only One File

The hierarchy of performed routines for the program of Figure 11.9
follows:

212

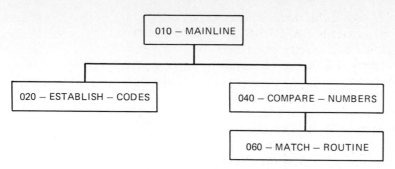

The heart of Figure 11.9 is in the comparison routine which is performed until there is no more data. Note well that HIGH-VALUES is moved to both OLD-MAST-ID and TRAN-ID on an end-of-file condition (COBOL lines 199 and 204), and that the comparison routine is performed until both IDs are equal to HIGH-VALUES (COBOL lines 161 and 162). The comparison routine (COBOL lines 181–208) is remarkable for its simplicity. In reality it consists of only a single nested IF plus two other simple IF

```
00001          IDENTIFICATION DIVISION.
00002          PROGRAM-ID.
00003             MERGE.
00004          AUTHOR.
00005             GRAUER.
00006          INSTALLATION.
00007             CITY UNIVERSITY OF NEW YORK
00008          DATE-WRITTEN.
00009             DECEMBER, 1976.
00010          REMARKS.
00011                 THIS PROGRAM PERFORMS A MATCH-MERGE OPERATION.  A TRANS-
00012             ACTION FILE AND AN OLD-MASTER FILE ARE MERGED TO PRODUCE A
00013             SINGLE PRINTED REPORT.  BOTH FILES ARE IN SEQUENTIAL ORDER.
00014                 ID NUMBERS APPEARING IN THE TRANSACTION FILE, BUT NOT THE
00015             MASTER FILE ARE FLAGGED AS ERRORS.  ID NUMBERS APPEARING IN
00016             THE MASTER FILE, BUT NOT THE TRANSACTION FILE ARE INACTIVE FOR
00017             THE PERIOD IN QUESTION.
00018
00019                 THIS LISTING STRONGLY PRESENTS THE ADVANTAGES OF A MODULAR
00020             APPROACH TO PROGRAMMING.

00022          ENVIRONMENT DIVISION.
00023          CONFIGURATION SECTION.
00024          SOURCE-COMPUTER.
00025             IBM-370.
00026          OBJECT-COMPUTER.
00027             IBM-370.
00028          SPECIAL-NAMES.
00029             C01 IS TOP-OF-PAGE.

00031          INPUT-OUTPUT SECTION.
00032          FILE-CONTROL.
00033             SELECT CODES-FILE
00034                 ASSIGN TO UT-S-CODES.
00035             SELECT OLD-MASTER-FILE
00036                 ASSIGN TO UT-S-OLDMAST.
00037             SELECT TRANS-FILE
00038                 ASSIGN TO UT-S-TRANS.
00039             SELECT PRINT-FILE
00040                 ASSIGN TO UT-S-PRINT.

00042          DATA DIVISION.
00043          FILE SECTION.

00045          FD  CODES-FILE
00046              RECORDING MODE IS F
00047              LABEL RECORDS ARE OMITTED
00048              RECORD CONTAINS 80 CHARACTERS
00049              DATA RECORD IS CODE-RECORD.
00050          01  CODE-RECORD                         PICTURE IS X(80).
```

Figure 11.9 Match/Merge Listing

```
00052      FD   OLD-MASTER-FILE
00053           RECORDING MODE IS F
00054           LABEL RECORDS ARE OMITTED
00055           RECORD CONTAINS 80 CHARACTERS.
00056           DATA RECORD IS OLD-MASTER-RECORD.
00057      01   OLD-MASTER-RECORD                   PICTURE IS X(80).

00059      FD   TRANS-FILE
00060           RECORDING MODE IS F
00061           LABEL RECORDS ARE OMITTED
00062           RECORD CONTAINS 80 CHARACTERS
00063           DATA RECORD IS TRANSACTION-RECORD.
00064      01   TRANSACTION-RECORD                  PICTURE IS X(80).

00066      FD   PRINT-FILE
00067           RECORDING MODE IS F
00068           LABEL RECORDS ARE OMITTED
00069           RECORD CONTAINS 133 CHARACTERS
00070           DATA RECORD IS PRINT-LINE.
00071      01   PRINT-LINE                          PICTURE IS X(133).


00073      WORKING-STORAGE SECTION.
00074      77   FILLER                              PICTURE IS X(14)
00075                          VALUE IS 'WS BEGINS HERE'.          ──── Established to facilitate
00076      77   WS-CODES-SWITCH                     PICTURE IS X(3)       subsequent debugging
00077                          VALUE IS SPACES.
00078      77   WS-TRANS-SWITCH                     PICTURE IS X(3)
00079                          VALUE IS SPACES.
00080      77   WS-OLD-MASTER-SWITCH                PICTURE IS X(3)
00081                          VALUE IS SPACES.
00082      77   WS-NUMBER-OF-CODES                  PICTURE IS S9(2)
00083                          VALUE IS ZEROS.
00084      77   WS-LINE-COUNT                       PICTURE IS S9(3)
00085                          VALUE IS +51.
00086      77   NEW-QOH                             PICTURE IS S9(6)
00087                          VALUE IS ZEROS.
00088      01   WS-CODE-RECORD.
00089           05   CARD-CODE                      PICTURE IS X(6).
00090           05   CARD-NAME                      PICTURE IS X(15).
00091           05   FILLER                         PICTURE IS X(59).
00092      01   WS-OLD-MAST-RECORD.
00093           05   OLD-MAST-ID                    PICTURE IS X(6).
00094           05   OLD-QOH                        PICTURE IS S9(6).
00095           05   FILLER                         PICTURE IS X(60).
00096      01   WS-TRANS-RECORD.
00097           05   TRAN-ID                        PICTURE IS X(6).
00098           05   FILLER                         PICTURE IS X(13).
00099           05   TRAN-RECEIVED                  PICTURE IS S9(4).
00100           05   FILLER                         PICTURE IS X(6).
00101           05   TRAN-SHIPPED                   PICTURE IS S9(4).
00102           05   FILLER                         PICTURE IS X(47).
00103      01   WS-PRINT-LINE.
00104           05   FILLER                         PICTURE IS XX.
00105           05   PRTR-NAME                      PICTURE IS X(15).
00106           05   FILLER                         PICTURE IS XX.
00107           05   PRTR-ID                        PICTURE IS X(6).
00108           05   FILLER                         PICTURE IS XX.
00109           05   PRTR-OLD-QOH                   PICTURE IS ZZZZZ9.
00110           05   FILLER                         PICTURE IS X(4).
00111           05   PRTR-RECEIVED                  PICTURE IS Z(8)9.
00112           05   FILLER                         PICTURE IS XXX.
00113           05   PRTR-SHIPPED                   PICTURE IS Z(8)9.
00114           05   FILLER                         PICTURE IS XXX.
00115           05   PRTR-NEW-QOH                   PICTURE IS Z(8)9.
00116           05   FILLER                         PICTURE IS XX.
00117           05   PRTR-BACKLOG                   PICTURE IS X(9).
00118           05   FILLER                         PICTURE IS X(52).
00119      01   HDG-LINE.
00120           05   FILLER      VALUE SPACES       PICTURE X(5).
00121           05   FILLER      VALUE 'PART'       PICTURE X(4).
00122           05   FILLER      VALUE SPACES       PICTURE X(9).
00123           05   FILLER      VALUE 'PART # '    PICTURE X(8).
00124           05   FILLER      VALUE 'OLD-AMT'    PICTURE X(7).
00125           05   FILLER      VALUE SPACES       PICTURE X(6).
00126           05   FILLER      VALUE 'RECEIVED'   PICTURE X(8).
00127           05   FILLER      VALUE SPACES       PICTURE X(7).
```

Figure 11.9 *(Continued)*

```
00128               05  FILLER     VALUE 'SHIPPED'        PICTURE X(7).
00129               05  FILLER     VALUE SPACES           PICTURE X(5).
00130               05  FILLER     VALUE 'NEW-AMT'        PICTURE X(7).
00131               05  FILLER     VALUE SPACES           PICTURE X(60).
```

┌─ Variable Length Table

```
00133          01  CODES-TABLE-VALUES.
00134              05  CODES  OCCURS 1 TO 10 TIMES
00135                  DEPENDING ON WS-NUMBER-OF-CODES
00136                  INDEXED BY CODE-INDEX.
00137                  10  CODE-VALUE                     PICTURE X(6).
00138                  10  CODE-NAME                      PICTURE X(15).

00140          PROCEDURE DIVISION.
00141
00142          010-MAINLINE.
00143              OPEN INPUT CODES-FILE,
00144                         TRANS-FILE,
00145                         OLD-MASTER-FILE,
00146                  OUTPUT PRINT-FILE.
00147
00148      *    ESTABLISH VALUES FOR CODE TABLE
00149              SET CODE-INDEX TO 1.
00150              READ CODES-FILE INTO WS-CODE-RECORD,
00151                  AT END MOVE HIGH-VALUES TO WS-CODES-SWITCH.
00152              PERFORM 020-ESTABLISH-CODES THRU 030-ESTABLISH-CODES-EXIT
00153                  UNTIL WS-CODES-SWITCH = HIGH-VALUES.
00154
00155      *    BEGIN MERGE PROCESS WITH TWO INITIAL READS
00156              READ TRANS-FILE INTO WS-TRANS-RECORD,
00157                  AT END MOVE HIGH-VALUES TO TRAN-ID.
00158              READ OLD-MASTER-FILE INTO WS-OLD-MAST-RECORD,
00159                  AT END MOVE HIGH-VALUES TO OLD-MAST-ID.
00160              PERFORM 040-COMPARE-NUMBERS THRU 050-COMPARE-NUMBERS-EXIT
00161                  UNTIL TRAN-ID = HIGH-VALUES,
00162                  AND OLD-MAST-ID = HIGH-VALUES.
00163              CLOSE CODES-FILE,
00164                    TRANS-FILE,
00165                    OLD-MASTER-FILE,
00166                    PRINT-FILE.
00167              STOP RUN.
```

┌─ Mainline Routine

┌─ Use of an index rather
│ than a subscript

```
00169          020-ESTABLISH-CODES.
00170              MOVE CARD-CODE TO CODE-VALUE (CODE-INDEX).
00171              MOVE CARD-NAME TO CODE-NAME (CODE-INDEX).
00172              SET CODE-INDEX UP BY 1.
00173              ADD 1 TO WS-NUMBER-OF-CODES.
00174              READ CODES-FILE INTO WS-CODE-RECORD,
00175                  AT END MOVE HIGH-VALUES TO WS-CODES-SWITCH.
00176
00177          030-ESTABLISH-CODES-EXIT.
00178              EXIT.
00179
```

└─ Routine to initialize variable length codes table

┌─ Nested IF statement to determine
│ which of three conditions apply

```
00181          040-COMPARE-NUMBERS.
00182
00183              IF OLD-MAST-ID < TRAN-ID,
00184                  DISPLAY 'NO ACTIVITY IN MASTER RECORD ', OLD-MAST-ID,
00185                  MOVE 'YES' TO WS-OLD-MASTER-SWITCH,
00186              ELSE
00187
00188                  IF OLD-MAST-ID = TRAN-ID,
00189                      MOVE 'YES' TO WS-OLD-MASTER-SWITCH
00190                      MOVE 'YES' TO WS-TRANS-SWITCH
00191                      PERFORM 060-MATCH-RTN THRU 070-MATCH-RTN-EXIT
00192                  ELSE,
00193                      DISPLAY '**ERROR - NO MATCH FOR TRAN-ID ' TRAN-ID,
00194                      MOVE 'YES' TO WS-TRANS-SWITCH.
00195
```

Figure 11.9 (Continued)

```
00196              IF WS-TRANS-SWITCH = 'YES'
00197                  MOVE 'NO' TO WS-TRANS-SWITCH
00198                  READ TRANS-FILE INTO WS-TRANS-RECORD,
00199                      AT END MOVE HIGH-VALUES TO TRAN-ID.
00200
00201              IF WS-OLD-MASTER-SWITCH = 'YES',
00202                  MOVE 'NO' TO WS-OLD-MASTER-SWITCH,
00203                  READ OLD-MASTER-FILE INTO WS-OLD-MAST-RECORD,
00204                      AT END MOVE HIGH-VALUES TO OLD-MAST-ID.
00205
00206          C50-COMPARE-NUMBERS-EXIT.
00207              EXIT.
00208
                                              ┌─ Page Heading Routine
00210          060-MATCH-RTN.                 │
00211              COMPUTE NEW-OOH = OLD-OOH /+ TRAN-RECEIVED - TRAN-SHIPPED.
00212
00213          ┌─────────────────────────────────────────────────────────┐
00214          │*CHECK IF HEADING IS NEEDED FOR PRINT REPORT              │
               │    IF WS-LINE-COUNT > 50,                                │
00215          │        MOVE ZEROS TO WS-LINE-COUNT,                      │
00216          │        WRITE PRINT-LINE FROM HDG-LINE AFTER ADVANCING    │
00217          │        TOP-OF-PAGE LINES.                                │
               └─────────────────────────────────────────────────────────┘
00218
00219          * ESTABLISH PRINT LINE
00220              MOVE SPACES TO WS-PRINT-LINE.
00221              SET CODE-INDEX TO 1.         ┌─ AT END condition checks for invalid code
00222              SEARCH CODES,                │
00223          ┌────────────────────────────────┴┐
               │    AT END MOVE 'UNKNOWN' TO PRTR-NAME,│
               └─────────────────────────────────┘
00224                  WHEN TRAN-ID = CODE-VALUE (CODE-INDEX)
00225                  MOVE CODE-NAME (CODE-INDEX) TO PRTR-NAME.
00226              MOVE OLD-OOH TO PRTR-OLD-OOH.
00227              MOVE TRAN-RECEIVED TO PRTR-RECEIVED.
00228              MOVE TRAN-SHIPPED TO PRTR-SHIPPED.
00229              MOVE NEW-OOH TO PRTR-NEW-OOH.
00230              MOVE TRAN-ID TO PRTR-ID.
00231              IF NEW-OOH < 0,
00232                  MOVE '*BACKLOG*' TO PRTR-BACKLOG.
00233              WRITE PRINT-LINE FROM WS-PRINT-LINE AFTER ADVANCING 2 LINES.
00234              ADD 1 TO WS-LINE-COUNT.
00235
00236          070-MATCH-RTN-EXIT.
00237              EXIT.
00238
```

Figure 11.9 *(Continued)*

statements. The nested IF determines which of three conditions apply; i.e., an inactive master record, a match, or an erroneous transaction. The simple IF statements test the value of two switches to determine which file(s) should be read for the next record.

It is truly remarkable to us how the structured approach simplifies the logic of this *nontrivial* problem. Indeed the only way to genuinely appreciate this accomplishment is for the reader to code the identical problem in a nonstructured manner. We can almost guarantee that the more traditional approach will be replete with logic errors.

Several other features of Figure 11.9 are worthy of mention. In particular, observe how a variable-length table for codes is defined in COBOL lines 133–138. Note further how this same table is initialized from a file in the ESTABLISH-CODES routine, and the use of an index rather than a subscript. Finally note the use of the AT END condition in the SEARCH verb (lines 222–225) to check for an invalid code.

Coding standards are used throughout. Record prefixing and paragraph sequencing are used as a matter of course. So too are uniform columns for PICTURE and VALUE clauses. Indentation is of particular importance in structured programs, particularly with nested IF statements. Note also the "stacking" technique for the OPEN and CLOSE verbs.

Summary

This chapter concludes the discussion of programming style begun in Chapter 6. Generality, efficiency, error checking, and ease of maintenance are essential characteristics of good commercial programs. Techniques for achieving these goals were presented as part of an overall discussion on programming style.

The material on structured programming was extended to include the case structure, pseudocode, and top-down development. Top-down development is closely tied to structured programming and requires that one concentrate on the highest levels of logic first and bring in the details later. It assumes that the top-level logic is the most crucial and therefore should receive the most testing. Programs developed in this manner can be read in sequence, from top to bottom without a lot of skipping around, and this makes it far easier to understand the overall program logic. Further, this style of programming has three distinct advantages:

1. Ease of changing programs. Changes in specific modules can be done independently of one another.

2. Interchangeability between programs. Frequently different programs can utilize the same modules, e.g., a print routine.

3. Ease of maintenance and debugging. Top-down programming seems to make a program's logic more apparent. Although initial development may take longer, maintenance and "logical" debugging are faster in structured programs.

One final point: This chapter contained what we believe are two excellent arguments for structured programming, i.e., the COBOL programs of Figures 11.6 and 11.9. However, the reader may not yet believe that the extra time to develop structured programs is worth the effort. If you are not convinced, we urge you to withhold judgment until after you have read Chapters 15 and 16 and reviewed the programs on file maintenance (Figures 15.12 and 16.9). As anyone who has ever written a maintenance program will attest, the logical requirements are imposing, yet the structured programs are remarkably simple. In conclusion, we believe the top-down structured approach facilitates program development to such an extent, that we can no longer code any other way.

PROBLEMS

1 XYZ Corporation stocks four sizes of widgets: small (S), medium (M), large (L), and extra large (X). 60% of all incoming orders are for medium widgets, 25% for large, 10% for small, and 5% for extra large.
(a) Rewrite the COBOL code below to reflect 88-level entries:

```
DATA DIVISION,
        .
        .
        .
    05  IN-CODE     PICTURE IS X.
        .
        .
        .
PROCEDURE DIVISION.
        .
        .
        .
    IF IN-CODE IS EQUAL TO 'S', PERFORM SMALL-SIZE.
    IF IN-CODE IS EQUAL TO 'M', PERFORM MEDIUM-SIZE.
    IF IN-CODE IS EQUAL TO 'L', PERFORM LARGE-SIZE.
    IF IN-CODE IS EQUAL TO 'X', PERFORM EXTRA-LARGE-SIZE.
```

(b) In a file of 10,000 transactions, how many comparisons would be saved if the IF statements were reordered to check for transactions in the order M, L, S, and X?

(c) What would have to be done in order to apply the GO TO DEPENDING in lieu of the series of IF statements?

2 Given the following COBOL code,

```
WORKING-STORAGE SECTION.
77  WS-PAY              PICTURE IS S9(3)V9.
77  SUB                 PICTURE IS 99.
01  PAYROLL-RECORD.
    05  NAME            PICTURE IS A(20).
    05  DAILY-PAY OCCURS 5 TIMES PICTURE 9(3).
        .
        .
        .
    PROCEDURE DIVISION.
        .
        .
        .
        ADD DAILY-PAY (SUB) TO WS-PAY.
```

what changes should be made to the 77-level entries in order for more efficient code to be generated?

3 Given the following COBOL code,

```
        .
        .
        .
    MAINLINE.
        READ CARD-FILE-ONE, AT END MOVE 'Y' TO EOF-1.
        READ CARD-FILE-TWO, AT END MOVE 'Y' TO EOF-2.
        PERFORM A-200 UNTIL EOF-1 = 'Y'.
        STOP RUN.
        .
        .
        .
    A-200.
        PERFORM B-200 4 TIMES.
        .
        .
        .
        READ CARD-FILE-ONE, AT END MOVE 'Y' TO EOF-1.
        .
        .
        .
    B-200 SECTION.
        .
        .
        .
        READ CARD-FILE-TWO, AT END MOVE 'Y' TO EOF-2.
        .
        .
        .
    B-250.
        ADD 5 TO COUNTER.
```

how many times is each paragraph (section) executed? (Assume that there are N cards in CARD-FILE-ONE and M cards in CARD-FILE-TWO and that $M = 4N$. Express your answers in terms of N and M where necessary.)

4 Construct pseudocode for the following:

(a)

(b)

(c)

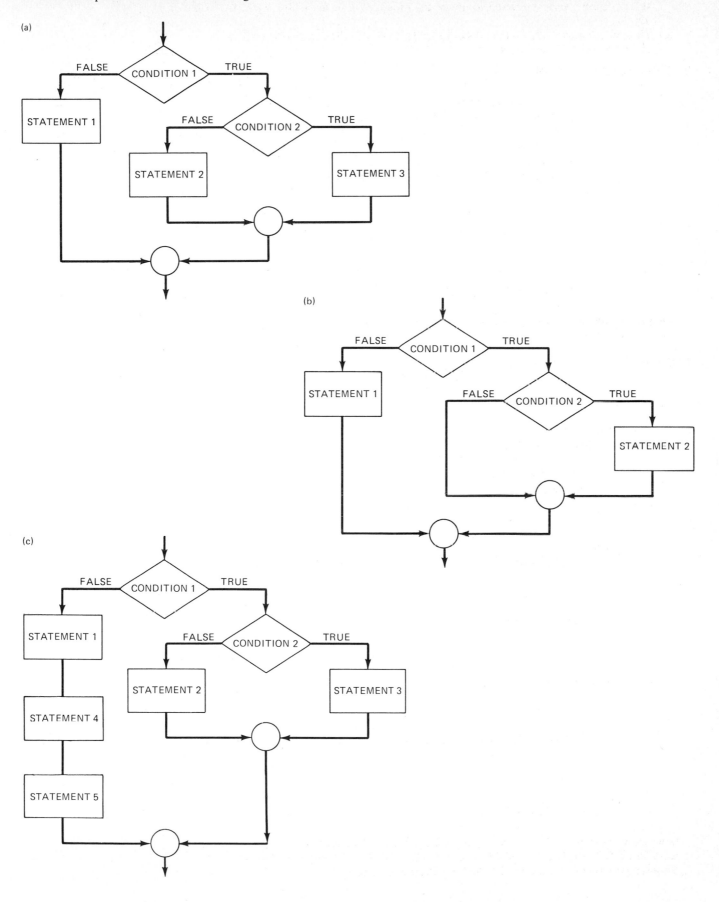

The Role of BAL in Deeper Understanding

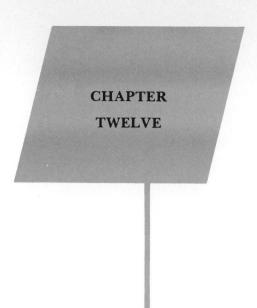

**CHAPTER
TWELVE**

Necessary Background

One of the reasons for using COBOL rather than a machine language is machine independence; i.e., a program written in ANS COBOL for an IBM system should run equally well, ideally with no modification, and practically with minimum modification on a Univac, Honeywell, or any other configuration. The concept of machine independence facilitates the learning of COBOL, or for that matter any other compiler language, in that knowledge of machine architecture is unnecessary. *Although the COBOL programmer need not know machine language, the authors are of the firm belief that even a superficial knowledge of the machine on which one is working greatly enhances the capabilities of the individual.* This is readily appreciated when one realizes the computer does not execute COBOL instructions per se but rather the machine language instructions generated by the COBOL compiler.

The next three chapters are designed to increase competence in COBOL through study of Assembler. In Chapter 12 we shall introduce number systems, base/displacement addressing, internal representation, and instruction formats. In Chapter 13 we shall develop elementary capability in dump reading and in Chapter 14 give an insight into the working of the COBOL compiler. The material may seem somewhat removed from COBOL, and perhaps it is. We maintain, however, that the best COBOL programmers are those who know a little more than COBOL.

Fundamental to the next three chapters is a thorough understanding of number systems. A number system is merely a set of symbols controlled by a well-defined set of rules for measuring quantities. The value of every digit is determined by its position; as one moves from right to left (i.e., away from the decimal point) each succeeding digit is multiplied by a higher power of the base in which one is working. For example, the number 1976 in base 10 is equal to:

$$1000 \quad + 900 \quad + 70 \quad + 6$$
$$= 1 \times 10^3 + 9 \times 10^2 + 7 \times 10^1 + 6 \times 10^0$$

We commonly use the decimal number system (base 10), but the choice of a base is actually quite arbitrary. Ten was picked a few thousand years ago, probably because man has ten fingers and ten toes. The advent of digital computers has forced consideration of bases other than 10, and that is what this section is all about.

Number systems are easily understood if one approaches the subject from existing knowledge, i.e., base 10. Everything about any other base can be related back to base 10. *All concepts are identical.* Thus, the decimal system has 10 digits, 0–9; the octal (base 8) system has 8 digits, 0–7; and the binary (base 2) system has 2 digits, 0 and 1; etc. Engineering considerations make it impractical to build a "base 10" computer because 10 different physical levels would be required to represent each of the 10 digits. On the other hand, a binary machine is very easy to build, as only two values are required. A current may be on or off, a switch up or down, a magnetic field right or left, etc. All computers are built as binary machines, and for this reason, we shall begin our study of number systems with base 2. To indicate which base we are talking about, we shall surround the number by (   )'s and use a subscript to indicate the base. If the parentheses are omitted, base 10 is assumed.

Binary

Base 2 has two digits, 0 and 1. The value of a digit is determined by its position, which represents some power of 2. The binary number $(10110)_2 = (22)_{10}$. The decimal value is obtained by expanding digits in the binary number by increasing powers of 2 as one moves away from the decimal point; thus,

$$(10110)_2$$

$$0 \times 2^0 = 0 \times 1 = 0$$
$$1 \times 2^1 = 1 \times 2 = 2$$
$$1 \times 2^2 = 1 \times 4 = 4$$
$$0 \times 2^3 = 0 \times 8 = 0$$
$$1 \times 2^4 = 1 \times 16 = 16$$
$$\overline{(22)_{10}}$$

Easy enough? Try the following examples as practice:

$$(11011)_2 = (27)_{10} \quad \text{and} \quad (100101)_2 = (37)_{10}$$

Decimal to Binary

The reader should now be able to convert from binary to decimal; how does one go from decimal to binary? For example, what does $(18)_{10}$ equal in binary? One approach is to determine by trial and error which powers of 2 make up 18.

After a few seconds, or minutes, we arrive at 16 and 2 and the binary number
10010. That approach is fine for small decimal numbers but doesn't work very
well for large numbers. A more systematic way to go from decimal to binary is
to repeatedly divide the decimal number by 2 until a quotient of zero is
reached. The remainders, read in reverse order, constitute the binary number.
Returning to the example, $(18)_{10} = (?)_2$:

$$
\begin{array}{ll}
2/\ 18 & \qquad\qquad \text{Answer} = (10010)_2 \\
2/\ \ 9 & \text{remainder of 0} \ \uparrow \\
2/\ \ 4 & \text{remainder of 1} \\
2/\ \ 2 & \text{remainder of 0} \\
2/\ \ 1 & \text{remainder of 0} \\
\ \ \ \ 0 & \text{remainder of 1}
\end{array}
$$

As practice, consider the examples

$$(35)_{10} = (100011)_2 \quad \text{and} \quad (71)_{10} = (1000111)_2$$

Binary Addition

Just as one adds in decimal, one can add in binary. Binary addition is no more
complicated than decimal addition; it just takes a little getting used to.
However, the principles of addition in either base are identical, and if one truly
understands decimal arithmetic, it should not be too difficult to work in binary,
or, for that matter, in any other base. Consider first the following addition in
base 10:

$$
\begin{array}{r}
38 \\
+46 \\
\hline
84
\end{array}
$$

If you add like most people, your thoughts begin with "8 + 6 = 14; write
down 4 and carry 1." Now analyze that statement. We are working in base 10
with valid digits 0–9. "14" cannot be written as a single digit; thus, we subtract
10 (i.e., the base) from 14, and the result of 4 is valid as a single digit; we
subtracted once and hence have a carry of 1. Involved? Yes, but that is
precisely the process we follow. Addition in base 10 has become so ingrained
over the years that we do all of that automatically. Now let's translate that
thought process to the binary system:

$$
\begin{array}{r}
(10)_2 \\
+(11)_2 \\
\hline
= \quad ?
\end{array}
$$

First, determine the result by converting each number to base 10, adding in
base 10, and then converting the sum back to binary:

$$
\begin{array}{r}
(10)_2 \ \text{-->} \ (2)_{10} \\
(11)_2 \ \text{-->} \ (3)_{10} \\
\hline
(101)_2 \ \text{<--} \ (5)_{10}
\end{array}
$$

We need, however, to be able to perform the addition directly in binary
without having to go through decimal, so let us add in binary, one column at a
time. First, $(0)_2 + (1)_2 = (1)_2$. In the next column, we add 1 and 1 to get 2,
except we can't write 2 as a single binary digit. Therefore, we subtract 2 from 2

and get zero, which is acceptable; we subtracted once and hence have a carry of 1. Returning to the initial example,

$$\begin{array}{r} \text{Carry} = 1 \\ (10)_2 \\ (11)_2 \\ \hline (101)_2 \end{array}$$

It takes a little getting used to. To check your understanding and also to gain a little practice, consider Table 12.1 in which the binary equivalents of the decimal numbers 1–10 are obtained through repeated addition.

Table 12.1 Binary and Decimal Equivalents

Decimal	Binary
1 ←----------→	1
	+ 1
2 ←---------→	10
	+ 1
3 ←---------→	11
	+ 1
4 ←---------→	100
	+ 1
5 ←---------→	101
	+ 1
6 ←---------→	110
	+ 1
7 ←---------→	111
	+ 1
8 ←---------→	1000
	+ 1
9 ←---------→	1001
	+ 1
10 ←---------→	1010

If you have been paying attention, you should now be able to convert from binary to decimal and from decimal to binary. You should also be able to do binary addition.

Hexadecimal

Although all computers function as binary machines, one never sees the internal contents displayed as binary numbers, simply because binary is too cumbersome. Nor does one see internal contents displayed as decimal numbers because binary-to-decimal conversion is time consuming and can be inexact with fractional numbers. The hexadecimal (base 16) number system solves both problems. It is much more concise than binary and provides direct and exact conversions to and from binary, i.e., four binary digits are exactly equal to one hex digit ($2^4 = 16$).

Just as base 10 has 10 digits, 0–9, base 16 has 16 digits, 0–15. The letter A represents 10, B represents 11, C is 12, D is 13, E is 14, and F is 15. In a decimal number each digit represents a power of 10; in a hex number each digit represents a power of 16. Consider the hex number $(12AB)_{16}$ and obtain its decimal equivalent:

$$(12AB)_{16}$$

$$B \times 16^0 = 11 \times \quad 1 = \quad 11$$
$$A \times 16^1 = 10 \times \quad 16 = \quad 160$$
$$2 \times 16^2 = \quad 2 \times \quad 256 = \quad 512$$
$$1 \times 16^3 = \quad 1 \times 4096 = 4096$$
$$(4779)_{10}$$

Decimal to Hexadecimal

Conversion from decimal to hex is accomplished much the same as conversion from decimal to binary, except that we divide by 16 instead of 2. For example, $(1000)_{10} = (?)_{16}$:

$$16 \underline{/\ 1000} \qquad\qquad\qquad \text{Answer} = (3E8)_{16}$$
$$16 \underline{/\quad 62} \quad \text{remainder of 8}$$
$$16 \underline{/\quad 3} \quad \text{remainder of } 14 = E$$
$$0 \quad \text{remainder of 3}$$

The remainders are read from the bottom up. Note that the remainder of 14 in decimal is converted to E in hex. As a check, we can convert $(3E8)_{16}$ to a decimal number and arrive at $(1000)_{10}$:

$$(3E8)_{16}$$

$$8 \times 16^0 = \quad 8 \times \quad 1 = \quad\quad 8$$
$$E \times 16^1 = 14 \times \quad 16 = \quad 224$$
$$3 \times 16^2 = \quad 3 \times 256 = \quad 768$$
$$(1000)_{10}$$

Hexadecimal Addition

Hexadecimal addition is made simple if we again use the thought processes of decimal arithmetic. Consider

$$\text{Carry} = 1$$
$$(39)_{16}$$
$$+ (59)_{16}$$
$$\overline{(92)_{16}}$$

Nine and 9 are 18; hex cannot express 18 as a single-digit number; therefore, subtract 16 and get 2. Two is valid; we subtracted once and hence have a carry of 1. It seems complicated only because we are so used to decimal arithmetic. The concepts of addition are identical in both bases, and it should only be a matter of time and practice to be comfortable in both.

Since hexadecimal includes some "strange-looking" digits, i.e., A, B, C, D, E, and F, perhaps another example will be helpful. Consider

$$\text{Carry} = 1$$
$$(AB)_{16}$$
$$+ (37)_{16}$$
$$\overline{(E2)_{16}}$$

B and 7 are 18 (remember, B denotes 11). Hex cannot express 18 as a single digit; thus subtract 16, get 2 and carry 1. Now A, 3, and 1 (the carry) equal 14, which is represented by E in hex.

Binary/Hexadecimal Conversion

A computer functions internally as a binary machine, but its contents are often displayed as hex numbers. How does the conversion take place? Consider

$$(10110100)_2 = (??)_{16}$$

One way is to convert the binary number to a decimal number by expanding powers of 2 and then to convert the decimal number to its hex equivalent by repeated division by 16. Thus, $(10110100)_2 = (180)_{10} = (B4)_2$.

There is, however, a shortcut. Since $2^4 = 16$, there are exactly four binary digits to one hex digit. Simply take the binary number and divide it into groups of four digits; begin at the decimal point and work right to left, i.e., 1011 0100. Then take each group of four digits and mentally convert to hex. Thus, $(0100)_2 = (4)_{10} = (4)_{16}$ and $(1011)_2 = (11)_{10} = (B)_{16}$. The answer is then B4 in hex, which was obtained earlier.

The process works in reverse as well. The hex number ABC can be immediately converted to the binary number 101010111100. As verification, convert ABC to decimal and then go from decimal to binary.

The advantages of hex notation should now be apparent. It is a more concise representation of the internal workings of a machine than binary, yet unlike decimal conversion, it is immediate and exact. It should also occur to you that octal (base 8) would also be suitable as a shorthand, and indeed several computers have used octal notation in lieu of hex.

The smallest addressable unit of storage is the *byte*. Each byte consists of 9 bits, 8 of which are used to represent data and a ninth bit, known as the parity bit, which is used for internal checking of data. The parity bit is of no concern to the programmer and is not discussed further.

Internal Data Representation

Three internal formats are of use to the COBOL programmer: EBCDIC, packed, and binary. Data represented according to EBCDIC (Extended Binary Coded Decimal Interchange Code) use specific byte combinations of 0's and 1's to denote different characters. Since a byte contains 8 data bits, each of which can assume either a 0 or 1, there are $2^8 = 256$ different combinations for a given byte. Table 12.2 displays the bit combinations for letters, numbers, and some special characters.

Yes, reader, there is a rhyme and reason to Table 12.2, at least where the letters and numbers are concerned. The 8 bits of a byte are divided into a zone and numeric portion as shown:

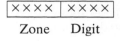

Zone   Digit

The 4 leftmost bits constitute the zone portion; the 4 rightmost bits make up the digit portion. Notice from Table 12.2 that the letters A–I all have the same zone (1100 in binary or C in hex). Note further that the letters J–R and S–Z and the digits 0–9 also have the same zones: D, E, and F, respectively.

Consider the word "COMPUTE" in EBCDIC. Since COMPUTE contains 7 characters, 7 bytes of storage are required. By Table 12.2, COMPUTE would appear internally as shown in Figure 12.1.

Table 12.2 EBCDIC Configuration for Letters, Numbers, and Some Special Characters

Letters Character	EBCDIC Binary	EBCDIC Hex
A	1100 0001	C1
B	1100 0010	C2
C	1100 0011	C3
D	1100 0100	C4
E	1100 0101	C5
F	1100 0110	C6
G	1100 0111	C7
H	1100 1000	C8
I	1100 1001	C9
J	1101 0001	D1
K	1101 0010	D2
L	1101 0011	D3
M	1101 0100	D4
N	1101 0101	D5
O	1101 0110	D6
P	1101 0111	D7
Q	1101 1000	D8
R	1101 1001	D9
S	1110 0010	E2
T	1110 0011	E3
U	1110 0100	E4
V	1110 0101	E5
W	1110 0110	E6
X	1110 0111	E7
Y	1110 1000	E8
Z	1110 1001	E9

Numbers Character	EBCDIC Binary	EBCDIC Hex
0	1111 0000	F0
1	1111 0001	F1
2	1111 0010	F2
3	1111 0011	F3
4	1111 0100	F4
5	1111 0101	F5
6	1111 0110	F6
7	1111 0111	F7
8	1111 1000	F8
9	1111 1001	F9

Special Characters Character	EBCDIC Binary	EBCDIC Hex
Blank	0100 0000	40
.	0100 1011	4B
(	0100 1101	4D
+	0100 1110	4E
$	0101 1011	5B
*	0101 1100	5C
)	0101 1101	5D
–	0110 0000	60
/	0110 0001	61
,	0110 1011	6B
'	0111 1101	7D
=	0111 1110	7E

(Binary)	11000011	11010110	11010100	11010111	11100100	11100011	11000101
(Hex)	C3	D6	D4	D7	E4	E3	C5

Figure 12.1 EBCDIC Representation of COMPUTE

Now suppose we wanted to represent the number "12345" in EBCDIC. This time, 5 bytes are required, and, again by Table 12.2, we get Figure 12.2.

(Binary)	11110001	11110010	11110011	11110100	11110101
(Hex)	F1	F2	F3	F4	F5

Figure 12.2 EBCDIC Representation of 12345

The "zone" portion of each byte is the same in Figure 12.2, and doesn't it seem inherently wasteful to use half of each byte for the zone when, in a numeric field, that zone is always 1111?

Packed Numbers

The packed format is used to represent numeric data more concisely. Essentially it stores two numeric digits in 1 byte by eliminating the zone. This is done throughout except in the rightmost byte, which contains a numeric digit in the zone portion and the sign of the entire number in the digit portion. A "C" or "F" denotes a positive number, and a "D" represents a negative number. Figure 12.3 shows both positive and negative packed representations of the numbers 12345 and 67. Only 3 bytes are required to represent the number 12345 in packed format compared to 5 bytes in EBCDIC in Figure 12.2. Note, however, that the packed representation of numbers with an even number of digits, e.g., 67, always contains an extra half byte of zeros.

Both the EBCDIC and packed formats are said to represent variable-length fields in that the number of bytes required depends on the data that are stored. "COMPUTE" requires 7 bytes for EBCDIC representation and "IBM" only 3 bytes. "12345" take 3 bytes in packed format but "67" only 2 bytes.

Positive configuration (12345)

00010010	00110100	01011100	(Binary)
12	34	5C	(Hex)

Negative configuration (12345)

00010010	00110100	01011101	(Binary)
12	34	5D	(Hex)

Positive configuration (67)

00000110	01111100	(Binary)
06	7C	(Hex)

Negative configuration (67)

00000110	01111101	(Binary)
06	7D	(Hex)

Figure 12.3 Packed Representation

Binary Numbers

Numeric data can also be stored in fixed-length units as binary numbers. Two bytes (half-word), 4 bytes (word), or 8 bytes (double-word) are used depending on the size of a decimal number according to the rule

Up to 4 decimal digits	2 bytes
5–9 decimal digits	4 bytes
10–18 decimal digits	8 bytes

Some explanation is in order. Consider a half-word (16 bits). The largest positive number which can be represented is a 0 and fifteen 1's (the high-order zero indicates a plus sign), which equals $2^{15} - 1$ or 32,767. Any four-digit decimal number will fit in a half-word since the largest four-digit decimal number is only 9999. However, not all five-digit numbers will fit and hence the limitation to four digits in a half-word.

The largest binary number which can be stored in a full word is $2^{31} - 1$, or 2,147,483,647 in decimal, and hence the limit of 9 decimal digits in a full-word. In similar fashion, a limit of 18 decimal digits is obtained for a double-word.

The sign of a binary number is indicated by its leftmost (high-order) bit. This is true regardless of whether the number occupies a half-word, word, or double-word. A "0" in the sign bit indicates a positive number; a "1" means the number is negative and stored in two's complement notation.

The two's complement of a number is obtained in two steps:

1. Reverse all bits; i.e., wherever there is a 0, make it 1, and wherever a 1 occurs, make it 0.

2. Add 1 to your answer from step 1.

For example, suppose we want the two's complement of 00101011:

Step 1: Reverse all bits   11010100
Step 2: Add 1 to answer from step 1   +   1
                                         _____
                                           11010101

Thus, the two's complement of 00101011 is 11010101. As a check on the answer, simply add the original number and its calculated complement. The result should be all 0's and a high-order carry of 1:

Check: 00101011
                                    +11010101
            High-order carry → 1/00000000

Now that we can determine the sign of a number in storage and calculate its two's complement if necessary, consider the following half-words in storage:

(a)   Sign
    ┌─────────────┬──────────┐
    │ 0 │ 0000000 │ 00110001 │
    └─────────────┴──────────┘

(b)   Sign
    ┌─────────────┬──────────┐
    │ 1 │ 1111111 │ 11001111 │
    └─────────────┴──────────┘

In the example (a), the number is positive, as indicated by the high-order bit. Accordingly, its decimal value is simply +49. Example (b), however, has a sign bit of 1, indicating a negative number and further that the number itself is stored in two's complement. To get its decimal value, we must first get the two's complement of the number and then put a minus sign in front of our answer. You should get −49.

The COBOL USAGE Clause and Data Formats

We have stated that the COBOL programmer is typically concerned with three types of data format: EBCDIC, packed, and binary. The COBOL USAGE clause allows the programmer to explicitly specify how data are to be stored internally. (Omission of the clause causes default to EBCDIC, which often results in inefficient object code, as explained in Chapter 14.) Consider the following COBOL entries:

```
77  FIELD-A              PICTURE IS S9(3)
                 USAGE IS DISPLAY            VALUE IS +1.

77  FIELD-B              PICTURE IS S9(3)
                 USAGE IS COMPUTATIONAL-3    VALUE IS +1.

77  FIELD-C              PICTURE IS S9(3)
                 USAGE IS COMPUTATIONAL      VALUE IS +1.
```

In each instance we define a numeric constant of +1; however, each entry has a different usage specified, and hence the fields will have very different internal formats. In particular USAGE IS DISPLAY indicates storage in zoned decimal (EBCDIC) format, COMPUTATIONAL-3 indicates packed format, and COMPUTATIONAL indicates binary format.

FIELD-A occupies 3 bytes of storage and stores the constant +1 in zoned decimal format, with high-order zeros. The internal representation of FIELD-A (shown in hex) is as follows:

F0	F0	C1

FIELD-B occupies 2 bytes of storage and stores the constant +1 in packed format, again with high-order zeros. Internal representation of FIELD-B (shown in hex) is as follows:

00	1C

FIELD-C is stored as a binary number with the number of bytes determined as per previous discussion. Thus, FIELD-C will occupy 2 bytes of storage as follows:

in binary:

00000000	00000001

in hex:

00	01

Base/Displacement Addressing

Since the byte is the smallest addressable unit of storage, every byte in main storage is assigned an address. System 360/370 is designed to reach a maximum address of 16,776,216, the equivalent of a 24-bit binary number. This implies that an instruction referencing two addresses in storage would require 6 bytes (48 bits) for the addresses alone, and clearly this is far too costly in terms of storage requirements. The solution is known as base/displacement addressing.

The addressing scheme uses the CPU's general-purpose registers (GPR's) to reduce storage requirements. A GPR is a hardware device capable of holding information during processing. Information is transferred to or from a register much faster than from main storage. There are 16 GPR's numbered from hex 0 to F. Each GPR contains 32 bits.

In the base/displacement method, memory is divided into units of 4096 (2^{12}) bytes. A 24-bit base address is loaded into a register, which is then designated as a base register. A 12-bit displacement is calculated for each location. (The displacement of a location is defined as the number of bytes higher, i.e., greater than the base address.) The address of a particular location is determined by specifying a base register and displacement from that base. Since it takes only 4 bits to designate a base register (0–F) and 12 bits for a displacement, we are effectively providing a 24-bit address in only 16 bits.

Consider the following example: GPR 7 has been designated as the base register. A program is to be stored beginning at core location $(8000)_{16}$, which is loaded into the 24 low-order bits of register 7 as the base address. It is required to reference core location $(8500)_{16}$. Given a base address of $(8000)_{16}$, the displacement for location $(8500)_{16}$ is calculated to be $(500)_{16}$. Now we have the 16 bits to specify the address of core location $(8500)_{16}$, as shown in Figure 12.4. Four bits are used to designate GPR 7, and 12 bits are used for the hex displacement 500.

There is another major advantage to the base/displacement method in addition to economy of space. All programs are easily relocatable; i.e., all addresses in a given program are easily changed by altering only the contents of the base register(s).

Assumptions:
1. GPR 7 is the base register.
2. $(8000)_{16}$ is the base address, which is loaded into register 7.
3. $(500)_{16}$ is the calculated displacement.

	Base	Displacement		
(Binary)	0111	0101	0000	0000
(Hex)	7	5	0	0

Figure 12.4 Base/Displacement Representation of Address $(8500)_{16}$

System 360/370 has different, but parallel, instructions for different data types. The instruction to add two packed numbers is different from the instruction to add two binary numbers; indeed the instruction to add binary half-words is different from that for binary full-words. The instruction set is designed in such a way that the instruction's length and format are dependent on the type and location of data on which it is to operate: Specifically, there are five types of instructions:

Instruction Formats

RR—Register to register (2 bytes long)
RX—Register to indexed storage (4 bytes long)
RS—Register to storage (4 bytes long)
SI—Storage immediate (4 bytes long)
SS—Storage to storage (6 bytes long)

Any of these instruction types provide the following information to the computer:

1. The operation to be performed, e.g., addition, subtraction, etc.;
2. The location of the operands, e.g., in registers, storage, or immediate (i.e., in the instruction), and
3. The nature of the data, i.e., fixed or variable in length, and if the latter, then the length of the data field(s).

Machine instruction formats are displayed in Figure 12.5. Although Figure 12.5 may not make much sense now, it will assume greater importance in Chapters 13 and 14 when *dump reading* and efficiency considerations are studied. An explanation of the notation of Figure 12.5 is helpful:

OP—Operation code
B—Base register
D—Displacement
X—Register designated as an index register (RX only)
R—Register designated as an operand
I—Immediate data; i.e., the operand is contained in the instruction itself (SI only)
L—Length used only for variable-length operands in SS format

In later chapters, it will become necessary to disect a machine instruction into its component parts. Consider the instruction D205A0103050.

Using Figure 12.5, we must somehow decipher this cryptic combination of characters. The key is the first byte of the instruction, which contains the op code, D2. Armed with this essential piece of information, we go to Appendix D, 360/370 Assembler Instructions, and find that D2 is the machine op code

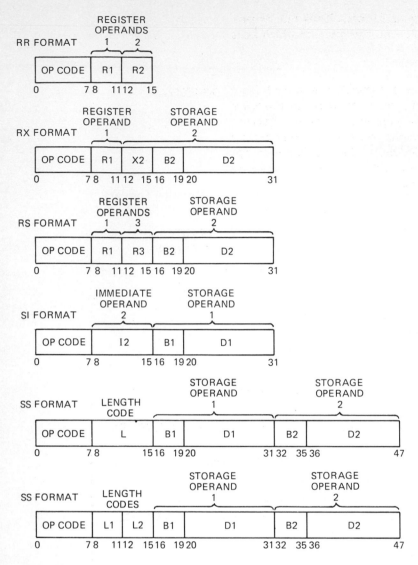

Figure 12.5 Instruction Formats

for MVC (move characters), an SS instruction. We are therefore able to separate the essential components of the instruction according to Figure 12.5:

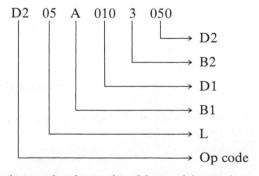

Essentially the instruction is moving 6 bytes (always 1 more than the length code) beginning at the address specified in the second operand to the address specified in the first operand. Both addresses are derived according to the base/displacement scheme.

The workings of several instructions are explained in the first part of Chapter 14. Appreciation for the different instruction formats comes from the realization that data are stored internally in varying formats. Thus the instruction to add two binary numbers is necessarily different from the one which adds two packed numbers.

Much of the material in this chapter may seem somewhat removed from COBOL. However, the groundwork developed here is essential to a deeper understanding of COBOL, especially since the computer does not execute COBOL instructions as such but rather the machine instructions generated by the COBOL compiler. It is imperative that the reader be familiar with the material on number systems, base/displacement addressing, and instruction formats before proceeding to Chapters 13 and 14.

Summary

REVIEW EXERCISES

TRUE	FALSE		
☐	☐	1	Every instruction must contain an op code.
☐	☐	2	Mathematically, there are 256 possible op codes.
☐	☐	3	The op code is the second byte in the instruction.
☐	☐	4	Instructions are 2, 4, 6, or 8 bytes in length.
☐	☐	5	Instructions are a half-word, word, or double-word in length.
☐	☐	6	There are 16 general-purpose registers in 360/370.
☐	☐	7	If the COBOL USAGE clause is omitted, the default is to COMPUTATIONAL.
☐	☐	8	Mathematically, there are 256 possible EBCDIC characters.
☐	☐	9	The EBCDIC character for the letter A is D1.
☐	☐	10	The displacement takes 12 bits in an instruction.
☐	☐	11	The base/displacement scheme provides for an effective address of 24 bits.
☐	☐	12	123 is a valid number in base 16.
☐	☐	13	123 is a valid number in base 3.
☐	☐	14	There are five different instruction types.
☐	☐	15	USAGE IS COMP-3 corresponds to the packed format.
☐	☐	16	Binary data are stored internally in 2, 4, or 6 bytes.
☐	☐	17	There are two formats for the SS instruction.
☐	☐	18	The high-order bit of a binary number denotes its sign.
☐	☐	19	The high-order 4 bits of a packed field denote its sign.
☐	☐	20	For packed numbers, either C or F indicates a plus sign.
☐	☐	21	For packed numbers, D indicates a minus sign.
☐	☐	22	A three-digit decimal number requires 2 bytes if USAGE is specified as COMPUTATIONAL or COMPUTATIONAL-3.
☐	☐	23	A five-digit decimal number requires 4 bytes if USAGE is specified as COMPUTATIONAL or COMPUTATIONAL-3.
☐	☐	24	The two's complement of a number is obtained just by switching 0's and 1's.

PROBLEMS

1 Indicate the instruction type which
(a) Has an operand contained in the instruction itself.
(b) Uses two registers to calculate a storage address.
(c) References two storage locations.

(d) Is 6 bytes long.
(e) Does not reference a storage location.
(f) Is 2 bytes long.
(g) Contains one length code.
(h) Contains two length codes.

2   Show internal representation for the following entries:

05	FIELD-A	PIC 9(5)	COMP	VALUE	67.
05	FIELD-B	PIC 9(5)	COMP-3	VALUE	67.
05	FIELD-C	PIC 9(5)	DISPLAY	VALUE	67.
05	FIELD-D	PIC 9(5)		VALUE	67.

3   What is the EBCDIC representation for "COBOL"? (Show both hex and binary configurations.)

4   What is wrong with the following entries?

05	FIELD-A	PIC 9(3)	COMP	VALUE '12'.
05	FIELD-C	PIC X(3)		VALUE 12.

5   (a) $(1001101)_2$
       $+(0111111)_2$
       _____
            ?

   (b) $(1001101)_2$
       $-(0111111)_2$
       _____
            ?

Check your answers to parts (a) and (b) by converting to decimal, performing the indicated operation, and converting the decimal answer back to binary.

6   (a) $(ABCD)_{16}$
       $+(1234)_{16}$
       _____
            ?

   (b) $(ABCD)_{16}$
       $-(1234)_{16}$
       _____
            ?

Check your answers as in Problem 5.

7   (a) $(1010110)_2 = (?)_{10} = (?)_{16}$.
   (b) $(?)_2 = (49)_{10} = (?)_{16}$.
   (c) $(?)_2 = (?)_{10} = (49)_{16}$.

8   Although we have studied only bases 2, 10, and 16, the concepts are applicable to any base. Accordingly, you should be able to do the following:
   (a) $(432)_5 = (?)_{10}$.
   (b) $(100)_{10} = (?)_6$.
   (c) $(2222)_3 = (?)_7$.
   (d) $(1100110)_2 = (?)_4 = (?)_8 = (?)_{16}$.
   (e) $(1234)_9$
       $+(5678)_9$
       _____
            ?

9   What is the decimal value of the following half-words in storage?
   (a) 11111111   11111111
   (b) 01111111   11111111
   (c) 10000000   00000000

10 Assume the contents of base register 3 are $(00001234)_{16}$ and the contents of base register 10 are $(00005678)_{16}$. Given the instruction D2023123A500:
   1. What is the effective address of the second operand?
   2. What is the effective address of the first operand?
   3. What is the nature of the instruction?

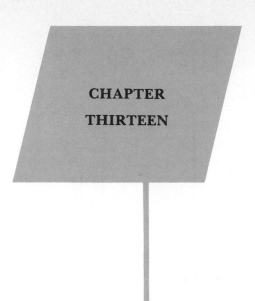

**CHAPTER
THIRTEEN**

Debugging, II

Should the COBOL applications programmer have a knowledge of Assembler **Overview**
language? We answer with an emphatic yes, but there are those who would
disagree. Although one can invariably find someone to debug a program,
self-sufficiency and complete understanding demand at least some knowledge
of Assembler and machine architecture.

As you have undoubtedly learned by now, there are many ways for your
program not to work. Errors can be broadly separated into those which occur
in compilation and those occurring during execution. The latter are further
divided into two classes:

1. Errors which do not prevent execution of the entire job but which produce
   calculated results different from what the programmer expected, and
2. Errors which result in the machine's inability to execute a particular
   instruction, thus causing an abnormal end (ABEND) of the job.

Chapter 5 dealt with compilation errors and execution errors of the first
kind. This chapter is devoted to debugging the second type of execution error
with emphasis placed on the *data exception*. We shall focus on two errors
commonly made by beginning programmers: (1) failure to initialize a 77-level
entry and (2) invalid input data.

When a program ABENDs, it is because the computer was instructed to do something it found impossible to perform. At that point, the COBOL program relinquishes control to the supervisor, which then prints a rather cryptic message indicating the reason for the ABEND. Unfortunately, that message is rarely enough to indicate the exact cause or location of the problem. One's primary recourse is to the core dump and related information. This type of debugging relies heavily on the concepts of number systems, base/displacement addressing, and instruction formats developed in Chapter 12. OS listings are used for all illustrations in this chapter, but the differences between OS and DOS are not great at the level of our discussion. The principal difference relates to finding the entry point of the main program, and this is discussed at the chapter's end.

The Core Dump

Figure 13.1 illustrates a dump. The contents of internal storage are strictly binary but are displayed in hex for conciseness. A dump appears somewhat foreboding to the uninitiated, but as with everything else, a little practice goes a long way. The essential thing to remember in analyzing Figure 13.1 is that a dump is merely a picture of memory contents at a given instant of time. The leftmost column of the dump indicates the internal location number. Subsequent digits are the contents of that location and others. Since the smallest addressable location is the byte (8 bits or 2 hex digits), every 2 hex digits indicate the contents of a particular byte.

Go down the first column in Figure 13.1 until you read 26CB20. The 2 hex digits immediately following are F5, indicating that the contents of byte 26CB20 are F5. The next 2 hex digits, F4, are the contents of the next sequential location, 26CB21. In similar fashion, F3 is the contents of 26CB22, F2 is the contents of 26CB23, etc. There are a total of 64 hex digits on the line beginning with 26CB20. Accordingly, the contents of 32 bytes beginning at 26CB20 and continuing to 26CB3F are shown on the same line. The first 2 hex digits on the next line will be the contents of location 26CB40.

Immediately following the 64 hex digits on a given line is the corresponding EBCDIC interpretation of those digits. According to the EBCDIC configurations of Table 12.2, F5 is the representation for 5, F4 for 4, and so forth. Many of the interpretation columns are blank because the contents of the corresponding locations are hex 40's, which is the internal representation of a blank.

Dump Reading: Example 1 (Failure to Initialize a 77-Level Entry)

Figure 13.2 is a close duplicate (only line 63 was altered) of the COBOL listing for the tuition billing example introduced in Chapter 4 and debugged in Chapter 5. Execution terminated after printing only the heading line and the message "COMPLETION CODE SYSTEM = 0C7," followed by pages of semiintelligible data culminating in a dump. Where do we go from here?

First look up the meaning of an "0C7" error in the IBM manual *IBM System/360 Operating System: Messages and Codes* and find that 0C7 is a data exception, indicating that an attempt was made to do arithmetic on invalid, i.e., nondecimal, data. Next, we turn to various aids supplied for these situations and try to determine the exact nature of the data exception. In particular, consider the data division map (Figure 13.3), register assignments (Figure 13.4), and procedure division map (Figure 13.5).

Figure 13.3 is a truncated data division map for Figure 13.2. A data division map lists all the data names in a given program and ties them to internal addresses by specifying a base locator (later tied to a base register) and a displacement. All data names within one file are assigned the same base locator. Thus, BL = 1 for all entries in CARD-FILE and BL = 2 for PRINT-FILE. All entries in working-storage are assigned BL = 3.

Figure 13.1 Illustrative Core Dump

```
00001          IDENTIFICATION DIVISION.
00002          PROGRAM-ID.  'TUITION'.
00003          AUTHOR.      THE BURSAR.
00004
00005
00006          ENVIRONMENT DIVISION.
00007
00008          CONFIGURATION SECTION.
00009          SOURCE-COMPUTER.  IBM-370.
00010          OBJECT-COMPUTER.  IBM-370.
00011          SPECIAL-NAMES.
00012              C01 IS TOP-OF-PAGE.
00013
00014          INPUT-OUTPUT SECTION.
00015          FILE-CONTROL.
00016              SELECT CARD-FILE ASSIGN TO UR-2540R-S-SYSIN.
00017              SELECT PRINT-FILE ASSIGN TO UR-1403-S-PRINT.
00018
00019
00020          DATA DIVISION.
00021          FILE SECTION.
00022          FD   CARD-FILE
00023              RECORDING MODE IS F
00024              LABEL RECORDS ARE OMITTED
00025              RECORD CONTAINS 80 CHARACTERS
00026              DATA RECORD IS STUDENT-CARD.
00027          01   STUDENT-CARD.
00028              05   STUDENT-NAME    PICTURE IS A(20).
00029              05   SOC-SEC-NO      PICTURE IS 9(9).
00030              05   CREDITS         PICTURE IS 9(2).
00031              05   UNION-MEMBER    PICTURE IS A.
00032              05   SCHOLARSHIP     PICTURE IS 9(4).
00033              05   FILLER          PICTURE IS X(44).
00034          FD   PRINT-FILE
00035              RECORDING MODE IS F
00036              LABEL RECORDS ARE OMITTED
00037              RECORD CONTAINS 133 CHARACTERS
00038              DATA RECORD IS PRINT-LINE.
00039          01   PRINT-LINE.
00040              05   FILLER                   PICTURE IS X.
00041              05   PRINT-STUDENT-NAME       PICTURE IS A(20).
00042              05   FILLER                   PICTURE IS X(2).
00043              05   PRINT-SOC-SEC-NO         PICTURE IS 999B99B9999.
00044              05   FILLER                   PICTURE IS X(4).
00045              05   PRINT-CREDITS            PICTURE IS 99.
00046              05   FILLER                   PICTURE IS X(3).
00047              05   PRINT-TUITION            PICTURE IS  $$$$,$$9.
00048              05   FILLER                   PICTURE IS X(1).
00049              05   PRINT-UNION-FEE          PICTURE IS  $$$$,$$9.
00050              05   FILLER                   PICTURE IS X(3).
00051              05   PRINT-ACTIVITY-FEE       PICTURE IS  $$$$,$$9.
00052              05   FILLER                   PICTURE IS X(3).
00053              05   PRINT-SCHOLARSHIP        PICTURE IS  $$$$,$$9.
00054              05   FILLER                   PICTURE IS X(5).
00055              05   PRINT-IND-BILL           PICTURE IS  $$$$,$$9.
00056              05   FILLER                   PICTURE IS X(38).
00057
00058          WORKING-STORAGE SECTION.
00059          77   TUITION            PICTURE IS 9(4)  VALUE IS ZEROS.
00060          77   ACTIVITY-FEE       PICTURE IS 9(2)  VALUE IS ZEROS.
00061          77   UNION-FEE          PICTURE IS 9(2)  VALUE IS ZEROS.
00062          77   INDIVIDUAL-BILL    PICTURE IS 9(4)  VALUE IS ZEROS.
00063          77   TOTAL-TUITION      PICTURE IS 9(6)
00064          77   TOTAL-SCHOLARSHIP  PICTURE IS 9(6)  VALUE IS ZEROS.
00065          77   TOTAL-ACTIVITY-FEE PICTURE IS 9(6)  VALUE IS ZEROS.
00066          77   TOTAL-UNION-FEE    PICTURE IS 9(6)  VALUE IS ZEROS.
00067          77   TOTAL-IND-BILL     PICTURE IS 9(6)  VALUE IS ZEROS.
00068          01   HEADER-LINE.
00069              05   FILLER         PICTURE IS X.
00070              05   HDG-NAME       PICTURE IS X(12) VALUE IS 'STUDENT NAME'.
00071              05   FILLER         PICTURE IS X(10) VALUE IS SPACES.
00072              05   HDG-SOC-SEC    PICTURE IS X(11) VALUE IS 'SOC SEC NUM'.
00073              05   FILLER         PICTURE IS X(2)  VALUE IS SPACES.
00074              05   HDG-CREDITS    PICTURE IS X(7)  VALUE IS 'CREDITS'.
00075              05   FILLER         PICTURE IS X(2)  VALUE IS SPACES.
00076              05   HDG-TUITION    PICTURE IS X(7)  VALUE IS 'TUITION'.
```

Figure 13.2 COBOL Listing for Tuition Problem

240

```
00077          05  FILLER             PICTURE IS X(2)  VALUE IS SPACES.
00078          05  HDG-UNION-FEE      PICTURE IS X(9)  VALUE IS 'UNION FEE'.
00079          05  FILLER             PICTURE IS X(2)  VALUE IS SPACES.
00080          05  HDG-ACTIVITY       PICTURE IS X(7)  VALUE IS 'ACT FEE'.
00081          05  FILLER             PICTURE IS X(2)  VALUE IS SPACES.
00082          05  HDG-SCHOLAR        PICTURE IS X(11) VALUE IS 'SCHOLARSHIP'.
00083          05  FILLER             PICTURE IS X(2)  VALUE IS SPACES.
00084          05  HDG-TOTAL-BILL     PICTURE IS X(10) VALUE IS 'TOTAL BILL'.
00085          05  FILLER             PICTURE IS X(36) VALUE IS SPACES.
00086
00087
00088      PROCEDURE DIVISION.
00089
00090      HOUSEKEEPING.
00091          OPEN INPUT CARD-FILE, OUTPUT PRINT-FILE.
00092          MOVE HEADER-LINE TO PRINT-LINE.
00093          WRITE PRINT-LINE AFTER ADVANCING TOP-OF-PAGE LINES.
00094          MOVE SPACES TO PRINT-LINE.
00095          MOVE '------------------------------------------------
00096        - '-------------------------------------' TO PRINT-LINE.
00097          WRITE PRINT-LINE AFTER ADVANCING 1 LINES.
00098
00099      READ-A-CARD.
00100          READ CARD-FILE AT END GO TO WRITE-UNIVERSITY-TOTALS.
00101          COMPUTE TUITION = 80 * CREDITS.
00102          IF UNION-MEMBER IS EQUAL TO 'Y' MOVE 25 TO UNION-FEE
00103              ELSE MOVE ZERO TO UNION-FEE.
00104          IF CREDITS IS GREATER THAN 6 GO TO MORE-THAN-6-CREDITS.
00105          MOVE 25 TO ACTIVITY-FEE.
00106          GO TO ADD-TOTAL-BILL.
00107
00108      MORE-THAN-6-CREDITS.
00109          IF CREDITS IS GREATER THAN 12 MOVE 75 TO ACTIVITY-FEE
00110          ELSE MOVE 50 TO ACTIVITY-FEE.
00111
00112      ADD-TOTAL-BILL.
00113          COMPUTE INDIVIDUAL-BILL = TUITION + UNION-FEE + ACTIVITY-FEE
00114              - SCHOLARSHIP.
00115
00116      UPDATE-UNIVERSITY-TOTALS.
00117          ADD TUITION TO TOTAL-TUITION.
00118          ADD UNION-FEE TO TOTAL-UNION-FEE.
00119          ADD ACTIVITY-FEE TO TOTAL-ACTIVITY-FEE.
00120          ADD INDIVIDUAL-BILL TO TOTAL-IND-BILL.
00121          ADD SCHOLARSHIP TO TOTAL-SCHOLARSHIP.
00122
00123      WRITE-DETAIL-LINE.
00124          MOVE SPACES TO PRINT-LINE.
00125          MOVE STUDENT-NAME       TO PRINT-STUDENT-NAME.
00126          MOVE SOC-SEC-NO         TO PRINT-SOC-SEC-NO.
00127          MOVE CREDITS            TO PRINT-CREDITS.
00128          MOVE TUITION            TO PRINT-TUITION.
00129          MOVE UNION-FEE          TO PRINT-UNION-FEE.
00130          MOVE ACTIVITY-FEE       TO PRINT-ACTIVITY-FEE.
00131          MOVE SCHOLARSHIP        TO PRINT-SCHOLARSHIP.
00132          MOVE INDIVIDUAL-BILL    TO PRINT-IND-BILL.
00133          WRITE PRINT-LINE AFTER ADVANCING 1 LINES.
00134          GO TO READ-A-CARD.
00135
00136      WRITE-UNIVERSITY-TOTALS.
00137          MOVE SPACES TO PRINT-LINE.
00138          MOVE '------------------------------------------------
00139        - '-------------------------------------' TO PRINT-LINE.
00140          WRITE PRINT-LINE AFTER ADVANCING 1 LINES.
00141          MOVE SPACES TO PRINT-LINE.
00142          MOVE TOTAL-TUITION      TO PRINT-TUITION.
00143          MOVE TOTAL-UNION-FEE    TO PRINT-UNION-FEE.
00144          MOVE TOTAL-ACTIVITY-FEE TO PRINT-ACTIVITY-FEE.
00145          MOVE TOTAL-SCHOLARSHIP  TO PRINT-SCHOLARSHIP.
00146          MOVE TOTAL-IND-BILL     TO PRINT-IND-BILL.
00147          WRITE PRINT-LINE AFTER ADVANCING 2 LINES.
00148
00149      END-OF-JOB-ROUTINE.
00150          CLOSE CARD-FILE, PRINT-FILE.
00151          STOP RUN.
```

Figure 13.2 (Continued)

```
COBOL                                    Pointer
level #      COBOL data name             to GPR   Displacement
 ↓  ↓↓                         ↓           ↓  ↓     ↓    ↓
LVL  SOURCE NAME                          BASE    DISPL
FD   CARD-FILE                            DCB=01
01   STUDENT-CARD                         BL=1    000
02   STUDENT-NAME                         BL=1    000
02   SOC-SEC-NO                           BL=1    014
02   CREDITS                              BL=1    01D
02   UNION-MEMBER                         BL=1    01F
02   SCHOLARSHIP                          BL=1    020
02   FILLER                               BL=1    024
FD   PRINT-FILE                           DCB=02
01   PRINT-LINE                           BL=2    000
02   FILLER                               BL=2    000
02   PRINT-STUDENT-NAME                   BL=2    001
02   FILLER                               BL=2    015
02   PRINT-SOC-SEC-NO                     BL=2    017
02   FILLER                               BL=2    022
02   PRINT-CREDITS                        BL=2    026
02   FILLER                               BL=2    028
02   PRINT-TUITION                        BL=2    02B
02   FILLER                               BL=2    033
02   PRINT-UNION-FEE                      BL=2    034
02   FILLER                               BL=2    03C
02   PRINT-ACTIVITY-FEE                   BL=2    03F
02   FILLER                               BL=2    047
02   PRINT-SCHOLARSHIP                    BL=2    04A
02   FILLER                               BL=2    052
02   PRINT-IND-BILL                       BL=2    057
02   FILLER                               BL=2    05F
77   TUITION                              BL=3    000
77   ACTIVITY-FEE                         BL=3    004
77   UNION-FEE                            BL=3    006
77   INDIVIDUAL-BILL                      BL=3    008
77   TOTAL-TUITION                        BL=3    00C
77   TOTAL-SCHOLARSHIP                    BL=3    012
77   TOTAL-ACTIVITY-FEE                   BL=3    018
77   TOTAL-UNION-FEE                      BL=3    01E
77   TOTAL-IND-BILL                       BL=3    024
```

Figure 13.3 Truncated Data Division Map for Figure 13.2

The base locators are tied to specific base registers by a table of register assignments shown in Figure 13.4. BL = 1 points to register 7, BL = 2 to register 8, and BL = 3 to register 6.

```
                    REGISTER ASSIGNMENT

                    REG 6    BL =3
                    REG 7    BL =1
                    REG 8    BL =2
```

Figure 13.4 Register Assignment for Figure 13.2

Figure 13.5 is a truncated procedure division map corresponding to Figure 13.2. It contains information about the actual machine language statements generated by the compiler. Reading from left to right in Figure 13.5, the four columns denote

1. The computer-generated COBOL statement number,

2. The COBOL verb referenced in the statement number,

3. The relative location, in hex, of the machine instruction, and

4. The actual machine instruction.

COBOL card #	COBOL verb	Relative location	Machine instruction					
113	COMPUTE	0007EA	F2	71	D	200	6	006
		0007F0	F2	73	D	208	6	000
		0007F6	FA	22	D	205	D	20D
		0007FC	F2	71	D	208	6	004
		000802	FA	22	D	20D	D	205
		000808	F2	73	D	200	7	020
		00080E	FB	22	D	20D	D	205
		000814	F3	32	6	008	D	20D
		00081A	96	F0	6	00B		
116	*UPDATE-UNIVERSITY-TOTALS							
117	ADD	00081E	F2	73	D	208	6	000
		000824	F2	75	D	200	6	00C
		00082A	FA	33	D	20C	D	204
		000830	F3	53	6	00C	D	20C
		000836	96	F0	6	011		
118	ADD	00083A	F2	71	D	208	6	006
		000840	F2	75	D	200	6	01E
		000846	FA	33	D	20C	D	204
		00084C	F3	53	6	01E	D	20C
		000852	96	F0	6	023		
119	ADD	000856	F2	71	D	208	6	004
		00085C	F2	75	D	200	6	018
		000862	FA	33	D	20C	D	204
		000868	F3	53	6	018	D	20C
		00086E	96	F0	6	01D		
120	ADD	000872	F2	73	D	208	6	008
		000878	F2	75	D	200	6	024
		00087E	FA	33	D	20C	D	204
		000884	F3	53	6	024	D	20C
		00088A	96	F0	6	029		
121	ADD	00088E	F2	73	D	208	7	020
		000894	F2	75	D	200	6	012
		00089A	FA	33	D	20C	D	204
		0008A0	F3	53	6	012	D	20C
		0008A6	96	F0	6	017		
123	*WRITE-DETAIL-LINE							
124	MOVE	0008AA	92	40	8	000		
		0008AE	D2	83	8	001	8	000
125	MOVE	0008B4	D2	13	8	001	7	000
126	MOVE	0008BA	F2	78	D	208	7	014
		0008C0	D2	0B	D	210	C	06B
		0008C6	DE	0B	D	210	D	20B
		0008CC	D2	0A	8	017	D	211

Figure 13.5 Truncated Procedure Division Map for Figure 13.2

Recall that the "instruction explosion" effect causes a single COBOL instruction to generate several machine language statements; e.g., COBOL statement 113 (COMPUTE) spawned nine machine language statements; statement 117 (ADD), five statements; etc.

A large amount of data is supplied in conjunction with a dump. The utility of this information varies with the experience of the individual, but certain portions are of immediate use. We have extracted some of the more essential information and grouped it into Figure 13.6, which contains (1) the cause of the ABEND, (2) the contents of the program status word (PSW) at ABEND, (3) the entry point address (EPA) of the COBOL program, and (4) the contents of the registers at ABEND.

We shall now begin the analysis of a dump. The last 3 bytes (6 hex digits) of the PSW provide the location of the interrupt. Subtraction of the entry point address (EPA) of the COBOL program, from the 3 bytes in the PSW, yields the relative address, i.e., the location within the COBOL program of the error. Thus, using Figure 13.6,

Address from PSW	24DEB0
−Entry point of COBOL program	−24D680
Relative address	830

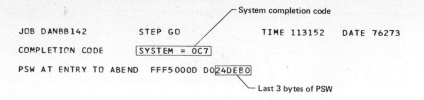

System completion code

Last 3 bytes of PSW

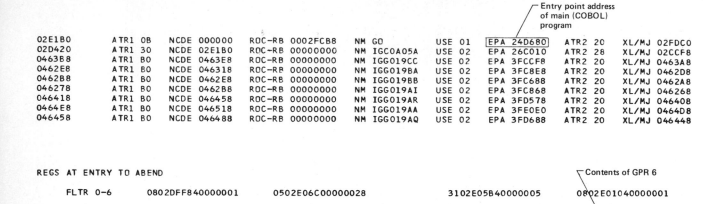

Entry point address of main (COBOL) program

02E1B0	ATR1 0B	NCDE 000000	ROC-RB 0002FCB8	NM GO	USE 01	EPA 24D680	ATR2 20	XL/MJ 02FDC0
02D420	ATR1 30	NCDE 02E1B0	ROC-RB 00000000	NM IGC0A05A	USE 02	EPA 26C010	ATR2 28	XL/MJ 02CCF8
0463B8	ATR1 B0	NCDE 0463E8	ROC-RB 00000000	NM IGG019CC	USE 02	EPA 3FCCF8	ATR2 20	XL/MJ 0463A8
0462E8	ATR1 B0	NCDE 046318	ROC-RB 00000000	NM IGG019BA	USE 02	EPA 3FC8E8	ATR2 20	XL/MJ 0462D8
0462B8	ATR1 B0	NCDE 0462E8	ROC-RB 00000000	NM IGG019BB	USE 02	EPA 3FC688	ATR2 20	XL/MJ 0462A8
046278	ATR1 B0	NCDE 0462B8	ROC-RB 00000000	NM IGG019AI	USE 02	EPA 3FC868	ATR2 20	XL/MJ 046268
046418	ATR1 B0	NCDE 046458	ROC-RB 00000000	NM IGG019AR	USE 02	EPA 3FD578	ATR2 20	XL/MJ 046408
0464E8	ATR1 B0	NCDE 046518	ROC-RB 00000000	NM IGG019AA	USE 02	EPA 3FE0E0	ATR2 20	XL/MJ 0464D8
046458	ATR1 B0	NCDE 046488	ROC-RB 00000000	NM IGG019AQ	USE 02	EPA 3FD688	ATR2 20	XL/MJ 046448

REGS AT ENTRY TO ABEND

Contents of GPR 6

```
    FLTR 0-6    0802DFF840000001    0502E06C00000028    3102E05B40000005    0802E01040000001

    REGS 0-7    00000001  0024DE6A  0024DE1C  5C02BA48    0024D878  0024DDF0  0024D708  0026CB58
    REGS 8-15   0024D930  0024E234  0024D680  0024D680    0024DC20  0024D9B8  4024DDDC  0024DE64
```

Contents of GPR 13

Figure 13.6 Information Associated with Core Dump

All addresses in a dump are specified in hexadecimal; thus the subtraction is also in hex. Now take the relative address (830) to the procedure division map and find that 830 occurs within COBOL statement 117, indicating that program execution terminated within this COBOL statement. The instruction at 830 is the next instruction that would have been executed had the ABEND not occurred; the instruction which caused the problem is the one immediately before at 82A. However, both machine instructions are contained within the COBOL ADD instruction of line 117.

To determine the exact cause of the error, we examine the machine language instruction at 82A which failed to execute. It has an op code of FA, and from the material on instruction formats in Chapter 12, we dissect the instruction as follows:

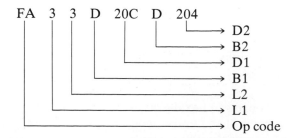

From Appendix D, we learn that FA is the op code for *add packed*. The instruction at 82A will add the contents of the second operand to the contents of the first operand and store the results in the first operand. The addresses of both operands are calculated in accordance with the base-displacement addressing scheme discussed in Chapter 12.

We see that both operands use general register D (i.e., GPR 13) as a base register. The first operand has a displacement of 20C and the second a displacement of 204. From Figure 13.6 the contents of register 13 is found to be 24D9B8. Simple addition (in hex) locates both operands:

$$
\begin{array}{ll}
\text{Contents of register 13} & = 24D9B8 \\
+\text{1st displacement} & = +\quad 20C \\
\hline
\text{Location of 1st operand} & = 24DBC4
\end{array}
$$

$$
\begin{array}{ll}
\text{Contents of register 13} & = 24D9B8 \\
+\text{2nd displacement} & = +\quad 204 \\
\hline
\text{Location of 2nd operand} & = 24DBBC
\end{array}
$$

The first operand begins at location 24DBC4. Its length code in the add packed instruction is 3, so that the first operand extends 3 bytes past 24DBC4; i.e., the first operand is in locations 24DBC4 through 24DBC7. (Remember, the actual number of bytes is always one more than the corresponding length code.) In similar fashion, the second operand is located in 24DBBC through 24DBBF.

The dump of Figure 13.7 is used to get the actual operands. The first, located in 24DBC4 through 24DBC7, has a value of 0001200F, a valid packed number. The second operand, located in 24DBBC through 24DBBF, is equal to 0700E832, an invalid packed field—hence the data exception and dump.

In effect, we have determined the precise cause of the ABEND, i.e., invalid data in the second operand, but it seems somewhat removed from the COBOL program. Let us examine the entire sequence of machine instructions generated for COBOL statement 117 and try to get a more satisfying explanation.

COBOL statement 117 and its associated machine language instructions through 830 (see Figure 13.5) are shown below:

ADD TUITION TO TOTAL-TUITION.

Location	Instruction
81E	F2 73 D 208 6 000
824	F2 75 D 200 6 00C
82A	FA 33 D 20C D 204
830	F3 53 6 00C D 20C

Data division entries for TUITION and TOTAL-TUITION are provided in COBOL statements 59 and 63 of Figure 13.2:

77 TUITION   PICTURE IS 9(4)   VALUE IS ZEROS.
77 TOTAL-TUITION PICTURE IS 9(6).

Consider the machine instructions generated for the COBOL statement. The programmer specifies that TUITION is to be added to TOTAL-TUITION. Since the data division entries for these data names do not specify a USAGE clause, both are taken as display. The compiler must, therefore, convert the incoming DISPLAY data to packed format prior to addition. Referring to Figure 12.5, instruction formats, we can break the first machine instruction into its component parts as shown:

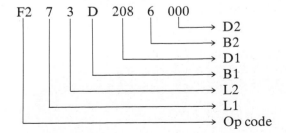

```
24D680   90ECD00C 185D05F0 4580F010 E3E4C9E3   C9D6D540 C1D5E2F4 0700989F F02407FF   *.....).0..0.TUITION ANS4....0...*
24D6A0   96021034 07FE41F0 000107FE 0024E234   0024D680 0024D680 0024DC20 0024D9B8   *.......0......S...0...0.......R.*
24D6C0   0024DD0A 0024E1F4 417701A4 50709148   4110D114 41000004 58F0C460 05EFD203   *.......4....&......J......0D-..K.*
24D6E0   9148D188 58E0C724 07FE45E0 F0385860   9023D350 1B334030 D34C4331 00001233   *..J...G.....0..-..L&.. .L<......*
24D700   4770F018 00000000 F1F2F0F0 F7F5F2F5   F1F3F0F0 4770F02E 9823F0F0 F0F0F0F0   *..0.....120075251300..0...000000*
24D720   F0F0F0F0 F0F0F0F0 F0F0F0F0 F0F0F0F0   F0F01923 47B0F04C 40E2E3E4 C4C5D5E3   *00000000000000000000....0< STUDENT*
24D740   40D5C1D4 C5404040 40404040 404040E2   D6C340E2 C5C340D5 E4D44040 C3D9C5C4   * NAME               SOC SEC NUM   CRED*
24D760   C9E3E240 40E3E4C9 E3C9D6D5 4040E4D5   C9D6D540 C6C5C540 40C1C3E3 40C6C5C5   *ITS  TUITION  UNION FEE  ACT FEE*
24D780   4040E2C3 C8D6D3C1 D9E2C8C9 D74040E3   D6E3C1D3 40C2C9D3 D3404040 40404040   *  SCHOLARSHIP  TOTAL BILL      *
24D7A0   40404040 40404040 40404040 40404040   40404040 40404040 40404040 40F0C454   *                             0D.*
24D7C0   45E0F034 00000000 00000000 00000000   00000000 0524F23A 0024D6A6 00000001   *..0..................2...0.....*
24D7E0   00000001 00000000 00000000 00000000   00000000 00000000 80000000 00000000   *................................*
24D800   00000000 00000000 00000002 00818300   0226CB00 00004000 00000001 4624DDEA   *..........................  ......*
24D820   8024D7C4 00CC4800 0002A60C 123FE0E0   003FD688 06000001 00090050 28012828   *..PD............0.........&....*
24D840   0026C9B8 0026CBA8 0026CB58 00000050   00C00001 00000000 003FCCF8 00000000   *..I............&...........8....*
24D860   00000000 00000000 00000000 00000000   00000000 00800000 00000000 00000000   *................................*
24D880   00000000 00000000 0524F23A 0024D6A6   00000001 00000001 00000000 00000000   *.........2...0..................*
24D8A0   00000000 00000000 00000000 80000000   00000000 00000000 00000000 00000001   *................................*
24D8C0   00818300 0226C9E8 00004000 00000001   46000001 8424D878 00B80048 00029AAC   *......IY.. ............Q........*
24D8E0   923FC868 003FD578 06000001 00090085   28012828 0026C958 0026CAFD 0026CAFD   *..H...N................I........*
24D900   00000085 00000001 00000000 003FCCF8   05EF0700 00000000 00000000 00000000   *..............8.................*
24D920   00000000 00000000 00840054 45E0F034   60606060 60606060 60606060 60606060   *..............0.----------------*
24D940   60606060 60606060 60606060 60606060   60606060 60606060 60606060 60606060   *--------------------------------*
      LINE 24D960 SAME AS ABOVE
24D980   60606060 60606060 60606060 60606060   60404040 40404040 40404040 40404040   *----------------                *
24D9A0   40404040 40404040 40404040 40404040   40404040 404E04C3 0030C4C2 0026CF68   *                      +DC..DB....*
24D9C0   0026CBB0 5024E23A 0024E4FA 4024DDDC   123FE0E0 00000038 0024D7FC 0024D7FC   *....&.S...U. ............P...P.*
24D9E0   5C02BA48 0024D878 5024E266 0024D708   0024D680 0024D930 403FE118 003FD688   **.....Q.&.S...P...0...R. .....0.*
24DA00   3022804B 00000000 00000000 0024DD0A   00000000 00000000 4024DDC4 0024F2DA   *.......................  ..D..2.*
24DA20   00000038 0024DBEC 0002A398 5C02BA48   0024D878 5024E266 0024D708 0024D680   *............*.....Q.&.S...P...0.*
24DA40   0024D930 0024E234 0024D680 0024D680   0024DC20 00010140 004807FF 48960270   *..R...S...0...0........ ........*
24DA60   10344807 FF4841F0 70000148 07FE4418   84300400 00441884 00040000 44188400   *.......0.........................*
24DA80   04000044 18843804 00004418 843C0400   0624EB38 0024EBC8 20008440 04000000   *........................TH... ....*
24DAA0   44188428 04000300 44246C04 00000000   00480700 48053048 18214841 1070002C   *..........%.....................*
24DAC0   481E1348 41107010 0048D707 70302870   30284850 10701000 48D20170 302A7020   *..........P.........&.....K.....*
24DAE0   9648D501 70302870 302A4807 8E484510   70303244 246C0400 00000044 246C0400   *..N..................%........%..*
24DB00   00000044 246C0220 00480A04 48181248   12FF4807 7E48D201 70204470 302A48D2   *.....%..................=.K........K*
24DB20   02702049 70302D48 07FE0048 50D07050   08485050 70D00448 50E070D0 54489120   *..............&..&...&&.....&.......*
24DB40   60040048 47E070F0 00000000 00000000   91406004 014847E0 70F02E48 96047000   *-.......0........ -.......0......*
24DB60   0024DDCA 4024D390 0024D680 00000580   0024E3C8 E2E8E2D6 E4E34040 E34847E0   *....  .L...0........THSYSOUT  T...*
24DB80   70F05E48 96207020 004818D5 4847F070   F08E4845 7070F050 44246C08 C9D3C2D6   *.0;..........N..0.0.......0&..%.ILBO*
24DBA0   C3D6D4F0 48410070 7000481B 0026CB58   0024D930 0024D708 00000000 0700E832   *COMO..................R...P.........Y.*
24DBC0   00000000 0001200F 70705648 96807020   00489610 60040048 00000000 00000000   *.........................-..........*
24DBE0   0024D7FC 8F24D8B0 00702008 1424D930   00000001 8024D8B0 70201048 00000001   *..P...Q.........R.......Q..........*
24DC00   00000B74 00000000 0024E29E 0024E3BB   0024E3C5 05EF4807 F9489120 60040048   *............S...T...TE.....9...-...*
24DC20   0024F75A 0024E4FA 0024F75A 0024E50A   0024F23A 0024F2DA 0024F75E 0024DDC4   *..7...U...7...V...2...2...7;...D*
24DC40   0024DE46 0024DE6A 0024E034 0024E152   0024DD82 0024DDEA 0024DDF0 0024DE1C   *.................................0....*
24DC60   0024DE22 0024DE3A 0024DE64 0024E02E   0024E076 0024E1EE 0024D7FC 0024D8B0   *..........................P...Q.*
24DC80   080CF2F5 F0F06C01 2CF7F5F0 21202040   20204020 20202040 205B2020 206B2021   *..2500%..750... .. .... .$...,..*
24DCA0   20480048 05EF0700 60606060 60606060   60606060 60606060 60606060 60606060   *........------------------------*
24DCC0   60606060 60606060 60606060 60606060   60606060 60606060 60606060 60606060   *--------------------------------*
```

Value of the first operand in add packed instruction

Value of TUITION before packing locations (24D708 – 24D70B)

Value of TOTAL-TUITION before packing locations (24D714 – 24D719)

Value of the second operand in the add packed instruction

Figure 13.7 Core Dump for Example 1

Appendix D, 360/370 Assembler Instructions, shows F2 to be the op code for PACK. A pack instruction converts data in the second operand to packed data and stores the result in the first operand. The second operand has a base register of 6 and a displacement of 000. From the data division map (Figure 13.3) and table of base register assignments (Figure 13.4), we conclude that the second operand is TUITION. Analogous reasoning shows that the next machine instruction packs TOTAL-TUITION into a second compiler work area.

The third instruction in the sequence, the one at relative location 82A, is the instruction which caused the ABEND. It has an op code of FA (add packed) and is supposed to add TUITION to TOTAL-TUITION and store the result in TOTAL-TUITION. Instead, it caused a data exception, which occurs only when an arithmetic field does not contain valid arithmetic data. The culprit is either TUITION or TOTAL-TUITION. We go into the dump (Figure 13.7) to find which of the two it is.

Both the data division map and first pack instruction show the address of TUITION as 6 000 (base register 6, displacement 000). The contents of GPR 6 at the time of the ABEND are 24D708. Since TUITION is 4 bytes, its value is found in the 4 bytes from 24D708 to 24D70B. Figure 13.7 shows TUITION to be F1F2F0F0. It is packed into a compiler work area via the instruction at 81E and becomes 1200F, a valid decimal number.

The first byte of TOTAL-TUITION is at 6 00C; its calculated address is, therefore, $(24D708)_{16} + (C)_{16} = (24D714)_{16}$. TOTAL-TUITION has a length of 6 bytes, so that its contents are found in the 6 bytes from 24D714 to 24D719 as 4770F02E9823. If these 6 bytes don't make sense to you, you're not alone; they don't make sense to the computer either, and that is the cause of the data exception. TOTAL-TUITION is defined in line 63 of the COBOL program as a 77-level entry. However, it was never initialized, either by a VALUE clause or by a MOVE ZEROS statement in the procedure division. The first time the computer went to access TOTAL-TUITION, it took whatever happened to be there, i.e., whatever was in locations 24D714 to 24D719. The field was not initialized, the contents were garbage, and the 0C7 resulted. The pack instruction at 824 inverted the low-order byte and put 2 into the sign bit. The add pack instruction at 82A failed to execute because 2 is an invalid sign.

Dump Reading: Example 2 (Bad Input Data)

The COBOL program of Figure 13.2 was rerun (after line 63 was amended to include a VALUE IS ZERO clause) but another 0C7 occurred, resulting in a second ABEND. Figures 13.2–13.5 from the first example are applicable for this example as well. Figure 13.8 shows the PSW, entry point, and contents of the GPR's for Example 2. Figure 13.9 shows the relevant portion of the dump. We shall follow the procedure used in Example 1.

First, subtract the entry point of the COBOL program from the address where the exception occurred:

Address from PSW	24B694
−Entry point of COBOL	−24AE80
Relative address	814

Next take the relative location 814, and using the procedure division map (Figure 13.5) establish which COBOL statement failed to execute. Location 814 is found to be within the COBOL COMPUTE statement of line 113. The instruction at 814 is the one which would have executed next if the ABEND did not occur. The instruction which actually caused the ABEND is the one

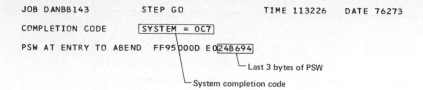

COMPLETION CODE   SYSTEM = 0C7

PSW AT ENTRY TO ABEND   FF95000D E024B694
                                        └── Last 3 bytes of PSW
                              └── System completion code

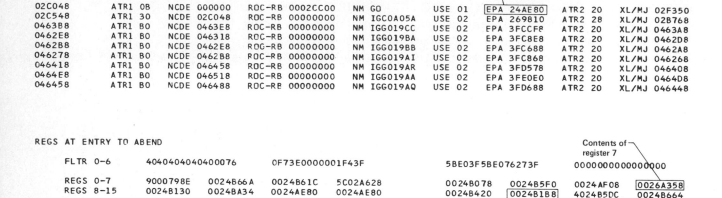

┌─ Entry point of main (COBOL)
│   program

02C048	ATR1 0B	NCDE 000000	ROC-RB 0002CC00	NM GO	USE 01	EPA 24AE80	ATR2 20	XL/MJ 02F350
02C548	ATR1 30	NCDE 02C048	ROC-RB 00000000	NM IGC0A05A	USE 02	EPA 269810	ATR2 28	XL/MJ 02B768
0463B8	ATR1 B0	NCDE 0463E8	ROC-RB 00000000	NM IGG019CC	USE 02	EPA 3FCCF8	ATR2 20	XL/MJ 0463A8
0462E8	ATR1 B0	NCDE 046318	ROC-RB 00000000	NM IGG019BA	USE 02	EPA 3FC8E8	ATR2 20	XL/MJ 0462D8
0462B8	ATR1 B0	NCDE 0462E8	ROC-RB 00000000	NM IGG019BB	USE 02	EPA 3FC688	ATR2 20	XL/MJ 0462A8
046278	ATR1 B0	NCDE 0462B8	ROC-RB 00000000	NM IGG019AI	USE 02	EPA 3FC868	ATR2 20	XL/MJ 046268
046418	ATR1 B0	NCDE 046458	ROC-RB 00000000	NM IGG019AR	USE 02	EPA 3FD578	ATR2 20	XL/MJ 046408
0464E8	ATR1 B0	NCDE 046518	ROC-RB 00000000	NM IGG019AA	USE 02	EPA 3FE0E0	ATR2 20	XL/MJ 0464D8
046458	ATR1 B0	NCDE 046488	ROC-RB 00000000	NM IGG019AQ	USE 02	EPA 3FD688	ATR2 20	XL/MJ 046448

REGS AT ENTRY TO ABEND   Contents of ─┐
                                                                                          register 7

FLTR 0-6   4040404040400076   0F73E0000001F43F   5BE03F5BE076273F   0000000000000000

REGS 0-7   9000798E   0024B66A   0024B61C   5C02A628   0024B078   0024B5F0   0024AF08   0026A358
REGS 8-15   0024B130   0024BA34   0024AE80   0024AE80   0024B420   0024B1B8   4024B5DC   0024B664
                                                                     └── Contents of
                                                                         register 13

Figure 13.8 Information Associated with Core Dump—Example 2

immediately preceding, i.e., the one at relative location 80E. The COMPUTE statement and machine instructions through 80E are repeated below:

COMPUTE INDIVIDUAL-BILL = TUITION + UNION-FEE + ACTIVITY-FEE − SCHOLARSHIP.

Location	Instruction
7EA	F2 71 D 200 6 006
7F0	F2 73 D 208 6 000
7F6	FA 22 D 205 D 20D
7FC	F2 71 D 208 6 004
802	FA 22 D 20D D 205
808	F2 73 D 200 7 020
80E	FB 22 D 20D D 205

The COBOL compiler adds and subtracts two fields at a time from left to right within the COMPUTE. TUITION is first added to UNION-FEE; ACTIVITY-FEE is added to that intermediate sum; finally, SCHOLARSHIP is subtracted. Since the USAGE clause was not specified in the definition of any of the operands, they are all packed prior to any arithmetic.

The first two machine instructions pack UNION-FEE and TUITION into compiler work areas, which are then added via the third instruction (op code FA—add packed). ACTIVITY-FEE is packed and added to the intermediate sum via the fourth and fifth instructions. SCHOLARSHIP is packed in instruction 6 (op code F2—pack) and subtracted from the intermediate sum in the seventh instruction where the data exception occurred. Everything worked well until the attempt to subtract SCHOLARSHIP.

The data division map (Figure 13.3) shows that SCHOLARSHIP is stored in the base register designated by BL = 1 (i.e., register 7), with displacement of hex 20. Figure 13.8 shows the contents of register 7 to be 26A358; thus, SCHOLARSHIP is stored in the 4 bytes beginning at location 26A378 (26A358 + 20). Figure 13.9 shows the contents of SCHOLARSHIP to be

SCHOLARSHIP after packing (locations 24B3BD – 24B3BF)

```
24B380   70F05E48 96207020 004818D5 4847F070   F08E4845 7070F050 44246C08 C9D3C2D6   *.0;........N..0.0.....0&..%.ILBO*
24B3A0   C3D6D4F0 48410070 7000481B 0026A358   0024B130 0024AF08 00000000 000C0004   *COMO............................*
24B3C0   00000000 0001515C 40404040 5BF16BF5   F1F5F3F4 60040048 00000000 000C0000   *.......*     $1,51534-..........*
24B3E0   0024AFFC 8F24B0B0 00702008 1424B130   00000001 8024B0B0 70201048 000C0001   *................................*
24B400   00000B74 00000000 0024BA9E 0024BBBB   0024BBC5 05EF4807 F9489120 6C040048   *.................E....9...-...*
24B420   0024CF5A 0024BCFA 0024CF5A 0024BD0A   0024CA3A 0024CADA 0024CF5E 0024B5C4   *...........................;...D*
24B440   0024B646 0024B66A 0024B834 0024B952   0024B5B2 0024B5EA 0024B5F0 0024B61C   *............................0...*
24B460   0024B622 0024B63A 0024B664 0024B82E   0024B876 0024B9EE 0024AFFC 0024B0B0   *................................*
24B480   080CF2F5 F0F06C01 2CF7F5F0 21202040   20204020 20202040 205B2020 206B2021   *..2500%..750... .. .... .$...,..*
24B4A0   20430048 05EF0700 60606060 60606060   60606060 60606060 60606060 60606060   *.......-------------------------*
24B4C0   60606060 60606060 60606060 60606060   60606060 60606060 60606060 60606060   *--------------------------------*
     LINE 24B4E0 SAME AS ABOVE
24B500   60606060 60606060 602458F0 C00C05EF   5810C058 D2011032 C0815840 1024D202   *---------..0........K....... ..K.*
24B520   4011C011 5010D228 9200D228 5810C05C   D2011032 C082D203 1060C084 5840C1024   * ...&.K...K....*K......K..-... ..*
24B540   D2024011 C0115010 D22C920F D22C9680   D22C4110 D2280A13 D2848000 603058F0   *K. ...&.K...K...K...K...K...-..0*
24B560   C00C05EF D203D234 D1F89254 D234D203   D23CC05C 9201D23B 4110D234 58F0C014   *....K.K.J8..K.K.K..*..K...K..0..*
24B580   05EF9240 8000D283 80018000 D2608000   C0889240 8061D222 80628061 58F0C00C   *... ..K.....K-..... ./K..../.0..*
24B5A0   05EFD203 D234D1F8 9214D234 D203D23C   C05C4110 C0015010 D2384110 D23458F0   *..K.K.J8...K.K.K..*....&.K...K..0*
24B5C0   C01405EF 58F0C00C 05EF5810 C0581821   D2022021 C03558F0 103005EF 5010D1F4   *.....0..........K......C....&.J4*
24B5E0   5870D1F4 5850C038 07F55810 C02807F1   F2710200 701DFC31 D204C060 F3326000   *..J4.&...5.....12.K......K..-3.-.*
24B600   D20596F0 60035820 C03C95E8 701F0772   D2016006 C0625810 C04007F1 D2016006   *K..0-......Y....K.-...... .1K.-.*


26A0A0   4126A0A0 7F00065D 02000000 7F269720   0026A0D0 0C000000 4026A0C8 C026A0D0   *....")...."........... ..H....*
26A0C0   00000000 00010000 012689A0 2000065D   00000000 00000000 00000000 C0000033   *..............)................*
26A0E0   00818300 00000001 00004000 00000001   04000001 54000000 00A40020 00020BD4   *..............................M*
26A100   923FC8E8 003FC688 06000001 00000660   28012828 4126A0A0 013FCCF8 003FCCF8   *..HY..F........-...........8...8*
26A120   0000007D 00000001 4126A158 7F000000   00000000 7F26A12C 0026A158 0C000000   *...'........."......."..........*
26A140   4026A150 0024B0B0 00000000 00010000   0126A1F0 20000085 4026A128 7F000000   * ..&...............0.... ..."...*
26A160   00000000 7F26A15C 0026A188 0C000000   4026A180 0024B0BC 00000000 00010000   *...."..*........ ...............*
26A180   0126A278 20000085 0126A1B8 41000000   04000000 4126A18C 0026A1B8 0D400050   *............................ .&*
26A1A0   4026A1B0 0024AFFC 27000000 00010000   0226A308 00000050 0026A188 7F000000   * ......................&....."...*
26A1C0   00000000 7F26A1BC 0026A1E8 0C000000   4026A1E0 0024AFFC 00000000 00010000   *...."......Y.... ...............*
26A1E0   0226A358 00000050 00000000 00020088   40D7C5C7 C7E840D1 D6D5C5E2 40404040   *.......&........ PEGGY JONES    *
26A200   40404040 404040F4 F5F640F4 F540F6F4   F5F64040 4040F1F5 40404040 405BF16B   *       456 45 6456     15    $1,*
26A220   F2F0F040 40404040 405BF2F5 40404040   40404040 5BF7F540 40404040 40404040   *200      $25          $75       *
26A240   5BF04040 40404040 405BF16B F3F0F040   40404040 40404040 40404040 40404040   *$0       $1,300                 *
26A260   40404040 40404040 40404040 40404040   40404040 40000000 40C84B40 C8C5C1E5   *                      ... H. HEAV*
26A280   E86CE6D6 D9D2C5D9 40404040 404040F7   F8F940F5 F240F1F2 F3F44040 4040F1F8   *Y-WORKER         789 52 1234    18*
26A2A0   40404040 405BF16B F4F4F040 40404040   40405BF0 40404040 4040404C 5BF7F540   *     $1,440       $0         $75 *
26A2C0   40404040 40404040 5BF04040 40404040   405BF16B F5F1F540 40404040 40404040   *        $0        $1,515        *
26A2E0   40404040 40404040 40404040 40404040   40404040 40404040 40404040 40E8E2C9   *                             YSI*
26A300   00000000 00020050 C84B40C8 C5C1E5E8   60E6D6D9 D2C5D940 40404040 F7F8F9F5   *.......&H. HEAVY-WORKER     7895*
26A320   F2F1F2F3 F4F1F8D5 F0F0F0F0 40404040   40404040 40404040 40404040 40404040   *21234l8N0000                    *
26A340   40404040 40404040 40404040 40404040   40404040 40404040 C2C5D5D1 C1D4C9D5   *                        BENJAMIN*
26A360   C540D3C5 C5404040 40404040 F8F7F6F8   F7F6F8F7 F6F1F8D5 40404040 40404040   *E LEE          87687687618N     *
26A380   40404040 40404040 40404040 40404040   40404040 40404040 40404040 40404040   *                                *
```

STUDENT-NAME (locations 26A358 – 26A36B)

SCHOLARSHIP before packing (locations 26A378 – 26A37B)

Figure 13.9 Core Dump—Example 2

40404040, which is EBCDIC for a blank field. We conclude that in the last data card that was processed SCHOLARSHIP was left blank.

Which student had the invalid data? STUDENT-NAME is 20 bytes in length and tied to BL = 1 (i.e., register 7) with displacement of 000. Hence, the name of student with the invalid data is found in the 20 bytes beginning at 26A358. Going into the dump, the bug is found to be in the data associated with BENJAMINE LEE.

One last point: We examined the value of SCHOLARSHIP as it resided in the input area. As a check, we should also observe its value after it has been packed into a compiler work area. The subtract instruction had as its second operand the 3 bytes beginning at location D 205. Thus, the beginning address is

Contents of register 13	24B1B8
+Displacement	+ 20 5
Address of first byte	24B3BD

Examining Figure 13.9, we see that the second operand contains 000004. (Reader, this is not an error. It is exactly what should be there as the result of a pack instruction on a blank field.) Since 4 is an invalid sign, the data exception occurred.

Extension to DOS

The examples in this chapter have been drawn from OS. At our level of discussion, everything about OS pertains to DOS as well with the exception of the COBOL program's entry point. Accordingly, DOS procedures for reading procedure and data division maps, core dumps, etc., are the same as those in this chapter.

Figure 13.10 illustrates the linkage editor map for DOS. Only the LABEL and REL-FR (relocation factor) columns are of interest here. The key to using Figure 13.10 is the PROGRAM-ID statement in the COBOL identification division. Assume, for example, the following COBOL statement in conjunction with Figure 13.10:

PROGRAM-ID. 'BILLING'.

To determine the entry point for the COBOL program BILLING, search the LABEL column in Figure 13.10 for BILLING and then read across under

03/31/76	PHASE	XFR-AD	LOCORE	HICORE	DSK-AD	ESD TYPE	LABEL	LOADED	REL-FR
	PHASE***	002DC4	002000	003DBF	5D 03 2	CSECT	IHD02200	002000	002000
						ENTRY	IHD02201	002000	
						CSECT	IJJCPD1	002018	002018
						ENTRY	IJJCPD1N	002018	
					* ENTRY	IJJCPD3	002018	
						CSECT	IHD02800	002210	002210
						ENTRY	IHD02801	002210	
						ENTRY	IHD02802	002246	
						CSECT	IHD03700	002388	002388
					* ENTRY	IHD03701	002388	
					* ENTRY	IHD03702	002398	
						ENTRY	IHD03704	002524	
						CSECT	BILLING	002640	002640
						CSECT	IJCFZII1	003C18	003C18
						CSECT	IJDFAPIZ	003CA8	003CA8
					* ENTRY	IJDFAZIZ	003CA8	

Figure 13.10 DOS Linkage Editor Map — ← **Entry point for COBOL program**

REL-FR and find 2640 as the entry point (in hex) of the COBOL program. *Chapter 13*
(The other, rather cryptic, names in the label column are IBM-supplied *Debugging, II*
programs which are required by the COBOL program. Most of these routines
are for I/O processing.)

Summary

The beginning programmer is often guilty of two practices which result in a
data exception:

1. Failure to initialize a 77-level entry (Example 1 in this chapter), and
2. Use of bad, i.e., nonnumeric, data as input (Example 2).

It is sound technique to always initialize a numeric 77-level entry to zero with
the VALUE clause regardless of whether or not the entry is initialized or
calculated in the procedure division. It is not as easy to eliminate the second
error. Incoming numeric fields are not allowed to contain decimal points,
commas, $ signs, or special characters. Further, high- and low-order zeros
should be punched and not left blank. Even after this is done, there is still the
possibility for error if data are punched in the wrong columns. The record
layout in the data division and the incoming data must correspond exactly. The
computer does not know what you intended; it only knows what you did.

   If a data exception does occur, the procedure to determine its exact cause is
summarized below:

1. Get the address of the data exception from the last 3 bytes of the PSW.
2. Get the entry point of the main program.
3. Subtract the address in #2 from the address in #1. The result is the
   relative location (within the COBOL program) of the next statement which
   would have been executed.
4. Use the procedure division map and relative location determined from #3
   to pinpoint the machine instruction causing the error.
5. Determine the COBOL instruction which contained the machine instruction
   that failed to execute.
6. Examine the operands in the COBOL instruction using the COBOL listing
   first (easy way out) or the dump if the answer is not readily apparent.
7. If steps 1–6 fail, ask for help.

PROBLEMS

1 Take a program that you have written and debugged and cause it to ABEND. (This
is best accomplished by failing to initialize a 77-level entry or blanking out a
numeric field in a data card.) Analyze the data and procedure division maps and the
dump, and find the cause of the error. After all, it is easiest to go through a dump if
you know what you are looking for, and this exercise is a good one to build
confidence. To have the appropriate material after an ABEND, the JCL is modified
as follows (the OS JCL may vary slightly at your facility):

> OS: (a) // EXEC COBUCLG,PARM.COB='PMAP,DMAP'
>   (replace existing EXEC card)
>
>   (b) //GO.SYSUDUMP DD SYSOUT=A
>   (new card before GO.SYSIN card)
>
> DOS: (a) // OPTION LINK,DUMP,SYM,LISTX
>   (replace existing OPTION card)

The meaning of these JCL modifications is covered in the chapters on JCL in the
next section.

```
02D240      ATR1 0B   NCDE 000000   ROC-RB 0002D9A8   NM GO        USE 01   EPA 22A680   ATR2 20   XL/MJ 029838
02D980      ATR1 30   NCDE 02D240   ROC-RB 00000000   NM IGC0A05A  USE 02   EPA 249010   ATR2 28   XL/MJ 02F350
0463B8      ATR1 B0   NCDE 0463E8   ROC-RB 00000000   NM IGG019CC  USE 02   EPA 3FCCF8   ATR2 20   XL/MJ 0463A8
0462E8      ATR1 B0   NCDE 046318   ROC-RB 00000000   NM IGG019BA  USE 02   EPA 3FC8E8   ATR2 20   XL/MJ 0462D8
0462B8      ATR1 B0   NCDE 0462E8   ROC-RB C0000000   NM IGG019BB  USE 02   EPA 3FC688   ATR2 20   XL/MJ 0462A8
046278      ATR1 BC   NCDE 0462B8   ROC-RB 00000000   NM IGG019AI  USE 02   EPA 3FC868   ATR2 20   XL/MJ 046268
046418      ATR1 B0   NCDE 046458   ROC-RB 00000000   NM IGG019AR  USE 02   EPA 3FD578   ATR2 20   XL/MJ 046408
0464E8      ATR1 B0   NCDE 046518   ROC-RB 00000000   NM IGG019AA  USE 02   EPA 3FE0E0   ATR2 20   XL/MJ 0464D8
046458      ATR1 B0   NCDE 046488   ROC-RB 00000000   NM IGG019AQ  USE 02   EPA 3FD688   ATR2 20   XL/MJ 046448


REGS AT ENTRY TO ABEND

     FLTR 0-6       0000000000000000        0000000000000000         0000000000000000         0000005800000000

     REGS 0-7       00000001   0022AE6A   0022AE1C   5C02B1D0       0022A878   0022ADF0   0022A708   00249B58
     REGS 8-15      0022A930   0022B234   0022A680   0022A680       0022AC20   0022A9B8   4022ADDC   0022AE64


22AB80   70F05E48 96207020 004818D5 4847F070    F08E4845 7070F050 44246C08 C9D3C2D6   *.0;........N..0.0.....0&..%.ILB0*
22ABA0   C3D6D4F0 48410070 7000481B 00249B58    0022A930 0022A708 00000000 00000004   *COM0.......................*
22ABC0   00000000 0001300C 40404040 40405BF2    F9F0F4F6 00000048 00000000 00000000   *........        $29046-.........*
22ABE0   0022A7FC 8F22A8B0 00702008 1422A930    00000001 8022AB80 70201048 00000001   *................................*
22AC00   00000B74 00000000 0022B29E 0022B3BB    0022B3C5 05EF4807 F9489120 60040048   *.................E....9...-..*
22AC20   0022C75A 0022B4FA 0022C75A 0022B50A    0022C23A 0022C2DA 0022C75E 0022ADC4   *..G......G.......B...B...G;..D*
22AC40   0022AE46 0022AE6A 0022B034 0022B152    0022AD82 0022ADEA 0022ADF0 0022AE1C   *........................0....*
22AC60   0022AE22 0022AE3A 0022AE64 0022B02E    0022B076 0022B1EE 0022A7FC 0022A8B0   *.........................0....*
22AC80   080CF2F5 F0F06C01 2CF7F5F0 21202040    20204020 20202040 205B2020 206B2021   *..2500%.750... .. ..... .$..,..*
22ACA0   20480048 05EF0700 60606060 60606060    60606060 60606060 60606060 60606060   *.....---------------------------*
22ACC0   60606060 60606060 60606060 60606060    60606060 60606060 60606060 60606060   *------------------------------*
         LINE 22ACE0 SAME AS ABOVE
22AD00   60606060 60606060 602458F0 C00C05EF    5810C058 D2011032 C0815840 1024D202   *---------..0.........K........ ..K.*
22AD20   4011C011 5010D228 9200D228 5810C05C    D2011032 C082D203 1060C084 58401024   * ...&.K...K... *K....K...-... .*
22AD40   D2024011 C0115010 D22C92CF D22C9680    D22C4110 D2280A13 D2848000 603058F0   *K....&.K...K...K...K....-...0*
22AD60   C00C05EF D203D234 D1F89254 D234D203    D23CC05C 9201D23B 4110D234 58F0C014   *....K.K.J8..K.K.K.*..K....K...0*
22AD80   05EF9240 8000D283 80018000 D2608000    C0889240 8061D222 80628061 58F0C00C   *... .K.......K-...K..../K....*.0..*
22ADA0   05EFD203 D234D1F8 9214D234 D203D23C    C05C4110 00015010 D2384110 D23458F0   *..K.K.J8..K.K..*..&.K...K..0*
22ADC0   C01405EF 58F0C00C 05EF5810 C0581821    D2022021 C03558F0 103005EF 5010D1F4   *......0.........K......O...&.J4*
22ADE0   5870D1F4 5850C038 07F55810 C02807F1    F271D200 701DFC31 D204C060 F3326000   *..J4.&...5....12.K...K..-3-..*
22AE00   D20596F0 60035820 C03C95E8 7C1F0772    D2016006 C0625810 C04007F1 D2016006   *K..0-.....Y...K.-..... .1K.-.*


2498A0   412498A0 7F00065D C2C00000 7F248F20    002498D0 0C000000 402498C8 0C2498D0   *....."..)...."............ ..H....*
2498C0   C0000000 00010000 012481A0 2000065D    00000000 00000000 C0000000 00000033   *................)............*
2498E0   00818300 00000001 00004000 00000001    04000001 54000000 00A4C020 03C2F48C   *.......................4.*
249900   923FC8E8 003FC688 00000660 00000660    28012828 412498A0 013FCCF8 003FCCF8   *..HY..F........-.....8...8*
249920   0000007D 0C000001 41249958 7F000000    00000000 7F24992C 00249958 0C000000   *................."........*
249940   40249950 0022A8B0 C0000000 00010000    012499F0 20000085 40249928 7F000000   * ..&........."......0....."..*
249960   00000000 7F24995C 00249988 00010000    40249980 0022A8B0 00000000 00010000   *......"......".........."..*
249980   01249A78 20000085 012499B8 7F000000    00000000 7F24998C 002499B8 0C000000   * ......."......"......*
2499A0   40249AB0 0022A7FC 00000000 00010000    02249B08 00000000 00249988 7F000000   * .................&..."...*
2499C0   00000000 7F2499BC 002499E8 C0000000    402499E0 0022A7FC 00000000 00310000   *......"...Y.............*
2499E0   02249B58 00000050 00000000 00020088    40E2E4E2 C1D5C0C2 C1D2C5D9 40404040   *......&......   SUSAN BAKER    *
249A00   40404040 404040F1 F1F140F2 F240F3F3    F3F34040 40400FF9 40404040 40405B40   *        111 22 3333      09      $*
249A20   F7F2F040 40404040 40405BF0 40404040    40404040 5BF5F040 40404040 40405BF5   *720      $0      $50      $5*
249A40   F0F04040 40404040 4040405B F2F7F040    40404040 40404040 40404040 40404040   *00      $270*
249A60   40404040 40404040 40000000 40D1D6C8    D5404040 40000000 40D1D6C8 D540D7C1   *        @....  JOHN PA*
249A80   D9F360E3 C9D4C5D9 40404040 404040F4    F5F640C2 F140F3F5 F4F64040 4040FCF3   *RT-TIMER      456 21 3546      03*
249AA0   40404040 40404040 F2F4F040 40404040    405BF2F5 40404040 40404040 5BF2F540   *        $240      $25      $25 *
249AC0   40404040 40404040 5BF04040 40404040    4040405B F2F9F040 40404040 40404040   *        $0      $290*
249AE0   40404040 40404040 40404040 40404040    40404040 40404040 40404040 40E8E2C9   *                              YSI*
249B00   00000000 00020050 C84B40C8 C5C1E5E8    60E6D6D9 D2C5D940 40404040 F7F8F9F5   *......&H. HEAVY-WORKER      7895*
249B20   F2F1F2F3 F4F1F8D5 F0F0F0F0 F0F0F0F0    40404040 40404040 40404040 40404040   *2123418N0000*
249B40   40404040 40404C40 40404040 40404040    40404C40 40404040 D7C5C7C7 E840D1D6   *                      PEGGY JO*
249B60   D5C5E240 40404040 40404040 F4F5F6F4    F5F6F4F5 F6F1F5E8 40404040 40404040   *NES      45645645615Y*
249B80   40404040 40404040 40404040 40404040    40404040 40404040 40404040 40404040   **
```

Figure 13.11

2 Use the COBOL listing, register assignments, and maps of Figures 13.2–13.5 with the accompanying dump (Figure 13.11) to determine the cause of the ABEND. A series of leading questions is provided to help.

   i. *Determine where the ABEND occurred.*

      a. At what machine location did the ABEND occur?

      b. At what location was the program loaded?

      c. What is the relative location within the COBOL program of the instruction which would have executed if there were no ABEND?

      d. What machine instruction is at that location?

      e. What is the actual machine address of the instruction in part d?

      f. What is the corresponding COBOL instruction?

   ii. *Examine the machine instruction which failed to execute.*

     The instruction which actually produced the ABEND is the one immediately before the instruction determined in part c.

      g. What is the machine instruction which actually caused the ABEND?

      h. What is its op code?

      i. Which base register is associated with the first operand?

      j. What is the displacement of the first operand?

      k. What is the effective address of the first operand?

      l. How many bytes are associated with the first operand (*careful*)?

      m. What are the internal contents of the first operand; are they valid as a decimal number?

      n. Which base register is associated with the second operand?

      o. What is the displacement of the second operand?

      p. How many bytes are associated with the second operand?

      q. What are the internal contents of the second operand; are they valid as a decimal number?

   iii. *Determine the data card which contained the invalid data.*

      r. Which base register is associated with CARD-FILE?

      s. What is the address contained in that base register when the ABEND occurred?

      t. What is the displacement of SCHOLARSHIP?

      u. What is the internal location of SCHOLARSHIP?

      v. What value was read from the card for SCHOLARSHIP?

      w. Which student had the invalid data?

Summarize why the dump occurred.

3 Explain how a data exception need not occur, even though a 77-level entry used as a counter was not initialized; specifically, consider the first example in this chapter in which TOTAL-TUITION was not set to zero. What would be the consequences of *not* getting a data exception, even if TOTAL-TUITION was not initialized?

4 a. A blank in a one-position numeric field causes a data exception, if arithmetic is performed in that field, and the USAGE for that field is DISPLAY. Assume that we define a four-position numeric field, with USAGE DISPLAY, that is also used in arithmetic calculations. Further assume that this four-position field has a valid low-order digit but is punched with leading (high-order) blanks. Will a data exception result? Why or why not?

b. Explain why an incoming numeric field (USAGE DISPLAY) will cause a data exception if a decimal point is actually punched in the field.

Note: A period is 4B in EBCDIC; a space is 40 in EBCDIC.

Insight into the COBOL Compiler

The COBOL compiler is a remarkably sophisticated program which translates COBOL into Assembler language. Unfortunately many practicing programmers know little more about the compiler. While such knowledge is unnecessary in terms of being able to write a COBOL program, it is invaluable in raising the overall capabilities of the individual.

The compiler-generated instructions to add two COMPUTATIONAL fields are different from those which add two COMPUTATIONAL-3 fields. Further, if COBOL operands are of different data types and/or decimal alignment, additional machine instructions are generated to convert and/or shift the data. How does this relate to COBOL since the programmer is permitted to mix data types or decimal alignments in the same COBOL instruction? The compiler, and not the programmer, is responsible for generating proper machine code to convert, shift, and do arithmetic. If the programmer is "lazy" or unaware, the compiler will bail him out. The COBOL programmer can, however, simplify the job of the compiler and thereby ensure more efficient machine code by specifying appropriate data types, decimal alignments, etc. That is the focus of this chapter. We shall examine in close detail machine language instructions generated by the COBOL compiler and see how apparently insignificant changes in COBOL code produce very different machine instructions. We shall show that even brief consideration of machine characteristics results in more efficient COBOL code and a better understanding of the COBOL logic.

The chapter begins with elementary coverage of some Assembler instructions. (We assume the material on instruction formats and machine architecture from Chapter 12 has been well digested.) A superficial level is maintained, for the present objective is to establish a link between COBOL and Assembler and not to provide in-depth coverage of BAL coding. As in previous chapters, emphasis is on IBM, but the concepts are applicable to any manufacturer. After the necessary Assembler has been covered, we shall concoct a COBOL program in which the procedure division consists entirely of ADD instructions for different data types, signs, and decimal alignments. We shall then examine the procedure and data division maps, associated with this program to accomplish our objective.

This chapter may appear somewhat removed from COBOL to the casual reader. We hope however, that the serious student finds these concepts well worth the effort as he/she progresses through advanced courses and perhaps an eventual career.

The reader may refer to Chapter 12 to review instruction formats and the addressing scheme. We shall begin with two instructions which convert from character to packed format and packed to character format, the PACK and UNPK instructions, respectively. First the PACK instruction:

Name	Pack
Mnemonic op code	PACK
Machine op code	F2
Type	SS
Assembler format	PACK D1(L1,B1),D2(L2,B2)

Essentially the PACK instruction takes the data in the second operand, packs them, and moves the result into the first operand. The contents of the second operand are unchanged.

Example 14.1

```
PACK   FIELDA,FIELDB
```

Before execution: FIELDA | ?? | ?? | ?? | FIELDB | F1 | F2 | F3 |

After execution: FIELDA | 00 | 12 | 3F | FIELDB | F1 | F2 | F3 |

Observe that since FIELDA was larger than necessary, high-order zeros are generated. The initial contents of FIELDA, i.e., the receiving field, are overwritten, and the final contents of FIELDB, i.e., the sending field, are not changed.

The UNPK (unpack) instruction is the reverse of the PACK instruction in that a packed field is converted to character format:

Name	Unpack
Mnemonic op code	UNPK
Machine op code	F3
Type	SS
Assembler format	UNPK D1(L1,B1),D2(L2,B2)

Example 14.2

Section IV
The Role of BAL
in Deeper Understanding

    UNPK   FIELDC,FIELDD

Before execution: FIELDC | ?? | ?? | ?? | FIELDD | 00 | 32 | 1F |

After execution: FIELDC | F3 | F2 | F1 | FIELDD | 00 | 32 | 1F |

As before, the final contents of the sending field, i.e., FIELDD, are unchanged, and the initial contents of the receiving field, i.e., FIELDC, are destroyed. Further note that the receiving field is usually larger than the sending field to accommodate the expanded results of the unpacking operation.

Next, consider two instructions which convert binary to decimal data (i.e., packed) and decimal to binary, namely the convert to decimal and convert to binary instructions:

Name	Convert to binary
Mnemonic op code	CVB
Machine op code	4F
Type	RX
Assembler format	CVB R1,D2(X2,B2)

The second operand must be in packed decimal format and located on a double word boundary. The result of the conversion is stored in the general register specified as R1.

Example 14.3

        CVB   8,FIELDC

Before execution: FIELDC | 00 | 00 | 00 | 00 | 00 | 00 | 12 | 3C | Note: FIELDC is aligned
                                                                            on a double word boundary.

                    Register 8 | ?? | ?? | ?? | ?? |

After execution: FIELDC | 00 | 00 | 00 | 00 | 00 | 00 | 12 | 3C | Note: $(123)_{10} = (7B)_{16}$.

                    Register 8 | 00 | 00 | 00 | 7B |

The convert to decimal (CVD) instruction works in reverse; i.e., it takes the contents of a general-purpose register and stores it as a packed field beginning on the double word boundary specified in the instruction:

Name	Convert to decimal
Mnemonic op code	CVD
Machine op code	4E
Type	RX
Assembler format	CVD R1,D2(X2,B2)

Example 14.4

        CVD   6,RESULT

Before execution: Register 6 | 00 | 00 | 00 | 23 |

                    RESULT | ?? | ?? | ?? | ?? | ?? | ?? | ?? | ?? |

After execution: Register 6 | 00 | 00 | 00 | 23 | Note: $(23)_{16} = (35)_{10}$.

                    RESULT | 00 | 00 | 00 | 00 | 00 | 00 | 03 | 5C |

Execution of the CVD instruction leaves the contents of the designated register unchanged. The original contents of the register are converted to a packed number and stored in the double word specified by the second operand.

Data are constantly transferred from one storage location to another, or from storage to a register, or from a register to storage. In this section three instructions are introduced which are used to move data, but there are several others in the complete instruction set.

Name	Move character
Mnemonic op code	MVC
Machine op code	D2
Type.	SS
Assembler format	MVC D1(L,B1),D2(B2)

The move character instruction (MVC) is a storage-to-storage instruction which moves data from the second operand to the first operand. The contents of the second operand are unchanged, and the original contents of the first operand are overwritten. Unlike the PACK and UNPK instructions which have two length fields, the MVC instruction has one length code, and the number of bytes which are moved is determined by the length of the first operand.

Example 14.5

    MVC   FIELDA,FIELDB

Before execution:	FIELDA	C1	C2	C3		FIELDB	D1	D2	D3

After execution:	FIELDA	D1	D2	D3		FIELDB	D1	D2	D3

The final contents of FIELDB are unchanged, and the original contents of FIELDA have been replaced by those of FIELDB.

Frequently data are to be transferred from register to storage and vice versa. Load instructions bring data from a storage location to a register, while store instructions transfer data from a register to storage. A load instruction does not alter the initial contents of the storage address. A store instruction does not change the contents of a register. We shall consider two instructions which manipulate a full word.

Name	Load
Mnemonic op code	L
Machine op code	58
Type	RX
Assembler format	L R1,D2(X2,B2)

Example 14.6

    L   5,FIELDA

Before execution:	Register 5	??	??	??	??		FIELDA	00	00	F0	F1

After execution:	Register 5	00	00	F0	F1		FIELDA	00	00	F0	F1

FIELDA is a full word, and after the load instruction has been executed, the contents of FIELDA are unchanged. The initial contents of register 5 have been replaced by the contents of FIELDA.

257

The store instruction causes the contents of a register to be placed in storage. The contents of the register are unaltered, and what was originally in storage is overwritten.

Name	Store
Mnemonic op code	ST
Machine op code	50
Type	RX
Assembler format	ST R1,D2(X2,B2)

Example 14.7

ST   6,FIELDB

Before execution: Register 6 | 00 | 00 | 12 | 34 | FIELDB | ?? | ?? | ?? | ?? |

After execution: Register 6 | 00 | 00 | 12 | 34 | FIELDB | 00 | 00 | 12 | 34 |

360/370 Add Instructions

Any one of several BAL instructions can be used to add data depending on the length, type, and location of the operands. The add packed (AP) instruction is for decimal data with both operands in storage. The add full word (A) instruction is for binary data when one operand is contained in a register and the other in a full word in storage. Consider the add packed instruction:

Name	Add packed
Mnemonic op code	AP
Machine op code	FA
Type	SS
Assembler format	AP D1(L1,B1),D2(L2,B2)

The contents of the second operand are added to the contents of the first operand, and the results are placed in the first operand. Both fields must be valid decimal fields, i.e., packed; otherwise a data exception will occur. The sum is in packed format, and its sign is stored in the low-order byte of the first operand.

Example 14.8

AP   FIELDA,FIELDB

Before execution: FIELDA | 01 | 23 | 4C | FIELDB | 05 | 67 | 8C |

After execution: FIELDA | 06 | 91 | 2C | FIELDB | 05 | 67 | 8C |

The initial contents of the first operand are overwritten, and the contents of the second operand are unchanged.

The add full word instruction adds (in binary) the contents of a full word in storage to the contents of a register and places the results in the designated register.

Name	Add full word
Mnemonic op code	A
Machine op code	5A
Type	RX
Assembler format	A R1,D2(X2,B2)

Example 14.9

Chapter 14
Insight into the
COBOL Compiler

    A 5,FIELDC

Before execution: Register 5 | 00 | 00 | 00 | 07 | FIELDC | 00 | 00 | 00 | 01 |

After execution: Register 5 | 00 | 00 | 00 | 08 | FIELDC | 00 | 00 | 00 | 01 |

The contents of FIELDC, a full word in storage, are added to the value of register 5, and the result is placed in register 5. (Note that both operands are binary.) The initial contents of register 5 are destroyed, and the contents of FIELDC are unaltered.

COBOL from the Viewpoint of BAL

The intent of Figure 14.1 is to illustrate a variety of COBOL and corresponding object formats for different data types, lengths, signs, decimal alignments, etc. The working-storage section defines 12 data names which are used in various combinations in the procedure division. Of primary interest in this example is the machine language code generated from the COBOL statements.

```
00001          IDENTIFICATION DIVISION.
00002          PROGRAM ID.    COBOLBAL.
00003          AUTHOR.  GRAUER AND CRAWFORD.
00004          ENVIRONMENT DIVISION.
00005          CONFIGURATION SECTION.
00006          SOURCE-COMPUTER.    IBM-370.
00007          OBJECT-COMPUTER.    IBM-370.
00008          DATA DIVISION.
00009          WORKING-STORAGE SECTION.
00010          77  BINARY-FIELD-ONE           PICTURE IS S9(3)
00011                  USAGE IS COMPUTATIONAL.
00012          77  BINARY-FIELD-TWO           PICTURE IS S9(5)
00013                  USAGE IS COMPUTATIONAL.
00014          77  BINARY-FIELD-UNSIGNED      PICTURE IS 9(3)
00015                  USAGE IS COMPUTATIONAL.
00016          77  BINARY-FIELD-WITH-POINT    PICTURE IS S9(3)V9
00017                  USAGE IS COMPUTATIONAL.
00018          77  ZONED-DECIMAL-FIELD-ONE    PICTURE IS S9(3)
00019                  USAGE IS DISPLAY.
00020          77  ZONED-DECIMAL-FIELD-TWO    PICTURE IS S9(5)
00021                  USAGE IS DISPLAY.
00022          77  ZONED-DECIMAL-UNSIGNED     PICTURE IS 9(3)
00023                  USAGE IS DISPLAY.
00024          77  ZONED-DECIMAL-WITH-POINT   PICTURE IS S9(3)V9
00025                  USAGE IS DISPLAY.
00026          77  PACKED-FIELD-ONE           PICTURE IS S9(3)
00027                  USAGE IS COMPUTATIONAL-3.
00028          77  PACKED-FIELD-TWO           PICTURE IS S9(5)
00029                  USAGE IS COMPUTATIONAL-3.
00030          77  PACKED-FIELD-UNSIGNED      PICTURE IS 9(3)
00031                  USAGE IS COMPUTATIONAL-3.
00032          77  PACKED-FIELD-WITH-POINT    PICTURE IS S9(3)V9
00033                  USAGE IS COMPUTATIONAL-3.
00034          PROCEDURE DIVISION.
00035
00036          *************************************************************************
00037          *     COMPARISON OF ADD INSTRUCTIONS FOR ALL COMBINATIONS OF DATA TYPES     *
00038          *     ALL DATA NAMES ARE SIGNED                                            *
00039          *     ALL DATA NAMES HAVE SIMILAR DECIMAL ALIGNMENTS                       *
00040          *************************************************************************
00041
00042
00043          *     COMBINING SIMILAR DATA TYPES
00044                ADD BINARY-FIELD-ONE TO BINARY-FIELD-TWO.
00045                ADD ZONED-DECIMAL-FIELD-ONE TO ZONED-DECIMAL-FIELD-TWO.
00046                ADD PACKED-FIELD-ONE TO PACKED-FIELD-TWO.
00047
00048
00049          * COMBINING PACKED FIELDS WITH ZONED DECIMAL FIELDS
```

Figure 14.1 COBOL Listing to Illustrate Efficiency Considerations

```
00050               ADD PACKED-FIELD-ONE TO ZONED-DECIMAL-FIELD-ONE.
00051               ADD ZONED-DECIMAL-FIELD-ONE TO PACKED-FIELD-ONE.
00052
00053          * COMBINING PACKED FIELDS WITH BINARY FIELDS
00054               ADD PACKED-FIELD-ONE TO BINARY-FIELD-ONE.
00055               ADD BINARY-FIELD-ONE TO PACKED-FIELD-ONE.
00056
00057          * COMBINING ZONED DECIMAL FIELDS WITH BINARY FIELDS
00058               ADD ZONED-DECIMAL-FIELD-ONE TO BINARY-FIELD-ONE.
00059               ADD BINARY-FIELD-ONE TO ZONED-DECIMAL-FIELD-ONE.
00060
00061          ***************************************************************************
00062          *     COMPARISON OF ADD INSTRUCTIONS FOR SIMILAR DATA TYPES            *
00063          *     ONE OPERAND IS UNSIGNED                                          *
00064          *     ALL DATA NAMES HAVE SIMILAR DECIMAL ALIGNMENTS                   *
00065          ***************************************************************************
00066
00067               ADD ZONED-DECIMAL-UNSIGNED TO ZONED-DECIMAL-FIELD-ONE.
00068               ADD ZONED-DECIMAL-FIELD-ONE TO ZONED-DECIMAL-UNSIGNED.
00069               ADD BINARY-FIELD-UNSIGNED TO BINARY-FIELD-ONE.
00070               ADD BINARY-FIELD-ONE TO BINARY-FIELD-UNSIGNED.
00071               ADD PACKED-FIELD-UNSIGNED TO PACKED-FIELD-ONE.
00072               ADD PACKED-FIELD-ONE TO PACKED-FIELD-UNSIGNED.
00073
00074          ***************************************************************************
00075          *     COMPARISON OF ADD INSTRUCTIONS FOR SIMILAR DATA TYPES            *
00076          *     ALL DATA NAMES ARE SIGNED                                        *
00077          *     DATA NAMES HAVE DIFFERENT DECIMAL ALIGNMENTS                     *
00078          ***************************************************************************
00079
00080               ADD ZONED-DECIMAL-WITH-POINT TO ZONED-DECIMAL-FIELD-ONE.
00081               ADD ZONED-DECIMAL-FIELD-ONE TO ZONED-DECIMAL-WITH-POINT.
00082               ADD BINARY-FIELD-ONE TO BINARY-FIELD-WITH-POINT.
00083               ADD BINARY-FIELD-WITH-POINT TO BINARY-FIELD-ONE.
00084               ADD PACKED-FIELD-ONE TO PACKED-FIELD-WITH-POINT.
00085               ADD PACKED-FIELD-WITH-POINT TO PACKED-FIELD-ONE.
00086               STOP RUN.
```

Figure 14.1 (*Continued*)

In the ensuing sections, we shall consider only a few of the COBOL statements in Figure 14.1, but the reader is well advised to consider the entire listing as an exercise.

Figure 14.2 shows the data division map, Figure 14.3 the literal pool and register assignment, and Figure 14.4 the procedure division map for Figure 14.1.

Data Division Map

Figure 14.2 is the data division map or glossary. A partial explanation of the various entries is given below, but the reader is referred to the *IBM COBOL Programmer's Guide* for a more detailed description.

INTERNAL NAME—The internal name generated by the compiler and used in the object code listing to represent data names in the source program. This column appears twice for legibility.

LEVEL NUMBER—A normalized level number in that the first level for any hierarchy is always kept at 01 but the other levels are incremented by 1. Levels 66, 77, and 88 are unaffected. Thus the level numbers in the data division map need not match those in the data division. (See Figures 13.2 and 13.3 for clarification.)

SOURCE NAME—Data name as it appears in the source program.

BASE—Contains information about the base register used for each data name. In general every file has its own base locator. In our example all 77-level entries have a base locator of 1 which is tied to register 6 in Figure 14.3.

```
INTRNL NAME   LVL  SOURCE NAME                    BASE   DISPL   INTRNL NAME   DEFINITION   USAGE       R  O  Q  M
DNM=1-032     77   BINARY-FIELD-ONE               BL=1   000     DNM=1-032     DS 2C        COMP
DNM=1-058     77   BINARY-FIELD-TWO               BL=1   002     DNM=1-058     DS 4C        COMP
DNM=1-084     77   BINARY-FIELD-UNSIGNED          BL=1   006     DNM=1-084     DS 2C        COMP
DNM=1-115     77   BINARY-FIELD-WITH-POINT        BL=1   008     DNM=1-115     DS 2C        COMP
DNM=1-148     77   ZONED-DECIMAL-FIELD-ONE        BL=1   00A     DNM=1-148     DS 3C        DISP-NM
DNM=1-181     77   ZONED-DECIMAL-FIELD-TWO        BL=1   00D     DNM=1-181     DS 5C        DISP-NM
DNM=1-214     77   ZONED-DECIMAL-UNSIGNED         BL=1   012     DNM=1-214     DS 3C        DISP-NM
DNM=1-246     77   ZONED-DECIMAL-WITH-POINT       BL=1   015     DNM=1-246     DS 4C        DISP-NM
DNM=1-280     77   PACKED-FIELD-ONE               BL=1   019     DNM=1-280     DS 2P        COMP-3
DNM=1-306     77   PACKED-FIELD-TWO               BL=1   01B     DNM=1-306     DS 3P        COMP-3
DNM=1-332     77   PACKED-FIELD-UNSIGNED          BL=1   01E     DNM=1-332     DS 2P        COMP-3
DNM=1-363     77   PACKED-FIELD-WITH-POINT        BL=1   020     DNM=1-363     DS 3P        COMP-3
```

Figure 14.2 Data Division Map

DISPL—Indicates the displacement, in hexadecimal, from the base register for each data name.

DEFINITION—Defines storage for each data item in Assembler-like terminology. Observe the various storage assignments and how they correspond to the specific COBOL USAGE and PICTURE clauses.

USAGE—Indicates the usage of the data name as defined in the COBOL program.

R O Q M—Four columns, each with special significance:
R—data name redefines another data name,
O—OCCURS clause has been specified,
Q—DEPENDING ON clause was specified,
M—format of the records in the file; fixed, variable, etc.

Literal Pool and Register Assignment

Figure 14.3 contains the literal pool and register assignment for Figure 14.1. The literal pool lists the collection of literals in the program. It includes those specified by the programmer as in a move statement and those generated by the compiler, e.g., those needed for decimal alignment. Use of these literals is made clearer in the section on nonaligned fields. The PGT, or program global table, contains the remaining addresses and literals used by the object program. Its use is not discussed further.

The register assignment shows that BL 1 (base locator 1) is assigned to general register 6.

```
002F8 (LIT + 0)       000A0000      0000000A


                      PGT                        002E0

               OVERFLOW CELLS                    002E0
               VIRTUAL CELLS                     002E0
               PROCEDURE NAME CELLS              002F4
               GENERATED NAME CELLS              002F4
               DCB ADDRESS CELLS                 002F8
               VNI CELLS                         002F8
               LITERALS                          002F8
               DISPLAY LITERALS                  00300

REGISTER ASSIGNMENT

      REG 6    BL = 1
```

Figure 14.3 Literal Pool and Register Assignment

The procedure division map (Figure 14.4) contains information about the generated object code. Reading from left to right, we see

1. Compiler generated statement number.

2. The COBOL verb referenced in the statement number under item 1.

3. The relative location, in hexadecimal, of the object instruction.

4. The actual object code instruction.

5. The object code instruction in a form that most closely resembles the Assembler language.

6. Compiler-generated information about the operands, including names and relative location of the literals.

```
44      ADD     000300                          START   EQU     *
                000300    48 30 6 000                   LH      3,000(0,6)          DNM=1-32
                000304    5A 30 6 002                   A       3,002(0,6)          DNM=1-58
                000308    50 30 6 002                   ST      3,002(0,6)          DNM=1-58
45      ADD     00030C    F2 72 D 1F8 6 00A             PACK    1F8(8,13),00A(3,6)   TS=01        DNM=1-148
                000312    F2 74 D 200 6 00D             PACK    200(8,13),00D(5,6)   TS=09        DNM=1-181
                000318    FA 32 D 1FC D 205             AP      1FC(4,13),205(3,13)  TS=05        TS=014
                00031E    F3 43 6 00D D 1FC             UNPK    00D(5,6),1FC(4,13)   DNM=1-181    TS=05
46      ADD     000324    FA 21 6 01B 6 019             AP      01B(3,6),019(2,6)    DNM=1-306    DNM=1-280
50      ADD     00032A    F2 72 D 200 6 00A             PACK    200(8,13),00A(3,6)   TS=09        DNM=1-148
                000330    FA 21 D 205 6 019             AP      205(3,13),019(2,6)   TS=014       DNM=1-280
                000336    F3 22 6 00A D 205             UNPK    00A(3,6),205(3,13)   DNM=1-148    TS=014
51      ADD     00033C    F2 72 D 200 6 00A             PACK    200(8,13),00A(3,6)   TS=09        DNM=1-148
                000342    FA 11 6 019 D 206             AP      019(2,6),206(2,13)   DNM=1-280    TS=015
54      ADD     000348    F8 71 D 200 6 019             ZAP     200(8,13),019(2,6)   TS=09        DNM=1-280
                00034E    4F 30 D 200                   CVB     3,200(0,13)          TS=09
                000352    4A 30 6 000                   AH      3,000(0,6)           DNM=1-32
                000356    40 30 6 000                   STH     3,000(0,6)           DNM=1-32
55      ADD     00035A    48 30 6 000                   LH      3,000(0,6)           DNM=1-32
                00035E    4E 30 D 200                   CVD     3,200(0,13)          TS=09
                000362    FA 11 6 019 D 206             AP      019(2,6),206(2,13)   DNM=1-280    TS=015
58      ADD     000368    F2 72 D 200 6 00A             PACK    200(8,13),00A(3,6)   TS=09        DNM=1-148
                00036E    4F 30 D 200                   CVB     3,200(0,13)          TS=09
                000372    4A 30 6 000                   AH      3,000(0,6)           DNM=1-32
                000376    40 30 6 000                   STH     3,000(0,6)           DNM=1-32
59      ADD     00037A    F2 72 D 200 6 00A             PACK    200(8,13),00A(3,6)   TS=09        DNM=1-148
                000380    48 30 6 000                   LH      3,000(0,6)           DNM=1-32
                000384    4E 30 D 1F8                   CVD     3,1F8(0,13)          TS=01
                000388    FA 21 D 1FD D 206             AP      1FD(3,13),206(2,13)  TS=06        TS=015
                00038E    F3 22 6 00A D 1FD             UNPK    00A(3,6),1FD(3,13)   DNM=1-148    TS=06
67      ADD     000394    F2 72 D 200 6 012             PACK    200(8,13),012(3,6)   TS=09        DNM=1-214
                00039A    F2 72 D 1F8 6 00A             PACK    1F8(8,13),00A(3,6)   TS=01        DNM=1-148
                0003A0    FA 21 D 205 D 1FE             AP      205(3,13),1FE(2,13)  TS=014       TS=07
                0003A6    F3 22 6 00A D 205             UNPK    00A(3,6),205(3,13)   DNM=1-148    TS=014
68      ADD     0003AC    F2 72 D 200 6 00A             PACK    200(8,13),00A(3,6)   TS=09        DNM=1-148
                0003B2    F2 72 D 1F8 6 012             PACK    1F8(8,13),012(3,6)   TS=01        DNM=1-214
                0003B8    FA 21 D 205 D 1FE             AP      205(3,13),1FE(2,13)  TS=014       TS=07
                0003BE    F3 22 6 012 D 205             UNPK    012(3,6),205(3,13)   DNM=1-214    TS=014
                0003C4    96 F0 6 014                   OI      014(6),X'F0'         DNM=1-214+2
69      ADD     0003C8    48 30 6 006                   LH      3,006(0,6)           DNM=1-84
                0003CC    4A 30 6 000                   AH      3,000(0,6)           DNM=1-32
                0003D0    40 30 6 000                   STH     3,000(0,6)           DNM=1-32
70      ADD     0003D4    48 30 6 000                   LH      3,000(0,6)           DNM=1-32
                0003D8    4A 30 6 006                   AH      3,006(0,6)           DNM=1-84
                0003DC    10 33                         LPR     3,3
                0003DE    40 30 6 006                   STH     3,006(0,6)           DNM=1-84
71      ADD     0003E2    FA 11 6 019 6 01E             AP      019(2,6),01E(2,6)    DNM=1-280    DNM=1-332
72      ADD     0003E8    FA 11 6 01E 6 019             AP      01E(2,6),019(2,6)    DNM=1-332    DNM=1-280
                0003EE    96 0F 6 01F                   OI      01F(6),X'0F'         DNM=1-332+1
80      ADD     0003F2    F2 73 D 200 6 015             PACK    200(8,13),015(4,6)   TS=09        DNM=1-246
                0003F8    F2 72 D 1F8 6 00A             PACK    1F8(8,13),00A(3,6)   TS=01        DNM=1-148
                0003FE    F0 20 D 1FD 0 001             SRP     1FD(3,13),001(0),0   TS=06
                000404    FA 22 D 205 D 1FD             AP      205(3,13),1FD(3,13)  TS=014       TS=06
                00040A    F1 76 D 200 D 200             MVO     200(8,13),200(7,13)  TS=09        TS=09
                000410    F3 22 6 00A D 205             UNPK    00A(3,6),205(3,13)   DNM=1-148    TS=014
81      ADD     000416    F2 72 D 200 6 00A             PACK    200(8,13),00A(3,6)   TS=09        DNM=1-148
                00041C    F2 73 D 1F8 6 015             PACK    1F8(8,13),015(4,6)   TS=01        DNM=1-246
                000422    F0 20 D 205 0 001             SRP     205(3,13),001(0),0   TS=014
                000428    FA 22 D 205 D 1FD             AP      205(3,13),1FD(3,13)  TS=014       TS=06
                00042E    F3 32 6 015 D 205             UNPK    015(4,6),205(3,13)   DNM=1-246    TS=014
82      ADD     000434    48 30 6 000                   LH      3,000(0,6)           DNM=1-32
                000438    4C 30 C 018                   MH      3,018(0,12)          LIT+0
                00043C    4A 30 6 008                   AH      3,008(0,6)           DNM=1-115
                000440    40 30 6 008                   STH     3,008(0,6)           DNM=1-115
```

Figure 14.4 Procedure Division Map

```
83    ADD    000444  48 30 6 000          LH    3,000(0,6)       DNM=1-32
             000448  4C 30 C 018          MH    3,018(0,12)      LIT+0
             00044C  4A 30 6 008          AH    3,008(0,6)       DNM=1-115
             000450  18 23                LR    2,3
             000452  8E 20 0 020          SRDA  2,020(0)
             000456  5D 20 C 01C          D     2,01C(0,12)      LIT+4
             00045A  40 30 6 000          STH   3,000(0,6)       DNM=1-32
84    ADD    00045E  F8 71 D 200 6 019    ZAP   200(8,13),019(2,6)   TS=09      DNM=1-280
             000464  F0 20 D 205 0 001    SRP   205(3,13),001(0),0   TS=014
             00046A  FA 22 6 020 D 205    AP    020(3,6),205(3,13)   DNM=1-363  TS=014
             000470  94 0F 6 020          NI    020(6),X'0F'         DNM=1-363
85    ADD    000474  F8 71 D 200 6 019    ZAP   200(8,13),019(2,6)   TS=09      DNM=1-280
             00047A  F0 20 D 205 0 001    SRP   205(3,13),001(0),0   TS=014
             000480  FA 22 D 205 6 020    AP    205(3,13),020(3,6)   TS=014     DNM=1-363
             000486  F1 76 D 200 D 200    MVO   200(8,13),200(7,13)  TS=09      TS=09
             00048C  F8 11 6 019 D 206    ZAP   019(2,6),206(2,13)   DNM=1-280  TS=014+1
86    STOP   000492  58 F0 C 00C          L     15,00C(0,12)         V(ILBODBG4)
             000496  05 EF                BALR  14,15
             000498          GN=01        EQU   *
             000498  58 F0 C 010          L     15,010(0,12)         V(ILBOSRV1)
             00049C  07 FF                BCR   15,15
             00049E  50 D0 5 008  INIT2   ST    13,008(0,5)
             0004A2  50 50 D 004          ST    5,004(0,13)
             0004A6  50 E0 D 054          ST    14,054(0,13)
             0004AA  91 20 D 048          TM    048(13),X'20'        SWT+0
             0004AE  47 E0 F 02E          BC    14,02E(0,15)
             0004B2  58 20 D 1B8          L     2,1B8(0,13)
             0004B6  91 40 D 049          TM    049(13),X'40'        SWT+1
             0004BA  47 E0 F 02E          BC    14,02E(0,15)
             0004BE  96 04 2 000          OI    000(2),X'04'
             0004C2  58 F0 2 038          L     15,038(0,2)
             0004C6  41 F0 F 004          LA    15,004(0,15)
             0004CA  07 FF                BCR   15,15
             0004CC  94 EF D 048          NI    048(13),X'EF'        SWT+0
             0004D0  58 F0 C 000          L     15,000(0,12)         VIR=1
             0004D4  05 EF                BALR  14,15
             0004D6  12 00                LTR   0,0
             0004D8  07 89                BCR   8,9
             0004DA  96 10 D 048          OI    048(13),X'10'        SWT+0
             0004DE  58 F0 C 004  INIT3   L     15,004(0,12)         VIR=2
```

Figure 14.4 (*Continued*)

DISPLAY TO DISPLAY: We return to Figure 14.1 and shall examine three COBOL add statements and generated object code. In each example both operands are signed, of the same data type, and have identical decimal alignment. Consider first COBOL statement 45, as well as statements 18–21 in the working-storage section.

COBOL Add Instructions with Similar Data Types

```
      ADD ZONED-DECIMAL-FIELD-ONE TO ZONED-DECIMAL-FIELD-TWO.

  77  ZONED-DECIMAL-FIELD-ONE      PICTURE IS S9(3)
         USAGE IS DISPLAY.

  77  ZONED-DECIMAL-FIELD-TWO      PICTURE IS S9(5)
         USAGE IS DISPLAY.
```

From the procedure division map, we extract four lines associated with COBOL statement 45:

```
  45  ADD   F2 72 D 1F8 6 00A   PACK ...  TS = 01      DNM = 1-148
            F2 74 D 200 6 00D   PACK ...  TS = 09      DNM = 1-181
            FA 32 D 1FC D 205   AP   ...  TS = 05      TS = 014
            F3 43 6 00D D 1FC   UNPK ...  DNM = 1-181  TS = 05
```

The COBOL programmer simply wants to add two numeric fields. However, since the fields are DISPLAY, i.e., stored as zoned decimal numbers, they must first be packed, and then after the addition, the sum must be unpacked. The first object instruction packs DNM = 1–148, i.e., ZONED-DECIMAL-FIELD-ONE (check the data division map), into a temporary storage area 8 bytes in length. In like manner, DNM = 1–181, i.e., ZONED-DECIMAL-FIELD-TWO, is packed into TS = 09, also a temporary storage area of 8 bytes. Notice how the length, base register, and displacement match the data division map. The contents of the two temporary storage areas are then added via the add packed instruction, and finally the sum is unpacked into DNM = 1–181, i.e., ZONED-DECIMAL-FIELD-TWO. (Observe the length codes associated with each instruction.)

PACKED TO PACKED: Consider now COBOL statement 46 and its relevant 77-level entries (lines 26–29).

```
            ADD PACKED-FIELD-ONE TO PACKED-FIELD-TWO.

    77  PACKED-FIELD-ONE                 PICTURE IS S9(3)
          USAGE IS COMPUTATIONAL-3.
    77  PACKED-FIELD-TWO                 PICTURE IS S9(5)
          USAGE IS COMPUTATIONAL-3.
```

This time only a single add packed instruction is generated by the compiler:

```
    46  ADD     FA 21 6 01B 6 019    AP  ...  DNM = 1–306    DNM = 1–280
```

Observe that the operands DNM = 1–306 and DNM = 1–280 correspond to PACKED-FIELD-TWO and PACKED-FIELD-ONE, respectively. Further note the displacement for each operand, 01B and 019, and the correspondence in the data division map. Finally the sum of the add packed instruction is stored in the first operand, i.e., DNM = 1–306 corresponding to PACKED-FIELD-TWO, as intended by the COBOL programmer. Compare this single instruction to the four instructions and 24 bytes of code required in the previous example. The saving is realized because the operands are defined as packed fields by the programmer; hence, there is no need for the compiler to pack and subsequently unpack.

BINARY TO BINARY: Addition of two binary operands is illustrated in COBOL statement 44 with the relevant 77-level entries defined in statements 10–13.

```
            ADD BINARY-FIELD-ONE TO BINARY-FIELD-TWO.

    77  BINARY-FIELD-ONE                 PICTURE IS S9(3)
          USAGE IS COMPUTATIONAL.
    77  BINARY-FIELD-TWO                 PICTURE IS S9(5)
          USAGE IS COMPUTATIONAL.
```

Object instructions generated by the compiler are shown below:

```
    44  ADD     48 30 6 000    LH  ...  DNM = 1–32
            5A 30 6 002    A   ...  DNM = 1–58
            50 30 6 002    ST  ...  DNM = 1–58
```

Since we are dealing with binary operands, the add packed instruction is no longer appropriate. Instead the compiler generates either an AH (add half-word) or A (add full word) instruction depending on the size of the binary operands. The LH (load half-word) instruction brings BINARY-FIELD-ONE into register 3. The A (add full word) instruction adds the value of BINARY-FIELD-TWO to register 3. Finally the store instruction moves the contents of register 3 to BINARY-FIELD-TWO.

Careful analysis of this section shows how three apparently similar COBOL instructions in Figure 14.1, statements 44, 45, and 46, produce vastly different object instructions. In each instance, the programmer was adding a three-position signed field to a five-position signed field of similar data type and decimal alignment. Addition of two COMPUTATIONAL-3 fields required one instruction (6 bytes); addition of two DISPLAY fields took four instructions (24 bytes); and addition of two COMPUTATIONAL fields took three instructions (12 bytes).

We shall concentrate on combinations of packed and binary data and leave the reader to work through other examples in Figure 14.1.

BINARY TO DECIMAL: BINARY-FIELD-ONE is added to PACKED-FIELD-ONE in COBOL statement 55. Both fields are defined as signed three-digit fields with no decimal point, as shown below:

```
        ADD BINARY-FIELD-ONE TO PACKED-FIELD-ONE.

   77   BINARY-FIELD-ONE              PICTURE IS S9(3)
           USAGE IS COMPUTATIONAL.
   77   PACKED-FIELD-ONE              PICTURE IS S9(3)
           USAGE IS COMPUTATIONAL-3.
```

Since a binary field is added to a packed field, it is necessary to first convert the binary data to packed data. Consider the three machine language statements generated:

```
   55  ADD    48 30 6 000        LH   ...  DNM = 1–32
              4E 30 D 200        CVD  ...  TS = 09
              FA 11 6 019 D 206  AP   ...  DNM = 1–280  TS = 015
```

BINARY-FIELD-ONE (i.e., DNM = 1–32) is loaded into register 3 via the load half word instruction. Next it is converted to a packed field and stored on a double word boundary by the CVD instruction. Finally the newly created packed field is added to DNM = 1–280, i.e., PACKED-FIELD-ONE, and the results are stored there. (The reader should question why the displacement associated with register D changed from 200 to 206 in the second and third instructions; if he didn't, then he is not paying attention.)

DECIMAL TO BINARY: COBOL statement 54 is identical to statement 55 except the results are stored in the binary field. The reasoning in the Assembler sequence is analogous to the previous example.

```
   54  ADD    F8 71 D 200 6 019  ZAP  ...  TS = 09      DNM = 1–280
              4F 30 D 200        CVB  ...  TS = 09
              4A 30 6 000        AH   ...  DNM = 1–32
              40 30 6 000        STH  ...  DNM = 1–32
```

The CVB instruction must operate on a double word boundary, and since PACKED-FIELD-ONE is only 2 bytes in length, it is necessary to fill the high-order bytes of the double word with zeros. The ZAP (zero and add packed) instruction takes the second operand DNM = 1–280, i.e., PACKED-FIELD-ONE; moves it to a double word boundary; and fills the high-order bytes with binary zeros. The newly moved decimal field is then converted to binary and stored in register 3. BINARY-FIELD-ONE is added to the contents of register 3, with the sum remaining in register 3. The sum is finally stored in BINARY-FIELD-ONE via the STH. Seem complicated? Yes, it is, but that is exactly the point. It is unnecessarily complex because the COBOL programmer, perhaps inadvertently, is adding a packed field to a binary field. Compare the four instructions and 18 bytes of code in this example to the single add packed instruction needed for addition of two decimal fields.

PACKED TO PACKED: When the data division and picture clause were first studied, we stated that any numeric field should be preceded by an "S" or otherwise the sign would be lost. That rule is still valid. Now let's learn what the compiler does. Consider COBOL statement 72 and relevant 77-level entries, lines 26, 27, 30, and 31.

77	PACKED-FIELD-ONE	PICTURE IS S9(3)
	USAGE IS COMPUTATIONAL-3.	
77	PACKED-FIELD-UNSIGNED	PICTURE IS 9(3)
	USAGE IS COMPUTATIONAL-3.	

Generated instructions are below:

```
72  ADD    FA 11 6 01E 6 019    AP ... DNM = 1–332      DNM = 1–280
        96 0F 6 01F          OI ... DNM = 1–332 + 1
```

The add packed instruction works exactly as the one generated by COBOL statement 46, considered earlier in the addition of packed fields. DNM = 1–332 is 2 bytes in length and stored in bytes 01E and 01F displaced from register 6. The AP instruction always produces a sign of "C" (plus) or "D" (minus) and stores it in the low-order byte of the sum, in this case byte 01F displaced from register 6.

The OI (or immediate) instruction is an SI instruction which takes the value of the "I" operand, "0F," and does a bit-by-bit *logical or* upon the storage address, altering the value of the storage location DNM = 1–332 + 1 (base register 6, displaced by 01F). In effect, it changes the sign from either "C" or "D" to "F" while the rest of the field remains undisturbed. Thus, since PACKED-FIELD-UNSIGNED was declared unsigned, an OI instruction was generated to remove the sign. This is not true in COBOL statement 71, as shown below:

ADD PACKED-FIELD-UNSIGNED TO PACKED-FIELD-ONE.

Generated instructions:

```
71  ADD  FA 11 6 019 6 01E    AP ... DNM = 1–280    DNM = 1–332
```

Here the sum is stored in PACKED-FIELD-ONE, which was declared as a signed field. Thus, there is only a single AP instruction generated, and the sign remains intact.

BINARY TO BINARY: Similar reasoning holds for binary operands, except a different instruction is used to remove the sign. Recall that the sign of a binary number is stored in the high-order bit. (A "0" indicates a positive number, and a "1" indicates a negative number stored in two's complement.) If the receiving field is unsigned, then an LPR (load positive register) instruction is generated in the series of instructions. Consider COBOL statement 70 and relevant 77-level entries 10, 11, 14, and 15.

ADD BINARY-FIELD-ONE TO BINARY-FIELD-UNSIGNED.

77	BINARY-FIELD-ONE	PICTURE IS S9(3)
	USAGE IS COMPUTATIONAL.	
77	BINARY-FIELD-UNSIGNED	PICTURE IS 9(3)
	USAGE IS COMPUTATIONAL.	

The generated instructions are shown below:

```
70  ADD    48 30 6 000    LH  ... DNM = 1–32
        4A 30 6 006    AH  ... DNM = 1–84
        10 33          LPR ...
        40 30 6 006    STH ... DNM = 1–84
```

These instructions parallel those generated for COBOL statement 44 except that an AH (add half-word) and STH (store half-word) are generated in lieu of an A (add full word) and ST (store full word), respectively. Why?

Further note the instruction LPR 3,3 after the addition. The effect of this instruction is to load the absolute value of register 3 into register 3, thereby destroying a minus sign if it were present.

COBOL statement 69 also involves an unsigned operand, except that it is not the receiving field; hence, there is no LPR instruction, and the generated code is comparable to that of COBOL statement 44.

Adding Operands that Are Not Aligned

The addition of operands with nonsimilar decimal alignment produces extensive and often confusing object code. COBOL statements 80–85 in Figure 14.1 illustrate several combinations for nonaligned fields. However, only statement 82 is covered in detail, as the others require introduction of several new instructions which go beyond the scope of this chapter. The reader should also realize that as complicated as the object instructions appear, they would be substantially more involved if different data types were mixed in the same instruction.

Consider COBOL statement 82 and relevant 77-level entries, statements 10, 11, 16, 17.

```
        ADD BINARY-FIELD-ONE TO BINARY-FIELD-WITH-POINT.

    77  BINARY-FIELD-ONE              PICTURE IS S9(3)
            USAGE IS COMPUTATIONAL.
    77  BINARY-FIELD-WITH-POINT       PICTURE IS S9(3)V9
            USAGE IS COMPUTATIONAL.
```

The generated object code is below:

```
    82  ADD    48 30 6 000   LH   ...  DNM = 1–32
               4C 30 C 018   MH   ...  LIT + 0
               4A 30 6 008   AH   ...  DNM = 1–115
               40 30 6 008   STH  ...  DNM = 1–115
```

Let us first consider conceptually what is and is not required. Both operands are binary, so there is no need for conversion of data type; both operands are signed, and thus no instructions need be generated to remove the sign. However, the decimal alignments are different, and they must first be made identical before addition can occur. BINARY-FIELD-WITH-POINT is the receiving field with an implied decimal point which in effect makes it larger by a factor of 10 than BINARY-FIELD-ONE; thus BINARY-FIELD-ONE will be multiplied by 10 prior to addition. (Note the presence of a divide instruction in the assembler sequence for COBOL statement 83 in which the same two operands are combined but where BINARY-FIELD-ONE is the receiving field.)

First DNM = 1–32, i.e., BINARY-FIELD-ONE, is loaded into register 3. The contents of register 3 are then multiplied by the contents of a half-word, beginning at LIT + 0, which equals "000A" in hexadecimal and "10" in decimal (see Figure 14.3). The results of the multiplication are stored in register 3. Next DNM = 1–115, i.e., BINARY-FIELD-WITH-POINT, is added to the contents of register 3, and the sum is placed in register 3. Finally the contents of register 3 are stored in BINARY-FIELD-WITH-POINT.

As can be seen from this example, the combination of nonaligned fields in a source program necessitates the generation of extra instructions in the object program. COBOL statements 80–85 present a sufficient variety of new BAL instructions to acquaint the reader with alignment logic. In actual practice situations arise in which incompatible formats are unavoidable. In such instances one must comply with the "specs" as given, and efficiency considerations are shunted aside.

The Assembler instructions listed below were introduced as background for efficiency considerations:

Summary

> PACK—Pack
> UNPK—Unpack
> CVB—Convert to binary
> CVD—Convert to decimal
> MVC—Move characters
> L—Load (full word)
> ST—Store (full word)
> AP—Add packed
> A—Add (full word)

Next, a COBOL program, consisting of ADD statements using various combinations of data types and decimal alignments, was used to illustrate basic workings of the COBOL compiler. The procedure and data division maps, register assignments, and literal pool were examined in detail. Several sets of COBOL and generated object instructions were compared. Initially both operands in the COBOL instruction were of the same data type and sign and were similarly aligned. Subsequently, these restrictions were removed to consider combinations of packed and binary data, nonaligned binary fields, and unsigned binary and decimal fields.

In conclusion, the COBOL programmer can and does function with no knowledge of the machine on which he is working. However, a little knowledge in this area goes a long way toward genuine understanding of debugging and efficiency considerations. We hope this point has been effectively made in both this chapter and the entire section. We have found that the best COBOL programmers are those who also know, or at least have a fundamental understanding of, Assembler as well.

REVIEW EXERCISES

TRUE	FALSE		
☐	☐	1	A load instruction changes the contents of a register.
☐	☐	2	A store instruction does not change the contents of a storage location.
☐	☐	3	DISPLAY data must be packed before they can be added.
☐	☐	4	Data must be in binary format before they can be added.
☐	☐	5	The COBOL programmer is not permitted to mix data types in the same COBOL instruction.
☐	☐	6	An add half-word instruction could be used in conjunction with packed data.
☐	☐	7	The CVD instruction converts binary data to packed format.
☐	☐	8	The CVB instruction changes the contents of a register.
☐	☐	9	The PACK instruction must operate on two fields of identical length.
☐	☐	10	The MVC instruction has only one length field.
☐	☐	11	AP (add packed) is a storage-to-storage instruction.
☐	☐	12	The CVB instruction works directly on DISPLAY data.
☐	☐	13	The addition of two COMPUTATIONAL-3 fields requires fewer machine instructions than the addition of two DISPLAY fields.
☐	☐	14	A minimum of four machine instructions is required to add two DISPLAY fields.

PROBLEMS

1 Consider the data division map of Figure 14.2. Show how the displacement and definition columns are consistent with the definitions in the working-storage section of Figure 14.1.

2 Consider the object instructions generated for COBOL statement 45. Show that the length codes in both the machine and Assembler instructions are consistent with the definitions in working-storage. Also show consistency of base registers and displacement between the machine and Assembler instructions.

3 Consider the following COBOL statement:

        ADD COMP3-DATA-NAME TO DISPLAY-DATA-NAME.

where

        77 COMP3-DATA-NAME PICTURE IS S9(4)
                USAGE IS COMPUTATIONAL-3.

and

        77 DISPLAY-DATA-NAME PICTURE IS S9(4).

are the definitions for the respective data names. The following statements were found in a procedure division map corresponding to the above:

        F2 F3 3168 A009   (PACK)
        FA F2 3168 A021   (AP)
        F3 3F A009 3168   (UNPK)

(a) Where is the compiler work area? How many bytes does it contain?
(b) What is the location associated with each COBOL data name? (*Do not guess*, but explain how the structure of the COBOL and BAL ADD statements gives you an unambiguous answer.)

4 Given the data division entries

        77 FIELD-A PIC 9(3)   VALUE 456.
        77 FIELD-B PIC 9(3)   VALUE 123.
        77 SUM1   PIC 9(3)   VALUE 0.
        77 SUM2   PIC S9(3)   VALUE 0.

and given the procedure division entries

        ADD FIELD-A, FIELD-B GIVING SUM1.
        ADD FIELD-A, FIELD-B GIVING SUM2.

explain why SUM1 would print as 579 but SUM2 would print as 57I. (Hint: Remember the *or immediate* instruction.)

5   Given the following data division entries:

```
01  FIRST-SET-OF-COUNTERS.
    05  COUNTER-A    DISPLAY    PIC 9(3).
    05  COUNTER-B    DISPLAY    PIC 9(3).
    05  COUNTER-C    DISPLAY    PIC 9(3).

01  SECOND-SET-OF-COUNTERS.
    05  COUNTER-D    COMP       PIC S9(4).
    05  COUNTER-E    COMP       PIC S9(4).
    05  COUNTER-F    COMP       PIC S9(4).

01  THIRD-SET-OF-COUNTERS.
    05  COUNTER-G    COMP-3     PIC 9(5).
    05  COUNTER-H    COMP-3     PIC 9(5).
    05  COUNTER-I    COMP-3     PIC 9(5).
```

Is there anything 'wrong' with the following?
(a) MOVE ZEROS TO FIRST-SET-OF-COUNTERS.
(b) MOVE ZEROS TO SECOND-SET-OF-COUNTERS.
(c) MOVE ZEROS TO THIRD-SET-OF-COUNTERS.

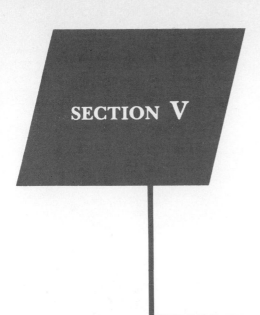

SECTION V

File Processing

CHAPTER

FIFTEEN

Magnetic Tape:
Concepts
and COBOL Implications

The punched card has enjoyed a long and successful reign since its introduction by Dr. Herman Hollerith. However, beginning in the late 1950s, as electronic computers gained in capability and acceptance, it became impractical to store entire files on cards. This is not to say that the punched card has outlived its usefulness, for even today it serves as a primary means of data input. Data are recorded on cards, but after initial entry are transferred to auxiliary storage such as tape or disk. In this chapter we shall discuss concepts of magnetic tape and associated COBOL implications.

Overview

This is a good place to distinguish between a reel of tape and a tape drive. The typical reel of magnetic tape is 2400 feet long, and $\frac{1}{2}$ inch wide and weighs about 4 pounds. The tape drive is the unit which reads (writes) information from the reel. The reel is easily portable; the drive is obviously confined to the machine room. See Figure 15.1.

Tapes are generally classified as either 7 or 9 track, depending on how data are stored internally. Recall from Chapter 12 that IBM systems use EBCDIC (an 8-bit code), whereas most other manufacturers use ASCII (a 6-bit code). Both codes employ parity checking and hence the extension to either 9 or 7 track. A 9-track tape can be viewed as having 9 rows extending for the entire length of the tape, i.e., 2400 feet. Each individual character is stored in a vertical

Tape Characteristics and Capacity

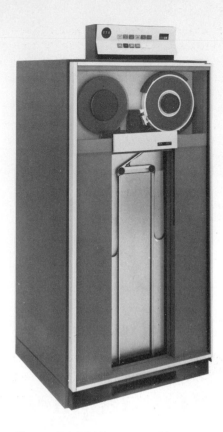

Figure 15.1 IBM Tape Drive (*Courtesy* IBM)

column. Each column contains 9 bits, one for each track. The individual bits may be "on" or "off," i.e., 1 or 0. The presence or absence of these bits in a particular column denotes a character much like the punched holes in a card column. Figure 15.2 shows schematics of 7- and 9-track tapes.

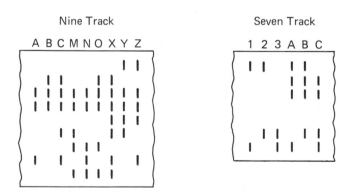

Figure 15.2 7- and 9-Track Schematics

The amount of data that can be stored on a given reel is dependent on three factors: tape density, blocking factor, and interrecord gap (also known as interblock gap). Tape density is a measure of how close the columns are to one another. It is usually specified as characters or bytes per inch (bpi). Common densities are 556, 800, 1600, and 6250 bpi.

The next time you are in the computer center, watch the operation of the tape drive and notice an uneven rather than smooth motion. This is produced by gaps, i.e., lengths of blank tape, between each record on the reel. These gaps are required for the system to distinguish between different physical records. In reality the tape drive continually stops and starts every time it encounters a gap, producing the irregular motion.

The interrecord gap (IRG) profoundly affects the storage capacity of a tape. It is typically anywhere from .3 to .75 inch. Consider a tape with a density of 1600 bpi and an IRG of $\frac{1}{2}$ inch. If we are recording card images, each tape record consists of 80 bytes and takes 80/1600 or 1/20 inch. However, an IRG of $\frac{1}{2}$ inch is present between each record. Thus we are left with the somewhat incongruous situation of having 10 times as much empty space as data.

Blocking offers a way out of this dilemma. If blocking is used, several records are grouped into one block (known as a physical record), and the entire block is read (written) at one time. The blocking factor is the number of logical records in one physical record. The interrecord gap is still required, but only between physical records. Figure 15.3 shows blocked and unblocked records, with an arbitrary blocking factor of 2 chosen for illustration.

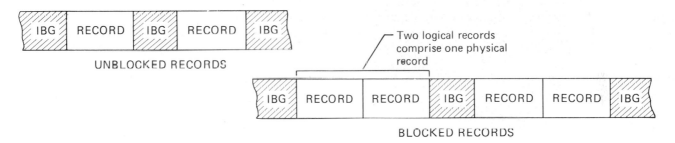

Figure 15.3 Blocked and Unblocked Records

To appreciate the effect of blocking on capacity, return to our example with card images, 1600 bpi and an IRG of $\frac{1}{2}$ inch, and assume a blocking factor of 5. Each physical record contains 400 bytes (5 × 80) and requires $\frac{1}{4}$ inch (400/1600). We have effected a fivefold improvement in terms of wasted space, but the tape still contains twice as much empty space as data.

Obviously blocking is a good thing. The higher the blocking factor, the more economical the tape storage. Why not increase the blocking factor to 10, 100, or 1000, or, better yet, consider the entire file as a single block. The limitation on blocking is determined by internal storage capacity. The entire block must be taken into storage at the same time. Card images, blocked by 100, would require an I/O area in storage of 8000 (80 × 100) bytes, which may not be available. Accordingly, the blocking factor is limited by storage considerations, and the programmer must operate within these constraints.

Example 15.1

How many card images can fit on a 2400-foot reel? Assume a density of 1600 bpi, IRG = $\frac{1}{2}$ inch, and a blocking factor of 30.

SOLUTION

1. Since the blocking factor is 30, there are 30 logical records to 1 physical record. Each physical record contains 30 × 80 = 2400 bytes.
2. Each physical record takes $1\frac{1}{2}$ inches (2400/1600).
3. Associated with each physical record is an IRG of $\frac{1}{2}$ inch. Thus we may say that each physical record requires 2 inches ($1\frac{1}{2}$ for data and $\frac{1}{2}$ for the IRG).
4. Since each physical record takes 2 inches, the entire tape can accommodate 14,400 physical records [(2400 ft/tape × 12 inches/ft) ÷ 2 inches/record].

5. Since there are 30 logical records per physical record, and since the tape holds 14,400 physical records, it can take 432,000 cards (14,400 × 30).

OBSERVATIONS

1. There are 2000 cards in a box. Thus a reel of tape with 432,000 cards is equivalent to 216 boxes. Which would you rather carry?
2. When stacked vertically, there are 140 cards to the inch. Thus a stack of 432,000 cards would stand approximately 252 feet tall [432,000/(140 × 12)] or the equivalent of a 25-story building.
3. Tapes with density of 6250 bpi and an IRG of .3 inch are commonly available. Consider these implications to items 1 and 2 above.

Example 15.2

The inventory file of ACME Wigdets, Inc. contains 36,000 records, each 400 bytes long. Determine whether the entire file will fit on a single 2400 foot reel of tape (use 800 bpi and IRG = .5 inch). Consider no blocking and then a blocking factor of 3.

SOLUTION: No Blocking

1. Each logical record takes $\frac{1}{2}$ inch (400/800).
2. Each record has an associated gap of $\frac{1}{2}$ inch. Since there is no blocking, each physical record requires 1 inch ($\frac{1}{2}$ for data and $\frac{1}{2}$ for the IRG).
3. The entire file of 36,000 records takes 36,000 inches or 3000 feet (36,000/12).
4. The entire file does not fit on one reel if blocking is not used.

SOLUTION: Blocking Factor of 3

1. Each logical record still takes $\frac{1}{2}$ inch.
2. Each physical record consists of three logical records or 1200 bytes (400 × 3). Each physical record takes $1\frac{1}{2}$ inches (1200/800).
3. Each physical record has an associated gap of $\frac{1}{2}$ inch. The total requirement for a physical record is 2 inches ($1\frac{1}{2}$ inches for data and $\frac{1}{2}$ inch for IRG).
4. 36,000 logical records in the file and a blocking factor of 3 means 12,000 physical records.
5. Since each physical record takes 2 inches, the entire file takes 24,000 inches or 2000 feet.
6. The entire file will fit on one reel if a blocking factor of 3 is used.

Vendors are constantly improving tape capabilities, and the numbers used herein may possibly be obsolete when you read them. However, that is immaterial. The concepts and methods of calculation are of primary importance; the actual numbers may add to the interest of the problem but are of secondary value from a pedagogical viewpoint.

Timing Considerations

For purposes of this discussion, reading and writing on tape are assumed to take equal amounts of time. The time required to pass a file (i.e., read or write) is dependent on two factors: transfer rate and start/stop time. Transfer rate is a function of the actual speed of the tape. Start/stop time is the time associated with passing an interrecord gap. The tape actually stops and starts everytime it encounters an IRG, producing the irregular motion noted earlier. These concepts are clarified in Example 15.3.

Chapter 15
Magnetic Tape:
Concepts and COBOL
Implications

Example 15.3

How long would it take to pass a file of 12,000 records, each record 400 bytes long? Use 800 bpi, a tape speed of 200 inches per second, and a start/stop time of 10 milliseconds (.01 second). Answer for both no blocking and a blocking factor of 3.

SOLUTION: No Blocking

1. A tape speed of 200 inches per second and a density of 800 bpi are equivalent to a transfer rate of 160,000 bytes per second (200 × 800).

2. The file contains a total of 4,800,000 bytes (12,000 records × 400 bytes per record).

3. 30 seconds are required for transfer time (4,800,000/160,000). This is the time to actually read the file; it does not include the time to pass the IRG's.

4. With no blocking, there are 12,000 IRG's, one for each record.

5. Since start/stop time is .01 second for 1 IRG, the start/stop time for the entire file is 120 seconds (.01 × 12,000).

6. The total time to pass the file is 150 seconds (transfer time of 30 seconds plus start/stop time of 120 seconds).

SOLUTION: Blocking Factor of 3

1. The transfer time of 30 seconds is unaffected by blocking; i.e., the file still contains 4,800,000 bytes, and the tape still moves at 200 inches per second.

2. Start/stop time is reduced. A blocking factor of 3 means there are now only 4000 IRG's (12,000/3). Start/stop time is now 40 seconds (.01 × 4000).

3. The total time is 70 seconds (30 seconds transfer plus 40 seconds start/stop).

OBSERVATION. A moderately fast card reader can process 1000 cards per minute. A file of 12,000 records, each record 400 bytes long, requires 5 cards per record or 60,000 cards total. At 1000 cards per minute, it would take 1 hour to read the entire file.

Identifying Files on Tape

The files contained on a tape are identified by means of internal labels, i.e., information stored on the tape before and after the file. Each reel contains a volume label, and each file contains both a header and trailer label. A given reel may contain several files (multifile volume), or a single file may stretch over several volumes (multivolume file). All volumes contain both a load point and end of tape marker, which are aluminum strips located 10 feet from either end. The load point signals where information begins, and the end of tape marker signals where information ends (see Figure 17.4 and the related discussion).

When the COBOL phrase LABEL RECORDS ARE STANDARD is included in the FD for a tape file, the system checks the internal labels of a file to assure that the proper volume has been mounted and that it contains the proper file. This is accomplished in conjunction with the JCL and is discussed in detail in Chapters 17 and 18, with the bulk of the discussion in Chapter 17.

COBOL Requirements

The COBOL statements for processing tape files are remarkably similar to those which process card and/or print files. Nevertheless, there are required extensions in the environment, data, and procedure divisions.

Our discussion of tape requirements revolves about the SELECT clause. (The reader should also consult a COBOL manual for variations in the I/O control paragraph.) The general format of the SELECT statement is

> <u>SELECT</u> file-name <u>ASSIGN</u> TO tape-unit-1[tape-unit-2] . . .
>
> [FOR <u>MULTIPLE REEL</u>]
>
> $$\left[\underline{\text{RESERVE}} \left\{ \begin{matrix} \text{integer} \\ \underline{\text{NO}} \end{matrix} \right\} \text{ALTERNATE} \left[\begin{matrix} \text{AREA} \\ \text{AREAS} \end{matrix} \right] \right]$$

Large files can extend over several reels (i.e., a multivolume file), and, in these instances, it is advantageous to assign multiple drives via the COBOL ASSIGN statement. If multiple units are specified, then after the first reel has been processed, the system automatically begins to read from the second; when the second is finished, control passes to the third; etc. If the ASSIGN clause specifies only one unit, the operator must wait for the first reel to rewind. He then removes the first reel and mounts the second before processing can continue. Obviously this is an unnecessary delay.

The RESERVE clause in the SELECT statement increases processing efficiency through overlap. Modern computer systems include hardware devices, called channels, which permit overlap, i.e., simultaneous processing and I/O (see Chapter 17). Under overlap the CPU processes data from one I/O area while the channel simultaneously operates on an alternate area called an I/O buffer. Unless instructed otherwise, most compilers reserve one alternate area to permit overlap. If the phrase RESERVE NO ALTERNATE AREAS is specified, overlap is prevented. Processing is substantially slowed, but an amount of core storage equal to the I/O buffer is saved. Usually RESERVE NO ALTERNATE AREAS is specified only on smaller systems if core storage is a problem. Two equivalent SELECT statements are

```
SELECT TAPE-FILE ASSIGN TO UT-2400-S-SYS010, UT-2400-S-SYS011
    FOR MULTIPLE REEL
    RESERVE 1 ALTERNATE AREA.

SELECT TAPE-FILE ASSIGN TO UT-2400-S-SYS010, UT-2400-S-SYS011.
```

As can be seen from the general format of the COBOL SELECT, the phrase FOR MULTIPLE REEL is optional and is used for documentation only. Multiple units are called for by the ASSIGN clause itself. Thus the omission of FOR MULTIPLE REEL in the second SELECT has no effect since two tape units are specified in the ASSIGN clause. As noted previously, one alternate area is typically reserved unless specification is to the contrary. If the phrase is omitted, as in the second example, one alternate area is still reserved under most compilers. Note also that the exact format of the system device, e.g., UT-2400-S-SYS010, varies from installation to installation; it is also possible to have device-independent SELECT statements as explained in Chapter 18.

Data Division

Extension from card and print files to tape centers around the COBOL FD, the general format of which is shown on the following page.

$$\left[\underline{BLOCK} \text{ CONTAINS} \left[\text{integer-1 } \underline{TO}\right] \text{ integer-2} \right] \begin{Bmatrix} \underline{RECORDS} \\ \underline{CHARACTERS} \end{Bmatrix}$$

[<u>RECORD</u> CONTAINS [integer-1 <u>TO</u>] integer-2 CHARACTERS]

[<u>RECORDING</u> MODE IS mode]

$$\text{LABEL} \begin{Bmatrix} \underline{RECORDS} \text{ ARE} \\ \underline{RECORD} \text{ IS} \end{Bmatrix} \begin{Bmatrix} \underline{STANDARD} \\ \underline{OMITTED} \end{Bmatrix}$$

$$\left[\underline{VALUE} \underline{OF} \text{ data-name-1 IS} \begin{Bmatrix} \text{data-name-2} \\ \text{literal-1} \end{Bmatrix} \left[\text{data-name-3 IS} \begin{Bmatrix} \text{data-name-4} \\ \text{literal-2} \dots \end{Bmatrix}\right]\right]$$

$$\left[\text{DATA} \begin{Bmatrix} \underline{RECORD} \text{ IS} \\ \underline{RECORDS} \text{ ARE} \end{Bmatrix} \text{record-name-1 [record-name-2]} \dots \right]$$

Until now, all records have been the same (i.e., fixed) length. Note, however, the variable lengths implied by RECORD (or BLOCK) CONTAINS integer-1 TO integer-2 CHARACTERS. In practice, records are often of varying length. For example, in a file of student records, a senior has completed more courses than a sophomore and requires a larger record to store his transcript. It is, of course, possible to provide a uniform maximum length for all, but this entails a large amount of wasted space. Accordingly, variable-length records are permitted and specified in the COBOL FD. Variable-length records can employ the OCCURS DEPENDING ON clause in the record description as shown in Figure 15.4.

```
FD   STUDENT-TRANSCRIPT-FILE
     RECORD CONTAINS 42 TO 342 CHARACTERS
     RECORDING MODE IS V
     LABEL RECORDS ARE STANDARD
     DATA RECORD IS STUDENT-RECORD.
01   STUDENT-RECORD.
     05   ST-NAME                              PIC X(30).
     05   ST-YEAR-IN-SCHOOL                    PIC X(10).
     05   ST-COURSES-COMPLETED                 PIC 99.
     05   ST-COURSE-GRADE OCCURS 0 TO 60 TIMES
          DEPENDING ON ST-COURSES-COMPLETED.
          10   ST-COURSE-NUMBER                PIC 9999.
          10   ST-GRADE                        PIC X.
```

Figure 15.4 Illustration of Variable-Length Record Description and OCCURS DEPENDING ON Clause

Every record contains a minimum of 42 characters (30 for name, 10 for year, and 2 for number of courses). If the student is an entering freshman, then no courses were completed, and the entire record consists of 42 characters. Records for upperclassmen contain an additional 5 bytes for every completed course. A maximum of 60 courses (300 bytes) is permitted in a record. There is considerable flexibility in the COBOL FD, and care must be taken to express one's exact intent. Thus the following pairs of entries are *not* equivalent:

```
         BLOCK CONTAINS 5 RECORDS
         RECORD CONTAINS 42 TO 342 CHARACTERS
                      vs.
         BLOCK CONTAINS 210 TO 1710 CHARACTERS
         RECORD CONTAINS 42 TO 342 CHARACTERS
```

The first pair states that the block contains exactly 5 records. The second pair states that the block contains from 210 to 1710 characters and thus could contain many more than 5 records if most of the records are of the smaller size. (Indeed the latter entry is misleading for still another reason. Use of the BLOCK CONTAINS CHARACTERS option requires that a 4-byte field for overall block length and additional 4-byte fields for individual record lengths be included in the computation of block size. This was *not* done and hence the latter entry is actually invalid.)

The RECORDING MODE specifies record type, e.g., fixed or variable length (RECORDING MODE is restricted to IBM compilers). Although this clause and several others are optional and need not be specified, we strongly endorse their use.

The LABEL RECORDS clause is the only required clause in the FD. LABEL RECORDS ARE STANDARD implies that standard labels are used and label processing is to be performed. LABEL RECORDS ARE OMITTED means either labels are omitted or they are nonstandard (i.e., user labels); in either case no label processing is to be performed (see Chapters 17 and 18).

When labels are used, the system must have additional information supplied to enable it to perform label processing. Under an IBM operating system, the information is specified in the JCL. In other systems it is supplied in the VALUE clause of the FD. Consider the entry

```
FD   TAPE-FILE
         .
         .
         .
     LABEL RECORDS ARE STANDARD
     VALUE OF IDENTIFICATION IS 123456.
```

VALUE OF IDENTIFICATION specifies that the header label for TAPE-FILE should contain a file ID of 123456, which will be checked in the label-processing routines. IBM systems treat the VALUE clause as documentation.

Procedure Division

Procedure division extensions involve the OPEN and CLOSE statements. General formats are shown below:

$$\underline{\text{OPEN}} \left[\underline{\text{INPUT}} \text{ file-name} \left[\begin{array}{c} \underline{\text{REVERSED}} \\ \text{WITH } \underline{\text{NO}} \ \underline{\text{REWIND}} \end{array} \right] \cdots \right]$$

$$[\underline{\text{OUTPUT}} \text{ file-name [WITH } \underline{\text{NO}} \ \underline{\text{REWIND}}] \ldots]$$

$$\underline{\text{CLOSE}} \text{ file-name} \left[\begin{array}{c} \underline{\text{REEL}} \\ \underline{\text{UNIT}} \end{array} \right] \left[\text{WITH} \left\{ \begin{array}{c} \underline{\text{NO}} \ \underline{\text{REWIND}} \\ \underline{\text{LOCK}} \end{array} \right\} \right] \cdots$$

The action of the OPEN and CLOSE verbs depends on the specifications of the LABEL RECORDS clause in the file FD. If standard labels are used, the OPEN initiates label processing. In an input file, the header label is checked against information in the JCL (IBM systems) or in the FD VALUE clause (non-IBM). When an output file is opened, an appropriate header label is written. The CLOSE initiates similar procedures for trailer labels; i.e., it checks the trailer label of an input file and causes a new trailer label to be written for an output file. No label processing is performed if the FD contains LABEL RECORDS ARE OMITTED.

The simplest form of an OPEN for an input file is OPEN INPUT file-name, which automatically causes the tape to be rewound. If NO REWIND is specified, the rewinding is suppressed. The latter is used when many files are contained on the same reel. The REVERSED option causes the file to be processed in reverse order, starting with the last record. (This is not possible on all tape drives.)

The simplest form of the CLOSE is CLOSE file-name, which automatically rewinds the tape at the end of processing. If LOCK is used, the reel is unloaded, which prevents further processing of that tape. (The LOCK option has no meaning under OS.) The NO REWIND option is used for multifile volumes and prevents the automatic rewinding associated with the CLOSE. The REEL or UNIT specification causes the volume, but not the file, to close and is used with multivolume files.

The READ and WRITE verbs are conceptually the same as for card files, but when blocking is used, the physical process is different. Assume, for illustration, a blocking factor of 5. When the first READ is executed, the entire block of 5 records is read into a storage buffer, but only the first record is made available to the program. The next time a READ is executed the second record is made available to the program, but no physical I/O takes place. In similar fashion, no physical I/O occurs for the 3rd, 4th, and 5th READ. The 6th, 11th, etc., execution of the READ all cause a new physical record to be brought into the I/O buffer, but there is no physical I/O for the 7th through 10th, 12th through 15th, etc., execution of the READ.

Record Formats

The remainder of the chapter is devoted to a discussion of COBOL examples. However, before proceeding further, it is useful to review the different record formats to which we shall refer.

FIXED UNBLOCKED—Every record in the file is the same length; there is one record per block.

FIXED BLOCKED—Every record in the file is the same length; there are many records per block.

VARIABLE UNBLOCKED—Records are of different length; there is one record per block.

VARIABLE BLOCKED—Records are of different length; there are many records per block.

Variable-length records require an additional 4-byte field prior to each record to indicate the length of each record. In addition, a 4-byte field denoting the length of the entire block is required at the beginning of each block (the latter field is redundant if variable-length records are unblocked). Thus if a block contains three variable-length records, a total of 16 additional bytes will be associated with each physical record or block. Consult a vendor's manual to determine when these bytes appear in the COBOL FD. Figure 15.5 summarizes record formats.

Card to Tape: Creating Variable-Length Records

Figure 15.6(a) contains a COBOL program to create variable-length tape records from a student card file. The number of cards per student varies with the number of courses taken last semester. The first card for each student is a master card ('M' in column 80) and contains student name and number, major, year in school, and number of courses taken. There is a separate course card (C in column 80) for each course, containing student number, course number, credits, semester, and grade.

Sample input for John Smith is shown in Figure 15.6(b).

Fixed Length Unblocked

Fixed Length Blocked

Variable Length Unblocked

Variable Length Blocked

Figure 15.5 Record Formats

```
00001              IDENTIFICATION DIVISION.
00002              PROGRAM-ID.  CARDTAPE.
00003              AUTHOR.  CRAWFORD.
00004              REMARKS.
00005                  THIS PROGRAM ILLUSTRATES CARD TO TAPE PROCESSING.  A FILE
00006                  OF STUDENT GRADE CARDS IS READ AND TRANSFERRED TO TAPE.
00007                  THERE IS A SINGLE MASTER CARD FOR EACH STUDENT AND A
00008                  VARIABLE NUMBER OF COURSE CARDS RESULTING IN VARIABLE
00009                  LENGTH RECORDS BEING OUTPUT TO TAPE.
00010              ENVIRONMENT DIVISION.
00011              CONFIGURATION SECTION.
00012              SOURCE-COMPUTER.    IBM-360.
00013              OBJECT-COMPUTER.    IBM-360.
00014              INPUT-OUTPUT SECTION.
00015              FILE-CONTROL.
00016                  SELECT CARD-FILE ASSIGN TO UR-2540R-S-SYSIN.
00017                  SELECT TAPE-FILE ASSIGN TO UT-2400-S-SYSTAPE.
00018              DATA DIVISION.
00019              FILE SECTION.
00020              FD  CARD-FILE
00021                  LABEL RECORDS ARE OMITTED
00022                  RECORDING MODE IS F
00023                  RECORD CONTAINS 80 CHARACTERS
00024                  DATA RECORD IS STUDENT-CARD.
00025              01  STUDENT-CARD                    PICTURE IS X(80).
00026              FD  TAPE-FILE
00027                  LABEL RECORDS ARE STANDARD
00028                  RECORDING MODE IS V
00029                  BLOCK CONTAINS 0 RECORDS
00030                  RECORD CONTAINS 60 TO 170 CHARACTERS
00031                  DATA RECORD IS TAPE-MASTER.
00032              01  TAPE-MASTER.
00033                  05  TP-STUDENT-NAME             PICTURE IS A(25).
00034                  05  TP-STUDENT-NUMBER           PICTURE IS 9(9).
00035                  05  TP-STUDENT-MAJOR            PICTURE IS A(15).
00036                  05  TP-STUDENT-YEAR             PICTURE IS A(9).
00037                  05  TP-NUMBER-COURSES           PICTURE IS 99.
```

Indicates block size will be entered in JCL

Figure 15.6(a) Creation of Variable-Length Tape Records

302

```
00038          05  TP-COMPLETED-COURSES OCCURS 0 TO 10 TIMES
00039              DEPENDING ON TP-NUMBER-COURSES.
00040              10   TP-COURSE-NUMBER           PICTURE IS 9(4).
00041              10   TP-CREDITS                 PICTURE IS 99.
00042              10   TP-SEMESTER                PICTURE IS X(4).
00043              10   TP-GRADE                   PICTURE IS A.
00044      WORKING-STORAGE SECTION.
00045      77  FILLER                             PICTURE IS X(14)
00046                               VALUE IS 'WS BEGINS HERE'.
00047      77  WS-SUB                             PICTURE IS 9(4)
00048              COMPUTATIONAL    VALUE IS ZERO.
00049      77  WS-EOF-INDICATOR                   PICTURE IS X(3)
00050                               VALUE IS SPACES.
00051      01  C1-STUDENT-MASTER.
00052          05  C1-STUDENT-NAME                PICTURE IS A(25).
00053          05  C1-STUDENT-NUMBER              PICTURE IS 9(9).
00054          05  C1-STUDENT-MAJOR               PICTURE IS A(15).
00055          05  C1-STUDENT-YEAR                PICTURE IS A(9).
00056          05  C1-NUMBER-OF-COURSES           PICTURE IS 99.
00057          05  FILLER                         PICTURE IS X(19).
00058          05  C1-TYPE-CARD                   PICTURE IS X.
00059      01  C2-STUDENT-COURSE-CARD.
00060          05  C2-STUDENT-NUMBER              PICTURE IS 9(9).
00061          05  FILLER                         PICTURE IS X(5).
00062          05  C2-COURSE-NUMBER               PICTURE IS 9(4).
00063          05  FILLER                         PICTURE IS X(5).
00064          05  C2-CREDITS                     PICTURE IS 9(2).
00065          05  FILLER                         PICTURE IS X(5).
00066          05  C2-SEMESTER                    PICTURE IS X(4).
00067          05  FILLER                         PICTURE IS X(5).
00068          05  C2-GRADE                       PICTURE IS A.
00069          05  FILLER                         PICTURE IS X(39).
00070          05  C2-TYPE-CARD                   PICTURE IS X.
00071              88  C2-STU-COURSE-CARD         VALUE 'C'.
00072              88  C2-STU-MASTER-CARD         VALUE 'M'.
00073      01  FILLER                             PICTURE IS X(12)
00074                               VALUE IS 'WS ENDS HERE'.
00075      PROCEDURE DIVISION.
00076          OPEN INPUT CARD-FILE
00077              OUTPUT TAPE-FILE.
00078          READ CARD-FILE INTO C1-STUDENT-MASTER
00079              AT END MOVE 'YES' TO WS-EOF-INDICATOR.
00080          IF C1-TYPE-CARD NOT = 'M'
00081              DISPLAY 'FIRST CARD IN IS NOT A MASTER CARD'
00082          ELSE
00083              PERFORM 100-PROCESS-MASTER THRU 100-PROCESS-MASTER-EXIT
00084                  UNTIL WS-EOF-INDICATOR = 'YES'.
00085          CLOSE CARD-FILE
00086                TAPE-FILE.
00087          STOP RUN.
00088
00089      100-PROCESS-MASTER.
00090
00091      *  RESET C2-TYPE-CARD
00092
00093          MOVE SPACE TO C2-TYPE-CARD
00094
00095      *  PROCESS MASTER
00096
00097          MOVE SPACES TO TAPE-MASTER.
00098          MOVE C1-STUDENT-NAME         TO TP-STUDENT-NAME.
00099          MOVE C1-STUDENT-NUMBER       TO TP-STUDENT-NUMBER.
00100          MOVE C1-STUDENT-MAJOR        TO TP-STUDENT-MAJOR.
00101          MOVE C1-STUDENT-YEAR         TO TP-STUDENT-YEAR.
00102          MOVE ZERO                    TO TP-NUMBER-COURSES.
00103          PERFORM 200-READ-GRADE-CARDS THRU 200-READ-GRADE-CARDS-EXIT
00104              VARYING WS-SUB FROM 1 BY 1
00105              UNTIL C2-STU-MASTER-CARD
00106              OR WS-EOF-INDICATOR = 'YES'.
00107          WRITE TAPE-MASTER.
00108
00109      100-PROCESS-MASTER-EXIT.
00110              EXIT.
```

Variable portion of tape record

Binary subscript

Checks that very first card is a master card

Reads course cards until a new master card (or end-of-file) is encountered

Figure 15.6(a) (Continued)

```
00111
00112        200-READ-GRADE-CARDS.
00113            READ CARD-FILE INTO C2-STUDENT-COURSE-CARD
00114                AT END MOVE 'YES' TO WS-EOF-INDICATOR
00115                GO TO 200-READ-GRADE-CARDS-EXIT.
00116            IF C2-STU-MASTER-CARD,
00117                MOVE C2-STUDENT-COURSE-CARD TO C1-STUDENT-MASTER
00118                GO TO 200-READ-GRADE-CARDS-EXIT.
00119        *
00120        *      COURSE CARD  FOR EXISTING MASTER CARD
00121        *
00122            MOVE C2-COURSE-NUMBER        TO TP-COURSE-NUMBER (WS-SUB).
00123            MOVE C2-CREDITS              TO TP-CREDITS (WS-SUB).
00124            MOVE C2-SEMESTER             TO TP-SEMESTER (WS-SUB).
00125            MOVE C2-GRADE                TO TP-GRADE (WS-SUB).
00126            ADD 1                        TO TP-NUMBER-COURSES.
00127        200-READ-GRADE-CARDS-EXIT.
00128            EXIT.
```

Figure 15.6(a) (Continued)

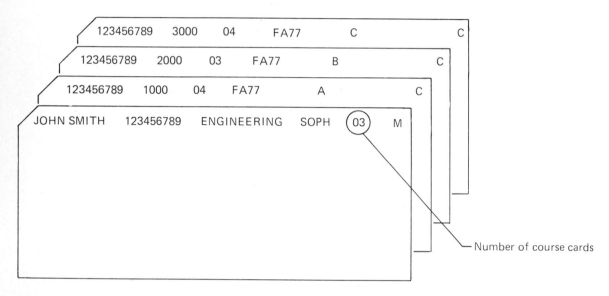

Figure 15.6(b) Sample Input Data to Create Variable-Length Tape Records

The COBOL FD for the output tape file (COBOL lines 26–31) describes the file characteristics. RECORDING MODE IS V denotes variable-length records. Each record has from 60 to 170 characters as per the RECORD CONTAINS clause in line 30. A maximum of 10 courses is allocated per student, with each course taking 11 bytes of information (COBOL lines 40–43). Thus there are anywhere from 0 to 110 bytes of course data, which, added to the 60 bytes of basic student data, establishes a record length of 60–170 bytes.

Note the clause BLOCK CONTAINS 0 RECORDS in COBOL line 29. This does not mean what it says literally but rather that the block size is to be entered via JCL. Omission of the BLOCK CONTAINS clause causes the compiler to assume unblocked records, i.e., 1 record per block (note that BLOCK CONTAINS 0 RECORDS is an IBM OS feature).

The procedure division of Figure 15.6(a) may at first appear unnecessarily complicated, but it contains a bit more logic than is implied in the above specifications. In particular, although the master card specifies the number of associated course cards (C1-NUMBER-OF-COURSES), *we cannot assume that the proper number of course cards will necessarily follow in the card file.* Accordingly, we use C2-TYPE-CARD as a switch and continue to read course cards for the current master card until a new master card is encountered.

Figure 15.6(a) contains many of the techniques and coding standards of Section II. The PERFORM statement of lines 103–106 is particularly interesting in that it combines an 88-level entry with a logical or. Also note the use of PERFORM THRU, READ INTO, and a COMPUTATIONAL subscript. Working-storage is delineated by the entries on lines 45–46 and 73–74 as an aid in debugging dumps. Finally, note the use of record prefixing and paragraph sequencing.

File Maintenance

A large proportion of data processing activity is devoted to file maintenance. Although printed reports are a more visible result of data processing, files must be maintained to reflect the changing nature of the physical environment. In a payroll system, for example, new employees can be added, while existing employees may be terminated or receive salary increases. Every physical system requires file maintenance, but the question of how often depends on the application. A file of student transcripts is updated only a few times a year. An airline reservation system, however, is continuously updated as seats on individual flights are booked.

Files can be processed either sequentially or nonsequentially. Sequential processing means that every single record is accessed in a given run. Nonsequential processing requires that only records which are actually changed be accessed. Tape processing is *always* sequential. Nonsequential processing is possible only with direct-access storage devices and is discussed in Chapter 16.

A sequential file update is shown schematically in Figure 15.7. Input to a sequential update consists of an old master file and a transaction file. Output will be a new master file and a series of printed reports reflecting the update. Figure 15.7 depicts both the old and new master files as being on tape. In actuality the files could be contained on magnetic disk as well, as long as they were organized sequentially. Finally, the transaction file need not be physically on cards provided it is in sequential order.

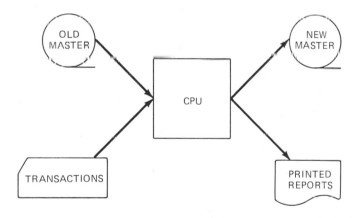

Figure 15.7 Sequential Update System Flowchart

Sequential maintenance is usually done periodically. Let us assume a payroll system is updated monthly and begin with a current master file on January 1. Transactions are collected (*batched*) during the month of January. Then, on February 1, we take the master file of January 1 (now the old master), the transactions accrued during January, and produce a new master as of February 1. The process continues from month to month. Transactions are collected during February. On March 1, we take the file created February 1 as the old master, run it against the February transactions, and produce a new master as of March 1. Figure 15.8 illustrates this discussion.

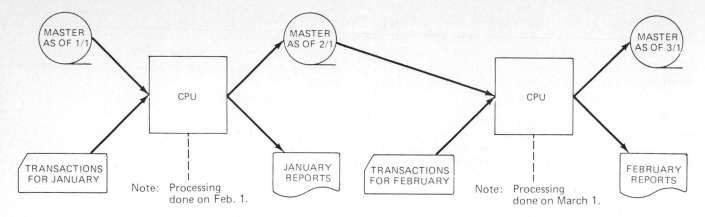

Figure 15.8 Two-Period Sequential Update

In Figure 15.8, the master files for January, February, and March are physically contained on different reels of tape. Further, since the January master gave rise to the February master, which in turn spawned the March master, the files are known as grandfather, father, and son, respectively.

Backup

Murphy's law states that "if something can go wrong, it will—and at the worst possible time." Data processing is certainly not exempt from this law, and it is absolutely essential that we provide as much backup as feasible. What if the tape containing the February master was inadvertently destroyed on February 27, just prior to the next update? If we were prudent enough to keep both the January 1 master and transactions for January, it is a simple matter to recreate the February 1 master file. A generally accepted practice is to keep at least the last three historical levels, i.e., the grandfather, father, and son.

How could information on tape be destroyed in the first place? The most likely way is that the operator incorrectly mounted a tape containing live data as a scratch tape. The file protect ring is a precautionary measure, designed to make the operator "think twice" before mounting a given reel as an output tape. The file protect ring fits into a groove on the tape. When it is in place either reading or writing can occur; when the ring is removed, only reading can take place. All reels containing live data should be stored without the file protect ring.

We shall now proceed to a COBOL program for a sequential update. The COBOL per se is not difficult, but the logic is as complex as anything we have yet tackled. Processing specifications are

1. Input: a master file and transaction file, both in ascending sequence by social security number.

2. Output: a master file and printed error report; the latter is to list invalid incoming transactions as described in item 5.

3. Each record in both master and transaction files contains three fields: name, social security number, and salary. In addition each transaction record contains a transaction code.

4. There are three types of transactions: additions, deletions, and salary changes, denoted by A, D, and C, respectively. Incoming transactions with a code of A are to be added to the file. Transactions with a code of D are to be removed from the master, and transactions with a code of C are to have the salary corrected.

5. The incoming data have been *scrubbed* via a previous edit program. Thus the transactions can be assumed to be in sequential order, to contain all

three fields, and to have a valid transaction code. However, the edit run could not check for two types of errors: (a) no matches in which a salary correction is indicated for a record not already in the file, and (b) duplicate additions for records already in the file. An appropriate error message is to be printed whenever either of these situations occur.

The structured programming techniques of Chapters 6 and 11 can be demonstrated to particularly good advantage in this application. Figure 15.9 is a flowchart of the mainline routine of the sequential update. Figure 15.10 contains the flowchart for the COMPARE-IDS routine. The entire program is coded in the top-down approach of structured programming as described below.

The mainline routine opens all files and reads the first record from both the transactions and old master files. It performs the COMPARE-IDS procedure until both files are out of data, after which all files are closed and processing is terminated.

The COMPARE-IDS procedure compares the social security numbers of the current records in both the old master and transaction files. If the former is lower, the COPY routine is performed. If the social security numbers are equal, the MATCH routine is performed; otherwise the ADD routine is

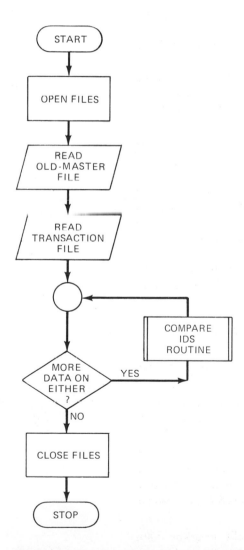

Figure 15.9 Mainline Routine for a Sequential Update

287

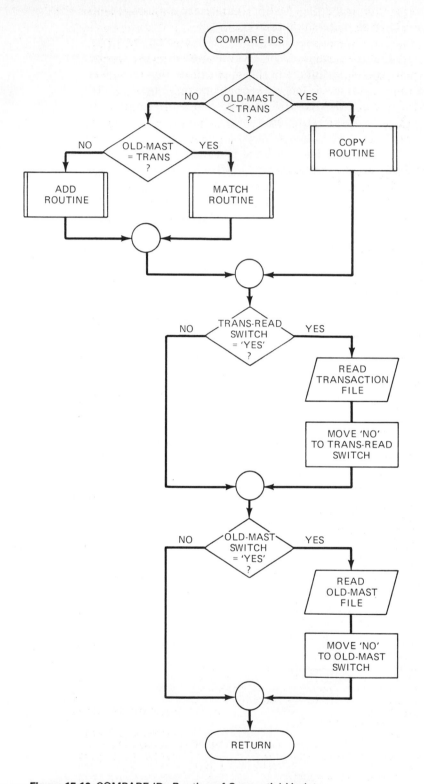

Figure 15.10 COMPARE IDs Routine of Sequential Update

performed. Regardless of which of the three routines is called, two switches are tested to determine from which file another record should be read.

Flowcharts are not shown for the COPY, MATCH, and ADD routines, as the logic is straightforward and easily seen from the COBOL program (Figure 15.11). The COPY routine copies an existing record from the old master as is and sets the switch to read another record from the old master. The MATCH routine checks for the type of transaction, A, D, or C, and processes accordingly. Note that a code of A in the MATCH routine causes an error message. Finally, the MATCH routine sets switches to read from both records. The ADD routine writes the incoming transaction record to the new master. If, however, the incoming code is not an A, an appropriate error message is printed. The ADD routine sets the switch to read another record from the transaction file.

The resulting COBOL program is shown in Figure 15.11, which utilizes standards advocated in Chapters 6 and 11. Observe the use of record prefixing, paragraph sequencing, and uniform columns for PICTURE, etc. The PERFORM section, READ INTO, and WRITE FROM options are used

```
00001          IDENTIFICATION DIVISION.
00002          PROGRAM-ID.      UPDATE.
00003          AUTHOR.          GRAUER.
00004          ENVIRONMENT DIVISION.
00005          CONFIGURATION SECTION.
00006          SOURCE-COMPUTER.      IBM-360.          ┌─ Program requires
00007          OBJECT-COMPUTER.      IBM-360.          /  four files
00008          INPUT-OUTPUT SECTION.
00009          FILE-CONTROL.
00010          SELECT TRANSACTION-FILE ASSIGN TO UR-2540R-S-SYSIN.
00011          SELECT ERROR-FILE ASSIGN TO UR-1403-S-SYSOUT.
00012          SELECT OLD-MASTER-FILE ASSIGN TO UT-2400-S-OLDMAST.
00013          SELECT NEW-MASTER-FILE ASSIGN TO UT-2400-S-NEWMAST.
00014          DATA DIVISION.
00015          FILE SECTION.
00016          FD  OLD-MASTER-FILE
00017              LABEL RECORDS ARE STANDARD ─────── Label processing - see
00018              RECORDING MODE IS F                 Chapters 17 and 18 on JCL
00019              BLOCK CONTAINS 3 RECORDS
00020              RECORD CONTAINS 40 CHARACTERS
00021              DATA RECORD IS OLD-MAST-RECORD.
00022          01  OLD-MAST-RECORD                    PICTURE IS X(40).
00023          FD  NEW-MASTER-FILE
00024              LABEL RECORDS ARE STANDARD
00025              RECORDING MODE IS F
00026              BLOCK CONTAINS 3 RECORDS
00027              RECORD CONTAINS 40 CHARACTERS
00028              DATA RECORD IS NEW-MAST-RECORD.
00029          01  NEW-MAST-RECORD                    PICTURE IS X(40).
00030          FD  TRANSACTION-FILE
00031              LABEL RECORDS ARE OMITTED
00032              RECORDING MODE IS F
00033              RECORD CONTAINS 80 CHARACTERS
00034              DATA RECORD IS TRANS-RECORD.
00035          01  TRANS-RECORD                       PICTURE IS X(80).
00036          FD  ERROR-FILE
00037              LABEL RECORDS ARE OMITTED
00038              RECORDING MODE IS F
00039              RECORD CONTAINS 132 CHARACTERS
00040              DATA RECORD IS ERROR-RECORD.
00041          01  ERROR-RECORD                       PICTURE IS X(132).
00042          WORKING-STORAGE SECTION.
00043          77  FILLER                             PICTURE IS X(14)
00044                              VALUE IS 'WS BEGINS HERE'.
00045        ┌─77  WS-OLD-MAST-READ-SWITCH            PICTURE IS X(3)
00046        │                     VALUE IS 'NO '.
00047        └─77  WS-TRANS-READ-SWITCH               PICTURE IS X(3)
00048        /                     VALUE IS 'NO '.
00049       /   01  WS-OLD-MAST-RECORD.
            └─ Switches to indicate which file is read next
```

Figure 15.11 COBOL Listing for Sequential Update

```
                        Use of conditional entries for transaction codes
00050                   05  WS-OLDMAST-ID                 PICTURE IS X(9).
00051                   05  WS-OLDMAST-NAME               PICTURE IS X(25).
00052                   05  WS-OLDMAST-SALARY             PICTURE IS 9(6).
00053               01  WS-NEW-MAST-RECORD.
00054                   05  WS-NEWMAST-ID                 PICTURE IS X(9).
00055                   05  WS-NEWMAST-NAME               PICTURE IS X(25).
00056                   05  WS-NEWMAST-SALARY             PICTURE IS 9(6).
00057               01  WS-TRANS-RECORD.
00058                   05  WS-TRANS-ID                   PICTURE IS X(9).
00059                   05  WS-TRANS-NAME                 PICTURE IS X(25).
00060                   05  WS-TRANS-SALARY               PICTURE IS 9(6).
00061                   05  FILLER                        PICTURE IS X(39).
00062                   05  WS-TRANS-CODE                 PICTURE IS X.
00063                       88  ADDITION   VALUE IS 'A'.
00064                       88  DELETION   VALUE IS 'D'.
00065                       88  UPDATE     VALUE IS 'C'.
00066               01  WS-ERROR-MESSAGE-1                PICTURE IS X(40)
00067                              VALUE IS ' RECORD ALREADY IN FILE '.
00068               01  WS-ERROR-MESSAGE-2                PICTURE IS X(40)
00069                              VALUE IS ' NO MATCH '.
00070               01  WS-PRINT-RECORD.
00071                   05  WS-PRINT-MESSAGE              PICTURE IS X(40).
00072                   05  WS-PRINT-ID                  PICTURE IS X(9).
00073                   05  FILLER                       PICTURE IS X(5)
00074                              VALUE IS SPACES.
00075                   05  WS-PRINT-NAME                PICTURE IS X(25).
00076                   05  FILLER                       PICTURE IS X(53)
00077                              VALUE IS SPACES.
00078               01  FILLER                           PICTURE IS X(12)
00079                              VALUE IS 'WS ENDS HERE'.
00080           PROCEDURE DIVISION.
00081               OPEN INPUT TRANSACTION-FILE
00082                          OLD-MASTER-FILE
00083                    OUTPUT NEW-MASTER-FILE
00084                           ERROR-FILE.
00085               READ TRANSACTION-FILE INTO WS-TRANS-RECORD
00086                   AT END MOVE HIGH-VALUES TO WS-TRANS-RECORD
00087                           MOVE 'NO ' TO WS-TRANS-READ-SWITCH.
00088               READ OLD-MASTER-FILE INTO WS-OLD-MAST-RECORD
00089   Mainline        AT END MOVE HIGH-VALUES TO WS-OLD-MAST-RECORD
00090   routine                 MOVE 'NO ' TO WS-OLD-MAST-READ-SWITCH.
00091               PERFORM 010-COMPARE-IDS
00092                   UNTIL WS-TRANS-ID = HIGH-VALUES
00093                   AND WS-OLDMAST-ID = HIGH-VALUES.
00094               CLOSE TRANSACTION-FILE
00095                     OLD-MASTER-FILE
00096                     NEW-MASTER-FILE
00097                     ERROR-FILE.
00098               STOP RUN.
00099
00100           010-COMPARE-IDS SECTION.
00101               IF WS-OLDMAST-ID < WS-TRANS-ID
00102                   PERFORM 050-COPY-OLD-REC
00103               ELSE
00104                   IF WS-OLDMAST-ID = WS-TRANS-ID
00105                       PERFORM 060-MATCH-ROUTINE
00106                   ELSE
00107                       PERFORM 070-NEW-RECORD.
00108               IF WS-TRANS-READ-SWITCH = 'YES'
00109                   MOVE 'NO ' TO WS-TRANS-READ-SWITCH
00110                   READ TRANSACTION-FILE INTO WS-TRANS-RECORD
00111                   AT END MOVE HIGH-VALUES TO WS-TRANS-RECORD.
00112
00113               IF WS-OLD-MAST-READ-SWITCH = 'YES'
00114                   MOVE 'NO ' TO WS-OLD-MAST-READ-SWITCH
00115                   READ OLD-MASTER-FILE INTO WS-OLD-MAST-RECORD
00116                   AT END MOVE HIGH-VALUES TO WS-OLD-MAST-RECORD.
00117
00118
00119           050-COPY-OLD-REC SECTION.
00120   COPY        WRITE NEW-MAST-RECORD FROM WS-OLD-MAST-RECORD.
00121   routine     MOVE 'YES' TO WS-OLD-MAST-READ-SWITCH.
00122
```

Figure 15.11 (*Continued*)

```
00123          ┌─ 060-MATCH-ROUTINE SECTION.
00124          │      IF ADDITION
00125          │          MOVE  WS-TRANS-NAME       TO WS-PRINT-NAME
00126          │          MOVE  WS-TRANS-ID         TO WS-PRINT-ID
00127          │          MOVE  WS-ERROR-MESSAGE-1  TO WS-PRINT-MESSAGE
00128          │          WRITE ERROR-RECORD FROM WS-PRINT-RECORD
00129          │          WRITE NEW-MAST-RECORD FROM WS-OLD-MAST-RECORD
00130          │          GO TO 060-MATCH-ROUTINE-EXIT.
00131  MATCH ─┤      IF DELETION
00132  routine │          GO TO 060-MATCH-ROUTINE-EXIT.
00133          │      IF UPDATE
00134          │          MOVE WS-TRANS-SALARY TO WS-OLDMAST-SALARY
00135          │          WRITE NEW-MAST-RECORD FROM WS-OLD-MAST-RECORD
00136          │          GO TO 060-MATCH-ROUTINE-EXIT.
00137          │
00138          │  060-MATCH-ROUTINE-EXIT.
00139          │      MOVE 'YES' TO WS-TRANS-READ-SWITCH.
00140          └─     MOVE 'YES' TO WS-OLD-MAST-READ-SWITCH.
00141
00142          ┌─ 070-NEW-RECORD SECTION.
00143          │      IF ADDITION
00144          │          WRITE NEW-MAST-RECORD FROM WS-TRANS-RECORD
00145  NEW   ─┤      ELSE MOVE WS-TRANS-NAME       TO WS-PRINT-NAME
00146  RECORD  │          MOVE WS-TRANS-ID         TO WS-PRINT-ID
00147  routine │          MOVE WS-ERROR-MESSAGE-2  TO WS-PRINT-MESSAGE
00148          │          WRITE ERROR-RECORD FROM WS-PRINT-RECORD.
00149          └─     MOVE 'YES' TO WS-TRANS-READ-SWITCH.
```

Figure 15.11 (*Continued*)

throughout. All ELSE clauses are aligned under the relevant IF. Finally, note the
use of 88-level conditional entries.

Figure 15.12 shows illustrative data for the program of Figure 15.11. The
new master file has NEW EMPLOYEE and NEW EMPLOYEE II since the
transaction file contained valid "adds" for these employees. SHERRY (social
security number 666666666) has been deleted from the new master, while
BAKER and BOROW had their salaries changed. The transaction for JONES
was invalid in that we attempted to change the salary of a record that was
absent from the old master. The transaction for JAMES was also invalid since
it tried to add a record already in the master file.

Summary

Magnetic tape was introduced as a medium for data storage. Several problems
were presented to illustrate tape capacity and timing. The necessary COBOL
extensions for tape processing were covered. The extensions per se are not
difficult, but the logic inherent in file maintenance can get very involved.

Four types of record formats were discussed: fixed-length blocked, fixed-
length unblocked, variable-length blocked, and variable-length unblocked. A
COBOL program to create blocked variable-length records was presented.

File maintenance is one of the more frequent data-processing applications.
The grandfather–father–son hierarchy was introduced as a means of backup. A
COBOL program for sequential updating was developed using techniques of
structured programming. The importance of checking incoming data was
emphasized.

One final word on the COBOL listings of Figures 15.6(a) and 15.11: The
procedure divisions of both programs are not unnecessarily complicated but
rather include substantial logic. Critics of structured programming are quick to
argue that these listings are very difficult to follow, but rarely do they offer
alternative solutions. We are not blind devotees of structured programming,
but we do believe these listings are as good a solution as any to the posed
problems. Before you object too strongly, *code and test* a nonstructured
solution, and see if, in fact, your approach is clearer than ours. We shall be glad
to listen.

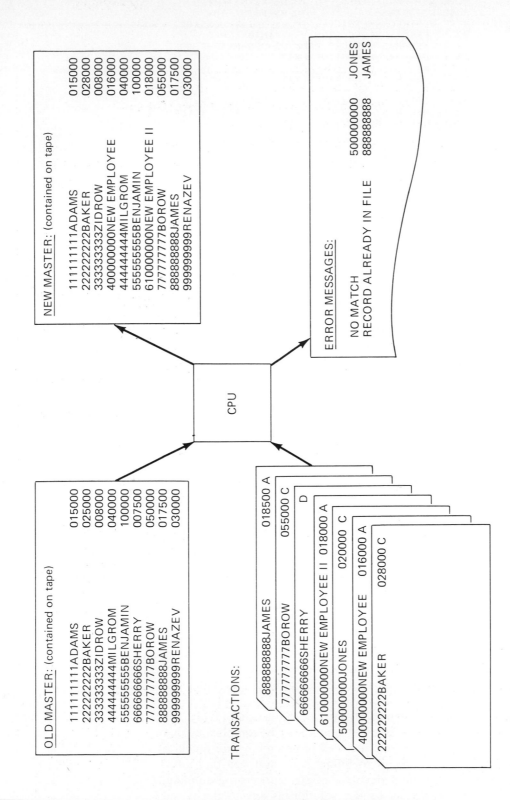

Figure 15.12. Illustrative Data for Sequential Update (Corresponds to System Flowchart in Figure 15.7)

True	False		
☐	☐	**1**	The capacity of a tape increases as the length of the IRG increases.
☐	☐	**2**	The capacity of a tape increases as the density increases.
☐	☐	**3**	A tape will start and stop many times as it processes a file.
☐	☐	**4**	30 is the absolute limit to the blocking factor.
☐	☐	**5**	Doubling the blocking factor will halve the transfer rate.
☐	☐	**6**	Doubling the blocking factor will halve the storage requirements of a file.
☐	☐	**7**	Density is commonly expressed in bytes per inch.
☐	☐	**8**	Doubling the blocking factor will halve the number of IRG's.
☐	☐	**9**	As the blocking factor increases, the start/stop time decreases.
☐	☐	**10**	More than one file can appear on a single reel of tape.
☐	☐	**11**	One file can stretch over several reels of tape.
☐	☐	**12**	There is more than one kind of internal label.
☐	☐	**13**	If the RESERVE clause is omitted in the SELECT statement, no alternate areas will be established.
☐	☐	**14**	The phrase FOR MULTIPLE REEL is required when multiple units are specified in a SELECT statement.
☐	☐	**15**	Every record must contain the same number of bytes.
☐	☐	**16**	The OPEN statement causes a tape to rewind unless specification is made to the contrary.
☐	☐	**17**	The CLOSE statement causes the tape to rewind unless specification is made to the contrary.
☐	☐	**18**	If blocking is used, every READ statement causes a new block to be taken from tape.
☐	☐	**19**	Both input and output files can be opened in the same statement.
☐	☐	**20**	The OPEN statement will always initiate label processing.
☐	☐	**21**	Variable-length records cannot be blocked.
☐	☐	**22**	Nonsequential processing is possible using magnetic tape.
☐	☐	**23**	The file protect ring must be on the reel to enable writing on a tape.
☐	☐	**24**	In a sequential update, the transaction file must be in the same sequence as the master file.

PROBLEMS

1 How many boxes of cards (2000 cards per box) are required for a file of 20,000 records, if each record contains 200 bytes? (Do *not* split records; i.e., one card cannot contain information for two different logical records.) How long will it take to read the entire file assuming the card reader can process 1000 cards per minute?

2 How much space on tape does the file of Problem 1 require? (Assume 800 bpi and IRG = .75 inches.) Answer for no blocking and a blocking factor of 5. Answer for 1600 bpi and IRG = .375.

3 How long will it take to pass the file of Problem 1? Assume a start/stop time of 10 milliseconds and a transfer rate of 200,000 bytes per second. Answer for no blocking and a blocking factor of 5.

4   Use the "old master" of Figure 15.12 and the transactions below:

```
111111111ADAMS     017000  ...A
222222222BAKER             ...D
300000000BROWN     028000  ...A
444444444MILGROM   045000  ...C
600000000SHERRY    010000  ...C
888888888JAMES     020000  ...C
```

Show the "new master" and error listing which would be produced using the COBOL program in Figure 15.11.

5   (a) Write a COBOL program to read in student cards from the tuition billing problem (Figure 4.8) and create a tape of student records. The tape is to have a blocking factor of 5.

(b) The same specifications as in part (a), except the tape is to contain the student records in ascending sequence by social security number.

6   Assume that two tape files exist: TAPE-FILE-1 and TAPE-FILE-2. Both files contain 80-byte records with the social security number in columns 10–18 on both. The blocking factor is 8 for both. Assume both files are in ascending sequence by social security number. Write a COBOL program to *merge* the two files and create TAPE-FILE-3, which will also have its records in social security sequence. Assume no duplicate records.

7   Same specifications as Problem 6 except duplicate records appear on TAPE-FILE-1 and TAPE-FILE-2. If this happens, display an error message and extract the record from TAPE-FILE-1 only.

8   Same specifications as Problem 6 except there are three input tape files. Assume no duplicate records.

CHAPTER SIXTEEN

Magnetic Disk: Concepts and COBOL Implications

In Chapter 15 we covered magnetic tape and sequential file organization. **Overview** Sequential processing is adequate when a significant number of records in a file have activity but totally impractical in situations where only a limited number of records are to be accessed. The physical characteristics of magnetic tape, however, dictate sequential processing as the only means of file organization possible with that device. One starts at the beginning of a file and interrogates every record (in sequential order) until the desired one is reached.

A direct capability can be provided only by devices with physical characteristics different from those of magnetic tape. Such units include the drum or data cell, but the most common device by far is the magnetic disk. This chapter begins with a discussion of the physical characteristics of the magnetic disk. Next, two types of file organization, indexed sequential (ISAM) and direct, are discussed and illustrated with appropriate listings. The chapter concludes with formal discussion of the necessary COBOL elements.

A disk pack is the device on which data are recorded. It consists of a series of **Magnetic Disk: Physical** platters (disks) permanently attached to a central spindle. The disk pack is **Characteristics** mounted on a disk drive, which is the unit that reads or writes information from the pack. Disk drives in turn can be grouped into a direct-access storage facility, shown in Figure 16.1.

Figure 16.1 Direct-Access Storage Facility (*Courtesy* IBM)

Figure 16.2 shows a 2314 disk pack, with 11 disks, enclosed in a protective cover. Data can be recorded on both sides of 9 of the 11 platters; it cannot be recorded on the top surface of the top disk or the bottom surface of the bottom disk, making a total of 20 surfaces on which data can be recorded.

Figure 16.2 IBM 2314 Disk Pack (*Courtesy* IBM)

All disk devices utilize a comb-type access mechanism as shown in Figure 16.3. Each recording surface (10 in all) has its own read/write head. Each pair of read/write heads (5 pairs in all) is attached to an access arm, which in turn is attached to an access assembly. Figure 16.3 illustrates the access mechanism of a 2311. Realize that the number of recording surfaces varies from device to device.

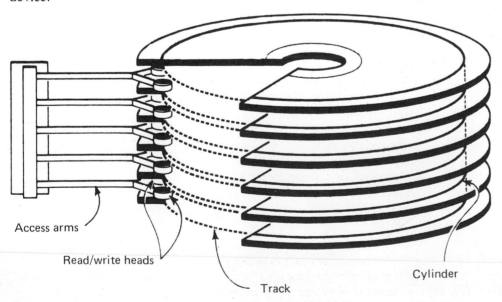

Access arms

Read/write heads

Track

Cylinder

Figure 16.3 Comb-Type Access Mechanism for 2311 (*Courtesy* IBM)

Every recording surface is divided into concentric circles, known as tracks, on which data are recorded (Figure 16.4). Interestingly enough, each track has *identical* storage capacity. Thus the innermost concentric circle (Track 202 in Figure 16.4) has the same capacity as the outermost concentric circle (Track 0).

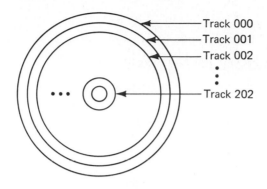

Figure 16.4 Tracks on a Disk Surface

The number of tracks which can be accessed in a single position of the access assembly is known as a cylinder. Figures 16.3 and 16.5 illustrate the cylinder concept for the 2311. The device has 10 recording surfaces or 10 tracks per cylinder. Each surface has 203 tracks, but only 200 are active at one time, with the remainder used as spares.

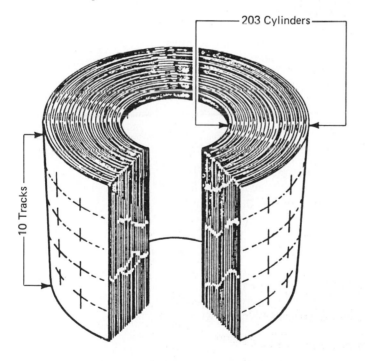

Figure 16.5 IBM 2311 Cylinders

Capacity

The maximum capacity of a disk pack is a function of three factors: (1) density (i.e., the number of bytes per track), (2) the number of recording surfaces (i.e., the number of tracks per cylinder), and (3) the number of tracks per surface (i.e., the number of cylinders). Capacity increases as any of these factors increases. As an illustration, consider the 2314 disk pack with density of 7294 bytes per track, 20 tracks per cylinder, and 200 cylinders. Maximum capacity is calculated to be

$$7294\frac{\text{bytes}}{\text{track}} \times 20\frac{\text{tracks}}{\text{cylinder}} \times 200\frac{\text{cylinders}}{\text{device}} = 29,176,000\frac{\text{bytes}}{\text{device}}$$

In similar fashion, the maximum capacity of a single-density 3330 pack is calculated as approximately 100 million bytes (13,030 bytes per track, 19 tracks per cylinder, and 404 cylinders). As with other calculations in this chapter and in Chapter 15, the numbers themselves are of secondary importance compared to the underlying concepts. The maximum capacity of devices other than the 2314 and 3330 is shown in Table 18.4.

In actual practice the achieved capacity is somewhat less than the calculated maximum. Each track requires certain fields to identify itself to the system, and these areas detract from the capacity available to the user. On the 2314, for example, each track can contain a maximum of 7294 bytes but the maximum *logical* record size is only 7188 bytes. Further, if more than one record is present per track, interrecord gaps are needed. Thus while one track of a 2314 can contain one 7188-byte record, it *cannot* contain two records of 3594 bytes but is restricted to two records of 3457 bytes. Effective track capacity is further reduced as the number of records per track increases, as can be seen in the table of track capacities (Table 16.1).

There is yet another factor which further reduces track capacity. Direct-access devices are designed to permit a straight path to a specified record but require that an additional field (key) be present. The key itself requires space and an additional gap that decreases capacity. Using Table 16.1, we find that when keys are used on a 2314 each track can contain two *physical* records of 3476 bytes each. This is contrasted to two records of 3521 bytes with no keys. Hopefully these concepts will be clarified by the examples below.

Example 16.1: Use of Track Capacity Table (2314)

Given physical records of 150 bytes each, how many such records, with and without keys, will fit on a single track of a 2314?

SOLUTION. From Table 16.1 we find that, with no keys, either 28 157-byte records or 29 148-byte records fit on a single track; i.e., 29 records will fit per track only if the record length is 148 bytes or less. Since this example is concerned with 150-byte records, each track will hold only 28 records.

With keys, 24 156-byte or 25 144-byte records fit per track. Thus 24 is the answer.

Example 16.2: Use of Track Capacity Table (3330)

Given physical records of 400 bytes each, how many such records, with and without keys, will fit on a single track of a 3330?

SOLUTION. Without keys, either 24 413-byte records or 25 391-byte records fit per track; thus 24 is the answer. With keys only 22 400-byte records will fit per track.

Example 16.3: Calculation of File Storage Requirements

Given a file of 6000 records, how many cylinders on a 2314 are required to store the file if records are formatted without keys? (There are 20 tracks per cylinder.) Assume no blocking and that each physical record is 2000 bytes.

Table 16.1 Track Capacity

Maximum Bytes Per Physical Record Formatted without Keys		Records Per Track	Maximum Bytes Per Physical Record Formatted with Keys	
2314	3330		2314	3330
7294	13030	1	7249	12974
3521	6447	2	3476	6391
2298	4253	3	2254	4197
1693	3156	4	1649	3100
1332	2498	5	1288	2442
1092	2059	6	1049	2003
921	1745	7	878	1689
793	1510	8	750	1454
694	1327	9	650	1271
615	1181	10	571	1125
550	1061	11	506	1005
496	962	12	452	906
450	877	13	407	821
411	805	14	368	749
377	742	15	333	686
347	687	16	304	631
321	639	17	277	583
298	596	18	254	540
276	557	19	233	501
258	523	20	215	467
241	491	21	198	435
226	463	22	183	407
211	437	23	168	381
199	413	24	156	357
187	391	25	144	335
176	371	26	133	315
166	352	27	123	296
157	335	28	114	279
148	318	29	105	262
139	303	30	96	247

Note: Calculation of track capacities requires the use of formulas to determine physical record size from logical record size. The material in this table is *not* intended as complete coverage; rather we present a mere taste of what is involved.

SOLUTION. Using Table 16.1, we find each track of a 2314 can hold three records, each 2298 bytes long, so that we can fit 3 records per track. Since there are 20 tracks per cylinder, each cylinder holds 60 (i.e. 20 × 3) records. A 6000-record file requires 100 (6000/60) cylinders.

Timing

Timing calculations are more complex with disk than with tape. Accordingly, we shall discuss timing from a conceptual viewpoint and shall not work any problems. Illustrative numbers are used for the 2314 to give an overall appreciation.

The time required to access data on a magnetic disk consists of four parts: access motion, head selection, rotational delay, and data transfer. (See Figure 16.3.) First, the access assembly is positioned over the proper cylinder. If the assembly is already over the proper cylinder, access time is zero. A movement of one cylinder on the 2314 requires 24 milliseconds; a movement of 200 cylinders takes 130 milliseconds. Access time requires an initial acceleration, but it is essentially a function of the number of cylinders moved. Once the arm is over the proper cylinder, a negligible time is required to activate the correct read/write head. Rotational delay is the time required for the data to rotate under the read/write head. This can range from 0 to 25 milliseconds. Finally data are transferred between the device and main storage at the rate of 312,000 bytes per second.

File Organization

Three types of file organization are commonly used with direct-access devices: sequential, direct, and indexed sequential (ISAM). In a sequential file, records are processed in the same order in which they appear; e.g., the 50th record is used only after the 49th, etc. Individual records cannot be located quickly, and as with magnetic tape, the entire file has to be rewritten when records are added or deleted. Thus sequential organization should be used only when a significant number of records in a file are to be processed. It is one of several methods commonly available on direct devices but the "only game in town" for magnetic tape.

Direct organization depends on a definitive relationship between the key of a record and its location on the device. It enables individual records to be directly accessed; e.g., the 50th record in the file can be accessed without processing the first 49. Direct organization is used when the time to locate individual records must be kept at an absolute minimum.

Indexed sequential organization permits both sequential and direct access. Sequential processing is less rapid than with strict sequential files, and location of individual records generally takes longer than with direct organization. ISAM files utilize a set of indexes, which allow new records to be added without rewriting the entire file and which provide its direct-access capability.

Sequential Processing

Although disk devices are capable of direct processing, they are frequently used for sequential processing as well. Indeed, the maintenance program of Figure 15.11 could be easily adapted to run with disk in lieu of tape. The only required modification is in the SELECT statements, and even this would not be necessary if the SELECT statements were written to be device independent. (See Chapter 18.) Consider the significance of the above statement: A COBOL program which processes sequential files can run on either tape or disk with no modification whatsoever. Obviously something has to change, but that something is the JCL submitted with the program.

The point we are trying to make is that sequential processing is conceptually the same whether the incoming files are contained on tape, disk, or even cards; i.e., the storage medium is immaterial to the COBOL program. Information on the type of file, its location, etc., is supplied through control cards submitted with the program.

Every program in the text to this point has involved sequential processing. We shall not present any examples of sequential processing using disk, simply because we have already covered this material. We shall concentrate instead on examples using ISAM and direct processing. Admittedly, the beginner is more comfortable with cards than with disk or tape, simply because he can touch his files; however, this reluctance to utilize mass storage devices is soon overcome.

Indexed Sequential (ISAM) Organization (IBM Implementation)

This method requires that records be loaded sequentially so that indexes can be established for direct access of individual records. There is one cylinder index for the entire file and many track indexes, one for each cylinder in the file. The cylinder index contains the key of the highest record contained in every cylinder in the file. The track index (for a given cylinder) contains the key of the highest record for every track in that cylinder. As an illustration, assume an ISAM file was loaded on cylinders 100–115 of a 2311. A hypothetical cylinder index (Table 16.2) for this file contains 16 entries (one for each cylinder in the file).

Table 16.2 Cylinder Index

Cylinder Number	Highest Key
100	130
101	249
102	800
103	1240
104	1410
105	1811
106	2069
107	2410
108	2811
109	3040
110	3400
111	3619
112	4511
113	4900
114	5213
115	6874

Although there are ten tracks per cylinder on a 2311, each track index conceptually has only seven entries. The first track, i.e., track 0, contains the track index itself. The last two tracks, tracks 8 and 9, are typically reserved as a cylinder overflow area, whose function is described in the next section. A hypothetical track index for cylinder 102 is shown in Table 16.3. Note that the highest key for all of cylinder 102 is 800, which occurs on track 7, and that this corresponds to the highest key for cylinder 102 in Table 16.2.

Table 16.3 Track Index for Cylinder 102

Track Number	Highest Key
1	312
2	346
3	449
4	598
5	642
6	717
7	800

Note: 1. Track 0 contains the track index.
2. Tracks 8 and 9 contain the cylinder overflow area.

Suppose we seek the record whose key is 400. The record key, 400, is first compared to entries in the cylinder index. Since an ISAM file is loaded sequentially, we conclude record 400 is on cylinder 102. (The highest key in cylinder 101 is 249, and the highest key in cylinder 102 is 800; therefore key 400 must be contained in cylinder 102.) Next we examine the track index for cylinder 102 (Table 16.3). Each entry in the track index contains the highest key for that track. We conclude that the key 400 is contained on track 3 of cylinder 102. We now know both the cylinder and track on which the record resides and may proceed directly to it.

When an ISAM file is accessed in a COBOL program, the I/O routines of the operating system perform the search for the programmer. The cylinder and track indexes are established automatically by the system when the file is loaded. The COBOL necessary to create and access ISAM files is straightforward and should present little difficulty when introduced later in this chapter.

Let us now consider what happens when a new record is added to an existing ISAM file. A major disadvantage of sequential organization is that the entire file has to be rewritten if even a single record is added. One might logically ask that since ISAM files are loaded sequentially, shouldn't a similar requirement pertain. Fortunately, the answer is no. ISAM solves the problem by establishing an overflow area and appropriate linkages. When an ISAM file is initially loaded, the programmer provides, through the JCL, a prime data area and an overflow area. (Usually two tracks of every cylinder are reserved as a cylinder overflow area as was done in Table 16.3. It is also possible to designate entire cylinders as an independent overflow area.)

Table 16.4 is an expanded version of Table 16.3 to reflect both prime and overflow areas for cylinder 102. In addition, we have appended the hypothetical record keys of every record in every track (assume four records per track).

Table 16.4 Track Index Plus Record Keys for Cylinder 102

Prime		Overflow					
Track	Key	Track	Key	Actual Record Keys			
1	312	1	312	251	269	280	312
2	346	2	346	318	327	345	346
3	449	3	449	377	394	400	449
4	598	4	598	469	500	502	598
5	642	5	642	617	619	627	642
6	717	6	717	658	675	700	717
7	800	7	800	722	746	748	800

The track index of Table 16.4 reflects the file immediately after creation; i.e., all records are stored in the prime data area, and the overflow area is entirely empty. This is denoted by identical entries in the overflow and prime portions of the track index.

What happens when a new record with key 410 is added to the file? The existing indexes indicate this record belongs in cylinder 102, track 3. ISAM places the new record with key 410 in its proper place and "bumps" record 449 to an overflow area. No change is required in the cylinder index, for the highest key in cylinder 102 is still 800. However, changes are made in the track index for cylinder 102. The highest record in the prime area of track 3 is no longer 449 but 410; the overflow area is no longer empty but contains record 449. The overflow entries for track 3 now contain a key of 449 and a pointer to the overflow area, namely, track 8, record 1.

Table 16.5 reflects the track index of Table 16.4 after three new records with keys 410, 730, and 289 were added in that order. The cylinder overflow area (tracks 8 and 9) contains the three bumped records in the order in which they were bumped. Thus the first record in track 8 is 449, the second is 800, and the last is 312.

Suppose another record, with key 380, is added to the file. Logically 380 belongs in track 3, and as in the previous example, it will bump a record in the prime area to overflow. The prime area for track 3 now consists of records 377,

Table 16.5 Track Index of Table 16.4 with Three Additions

	Prime		Overflow		Actual Record Keys			
	Track	Key	Track	Key				
	1	289	T8, R3	312	251	269	280	289
	2	346	2	346	318	327	345	346
	3	410	T8, R1	449	377	394	400	410
	4	598	4	598	469	500	502	598
	5	642	5	642	617	619	627	642
	6	717	6	717	658	675	700	717
	7	748	T8, R2	800	722	730	746	748
Overflow	8	No entries			449	800	312	
	9	No entries			No entries			

380, 394, and 400. The bumped record, key 410, is written in the first available space in overflow, i.e., track 8, record 4. Consider carefully the contents of the overflow area: records 449, 800, 312, and 410. Both 449 and 410 logically belong to track 3. They are physically separated from track 3 and indeed from each other. They must be logically reconnected, and this is done via link fields in the overflow area. Each record in overflow has an associated link field which points to the next logical record in the track. Table 16.6 is an updated version of Table 16.5 to reflect the addition of record 380 to track 3 and the linkage fields in overflow. (Table 16.6 also contains two new additions, records 311 and 635, as additional examples.)

Table 16.6 Track Index Plus Overflow Linkages

	Prime		Overflow		Actual Record Keys			
	Track	Key	Track	Key				
	1	200	T9, R1	312	251	269	280	289
	2	346	2	346	318	327	345	346
	3	400	T8, R4	449	377	380	394	400
	4	598	4	598	469	500	502	598
	5	635	T9, R2	642	617	619	627	635
	6	717	6	717	658	675	700	717
	7	748	T8, R2	800	722	730	746	748

		Key	Link	Key	Link	Key	Link	Key	Link
Overflow	8	449	***	800	***	312	***	410	T8, R1
	9	311	T8, R3	642	***				

Let us trace through track 3 in Table 16.6. The prime area contains keys 377, 380, 394, and 400. The overflow area begins on track 8, record 4, i.e., key 410. This in turn has a link field to track 8, record 1, key 449. The link associated with key 449 is ***, indicating the logical end of the chain.

As more and more records are added to the file, the overflow area becomes increasingly full and processing necessarily slows. Periodically the file will be reorganized. It is read sequentially, i.e., via overflow linkages, and then rewritten to a work file. Finally the work file is reloaded as a new ISAM file, with all records in strict physical order and overflow areas empty.

```
00001          IDENTIFICATION DIVISION.
00002          PROGRAM-ID.     CREATE.
00003          AUTHOR.         GRAUER.
00004          ENVIRONMENT DIVISION.
00005          CONFIGURATION SECTION.
00006          SOURCE-COMPUTER.  IBM-360.
00007          OBJECT-COMPUTER.  IBM-360.
00008          INPUT-OUTPUT SECTION.
00009          FILE-CONTROL.
00010              SELECT TRANSACTION-FILE ASSIGN TO UR-2540R-S-SYSIN.
00011          ┌── SELECT NEW-MASTER-FILE ASSIGN TO DA-I-NEWMAST ──┐
00012          │      ACCESS IS SEQUENTIAL                          │
00013          └──    RECORD KEY IS ISAM-ID-NUMBER.               ──┘
00014          DATA DIVISION.                            └── SELECT statement
00015          FILE SECTION.
00016          FD   NEW-MASTER-FILE
00017               LABEL RECORDS ARE STANDARD
00018               RECORDING MODE IS F
00019               BLOCK CONTAINS 3 RECORDS
00020               RECORD CONTAINS 41 CHARACTERS
00021               DATA RECORD IS ISAM-MAST-RECORD.
00022          01   ISAM-MAST-RECORD.
00023          ┌── 05   ISAM-DELETE-CODE      PIC X. ──┐
00024          └── 05   ISAM-ID-NUMBER        PIC X(9).
00025              05   ISAM-NAME             PIC X(25).
00026              05   ISAM-SALARY           PIC X(6).
00027          FD   TRANSACTION-FILE                   └── 1 byte field to indicate
00028               LABEL RECORDS ARE OMITTED              active records
00029               RECORDING MODE IS F
00030               RECORD CONTAINS 80 CHARACTERS
00031               DATA RECORD IS TRANS-RECORD.
00032          01   TRANS-RECORD.
00033               05   TR-ID-NUMBER         PIC X(9).
00034               05   TR-NAME              PIC X(25).
00035               05   TR-SALARY            PIC X(6).
00036               05   FILLER               PIC X(40).
00037          WORKING-STORAGE SECTION.
00038          77  WS-EOF-INDICATOR           PIC X(3)  VALUE 'NO '.
00039
00040          PROCEDURE DIVISION.
00041              OPEN INPUT TRANSACTION-FILE,
00042                   OUTPUT NEW-MASTER-FILE.
00043              READ TRANSACTION-FILE,
00044                   AT END MOVE 'YES' TO WS-EOF-INDICATOR.
00045              PERFORM 010-READ-A-CARD
00046                   UNTIL WS-EOF-INDICATOR = 'YES'.
00047              CLOSE TRANSACTION-FILE, NEW-MASTER-FILE.
00048              STOP RUN.
00049
00050          010-READ-A-CARD.
00051          ┌── MOVE LOW-VALUES    TO ISAM-DELETE-CODE. ──┐── Denotes an active record
00052              MOVE TR-ID-NUMBER TO ISAM-ID-NUMBER.
00053              MOVE TR-NAME      TO ISAM-NAME.
00054              MOVE TR-SALARY    TO ISAM-SALARY.
00055              WRITE ISAM-MAST-RECORD
00056          ┌── INVALID KEY DISPLAY 'RECORD OUT OF SEQUENCE OR ',
00057          │       'DUPLICATE', TR-ID-NUMBER.                   │
00058              READ TRANSACTION-FILE,
00059                   AT END MOVE 'YES' TO WS-EOF-INDICATOR.

                                              INVALID KEY clause in ──
                                              WRITE statement
```

Figure 16.6 Creation of an ISAM File

Very little in the way of additional COBOL is required to process ISAM files. We have included three COBOL listings to illustrate considerations of ISAM processing. Figure 16.6 creates an ISAM file from cards, Figure 16.7 shows sequential access, and Figure 16.9 demonstrates random (direct) access of an ISAM file.

Creation of an ISAM File

Figure 16.6 contains a COBOL program to create an ISAM file. The only new material is in the SELECT statement (lines 11–13), the MOVE statement (line 51), and the WRITE statement (lines 55–57). The program utilizes two files. It reads an incoming transaction file and creates an ISAM file as output. *The incoming file must be in sequential order.*

The SELECT statement contains the clause ACCESS IS SEQUENTIAL (line 12), indicating that in this particular run we are accessing the ISAM file sequentially. It also contains a RECORD KEY clause (line 13), which specifies the field within the ISAM record that serves as a key. Note that ISAM-ID-NUMBER, the field specified in the RECORD KEY, *must* be defined within the ISAM record itself.

ISAM files do not physically delete inactive records. Instead a 1-byte field is established at the beginning of each record (line 23) with the convention that LOW-VALUES denote an active record and HIGH-VALUES an inactive record. When a file is created, all records are initially active—thus the MOVE statement of line 51. Subsequent processing, e.g., file maintenance, may "delete" specified records by moving HIGH-VALUES to this field (see Figure 16.9).

The WRITE statement (lines 55–57) contains an INVALID KEY clause. As was explained earlier, the key of every record in a file must be unique. Further, ISAM files must be written in *logical* sequential order. The INVALID KEY clause is a check on these two conditions; i.e., it ensures that the RECORD KEY of the present record is not a duplicate and, further, that it is higher than the key of the previous record.

Sequential Access of an ISAM File

Figure 16.7 contains a COBOL program to print active records from an ISAM file. The logic is straightforward; read a record and test that the record is active (i.e., LOW-VALUES are present in the first byte). If the record is active, print; if inactive, bypass. The IF statement of lines 73–74 is *not* actually required as the system automatically bypasses inactive records. It is included, however, to remind the student that not all physical records are logically active. The COBOL program is really quite simple. It contains the clause, ACCESS IS SEQUENTIAL (line 15) to indicate sequential access. Other than that there is no new material.

Figure 16.7 also contains the page heading routine first shown in the car billing problem of Figure 7.8. While that material is not new, it is worth repeating. Note the use of a line counter and page counter (defined in lines 45–46). Also note the use of CURRENT-DATE, which appears at the top of every page in the report.

Random (Direct) Access of an ISAM File

In Chapter 15 we introduced the concepts of file maintenance and sequential processing; in particular Figure 15.11 contained a maintenance program to take a transaction file and an old master file as input and create a new master

```
00001          IDENTIFICATION DIVISION.
00002          PROGRAM-ID.     ISAMPRNT.
00003          AUTHOR.         GRAUER.
00004
00005          ENVIRONMENT DIVISION.
00006          CONFIGURATION SECTION.
00007          SOURCE-COMPUTER.  IBM-360.
00008          OBJECT-COMPUTER.  IBM-360.
00009          SPECIAL-NAMES.
00010              CO1 IS TOP-OF-PAGE.
00011          INPUT-OUTPUT SECTION.
00012          FILE-CONTROL.
00013              SELECT PRINT-FILE ASSIGN TO UR-1403-S-SYSPRINT.
00014              SELECT NEW-MASTER-FILE ASSIGN TO DA-I-NEWMAST
00015                  ACCESS IS SEQUENTIAL
00016                  RECORD KEY IS ISAM-ID-NUMBER.
00017                                        └── SELECT statement
00018          DATA DIVISION.
00019          FILE SECTION.
00020          FD  NEW-MASTER-FILE
00021              LABEL RECORDS ARE STANDARD
00022              RECORDING MODE IS F
00023              BLOCK CONTAINS 3 RECORDS
00024              RECORD CONTAINS 41 CHARACTERS
00025              DATA RECORD IS ISAM-MAST-RECORD.
00026          01  ISAM-MAST-RECORD.
00027              05  ISAM-DELETE-CODE      PIC X.
00028              05  ISAM-ID-NUMBER        PIC X(9).
00029              05  ISAM-NAME             PIC X(25).
00030              05  ISAM-SALARY           PIC X(6).
00031          FD  PRINT-FILE
00032              LABEL RECORDS ARE OMITTED
00033              RECORDING MODE IS F
00034              RECORD CONTAINS 133 CHARACTERS
00035              DATA RECORD IS PRINT-LINE.
00036          01  PRINT-LINE.
00037              05  FILLER                PIC X.
00038              05  PR-ID-NUMBER          PIC X(9).
00039              05  FILLER                PIC X(3).
00040              05  PR-NAME               PIC X(25).
00041              05  FILLER                PIC X(3).
00042              05  PR-SALARY             PIC X(6).
00043              05  FILLER                PIC X(86).
00044          WORKING-STORAGE SECTION.
00045          77  WS-LINE-COUNT             PIC S99   VALUE 52.
00046          77  WS-PAGE-COUNT             PIC S99   VALUE ZEROS.
00047          77  WS-EOF-INDICATOR          PIC X(3)  VALUE 'NO '.
00048          01  HDG-LINE-ONE.
00049              05  FILLER                PIC X(20) VALUE SPACES.
00050              05  HDG-DATE              PIC X(8).
00051              05  FILLER                PIC X(10) VALUE SPACES.
00052              05  FILLER                PIC X(5)  VALUE 'PAGE '.
00053              05  HDG-PAGE              PIC ZZ9.
00054              05  FILLER                PIC X(87) VALUE SPACES.
00055          01  HDG-LINE-TWO.
00056              05  FILLER                PIC X(8)  VALUE '    ID #'.
00057              05  FILLER                PIC X(10) VALUE SPACES.
00058              05  FILLER                PIC X(4)  VALUE 'NAME'.
00059              05  FILLER                PIC X(19) VALUE SPACES.
00060              05  FILLER                PIC X(6)  VALUE 'SALARY'.
00061              05  FILLER                PIC X(86) VALUE SPACES.
00062
00063          PROCEDURE DIVISION.
00064              OPEN INPUT NEW-MASTER-FILE, OUTPUT PRINT-FILE.
00065              READ NEW-MASTER-FILE,
00066                  AT END MOVE 'YES' TO WS-EOF-INDICATOR.
00067              PERFORM 010-READ-A-RECORD THRU 015-READ-EXIT
00068                  UNTIL WS-EOF-INDICATOR = 'YES'.
00069              CLOSE NEW-MASTER-FILE, PRINT-FILE.
00070              STOP RUN.
00071
00072          010-READ-A-RECORD.
```

Figure 16.7 Sequential Access of an ISAM File

306

```
00073        IF ISAM-DELETE-CODE IS NOT EQUAL TO LOW-VALUES,
00074            GO TO 015-READ-EXIT.
00075        IF WS-LINE-COUNT > 51
00076            PERFORM 030-PAGE-HEADING.                      ── Test for active
00077        MOVE SPACES          TO PRINT-LINE.                   record
00078        MOVE ISAM-ID-NUMBER TO PR-ID-NUMBER.
00079        MOVE ISAM-NAME       TO PR-NAME.
00080        MOVE ISAM-SALARY     TO PR-SALARY.
00081        WRITE PRINT-LINE AFTER ADVANCING 1 LINES.
00082        ADD 1 TO WS-LINE-COUNT.
00083
00084    015-READ-EXIT.
00085        READ NEW-MASTER-FILE,
00086            AT END MOVE 'YES' TO WS-EOF-INDICATOR.
00087
00088    030-PAGE-HEADING.
00089        MOVE ZEROS TO WS-LINE-COUNT.
00090        ADD 1 TO WS-PAGE-COUNT.
00091        MOVE CURRENT-DATE TO HDG-DATE.
00092        MOVE WS-PAGE-COUNT TO HDG-PAGE.
00093        WRITE PRINT-LINE FROM HDG-LINE-ONE
00094            AFTER ADVANCING TOP-OF-PAGE LINES.
00095        WRITE PRINT-LINE FROM HDG-LINE-TWO
00096            AFTER ADVANCING 2 LINES.
```

Figure 16.7 *(Continued)*

file as output. Since processing was strictly sequential, every record in the old master had to be read and rewritten regardless of whether or not it was changed. Obviously if only a "small" percentage of records is changed, sequential processing is an inefficient means of file maintenance. ISAM files provide the capability to do file maintenance on a direct basis; i.e., only new or changed records are written—unchanged records are left alone. Thus while sequential processing required two distinct master files, an old and a new, direct processing uses a single master file from which records are both read and written to.

Figure 16.8 contains a flowchart for the mainline logic of a direct update. Figure 16.9 has the corresponding COBOL listing. As stated earlier in Chapter 15, the logic for file maintenance is somewhat involved; however, we believe the structured approach of Figures 16.8 and 16.9 goes a long way toward simplifying program logic. As such it is a strong argument for the advantages of structured programming in program development, maintenance, and documentation.

Figure 16.9 contains only three files: an input transaction file, an output error file, and an ISAM file, which is used for both input and output. As such it is opened as an I/O file (lines 79–80). Note that updated records are written to this file via a REWRITE verb (line 118). The SELECT statement for this file has three clauses: ACCESS IS RANDOM, NOMINAL KEY, and RECORD KEY. The NOMINAL KEY denotes a field in working-storage, whereas RECORD KEY specifies the key of each ISAM record and as such is contained in the record itself.

After a record is read from the transaction file, its ID number is moved to the NOMINAL KEY (MOVE statement in line 92). The ISAM file is accessed by the READ statement in lines 93–94. Note the INVALID KEY clause in line 94, which is activated only if the ISAM file does not contain the NOMINAL KEY. (Under random access of an ISAM file however, the system will return 'deleted' records; i.e. those records with HIGH-VALUES in the first byte. An additional routine could be inserted in Figure 16.9 to check for

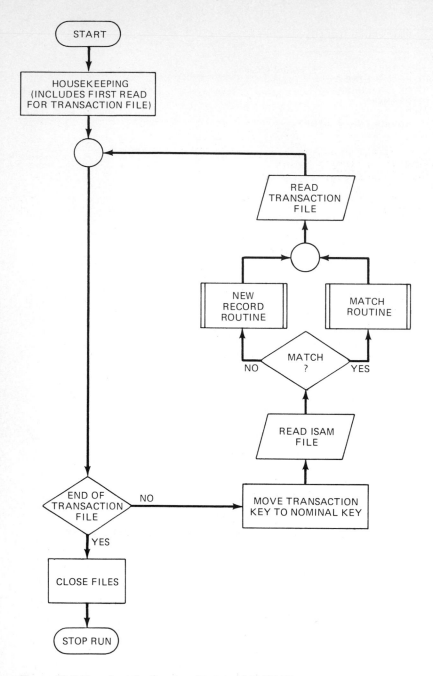

Figure 16.8 Flowchart for Random Update of ISAM File

this possibility.) If the INVALID KEY is activated, it means either a new record or a "no match." Either way it causes a perform of 070-NEW-RECORD. If INVALID KEY is not activated, then 060-MATCH-ROUTINE is performed instead. In other words the data name contained in the NOMINAL KEY clause (WS-MATCH-NUMBER) holds the key of the current transaction, i.e., the record we are trying to find. When an ISAM file is read, the COBOL program searches the ISAM file to find an existing record which has a RECORD KEY that matches the NOMINAL KEY.

Figure 16.9 utilizes many of the procedure division techniques advocated in Chapter 11. In particular, note the use of READ INTO, WRITE FROM, and PERFORM THRU. Figure 16.9 was tested with the same data used for Figure 15.12 and, as expected, produced identical results (see Figure 15.12).

```
00001          IDENTIFICATION DIVISION.
00002          PROGRAM-ID.    UPDATE.
00003          AUTHOR.        GRAUER.
00004          ENVIRONMENT DIVISION.
00005          CONFIGURATION SECTION.
00006          SOURCE-COMPUTER.    IBM-360.
00007          OBJECT-COMPUTER.    IBM-360.
00008          INPUT-OUTPUT SECTION.
00009          FILE-CONTROL.
00010              SELECT TRANSACTION-FILE ASSIGN TO UR-2540R-S-SYSIN.
00011              SELECT ERROR-FILE ASSIGN TO UR-1403-S-SYSOUT.
00012              SELECT ISAM-FILE ASSIGN TO DA-I-NEWMAST
00013                  ACCESS IS RANDOM
00014                  NOMINAL KEY IS WS-MATCH-NUMBER
00015                  RECORD KEY IS ISAM-ID-NUMBER.
00016          DATA DIVISION.                              ┌── SELECT statement
00017          FILE SECTION.                                   for ISAM file
00018          FD  ISAM-FILE
00019              LABEL RECORDS ARE STANDARD
00020              RECORDING MODE IS F
00021              BLOCK CONTAINS 3 RECORDS
00022              RECORD CONTAINS 41 CHARACTERS
00023              DATA RECORD IS ISAM-RECORD.        ┌── RECORD KEY
00024          01  ISAM-RECORD.
00025              05   ISAM-DELETE-CODE              PICTURE IS X.
00026              05   ISAM-ID-NUMBER                PICTURE IS X(9).
00027              05   ISAM-NAME                     PICTURE IS X(25).
00028              05   ISAM SALARY                   PICTURE IS X(6).
00029          FD  TRANSACTION-FILE
00030              LABEL RECORDS ARE OMITTED
00031              RECORDING MODE IS F
00032              RECORD CONTAINS 80 CHARACTERS
00033              DATA RECORD IS TRANS-RECORD.
00034          01  TRANS-RECORD                       PICTURE IS X(80).
00035          FD  ERROR-FILE
00036              LABEL RECORDS ARE OMITTED
00037              RECORDING MODE IS F
00038              RECORD CONTAINS 133 CHARACTERS
00039              DATA RECORD IS ERROR-RECORD.
00040          01  ERROR-RECORD                       PICTURE IS X(133).
00041          WORKING-STORAGE SECTION.
00042          77  FILLER                             PICTURE IS X(14)
00043                            VALUE IS 'WS BEGINS HERE'.
00044          77  WS-MATCH-NUMBER                    PICTURE IS X(9).──── Definition of NOMINAL KEY
00045          77  WS-EOF-INDICATOR                   PICTURE IS X(3)       in working-storage
00046                            VALUE IS 'NO '.
00047          77  WS-INVALID-SWITCH                  PICTURE IS X(3).
00048              88   NO-MATCH-OR-NEW-RECORD        VALUE IS 'YES'.
00049          01  WS-TRANS-RECORD.
00050              05   WS-TRANS-ID                   PICTURE IS X(9).
00051              05   WS-TRANS-NAME                 PICTURE IS X(25).
00052              05   WS-TRANS-SALARY               PICTURE IS 9(6).
00053              05   FILLER                        PICTURE IS X(39).
00054              05   WS-TRANS-CODE                 PICTURE IS X.
00055                   88   ADDITION     VALUE IS 'A'.
00056                   88   DELETION     VALUE IS 'D'.
00057                   88   UPDATE       VALUE IS 'C'.
00058          01  WS-ERROR-MESSAGE-1                 PICTURE IS X(40)
00059                            VALUE IS ' RECORD ALREADY IN FILE '.
00060          01  WS-ERROR-MESSAGE-2                 PICTURE IS X(40)
00061                            VALUE IS ' NO MATCH '
00062          01  WS-PRINT-RECORD.
00063              05   WS-PRINT-MESSAGE              PICTURE IS X(40).
00064              05   WS-PRINT-ID                   PICTURE IS X(9).
00065              05   FILLER                        PICTURE IS X(5)
00066                            VALUE IS SPACES.
00067              05   WS-PRINT-NAME                 PICTURE IS X(25).
00068              05   FILLER                        PICTURE IS X(53)
00069                            VALUE IS SPACES.
00070          01  WS-ISAM-RECORD.
00071              05   WS-ISAM-DELETE-CODE           PICTURE IS X.
00072              05   WS-ISAM-ID                    PICTURE IS X(9).
00073              05   WS-ISAM-NAME                  PICTURE IS X(25).
00074              05   WS-ISAM-SALARY                PICTURE IS X(6).
```

Figure 16.9 Random Access of ISAM File

```
00075        01  FILLER                           PICTURE IS X(12)
00076                                   VALUE IS 'WS ENDS HERE'.
00077            PROCEDURE DIVISION.
00078                MOVE 'NO.' TO WS-INVALID-SWITCH.
00079                OPEN INPUT TRANSACTION-FILE,
00080                    ┌─I-O ISAM-FILE─┐──────── ISAM file opened as I-O
00081                      OUTPUT ERROR-FILE.
00082                READ TRANSACTION-FILE INTO WS-TRANS-RECORD
00083                    AT END MOVE 'YES' TO WS-EOF-INDICATOR.
00084                PERFORM 010-READ-ISAM-FILE THRU 010-READ-ISAM-FILE-EXIT
00085                    UNTIL WS-EOF-INDICATOR = 'YES'.
00086                CLOSE TRANSACTION-FILE
00087                      ISAM-FILE
00088                      ERROR-FILE.
00089                STOP RUN.                    ┌─ Transaction key moved
00090                                             │   to NOMINAL KEY
00091            010-READ-ISAM-FILE.                         ┌─ INVALID KEY clause
00092                ┌─MOVE WS-TRANS-ID TO WS-MATCH-NUMBER.─┐│    in ISAM READ
00093                READ ISAM-FILE INTO WS-ISAM-RECORD      │
00094                    ┌─INVALID KEY MOVE  'YES' TO WS-INVALID-SWITCH.─┐
00095                IF NO-MATCH-OR-NEW-RECORD
00096                    PERFORM 070-NEW-RECORD THRU 070-NEW-RECORD-EXIT
00097                ELSE
00098                    PERFORM 060-MATCH-ROUTINE THRU 060-MATCH-ROUTINE-EXIT.
00099                READ TRANSACTION-FILE INTO WS-TRANS-RECORD
00100                    AT END MOVE 'YES' TO WS-EOF-INDICATOR.
00101
00102            010-READ-ISAM-FILE-EXIT.
00103                EXIT.
00104
00105            060-MATCH-ROUTINE.
00106                IF ADDITION
00107                    MOVE WS-TRANS-NAME       TO WS-PRINT-NAME
00108                    MOVE WS-TRANS-ID         TO WS-PRINT-ID
00109                    MOVE WS-ERROR-MESSAGE-1 TO WS-PRINT-MESSAGE
00110                    WRITE ERROR-RECORD FROM WS-PRINT-RECORD
00111                    GO TO 060-MATCH-ROUTINE-EXIT.
00112                IF DELETION
00113                    MOVE HIGH-VALUES TO WS-ISAM-DELETE-CODE
00114                    REWRITE ISAM-RECORD FROM WS-ISAM-RECORD
00115                    GO TO 060-MATCH-ROUTINE-EXIT.
00116                IF UPDATE
00117                    MOVE WS-TRANS-SALARY TO WS-ISAM-SALARY
00118                    ┌─REWRITE ISAM-RECORD FROM WS-ISAM-RECORD.─┐
00119
00120            060-MATCH-ROUTINE-EXIT.          └─ REWRITE statement
00121                EXIT.
00122
00123          ┌─070-NEW-RECORD.
00124                MOVE 'NO ' TO WS-INVALID-SWITCH.
00125                IF ADDITION
00126                    MOVE LOW-VALUES         TO WS-ISAM-DELETE-CODE
00127                    MOVE WS-TRANS-ID        TO WS-ISAM-ID
00128                    MOVE WS-TRANS-NAME      TO WS-ISAM-NAME
00129                    MOVE WS-TRANS-SALARY    TO WS-ISAM-SALARY
00130                    WRITE ISAM-RECORD FROM WS-ISAM-RECORD
00131                ELSE MOVE WS-TRANS-NAME     TO WS-PRINT-NAME
00132                    MOVE WS-TRANS-ID        TO WS-PRINT-ID
00133                    MOVE WS-ERROR-MESSAGE-2 TO WS-PRINT-MESSAGE
00134                    WRITE ERROR-RECORD FROM WS-PRINT-RECORD.
00135
00136          └─070-NEW-RECORD-EXIT.
00137                EXIT.
```

└─ Routine to process new records or no matches

Figure 16.9 (*Continued*)

Direct or random organization requires a predictable relationship between a key and its address, i.e., the track and cylinder on which the record is found. There are several ways to supply this relationship, but the division/remainder algorithm is the most common. This method first determines the relative track within the file where the record is located; it then converts the relative track to a cylinder and track address.

Direct (Random) Organization

The relative track is calculated through division of the record key by the prime number closest to the number of tracks allocated to the file. [A prime number is a number that can be divided evenly only by itself and 1. Thus 1, 2, 3, 5, 7, 11, 13, and 17 are prime numbers (4, 6, 8, 9, 10, 12, 14, 15, and 16 are nonprime numbers).] The quotient is discarded, and the remainder is the relative track. The remainder is then divided by the number of tracks per cylinder to supply a cylinder and track address, as illustrated in Example 16.4.

Example 16.4

Calculate the cylinder and track address for key 12345, using the division/remainder method. The entire file is stored on cylinders 100–124 of a 2314, with 20 tracks per cylinder.

SOLUTION

1. 500 tracks are allocated to the file (25 cylinders × 20 tracks per cylinder).
2. 499 is the prime number closest to 500 (without exceeding 500).
3. Divide the key, 12345, by 499. The quotient is 24; the remainder is 369. Only the remainder, 369, is significant; it is the relative track on which the record is located.
4. Divide the relative track, 369, by the number of tracks per cylinder (20 on a 2314). The quotient is 18; the remainder is 9.
5. Record 12345 will be located on cylinder 118, track 9. (Take the quotient from step 4 and add it to the beginning cylinder of the file; the remainder from step 4 provides the track within the cylinder.)

OBSERVATION. Using the same procedure, determine the cylinder and track address for the record whose key is 98765. You should get cylinder 123, track 2.

The division/remainder method, and indeed any algorithm used to establish a direct file, inevitably creates synonyms, two records which randomize to the same track and cylinder. In the specification for Example 16.4 records 12345 and 50269 would be synonyms since both randomize to cylinder 118, track 9. If the record length is such that every track can hold ten records, then the first ten synonyms will fit on the calculated address. Additional records, however, will have to be written in an overflow area. Provision for overflow and a simultaneous reduction in the occurrence of synonyms is accomplished by allocating more space to the file than is absolutely required from track capacity calculations, as shown in Example 16.5.

Example 16.5

How many cylinders are required for a file of 5000 records loaded as a direct file. Each physical record is 160 bytes long and is formatted with keys. Use an 80% packing factor (i.e., only 80% of the space allocation is to be filled). Answer for a 2314.

SOLUTION

1. By Table 16.1, 23 records will fit per track.
2. An 80% packing factor implies that space is to be allocated for 6250 records (5000/.80).
3. 272 tracks are necessary for the entire file (6250/23).
4. 14 cylinders are required (272/20; the 2314 has 20 tracks per cylinder).

The division/remainder method creates a valid cylinder and track number for each key but by no means assures optimal file organization. In a given file several records may randomize to the same cylinder and track (synonyms), while other tracks may be completely empty. How well the method works in practice depends on the distribution of keys in the file. Often the systems analyst will be forced to use different methods of randomization for different files. Another disadvantage is that the method is device dependent because the generated address is a function of the number of tracks per cylinder.

COBOL Implications

Figure 16.10 contains a COBOL program to create a direct-access file from cards. We assume that 100 tracks have been allocated to the file. Thus 97 is the prime number which will be used in the division/remainder algorithm. The SELECT statement of lines 9-11 contains two required clauses. The first clause, ACCESS IS RANDOM, specifies direct access. The second clause, ACTUAL KEY, denotes a data name, WS-ACT-KEY, in working-storage which consists of two fields, WS-TRACK-ID and WS-REC-ID. The first field contains the calculated relative track, and the second field holds the record key (the format of the ACTUAL KEY varies from manufacturer to manufacturer—check with your installation).

Consider the logic of Figure 16.10. The mainline consists of lines 46–53 and is the format followed throughout the text. The paragraph 010-READ-A-CARD contains the logic to determine the record address. Lines 59-60 move the incoming key, CD-PART-NUM, to two fields, WS-WORK-FIELD and WS-REC-ID. (Notice how a single MOVE statement can move the same source field to two receiving fields.) WS-WORK-FIELD is next divided by 97 (the largest prime number less than 100), and the remainder is kept in WS-TRACK-ID. Thus the two fields in WS-ACT-KEY (i.e., the ACTUAL KEY) are now filled. WS-TRACK-ID has been determined by the remainder clause in line 62, and WS-REC-ID was specified by the MOVE statement of lines 59–60.

The WRITE statement of lines 66–67 contains the INVALID KEY clause. The latter is activated if the calculated relative track is beyond the file limits. It can also be activated if we are processing an existing direct file and fail to find an incoming key.

Summary

Much of the discussion in this chapter revolved around the COBOL listings for indexed sequential and direct organization. The programs were presented in conjunction with concepts of file organization and little attention was paid to the COBOL syntax per se. Accordingly, a formal presentation of the requisite COBOL should serve as an effective review.

Note that each COBOL statement is presented only once as it would appear in a manufacturer's manual; e.g., we shall not present three different SELECT statements (one for each type of file organization) as is done in some texts. Further, we shall omit most of the more esoteric clauses; the reader is directed to a reference manual for additional discussion.

Environment Division. COBOL requirements for direct access files (i.e., both direct and ISAM organization) center around the SELECT statement in the file-control paragraph. Additional options are present in the APPLY statement of the I-O-Control paragraph. There is considerable variation in these statements from manufacturer to manufacturer and indeed from OS to DOS. Check carefully at your installation for the exact syntax. The OS syntax with commonly used clauses is shown on page 314.

```
00001          IDENTIFICATION DIVISION.
00002          PROGRAM-ID.  DIRECT.
00003          ENVIRONMENT DIVISION.
00004          CONFIGURATION SECTION.
00005          SOURCE-COMPUTER.  IBM-370.
00006          OBJECT-COMPUTER.  IBM-370.
00007          INPUT-OUTPUT SECTION.                     ⌐SELECT statement
00008          FILE-CONTROL.
00009              ┌SELECT DIRECT-FILE ASSIGN DA-2314-D-MASTER
00010              │   ACCESS IS RANDOM
00011              │   ACTUAL KEY IS WS-ACT-KEY.                   │
00012              └SELECT CARD-FILE ASSIGN TO UR-2540R-S-SYSIN.───┘
00013          DATA DIVISION.
00014          FILE SECTION.
00015          FD  DIRECT-FILE
00016              RECORDING MODE IS F
00017              LABEL RECORDS ARE STANDARD
00018              RECORD CONTAINS 80 CHARACTERS
00019              DATA RECORD IS DIRECT-RECORD.
00020          01  DIRECT-RECORD.
00021              05  DR-PART-NUM              PIC IS 9(8).
00022              05  DR-NUMBER-IN-STOCK       PIC IS 9(4).
00023              05  DR-PRICE                 PIC IS 9(5)V99.
00024              05  FILLER                   PIC IS X(61).
00025          FD  CARD-FILE
00026              RECORDING MODE IS F
00027              LABEL RECORDS ARE OMITTED
00028              RECORD CONTAINS 80 CHARACTERS
00029              DATA RECORD IS CARD-RECORD.
00030          01  CARD-RECORD.
00031              05  CD-PART-NUM              PIC IS 9(8).
00032              05  CD-NUMBER-IN-STOCK       PIC IS 9(4).
00033              05  CD-PRICE                 PIC IS 9(5)V99.
00034              05  FILLER                   PIC IS X(61).
00035          WORKING-STORAGE SECTION.
00036          77  WS-EOF-INDICATOR             PIC IS X(3) VALUE 'NO '.
00037          77  WS-WORK-FIELD                PIC IS S9(8)
00038              USAGE IS COMPUTATIONAL       SYNC.
00039          77  WS-QUOTIENT                  PIC IS S9(5)
00040              USAGE IS COMPUTATIONAL       SYNC.            ⌐Relative
00041          01  WS-ACT-KEY.                                  │  track
00042              ┌05  WS-TRACK-ID             PIC IS S9(5)│
00043              │    USAGE IS COMPUTATIONAL  SYNC.        │
00044              └05  WS-REC-ID               PIC IS X(8).─┘
00045          PROCEDURE DIVISION.                             └─Record key
00046              OPEN INPUT CARD-FILE,
00047                   OUTPUT DIRECT-FILE.
00048              READ CARD-FILE,
00049                  AT END MOVE 'YES' TO WS-EOF-INDICATOR.
00050              PERFORM 010-READ-A-CARD THRU 030-READ-EXIT
00051                  UNTIL WS-EOF-INDICATOR = 'YES'.
00052              CLOSE CARD-FILE, DIRECT-FILE.
00053              STOP RUN.
00054
00055          010-READ-A-CARD.
00056              MOVE CD-PART-NUM          TO DR-PART-NUM.
00057              MOVE CD-NUMBER-IN-STOCK   TO DR-NUMBER-IN-STOCK.
00058              MOVE CD-PRICE             TO DR-PRICE.
00059              MOVE CD-PART-NUM          TO WS-WORK-FIELD
00060                                           WS-REC-ID.
00061              ┌DIVIDE WS-WORK-FIELD BY 97 GIVING WS-QUOTIENT│  Implementation of
00062              │                    REMAINDER WS-TRACK-ID.   │  division remainder
00063                                                               algorithm
00064          020-WRITE-A-RECORD.
00065              EXHIBIT NAMED WS-TRACK-ID, CD-PART-NUM.
00066              ┌WRITE DIRECT-RECORD
00067              │   INVALID KEY DISPLAY 'INVALID KEY  ', WS-TRACK-ID, WS-REC-ID.│
00068
00069          030-READ-EXIT.                                 └─INVALID KEY clause in WRITE statement
00070              READ CARD-FILE,
00071                  AT END MOVE 'YES' TO WS-EOF-INDICATOR.
```

Figure 16.10 Creation of a Direct File

```
ENVIRONMENT DIVISION.
    FILE-CONTROL.
        SELECT file-name ASSIGN TO system-name-1 [system-name-2] ...
        ACCESS MODE IS  {SEQUENTIAL}
                        {RANDOM    }
        ACTUAL KEY IS data-name
        NOMINAL KEY IS data-name
        RECORD KEY IS data-name
    I-O-CONTROL.
        APPLY CORE-INDEX ON file-name-1 [file-name-2]
```

Every file in a COBOL program requires a SELECT statement to link a programmer-chosen file name to a system name. Under OS the system name has the form

class[-device]-organization-name.

Class may assume one of the three values: UR (unit record), UT (utility), or DA (direct access). The device type is optional and is often omitted to achieve device independence, although this was not done in most of the illustrative programs in the text. (See Chapter 18.) Organization commonly assumes one of three values: S(sequential), D(direct), or I (indexed).

The following are valid system names:

UR-2540R-S-SYSIN
UT-S-SYSIN
DA-3330-I-ISAM
DA-2314-D-DIRECT
UT-2400-S-TAPE
UT-S-TAPE

The ACCESS MODE clause indicates how a file is accessed. If it is not specified, ACCESS IS SEQUENTIAL is assumed. Thus ACCESS IS RANDOM is required for both direct files and random access of ISAM files. If ACCESS IS RANDOM is specified, then ACTUAL KEY must also be specified for direct files. Both NOMINAL and RECORD KEY clauses would be required for random access of an ISAM file.

There are several options for the APPLY clause, only one of which is shown. APPLY CORE-INDEX can be specified only for an ISAM file whose access mode is random. It causes the highest-level index to be retained in core and results in increased efficiency. Our discussion referenced only two indexes: cylinder and track. It is possible, however, to obtain a third level, known as a master index. If the latter is present, APPLY CORE-INDEX will cause the master index to remain in core; if a master index is not present, then the cylinder index will be kept in core.

Data Division. There were no new clauses explicitly introduced for direct-access files. Realize, however, that disk files, like those on tape, are likely to contain blocked and/or variable-length records. Thus the discussion in Chapter 15 on FD formats is applicable here as well. The BLOCK CONTAINS clause is applicable to both sequential and indexed sequential files. It should not be used with direct files.

Procedure Division. Direct-access files required additional clauses for the OPEN, READ, and WRITE statements. In addition, the REWRITE statement was introduced.

An OPEN statement is required for every file in a program. Each file is opened as either input, output, or I/O. We are familiar with the first two and have used them throughout the text. An example of an I/O file was presented in Figure 16.9 in which the same file is both read from and written to. When a direct-access file is updated, we are not required to write every single record, as is the case in a sequential file. Instead only new and/or changed records are

314

written, and these are written to the original file. Hence the same file is both input and output. Further, the altered records are in effect rewritten; i.e., they were present in the original file and thus the necessity of the REWRITE statement. The REWRITE statement will replace a logical record if the ACTUAL KEY or NOMINAL KEY is valid. The reader should realize that the I/O and REWRITE options make sense for both direct-access and ISAM files; however, they are not permitted with strict sequential organization.

The general form of the REWRITE verb is

REWRITE record-name [FROM identifier] [INVALID KEY imperative statement]

Consider now the WRITE statement:

WRITE record-name [FROM identifier] [INVALID KEY imperative statement]

Both WRITE and REWRITE allow the FROM option, which we encourage. The INVALID KEY clause should be used with any file on disk and is activated for a variety of reasons. It is activated if an ISAM file is processed sequentially and either a duplicate record exists or the incoming records are not in sequential order. It is activated if a sequential file (used as output) does not have sufficient space to write a record. It is activated if a direct file calculated a relative track outside the limits of the file.

The READ statement also contains an INVALID KEY clause, which must be used for direct files or ISAM files processed randomly. The option is activated for ISAM files if no record exists whose RECORD KEY matches the NOMINAL KEY. It is activated for direct files when no match is found for ACTUAL KEY. The general format is

READ file name [INTO identifier]
$\begin{Bmatrix} \text{AT END} \\ \text{INVALID KEY} \end{Bmatrix}$ imperative statement

One final point on file organization: the inherent characteristics of a file should determine its method of organization. Perhaps the most important consideration is file activity. If the file is inactive, i.e., a "low" percentage of records are processed in a given run, then file organization should permit individual records to be located quickly. Alternatively, a highly active file should be processed sequentially. Unfortunately quantitative guidelines as to the percentage of activity which constitutes an active file are difficult to define.

REVIEW EXERCISES

TRUE	FALSE		
☐	☐	1	The number of cylinders on a disk pack is equal to the number of tracks on a recording surface.
☐	☐	2	The number of read/write heads on the assembly arm is equal to the number of tracks per cylinder.
☐	☐	3	An increase in the density per track decreases the overall capacity of the disk pack.
☐	☐	4	If one track on a disk device can hold a single 10,000 byte record, it is logical to assume it could hold two records each of 5000 bytes.
☐	☐	5	Sequential organization is not possible on a direct-access device.
☐	☐	6	An ISAM file can be accessed either sequentially or directly.
☐	☐	7	Head selection is the most time consuming process in retrieving a record from a disk pack.

TRUE	FALSE		
☐	☐	8	If two records are located on the same cylinder, access time for the second will be zero.
☐	☐	9	If two records are located on different tracks of the same recording surface, access time for the second will be zero.
☐	☐	10	It is not possible to have a zero rotational delay.
☐	☐	11	The division/remainder algorithm is used to calculate addresses for an ISAM file.
☐	☐	12	An ISAM file has more than one track index.
☐	☐	13	In an ISAM file, records are physically in sequential order.
☐	☐	14	If two records randomize to the same cylinder, they are called synonyms.
☐	☐	15	The division/remainder method will produce the same track and cylinder for a given key, independent of device.
☐	☐	16	It is not possible to have a packing factor greater than 100%.
☐	☐	17	Device type must be specified in a SELECT statement.
☐	☐	18	The REWRITE verb can be used only on a file that was opened as I/O.
☐	☐	19	The ACTUAL KEY is required for direct-access files.
☐	☐	20	The ACCESS clause must always be specified.
☐	☐	21	The NOMINAL KEY is always required for ISAM files.
☐	☐	22	LOW-VALUES commonly denote active records for ISAM files.
☐	☐	23	WRITE and REWRITE may be used interchangeably.
☐	☐	24	The INVALID KEY clause of the WRITE statement cannot be used for sequential files.
☐	☐	25	A given READ statement can contain both the INVALID KEY and AT END clauses.

PROBLEMS

1 Calculate the maximum storage capacity of a hypothetical disk device with 16 recording surfaces, 400 cylinders, and a recording density of 10,000 bytes per track.

2 Consider a file of 10,000 physical records, each 400 bytes long. How many cylinders are required to store the file (sequentially with no keys) on a 2314? On a 3330?

3 Consider the file of Problem 2, i.e., 10,000 records, each 400 bytes long. This time assume keys and determine how many cylinders are required to store this file as an ISAM file on both a 2314 and a 3330. Further assume that one track in each cylinder is used for the track index and two additional tracks are used for overflow.

4 Consider the file of Problems 2 and 3. How many cylinders are required to store this as a direct file (with keys) on a 2314? On a 3330? Assume an 80% packing factor in both cases.

5 A file of student records is organized as a direct file and is stored on cylinders 80–100 on a 2314. Use the division/remainder algorithm to calculate the cylinder and track address for records whose keys are 12345 and 54321.

6 Extend Table 16.6 to reflect the addition of record keys 747 and 701.

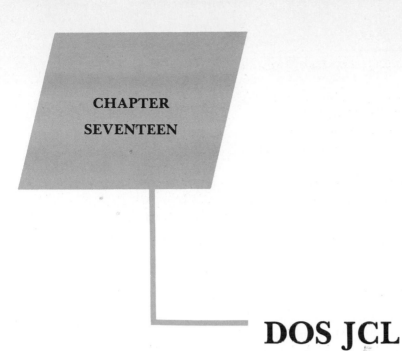

DOS JCL

An operating system is a complex set of programs, supplied by the mainframe manufacturer, to improve the effectiveness of a computer. Communication with the operating system is accomplished through user-prepared control cards known as job control language, or simply JCL. Chapters 17 and 18 are directed at the COBOL programmer (in an "IBM shop") who continually utilizes the facilities of an operating system but whose knowledge of JCL is typically below his COBOL capability. "Just give me the control cards" is a phrase heard far too often.

In this chapter and the next we shall discuss the two most widely used operating systems, DOS and OS. The chapters may be read independently of one another, and we suggest you concentrate on the operating system in use at your installation. Each chapter begins with an overview of the programs constituting the operating system. This is followed by substantial coverage of JCL. At the conclusion of either chapter the reader should have acquired sufficient JCL to manipulate tape and disk files in conjunction with the COBOL covered in Chapters 15 and 16.

Overview

The disk operating system is composed of three sets of programs: control programs, language translators, and service programs (Table 17.1).

DOS Components

317

Table 17.1 Programs Comprising DOS

I. Control programs
    Supervisor
    Job control
    Initial program loader (IPL)
II. Language translators
    Assembler (BAL)
    COBOL
    FORTRAN
    PL/I
    RPG
III. Service programs
    Linkage-editor
    Librarian
    Sort/merge
    Utilities
    Autotest

Control programs supervise the execution of all other programs as well as controlling the location, storage, and retrieval of data. The initial program loader (IPL) loads the supervisor into main storage when the system is initiated. It is used only at the start of operations or after a *system crash* when the system has to be reinitiated. The supervisor is the most important control program, and part of it resides in main storage at all times. It handles all I/O operations, program interrupts, and any other functions required by a problem program. Job control interprets JCL statements and provides for continuity between jobs and job steps. It is called by the supervisor whenever necessary.

A language translator accepts statements in a higher-level language and translates them into machine language. We are familiar with COBOL and Assembler. FORTRAN is a widely used language which is best suited to problems with a large amount of calculations and limited I/O. PL/I is a general-purpose language which combines features of COBOL, FORTRAN, and other languages. RPG is a report program generator designed especially for report writing and file maintenance applications.

Service programs perform a variety of functions required by the user. The linkage-editor combines object modules (i.e., the output of a language translator) with modules from a system library to produce an executable program. The sort/merge programs allow the user to sort a file of randomly ordered records or to merge several sequenced files into one. Autotest provides aid in testing and debugging programs. Utility programs are used to copy files from one device to another, e.g., tape to disk, card to tape, etc.

The librarian is used to maintain the three system libraries. A given program can be stored (cataloged) in a different form in all three libraries. The *source statement library* contains programs in the form in which they were written. The *relocatable library* contains object modules which are the results of a compilation. Programs in the relocatable library have been translated into machine language but have not yet been tied to specific addresses or combined with other required modules; hence they are not yet executable. The *core image library* contains fully executable programs. Each program in this library has been processed by the linkage editor.

We proceed to a discussion of DOS JCL.

The JCL to compile, link-edit, and execute a COBOL program is shown in Figure 17.1.

A Basic Job Stream

All JCL statements consist of up to four components, with blanks as the delimeters between components. Every statement begins with // in columns 1

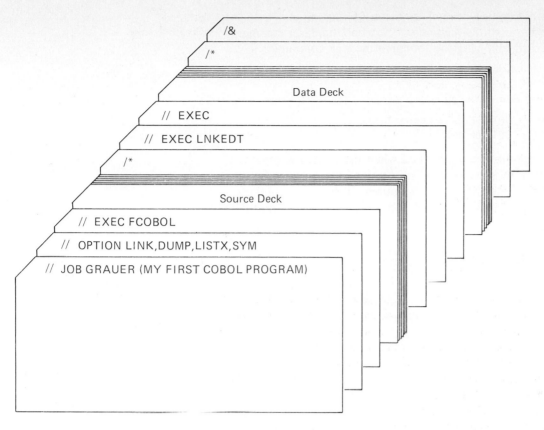

```
                                    /&
                                 /*
                        Data Deck
                   // EXEC
                // EXEC LNKEDT
             /*
                  Source Deck
          // EXEC FCOBOL
       // OPTION LINK,DUMP,LISTX,SYM
    // JOB GRAUER (MY FIRST COBOL PROGRAM)
```

Figure 17.1 Basic DOS JCL

and 2 with the exception of /*, denoting end of file, and /&, denoting end of job. The second component indicates the operation, e.g., EXEC, OPTION, etc., and may be up to eight characters long. Operands follow next. A statement may have none, e.g., the last EXEC card, or several, as in the OPTION statement. Comments are last and follow the last operand, as illustrated in the JOB statement.

Presentation of JCL statements is facilitated through notation similar to that used in explaining COBOL. Thus,

UPPERCASE LETTERS—are required to appear in a JCL statement exactly as shown in the sample format.

LOWERCASE LETTERS—denote generic terms that are replaced in the actual JCL statement.

[ ]—indicate an optional specification; i.e., the contents of the brackets appear at the discretion of the programmer in conjunction with his requirements.

{ }—require that a choice be made among the items stacked within.

. . .—denote repetition, at programmer discretion, of the last syntactical element.

We proceed to an explanation of the JOB, OPTION, EXEC, /*, and /& statements.

JOB Statement

Format: // JOB jobname
Example: // JOB GRAUER (MY FIRST COBOL PROGRAM)

319

The jobname is a programmer-defined name consisting of one to eight alphanumeric characters, the first of which must be alphabetic. User comments may appear on the JOB card following the jobname through column 72.

OPTION Statement

Format: // OPTION option1,option2,option3...
Example: // OPTION LINK

Default values for all options are established when the system is generated (SYSGEN time). The OPTION statement permits one to temporarily, i.e., for the duration of the job, override the standard options. Table 17.2 contains a partial list of DOS options, which are listed for the most part in mutually exclusive pairs, e.g., DUMP and NODUMP.

Table 17.2   Partial List of DOS Options

DUMP	Causes a dump of main storage and registers to be printed in case of abnormal program termination, e.g., a data exception.
NODUMP	Suppresses the DUMP option.
LINK	Indicates the object module is to be link-edited. This option must be present prior to the EXEC LNKEDT statement.
NOLINK	Suppresses the LINK option.
DECK	Causes the compiler to punch an object deck.
NODECK	Suppresses the DECK option.
LISTX	Generates a procedure division map. In addition, other information, such as register assignments and the literal pool, is also printed.
NOLISTX	Suppresses the LISTX option.
XREF	Provides a cross-reference list.
NOXREF	Suppresses the XREF option.
SYM	Generates a data division map. In addition, other information, such as register assignments and the literal pool, is also printed.
NOSYM	Suppresses the SYM option.
ERRS	Causes compiler diagnostics to be listed.
NOERRS	Suppresses the ERRS option.
CATAL	Causes the cataloging of the program in the core image library.

Note: The LINK and CATAL options may *not* appear in the same statement.

The CATAL option does not appear in a mutually exclusive pair. This option will *catalog* a program in the core image library. If the option is not specified, no cataloging will take place; however, it is *incorrect* to say NOCATAL.

As an illustration, assume we want data and procedure division maps, a dump in the event of ABEND, and for the object module to be link-edited. All this is accomplished by the statement

// OPTION LISTX,SYM,DUMP,LINK

Options may be listed in any order. What about the options of Table 17.2 not specified in the option statement; i.e., which is, in effect, DECK or NODECK, ERRS or NOERRS, etc.? The answer depends on the options included in the system generation. Typically NODECK and ERRS are default options, and hence there is no reason to specify them explicitly. The purpose of the OPTION card is to *temporarily* override the default options. Common practice therefore is to specify only those options which differ from the SYSGEN, but it is certainly not incorrect to explicitly specify all options.

Format: // EXEC prog-name
Example: // EXEC FCOBOL

The EXEC statement causes the execution of a program. A given job stream can contain several EXEC statements, each of which produces a job step. The program-name field must be specified when the program to be executed is in the core image library, e.g., FCOBOL or LNKEDT. It is not specified if the COBOL program was freshly compiled and link-edited as in the third EXEC statement of Figure 17.1.

/* (Slash Asterisk) Statement

The /* control card signifies that the end of data has been reached. It appears after the COBOL source deck in Figure 17.1 since the COBOL source deck is the data for the COBOL compiler. It also appears after the data cards.

/& (Slash Ampersand) Statement

This statement denotes the end of a job, and it is the last statement in a job stream. A given job may contain several /* statements, but it must contain one and only one /& card.

Device Assignments

A computer is connected to its I/O devices through a channel which is a hardware device with limited logic circuitry. It permits overlap, i.e., simultaneous I/O and processing, and is therefore essential to maximize overall utilization of a system's resources. Each I/O device is attached to a channel through a control unit. There can be several control units hooked to one channel and several I/O devices tied to one control unit. Each type of I/O device, however, requires its own control unit. To the user the functions of the control unit are indistinguishable from the functions of the I/O device itself. Indeed, some control units (e.g., printer) are physically housed within the device itself; others (e.g., tape drives) require a separate piece of equipment in the machine room.

The JCL ASSGN statement ties an I/O device to a symbolic address. The COBOL SELECT statement links the programmer-defined file name to the symbolic address of an I/O device. The two statements in combination relate COBOL-defined file names to specific I/O devices. (Disk files require an additional JCL statement, the EXTENT statement, covered in a later section in this chapter, to specify the exact location of a file on the disk pack.)

A three-digit number of the form 'cuu' is used in the ASSGN statement to specify the address of the I/O device. 'c' denotes the channel number; the first 'u' denotes the control unit, and the second 'u' the device. Figure 17.2 is a schematic diagram of an installation with four tape drives, four disk drives, a card reader and punch, printer, and keyboard. Note the boxes denoting the tape and disk drive control units. Further note that the tapes and disks are all on one channel. There are two control units hooked to the same channel, one for the tape drives and one for the disk drives. The card reader, punch, printer, and keyboard are all on a second channel. No separate boxes are shown for the control units for these devices, as they are housed within the devices themselves.

The four tape drives are addressed by 181, 182, 183, and 184, respectively. Each of these drives is on channel 1. The disk drives are 191, 192, 193 and 194 and are all on channel 1. The card reader, punch, printer, and keyboard are 00C, 00D, 00E, and 01F, respectively.

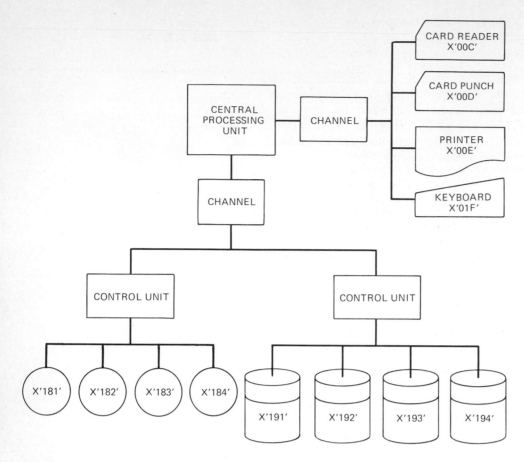

Figure 17.2 Schematic Illustration of a Typical Installation

The COBOL programmer does not refer to an I/O device by its address. Instead he uses a symbolic name which causes programs to be dependent on a device type rather than a particular device. At execution time, the symbolic name is tied to the specific device by a table of permanent assignments established at SYSGEN or by individual ASSGN statements which override permanent assignments. Symbolic names are divided into system and programmer units, as shown in Table 17.3.

We have discussed the symbolic addresses and permanent assignments of I/O devices. Both are tied to COBOL through the SELECT statement. Consider

SELECT INPUT-FILE ASSIGN TO SYS004-UR-2540R-S.

The programmer specifies that INPUT-FILE is to come from SYS004 and further that SYS004 is a card reader. According to Table 17.3, SYS004 is permanently assigned to the card reader, and there is no need for further JCL. We could, however, optionally provide an ASSGN card, which temporarily (for the duration of the JOB or until another ASSGN card is read) overrides the permanent assignment of Table 17.3.

ASSGN Statement

Format: // ASSGN SYSnnn,X'cuu'
Example: // ASSGN SYS004,X'00C'

In this example SYS004 is assigned to the device whose address is 00C. Since the temporary and permanent assignments match, the ASSGN card has

Table 17.3 Typical Permanent Device Assignments

	Symbolic Name	Address	Device Type
Programmer	SYS004	X'00C'	Card reader
logical	SYS005	X'00D'	Card punch
units	SYS006	X'00E'	Printer
	SYS010	X'181'	Tape drive
	SYS011	X'182'	Tape drive
	SYS012	X'183'	Tape drive
	SYS013	X'184'	Tape drive
	SYS014	X'191'	Disk drive
	SYS015	X'192'	Disk drive
	SYS016	X'193'	Disk drive
	SYS017	X'194'	Disk drive

	Symbolic Name	Address	Function
System	SYSRDR	X'00C'	Input for JCL
logical	SYSIPT	X'00C'	Input for programs
units	SYSPCH	X'00D'	Punched output
	SYSLST	X'00E'	Printed output
	SYSLOG	X'01F'	Operator messages
	SYSLNK	X'191'	Input to linkage editor
	SYSRES	X'192'	Contains operating system

Note: These assignments are representative of permanent assignments established at system generation. They will, of course, vary from installation to installation.

no effect. It is common practice, however, to explicitly specify all assignments in the JCL to avoid any ambiguity. Moreover, in a majority of instances, ASSGN statements are mandatory rather than optional, as illustrated below:

COBOL:
```
    SELECT OLD-TAPE-MASTERFILE ASSIGN TO SYS010-UT-2400-S.
    SELECT NEW-TAPE-MASTERFILE ASSIGN TO SYS011-UT-2400-S.
```

The programmer specifies SYS010 and SYS011 for OLD-TAPE-MASTERFILE and NEW-TAPE-MASTERFILE, respectively. These symbolic names are permanently assigned to tape drives 181 and 182. Assume, however, that one of these drives, 181, is unavailable. Are we to wait until it becomes available before our program can be executed? That would hardly be practical. We bypass the problem by assigning SYS010 to an available drive via an ASSGN statement: //ASSGN SYS010, X'183'.

PAUSE Statement

```
    Format:  // PAUSE  comments
    Example: // PAUSE  MOUNT TAPE REEL # 1234 ON 183
```

The PAUSE statement allows one to instruct the operator between job steps. It is a convenient way to request that a particular reel of tape, disk pack, print form, etc., be mounted. The above example requests the operator to mount reel # 1234 from the tape library on 183. (Of course the programmer must coordinate his PAUSE, SELECT, and ASSGN statements.)

When a PAUSE statement is encountered by the operating system, its message prints on the keyboard, and processing is suspended. The operator complies with the request, then hits the end-of-block key on the console, whereupon processing resumes. A variety of messages can be given via the PAUSE statement. Most commonly, instructions are given to mount specific volumes (tape reels or disk packs) and special forms for the printer (e.g., payroll checks, multiple part paper, etc.).

The tape library of a typical installation consists of hundreds or even thousands of reels. When the programmer requests a specific reel via a PAUSE statement or other instruction, he is referring to an *external* label, i.e., a piece of paper pasted on the reel of tape for visual identification. Unfortunately, it is far too easy to inadvertently mount the wrong reel, and the consequences of such an action can be disastrous. *Internal* labels, consisting of information written on the tape itself, are used as a precaution.

There are three standard DOS labels: volume, header, and trailer. The volume label appears at the beginning of each volume (i.e., reel) and contains a six-digit serial number to uniquely identify the volume. A header label is an 80-byte record which appears before each file on the tape. The trailer label also 80 bytes, appears at the end of each file. The header and trailer labels contain identical information, with the exception of a block count field (in the trailer label) that indicates the number of records contained in the file.

Every volume contains one and only one volume label. It can contain several sets of header and trailer labels depending on the number and size of the files on the reel. The COBOL programmer indicates label processing is desired by the clause "LABEL RECORDS ARE STANDARD" in the FD for the file. If this clause is included for a tape file, then supporting JCL, namely the LBLTYP and TLBL statements, are also required.

Volume, header, and trailer labels are illustrated schematically in Figure 17.3. Figure 17.3 is an example of a multifile volume; i.e., several files are contained on the same volume (reel). It is also possible to have a multivolume file in which the same file extends over several volumes.

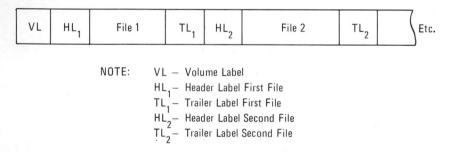

NOTE: VL – Volume Label
HL$_1$– Header Label First File
TL$_1$– Trailer Label First File
HL$_2$– Header Label Second File
TL$_2$– Trailer Label Second File

Figure 17.3 Volume, Header, and Trailer Labels

LBLTYP Statement

Format: // LBLTYP $\begin{Bmatrix} \text{TAPE} \\ \text{NSD(nn)} \end{Bmatrix}$

Example: // LBLTYP TAPE

The NSD (nonsequential disk) option is used only when processing nonsequential disk files and is discussed in that section. The LBLTYP statement must appear immediately before the // EXEC LNKEDT statement. It specifies that an amount of storage is to be allocated for label processing.

Format: // TLBL filename,['file-identifier'],[date],
        [file-serial-number],[volume-sequence-number],
        [file-sequence-number],[generation-number],
        [version-number]
Example: // TLBL SYS010,,99/365,111111

The TLBL statement is used when tape label processing is desired. It is a complex statement in that a number of parameters may optionally be specified. Observe that only one parameter, the file name (derived from the COBOL SELECT statement), is mandatory. If a parameter is omitted and others follow, an extra comma is used. In the above example, file-identifier was skipped; thus two commas follow the file name. If, however, a parameter is omitted and no further parameters appear to its right, the extra commas are not used. Since file-serial-number was the last specified parameter, all other commas were skipped. Each of the entries in the TLBL statement are explained below:

FILENAME—From 1–7 characters in length. It identifies the file to the control program and is taken directly from the COBOL SELECT statement. If SELECT TAPE-FILE ASSIGN TO SYS010-UT-2400-S appears in the COBOL program, then SYS010 must be the file name in the TLBL statement.

FILE-IDENTIFIER—Consists of 1–17 characters and is contained within apostrophes. If omitted on output files, then the file name is used. If it is omitted on input files, no checking is done.

DATE—Consists of 1–6 characters in the form yy/ddd indicating the expiration date of the file. Output files may specify an alternative format, dddd, indicating the number of days the file is to be retained.

FILE-SERIAL-NUMBER—Consists of 1–6 characters indicating the volume serial number of the first (often only) reel of the file.

VOLUME-SEQUENCE-NUMBER—Consists of 1–4 characters indicating the sequence number of a multivolume file (i.e., a large file extending over several reels).

FILE-SEQUENCE-NUMBER—Consists of 1–4 characters indicating the sequence number of the file on a multifile volume (i.e., several short files contained on one volume).

GENERATION-NUMBER—Consists of 1–4 digits indicating the number of a particular edition of the file.

VERSION-NUMBER—Consists of 1 or 2 digits which modify the generation-number.

All parameters in the TLBL card correspond directly to entries in the standard tape labels shown in Figure 17.4. Header and trailer labels for a given file are identical except for the label identifier (indicating the type of label) and the block count field (showing the number of physical records in the file). If an

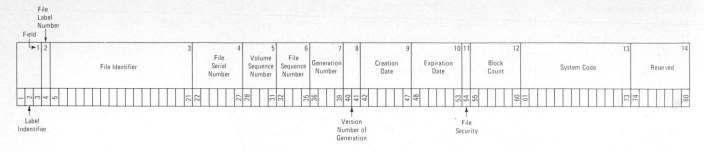

Figure 17.4 Standard Tape Label (*Courtesy* IBM)

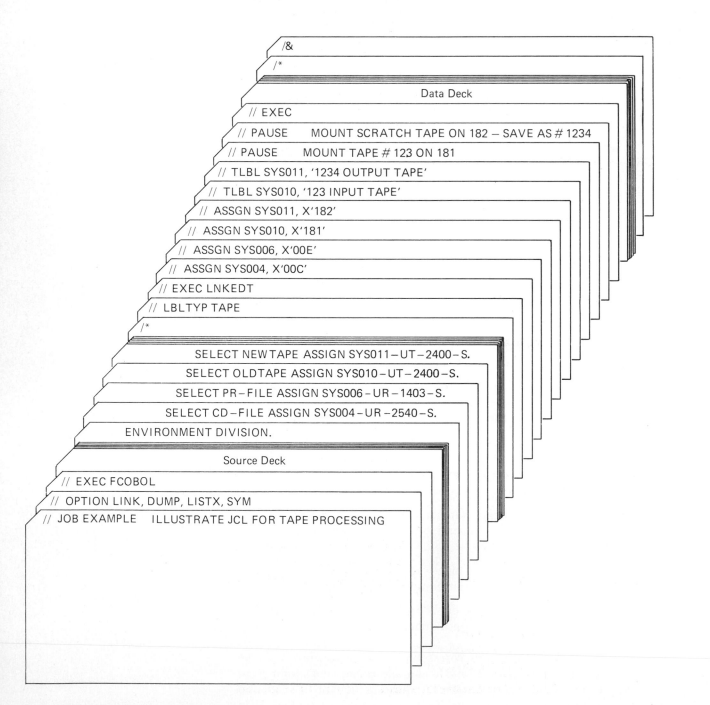

```
/&
/*
                              Data Deck
// EXEC
// PAUSE      MOUNT SCRATCH TAPE ON 182 – SAVE AS # 1234
// PAUSE      MOUNT TAPE # 123 ON 181
// TLBL SYS011, '1234 OUTPUT TAPE'
// TLBL SYS010, '123 INPUT TAPE'
// ASSGN SYS011, X'182'
// ASSGN SYS010, X'181'
// ASSGN SYS006, X'00E'
// ASSGN SYS004, X'00C'
// EXEC LNKEDT
// LBLTYP TAPE
/*
          SELECT NEWTAPE ASSIGN SYS011–UT–2400–S.
          SELECT OLDTAPE ASSIGN SYS010–UT–2400–S.
          SELECT PR–FILE ASSIGN SYS006–UR–1403–S.
          SELECT CD–FILE ASSIGN SYS004–UR–2540–S.
     ENVIRONMENT DIVISION.
                Source Deck
// EXEC FCOBOL
// OPTION LINK, DUMP, LISTX, SYM
// JOB EXAMPLE    ILLUSTRATE JCL FOR TAPE PROCESSING
```

Figure 17.5 Job Stream for Tape Processing

output file is processed, header and trailer labels are written on the tape according to specifications in the TLBL card. If an input file is processed, the label information on the tape is checked against the TLBL card to ensure that the proper reel has been mounted.

Information on tape processing is summarized via Figure 17.5. It shows JCL for a COBOL program to update an existing tape file from transactions punched on cards. The program creates a new tape file and a printed exception report. Label processing is done for both input and output tapes. The OPTION card provides for the linkage-editor, procedure and data division maps, and a dump in the event of an ABEND. Label processing is called for by the phrase "LABEL RECORDS ARE STANDARD" in the COBOL program. Note the tie between the COBOL SELECT and the ASSGN and TLBL statements. Finally, note the use of the PAUSE statements to provide instructions to the operator.

Processing Disk Files

The concepts of label processing are applicable to disk as well as tape. Just as there is a TLBL statement, there is a DLBL statement. There is also one major extension for disk files. Tape processing is strictly sequential, whereas disk processing may be either sequential or nonsequential. Thus the DLBL statement contains an additional parameter indicating the type of file organization. In addition, the EXTENT statement, required for disk files, specifies the address of the file on the disk device by providing a cylinder and track number where the first record in the file may be found. The EXTENT statement also specifies the size (extent) of the file by stating the number of tracks allocated for its storage.

DLBL Statement

> Format: `// DLBL filename [,'file-identifier'][,date][,codes]`
> Example: `// DLBL SYS013,'THIS IS DISK FILE',99/365,SD`

The DLBL statement provides the necessary information for processing disk labels. As with tape processing, if an input file is referenced, label checking is done to ensure that the proper volume was mounted. If an output file is specified, a disk label is created in accordance with Figure 17.6. Only the filename parameter is required on the DLBL card; and it is tied to the COBOL SELECT, as was the filename in the TLBL statement. All parameters are explained below:

FILENAME—Consists of 1–7 characters in length and is tied directly to the SELECT statement; i.e., the SYS number matches in both statements. However, the filename in the DLBL card need not match the symbolic name on the ASSGN or EXTENT statements (more on this in the next section).

FILE-IDENTIFIER—Filename as it appears in the volume label; consists of 1-44 characters.

DATE—One of two formats as in the TLBL statement. Omission of this parameter causes the file to be retained for seven days.

CODES—A 2- or 3-character field indicating the type of file as follows:

> SD—sequential disk
> DA—direct access
> ISC—create ISAM file
> ISE—existing ISAM file

Omission of this parameter causes a default to sequential disk.

327

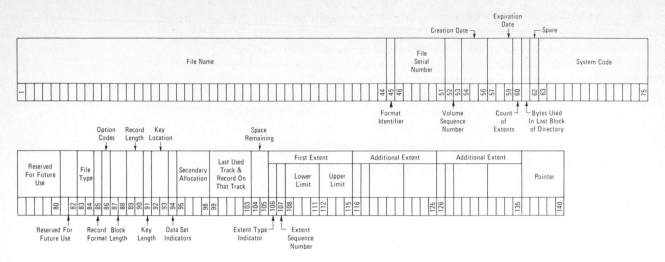

Figure 17.6 Standard Disk Label (*Courtesy* IBM)

EXTENT Statement

> Format: // EXTENT[symbolic-unit],[serial-number],[type],
> [sequence-number],[relative-track],[number-of-tracks],
> [split-cylinder-track],[B-bins]
> Example: // EXTENT SYS014,111111,1,,200,20

The EXTENT statement specifies the exact location of a file, the number of tracks in the file, and other information associated with the file. One or more EXTENT statements *must* follow the corresponding DLBL card. Parameters are described below:

SYMBOLIC-UNIT—The SYS number of the device on which the file is physically located. It must match the symbolic name on the ASSGN card (or standard assignment) and may, but is not required to, match the SYS number on the COBOL SELECT and corresponding DLBL card. (Stay with us—we shall clarify the statement in ensuing examples.)

SERIAL-NUMBER—Consists of 1–6 characters specifying the volume serial number. If omitted, the volume serial number of the preceding EXTENT card is used. If omitted entirely, the serial number is not checked, and the programmer runs the risk of processing the wrong volume.

TYPE—A 1-character field indicating the type of extent as follows:

> 1—data area
> 2—overflow area (ISAM)
> 4—index area (ISAM)
> 8—split cylinder data area (split cylinders are not covered in the text)

SEQUENCE-NUMBER—One to three digits indicating the sequence number of the extent within a multi-extent file. Its use is optional for sequential (code = SD on DLBL) or direct-access (code = DA on DLBL) files but mandatory for ISAM files.

328

RELATIVE-TRACK—A 1–5 digit number indicating the sequential number of the track (relative to zero) where the file begins. A simple calculation is required to convert a cylinder and track address to a relative track. The calculation is device dependent and is shown in Table 17.4.

NUMBER-OF-TRACKS—A 1- to 5-digit number specifying the number of tracks allocated to the file.

Split cylinder and bin parameters are not discussed further in the text. (The reader is referred to the *DOS Programmer's Guide* for information.)

Table 17.4 Conversion of Cylinder and Track Address to Relative Track

The formula is device dependent as shown:

Device	Formula	
2311		$10 * \text{cylinder} + \text{track}$
2314	Relative track =	$20 * \text{cylinder} + \text{track}$
3330		$19 * \text{cylinder} + \text{track}$
3340		$12 * \text{cylinder} + \text{track}$

Sometimes it is necessary to go in reverse, i.e., calculate a cylinder and track address given a relative track. Again, the formula is device dependent as shown:

Device	Formula	
2311	(Relative track)/10	
2314	(Relative track)/20	quotient = cylinder, remainder = track
3330	(Relative track)/19	
3340	(Relative track)/12	

Sequential Processing

Figure 17.7 shows the JCL necessary to update a sequential disk file from card transactions. A new master file is created, as is a printed exception report. Both disk files are stored on the same pack. Among other points, the example emphasizes relationships among the SELECT, ASSGN, DLBL, and EXTENT statements.

OLD-MASTER and NEW-MASTER are assigned to SYS014 and SYS016, respectively, via COBOL SELECT statements. There are corresponding DLBL statements for each of these file names. Both DLBL cards are followed by EXTENT statements specifying the physical device where the file is located, in this instance SYS010 for both. Both files are on the same device, SYS010, which in turn is assigned to X'291' by the ASSGN statement. The file NEW-MASTER will be retained until the last day of 1999 as per the entry on its DLBL statement. It begins on relative track 1000 and continues for 100 tracks (EXTENT statement).

Label processing will be performed, but the LBLTYP card is omitted, as that statement is not used with sequential disk files. The ASSGN statements have been omitted for CARD-FILE and PRINT-FILE since those SELECT statements match the permanent assignments in Table 17.3.

ISAM Reorganization

ISAM processing becomes less efficient as new records are added and old records are logically deleted (ISAM organization was discussed in Chapter 16). Accordingly, an ISAM file is periodically reorganized whereby the logically deleted records are physically dropped from the file, and the additions are

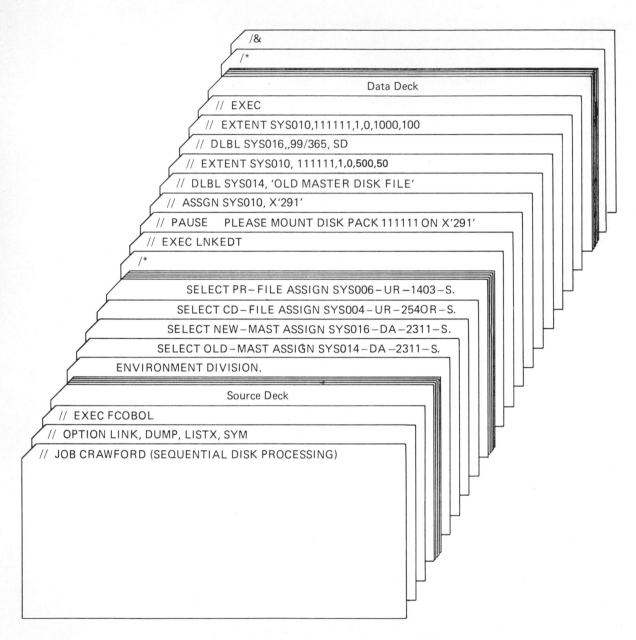

Figure 17.7 JCL for Sequential Disk Processing

The cards in the deck read (from top to back):

```
/&
/*
Data Deck
// EXEC
// EXTENT SYS010,111111,1,0,1000,100
// DLBL SYS016,,99/365, SD
// EXTENT SYS010, 111111,1,0,500,50
// DLBL SYS014, 'OLD MASTER DISK FILE'
// ASSGN SYS010, X'291'
// PAUSE    PLEASE MOUNT DISK PACK 111111 ON X'291'
// EXEC LNKEDT
/*
SELECT PR–FILE ASSIGN SYS006–UR–1403–S.
SELECT CD–FILE ASSIGN SYS004–UR–2540R–S.
SELECT NEW–MAST ASSIGN SYS016–DA–2311–S.
SELECT OLD–MAST ASSIGN SYS014–DA–2311–S.
ENVIRONMENT DIVISION.
Source Deck
// EXEC FCOBOL
// OPTION LINK, DUMP, LISTX, SYM
// JOB CRAWFORD (SEQUENTIAL DISK PROCESSING)
```

transferred from the overflow to the prime data area. The decision of how often this is to be done is made by a systems analyst and is not discussed here.

Reorganization is generally a two-step process. First the ISAM file is read sequentially and dumped on tape. Next the newly created tape is used as input to a second COBOL (or utility) program which restores the ISAM file on disk. The restored file is logically equivalent to the original; however, its records have been physically rearranged to make processing more efficient. Figure 17.8 shows the JCL needed for the first step.

Much of Figure 17.8 has already been reviewed in Figures 17.5 and 17.7, and that discussion will not be repeated here. Note, however, the NSD parameter in the LBLTYP statement. The 02 in parentheses indicates the number of EXTENT cards associated with the nonsequential disk file. The type and sequence parameters in the EXTENT statements assume importance. In this example, the first EXTENT has a type of 4, indicating the EXTENT for the cylinder index. The second EXTENT has a type of 1, indicating EXTENTS for the prime data area.

Summary

Job control language (JCL) is the means whereby the programmer communicates with an operating system. Sufficient JCL for DOS was presented to enable the programmer to do basic file processing. A synopsis of the various statements and their functions is listed below:

JOB—Indicates a new job and its job name.

OPTION—Specifies the options to be in effect for the duration of the job. Any options included in this statement override those established at SYSGEN. Any omitted options default to those of the SYSGEN.

EXEC—Causes the execution of a program.

/*—Indicates the end of a file or data set. (This statement appears at the end of a COBOL deck because the COBOL deck is the data for the program FCOBOL.)

/&—Indicates the end of a job.

ASSGN—Links a symbolic device to a physical device. It is required only if the temporary assignment is different from the permanent assignment.

PAUSE—Temporarily suspends execution; it enables the programmer to make requests of the operator, such as mounting a particular volume.

LBLTYP—Required for label processing of tape and nonsequential disk files. It is not used when processing sequential disk files.

TLBL—Contains information for the label processing of tape files.

DLBL—Contains information for the label processing of disk files.

EXTENT—Specifies the exact location(s) of a file on disk.

The link between the TLBL, DLBL, and COBOL SELECT statements was discussed, as were elementary concepts of the disk operating system. DOS JCL is relatively easy, and only a little practice is necessary to become thoroughly comfortable with it. You should expect, however, to make several errors, especially in the beginning. As a guide to understanding your mistakes, and also as a teaching aid, we offer a list of JCL *errors to avoid*:

1. Incorrect format: *All* statements (except for /* and /&) require // in columns 1 and 2 and a space in column 3. Too often, this simple rule is violated, as in //JOB.

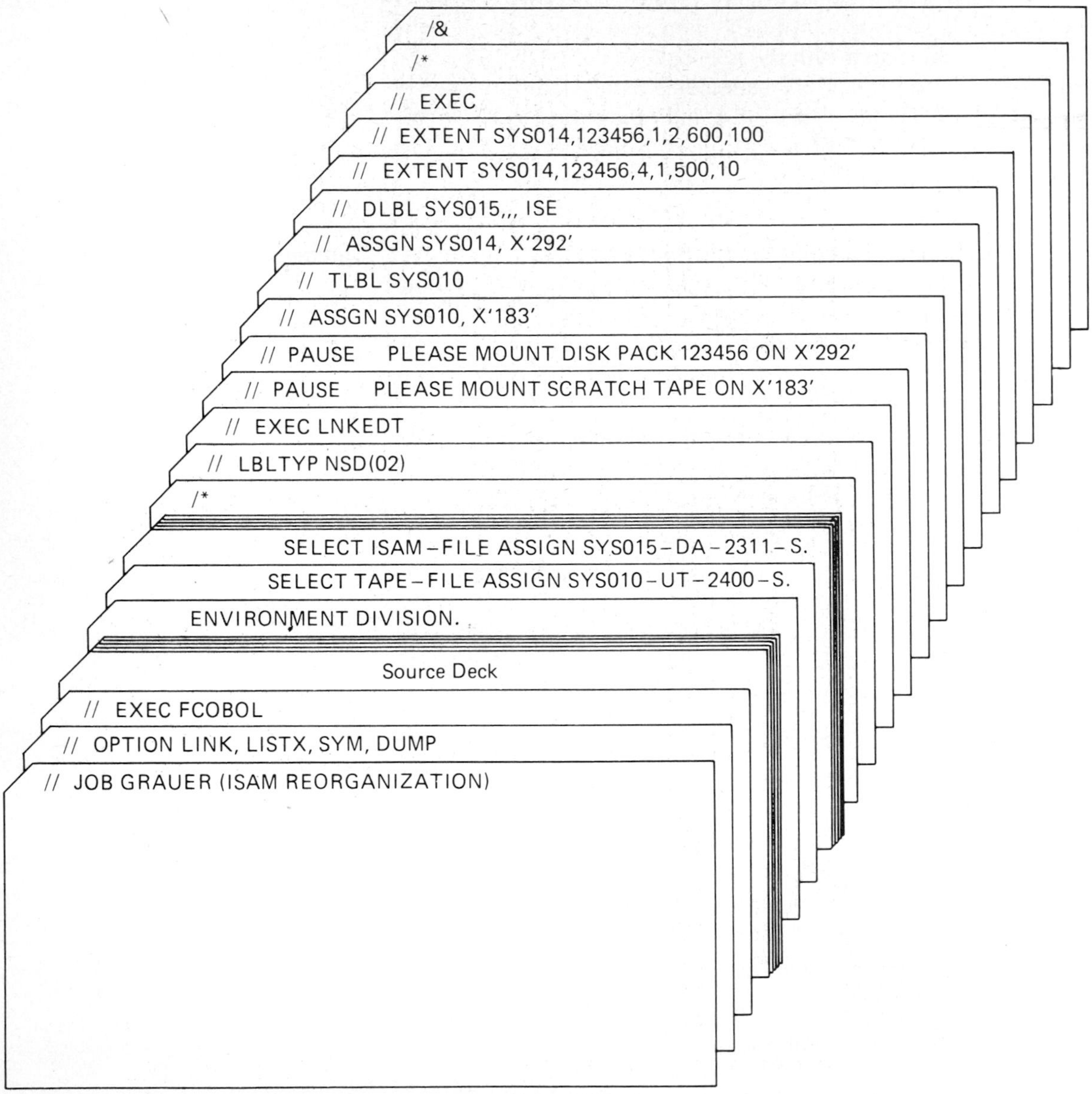
/&
/*
// EXEC
// EXTENT SYS014,123456,1,2,600,100
// EXTENT SYS014,123456,4,1,500,10
// DLBL SYS015,,, ISE
// ASSGN SYS014, X'292'
// TLBL SYS010
// ASSGN SYS010, X'183'
// PAUSE PLEASE MOUNT DISK PACK 123456 ON X'292'
// PAUSE PLEASE MOUNT SCRATCH TAPE ON X'183'
// EXEC LNKEDT
// LBLTYP NSD(02)
/*
SELECT ISAM-FILE ASSIGN SYS015-DA-2311-S.
SELECT TAPE-FILE ASSIGN SYS010-UT-2400-S.
ENVIRONMENT DIVISION.
Source Deck
// EXEC FCOBOL
// OPTION LINK, LISTX, SYM, DUMP
// JOB GRAUER (ISAM REORGANIZATION)

Figure 17.8 JCL for ISAM Reorganization

2. Misspelling of key words: TLBL, DLBL, ASSGN, LNKEDT, and LBLTYP are correct spellings. Beginners, and accomplished programmers as well, are guilty of many variations.

3. Incomplete information for label processing: A TLBL or DLBL statement is required for label processing of tape and disk files, respectively. The LBLTYP card is also required for tape and nonsequential disk files. Finally, the phrase "LABEL RECORDS ARE STANDARD" must be present in the COBOL FD if label processing is desired.

4. Incorrect placement of LBLTYP: This statement, if present, must immediately precede the EXEC LNKEDT card.

5. Incorrect correspondence between COBOL SELECT and JCL: The SYS number in the COBOL SELECT must match with appropriate TLBL and DLBL statements.

6. Invalid extents: All disk files require one or more EXTENT statements, and frequently this information is incorrect or miscopied. This error may produce a cryptic message "LOGICAL TRANSIENT AREA NOT ASSIGNED."

7. Incorrect volume (i.e., tape reel or disk pack): This can result from several causes. The programmer might request the wrong volume, or the operator may fail to mount the volume requested by the programmer. Even if neither of these situations occur, the system may still think it has the wrong volume because incorrect (i.e., nonmatching) label information was supplied in the TLBL or DLBL statement.

8. Omission of OPTION LINK with EXEC LNKEDT: NOLINK is usually established as the default option at SYSGEN. Thus if a program is to be link-edited after compilation, OPTION LINK must be specified.

9. Omission of ASSGN statement(s): An ASSGN statement is not necessary if the temporary assignment matches the permanent assignment. In the majority of instances, this is not the case, and a separate ASSGN card is required for every device where the assignments do not match.

REVIEW EXERCISES

TRUE	FALSE		
☐	☐	1	Every JCL statement begins with // in columns 1 and 2.
☐	☐	2	Every job stream must contain one and only one /& card.
☐	☐	3	Every job stream must contain one and only one /* card.
☐	☐	4	There may be more than one EXEC statement within a job stream.
☐	☐	5	The /* statement is the last card in a deck.
☐	☐	6	Comments are not permitted on JCL statements.
☐	☐	7	The PAUSE statement suspends processing for two minutes.
☐	☐	8	The LBLTYP statement must be present whenever label processing is performed.
☐	☐	9	The ASSGN statement is required only when a permanent assignment matches a temporary assignment.
☐	☐	10	The COBOL SELECT statement matches the SYS number in a DLBL or TLBL card.
☐	☐	11	A TLBL card is mandatory whenever a tape file is processed.

TRUE	FALSE		
☐	☐	**12**	The SYS number in the DLBL statement must match the SYS number in the EXTENT card which follows it.
☐	☐	**13**	A given file can have more than one EXTENT statement.
☐	☐	**14**	The formula to calculate the relative track from a cylinder and track address is device dependent.
☐	☐	**15**	The expiration date of a file is specified on its EXTENT card.
☐	☐	**16**	The ASSGN statement equates a logical (symbolic) device to a physical device.
☐	☐	**17**	There is only one type of internal label.
☐	☐	**18**	The LBLTYP statement (if required) immediately follows the EXEC LNKEDT statement.
☐	☐	**19**	The code parameter in the DLBL card must always be specified.
☐	☐	**20**	The COBOL compiler is considered a "control program."
☐	☐	**21**	The job control program remains in main storage at all times.
☐	☐	**22**	DOS has three distinct system libraries.
☐	☐	**23**	The FORTRAN compiler is not a part of the disk operating system.
☐	☐	**24**	A multivolume tape file extends over several reels.
☐	☐	**25**	Parameters in the OPTION statement may be listed in any order.
☐	☐	**26**	Parameters in the TLBL statement may be listed in any order.

1 Show the DOS JCL to compile, link-edit, and execute a COBOL program. The **PROBLEMS** program reads a deck of cards (CARD-FILE) and writes them on tape (TAPE-FILE). Your JCL must accommodate all the following:

1. Suppress procedure data division maps as well as the COBOL listing. A dump is required in the event of ABEND.

2. Perform label processing as follows:
   a. Assign an expiration date of 1/1/80 to the tape file,
   b. Assign file and volume identifiers of "NEW TAPE MASTER" and 123456, respectively.

3. Cause the operator to mount a scratch tape which will be saved as student tape # 1 (external label).

4. Use 00C and 183 as the addresses of the card reader and tape drive, respectively.

5. Show appropriate COBOL SELECT statements.

2 Show the DOS JCL to compile, link-edit, and execute a COBOL program which will create an ISAM file from cards. You are to accommodate all the following:

1. Procedure division and data division maps are required, as is a dump in the event of an unplanned termination.

2. An object deck is to be produced.

3. *Show* COBOL SELECTS for CARD-FILE, PRINT-FILE, and DISK-FILE; the latter is the ISAM file to be created.

4. The cylinder index is to be the first five tracks of cylinder 60. Independent overflow is to take all of cylinders 61 and 62. The prime data area is to extend for all cylinders 63–72. (Volume ID is 222222.) Assume a 2311.

5. 00C, 00F, and 191 are the addresses of the card reader, printer, and disk device, respectively.

6. Retain the newly created ISAM file for two weeks.

7. Create standard labels (supply necessary DLBL parameters).

3 Show the DOS JCL to execute a COBOL program UPDATE, which has been cataloged in the core image library. The program UPDATE merges transactions

from a tape file (SYS010) and a sequential disk file (SYS014) to create a new
sequential disk file (SYS015). Accommodate all the following:

1. Produce a dump in the event of an ABEND.

2. Perform label processing:
   a. Existing tape file: File serial number is 111111.
   b. Existing disk file: Volume serial number is 222222.
                           File identifier is 'DISK-MASTER'.
   c. New disk file: File identifier is 'NEW-FILE'.
                      Retain 100 days.
                      Volume serial number is 222222.

3. The old disk file begins at cylinder 30, track 0, and goes for 100 tracks. The new disk file begins at cylinder 60 and goes for 110 tracks. (Assume a 2314 device.)

4. Use 181 and 281 as the tape and disk address, respectively.

5. Instruct the operator to mount tape 123 and disk pack 456.

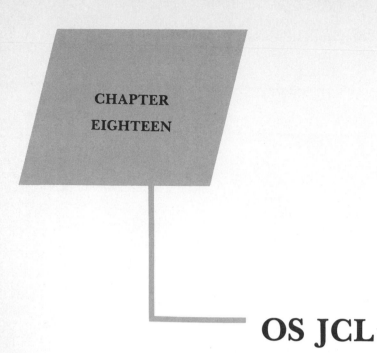

CHAPTER EIGHTEEN

OS JCL

Overview

An effective COBOL programmer is thoroughly comfortable with the job control language. Unfortunately OS JCL retains a mystique which too often makes both students and practicing programmers shy away. Admittedly the multipage collection of /'s, X's, etc., is somewhat foreboding, but given half a chance, it becomes thoroughly understandable. In this chapter we shall attempt to remove this apprehension and instill in the reader an appreciation for OS JCL.

The chapter begins with an overview of OS. Next we shall consider syntactical rules, basic statements (JOB, EXEC, DD, /*, and //), key-word and positional parameters, and system output. Our objective is to develop JCL capability corresponding to the COBOL of Chapters 15 and 16. Job streams, parallel to those developed for DOS in Chapter 17, are used as illustrations.

OS Components

The operating system (OS) is composed of three sets of programs, as shown in Table 18.1.

Job management is responsible for scheduling work to be processed on the computer system. It has two components: the master scheduler and the job scheduler. The master scheduler directs communication with the operator. The job scheduler prepares individual jobs for execution. It interprets JCL

Table 18.1 Programs Comprising OS

Chapter 18
OS JCL

I. Control programs
   Job management
   Data management
   Task management
II. Language translators
   ALGOL
   Assembler (BAL)
   COBOL
   FORTRAN
   PL/I
   RPG
III. Service programs
   Linkage editor
   Utilities
   Sort/merge

statements and places incoming jobs on a work queue. It initiates jobs from the work queue and terminates jobs when they are completed.

Task management allocates the resources of the CPU and supervises the execution of individual tasks. (A task is the smallest unit of work that can be performed.) Task management decides what is to be processed and when it should be done. It is responsible for interrupt handling and decides which of the several tasks in contention for a CPU resource is to gain control.

Data management is responsible for all I/O functions and governs the movement of data between main storage and peripheral devices. Data management also allocates space on direct-access storage devices. It is responsible for cataloging and locating data sets, for protecting data sets against unauthorized use, and for handling errors which occur during I/O operations.

Language translators accept statements in a higher-level language and translate them into machine language. COBOL, FORTRAN, PL/I, RPG, and BAL were discussed under DOS in Chapter 17. ALGOL is a scientific language used mainly outside the United States.

There are several other service programs in addition to the ones shown in Table 18.1. Concerning those listed, the linkage editor combines object modules into a single program (known as a load module) which is ready for execution. The sort/merge programs under OS are conceptually the same as those in DOS. However, there are fewer restrictions in OS, and consequently these programs are usually faster and more flexible than their DOS counterparts.

Utility programs are of two types. Data set utility programs are used to copy and/or edit data sets from one storage medium to another. These utilities are used frequently by the applications programmer. System utilities are used by the systems programmer to alter or extend the system libraries. These utilities can also print an inventory of the data and programs in the system libraries.

OS configurations generally fall into two categories: MFT (multiprogramming with fixed number of tasks) and MVT (multiprogramming with variable number of tasks). Multiprogramming is the concurrent, *not* simultaneous, execution of two or more programs. It is designed to make maximum use of the system resources by having several programs reside in main storage simultaneously. Under multiprogramming, when one program suspends execution, e.g., for an I/O operation, control immediately passes to another program, which then begins (or continues) execution. At any given instant of time the CPU is executing only one instruction, although several programs reside simultaneously in main storage.

In MFT, main storage is divided into an area for the control program and as many as 15 predefined areas of contiguous core called partitions. Individual programs are loaded into specific partitions. Under MVT, a portion of main storage is allocated for control programs, and the remainder is considered a dynamic storage area. MVT dynamically allocates core storage for each job as it is run. Storage space in MVT is determined by individual program requirements rather than by predefined partition sizes as in MFT.

Figure 18.1 is a typical job stream to compile, link-edit, and execute a COBOL program. It also illustrates key-word and positional parameters, rules for continuation of JCL, and placement of comments. The discussion uses the words *file* and *data set* interchangeably.

Basic Job Stream

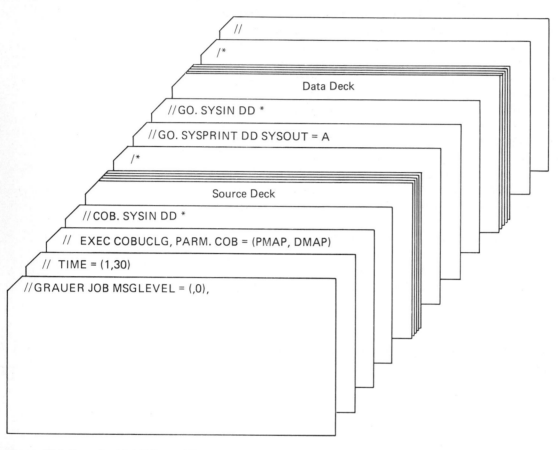

Figure 18.1 Compile, Link-Edit, and Execute a COBOL Program

Figure 18.1 contains five types of statements: JOB, EXEC, DD, /*, and //. Our entire discussion of OS JCL revolves around variation in the first three. The JOB, EXEC, and DD statements each consist of up to five parts in specified order: //, name, operation, parameter, and comments. If the name is supplied, it must begin in column 3 immediately following //. Whether or not a name is used depends on the type of statement and whether subsequent references are made back to the statement. In Figure 18.1, names are given to the JOB and three DD statements but not to the EXEC statement. The operation (i.e., JOB, EXEC, or DD) follows next. Optional parameters (e.g., MSGLEVEL or PARM) follow the operation. A blank separates the name, operation, and parameter fields. However, if the name is omitted, as in the EXEC statement, then a blank separates the // and operation. A comma delineates individual parameters. Comments may follow the last parameter.

Parameters are of two types: *key-word* and *positional*. Key-word parameters may appear in any order within a statement; it is the key word itself which conveys meaning to the system. Positional parameters, as the name implies, are required to appear in a specified order. If a positional parameter is omitted, its absence must be denoted by a comma, unless no additional positional parameters follow in the statement.

The JOB statement in Figure 18.1 contains both key-word and positional parameters. MSGLEVEL and TIME are key words, and their order could be reversed. However, the subparameters appearing in parentheses are positional and must appear in the order shown. (1,30) indicates 1 minute and 30 seconds. If the minute's parameter were omitted, i.e., if only 30 seconds were desired, then the comma would still be required (,30). This is further discussed under the JOB statement.

The JOB statement also illustrates the rules for continuation. Coding begins in column 1 and continues up to and including column 71. If additional space is needed, one stops somewhere before column 71 and continues on a second, third, etc., card. The continued card (all cards but the first) require // in columns 1 and 2 and a blank in column 3. Coding on the continued card must begin between columns 4 and 16. The statement which was continued, i.e., the first card, must end with a comma. Earlier versions of OS also required that a nonblank character be inserted in column 72 of the first card, but this is not shown in Figure 18.1.

The EXEC statement of Figure 18.1 invokes the procedure COBUCLG, which will compile, link-edit, and execute a COBOL program. (The procedure concept is explained in the next section.) The PARM parameter in this statement will generate procedure and data division maps with the COBOL compilation.

There are three DD (data definition) statements in Figure 18.1, each of which supplies information about an input or output file. The * is a positional parameter which means the file immediately follows in the job stream. Thus COBOL source and data decks follow the COB.SYSIN and GO.SYSIN DD cards, respectively. In the DD statement for SYSPRINT, SYSOUT=A means the file is to appear on a class A output device, i.e., a printer. The /* denotes the end of a data set and appears after both the COBOL source deck and input data cards. It serves the identical function in DOS. The // statement denotes end of job and is analogous to /& in DOS.

System Output and the Procedure Concept

A COBOL program which merely goes "card to print" typically results in the series of messages shown in Figure 18.2. The reaction of most beginners is to bypass Figure 18.2 as quickly as possible and turn immediately to the COBOL listing. We try to do better. We do, however, avoid line-by-line detailed explanations and instead aim at an overall level of conceptual understanding.

Figure 18.2 consists primarily of lines beginning with XX, //, or IEF. Any statement that starts with // means the line originated in the programmer-supplied JCL. Any statement beginning with XX indicates a JCL statement pulled from the procedure COBUCLG. (XX represents // in the JCL statement as it appears in the procedure.) The letters IEF are the first three characters in a system message indicating a particular action the system has taken.

The programmer-supplied EXEC statement of Figure 18.2 specifies execution of the procedure COBUCLG, which in turn consists of three job steps: compile (step name COB), link-edit (step name LKED), and execute (step name GO). Subsequent JCL statements will reference these step names; for example, see the discussion of PARM.COB in the EXEC statement. Each job

```
//DANBB142 JOB  TIME=(1,30)                          ┌─ Programmer supplied
// EXEC COBUCLG,PARM.COB=(PMAP,DMAP)    ─────────────┘  EXEC statement
XXCOBUCLG PROC SUT1=15,SOBJ=15,SLUT1=50,SLUT2=20,SLMOD1=50,SLMOD2=20,      00000100
XX             ADDLIB='SYS1.ADDLIB',STEPLIB='SYS1.ADDLIB'                  00000200
XXCOB      ┌─ EXEC PGM=IKFCBL00 ─┐                                         00000300
XXSYSPRINT DD  SYSOUT=A,DCB=BLKSIZE=1936  ── IBM program - COBOL compiler  00000400
XXSYSUT1   DD  UNIT=3330,SPACE=(TRK,(&SUT1,5))                             00000500
IEF653I SUBSTITUTION JCL - UNIT=3330,SPACE=(TRK,(15,5))
XXSYSUT2   DD  UNIT=3330,SPACE=(TRK,(&SUT1,5))                             00000600
IEF653I SUBSTITUTION JCL - UNIT=3330,SPACE=(TRK,(15,5))
XXSYSUT3   DD  UNIT=3330,SPACE=(TRK,(&SUT1,5))                             00000700
IEF653I SUBSTITUTION JCL - UNIT=3330,SPACE=(TRK,(15,5))
XXSYSUT4   DD  UNIT=3330,SPACE=(TRK,(&SUT1,5))                             00000800
IEF653I SUBSTITUTION JCL - UNIT=3330,SPACE=(TRK,(15,5))
XXSYSUT5   DD  UNIT=3330,SPACE=(TRK,(&SUT1,5)),DISP=(,PASS)                00000900
IEF653I SUBSTITUTION JCL - UNIT=3330,SPACE=(TRK,(15,5)),DISP=(,PASS)
XXSYSLIN   DD  DSNAME=&LOADSET,DCB=BLKSIZE=3120,DISP=(MOD,PASS),           00001000
XX             UNIT=3330,SPACE=(6400,(&SOBJ,10))                           00001100
IEF653I SUBSTITUTION JCL - UNIT=3330,SPACE=(6400,(15,10))
//COB.SYSIN DD UNIT=(CTC,,DEFER),DSN=&&ASPI0001,VOL=SER=016948,         *
// DISP=(OLD,DELETE),DCB=(LRECL=80,BLKSIZE=80,RECFM=F)
IEF236I ALLOC. FOR DANBB142 COB
IEF237I 77E   ALLOCATED TO SYSPRINT          ┌─ Step name — COB
IEF237I 268   ALLOCATED TO SYSUT1            │  (Beginning of compile step)
IEF237I 268   ALLOCATED TO SYSUT2
IEF237I 268   ALLOCATED TO SYSUT3
IEF237I 268   ALLOCATED TO SYSUT4
IEF237I 269   ALLOCATED TO SYSUT5
IEF237I 268   ALLOCATED TO SYSLIN
IEF237I 784   ALLOCATED TO SYSIN
IEF142I - STEP WAS EXECUTED - COND CODE 0004 ─── End of compile step
IEF285I    SYS76273.T113030.RV001.DANBB142.ASP0A001    DELETED
IEF285I    VOL SER NOS= ASP77E.
IEF285I    SYS76273.T113030.RV001.DANBB142.R0002648    DELETED
IEF285I    VOL SER NOS= SCR001.
IEF285I    SYS76273.T113030.RV001.DANBB142.R0002649    DELETED
IEF285I    VOL SER NOS= SCR001.
IEF285I    SYS76273.T113030.RV001.DANBB142.R0002650    DELETED
IEF285I    VOL SER NOS= SCR001.
IEF285I    SYS76273.T113030.RV001.DANBB142.R0002651    DELETED
IEF285I    VOL SER NOS= SCR001.
IEF285I    SYS76273.T113030.RV001.DANBB142.R0002652    PASSED
IEF285I    VOL SER NOS= SCR002.
IEF285I    SYS76273.T113030.RV001.DANBB142.LOADSET     PASSED
IEF285I    VOL SER NOS= SCR001.
IEF285I    SYS76273.T113030.RV001.DANBB142.ASPI0001    DELETED
IEF285I    VOL SER NOS= 016948.

 ** START - STEP=COB       JOB=DANBB142   DATE= 9/29/76   CLOCK=11.30.40   PGM=IKFCBL00
 ** END -                                 DATE= 9/29/76   CLOCK=11.31.18   CPU=    0.81 SEC;  CC =    4  **
 ** EXCPS - DISK=   240,   CTC=    210,   TAPE=     0,   TOTAL=   450;   REGION USED=  120K OF  130K  **

      DDNAME      EXCP COUNT    PCI COUNT
      LINK/SVC:       78          447
      SYSPRINT:       53
      SYSUT1  :       31
      SYSUT2  :       37
      SYSUT3  :       50
      SYSUT4  :       32
      SYSUT5  :        0      ┌─ Step name — LKED
      SYSLIN  :       12      │  (Beginning of link step)
      SYSIN   :      157                       ┌─ Cond parameter tests
                                               │  results of compile step
XXLKED     EXEC PGM=IEWL,PARM='LIST,XREF,LET', COND=(5,LT,COB)             00001200
XXSYSLIN   DD  DSNAME=&LOADSET,DISP=(OLD,DELETE)                           00001300
XX         DD  DDNAME=SYSIN                                                00001400
XXSYSLMOD  DD  DSNAME=&&GOSET(GO),DISP=(NEW,PASS),UNIT=3330,               00001500
XX             SPACE=(1024,(&SLMOD1,&SLMOD2,1))                            00001600
IEF653I SUBSTITUTION JCL - SPACE=(1024,(50,20,1))
XXSYSLIB   DD  DSNAME=&ADDLIB,DISP=SHR                                     00001700
IEF653I SUBSTITUTION JCL - DSNAME=SYS1.ADDLIB,DISP=SHR
XX         DD  DSNAME=SYS1.COBLIB,DISP=SHR                                 00001800
XXSYSUT1   DD  UNIT=(3330,SEP=(SYSLIN,SYSLMOD)),                           00001900
XX             SPACE=(1024,(&SLUT1,&SLUT2))                                00002000
IEF653I SUBSTITUTION JCL - SPACE=(1024,(50,20))
XXSYSPRINT DD  SYSOUT=A,DCB=BLKSIZE=1936                                   00002100
IEF236I ALLOC. FOR DANBB142 LKED
IEF237I 268   ALLOCATED TO SYSLIN
IEF237I 268   ALLOCATED TO SYSLMOD
IEF237I 251   ALLOCATED TO SYSLIB
IEF237I 251   ALLOCATED TO
IEF237I 269   ALLOCATED TO SYSUT1       ┌─ End of linkage editor step
IEF237I 77E   ALLOCATED TO SYSPRINT     │
IEF142I - STEP WAS EXECUTED - COND CODE 0000
IEF285I    SYS76273.T113030.RV001.DANBB142.LOADSET     DELETED
IEF285I    VOL SER NOS= SCR001.
```

Figure 18.2 System Output for COBUCLG Procedure

```
IEF285I    SYS76273.T113030.RV001.DANBB142.GOSET              PASSED
IEF285I       VOL SER NOS= SCR001.
IEF285I    SYS1.ADDLIB                                        KEPT
IEF285I       VOL SER NOS= SYS002.
IEF285I    SYS1.COBLIB                                        KEPT
IEF285I       VOL SER NOS= SYS002.
IEF285I    SYS76273.T113030.RV001.DANBB142.R0002653           DELETED
IEF285I       VOL SER NOS= SCR002.
IEF285I    SYS76273.T113030.RV001.DANBB142.ASPOA002           DELETED
IEF285I       VOL SER NOS= ASP77E.

  ** START - STEP=LKED       JOB=DANBB142    DATE= 9/29/76   CLOCK=11.31.18   PGM=IEWL
  ** END  -                                  DATE= 9/29/76   CLOCK=11.31.47   CPU=    0.15 SEC;  CC=    0   **
  ** EXCPS - DISK=     116,   CTC=    11,   TAPE=    0,   TOTAL=    127;   REGION USED=  128K OF  130K   **

       DDNAME      EXCP COUNT   PCI COUNT
       LINK/SVC:       10          15
       SYSLIN  :       10
       SYSLMOD :       15
       SYSLIB  :       81
         "     :        0
       SYSUT1  :        0 ———— Step name — GO
       SYSPRINT:       11        (Beginning of execute step)
```

```
XXGO        EXEC PGM=*.LKED.SYSLMOD,COND=((5,LT,COB),(5,LT,LKED))        00002200
XXSTEPLIB  DD  DSNAME=SYS1.COBLIB,DISP=SHR                               00002300
XX         DD  DSNAME=&STEPLIB,DISP=SHR                                  00002400
IEF653I SUBSTITUTION JCL - DSNAME=SYS1.ADDLIB,DISP=SHR
XXSYSUT5   DD  DSN=*.COB.SYSUT5,DISP=(OLD,DELETE)                        00002500
XXSYSDBOUT DD  SYSOUT=A,DCB=BLKSIZE=1936                                 00002600
XXDISPLAY  DD  SYSOUT=A,DCB=(RECFM=FA,LRECL=121,BLKSIZE=121,BUFNO=1)     00002700
XXDELETE   DD  DSN=&&GOSET,DISP=(OLD,DELETE,DELETE)                      00002800
//GO.SYSUDUMP DD SYSOUT=A
//GO.PRINT DD SYSOUT=A
//GO.SYSIN DD UNIT=(CTC,,DEFER),DSN=&&ASPIO002,VOL=SER=026948,          *
// DISP=(OLD,DELETE),DCB=(LRECL=80,BLKSIZE=80,RECFM=F)
//
IEF236I ALLOC. FOR DANBB142 GO
IEF237I 268   ALLOCATED TO PGM=*.DD
IEF237I 251   ALLOCATED TO STEPLIB
IEF237I 251   ALLOCATED TO
IEF237I 269   ALLOCATED TO SYSUT5
IEF237I 778   ALLOCATED TO SYSDBOUT
IEF237I 779   ALLOCATED TO DISPLAY
IEF237I 268   ALLOCATED TO DELETE          ———— Completion code for GO step
IEF237I 778   ALLOCATED TO SYSUDUMP             indicates ABEND
IEF237I 77C   ALLOCATED TO PRINT
IEF237I 77D   ALLOCATED TO SYSIN
COMPLETION CODE - SYSTEM=0C7  USER=0000
IEF285I    SYS76273.T113030.RV001.DANBB142.GOSET              PASSED
IEF285I       VOL SER NOS= SCR001.
IEF285I    SYS1.COBLIB                                        KEPT
IEF285I       VOL SER NOS= SYS002.
IEF285I    SYS1.ADDLIB                                        KEPT
IEF285I       VOL SER NOS= SYS002.
IEF285I    SYS76273.T113030.RV001.DANBB142.R0002652           DELETED
IEF285I       VOL SER NOS= SCR002.
IEF285I    SYS76273.T113030.RV001.DANBB142.ASPOA003           DELETED
IEF285I       VOL SER NOS= ASP778.
IEF285I    SYS76273.T113030.RV001.DANBB142.GOSET              DELETED
IEF285I       VOL SER NOS= SCR001.
IEF285I    SYS76273.T113030.RV001.DANBB142.ASPOA005           DELETED
IEF285I       VOL SER NOS= ASP77B.
IEF285I    SYS76273.T113030.RV001.DANBB142.ASPOA006           DELETED
IEF285I       VOL SER NOS= ASP77C.
IEF285I    SYS76273.T113030.RV001.DANBB142.ASPIO002           DELETED
IEF285I       VOL SER NOS= 026948.

  ** START - STEP=GO         JOB=DANBB142    DATE= 9/29/76   CLOCK=11.31.47   PGM=PGM=*.DD
  ** END  -                                  DATE= 9/29/76   CLOCK=11.31.55   CPU=    0.24 SEC;  CC= SOC7   **
  ** EXCPS - DISK=       8,   CTC=    77,   TAPE=    0,   TOTAL=     85;   REGION USED=   22K OF  130K   **

       DDNAME      EXCP COUNT   PCI COUNT
       LINK/SVC:        2
       PGM=*.DD:        3           1
       STEPLIB :        3           1
         "     :        0
       SYSUT5  :        0
       SYSDBOUT:        9
       DISPLAY :        0
       DELETE  :        0
       SYSUDUMP:       61
       PRINT   :        3
       SYSIN   :        4
  ** START - JOB=DANBB142   DATE= 9/29/76   CLOCK=11.30.40
  **   END  -               DATE= 9/29/76   CLOCK=11.31.55   ACCOUNTING TIME= 16.06 SECONDS;   MAX REGION USED= 128K   **
```

Figure 18.2 (Continued)

341

step is denoted by an XX EXEC (really // EXEC) statement requesting execution of a program, e.g., IKFCBL00 for the compile (COB) step.

At the conclusion of each job step a completion message, perhaps of the form "STEP WAS EXECUTED—COND CODE 0000", appears. The value of the condition code indicates the success encountered during that step. In the compile step, for example, a condition code of 0000 indicates no diagnostics, a code of 0004 indicates that a warning was the most severe level of error, 0008 means a C-level diagnostic, and 0012 an E-level diagnostic. If a step is abnormally terminated, i.e., ABEND, the condition code is replaced by a completion code stating the reason for the termination. In Figure 18.2 the first two steps executed with condition codes of 0004 and 0000, respectively. The GO step ABENDed due to a data exception (completion code OC7). Thus by examining the system output, we can tell the highest severity error encountered during the execution of each job step. We can also tell how far the COBOL program went in the compile, link-edit, and execute sequence.

The DD statements of Figure 18.1 are also made clearer by a conceptual understanding of Figure 18.2. Consider the components of the statement //GO.SYSIN DD *. // is followed by the step-name.file-name, i.e., GO.SYSIN. GO is the step name for the execute step of COBUCLG, SYSIN indicates the file name and is tied to the COBOL SELECT statement, DD indicates the operation, and * says the file (i.e., data cards) follows immediately in the job stream.

The concept of a procedure (or proc) is fundamental to OS. It is perfectly permissible, albeit impractical, for the COBOL programmer to submit the entire job stream, i.e., procedure, with his program. Common practice is to catalog the necessary JCL into a procedure and then call the procedure. In this way the job of the individual is simplified, and every programmer has convenient access to identical job streams. Installations usually establish a procedure library, with many of the actual procs supplied by IBM, e.g., COBUCLG.

JOB Statement

```
Format:     //jobname JOB   (Acct information),programmer-name,
            //  keyword parameters
            Note: Continuation on a second card may be required.
Useful key words:  CLASS
            REGION
            MSGLEVEL
            TIME
Example:    //GRAUER JOB MSGLEVEL=(,0),
            //    TIME=(1,30)
```

The JOB statement may contain some or all of the following information: job name, accounting information, programmer's name, indication of whether or not control statements and allocation messages are to be printed, priority, and region size.

It has two positional parameters: accounting information and programmer name. In addition several of the key-word parameters have subparameters which are positional in nature.

The job name must begin with an alphabetic (A–Z) or national (#, @, $) character and may be up to eight alphanumeric characters in length.

If accounting information is supplied, it must be coded prior to any other parameters. It can consist of only an account number or other additional parameters required by the installation's accounting system. If more than one account parameter is supplied, all such parameters are enclosed in parentheses. If there is only one parameter, parentheses are omitted.

The programmer name is a positional parameter which follows the accounting information. Since it is the last positional parameter, its omission does not require a comma. In Figure 18.1 both positional parameters (i.e., accounting information and programmer-name) are omitted, and hence no comma is used.

Key-word parameters are explained below:

REGION = NNNK—NNN specifies the amount of main storage (in units of 1024 bytes; i.e., 1K = 1024 bytes) that is to be allocated to the entire job.

MSGLEVEL = (S,M)—

S = 0 if only job statement is to be printed,
1 if input job control and all catalogued procedure statements are to be printed,
2 if only input JCL is to be printed.

M = 0 if no allocation messages are to be printed,
1 if all allocation messages are to be printed.

Note that S and M are positional subparameters. Omission of S requires a comma, as shown in Figure 18.1.

TIME = (MM,SS)—MM time in minutes.
SS time in seconds.
These parameters need not be in parentheses if only minutes are specified. They are both positional subparameters.

CLASS = X—Where X may be any letter from A to O indicating the class of a job. The meaning of each class is determined by the individual installation. Job class specifies the region (MVT) or partition (MFT), which in turn determines a priority relative to other jobs.

EXEC Statement

Format: //stepname EXEC operands comments
Useful key words: PARM
                    COND
                    REGION
                    TIME
Example: //STEP1 EXEC COBUCLG,PARM.COB='PMAP,DMAP'   CREATES MAPS

The EXEC statement is used to execute either a single program or a procedure. If a program is to be executed, the key word PGM must be specified, e.g., // EXEC PGM = IKFCBL00. If a procedure is to be executed, the key word PROC can either be specified or omitted. Both statements below are valid:

                // EXEC PROC=COBUCLG
                // EXEC COBUCLG

The step name is optional in the EXEC statement. If used, it must begin in column 3 immediately following the //; if omitted, a space is required in column 3. Accordingly, both statements below are valid:

        //STEP1 EXEC COBUCLG   (stepname—STEP1)
        // EXEC COBUCLG   (stepname not supplied)

The PARM parameter requests options for a job step and overrides any defaults that were established at system generation. The key word PARM is followed by a period and the step name for which the options are to apply.

PARM.COB='PMAP, DMAP' supplies procedure and data division maps for the step name COB (the compile step). Remember, the procedure COBUCLG consists of three separate steps: compile, link-edit, and execute with step names COB, LKED, and GO, respectively. Other compiler options are shown in Table 18.2.

Table 18.2 Compilation Parameters

SOURCE	Prints the source listing (suppressed by NOSOURCE).
CLIST	Produces a condensed listing of the procedure division map; only the first machine language statement of every COBOL statement is shown (suppressed by NOCLIST—cannot be used simultaneously with PMAP).
DMAP	Produces a data division map (suppressed by NODMAP).
PMAP	Produces a procedure division map (suppressed by NOPMAP—cannot be used simultaneously with CLIST).
LIB	Indicates that a COPY statement appears in the COBOL program (NOLIB indicates that COPY statements are not present and also provides more efficient compilation).
VERB	Prints procedure and verb names on the procedure division map (suppressed by NOVERB).
LOAD	Stores object program on direct-access device for input to the linkage editor or loader programs (suppressed by NOLOAD).
DECK	Punches object deck (suppressed by NODECK).
SEQ	Checks incoming COBOL statements for proper sequence in columns 1–6 (suppressed by NOSEQ).
LINECNT=nn	Specifies the number of lines to be printed on each page of output listing (60 is default).
FLAGW	Prints all diagnostic messages.
FLAGE	Prints C-, E-, and D-level diagnostics; suppresses W-level diagnostics.
SUPMAP	Suppresses the PMAP option if an E-level diagnostic was present (suppressed by NOSUPMAP).
QUOTE	Specifies that quotation marks (") will enclose nonnumeric literals.
APOST	Specifies the apostrophe (') will enclose nonnumeric literals.
XREF	Generates a cross-reference listing (suppressed by NOXREF).

The COND (condition) parameter avoids unnecessary usage of computer time by suppressing execution of specified job steps. Essentially it ties execution of the present job step to the results of a previous step. Consider its use in the procedure COBUCLG shown in Figure 18.2:

```
//LKED EXEC PGM=IEWL,PARM='LIST,XREF,LET',COND=(5,LT,COB)
```

The COND parameter permits execution of the link-edit step (step name LKED) if and only if the system return code of the compile step (COB) was not greater than 4. This makes considerable sense if we recall that a condition code of 4 indicates a warning, while higher condition codes indicate C- or E-level diagnostics. Subsequent execution would most likely be incorrect if either of the last two were present; a warning need not necessarily cause incorrect execution, and therefore it is allowed.

The precise format of the COND parameter is shown below:

```
COND=(code,operator,stepname)
```

Permissible operators are

LT	less than
LE	less than or equal
EQ	equal
NE	not equal
GT	greater than
GE	greater than or equal

The operator specifies the comparison to be made between the specified code in the COND parameter and the system return code. The code in the COND parameter is compared to the system return code. If the relationship is true, the step is bypassed. Assume, for example, a return code of 8 after the compile step (i.e., a C-level diagnostic). The comparison is (5, LT, 8), which is true, and hence the step LKED would be bypassed.

The REGION and TIME parameters are used in the EXEC statement in much the same way as in the JOB statement. The REGION parameter specifies the amount of core to be allowed to a particular job step, e.g.,

```
//STEP1 EXEC PGM=PROGA,REGION=128K
```

The TIME parameter specifies the maximum amount of CPU time (minutes, seconds) for a job step:

```
//STEP1 EXEC PGM=PROGA,TIME=(1,30)
```

Both REGION and TIME are key-word parameters and can appear in the same EXEC statement in any order.

DD Statement

```
Format:  //DDname DD operands
Example: //GO.SYSIN DD *
         //GO.PRINT DD SYSOUT=A
```

The data definition (DD) statement appears more often than any other. Every data set requires its own DD statement, either as part of a proc or in the programmer-supplied job stream. The DD statement encompasses the functions of the DOS TLBL, DLBL, EXTENT, and LBLTYP statements (see Chapter 17). It may contain both key-word and positional parameters.

Recall that the procedure COBUCLG consists of three separate steps: compile, link-edit, and execute. The DD statements of the execute (GO) step are tied to the COBOL SELECT statement. Consider

```
COBOL:
        SELECT PRINT-FILE ASSIGN TO UR-1403-S-PRINT.
        SELECT CARD-FILE ASSIGN TO UR-2540R-S-SYSIN.

JCL:
        //GO.PRINT DD SYSOUT=A
        //GO.SYSIN DD *
```

The COBOL SELECT links a programmer-defined file name to a system device; the DD statement provides information as to the location and disposition of that file. *The last entry in the SELECT must match the DD name—thus the appearance of PRINT and SYSIN in both SELECT and DD statements.* In the COBOL program, PRINT-FILE is tied to the system device PRINT. The corresponding DD statement causes PRINT to be assigned to a printer via SYSOUT=A. CARD-FILE is linked to SYSIN in COBOL. The * in the matching DD statement means that the data set for SYSIN follows in the job stream; i.e., it is a card file.

SYSIN and PRINT are commonly used DD names for the card reader and printer, respectively. However, the programmer may supply any other suitable names as long as consistency is maintained. The DD name can be up to eight characters in length, the first of which must be alphabetic. Thus the following pair is perfectly acceptable:

```
COBOL:
        SELECT CARD-FILE ASSIGN TO UR-2540R-S-INCARDS.

JCL:
        //GO.INCARDS DD *
```

More than one printer and/or card reader can be conceptually specified via multiple pairs of DD and SELECT statements. Suppose that we are processing a series of card transactions, several of which are in error. The erroneous transactions are randomly scattered throughout the input deck, but the requirements of the problem call for separate reports for the valid and invalid transactions. This is easily accomplished by creating two print files:

<u>COBOL</u>:
```
        SELECT VALID-FILE ASSIGN TO UR-1403-S-PRINT.
        SELECT ERROR-FILE ASSIGN TO UR-1403-S-ERROR.
```

<u>JCL</u>:
```
        //GO.PRINT DD SYSOUT=A
        //GO.ERROR DD SYSOUT=A
```

In the COBOL program, valid transactions are output to the file VALID-FILE. Invalid transactions are written to ERROR-FILE. The two DD statements specify that both PRINT and ERROR are assigned to a printer, and the reports will list separately.

Device Independence and the SELECT Statement

The SELECT statement has the general format

<u>SELECT</u> file-name <u>ASSIGN</u> TO system-name

The system name in turn has the format

Class [-device]-organization-name

The SELECT statement below is typical for card files:

```
    SELECT CARD-FILE ASSIGN TO UR-2540R-S-SYSIN.
```

Let us analyze the system name UR-2540R-S-SYSIN. UR is the device class and denotes unit record, 2540R signifies a 2540 card reader, S denotes sequential organization, and SYSIN matches the DD name in a JCL statement. However, the device is optional in the SELECT statement. Indeed, it may be preferable to omit the device entirely and thereby obtain device independence. (If device is omitted, class must be specified as UT—see the summary discussion in Chapter 16.) Thus,

```
    SELECT CARD-FILE ASSIGN TO UT-S-SYSIN.
```

is a perfectly valid SELECT statement. (How will the system know that the file SYSIN is contained on cards?)

In the following sections on tape and disk files we shall omit the device in the COBOL SELECT and supply this information through the DD unit parameter.

Additional DD Statements

Two other DD statements are frequently associated with COBOL jobs:

```
        //COB.SYSLIB DD DSN=USERLIB,DISP=SHR
        //GO.SYSUDUMP DD SYSOUT=A
```

SYSUDUMP specifies a core dump in the event of an ABEND and causes
the dump to appear on a class A output device (i.e., a printer). A DD
statement for SYSLIB is required when the COBOL source program contains
a COPY statement. (See examples in Chapter 8.) This statement specifies the
name of the data set, e.g., USERLIB.

We have covered the basic JCL needed for COBOL compilation and
execution using only card input and printer output. Extension to tape and disk
requires additional parameters for the DD statement. Table 18.3 summarizes
these parameters, which are discussed further in the subsequent sections.

Table 18.3 A Summary of Common DD Parameters

*	Indicates that a card file immediately follows in the job stream.
SYSOUT	Indicates a unit record (printer or punch) output device. SYSOUT=A and SYSOUT=B typically denote the printer (stock paper) and punch, respectively. Special forms are indicated by different letters established at the installation.
DSNAME or DSN	Indicates the name by which a data set is identified to the system.
UNIT	Specifies the device used by a data set.
VOL=SER=	Specifies the volume serial number of a data set; causes a mount message to be printed if the volume is not already available.
DISP	Indicates whether the file already exists and its disposition in the event of a successful completion or abnormal termination of the job step.
SPACE	Requests a space allocation for a new file.
DCB	Specifies characteristics of a file such as record length, blocking factor, fixed- or variable-length records, etc. This parameter can supply information not contained in the COBOL FD and hence provide a higher degree of flexibility.
LABEL	Specifies the type of labels used (if any), the retention period for a new file, and the location of an existing file on a tape containing several files.

The concept of label processing was discussed in Chapter 17. Standard tape **Processing Tape Files**
labels consist of volume, header, and trailer labels. The volume label appears at
the beginning of each reel and contains information to verify that the correct
tape has been mounted. Header labels appear before each file on a volume;
trailer labels appear after the file. These labels contain almost identical
information to identify the data set, creation date, expiration date, and much
more. In addition, the trailer label contains a block count field which contains
the number of physical records recorded for the file. Label-processing routines
ensure that the proper volume is mounted. They create new labels for output
data sets and can prevent accidental overwriting of vital data sets. Installations
also have the opportunity to develop their own label (user labels) and label-
processing routines.

Information required for tape processing is supplied on a DD statement
with additional parameters as shown in Figure 18.3.

```
//GO.ddname   DD   DISP=(current status,normal disposition,cond disposition),
//     VOL=SER=nnnnnn,DSN=dsname,
//     LABEL=(data-set-sequence- # ,SL,⎡EXPDT=yyddd⎤),
                                      ⎣RETPD=DDDD ⎦
              ⎧unit-address⎫
//     UNIT=⎨device-type ⎬
              ⎩group-name ⎭
```

Figure 18.3 DD Parameters

347

The DISP parameter indicates the status of the data set at the start and conclusion of processing. It has three positional subparameters, with possible values shown below:

$$DISP = \left(\begin{bmatrix} NEW \\ OLD \\ SHR \\ MOD \end{bmatrix}, \begin{bmatrix} DELETE \\ KEEP \\ PASS \\ CATLG \\ UNCATLG \end{bmatrix}, \begin{bmatrix} DELETE \\ KEEP \\ CATLG \\ UNCATLG \end{bmatrix} \right)$$

The first parameter indicates the status of a data set at the start of the job step. NEW specifies the data set is to be created, whereas OLD means it already exists. SHR means the data set already exists and may be used simultaneously (shared) with other jobs. (Use of SHR is restricted to disk files.) MOD states the data set is to be added to (modified) and causes the read/write mechanism to be positioned after the last record in the data set.

The second positional parameter specifies the disposition at the normal conclusion of the job step. KEEP means the data set is to be retained. It causes the tape to be rewound and unloaded and a message to be sent to the operator directing him to retain the tape. PASS causes the data set to be passed for use by a subsequent job step. (The final disposition of a passed data set should be indicated in the last DD statement referring to that data set.) It causes the tape to be rewound but not unloaded. DELETE states the data set is no longer needed and allows it to be scratched. CATLG causes the data set to be retained and establishes an entry in the system catalog pointing to the data set. UNCATLG also causes the data set to be retained but removes the entry in the catalog. Omission of the second positional parameter causes new data sets to be deleted and existing (old) data sets to be retained.

The third subparameter specifies disposition if the job terminates abnormally. If this parameter is omitted, disposition defaults to that specified for normal processing. Some examples:

1. DISP=(NEW,KEEP,DELETE)
   Explanation: Creates a new data set, keeps it if job step successfully executes, deletes it if the step ABENDs.
2. DISP=(SHR,KEEP)
   Explanation: Allows an existing data set to be used simultaneously by other jobs; retains it under all circumstances. (SHR is restricted to disk files.)
3. DISP=OLD
   Explanation: Specifies an existing data set to be retained under both normal and abnormal termination. Note parentheses are not required since only the first positional parameter was specified.
4. DISP=(NEW,CATLG,DELETE)
   Explanation: Creates a new data set, catalogs it if job step executes successfully, deletes it if step ABENDs.

UNIT Parameter

The UNIT parameter indicates the physical device on which the data set is to be processed. It is specified in one of three ways: unit address, device type, or group name. Specification of the unit address UNIT=185 explicitly specifies the device, i.e., tape drive 185. This is not a particularly good way of indicating the unit since the system must wait for the particular tape drive even if others are available. The device type indicates the class of tape drive, e.g., UNIT=2400, which calls for a series 2400 tape drive to be used. The system determines which 2400 units are available, selects one, and issues the appropriate message in conjunction with the VOL parameter. UNIT=TAPE illustrates how a group name is specified. This instructs the system to use any available tape device. Often this corresponds exactly to specification of a device type as in the case where only 2400 series drives are present. However, the group name can provide greater flexibility if all sequential devices (tape and disk) are combined under SYSSQ and the request is for UNIT=SYSSQ. Of course, such specification is not always feasible.

VOL (Volume) Parameter

The VOL parameter specifies the tape volume which contains the data set. VOL=SER=123456 causes a message to be printed directing the operator to mount tape 123456. (The physical device is determined by the UNIT parameter.) In addition, when standard labels are used, the VOL parameter causes IOCS to verify that 123456 is the volume serial number present in the volume label of the mounted tape. When an output data set is created on tape, the VOL parameter is typically omitted. In that instance the system will tell the operator to mount a scratch tape (i.e., a tape with nothing of value on it). After the job is completed, the volume serial number of the scratch tape is noted for future reference. It should be obvious that the VOL parameter is required for input data sets or else the system would not be able to locate the specified files.

LABEL Parameter

The LABEL parameter uses two positional subparameters to specify the type of label processing and the location of a data set on a volume. The first entry specifies the relative position of a data set on the reel. The second parameter indicates if labels are used and the type of label processing, e.g., SL—standard labels, NL—no labels, etc. Retention period is specified by keyword parameters in one of two ways. Either an explicit number of days is indicated with the key word RETPD or an explicit expiration date is specified via EXPDT. RETPD=1000 retains a file for 1000 days. EXPDT=99365 retains a file until the last day of 1999.

DSN (DSNAME or Data Set Name) Parameter

The DSN parameter specifies the actual name of the data set. It may be up to eight characters, the first of which is alphabetic (qualified names which may be longer than eight characters are discussed in conjunction with Figure 18.5). The parameter is required if the data set is to be cataloged or passed to another job step. Its name is independent of all other names used in the program.

The information on tape processing is summarized via Figure 18.4, which contains the JCL for the sequential update of Chapter 15. Information for the COBOL files OLD-MASTER and NEW-MASTER is provided in the DD statements for OLDTAPE and NEWTAPE, respectively. Both files use standard labels. The OLD-MASTER file is the third data set on volume number 001234 (LABEL and VOL parameters). The NEW-MASTER file will be retained for 365 days after the job completes execution, or else it will be deleted (see LABEL and DISP parameters). Note that the VOL parameter is

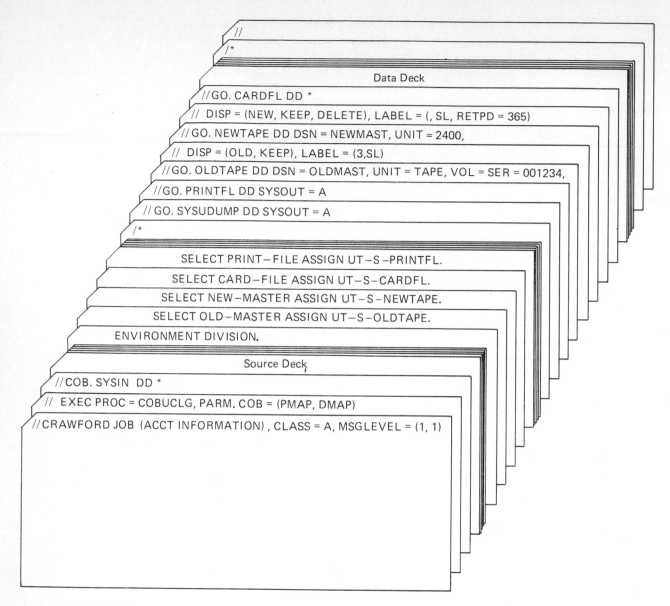

```
//
/*
                        Data Deck
//GO. CARDFL DD *
//  DISP = (NEW, KEEP, DELETE), LABEL = (, SL, RETPD = 365)
//GO. NEWTAPE DD DSN = NEWMAST, UNIT = 2400,
//  DISP = (OLD, KEEP), LABEL = (3,SL)
//GO. OLDTAPE DD DSN = OLDMAST, UNIT = TAPE, VOL = SER = 001234,
//GO. PRINTFL DD SYSOUT = A
// GO. SYSUDUMP DD SYSOUT = A
/*
          SELECT PRINT—FILE ASSIGN UT—S—PRINTFL.
          SELECT CARD—FILE ASSIGN UT—S—CARDFL.
          SELECT NEW—MASTER ASSIGN UT—S—NEWTAPE.
          SELECT OLD—MASTER ASSIGN UT—S—OLDTAPE.
       ENVIRONMENT DIVISION.
                        Source Deck
//COB. SYSIN  DD *
//  EXEC PROC = COBUCLG, PARM. COB = (PMAP, DMAP)
//CRAWFORD JOB (ACCT INFORMATION) , CLASS = A, MSGLEVEL = (1, 1)
```

Figure 18.4 OS Job Stream for Tape Processing

omitted for the output data set, denoting a scratch tape. A dump is printed in the event of an ABEND via the DD statement for SYSUDUMP.

Processing Files on Direct-Access Devices

A major difference in the organization of direct-access volumes is that, unlike tape, disk packs are not organized sequentially. The volume label of a direct-access device always appears on cylinder 0, track 0 and contains information similar to that in a tape volume label. In addition, it contains a pointer to the VTOC (volume table of contents), which is a separate data set, contained somewhere on the disk. The VTOC contains information about every data set on the volume, and it is through the VTOC that the system is able to locate data sets specified by the DSN parameter. The VTOC contains information analogous to the header and trailer labels of tape, namely creation date, expiration date, etc.

The OS JCL we present for disk processing is essentially the same as that for tape processing with one exception. Newly created direct-access data sets require a SPACE parameter in the DD statement to indicate the size of the file. In addition we shall introduce the DCB parameter in this discussion;

however, most of what we say about the DCB is applicable to the other data sets as well (i.e., tape, card, print, and punch). We shall discuss qualification in the DSNAME parameter and also changes in the UNIT parameter to cover direct-access devices.

SPACE Parameter

The SPACE parameter is required when creating data sets on direct-access devices. Its symbolic format is

$$\text{SPACE} = \left(\left\{ \begin{array}{l} \text{TRK} \\ \text{CYL} \\ \text{blocklength} \end{array} \right\}, \text{(primary-quantity,secondary-quantity),[RLSE],[CONTIG]} \right)$$

Subparameters, other than those above, are also available but beyond the scope of this discussion. The SPACE parameter indicates how much space is required for an output data set. It is not used for an input data set since the file already exists, and such information would be superfluous.

The SPACE parameter requests space on a direct-access device in terms of tracks, cylinders, or blocks. SPACE=(TRK,400) requests 400 tracks, SPACE=(CYL,100) requests 100 cylinders, and SPACE=(1000,3000) specifies space for 3000 blocks, each 1000 bytes. It should be obvious that the number of tracks or cylinders required for a given data set varies with the device. However, the number of blocks is a function of the file itself and is device independent. Capacities of various IBM direct-access devices are shown in Table 18.4.

Table 18.4 IBM Direct-Access Capacities

Device	Track Capacity	Tracks Per Cylinder	Number of Cylinders
2311 disk	3,625	10	200
2314 disk	7,294	20	200
3330 disk	13,030	19	404 or 808
3340 disk	8,368	12	348 or 696
2301 drum	20,483	8	25
2302 drum	4,892	10	80
2321 data cell	2,000	20	980

Table 18.4 is essential for determining the space requirements of a data set. Obviously the same file requires fewer tracks on a 3330 than a 2311 (see Problem 2).

The SPACE parameter can also provide for a secondary allocation if the primary allocation is insufficient. SPACE=(TRK,(100,20)) specifies a primary allocation of 100 tracks and a secondary amount of 20 tracks. In this example, OS will add an additional 20 tracks to the data set if the primary allocation is insufficient. It will do this up to 15 times (total = 300 tracks), at which time the job step terminates if space is still inadequate.

Two additional subparameters, RLSE and CONTIG, are frequently specified. RLSE returns any unused portion of the primary or secondary allocation, a highly desirable practice. The CONTIG subparameter requires that the primary allocation be contiguous. A contiguous allocation generally speeds up subsequent I/O since the access delay (seek time) is reduced. However, the programmer must be sure that sufficient contiguous space is available or else execution will be delayed and perhaps terminated.

The UNIT parameter serves the same purpose with direct-access devices as with tape. Reference may be by unit address, device type, or group name. Device types for disks include 2311, 2314, 3330, 3340, and 3350. Other direct-access device types are drums (2301, 2302, and 2305) and the 2321 data cell. Group names are installation dependent, but UNIT=DISK or UNIT=SYSDA is used almost universally to specify a disk device.

The information on sequential disk processing is summarized in Figure 18.5. Very little, except for the SPACE parameter, is different from the job stream for tape processing in Figure 18.4. The EXEC statement invokes the procedure COBUCLG with procedure and data division maps and a cross-reference listing (Table 18.2). A dump is specified in the event of an ABEND via the DD statement for SYSUDUMP. Note the correspondence between the four COBOL SELECT statements and the JCL DD statements.

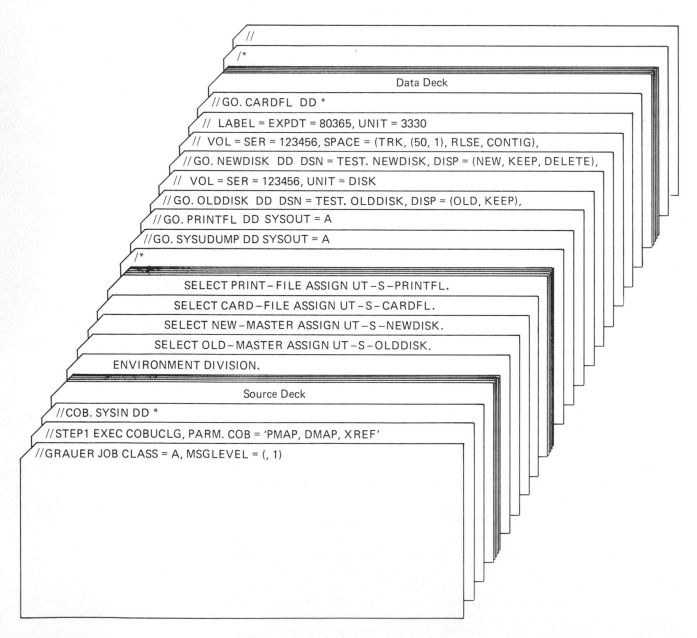

```
//
/*
                              Data Deck
//GO. CARDFL  DD *
//   LABEL = EXPDT = 80365, UNIT = 3330
//   VOL = SER = 123456, SPACE = (TRK, (50, 1), RLSE, CONTIG),
//GO. NEWDISK  DD  DSN = TEST. NEWDISK, DISP = (NEW, KEEP, DELETE),
//   VOL = SER = 123456, UNIT = DISK
//GO. OLDDISK  DD  DSN = TEST. OLDDISK, DISP = (OLD, KEEP),
//GO. PRINTFL DD SYSOUT = A
//GO. SYSUDUMP DD SYSOUT = A
/*
       SELECT PRINT-FILE ASSIGN UT-S-PRINTFL.
       SELECT CARD-FILE ASSIGN UT-S-CARDFL.
       SELECT NEW-MASTER ASSIGN UT-S-NEWDISK.
       SELECT OLD-MASTER ASSIGN UT-S-OLDDISK.
       ENVIRONMENT DIVISION.
                             Source Deck
//COB. SYSIN DD *
//STEP1 EXEC COBUCLG, PARM. COB = 'PMAP, DMAP, XREF'
//GRAUER JOB CLASS = A, MSGLEVEL = (, 1)
```

Figure 18.5 OS Job Stream for Sequential Disk Processing

The DD statements for the two disk files do contain some new material. A SPACE parameter is provided for the COBOL file NEW-MASTER. The primary allocation is 50 tracks, which must be contiguous. Any unused amount will be returned to the system due to the RLSE subparameter. The SPACE parameter is omitted for the COBOL file OLD-MASTER since that file already exists (DISP=OLD). The newly created data set, TEST.NEWDISK, will be deleted if the job ABENDs; else it will be retained until the last day of 1980.

The DSN parameter in the DD statements illustrates qualification. Qualification is used because a given installation may contain hundreds or even thousands of data sets, each of which must have a unique name. When the DSN parameter was first introduced, we stated it was limited to 8 characters. Qualification helps to ensure uniqueness and also provides more meaningful names. A qualified dataset name consists of two or more levels, separated by a period, in much the same way the hyphen is used in ordinary COBOL data names. The entire qualified data name cannot exceed 44 characters, and the individual levels (i.e., entries between the periods) cannot exceed 8 characters. TEST.NEWDISK and TEST.OLDDISK are examples of qualified data set names.

DCB Parameter

Every file in a COBOL program requires its own DCB macro to be completed before execution can take place. The DCB macro contains information about file characteristics such as record length, block size, record format, file organization, etc. The information may come from a combination of three sources: (1) the COBOL FD, (2) the DCB parameter on the DD statement, or (3) the data set header label. Further, there is a specified hierarchy for extracting information and building the DCB. The information in the COBOL FD has first priority, followed by the DCB parameter on the DD statement, and finally information on the header label. Consider the code below:

```
COBOL:
        SELECT TAPE-FILE ASSIGN TO UT-S-TAPEFILE.
        .
        .
        .
    FD TAPE-FILE
        LABEL RECORDS ARE STANDARD
        RECORDING MODE IS F
        BLOCK CONTAINS 0 CHARACTERS
        RECORD CONTAINS 0 CHARACTERS
        DATA RECORD IS TAPE-INFORMATION.
JCL:
    //GO.TAPEFILE DD DISP=(OLD,KEEP),UNIT=2400,VOL=SER=000123,
    //  LABEL=(3,SL),DCB=(LRECL=100,BLKSIZE=500)
```

The COBOL FD implies that TAPE-FILE has standard labels and fixed-length records. It specifies block and record size of zero characters each, which means this information is provided through appropriate key-word subparameters in the DCB key-word parameter. Record length is 100 bytes (LRECL=100) and block size is 500 bytes (BLKSIZE=500). The reader is advised to consult the *OS Programmer's Guide for ANS COBOL* for a complete discussion of available DCB subparameters.

What is to be gained by using the DCB over the COBOL FD? The answer, in a word, is flexibility. Often the same COBOL program may be used to process different files. If record length and block size are not specified in the COBOL FD, the only necessary modification would be in the execution time JCL, but the program need not be recompiled. The DCB parameter can be specified for any file type, i.e., tape, card, etc. It is optional in all cases except for ISAM files, which require the entry DCB=DSORG=IS (data set organization = indexed sequential). Figure 18.6 contains the JCL to load an ISAM file from tape. All statements have already been discussed in relation to Figures 18.4 and 18.5.

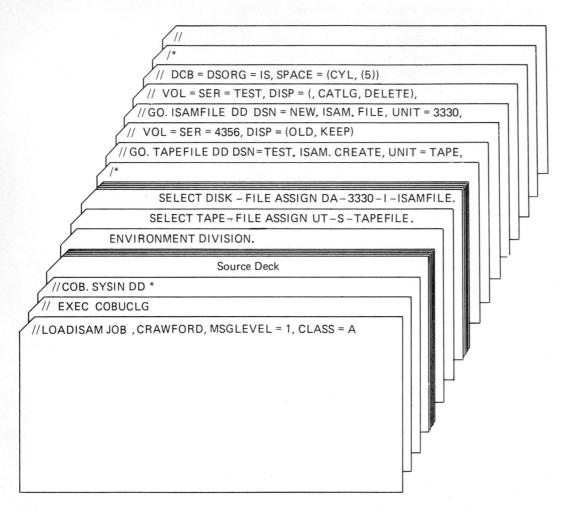

Figure 18.6 OS Job Stream to Load an ISAM File

The discussion of OS JCL revolved about three basic statements: JOB, EXEC, and DD, with emphasis on the latter. The key-word and positional parameters which were discussed are listed below: **Summary**

JOB:

CLASS	—Assigns a class to a job.
REGION	—Assigns an amount of core for the job (MVT only).
MSGLEVEL	—Controls system output.
TIME	—Assigns a maximum time allocation to a job.

EXEC:

PARM	—Controls job step parameters.
COND	—Prevents unnecessary job steps from execution.
REGION	—Assigns an amount of core for a job step (MVT only).
TIME	—Assigns a maximum time for a job step.

*	—Indicates the file follows immediately in the job stream.
SYSOUT	—Directs an output data set to a printer or punch.
DSN	—Specifies the data set name.
UNIT	—Specifies the unit to process the data set.
DCB	—Supplements the COBOL FD.
DISP	—Specifies disposition of data sets.
SPACE	—Assigns space for an output data set on a direct access device.
VOLUME	—Directs the operator to mount a specified volume; also used in label checking.
LABEL	—Specifies type of label processing, location of a data set on a volume (tape only), and retention period.

As often as not, a COBOL program fails in execution due to JCL-associated errors. Such mistakes are particularly irksome to the COBOL programmer who may incorrectly feel that JCL is not his province. We have tried to make it clear that working knowledge of JCL is very definitely in the realm of programmer responsibility and, further, that such knowledge is not difficult to achieve. As a pedagogic aid, we offer the following list of *errors to avoid*:

1. Improper format for EXEC statement: The syntactical rules for this statement are simple: // in columns 1 and 2 and a blank in column 3 if the job step is unnamed. If the step is named, then the step name begins in column 3 and is followed by a blank and then the word EXEC. Valid and invalid statements are shown below:

    ```
    Valid:   // EXEC COBUCLG
    Valid:   //STEP1 EXEC PGM=PROGA

    Invalid: //EXEC COBUCLG
    Invalid: //  STEP1 EXEC PGM=PROGA
    ```

2. Improper format for JOB statement: The job name begins in column 3, followed by a blank and the word JOB. (Other information is installation dependent and follows JOB.) Examples are shown:

    ```
    Valid:   //JONES JOB
    Invalid: //  JONES JOB
    ```

3. Invalid continuation: The card to be continued (i.e., the first card) must end on a comma. Continued cards begin with // in columns 1 and 2 and a space in 3 and then continue anywhere in columns 4–16.

4. Misspelled procedure name: Procedure names are chosen for uniqueness, not necessarily mnemonic significance. Copy the name correctly and completely.

5. Misspelled key-word parameters: Misspellings, either through keypunch or programmer error, are far too common. BLKSIZE, LRECL, DSORG, LABEL, CATLG, SHR, and MSGLEVEL are *correct* spellings of frequently abused parameters.

6. Omission of // at end of job stream: While not technically an error, it can have serious consequences. Omission of the null (//) statement means that subsequent cards can be taken as part of your job stream. Thus if the job after yours contains a JOB card JCL error, your job may "flush" through no fault of your own.

7. Omission of a positional parameter or associated comma: Positional parameters derive their meaning from a specified order. If omitted, their absence must be indicated by a comma.

8. Incorrect order of JCL statements: Occurs frequently when using a proc. In COBUCLG, for example, the COB step precedes the GO step. Thus all DD statements for the former (e.g., //COB.SYSIN DD *) must precede those of the latter (e.g., //GO.SYSIN DD *).

9. Omission of a DD statement: Every file, in every job step, requires a DD statement. Make sure you have them all.

10. Incorrect or omitted DSN for an input file: The purpose of the DSN parameter in the DD statement is to identify a data set. If this parameter is left out or misspelled, the system will not be able to locate the proper file on which to operate.

11. Incorrect or omitted VOL=SER parameter: This parameter causes a message to be printed informing the operator of the proper volume. Obviously, incorrect specification makes it difficult for the operator to comply with the request.

REVIEW EXERCISES

TRUE	FALSE		
☐	☐	1	A given DD statement may contain either positional or key-word parameters but not both.
☐	☐	2	Every job stream must contain one and only one /* statement.
☐	☐	3	A procedure may contain more than one EXEC statement.
☐	☐	4	The DD and EXEC statements must have a blank in column 3.
☐	☐	5	It is possible to continue any JCL statement to a second card.
☐	☐	6	Comments are not permitted on any JCL statement.
☐	☐	7	The job scheduler and master scheduler are both part of the data management routines.
☐	☐	8	Data management is responsible for I/O operations.
☐	☐	9	Under multiprogramming, the CPU may execute instructions from two different programs simultaneously.
☐	☐	10	The /* statement is the last statement in a job stream.
☐	☐	11	The omission of a positional parameter *always* requires a comma.
☐	☐	12	There are no positional parameters or subparameters on the JOB statement.
☐	☐	13	The EXEC statement does not require a step name.
☐	☐	14	The procedure COBUCLG will *always* attempt to execute the compiled program.
☐	☐	15	The same DD name may appear in two different steps of a procedure.
☐	☐	16	The MOUNT parameter *always* causes a message to be printed, directing the operator to mount a specific volume.
☐	☐	17	The VOL parameter is optional.
☐	☐	18	The SPACE parameter is required for input data sets.
☐	☐	19	The DISP parameter has three positional subparameters.
☐	☐	20	The SPACE parameter must specify required space in terms of tracks.
☐	☐	21	VOL=SER= is required if UNIT is specified.
☐	☐	22	The secondary space allocation in the SPACE parameter is attempted only once.
☐	☐	23	A card file must have an * on its DD statement.
☐	☐	24	DD statements precede the EXEC card.
☐	☐	25	Certain parameters may appear on either the JOB or EXEC statement.

TRUE	FALSE		
☐	☐	26	The DCB parameter overrides information in the COBOL FD.
☐	☐	27	The UNIT parameter is not required for a print file.
☐	☐	28	If the normal disposition of an existing data set is not specified, the data set is deleted at the end of the job step.
☐	☐	29	A data set name may consist of more than eight characters if it is qualified.
☐	☐	30	The DCB parameter is not permitted for a card file.

31 Given the DD specification

```
//GO.TAPEFILE DD DISP=(OLD,KEEP),LABEL=(2,SL),
// DSN=TESTFILE,VOL=SER=123456,UNIT=2400
```

answer true or false:

TRUE	FALSE		
☐	☐	(a)	TAPEFILE is the entry on the COBOL SELECT statement.
☐	☐	(b)	TESTFILE is the first file on the tape.
☐	☐	(c)	The operator will be directed to mount the tape with an external label "TESTFILE".
☐	☐	(d)	The tape will be scratched if the job ABENDs.
☐	☐	(e)	The tape will be mounted on any available tape drive.

32 Given the DD specifications

```
//GO.NEWFILE DD DISP=(NEW,KEEP),SPACE=(CYL,20),
// DSN=OUTPUT,UNIT=DISK,LABEL=EXPDT=99365,
// VOL=SER=123456
```

answer true or false:

TRUE	FALSE		
☐	☐	(a)	OUTPUT is the entry in the COBOL SELECT statement.
☐	☐	(b)	The file will be retained indefinitely if the job executes successfully.
☐	☐	(c)	The file will be deleted if the job ABENDs.
☐	☐	(d)	The job will terminate if more than 20 cylinders are required.
☐	☐	(e)	The file will be stored in contiguous cylinders.
☐	☐	(f)	Any available disk device may be used.
☐	☐	(g)	A message to mount volume number 123456 will definitely be issued.

PROBLEMS

1 Complete the table below; indicate whether the job step is executed or bypassed:

Code in COND Parameter	Operation	System Return Code from Last Step	Executed or Bypassed
5	LT	4	
9	GT	8	
5	LT	(C-Level diagnostic)	
5	LT	(W-Level diagnostic)	
12	EQ	(E-Level diagnostic)	
12	NE	12	

2 Complete the SPACE parameters for an output data set of 3300 blocks. Each block is 1000 bytes in length. (Assume that 3, 6, and 11 are the number of blocks per track for the 2311, 2314, and 3330, respectively.) In each case provide a secondary allocation equal to 10% of the primary allocation:

(a) //GO.OUTDISK DD   UNIT=2311,SPACE=(TRK,(   ))
(b) //GO.OUTDISK DD   UNIT=2311,SPACE=(CYL,(   ))
(c) //GO.OUTDISK DD   UNIT=2314,SPACE=(TRK,(   ))
(d) //GO.OUTDISK DD   UNIT=2314,SPACE=(CYL,(   ))
(e) //GO.OUTDISK DD   UNIT=3330,SPACE=(1000,(   ))

3 Show OS JCL necessary to compile, link-edit, and execute a COBOL program. The *Section V* program reads a deck of cards and produces a tape. Your JCL must accommodate *File Processing* all the following:

1. Produce procedure and data division maps and a dump in the event of an ABEND.
2. Store the data set as the second file on tape.
3. Retain the newly created tape file for 100 days if the job executes successfully; if the job ABENDs, scratch the tape.
4. Use any available tape drive.
5. Provide a DCB parameter for the tape file to show a logical record of 80 bytes and a blocking factor of 10.
6. Store the newly created data set on tape volume 001234 as NEW.TAPE.
7. Show a corresponding COBOL SELECT for every DD statement.

4 Repeat Problem 3 except that the newly created data set is to appear as a sequential file on a 2314 device. (Assume 10 cylinders for the file.)

5 Repeat Problem 3 except that the newly created data set is to appear as an ISAM file on a 3330 device. (Assume 30 cylinders for the file.)

Appendices

APPENDIX A

SPLICE:
A COBOL Precompiler

Almost since the very inception of COBOL, critics have complained that its advantage of self-documentation is entirely offset by its verbosity. Yet today, almost 20 years later, COBOL remains "on top of the heap" and is by far the most widely used business language. Further, the problem of writer's cramp has effectively been eliminated through the advent of COBOL precompilers. This subject is usually not covered in the university. The authors, however, have chosen to include precompilers because of the increasing acceptance in industry of this concept and because of their belief that an effective and available precompiler can facilitate COBOL instruction.

Simply stated, the objective of a COBOL precompiler is a quick way to code COBOL. A precompiler accepts abbreviations, shortcuts, etc., as input and uses the computer to expand the shorthand program into a complete COBOL program prior to compilation. Savings vary according to the particular product, but results of 50% and higher are commonly achieved with the better ones. (A saving of 50% implies that a precompiler consisting of X statements generates a COBOL program of 2X statements.)

In this appendix we shall introduce the reader to the capabilities of a sophisticated precompiler. Focus is on SPLICE (Shorthand Programming Language In a COBOL Environment), which was developed by the authors and is in commercial use. The reader should also seek additional information on METACOBOL by Applied Data Research and WORK TEN by National Computing Industries. Indeed, there are several other lesser known products, and the authors estimate that there are well over 1000 installations employing some type of shorthand.

The authors will gladly make SPLICE available to educational institutions for a maintenance fee. Interested readers should contact Professor Robert Grauer, Department of Management Science, University of Miami, Coral Gables, Florida 33124. However, the authors *do not* believe that SPLICE should be used in an introductory course, since students must first go through the "pain" of learning COBOL. SPLICE can be made available to students on an optional basis in the second semester. Used in this manner, SPLICE provides the potential for exposing the student to more problems since the clerical problems of COBOL are reduced and/or eliminated.

SPLICE should not be considered a new language but rather a quicker way to develop COBOL programs. An individual writes in SPLICE, which in turn generates COBOL source code. The implicit documentation is retained, but the associated drudgery of coding is eliminated.

Overview of SPLICE

SPLICE has seven features whereby a programmer can reduce coding effort:

1. Procedure division abbreviations
2. Data division abbreviations
3. User-defined abbreviations
4. One-line identification division
5. Creation of COBOL FD's
6. Creation and initialization of 77-level entries
7. Relative addressing

Procedure and data division abbreviations are apt to be found in all shorthands, whereas features such as relative addressing are unique to SPLICE. Items 1–4 are elementary; items 5–7 are more advanced in the sense they take longer to learn. The beauty of SPLICE is that the COBOL programmer need not use all seven techniques. He can select only those which appeal to him, but naturally the more he uses, the greater his savings. Further, SPLICE accepts any COBOL statement, and this enables one to submit an "off-the-shelf" COBOL program to SPLICE. In these instances, the savings are considerably less than in programs developed from scratch, but this capability allows SPLICE to be applied to maintenance as well as developmental programs.

By way of illustration, we have coded a SPLICE program which substantially reproduces the COBOL program of Chapter 4. Observe that an 85-statement SPLICE program (Figure A.1) expanded to 180 COBOL statements (Figure A.2), a savings of approximately two to one. The seven features of SPLICE are discussed by repeated reference to these listings.

Procedure Division Abbreviations

All COBOL verbs, plus other key reserved words, are assigned SPLICE abbreviations for use in the procedure division (Table A.1). Consider SPLICE line 28, which expands to COBOL line 11500:

SPLICE:
W PRINT-LINE AA TOP-OF-PAGE LN.

COBOL:
WRITE PRINT-LINE AFTER ADVANCING TOP-OF-PAGE LINES.

```
 1              TUITION        THE BURSAR.      1 Line Identification Division
 2          S-N
 3              CO1 IS TOP-OF-PAGE.
 4          CSEL CARD-FILE UR-2540R-S-SYSIN.
 5          PSEL PRINT-FILE UR-1403-S-SYSOUT RF LO RE 133 PRTR.    Creation of COBOL FD
 6          W-S
 7          01  HEADER-LINE.
 8              05  F                    P  X.
 9              05  HDG-NAME             P  X(12) V 'STUDENT NAME'.
10              05  F                    P  X(10) V S.      Use of data
11              05  HDG-SOC-SEC          P  X(11) V 'SOC SEC NUM'.   division
12              05  F                    P  X(2)  V S.      abbreviations
13              05  HDG-CREDITS          P  X(7)  V 'CREDITS'.
14              05  F                    P  X(2)  V S.
15              05  HDG-TUITION          P  X(7)  V 'TUITION'.
16              05  F                    P  X(2)  V S.
17              05  HDG-UNION-FEE        P  X(9)  V 'UNION FEE'.
18              05  F                    P  X(2)  V S.
19              05  HDG-ACTIVITY         P  X(7)  V 'ACT FEE'.
20              05  F                    P  X(2)  V S.
21              05  HDG-SCHOLAR          P  X(11) V 'SCHOLARSHIP'.
22              05  F                    P  X(2)  V S.
23              05  HDG-TOTAL-BILL       P  X(10) V 'TOTAL BILL'.
24              05  F                    P  X(36) V S.
25          P-D     Beginning of procedure division
26              O IP CARD-FILE, OP PRINT-FILE.
27              M HEADER-LINE TO PRTR.
28              W PRINT-LINE AA TOP-OF-PAGE LN.      Use of procedure division
29              MS PRTR.                              abbreviations
30              MOVE '--------------------------------------------------------
31              '-----------------------------------------' T PRTR.
32              WRITE PRINT-LINE AFTER ADVANCING 1 LINES.
33          R-A-C.
34              R CARD-FILE, AE GT WRITE-UNIVERSITY-TOTALS.
35              CP TUITION(4)U = 80 * CREDITS.
36              IF CARD-32-32-A E UNION-MEMBER IE 'Y' M 25 T U-F,
37              ES MZ U-F(2)U.
38              IF CREDITS IG 6 GT MORE-THAN-6-CREDITS.
39              M 25 T A-F(2)U.
40              GT ADD-TOTAL-BILL.                Creation of 77 level
41          MORE-THAN-6-CREDITS.                  entry for tuition
42              IF CREDITS IG 12 M 75 T A-F, ES M 50 T A-F.
43          ADD-TOTAL-BILL.
44              CP IND(4)U = TUITION + U-F + A-F - SCH.
45          UPDATE-UNIVERSITY-TOTALS.
46              AD TUITION T TOTAL-TUITION(6)U.
47              AD U-F T TOTAL-UNION-FEE(6)U.
48              AD A-F T TOT-AF(6)U.
49              AD IND T TOTAL-IND-BILL(6)U.
50              AD SCH T TOT-SC(6)U.
51          WRITE-DETAIL-LINE.
```

```
52              MS PRTR.                    Relative addressing with equate
53              M CARD-1-20 E STUDENT-NAME T PRTR-2-21 E PRINT-STUDENT-NAME.
54  Relative    M CARD-21-29-U T PRTR-24-34-R 999B99B9999 E PRINT-SOC-SEC-NO.
55  addressing  M CARD-30-31-U E CREDITS T PRTR-39-40-U E PRINT-CREDITS.
56  for card    M TUITION T PRINT-TUITION.
57  record      M U-F T PRINT-UNION-FEE.
58              M A-F T PRINT-ACTIVITY-FEE.
59              M CARD-33-36-U E SCH T PRINT-SCHOLARSHIP.
60              M IND T PRINT-IND-BILL.
61              W PRTR AA 1 LN.
62              GT R-A-C.
63          WRITE-UNIVERSITY-TOTALS.
64              MS PRTR.
65              MOVE '--------------------------------------------------------
66              '-----------------------------------------' T PRTR.
67              W PRTR AA 1 LN.
68              MS PRTR.
69              M TOTAL-TUITION T PRTR-44-51-R $$$$,$$9 E PRINT-TUITION.
70              M TOTAL-UNION-FEE T PRTR-53-60-R $$$$,$$9 E PRINT-UNION-FEE.
71              M TOT-AF T PRTR-64-71-R $$$$,$$9 E PRINT-ACTIVITY-FEE.
72              M TOT-SC T PRTR-75-82-R $$$$,$$9 E PRINT-SCHOLARSHIP.
```

Figure A.1 85-Statement SPLICE Listing

```
73          M TOTAL-IND-BILL T PRTR-88-95-R $$$$,$$9 E PRINT-IND-BILL.
74          W PRTR AA 2 LN.
75       END-OF-JOB-ROUTINE.
76          C CARD-FILE, PRINT-FILE.  SR.
77     S CARD-21-29-U    SOC-SEC-NUM
78     S PRTR            PRINT-LINE
79     S R-A-C           READ-A-CARD                  — User-defined abbreviations
80     S A-F             ACTIVITY-FEE
81     S TOT-AF          TOTAL-ACTIVITY-FEE
82     S U-F             UNION-FEE
83     S IND             INDIVIDUAL-BILL
84     S SCH             SCHOLARSHIP
85     S TOT-SC          TOTAL-SCHOLARSHIP

     85 SPLICE STATEMENTS
```

Figure A.1 (Continued)

```
000100 IDENTIFICATION DIVISION.                                       TUITION
000200 PROGRAM-ID.                                                    TUITION
000300      TUITION.                                                  TUITION
000400 AUTHOR.                                                        TUITION
000500      THE BURSAR.                                               TUITION
000600 INSTALLATION.                                                  TUITION
000700      CITY UNIVERSITY OF NEW YORK.                              TUITION
000800 DATE-WRITTEN.                                                  TUITION
000900      SEPTEMBER, 1976.                                          TUITION
001000      SKIP3                                                     TUITION
001100 ENVIRONMENT DIVISION.                                          TUITION
001200 CONFIGURATION SECTION.                                         TUITION
001300 SOURCE-COMPUTER.                                               TUITION
001400      IBM-370.                                                  TUITION
001500 OBJECT-COMPUTER.                                               TUITION
001600      IBM-370.                                                  TUITION
001700 SPECIAL-NAMES.                                                 TUITION
001800                                                                TUITION
001900      C01 IS TOP-OF-PAGE.                                       TUITION
002000      SKIP2                                                     TUITION
002100 INPUT-OUTPUT SECTION.                                          TUITION
002200 FILE-CONTROL.                                                  TUITION
002300      SELECT CARD-FILE                                          TUITION
002400          ASSIGN TO UR-2540R-S-SYSIN.                           TUITION
002500      SELECT PRINT-FILE                                         TUITION
002600          ASSIGN TO UR-1403-S-SYSOUT.                           TUITION
002700      SKIP3                                                     TUITION
002800 DATA DIVISION.                                                 TUITION
002900 FILE SECTION.                                                  TUITION
003000      SKIP2                                                     TUITION
003100 FD   CARD-FILE                                                 TUITION
003200      RECORDING MODE IS F                                       TUITION
003300      LABEL RECORDS ARE OMITTED                                 TUITION
003400      RECORD CONTAINS 80 CHARACTERS                             TUITION
003500      DATA RECORD IS CARD.                                      TUITION
003600      SKIP1                                                     TUITION
003700 01   CARD.                                                     TUITION
003800      05   CARD-R     PICTURE IS X(80).                         TUITION
003900      05   FILLER REDEFINES CARD-R.                             TUITION
004000         10   STUDENT-NAME          PICTURE IS X(20).           TUITION
004100         10   SOC-SEC-NUM           PICTURE IS 9(9).            TUITION
004200         10   CREDITS               PICTURE IS 9(2).            TUITION
004300         10   UNION-MEMBER          PICTURE IS A(1).            TUITION
004400         10   SCHOLARSHIP           PICTURE IS 9(4).            TUITION
004500         10   FILLER                PICTURE IS X(44).           TUITION
004600      SKIP2                                                     TUITION
004700 FD   PRINT-FILE                                                TUITION
004800      RECORDING MODE IS F                                       TUITION
004900      LABEL RECORDS ARE OMITTED                                 TUITION
005000      RECORD CONTAINS 133 CHARACTERS                            TUITION
005100      DATA RECORD IS PRINT-LINE.                                TUITION
005200      SKIP1                                                     TUITION
005300 01   PRINT-LINE.                                               TUITION
005400      05   PRTR-R     PICTURE IS X(133).                        TUITION
005500      05   FILLER REDEFINES PRTR-R.                             TUITION
005600         10   FILLER                PICTURE IS X.               TUITION
```

Figure A.2 COBOL Statements Generated by SPLICE

```
005700          10   PRINT-STUDENT-NAME          PICTURE IS X(20).          TUITION
005800          10   FILLER                      PICTURE IS XX.             TUITION
005900          10   PRINT-SOC-SEC-NO            PICTURE 999B99B9999.       TUITION
006000          10   FILLER                      PICTURE IS X(4).           TUITION
006100          10   PRINT-CREDITS               PICTURE IS 9(2).           TUITION
006200          10   FILLER                      PICTURE IS XXX.            TUITION
006300          10   PRINT-TUITION               PICTURE $$$$,$$9.          TUITION
006400          10   FILLER                      PICTURE IS X.              TUITION
006500          10   PRINT-UNION-FEE             PICTURE $$$$,$$9.          TUITION
006600          10   FILLER                      PICTURE IS XXX.            TUITION
006700          10   PRINT-ACTIVITY-FEE          PICTURE $$$$,$$9.          TUITION
006800          10   FILLER                      PICTURE IS XXX.            TUITION
006900          10   PRINT-SCHOLARSHIP           PICTURE $$$$,$$9.          TUITION
007000          10   FILLER                      PICTURE IS X(5).           TUITION
007100          10   PRINT-IND-BILL              PICTURE $$$$,$$9.          TUITION
007200          10   FILLER                      PICTURE IS X(38).          TUITION
007300 WORKING-STORAGE SECTION.                                            TUITION
007400 77   TUITION                        PICTURE IS   9(4)               TUITION
007500                                     VALUE IS ZEROS.                 TUITION
007600 77   UNION-FEE                      PICTURE IS   9(2)               TUITION
007700                                     VALUE IS ZEROS.                 TUITION
007800 77   ACTIVITY-FEE                   PICTURE IS   9(2)               TUITION
007900                                     VALUE IS ZEROS.                 TUITION
008000 77   INDIVIDUAL-BILL                PICTURE IS   9(4)               TUITION
008100                                     VALUE IS ZEROS.                 TUITION
008200 77   TOTAL-TUITION                  PICTURE IS   9(6)               TUITION
008300                                     VALUE IS ZEROS.                 TUITION
008400 77   TOTAL-UNION-FEE                PICTURE IS   9(6)               TUITION
008500                                     VALUE IS ZEROS.                 TUITION
008600 77   TOTAL-ACTIVITY-FEE             PICTURE IS   9(6)               TUITION
008700                                     VALUE IS ZEROS.                 TUITION
008800 77   TOTAL-IND-BILL                 PICTURE IS   9(6)               TUITION
008900                                     VALUE IS ZEROS.                 TUITION
009000 77   TOTAL-SCHOLARSHIP              PICTURE IS   9(6)               TUITION
009100                                     VALUE IS ZEROS.                 TUITION
009200 01   HEADER-LINE.                                                   TUITION
009300      05   FILLER              PICTURE X.                            TUITION   *
009400      05   HDG-NAME            PICTURE X(12) VALUE 'STUDENT NAME'.   TUITION   *
009500      05   FILLER              PICTURE X(10) VALUE SPACES.           TUITION   *
009600      05   HDG-SOC-SEC         PICTURE X(11) VALUE 'SOC SEC NUM'.    TUITION   *
009700      05   FILLER              PICTURE X(2) VALUE SPACES.            TUITION   *
009800      05   HDG-CREDITS         PICTURE X(7) VALUE 'CREDITS'.         TUITION   *
009900      05   FILLER              PICTURE X(2) VALUE SPACES.            TUITION   *
010000      05   HDG-TUITION         PICTURE X(7) VALUE 'TUITION'.         TUITION   *
010100      05   FILLER              PICTURE X(2) VALUE SPACES.            TUITION   *
010200      05   HDG-UNION-FEE       PICTURE X(9) VALUE 'UNION FEE'.       TUITION   *
010300      05   FILLER              PICTURE X(2) VALUE SPACES.            TUITION   *
010400      05   HDG-ACTIVITY        PICTURE X(7) VALUE 'ACT FEE'.         TUITION   *
010500      05   FILLER              PICTURE X(2) VALUE SPACES.            TUITION   *
010600      05   HDG-SCHOLAR         PICTURE X(11) VALUE 'SCHOLARSHIP'.    TUITION   *
010700      05   FILLER              PICTURE X(2) VALUE SPACES.            TUITION   *
010800      05   HDG-TOTAL-BILL      PICTURE X(10) VALUE 'TOTAL BILL'.     TUITION   *
010900      05   FILLER              PICTURE X(36) VALUE SPACES.           TUITION   *
011000      SKIP3                                                         TUITION
011100 PROCEDURE DIVISION.                                               TUITION
011200      OPEN INPUT CARD-FILE,                                         TUITION   *
011300           OUTPUT PRINT-FILE.                                       TUITION   *
011400      MOVE HEADER-LINE TO PRINT-LINE.                              TUITION   *
011500      WRITE PRINT-LINE AFTER ADVANCING TOP-OF-PAGE LINES.          TUITION   *
011600      MOVE SPACES TO PRINT-LINE.                                   TUITION   *
011700      MOVE '-------------------------------------------------------TUITION
011800-           -----------------------------------' TO                TUITION   *
011900          PRINT-LINE.                                              TUITION
012000      WRITE PRINT-LINE AFTER ADVANCING 1 LINES.                    TUITION
012100                                                                   TUITION
012200 READ-A-CARD.                                                      TUITION
012300      READ CARD-FILE,                                              TUITION   *
012400           AT END GO TO WRITE-UNIVERSITY-TOTALS.                   TUITION   *
012500      COMPUTE TUITION = 80 * CREDITS.                              TUITION   *
012600                                                                   TUITION
012700      IF UNION-MEMBER IS EQUAL TO 'Y' MOVE 25 TO UNION-FEE,        TUITION   *
012800          ELSE MOVE ZEROS TO UNION-FEE.                            TUITION   *
012900                                                                   TUITION
013000      IF CREDITS IS GREATER THAN 6 GO TO MORE-THAN-6-CREDITS.      TUITION   *
013100      MOVE 25 TO ACTIVITY-FEE.                                     TUITION   *
013200      GO TO ADD-TOTAL-BILL.                                        TUITION   *
```

Figure A.2 (*Continued*)

```
013300                                                                  TUITION
013400 MORE-THAN-6-CREDITS.                                             TUITION
013500                                                                  TUITION
013600      IF CREDITS IS GREATER THAN 12 MOVE 75 TO ACTIVITY-FEE,      TUITION  *
013700           ELSE MOVE 50 TO ACTIVITY-FEE.                          TUITION  *
013800                                                                  TUITION
013900 ADD-TOTAL-BILL.                                                  TUITION
014000      COMPUTE INDIVIDUAL-BILL = TUITION + UNION-FEE + ACTIVITY-FEE TUITION  *
014100           - SCHOLARSHIP.                                         TUITION
014200                                                                  TUITION
014300 UPDATE-UNIVERSITY-TOTALS.                                        TUITION
014400      ADD TUITION TO TOTAL-TUITION.                               TUITION  *
014500      ADD UNION-FEE TO TOTAL-UNION-FEE.                           TUITION  *
014600      ADD ACTIVITY-FEE TO TOTAL-ACTIVITY-FEE.                     TUITION  *
014700      ADD INDIVIDUAL-BILL TO TOTAL-IND-BILL.                      TUITION  *
014800      ADD SCHOLARSHIP TO TOTAL-SCHOLARSHIP.                       TUITION  *
014900                                                                  TUITION
015000 WRITE-DETAIL-LINE.                                               TUITION
015100      MOVE SPACES TO PRINT-LINE.                                  TUITION  *
015200      MOVE STUDENT-NAME TO PRINT-STUDENT-NAME.                    TUITION  *
015300      MOVE SOC-SEC-NUM  TO PRINT-SOC-SEC-NO.                      TUITION  *
015400      MOVE CREDITS TO PRINT-CREDITS.                              TUITION  *
015500      MOVE TUITION TO PRINT-TUITION.                              TUITION  *
015600      MOVE UNION-FEE TO PRINT-UNION-FEE.                          TUITION  *
015700      MOVE ACTIVITY-FEE TO PRINT-ACTIVITY-FEE.                    TUITION  *
015800      MOVE SCHOLARSHIP TO PRINT-SCHOLARSHIP.                      TUITION  *
015900      MOVE INDIVIDUAL-BILL TO PRINT-IND-BILL.                     TUITION  *
016000      WRITE PRINT-LINE AFTER ADVANCING 1 LINES.                   TUITION  *
016100      GO TO READ-A-CARD.                                          TUITION  *
016200                                                                  TUITION
016300 WRITE-UNIVERSITY-TOTALS.                                         TUITION
016400      MOVE SPACES TO PRINT-LINE.                                  TUITION  *
016500      MOVE '----------------------------------------------------TUITION
016600-         '-----------------------------------------' TO          TUITION  *
016700           PRINT-LINE.                                            TUITION
016800      WRITE PRINT-LINE AFTER ADVANCING 1 LINES.                   TUITION  *
016900      MOVE SPACES TO PRINT-LINE.                                  TUITION  *
017000      MOVE TOTAL-TUITION TO PRINT-TUITION.                        TUITION  *
017100      MOVE TOTAL-UNION-FEE TO PRINT-UNION-FEE.                    TUITION  *
017200      MOVE TOTAL-ACTIVITY-FEE TO PRINT-ACTIVITY-FEE.              TUITION  *
017300      MOVE TOTAL-SCHOLARSHIP TO PRINT-SCHOLARSHIP.                TUITION  *
017400      MOVE TOTAL-IND-BILL TO PRINT-IND-BILL.                      TUITION  *
017500      WRITE PRINT-LINE AFTER ADVANCING 2 LINES.                   TUITION  *
017600                                                                  TUITION
017700 END-OF-JOB-ROUTINE.                                              TUITION
017800      CLOSE CARD-FILE,                                            TUITION  *
017900           PRINT-FILE.                                            TUITION
018000      STOP RUN.                                                   TUITION  *
```

180 CARDS GENERATED FROM SPLICE INPUT   NO SPLICE ERRORS

Figure A.2 (*Continued*)

"W" is expanded to "WRITE," "AA" to "AFTER ADVANCING," and "LN" to "LINES." Procedure division abbreviations are listed in Table A.1. Consider also SPLICE statement 26, which expands to COBOL statements 11200 and 11300:

SPLICE:
    O IP CARD-FILE, OP PRINT-FILE.

COBOL:
    OPEN INPUT CARD-FILE,
         OUTPUT PRINT-FILE.

In addition to expansion for the abbreviations "O," "IP," and "OP," the COBOL output has been reformatted on two lines, as SPLICE automatically causes a new line to begin in column 16 after a comma is encountered. A new line will also begin in column 12 after a period is encountered. SKIP statements are inserted prior to DIVISION headers, FD's, and 01's to further enhance legibility.

Table A.1 Splice Procedure Division Abbreviations

A	ALTER	HV	HIGH-VALUES	R	READ
AA	AFTER ADVANCING			RD	READY TRACE
AC	ACCEPT	I	INTO	RE	RELEASE
AD	ADD	IC	INCLUDE	RF	REPLACING FIRST
AE	AT END	IE	IS EQUAL TO	RL	REEL
AF	AFTER	IG	IS GREATER THAN	RN	ROUNDED
AK	ASCENDING KEY	IK	INVALID KEY	RP	REPLACING
AL	IS ALPHABETIC	IL	IS LESS THAN	RS	RESET TRACE
AP	AFTER POSITIONING	IP	INPUT	RT	RETURN
AY	AND EVERY	IZ	IS ZERO	RV	REVERSED
				RW	REWRITE
B	BLANK	L	LEADING		
BA	BEFORE ADVANCING	LB	LABELS	S	SPACE
BG	BEGINNING	LN	LINES	SE	STANDARD ERROR
		LV	LOW-VALUES	SP	UPON SYSPUNCH
C	CLOSE			SR	STOP RUN
CA	CALL	M	MOVE	ST	STOP
CG	CHANGED	MP	MULTIPLY	SU	SUBTRACT
CH	CHARACTERS	MS	MOVE SPACES TO	SZ	ON SIZE
CK	CHECKING	MZ	MOVE ZEROES TO		
CN	CONSOLE			T	TO
CO	CORRESPONDING	N	NAMED	TA	THAN
CP	COMPUTE	NA	NOT ALPHABETIC	TE	THEN
CR	CREATING	NE	IS NOT EQUAL TO	TF	TRANSFORM
		NG	IS NOT GREATER	TL	TALLYING
DK	DESCENDING KEY	NL	IS NOT LESS	TM	TIMES
DP	DEPENDING ON	NN	IS NOT NUMERIC	TP	TO PROCEED TO
DS	DISPLAY	NP	IS NOT POSITIVE	TU	THRU
DV	DIVIDE	NR	WITH NO REWIND		
		NS	NEXT SENTENCE	U	USE
EB	ENDING LABELS	NT	IS NEGATIVE	UA	USE AFTER
EC	ENTER COBOL	NU	IS NUMERIC	UC	UPON CONSOLE
EH	EXHIBIT	NX	IS NOT NEGATIVE	UE	USE AFTER ERROR
EL	ENTER LINKAGE	NZ	IS NOT ZERO	UF	UNTIL FIRST
EM	EXAMINE			UN	UNTIL
EN	ENTRY	O	OPEN	US	USING
ES	ELSE	OP	OUTPUT	UT	UNIT
EV	EVERY	OT	OTHERWISE	UX	UPON
EX	EXIT				
		P	PERFORM	V	VARYING
F	FROM	PR	PROCEDURE		
FC	FROM CONSOLE	PS	IS POSITIVE	W	WRITE
				WL	WITH LOCK
G	GIVING	Q	QUOTE		
GT	GO TO			Z	ZERO

The user has the option of using either the SPLICE abbreviations or the nonabbreviated COBOL form. SPLICE line 28 utilizes abbreviations, while line 32 does not.

Data Division Abbreviations

Although the SPLICE programmer can create much of the data division directly in the procedure division, as will be explained in subsequent sections, data division abbreviations are provided as well (Table A.2). Consider SPLICE lines 8 and 9, which expand to COBOL statements 9300 and 9400:

```
SPLICE:
  05  F          P X.
  05  HDG-NAME   P X(12) V 'STUDENT NAME'.

COBOL:
  05  FILLER     PICTURE X.
  05  HDG-NAME   PICTURE X(12) VALUE 'STUDENT NAME'.
```

Table A.2 Splice Data Division Abbreviations

BZ	BLANK WHEN ZERO	LV	LOW-VALUES
C	COMPUTATIONAL	OC	OCCURS
C1	COMPUTATIONAL-1	P	PICTURE
C2	COMPUTATIONAL-2	Q	QUOTES
C3	COMPUTATIONAL-3	R	REDEFINES
DP	DEPENDING ON	S	SPACES
DS	DISPLAY	TM	TIMES
F	FILLER	V	VALUE
HV	HIGH-VALUES	Z	ZEROS
JR	JUSTIFIED RIGHT		

User-Defined Abbreviations

In theory, COBOL allows data names up to 30 characters. In practice, most programmers find it cumbersome to code such extended data names and revert to more cryptic abbreviations, thus defeating the intent of self-documentation. To fully document programs and to simultaneously accommodate the programmer, SPLICE provides user-defined abbreviations in addition to its predefined procedure and data division abbreviations. The programmer codes an "S" (for substitute) in column 7, leaves at least one space, codes his abbreviation, again leaves at least one space, and finally codes the extended COBOL data name. This sequence may go anywhere in the procedure division, and expansion occurs for all instances in both the procedure and data divisions.

In our example we have grouped the substitute statements at the end of the procedure division. Consider SPLICE line 78:

```
SPLICE:
  S  PRTR    PRINT-LINE
```

Everytime "PRTR" is encountered, in either the procedure or data division, it is expanded to "PRINT-LINE". This happens in several places, e.g., SPLICE line 64 and COBOL line 16400:

```
SPLICE:
  MS  PRTR.

COBOL:
  MOVE SPACES TO PRINT-LINE.
```

User-defined abbreviations are applicable to paragraph and file names as well; SPLICE line 79 reads

```
SPLICE:
S    R-A-C    READ-A-CARD
```

The character string "R-A-C" in the SPLICE listing is expanded to "READ-A-CARD" everywhere in the COBOL program, as in COBOL lines 12200 and 16100.

One-Line Identification Division

A single SPLICE statement generates the entire COBOL identification division. One need specify only the program name beginning in column 12 (TUITION) and the author's name beginning in column 24 (THE BURSAR). Remarks are optional and appear in the COBOL program exactly as they do in the SPLICE program.

The resulting COBOL identification division is shown below, as are the SPLICE statements which generated it:

```
SPLICE:
        TUITION    THE BURSAR.

COBOL:
    IDENTIFICATION DIVISION.
    PROGRAM-ID.
        TUITION.
    AUTHOR.
        THE BURSAR.
    INSTALLATION.
        CITY UNIVERSITY OF NEW YORK.
    DATE-WRITTEN.
        SEPTEMBER, 1975.
```

Creating COBOL FD's

The SPLICE select statement is used to create both the COBOL select statement and the corresponding COBOL FD. The format of the SPLICE statement is quite rigid, and the user must adhere exactly. In column 7, enter a C, X, P, T, or D depending on whether the file is card, punch, printer, tape, or disk, respectively. Code "SEL" in columns 8–10. The remainder of the statement is coded in the following order beginning in column 12: file-name, system-name, FD abbreviations, and record name(s).

Consider SPLICE statement 5, which generates COBOL statements 2500 and 2600 and statements 4700–5100:

```
SPLICE:
PSEL PRINT-FILE UR-1403-S-SYSOUT RF LO RE 133 PRTR.

COBOL:
    SELECT PRINT-FILE
        ASSIGN TO UR-1403-S-SYSOUT.

FD    PRINT-FILE
    RECORDING MODE IS F
    LABEL RECORDS ARE OMITTED
    RECORD CONTAINS 133 CHARACTERS
    DATA RECORD IS PRINT-LINE.
```

FD abbreviations are provided in Table A.3. Observe that PRTR is coded in the SPLICE select statement and PRINT-LINE is in the generated COBOL FD. (Remember SPLICE line 78 and user-defined abbreviations.)

Table A.3 FD Abbreviations

RE	nn		RECORD CONTAINS nn CHARACTERS
RE2	nn	nn	RECORD CONTAINS nn TO nn CHARACTERS
BC	nn		BLOCK CONTAINS nn CHARACTERS
BC2	nn	nn	BLOCK CONTAINS nn TO nn CHARACTERS
BR	nn		BLOCK CONTAINS nn RECORDS
BR2	nn	nn	BLOCK CONTAINS nn TO nn RECORDS
LO			LABEL RECORDS ARE OMITTED
LS			LABEL RECORDS ARE STANDARD
RF			RECORDING MODE IS F
RS			RECORDING MODE IS S
RU			RECORDING MODE IS U
RV			RECORDING MODE IS V

Examine SPLICE line 4, which established the FD for CARD-FILE and COBOL statements 3100–3500. There were no FD abbreviations coded, yet appropriate entries were generated in the COBOL FD. Default values are established in Table A.4 and are a function of the letter coded in column 7:

SPLICE:
CSEL CARD-FILE UR-2540R-S-SYSIN.

COBOL:
        SELECT CARD-FILE
            ASSIGN TO UR-2540R-S-SYSIN.

    FD CARD-FILE
        RECORDING MODE IS F
        LABEL RECORDS ARE OMITTED
        RECORD CONTAINS 80 CHARACTERS
        DATA RECORD IS CARD.

Table A.4 Default Values Generated for FD Entries

Code in Column 7 of SEL Statement	Default FD Values (may be overridden)				Default Record Name used in relative addressing (may be overridden)
	Record Contains	Block Contains	Recording Mode	Label Records	
C	RE 80	BR 1	RF	LO	CARD
X	RE 80	BR 1	RF	LO	PCRD
P	RE 133	BR 1	RF	LO	PRTR
T	RE 80	BR 1	RF	LS	TAPP*
D	RE 80	BR 1	RF	LS	DISK

*Note: DOS default is TPnn where nn stems from the SYS number.

Creating 77-Level Entries

77-Level entries may be created dynamically in the procedure division. This is accomplished by following the data name immediately with ( )'s and indicating the length and type of data name intended according to Table A.5. If no specific type is given, the data are assumed to be alphanumeric. All numeric entries are initialized to zero and all nonnumeric entries to spaces. As an example, consider SPLICE statement 35, which generates COBOL statement 12500, and also statements 7400–7500:

SPLICE:

    CP TUITION(4)U = 80 * CREDITS.

COBOL:

    77 TUITION   PICTURE IS 9(4)
                      VALUE IS ZEROS.

    COMPUTE TUITION = 80 * CREDITS.

Realize it is absolutely essential that the ( ) immediately follow the data name and that there is no confusion between a SPLICE-defined 77-level entry and a COBOL subscripted variable, as the latter requires a space between the data name and left parenthesis.

Table A.5 Usage Abbreviations for 77-Level Entries and
                     Relative Addressing

A	Alphabetic
B	Computational
C	Computational-3 (unsigned)
P	Computational-3 (signed)
R	Report (relative addressing only—permits edit picture formats)
S	Display numeric (signed)
U	Display numeric (unsigned)

Note: Default is alphanumeric.

**Relative Addressing
and the Equate Feature**

Relative addressing is one of the more powerful features of SPLICE and the one which best distinguishes it from other precompilers. By employing this technique, the user can create the greater part of the data division directly in the procedure division, and since the data division tends to be the most cumbersome, relative addressing eliminates much of the drudgery in COBOL coding. Relative addressing is a technique which generates COBOL record descriptions by referencing only the relevant positions in the record. The equate and substitute features can be used in conjunction with relative addressing to provide more meaningful data names.

Consider the record description for CARD. Recall that the FD for CARD-FILE was generated by the SPLICE select statement and that CARD was specified to contain 80 characters. The SPLICE precompiler scans the procedure division for all occurrences of the data name CARD and finds

IF CARD-32-32-A E UNION-MEMBER...	(statement 36)
M CARD-1-20 E STUDENT-NAME...	(statement 53)
M CARD-21-29-U T PRTR...	(statement 54)
M CARD-30-31-U E CREDITS...	(statement 55)
M CARD-33-36-U E SCH...	(statement 59)

Since CARD has been specified to contain 80 characters, it is now possible to define the complete record description by inserting appropriate FILLER entries. The programmer also has the option of the equate feature in which a different name is assigned to particular positions in the record. Thus in statement 53, card positions 1–20 are equated to STUDENT-NAME. (Follow the relative addressing entry with E and the equated name.) Subsequent references may be either the equated name or the particular positions mentioned; either or both may be expanded via the substitute feature. Thus statement 59 equates positions 33–36 to SCH, which in turn is expanded to SCHOLARSHIP via the substitute command in line 84. The type of picture is determined according to Table A.5 in a manner similar to that for 77-level

entries. The COBOL record description for CARD in statements 3700–4500 is
reproduced below:

```
01  CARD.
    05  CARD-R     PICTURE IS X(80).
    05  FILLER REDEFINES CARD-R.
        10  STUDENT-NAME      PICTURE IS X(20).
        10  SOC-SEC-NUM       PICTURE IS 9(9).
        10  CREDITS           PICTURE IS 9(2).
        10  UNION-MEMBER      PICTURE IS A(1).
        10  SCHOLARSHIP       PICTURE IS 9(4).
        10  FILLER            PICTURE IS X(44).
```

Usage is indicated according to Table A.5 in the same way as for 77-level entries.

An additional benefit of SPLICE is its support of structured programming. *Specifically SPLICE will realign COBOL programs so that the ELSE appears under the relevant IF according to compiler rather than programmer interpretation. Further, nested IF's are successively indented by four columns, and all detail lines are indented four columns from the appropriate IF or ELSE.* Benefits are:

Support of Structured Programming

1. Documentation of new or existing programs where no programmer alignment was attempted.
2. Detection of logic errors where indentation was incorrectly applied.

Two examples follow.

Input to SPLICE

Example 1: No Attempted Programmer Alignment

```
IF NOT FULL-SIZE AND NOT COMPACT AND NOT INTERMEDIATE
    DISPLAY ' ERROR IN DATA ' NAME-FIELD
    MOVE 'YES' TO ERROR-SWITCH ELSE
IF MILES-DRIVEN OF WS-CARD-IN IS NOT POSITIVE
    DISPLAY ' ERROR IN DATA ' NAME-FIELD
    MOVE 'YES' TO ERROR-SWITCH ELSE
IF DAYS-RENTED OF WS-CARD-IN IS NOT POSITIVE
    DISPLAY ' ERROR IN DATA ' NAME-FIELD
    MOVE 'YES' TO ERROR-SWITCH.
```

Output from SPLICE

```
IF NOT FULL-SIZE AND NOT COMPACT AND NOT INTERMEDIATE
    DISPLAY ' ERROR IN DATA ' NAME-FIELD
    MOVE 'YES' TO ERROR-SWITCH
ELSE
    IF MILES-DRIVEN OF WS-CARD-IN IS NOT POSITIVE
        DISPLAY ' ERROR IN DATA ' NAME-FIELD
        MOVE 'YES' TO ERROR-SWITCH
    ELSE
        IF DAYS-RENTED OF WS-CARD-IN IS NOT POSITIVE
            DISPLAY ' ERROR IN DATA ' NAME-FIELD
            MOVE 'YES' TO ERROR-SWITCH.
```

```
IF NOT COMPANY-EXECUTIVE,
    IF COMPACT
        MOVE .08 TO WS-MILEAGE-RATE
        MOVE 7.00 TO WS-DAILY-RATE
    ELSE IF INTERMEDIATE
            MOVE .10 TO WS-MILEAGE-RATE
            MOVE 8.00 TO WS-DAILY-RATE
        ELSE IF FULL-SIZE
                MOVE .12 TO WS-MILEAGE-RATE
                MOVE 10.00 TO WS-DAILY-RATE
ELSE
    DISPLAY 'CO EXEC' NAME-FIELD
    MOVE ZERO TO WS-MILEAGE-RATE
    MOVE ZERO TO WS-DAILY-RATE.
```

Output from SPLICE

```
IF NOT COMPANY-EXECUTIVE,
    IF COMPACT
        MOVE .08 TO WS-MILEAGE-RATE
        MOVE 7.00 TO WS-DAILY-RATE
    ELSE
        IF INTERMEDIATE
            MOVE .10 TO WS-MILEAGE-RATE
            MOVE 8.00 TO WS-DAILY-RATE
        ELSE
            IF FULL-SIZE
                MOVE .12 TO WS-MILEAGE-RATE
                MOVE 10.00 TO WS-DAILY-RATE
            ELSE
                DISPLAY 'CO EXEC' NAME-FIELD
                MOVE ZERO TO WS-MILEAGE-RATE
                MOVE ZERO TO WS-DAILY-RATE.
```

Summary

One of the reasons for the wide use of COBOL is its easy legibility and inherent documentation. This capability is especially important in industry since individuals are frequently asked to maintain programs they did not write, and documentation in these instances is crucial. However, the legibility of a COBOL program is regarded as both an advantage and disadvantage. It is a big plus to the programmer called on to modify someone else's program but a disadvantage to a person who codes the initial program and too often complains of writer's cramp, particularly the individual who is used to FORTRAN or PL/I. The notion of a COBOL shorthand or precompiler is an attempt to capture the best of both worlds. Essentially a programmer codes in the shorthand language which in turn expands to a COBOL program.

Illustration of the precompiler concept was accomplished through specific examples from SPLICE, a product developed by the authors. *SPLICE is available to educational institutions. Additional information, including reference cards and User's Manuals, may be obtained from the authors as described in the beginning of this appendix.* SPLICE is currently running on IBM 360/370 (both OS and DOS), Spectra 70, and Univac Series 90.

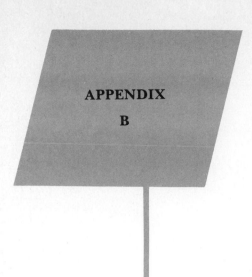

COBOL Reserved Words

ACCEPT	ASCENDING
ACCESS	ASSIGN
ACTUAL	AT
ADD	AUTHOR
ADDRESS	
ADVANCING	* BASIS
AFTER	BEFORE
ALL	BEGINNING
ALPHABETIC	BLANK
ALPHANUMERIC	BLOCK
ALPHANUMERIC-EDITED	BY
ALTER	
ALTERNATE	* CALL
AND	* CANCEL
* APPLY	* CBL
ARE	* CD
AREA	CF
AREAS	CH
	* CHANGED

Note: *'s denote entries restricted to IBM compilers.

* CHARACTER
CHARACTERS
CLOCK-UNITS
CLOSE
COBOL
CODE
COLUMN
* COM-REG
COMMA
COMP
* COMP-1
* COMP-2
* COMP-3
* COMP-4
COMPUTATIONAL
* COMPUTATIONAL-1
* COMPUTATIONAL-2
* COMPUTATIONAL-3
* COMPUTATIONAL-4
COMPUTE
CONFIGURATION
* CONSOLE
CONSTANT
CONTAINS
CONTROL
CONTROLS
COPY
* CORE-INDEX
CORR
CORRESPONDING
* COUNT
* CSP
CURRENCY
* CURRENT-DATE
* CYL-INDEX
* CYL-OVERFLOW
* C01
* C02
* C03
* C04
* C05
* C06
* C07
* C08
* C09
* C10
* C11
* C12

DATA
* DATE
DATE-COMPILED
DATE-WRITTEN
* DAY
DE
* DEBUG

DEBUG-CONTENTS
DEBUG-ITEM
DEBUG-SUB-1
DEBUG-SUB-2
DEBUG-SUB-3
DEBUG-NAME
DEBUGGING
DECIMAL-POINT
DECLARATIVES
* DELETE
* DELIMITED
* DELIMITER
DEPENDING
* DEPTH
DESCENDING
* DESTINATION
DETAIL
DISABLE
* DISP
DISPLAY
DISPLAY-n
* DISPLAY-ST
DIVIDE
DIVISION
DOWN

* EJECT
ELSE
* EMI
ENABLE
END
END-OF-PAGE
* ENDING
ENTER
* ENTRY
ENVIRONMENT
* EOP
EQUAL
EQUALS
ERROR
* ESI
* ETI
EVERY
EXAMINE
EXCEEDS
* EXHIBIT
EXIT
* EXTENDED-SEARCH

FD
FILE
FILE-CONTROL
FILE-LIMIT
FILE-LIMITS
FILLER
FINAL
FIRST

FOOTING
FOR
FROM

GENERATE
GIVING
GO
* GOBACK
GREATER
GROUP

HEADING
HIGH-VALUE
HIGH-VALUES
HOLD

I-O
I-O-CONTROL
* ID
IDENTIFICATION
IF
IN
INDEX
INDEX-N
INDEXED
INDICATE
INITIAL
INITIATE
INPUT
INPUT-OUTPUT
* INSERT
INSPECT
INSTALLATION
INTO
INVALID
IS

JUST
JUSTIFIED

KEY
KEYS

LABEL
* LABEL-RETURN
LAST
LEADING
* LEAVE
LEFT
* LENGTH
LESS
LIBRARY
LIMIT
LIMITS
LINAGE
LINAGE-COUNTER
LINE
LINE-COUNTER

LINES
* LINKAGE
LOCK
LOW-VALUE
LOW-VALUES
LOWER-BOUND
LOWER-BOUNDS

* MASTER-INDEX
MEMORY
MERGE
* MESSAGE
MODE
MODULES
* MORE-LABELS
MOVE
MULTIPLE
MULTIPLY

* NAMED
NEGATIVE
NEXT
NO
* NOMINAL
NOT
NOTE
* NSTD-REELS
NUMBER
NUMERIC
* NUMERIC-EDITED

OBJECT-COMPUTER
OBJECT-PROGRAM
OCCURS
OF
OFF
* OH
OMITTED
ON
OPEN
OPTIONAL
OR
* OTHERWISE
OUTPUT
OV
* OVERFLOW

PAGE
PAGE-COUNTER
PERFORM
PF
PH
PIC
PICTURE
PLUS
* POINTER
POSITION
* POSITIONING

POSITIVE
PREPARED
* PRINT-SWITCH
PRINTING
PRIORITY
PROCEDURE
PROCEDURES
PROCEED
PROCESS
PROCESSING
* PROGRAM
PROGRAM-ID

* QUEUE
QUOTE
QUOTES

RANDOM
RANGE
RD
READ
* READY
* RECEIVE
RECORD
* RECORD-OVERFLOW
* RECORDING
RECORDS
REDEFINES
REEL
REFERENCES
RELEASE
* RELOAD
REMAINDER
REMARKS
RENAMES
* REORG-CRITERIA
REPLACING
REPORT
REPORTING
REPORTS
* REREAD
RERUN
RESERVE
RESET
RETURN
* RETURN-CODE
REVERSED
REWIND
* REWRITE
RF
RH
RIGHT
ROUNDED
RUN

SA
SAME

SD
SEARCH
SECTION
SECURITY
SEEK
* SEGMENT
SEGMENT-LIMIT
SELECT
SELECTED
* SEND
SENTENCE
* SEPARATE
SEQUENTIAL
* SERVICE
SET
SIGN
SIZE
* SKIP1
* SKIP2
* SKIP3
SORT
* SORT-CORE-SIZE
* SORT-FILE-SIZE
SORT-MERGE
* SORT-MESSAGE
* SORT-MODE-SIZE
* SORT-RETURN
SOURCE
SOURCE-COMPUTER
SPACE
SPACES
SPECIAL-NAMES
STANDARD
* START
STATUS
STOP
* STRING
* SUB-QUEUE-1
* SUB-QUEUE-2
* SUB-QUEUE-3
SUBTRACT
SUM
SUPERVISOR
* SUPPRESS
SUSPEND
* SYMBOLIC
SYNC
SYNCHRONIZED
* SYSIN
* SYSIPT
* SYSLST
* SYSOUT
* SYSPCH
* SYSPUNCH
* S01
* S02

* TABLE
TALLY
TALLYING
TAPE
TERMINAL
TERMINATE
* TEXT
THAN
* THEN
THROUGH
THRU
* TIME
* TIME-OF-DAY
TIMES
TO
* TOTALED
* TOTALING
* TRACE
* TRACK
* TRACK-AREA
* TRACK-LIMIT
* TRACKS
* TRAILING
* TRANSFORM
TYPE

UNEQUAL
UNIT
* UNSTRING
UNTIL

UP
UPON
UPPER-BOUND
UPPER-BOUNDS
* UPSI-0
* UPSI-1
* UPSI-2
* UPSI-3
* UPSI-4
* UPSI-5
* UPSI-6
* UPSI-7
USAGE
USE
USING

VALUE
VALUES
VARYING

WHEN
WITH
WORDS
WORKING-STORAGE
WRITE
* WRITE-ONLY
* WRITE-VERIFY

ZERO
ZEROES
ZEROS

IBM
Full American Standard
COBOL Format Summary

IDENTIFICATION DIVISION — BASIC FORMATS

{ IDENTIFICATION DIVISION. }
{ ID DIVISION. }

PROGRAM-ID. *program-name.*

AUTHOR. [*comment-entry*] . . .

INSTALLATION. [*comment-entry*] . . .

DATE-WRITTEN. [*comment-entry*] . . .

DATE-COMPILED. [*comment-entry*] . . .

SECURITY. [*comment-entry*] . . .

REMARKS. [*comment-entry*] . . .

ENVIRONMENT DIVISION — BASIC FORMATS

ENVIRONMENT DIVISION.

CONFIGURATION SECTION.

SOURCE-COMPUTER. *computer-name.*

OBJECT-COMPUTER. *computer-name* [MEMORY SIZE *integer* { WORDS / CHARACTERS / MODULES }]

    [SEGMENT-LIMIT IS *priority-number*].

SPECIAL-NAMES. [*function-name* IS *mnemonic-name*] . . .

    [CURRENCY SIGN IS *literal*]

    [DECIMAL-POINT IS COMMA].

INPUT-OUTPUT SECTION.

FILE-CONTROL.

    {SELECT [OPTIONAL] *file name*

    ASSIGN TO [*integer-1*] *system-name-1* [*system-name-2*] . . .

        [FOR MULTIPLE { REEL / UNIT }]

    RESERVE { NO / *integer-1* } ALTERNATE [AREA / AREAS]

    { FILE-LIMIT IS / FILE-LIMITS ARE } { *data-name-1* / *literal-1* } THRU { *data-name-2* / *literal-2* }

    [{ *data-name-3* / *literal-3* } THRU { *data-name-4* / *literal-4* }] . . .

    ACCESS MODE IS { SEQUENTIAL / RANDOM }

    PROCESSING MODE IS SEQUENTIAL

    ACTUAL KEY IS *data-name*

    NOMINAL KEY IS *data-name*

    RECORD KEY IS *data-name*

    TRACK-AREA IS { *data-name* / *integer* } CHARACTERS

    TRACK-LIMIT IS *integer* [TRACK / TRACKS] .} . . .

I-O-CONTROL.

    RERUN ON *system-name* EVERY [*integer* RECORDS / [END OF] { REEL / UNIT }] OF *file-name*

    SAME [RECORD / SORT] AREA FOR *file-name-1* {*file-name-2*} . . .

    MULTIPLE FILE TAPE CONTAINS *file-name-1* [POSITION *integer-1*]

        [*file-name-2* [POSITION *integer-2*]] . . .

    APPLY WRITE-ONLY ON *file-name-1* [*file-name-2*] . . .

    APPLY CORE-INDEX ON *file-name-1* [*file-name-2*] . . .

    APPLY RECORD-OVERFLOW ON *file-name-1* [*file-name-2*] . . .

    APPLY REORG-CRITERIA TO *data-name* ON *file-name* . . . .

NOTE: Format 2 of the RERUN Clause (for Sort Files) is included with Formats for the SORT feature.

DATA DIVISION — BASIC FORMATS

DATA DIVISION.

FILE SECTION.

FD *file-name*

    BLOCK CONTAINS [*integer-1* TO] *integer-2* { CHARACTERS / RECORDS }

    RECORD CONTAINS [*integer-1* TO] *integer-2* CHARACTERS

    RECORDING MODE IS *mode*

    LABEL { RECORD IS / RECORDS ARE } { OMITTED / STANDARD / *data-name-1* [*data-name-2*] . . . [TOTALING AREA IS *data-name-3* TOTALED AREA IS *data-name-4*] }

    VALUE OF *data-name-1* IS { *literal-1* / *data-name-2* } [*data-name-3* IS { *literal-2* / *data-name-4* }] . . .

    DATA { RECORD IS / RECORDS ARE } *data-name-1* [*data-name-2*] . . . .

NOTE: Format for the REPORT Clause is included with Formats for the REPORT WRITER feature.

01-49 { *data-name-1* / FILLER }

    REDEFINES *data-name-2*

    BLANK WHEN ZERO

    { JUSTIFIED / JUST } RIGHT

    { PICTURE / PIC } IS *character string*

    [SIGN IS] { LEADING / TRAILING } [SEPARATE CHARACTER] (Version 3 & 4)

    { SYNCHRONIZED / SYNC } [LEFT / RIGHT]

    [USAGE IS] { INDEX / DISPLAY / COMPUTATIONAL / COMP / COMPUTATIONAL-1 / COMP-1 / COMPUTATIONAL-2 / COMP-2 / COMPUTATIONAL-3 / COMP-3 / COMPUTATIONAL-4 / COMP-4 / DISPLAY-ST } (Version 3 & 4)

88 *condition-name* { VALUE IS / VALUES ARE } *literal-1* [THRU *literal-2*]

    [*literal-3* [THRU *literal-4*]] . . .

66 *data-name-1* RENAMES *data-name-2* [THRU *data-name-3*].

NOTE: Formats for the OCCURS Clause are included with Formats for the TABLE HANDLING feature.

WORKING-STORAGE SECTION.

77 *data-name-1*

01-49 { *data-name-1* / FILLER }

    REDEFINES *data-name-2*

    BLANK WHEN ZERO

    { JUSTIFIED / JUST } RIGHT

    { PICTURE / PIC } IS *character string*

    [SIGN IS] { LEADING / TRAILING } [SEPARATE CHARACTER] (Version 3 & 4)

    { SYNCHRONIZED / SYNC } [LEFT / RIGHT]

Note: Shaded entries denote IBM extensions

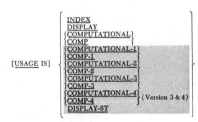

$$[\underline{\text{USAGE}} \text{ IS}] \left\{ \begin{array}{l} \underline{\text{INDEX}} \\ \underline{\text{DISPLAY}} \\ \underline{\text{COMPUTATIONAL}} \\ \underline{\text{COMP}} \\ \underline{\text{COMPUTATIONAL-1}} \\ \underline{\text{COMP-1}} \\ \underline{\text{COMPUTATIONAL-2}} \\ \underline{\text{COMP-2}} \\ \underline{\text{COMPUTATIONAL-3}} \\ \underline{\text{COMP-3}} \\ \underline{\text{COMPUTATIONAL-4}} \\ \underline{\text{COMP-4}} \\ \underline{\text{DISPLAY-ST}} \end{array} \right\} \text{(Version 3 \& 4)}$$

$\underline{\text{VALUE}}$ IS literal

88 condition-name $\left\{ \begin{array}{l} \underline{\text{VALUE}} \text{ IS} \\ \underline{\text{VALUES}} \text{ ARE} \end{array} \right\}$ literal-1 [$\underline{\text{THRU}}$ literal-2]

                [literal-3 [$\underline{\text{THRU}}$ literal-4]] . . .

66 data-name-1 $\underline{\text{RENAMES}}$ data-name-2 [$\underline{\text{THRU}}$ data-name-3].

NOTE: Formats for the OCCURS Clause are included with Formats for the TABLE HANDLING feature.

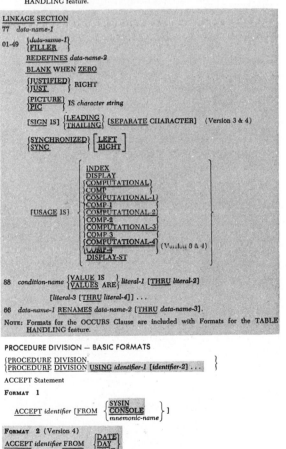

LINKAGE SECTION

77 data-name-1

01-49 $\left\{ \begin{array}{l} \text{data-name-1} \\ \underline{\text{FILLER}} \end{array} \right\}$

  $\underline{\text{REDEFINES}}$ data-name-2

  $\underline{\text{BLANK}}$ WHEN $\underline{\text{ZERO}}$

  $\left\{ \begin{array}{l} \underline{\text{JUSTIFIED}} \\ \underline{\text{JUST}} \end{array} \right\}$ RIGHT

  $\left\{ \begin{array}{l} \underline{\text{PICTURE}} \\ \underline{\text{PIC}} \end{array} \right\}$ IS character string

  [$\underline{\text{SIGN}}$ IS] $\left\{ \begin{array}{l} \underline{\text{LEADING}} \\ \underline{\text{TRAILING}} \end{array} \right\}$ [$\underline{\text{SEPARATE}}$ CHARACTER] (Version 3 & 4)

  $\left\{ \begin{array}{l} \underline{\text{SYNCHRONIZED}} \\ \underline{\text{SYNC}} \end{array} \right\} \left\{ \begin{array}{l} \underline{\text{LEFT}} \\ \underline{\text{RIGHT}} \end{array} \right\}$

$$[\underline{\text{USAGE}} \text{ IS}] \left\{ \begin{array}{l} \underline{\text{INDEX}} \\ \underline{\text{DISPLAY}} \\ \underline{\text{COMPUTATIONAL}} \\ \underline{\text{COMP}} \\ \underline{\text{COMPUTATIONAL-1}} \\ \underline{\text{COMP-1}} \\ \underline{\text{COMPUTATIONAL-2}} \\ \underline{\text{COMP-2}} \\ \underline{\text{COMPUTATIONAL-3}} \\ \underline{\text{COMP-3}} \\ \underline{\text{COMPUTATIONAL-4}} \\ \underline{\text{COMP-4}} \\ \underline{\text{DISPLAY-ST}} \end{array} \right\} \text{(Version 3 \& 4)}$$

88 condition-name $\left\{ \begin{array}{l} \underline{\text{VALUE}} \text{ IS} \\ \underline{\text{VALUES}} \text{ ARE} \end{array} \right\}$ literal-1 [$\underline{\text{THRU}}$ literal-2]

                [literal-3 [$\underline{\text{THRU}}$ literal-4]] . . .

66 data-name-1 $\underline{\text{RENAMES}}$ data-name-2 [$\underline{\text{THRU}}$ data-name-3].

NOTE: Formats for the OCCURS Clause are included with Formats for the TABLE HANDLING feature.

PROCEDURE DIVISION — BASIC FORMATS

$\left\{ \begin{array}{l} \underline{\text{PROCEDURE}} \ \underline{\text{DIVISION}}. \\ \underline{\text{PROCEDURE}} \ \underline{\text{DIVISION}} \ \underline{\text{USING}} \text{ identifier-1 [identifier-2]} . . . \end{array} \right\}$

ACCEPT Statement

FORMAT 1

$\underline{\text{ACCEPT}}$ identifier [$\underline{\text{FROM}}$ $\left\{ \begin{array}{l} \underline{\text{SYSIN}} \\ \underline{\text{CONSOLE}} \\ \text{mnemonic-name} \end{array} \right\}$]

FORMAT 2 (Version 4)

$\underline{\text{ACCEPT}}$ identifier $\underline{\text{FROM}}$ $\left\{ \begin{array}{l} \underline{\text{DATE}} \\ \underline{\text{DAY}} \\ \underline{\text{TIME}} \end{array} \right\}$

ADD Statement

FORMAT 1

$\underline{\text{ADD}}$ $\left\{ \begin{array}{l} \text{identifier-1} \\ \text{literal-1} \end{array} \right\}$ $\left[\begin{array}{l} \text{identifier-2} \\ \text{literal-2} \end{array} \right]$ . . . $\underline{\text{TO}}$ identifier-m [$\underline{\text{ROUNDED}}$]

      [identifier-n [$\underline{\text{ROUNDED}}$]] . . . [ON $\underline{\text{SIZE}}$ $\underline{\text{ERROR}}$ imperative-statement]

FORMAT 2

$\underline{\text{ADD}}$ $\left\{ \begin{array}{l} \text{identifier-1} \\ \text{literal-1} \end{array} \right\}$ $\left\{ \begin{array}{l} \text{identifier-2} \\ \text{literal-2} \end{array} \right\}$ $\left[\begin{array}{l} \text{identifier-3} \\ \text{literal-3} \end{array} \right]$ . . . $\underline{\text{GIVING}}$

      identifier-m [$\underline{\text{ROUNDED}}$] [ON $\underline{\text{SIZE}}$ $\underline{\text{ERROR}}$ imperative-statement]

FORMAT 3

$\underline{\text{ADD}}$ $\left\{ \begin{array}{l} \underline{\text{CORRESPONDING}} \\ \underline{\text{CORR}} \end{array} \right\}$ identifier-1 $\underline{\text{TO}}$ identifier-2 [$\underline{\text{ROUNDED}}$]

      [ON $\underline{\text{SIZE}}$ $\underline{\text{ERROR}}$ imperative-statement]

ALTER Statement

$\underline{\text{ALTER}}$ procedure-name-1 $\underline{\text{TO}}$ [$\underline{\text{PROCEED}}$ $\underline{\text{TO}}$] procedure-name-2

        [procedure-name-3 $\underline{\text{TO}}$ [$\underline{\text{PROCEED}}$ $\underline{\text{TO}}$] procedure-name-4] . . .

CALL Statement

FORMAT 1

$\underline{\text{CALL}}$ literal-1 [$\underline{\text{USING}}$ identifier-1 [identifier-2] . . .]

FORMAT 2 (Version 4)

$\underline{\text{CALL}}$ identifier-1 [$\underline{\text{USING}}$ identifier-2 [identifier-3] . . .]

CANCEL Statement (Version 4)

$\underline{\text{CANCEL}}$ $\left\{ \begin{array}{l} \text{literal-1} \\ \text{identifier-1} \end{array} \right\}$ $\left[\begin{array}{l} \text{literal-2} \\ \text{identifier-2} \end{array} \right]$ . . .

CLOSE Statement

FORMAT 1

$\underline{\text{CLOSE}}$ file-name-1 $\left[\begin{array}{l} \underline{\text{REEL}} \\ \underline{\text{UNIT}} \end{array} \right]$ [WITH $\left\{ \begin{array}{l} \underline{\text{NO}} \ \underline{\text{REWIND}} \\ \underline{\text{LOCK}} \end{array} \right\}$]

    [file-name-2 $\left[\begin{array}{l} \underline{\text{REEL}} \\ \underline{\text{UNIT}} \end{array} \right]$ [WITH $\left\{ \begin{array}{l} \underline{\text{NO}} \ \underline{\text{REWIND}} \\ \underline{\text{LOCK}} \end{array} \right\}$]] . . .

FORMAT 2

$\underline{\text{CLOSE}}$ file-name-1 [WITH $\left\{ \begin{array}{l} \underline{\text{NO}} \ \underline{\text{REWIND}} \\ \underline{\text{LOCK}} \\ \underline{\text{DISP}} \end{array} \right\}$]

    [file-name-2 [WITH $\left\{ \begin{array}{l} \underline{\text{NO}} \ \underline{\text{REWIND}} \\ \underline{\text{LOCK}} \\ \underline{\text{DISP}} \end{array} \right\}$]] . . .

FORMAT 3

$\underline{\text{CLOSE}}$ file-name-1 $\left\{ \begin{array}{l} \underline{\text{REEL}} \\ \underline{\text{UNIT}} \end{array} \right\}$ [WITH $\left\{ \begin{array}{l} \underline{\text{NO}} \ \underline{\text{REWIND}} \\ \underline{\text{LOCK}} \\ \underline{\text{POSITIONING}} \end{array} \right\}$]

    [file-name-2 $\left\{ \begin{array}{l} \underline{\text{REEL}} \\ \underline{\text{UNIT}} \end{array} \right\}$ [WITH $\left\{ \begin{array}{l} \underline{\text{NO}} \ \underline{\text{REWIND}} \\ \underline{\text{LOCK}} \\ \underline{\text{POSITIONING}} \end{array} \right\}$]] . . .

COMPUTE Statement

COMPUTE identifier-1 [ROUNDED] = $\left\{\begin{array}{l} arithmetic\text{-}expression \\ identifier\text{-}2 \\ literal\text{-}1 \end{array}\right\}$

    [ON SIZE ERROR imperative-statement]

DECLARATIVE Section

PROCEDURE DIVISION.

DECLARATIVES.

{section-name SECTION. USE sentence.

{paragraph-name. {sentence} ...} ... } ...

END DECLARATIVES.

DISPLAY Statement

DISPLAY $\left\{\begin{array}{l} identifier\text{-}1 \\ literal\text{-}1 \end{array}\right\}$ $\left[\begin{array}{l} identifier\text{-}2 \\ literal\text{-}2 \end{array}\right]$ ... [UPON $\left\{\begin{array}{l} CONSOLE \\ SYSPUNCH \\ SYSOUT \\ mnemonic\text{-}name \end{array}\right\}$]

DIVIDE Statement

FORMAT 1

DIVIDE $\left\{\begin{array}{l} identifier\text{-}1 \\ literal\text{-}1 \end{array}\right\}$ INTO identifier-2 [ROUNDED]

    [ON SIZE ERROR imperative-statement]

FORMAT 2

DIVIDE $\left\{\begin{array}{l} identifier\text{-}1 \\ literal\text{-}1 \end{array}\right\}$ $\left\{\begin{array}{l} INTO \\ BY \end{array}\right\}$ $\left\{\begin{array}{l} identifier\text{-}2 \\ literal\text{-}2 \end{array}\right\}$ GIVING identifier-3

    [ROUNDED] [REMAINDER identifier-4] [ON SIZE ERROR imperative-statement]

ENTER Statement

ENTER language-name [routine-name]

ENTRY Statement

ENTRY literal-1 [USING identifier-1 [identifier-2] ...]

EXAMINE Statement

FORMAT 1

EXAMINE identifier TALLYING $\left\{\begin{array}{l} UNTIL\ FIRST \\ ALL \\ LEADING \end{array}\right\}$ literal-1

    [REPLACING BY literal-2]

FORMAT 2

EXAMINE identifier REPLACING $\left\{\begin{array}{l} ALL \\ LEADING \\ FIRST \\ UNTIL\ FIRST \end{array}\right\}$ literal-1 BY literal-2

EXIT Statement

paragraph-name. EXIT [PROGRAM]

GOBACK Statement

GOBACK.

GO TO Statement

FORMAT 1

GO TO procedure-name-1

FORMAT 2

GO TO procedure-name-1 [procedure-name-2] ... DEPENDING ON identifier

FORMAT 3

GO TO.

IF Statement

IF condition THEN $\left\{\begin{array}{l} statement\text{-}1 \\ NEXT\ SENTENCE \end{array}\right\}$ $\left\{\begin{array}{l} ELSE \\ OTHERWISE \end{array}\right\}$ $\left\{\begin{array}{l} statement\text{-}2 \\ NEXT\ SENTENCE \end{array}\right\}$

MOVE Statement

FORMAT 1

MOVE $\left\{\begin{array}{l} identifier\text{-}1 \\ literal\text{-}1 \end{array}\right\}$ TO identifier-2 [identifier-3] ...

FORMAT 2

MOVE $\left\{\begin{array}{l} CORRESPONDING \\ CORR \end{array}\right\}$ identifier-1 TO identifier-2

MULTIPLY Statement

FORMAT 1

MULTIPLY $\left\{\begin{array}{l} identifier\text{-}1 \\ literal\text{-}1 \end{array}\right\}$ BY identifier-2 [ROUNDED]

    [ON SIZE ERROR imperative-statement]

FORMAT 2

MULTIPLY $\left\{\begin{array}{l} identifier\text{-}1 \\ literal\text{-}1 \end{array}\right\}$ BY $\left\{\begin{array}{l} identifier\text{-}2 \\ literal\text{-}2 \end{array}\right\}$ GIVING identifier-3

    [ROUNDED] [ON SIZE ERROR imperative-statement]

NOTE Statement

NOTE character string

OPEN Statement

FORMAT 1

OPEN [INPUT {file-name $\left[\begin{array}{l} REVERSED \\ WITH\ NO\ REWIND \end{array}\right]$ } ...]

    [OUTPUT {file-name [WITH NO REWIND] } ...]

    [I-O {file-name} ...]

FORMAT 2

OPEN [INPUT {file-name $\left[\begin{array}{l} REVERSED \\ WITH\ NO\ REWIND \end{array}\right]$ $\left[\begin{array}{l} LEAVE \\ REREAD \\ DISP \end{array}\right]$ } ...]

    [OUTPUT {file-name [WITH NO REWIND] $\left[\begin{array}{l} LEAVE \\ REREAD \\ DISP \end{array}\right]$ } ...]

    [I-O {file-name} ...]

PERFORM Statement

FORMAT 1

$\underline{PERFORM}$ procedure-name-1 [$\underline{THRU}$ procedure-name-2]

FORMAT 2

$\underline{PERFORM}$ procedure-name-1 [$\underline{THRU}$ procedure-name-2] $\begin{Bmatrix} identifier-1 \\ integer-1 \end{Bmatrix}$ $\underline{TIMES}$

FORMAT 3

$\underline{PERFORM}$ procedure-name-1 [$\underline{THRU}$ procedure-name-2] $\underline{UNTIL}$ condition-1

FORMAT 4

$\underline{PERFORM}$ procedure-name-1 [$\underline{THRU}$ procedure-name-2]

$\underline{VARYING}$ $\begin{Bmatrix} index\text{-}name\text{-}1 \\ identifier\text{-}1 \end{Bmatrix}$ $\underline{FROM}$ $\begin{Bmatrix} index\text{-}name\text{-}2 \\ literal\text{-}2 \\ identifier\text{-}2 \end{Bmatrix}$ $\underline{BY}$ $\begin{Bmatrix} literal\text{-}3 \\ identifier\text{-}3 \end{Bmatrix}$ $\underline{UNTIL}$ condition-1

[$\underline{AFTER}$ $\begin{Bmatrix} index\text{-}name\text{-}4 \\ identifier\text{-}4 \end{Bmatrix}$ $\underline{FROM}$ $\begin{Bmatrix} index\text{-}name\text{-}5 \\ literal\text{-}5 \\ identifier\text{-}5 \end{Bmatrix}$ $\underline{BY}$ $\begin{Bmatrix} literal\text{-}6 \\ identifier\text{-}6 \end{Bmatrix}$ $\underline{UNTIL}$ condition-2

[$\underline{AFTER}$ $\begin{Bmatrix} index\text{-}name\text{-}7 \\ identifier\text{-}7 \end{Bmatrix}$ $\underline{FROM}$ $\begin{Bmatrix} index\text{-}name\text{-}8 \\ literal\text{-}8 \\ identifier\text{-}8 \end{Bmatrix}$ $\underline{BY}$ $\begin{Bmatrix} literal\text{-}9 \\ identifier\text{-}9 \end{Bmatrix}$ $\underline{UNTIL}$ condition-3]]

READ Statement

$\underline{READ}$ file-name RECORD [$\underline{INTO}$ identifier]

$\begin{Bmatrix} \underline{AT\ END} \\ \underline{INVALID}\ KEY \end{Bmatrix}$ imperative-statement

REWRITE Statement

$\underline{REWRITE}$ record-name [$\underline{FROM}$ identifier] [$\underline{INVALID}$ KEY imperative-statement]

SEEK Statement

$\underline{SEEK}$ file-name RECORD

START Statement

FORMAT 1

$\underline{START}$ file-name [$\underline{INVALID}$ KEY imperative-statement]

FORMAT 2 (Version 3 & 4)

$\underline{START}$ file-name

$\underline{USING}$ KEY data-name $\begin{Bmatrix} \underline{EQUAL\ TO} \\ = \end{Bmatrix}$ identifier

[$\underline{INVALID}$ KEY imperative-statement]

STOP Statement

$\underline{STOP}$ $\begin{Bmatrix} \underline{RUN} \\ literal \end{Bmatrix}$

SUBTRACT Statement

FORMAT 1

$\underline{SUBTRACT}$ $\begin{Bmatrix} identifier-1 \\ literal-1 \end{Bmatrix}$ $\begin{bmatrix} identifier-2 \\ literal-2 \end{bmatrix}$ ... $\underline{FROM}$ identifier-m [$\underline{ROUNDED}$]

[identifier-n [$\underline{ROUNDED}$]] ... [$\underline{ON}$ $\underline{SIZE}$ $\underline{ERROR}$ imperative-statement]

FORMAT 2

$\underline{SUBTRACT}$ $\begin{Bmatrix} identifier-1 \\ literal-1 \end{Bmatrix}$ $\begin{bmatrix} identifier-2 \\ literal-2 \end{bmatrix}$ ... $\underline{FROM}$ $\begin{Bmatrix} identifier-m \\ literal-m \end{Bmatrix}$ $\underline{GIVING}$ identifier-n

[$\underline{ROUNDED}$] [$\underline{ON}$ $\underline{SIZE}$ $\underline{ERROR}$ imperative-statement]

FORMAT 3

$\underline{SUBTRACT}$ $\begin{Bmatrix} \underline{CORRESPONDING} \\ \underline{CORR} \end{Bmatrix}$ identifier-1 $\underline{FROM}$ identifier-2 [$\underline{ROUNDED}$]

[$\underline{ON}$ $\underline{SIZE}$ $\underline{ERROR}$ imperative-statement]

TRANSFORM Statement

$\underline{TRANSFORM}$ identifier-3 CHARACTERS $\underline{FROM}$ $\begin{Bmatrix} figurative\text{-}constant\text{-}1 \\ nonnumeric\text{-}literal\text{-}1 \\ identifier\text{-}1 \end{Bmatrix}$

$\underline{TO}$ $\begin{Bmatrix} figurative\text{-}constant\text{-}2 \\ nonnumeric\text{-}literal\text{-}2 \\ identifier\text{-}2 \end{Bmatrix}$

USE Sentence

FORMAT 1

Option 1:

$\underline{USE}$ $\begin{Bmatrix} \underline{BEFORE} \\ \underline{AFTER} \end{Bmatrix}$ $\underline{STANDARD}$ [$\underline{BEGINNING}$] $\begin{bmatrix} \underline{REEL} \\ \underline{FILE} \\ \underline{UNIT} \end{bmatrix}$

$\underline{LABEL}$ $\underline{PROCEDURE}$ ON $\begin{Bmatrix} \{file\text{-}name\} ... \\ \underline{OUTPUT} \\ \underline{INPUT} \\ \underline{I\text{-}O} \end{Bmatrix}$.

Option 2:

$\underline{USE}$ $\begin{Bmatrix} \underline{BEFORE} \\ \underline{AFTER} \end{Bmatrix}$ STANDARD [$\underline{ENDING}$] $\begin{bmatrix} \underline{REEL} \\ \underline{FILE} \\ \underline{UNIT} \end{bmatrix}$

$\underline{LABEL}$ $\underline{PROCEDURE}$ ON $\begin{Bmatrix} \{file\text{-}name\} ... \\ \underline{OUTPUT} \\ \underline{INPUT} \\ \underline{I\text{-}O} \end{Bmatrix}$.

FORMAT 2

$\underline{USE}$ $\underline{AFTER}$ STANDARD $\underline{ERROR}$ $\underline{PROCEDURE}$

ON $\begin{Bmatrix} \{file\text{-}name\text{-}1\}\ [file\text{-}name\text{-}2] ... \\ [\underline{GIVING}\ data\text{-}name\text{-}1,\ data\text{-}name\text{-}2] \\ \underline{INPUT} \\ \underline{OUTPUT} \\ \underline{I\text{-}O} \end{Bmatrix}$

NOTE: Format 3 of the USE Sentence is included in Formats for the REPORT WRITER feature.

WRITE Statement

FORMAT 1

$\underline{WRITE}$ record name [$\underline{FROM}$ identifier-1] [$\begin{Bmatrix} \underline{BEFORE} \\ \underline{AFTER} \end{Bmatrix}$ ADVANCING

$\begin{Bmatrix} identifier\text{-}2\ LINES \\ integer\ LINES \\ mnemonic\text{-}name \end{Bmatrix}$] [AT $\begin{Bmatrix} \underline{END\text{-}OF\text{-}PAGE} \\ \underline{EOP} \end{Bmatrix}$ imperative-statement]

FORMAT 2

$\underline{WRITE}$ record-name [$\underline{FROM}$ identifier-1] $\underline{AFTER}$ $\underline{POSITIONING}$ $\begin{Bmatrix} identifier\text{-}2 \\ integer \end{Bmatrix}$ LINES

[AT $\begin{Bmatrix} \underline{END\text{-}OF\text{-}PAGE} \\ \underline{EOP} \end{Bmatrix}$ imperative-statement]

FORMAT 3

$\underline{WRITE}$ record-name [$\underline{FROM}$ identifier-1] $\underline{INVALID}$ KEY imperative-statement

SORT — BASIC FORMATS

Environment Division Sort Formats

FILE-CONTROL PARAGRAPH — SELECT SENTENCE

SELECT Sentence (for GIVING option only)

$\underline{SELECT}$ file-name

$\underline{ASSIGN}$ TO [integer-1] system-name-1 [system-name-2] ...

$\underline{OR}$ system-name-3 [FOR $\underline{MULTIPLE}$ $\begin{Bmatrix} \underline{REEL} \\ \underline{UNIT} \end{Bmatrix}$]

[$\underline{RESERVE}$ $\begin{Bmatrix} integer\text{-}2 \\ \underline{NO} \end{Bmatrix}$ ALTERNATE $\begin{bmatrix} AREA \\ AREAS \end{bmatrix}$].

383

SELECT Sentence (for Sort Work Files)

    SELECT sort-file-name

        ASSIGN TO [integer] system-name-1 [system-name-2] . . .

I-O-CONTROL PARAGRAPH

RERUN Clause

    RERUN ON system-name

SAME RECORD/SORT AREA Clause

    SAME $\begin{Bmatrix} \text{RECORD} \\ \text{SORT} \end{Bmatrix}$ AREA FOR file-name-1 {file-name-2} . . .

Data Division Sort Formats

SORT-FILE DESCRIPTION

    SD sort-file-name

        RECORDING MODE IS mode

        DATA $\begin{Bmatrix} \text{RECORD IS} \\ \text{RECORDS ARE} \end{Bmatrix}$ data-name-1 [data-name-2] . . .

        RECORD CONTAINS [integer-1 TO] integer-2 CHARACTERS.

Procedure Division Sort Formats

RELEASE Statement

    RELEASE sort-record-name [FROM identifier]

RETURN Statement

    RETURN sort-file-name RECORD [INTO identifier]

        AT END imperative-statement

SORT Statement

    SORT file-name-1 ON $\begin{Bmatrix} \text{DESCENDING} \\ \text{ASCENDING} \end{Bmatrix}$ KEY {data-name-1} . . .

    [ON $\begin{Bmatrix} \text{DESCENDING} \\ \text{ASCENDING} \end{Bmatrix}$ KEY {data-name-2} . . .] . . .

    $\begin{Bmatrix} \text{INPUT PROCEDURE} \text{ IS } section\text{-}name\text{-}1 \text{ [THRU } section\text{-}name\text{-}2] \\ \text{USING } file\text{-}name\text{-}2 \end{Bmatrix}$

    $\begin{Bmatrix} \text{OUTPUT PROCEDURE} \text{ IS } section\text{-}name\text{-}3 \text{ [THRU } section\text{-}name\text{-}4] \\ \text{GIVING } file\text{-}name\text{-}3 \end{Bmatrix}$

REPORT WRITER — BASIC FORMATS

Data Division Report Writer Formats

NOTE: Formats that appear as Basic Formats within the general description of the Data Division are illustrated there.

FILE SECTION — REPORT Clause

    $\begin{Bmatrix} \text{REPORT IS} \\ \text{REPORTS ARE} \end{Bmatrix}$ report-name-1 [report-name-2] . . .

REPORT SECTION

    REPORT SECTION.

    RD report-name

        WITH CODE mnemonic-name

        $\begin{Bmatrix} \text{CONTROL IS} \\ \text{CONTROLS ARE} \end{Bmatrix}$ $\begin{Bmatrix} \text{FINAL} \\ identifier\text{-}1 \text{ [}identifier\text{-}2] \dots \\ \text{FINAL } identifier\text{-}1 \text{ [}identifier\text{-}2] \dots \end{Bmatrix}$

        PAGE $\begin{bmatrix} \text{LIMIT IS} \\ \text{LIMITS ARE} \end{bmatrix}$ interger-1 $\begin{Bmatrix} \text{LINE} \\ \text{LINES} \end{Bmatrix}$

        [HEADING integer-2]

        [FIRST DETAIL integer-3]

        [LAST DETAIL integer-4]

        [FOOTING integer-5]

REPORT GROUP DESCRIPTION ENTRY

FORMAT 1

    01 [data-name-1]

        LINE NUMBER IS $\begin{Bmatrix} integer\text{-}1 \\ \text{PLUS } integer\text{-}2 \\ \text{NEXT PAGE} \end{Bmatrix}$

        NEXT GROUP IS $\begin{Bmatrix} integer\text{-}1 \\ \text{PLUS } integer\text{-}2 \\ \text{NEXT PAGE} \end{Bmatrix}$

        TYPE IS $\begin{Bmatrix} \text{REPORT HEADING} \\ \text{RH} \\ \text{PAGE HEADING} \\ \text{PH} \\ \text{CONTROL HEADING} \\ \text{CH} \\ \text{DETAIL} \\ \text{DE} \\ \text{CONTROL FOOTING} \\ \text{CF} \\ \text{PAGE FOOTING} \\ \text{PF} \\ \text{REPORT FOOTING} \\ \text{RF} \end{Bmatrix}$ $\begin{Bmatrix} identifier\text{-}n \\ \text{FINAL} \end{Bmatrix}$ $\begin{Bmatrix} identifier\text{-}n \\ \text{FINAL} \end{Bmatrix}$

    USAGE Clause.

FORMAT 2

    nn [data-name-1]

        LINE Clause — See Format 1

        USAGE Clause.

FORMAT 3

    nn [data-name-1]

        COLUMN NUMBER IS integer-1

        GROUP INDICATE

        JUSTIFIED Clause

        LINE Clause — See Format 1

        PICTURE Clause

        RESET ON $\begin{Bmatrix} identifier\text{-}1 \\ \text{FINAL} \end{Bmatrix}$

        BLANK WHEN ZERO Clause

        SOURCE IS $\begin{Bmatrix} \text{TALLY} \\ identifier\text{-}2 \end{Bmatrix}$

        SUM $\begin{Bmatrix} \text{TALLY} \\ identifier\text{-}3 \end{Bmatrix}$ $\begin{Bmatrix} \text{TALLY} \\ identifier\text{-}4 \end{Bmatrix}$ . . . [UPON data-name]

        VALUE IS literal-1

        USAGE Clause.

FORMAT 4

01 *data-name-1*

BLANK WHEN ZERO Clause

COLUMN Clause — See Format 2

GROUP Clause — See Format 2

JUSTIFIED Clause

LINE Clause — See Format 1

NEXT GROUP Clause — See Format 1

PICTURE Clause

RESET Clause — See Format 2

$\left\{\begin{array}{l}\text{SOURCE Clause}\\ \text{SUM Clause}\\ \text{VALUE Clause}\end{array}\right\}$ See Format 2

TYPE Clause — See Format 1

USAGE Clause.

Procedure Division Report Writer Formats

GENERATE Statement

GENERATE *identifier*

INITIATE Statement

INITIATE *report-name-1* [*report-name-2*] . . .

TERMINATE Statement

TERMINATE *report-name-1* [*report-name-2*] . . .

USE Sentence

USE BEFORE REPORTING *data-name*.

TABLE HANDLING — BASIC FORMATS
Data Division Table Handling Formats

OCCURS Clause

FORMAT 1

OCCURS *integer-2* TIMES

[$\left\{\begin{array}{l}\text{ASCENDING}\\ \text{DESCENDING}\end{array}\right\}$ KEY IS *data-name-2* [*data-name-3* . . .] . . .

[INDEXED BY *index-name-1* [*index-name-2*] . . .]

FORMAT 2

OCCURS *integer-1* TO *integer-2* TIMES [DEPENDING ON *data-name-1*]

[$\left\{\begin{array}{l}\text{ASCENDING}\\ \text{DESCENDING}\end{array}\right\}$ KEY IS *data-name-2* [*data-name-3*] . . .] . . .

[INDEXED BY *index-name-1* [*index-name-2*] . . .]

FORMAT 3

OCCURS *integer-2* TIMES [DEPENDING ON *data-name-1*]

[$\left\{\begin{array}{l}\text{ASCENDING}\\ \text{DESCENDING}\end{array}\right\}$ KEY IS *data-name-2* [*data-name-3*] . . .] . . .

[INDEXED BY *index-name-1* [*index-name-2*] . . .]

USAGE Clause

[USAGE IS] INDEX

Procedure Division Table Handling Formats

SEARCH Statement

FORMAT 1

SEARCH *identifier-1* [VARYING $\left\{\begin{array}{l}\text{*index-name-1*}\\ \text{*identifier-2*}\end{array}\right\}$]

[AT END *imperative-statement-1*]

WHEN *condition-1* $\left\{\begin{array}{l}\text{*imperative-statement-2*}\\ \text{NEXT SENTENCE}\end{array}\right\}$

[WHEN *condition-2* $\left\{\begin{array}{l}\text{*imperative-statement-3*}\\ \text{NEXT SENTENCE}\end{array}\right\}$] . . .

FORMAT 2

SEARCH ALL *identifier-1* [AT END *imperative-statement-1*]

WHEN *condition-1* $\left\{\begin{array}{l}\text{*imperative-statement-2*}\\ \text{NEXT SENTENCE}\end{array}\right\}$

SET Statement

FORMAT 1

SET $\left\{\begin{array}{l}\text{*index-name-1* [*index-name-2*]}\\ \text{*identifier-1* [*identifier-2*]}\end{array}\right\}$ . . . TO $\left\{\begin{array}{l}\text{*index-name-3*}\\ \text{*identifier-3*}\\ \text{*literal-1*}\end{array}\right\}$

FORMAT 2

SET *index-name-4* [*index-name-5*] . . . $\left\{\begin{array}{l}\text{UP BY}\\ \text{DOWN BY}\end{array}\right\}$ $\left\{\begin{array}{l}\text{*identifier-4*}\\ \text{*literal-2*}\end{array}\right\}$

SEGMENTATION — BASIC FORMATS
Environment Division Segmentation Formats

OBJECT-COMPUTER PARAGRAPH
SEGMENT-LIMIT Clause

SEGMENT-LIMIT IS *priority-number*

Procedure Division Segmentation Formats
Priority Numbers
section-name SECTION [*priority-number*].

SOURCE PROGRAM LIBRARY FACILITY

COPY Statement

COPY *library-name* [SUPPRESS]

[REPLACING *word-1* BY $\left\{\begin{array}{l}\text{*word-2*}\\ \text{*literal-1*}\\ \text{*identifier-1*}\end{array}\right\}$ *word-3* BY $\left\{\begin{array}{l}\text{*word-4*}\\ \text{*literal-2*}\\ \text{*identifier-2*}\end{array}\right\}$] . . .] .

Assembler Formats

NAME	MNEMONIC	OP CODE	FORMAT	OPERANDS
Add (c)	AR	1A	RR	R1,R2
Add (c)	A	5A	RX	R1,D2(X2,B2)
Add Decimal (c)	AP	FA	SS	D1(L1,B1),D2(L2,B2)
Add Halfword (c)	AH	4A	RX	R1,D2(X2,B2)
Add Logical (c)	ALR	1E	RR	R1,R2
Add Logical (c)	AL	5E	RX	R1,D2(X2,B2)
AND (c)	NR	14	RR	R1,R2
AND (c)	N	54	RX	R1,D2(X2,B2)
AND (c)	NI	94	SI	D1(B1),I2
AND (c)	NC	D4	SS	D1(L,B1),D2(B2)
Branch and Link	BALR	05	RR	R1,R2
Branch and Link	BAL	45	RX	R1,D2(X2,B2)
Branch on Condition	BCR	07	RR	M1,R2
Branch on Condition	BC	47	RX	M1,D2(X2,B2)
Branch on Count	BCTR	06	RR	R1,R2
Branch on Count	BCT	46	RX	R1,D2(X2,B2)
Branch on Index High	BXH	86	RS	R1,R3,D2(B2)
Branch on Index Low or Equal	BXLE	87	RS	R1,R3,D2(B2)
Clear I/O (c,p)	CLRIO	9D01	S	D2(B2)
Compare (c)	CR	19	RR	R1,R2
Compare (c)	C	59	RX	R1,D2(X2,B2)
Compare and Swap (c)	CS	BA	RS	R1,R3,D2(B2)
Compare Decimal (c)	CP	F9	SS	D1(L1,B1),D2(L2,B2)
Compare Double and Swap (c)	CDS	BB	RS	R1,R3,D2(B2)
Compare Halfword (c)	CH	49	RX	R1,D2(X2,B2)
Compare Logical (c)	CLR	15	RR	R1,R2
Compare Logical (c)	CL	55	RX	R1,D2(X2,B2)
Compare Logical (c)	CLC	D5	SS	D1(L,B1),D2(B2)
Compare Logical (c)	CLI	95	SI	D1(B1),I2
Compare Logical Characters under Mask (c)	CLM	BD	RS	R1,M3,D2(B2)
Compare Logical Long (c)	CLCL	0F	RR	R1,R2
Convert to Binary	CVB	4F	RX	R1,D2(X2,B2)
Convert to Decimal	CVD	4E	RX	R1,D2(X2,B2)
Diagnose (p)		83		Model-dependent
Divide	DR	1D	RR	R1,R2
Divide	D	5D	RX	R1,D2(X2,B2)
Divide Decimal	DP	FD	SS	D1(L1,B1),D2(L2,B2)
Edit (c)	ED	DE	SS	D1(L,B1),D2(B2)
Edit and Mark (c)	EDMK	DF	SS	D1(L,B1),D2(B2)
Exclusive OR (c)	XR	17	RR	R1,R2
Exclusive OR (c)	X	57	RX	R1,D2(X2,B2)
Exclusive OR (c)	XI	97	SI	D1(B1),I2
Exclusive OR (c)	XC	D7	SS	D1(L,B1),D2(B2)
Execute	EX	44	RX	R1,D2(X2,B2)
Halt I/O (c,p)	HIO	9E00	S	D2(B2)
Halt Device (c,p)	HDV	9E01	S	D2(B2)
Insert Character	IC	43	RX	R1,D2(X2,B2)
Insert Characters under Mask (c)	ICM	BF	RS	R1,M3,D2(B2)
Insert PSW Key (p)	IPK	B20B	S	
Insert Storage Key (p)	ISK	09	RR	R1,R2
Load	LR	18	RR	R1,R2
Load	L	58	RX	R1,D2(X2,B2)
Load Address	LA	41	RX	R1,D2(X2,B2)
Load and Test (c)	LTR	12	RR	R1,R2
Load Complement (c)	LCR	13	RR	R1,R2
Load Control (p)	LCTL	B7	RS	R1,R3,D2(B2)
Load Halfword	LH	48	RX	R1,D2(X2,B2)
Load Multiple	LM	98	RS	R1,R3,D2(B2)
Load Negative (c)	LNR	11	RR	R1,R2
Load Positive (c)	LPR	10	RR	R1,R2
Load PSW (n,p)	LPSW	82	S	D2(B2)
Load Real Address (c,p)	LRA	B1	RX	R1,D2(X2,B2)
Monitor Call	MC	AF	SI	D1(B1),I2
Move	MVI	92	SI	D1(B1),I2
Move	MVC	D2	SS	D1(L,B1),D2(B2)
Move Long (c)	MVCL	0E	RR	R1,R2
Move Numerics	MVN	D1	SS	D1(L,B1),D2(B2)
Move with Offset	MVO	F1	SS	D1(L1,B1),D2(L2,B2)
Move Zones	MVZ	D3	SS	D1(L,B1),D2(B2)
Multiply	MR	1C	RR	R1,R2
Multiply	M	5C	RX	R1,D2(X2,B2)
Multiply Decimal	MP	FC	SS	D1(L1,B1),D2(L2,B2)
Multiply Halfword	MH	4C	RX	R1,D2(X2,B2)
OR (c)	OR	16	RR	R1,R2

NAME	MNEMONIC	OP CODE	FORMAT	OPERANDS
OR (c)	O	56	RX	R1,D2(X2,B2)
OR (c)	OI	96	SI	D1(B1),I2
OR (c)	OC	D6	SS	D1(L,B1),D2(B2)
Pack	PACK	F2	SS	D1(L1,B1),D2(L2,B2)
Purge TLB (p)	PTLB	B20D	S	
Read Direct (p)	RDD	85	SI	D1(B1),I2
Reset Reference Bit (c,p)	RRB	B213	S	D2(B2)
Set Clock (c,p)	SCK	B204	S	D2(B2)
Set Clock Comparator (p)	SCKC	B206	S	D2(B2)
Set CPU Timer (p)	SPT	B208	S	D2(B2)
Set Prefix (p)	SPX	B210	S	D2(B2)
Set Program Mask (n)	SPM	04	RR	R1
Set PSW Key from Address (p)	SPKA	B20A	S	D2(B2)
Set Storage Key (p)	SSK	08	RR	R1,R2
Set System Mask (p)	SSM	80	S	D2(B2)
Shift and Round Decimal (c)	SRP	F0	SS	D1(L1,B1),D2(B2),I3
Shift Left Double (c)	SLDA	8F	RS	R1,D2(B2)
Shift Left Double Logical	SLDL	8D	RS	R1,D2(B2)
Shift Left Single (c)	SLA	8B	RS	R1,D2(B2)
Shift Left Single Logical	SLL	89	RS	R1,D2(B2)
Shift Right Double (c)	SRDA	8E	RS	R1,D2(B2)
Shift Right Double Logical	SRDL	8C	RS	R1,D2(B2)
Shift Right Single (c)	SRA	8A	RS	R1,D2(B2)
Shift Right Single Logical	SRL	88	RS	R1,D2(B2)
Signal Processor (c,p)	SIGP	AE	RS	R1,R3,D2(B2)
Start I/O (c,p)	SIO	9C00	S	D2(B2)
Start I/O Fast Release (c,p)	SIOF	9C01	S	D2(B2)
Store	ST	50	RX	R1,D2(X2,B2)
Store Channel ID (c,p)	STIDC	B203	S	D2(B2)
Store Character	STC	42	RX	R1,D2(X2,B2)
Store Characters under Mask	STCM	BE	RS	R1,M3,D2(B2)
Store Clock (c)	STCK	B205	S	D2(B2)
Store Clock Comparator (p)	STCKC	B207	S	D2(B2)
Store Control (p)	STCTL	B6	RS	R1,R3,D2(B2)
Store CPU Address (p)	STAP	B212	S	D2(B2)
Store CPU ID (p)	STIDP	B202	S	D2(B2)
Store CPU Timer (p)	STPT	B209	S	D2(B2)
Store Halfword	STH	40	RX	R1,D2(X2,B2)
Store Multiple	STM	90	RS	R1,R3,D2(B2)
Store Prefix (p)	STPX	B211	S	D2(B2)
Store Then AND System Mask (p)	STNSM	AC	SI	D1(B1),I2
Store Then OR System Mask (p)	STOSM	AD	SI	D1(B1),I2
Subtract (c)	SR	1B	RR	R1,R2
Subtract (c)	S	5B	RX	R1,D2(X2,B2)
Subtract Decimal (c)	SP	FB	SS	D1(L1,B1),D2(L2,B2)
Subtract Halfword (c)	SH	4B	RX	R1,D2(X2,B2)
Subtract Logical (c)	SLR	1F	RR	R1,R2
Subtract Logical (c)	SL	5F	RX	R1,D2(X2,B2)
Supervisor Call	SVC	0A	RR	I
Test and Set (c)	TS	93	S	D2(B2)
Test Channel (c,p)	TCH	9F00	S	D2(B2)
Test I/O (c,p)	TIO	9D00	S	D2(B2)
Test under Mask (c)	TM	91	SI	D1(B1),I2
Translate	TR	DC	SS	D1(L,B1),D2(B2)
Translate and Test (c)	TRT	DD	SS	D1(L,B1),D2(B2)
Unpack	UNPK	F3	SS	D1(L1,B1),D2(L2,B2)
Write Direct (p)	WRD	84	SI	D1(B1),I2
Zero and Add Decimal (c)	ZAP	F8	SS	D1(L1,B1),D2(L2,B2)

Floating-Point Instructions

NAME	MNEMONIC	OP CODE	FORMAT	OPERANDS
Add Normalized, Extended (c,x)	AXR	36	RR	R1,R2
Add Normalized, Long (c)	ADR	2A	RR	R1,R2
Add Normalized, Long (c)	AD	6A	RX	R1,D2(X2,B2)
Add Normalized, Short (c)	AER	3A	RR	R1,R2
Add Normalized, Short (c)	AE	7A	RX	R1,D2(X2,B2)
Add Unnormalized, Long (c)	AWR	2E	RR	R1,R2
Add Unnormalized, Long (c)	AW	6E	RX	R1,D2(X2,B2)
Add Unnormalized, Short (c)	AUR	3E	RR	R1,R2
Add Unnormalized, Short (c)	AU	7E	RX	R1,D2(X2,B2)

c. Condition code is set. p. Privileged instruction.
n. New condition code is loaded. x. Extended precision floating-point.

Floating-Point Instructions (Contd)

(4)

NAME	MNEMONIC	OP CODE	FORMAT	OPERANDS
Compare, Long (c)	CDR	29	RR	R1,R2
Compare, Long (c)	CD	69	RX	R1,D2(X2,B2)
Compare, Short (c)	CER	39	RR	R1,R2
Compare, Short (c)	CE	79	RX	R1,D2(X2,B2)
Divide, Long	DDR	2D	RR	R1,R2
Divide, Long	DD	6D	RX	R1,D2(X2,B2)
Divide, Short	DER	3D	RR	R1,R2
Divide, Short	DE	7D	RX	R1,D2(X2,B2)
Halve, Long	HDR	24	RR	R1,R2
Halve, Short	HER	34	RR	R1,R2
Load and Test, Long (c)	LTDR	22	RR	R1,R2
Load and Test, Short (c)	LTER	32	RR	R1,R2
Load Complement, Long (c)	LCDR	23	RR	R1,R2
Load Complement, Short (c)	LCER	33	RR	R1,R2
Load, Long	LDR	28	RR	R1,R2
Load, Long	LD	68	RX	R1,D2(X2,B2)
Load Negative, Long (c)	LNDR	21	RR	R1,R2
Load Negative, Short (c)	LNER	31	RR	R1,R2
Load Positive, Long (c)	LPDR	20	RR	R1,R2
Load Positive, Short (c)	LPER	30	RR	R1,R2
Load Rounded, Extended to Long (x)	LRDR	25	RR	R1,R2
Load Rounded, Long to Short (x)	LRER	35	RR	R1,R2
Load, Short	LER	38	RR	R1,R2
Load, Short	LE	78	RX	R1,D2(X2,B2)
Multiply, Extended (x)	MXR	26	RR	R1,R2
Multiply, Long	MDR	2C	RR	R1,R2
Multiply, Long	MD	6C	RX	R1,D2(X2,B2)
Multiply, Long/Extended (x)	MXDR	27	RR	R1,R2
Multiply, Long/Extended (x)	MXD	67	RX	R1,D2(X2,B2)
Multiply, Short	MER	3C	RR	R1,R2
Multiply, Short	ME	7C	RX	R1,D2(X2,B2)
Store, Long	STD	60	RX	R1,D2(X2,B2)
Store, Short	STE	70	RX	R1,D2(X2,B2)
Subtract Normalized, Extended (c,x)	SXR	37	RR	R1,R2
Subtract Normalized, Long (c)	SDR	2B	RR	R1,R2
Subtract Normalized, Long (c)	SD	6B	RX	R1,D2(X2,B2)
Subtract Normalized, Short (c)	SER	3B	RR	R1,R2
Subtract Normalized, Short (c)	SE	7B	RX	R1,D2(X2,B2)
Subtract Unnormalized, Long (c)	SWR	2F	RR	R1,R2
Subtract Unnormalized, Long (c)	SW	6F	RX	R1,D2(X2,B2)
Subtract Unnormalized, Short (c)	SUR	3F	RR	R1,R2
Subtract Unnormalized, Short (c)	SU	7F	RX	R1,D2(X2,B2)

EXTENDED MNEMONIC INSTRUCTIONS†

Use	Extended Code* (RX or RR)	Meaning	Machine Instr.* (RX or RR)
General	B or BR	Unconditional Branch	BC or BCR 15,
	NOP or NOPR	No Operation	BC or BCR 0,
After	BH or BHR	Branch on A High	BC or BCR 2,
Compare	BL or BLR	Branch on A Low	BC or BCR 4,
Instructions	BE or BER	Branch on A Equal B	BC or BCR 8,
(A:B)	BNH or BNHR	Branch on A Not High	BC or BCR 13,
	BNL or BNLR	Branch on A Not Low	BC or BCR 11,
	BNE or BNER	Branch on A Not Equal B	BC or BCR 7,
After	BO or BOR	Branch on Overflow	BC or BCR 1,
Arithmetic	BP or BPR	Branch on Plus	BC or BCR 2,
Instructions	BM or BMR	Branch on Minus	BC or BCR 4,
	BNP or BNPR	Branch on Not Plus	BC or BCR 13,
	BNM or BNMR	Branch on Not Minus	BC or BCR 11,
	BNZ or BNZR	Branch on Not Zero	BC or BCR 7,
	BZ or BZR	Branch on Zero	BC or BCR 8,
After Test	BO or BOR	Branch if Ones	BC or BCR 1,
under Mask	BM or BMR	Branch if Mixed	BC or BCR 4,
Instruction	BZ or BZR	Branch if Zeros	BC or BCR 8,
	BNO or BNOR	Branch if Not Ones	BC or BCR 14,

*Second operand not shown; in all cases it is D2(X2,B2) for RX format or R2 for RR format.

†For OS/VS and DOS/VS; source: GC33-4010.

EDIT AND EDMK PATTERN CHARACTERS (in hex)

20—digit selector	40—blank	5C—asterisk
21—start of significance	4B—period	6B—comma
22—field separator	5B—dollar sign	C3D9—CR

Index